John Chamberlain

A Catalogue Raisonné of the Sculpture 1954–1985

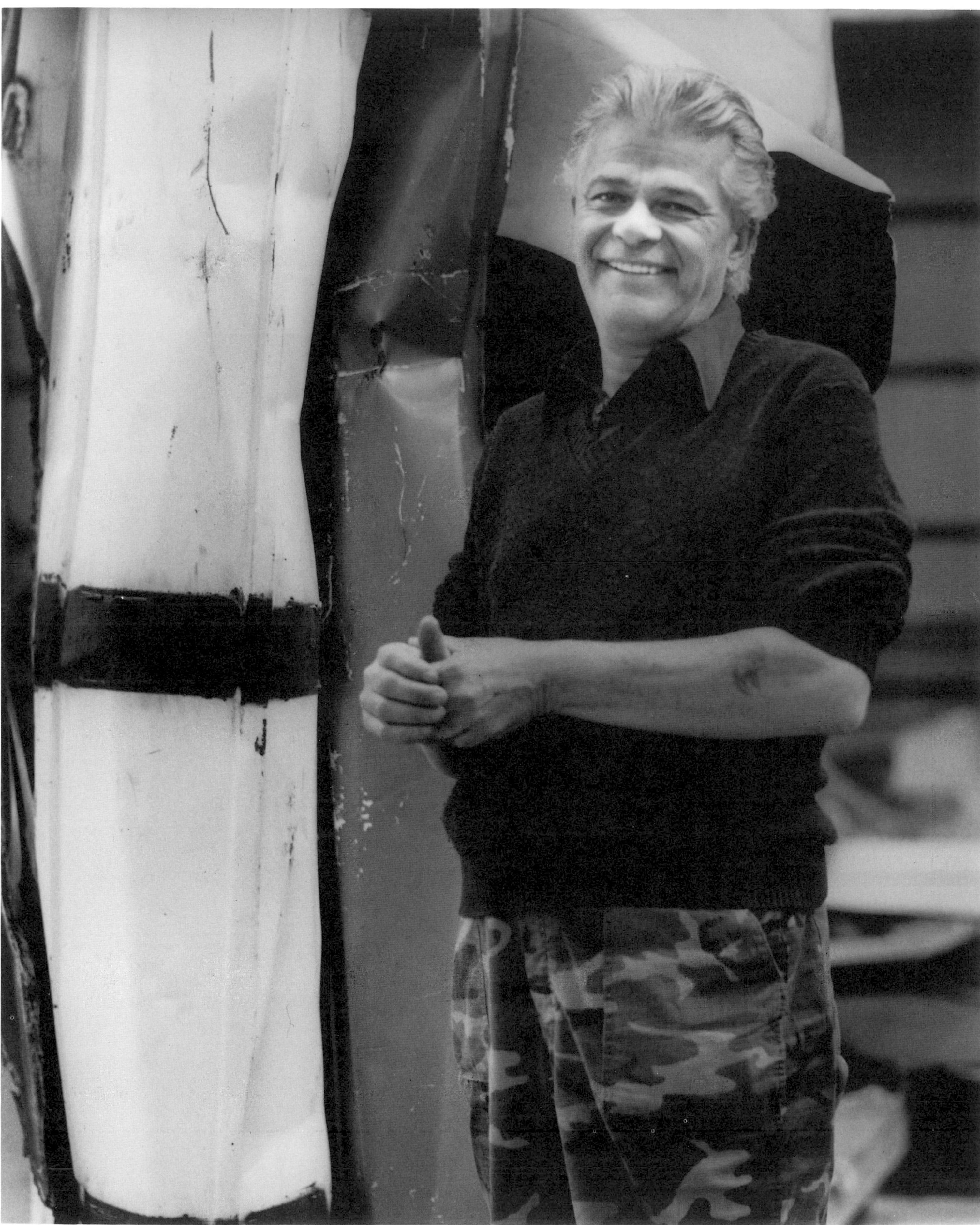

John Chamberlain

A Catalogue Raisonné of the Sculpture 1954–1985

Julie Sylvester

With an Essay by
Klaus Kertess

Hudson Hills Press,
New York

In Association with
The Museum of
Contemporary Art,
Los Angeles

For Jeffrey Krass

First Edition

Published in the United States by Hudson Hills Press, Inc., Suite 1308, 230 Fifth Avenue, New York, NY 10001-7704.

Distributed in the United States, its territories and possessions, Mexico, and Central and South America by Rizzoli International Publications, Inc.

Distributed in Canada by Irwin Publishing Inc.

Distributed in the United Kingdom, Eire, Europe, Israel, and the Middle East by Phaidon Press Limited.

Distributed in Japan by Yohan (Western Publications Distribution Agency).

Editor and Publisher: Paul Anbinder

Copy editor: Eve Sinaiko

Designer: Betty Binns Graphics/Betty Binns and David Skolkin

Index: Gisela S. Knight

Composition: Trufont Typographers

Manufactured in Japan by Toppan Printing Company

Library of Congress Cataloguing-in-Publication Data
Sylvester, Julie, 1954–
John Chamberlain : a catalogue raisonné of the sculpture, 1954–1985.

"In association with the Museum of Contemporary Art, Los Angeles."
Bibliography: p.
Includes index.
1. Chamberlain, John, 1927– —Catalogues raisonnés. 2. Abstract expressionism—United States.
I. Chamberlain, John, 1927– II. Museum of Contemporary Art (Los Angeles, Calif.) III. Title.
NB237.C43A4 1986 730′.92′4 86-3090
ISBN 0-933920-58-X

Photo credits

Most of the photographs reproduced in this volume have been provided by the museums, galleries, foundations, and private collectors noted in the catalogue raisonné. We thank them for supplying the necessary photographs and for their generous permission to reproduce them. In addition, we wish to thank the following photographers:

Jon Abbott: cat. nos. 35, 448, 452, 519, 522, 563, 603, 608, 611, 612, 614, 615, 618, 620–624, 645, 646, 659 (left), 664, 678
Oliver Baker: 12, 13, 57, 58
Rudolph Burckhardt: 15, 185, 299, 305, 312, 338
Balthazar Burkhard
Suzan Campbell: XXIII
Bob Cavin
A. C. Cooper Ltd.: 154
Ivan Dalla Tana: 784, 785, 792, 794, 797
Bevan Davies
D. James Dee: 125
Dick Dickinson: 699
eeva-inkeri
Michael Goodman
Carmelo Guadagno: 111, 257
John Hearon: 739
R. H. Hensleigh: 740
Al Jung
Balthazar Korab: 747
Joel Leivick: 141
Marjorie Lenk: 26
David J. Lorczak: 3
J. B. McCourtney: 681, 683, 684, 686, 687, 690, 694–696, 700, 702, 724, 726–730
Robert McKeever: 209, 226
Edward Meneeley: 32
Douglas M. Parker Studio: 725, 765
Herb Peck
Eric Pollitzer: 21, 124, 133, 191, 294, 298, 317, 339, 340, 390, 391, 396, 400, 414, 486, 507, 518, p. 221
Jules Porter: 757
David Reynolds: 422, 524, 534
Jimm Roberts: frontispiece
Friedrich Rosenstiel: 606
Dennis Ryan
San Ries/Esto, © 1983: 717
John D. Schiff
Ken Schowell
Harry Shunk: 303, 323
Shunk-Kender: 295, 353, p. 100 (installation)
Steven Sloman
Glenn Steigelman, Inc.: 27
Bill J. Strehorn
Nic Tenwiggenhorn
Tim Thayer
Frank J. Thomas: 146
Jon Thompson
Ronald Ian Unruh: 43, 533
Tom Vinetz
John F. Waggaman: 155, 163, 165, 187
Dan Walworth: 15, 95, 112, 116, 153, 314, 328, 334, 335, 343, 352, 380–388, 393, 448, 450, 451, 557, 560, 566, 568, 590, 594, 609, 643, 650, 652–657, 659 (right), 660, 661, 663, 665, 667–670, 688, 694, 699

Cover illustration: *Three-Cornered Desire*, 1979 (cat. no. 620, detail).

Contents

Acknowledgments

The catalogue raisonné was begun in June 1981. The initial stages of this undertaking were realized through the encouragement and essential support of Heiner and Philippa Friedrich. The Leo Castelli Gallery and the Dia Art Foundation made their considerable resources available to me. Randi Semler de Jong assisted in seeing the project to completion with a spirit and ability that were integral to it.

I am grateful to Richard Koshalek and Julia Brown Turrell of The Museum of Contemporary Art in Los Angeles for their recognition of the significance of the catalogue raisonné and retrospective of John Chamberlain's sculpture. Paul Anbinder's sensitivity as a publisher has been greatly appreciated. The participation of Xavier Fourcade has been a significant contribution to this publication.

The catalogue raisonné has been enriched by the writing of Klaus Kertess, and I have thoroughly enjoyed working with him. Thordis Moeller's commitment to John Chamberlain's work and her daily involvement in this endeavor have been important to me. I wish to thank her for her advice and invaluable friendship.

Finally, I am grateful to John Chamberlain for his enthusiasm, criticism, and friendship throughout these years. I continue to admire John's humor, wisdom, and great generosity.

Julie Sylvester

Foreword

It is a great pleasure for The Museum of Contemporary Art to present this retrospective of the work of John Chamberlain and to be a partner in the publication of the catalogue raisonné of his sculpture. Well deserved and overdue, these endeavors celebrate the work and thought of one of this country's most important sculptors.

John Chamberlain is an artist who breathes life and poetry into everyday materials, making the common uncommon and imbuing materials with movement and feeling. He has infused sculpture with color, both found and applied, and has worked both on the wall plane and in the round to create a tangible sense of simultaneous inside and outside. This exhibition and publication, which have been many years in the making, trace the evolution of his work from the 1950s to the present: from the early assemblages made from welded steel, through works incorporating automobile-body parts and others of urethane foam, to the coated Plexiglas pieces and painted steel works of the 1970s and 1980s.

This catalogue raisonné provides a comprehensive record of the artist's sculpture, an oeuvre consisting of over eight hundred works to date. It offers, too, the special opportunity to present a critical essay on the art of John Chamberlain by Klaus Kertess and extensive interviews with the artist by Julie Sylvester.

Author and compiler of this catalogue raisonné, Julie Sylvester is also Guest Curator of the retrospective exhibition. Her commitment to, and involvement with, the work of John Chamberlain are of long standing, and the Museum gratefully acknowledges her crucial role in this project. We greatly appreciate the involvement of Paul Anbinder and Hudson Hills Press as publishers of this book in association with the Museum, and of designers Betty Binns and David Skolkin, who have given visual coherence to a mass of information.

We are very appreciative of the generosity of the lenders to this exhibition and gratefully acknowledge the support of the National Endowment for the Arts in making this project possible. The assistance of Xavier Fourcade in the realization of the catalogue raisonné is also appreciated.

I wish to thank the Museum's dedicated staff, in particular Jacqueline Crist, Assistant Curator and Project Director for the exhibition; Howard Singerman, Publications Coordinator; Mo Shannon, Registrar, and her staff; John Bowsher, Chief Preparator and Installation Designer, and his staff; and Susan Jenkins and Diana Schwab, Curatorial Secretaries, who have all been integral partners in bringing this project to fruition. I also would like to thank Sherri Geldin, Associate Director, and Kerry J. Buckley, Director of Development, for their crucial support.

We thank the Board of Trustees and its Program Committee for lending their support to this ambitious endeavor, and particularly Director Richard Koshalek, whose enthusiastic support and commitment have made the Museum's program a reality.

In closing, we thank John Chamberlain for his work and for his help and good-natured cooperation in all aspects of this project. It has been a special experience for the Museum.

Julia Brown Turrell
Senior Curator

Auto / Bio

Conversations with John Chamberlain

JULIE SYLVESTER: You were born in Rochester, Indiana, on April 16, 1927. Did you spend your childhood there?

JOHN CHAMBERLAIN: Well, some of it. I was born over a meat market in a second-floor apartment at the corner of Ninth and Main in Rochester, Indiana, on April 16, 1927. Which is not the same year but is the same day as Charles Chaplin and Merce Cunningham and probably Lew Alcindor, who became a Moslem and something of a basketball player. It also is a square-root birthday: 4/16.

JS: How long did you live in Rochester?

JC: Long enough to know that I was probably going to have to leave. It made me break the family tradition of being a saloon keeper, which, for this country, was a long tradition. I think we had six generations of saloon-keepers. Really. I've kept up with saloonism, however. It's in the best tradition of English or Irish hanging out, where you meet—it's the clubhouse effect. But you're not here to talk about saloons.

JS: Would you say you had a rather conventional childhood in Rochester?

JC: Actually it was very lonely. I never really found the clubhouse until I was about thirty. I spent my time until then sniffing around for whatever was compatible. When I went to Black Mountain College, when I was something like twenty-nine, that was the first time I found a group of people, a compatibleness. But then, I had held out for a long time without reducing my demand. Had I reduced my demand, I'd be a saloon keeper today. I wasn't a—as they say—spirited horse that was broken or tamed. I kept my spirit until I found what it was I identified with.

JS: You were something of an inventor as a child, designing aircraft and discovering radar.

JC: Not knowing that radar had already been discovered. The design I thought of has become known as "omni," which is a three-point receiver. But the crucial part is that I wanted to leave home badly enough to invent radar. Up to the time when I was about eleven and a half, I was very interested in being an aeronautical engineer. I saw it as something that would get me out of town. When I was twelve I discovered Schubert. The poetics and the agony of Schubert were so impressive to me; I've never forgotten. To this day, when I hear the *Unfinished* Symphony, I still cry.

JS: Why did you want to leave Rochester so badly?

JC: Have you ever been there? I found that no one agreed with me about scale. I remember that I always played with toys that had wheels. I remember a dirigible with wheels that I sat on and rode up and down the sidewalk, and I had a wagon that had a stake body—just a flat wagon with stakes in it. Then the block became the world, and I investigated the block and the world as the block. Then there came other blocks, and much later I decided that the world is measured in blocks. I was very curious. When I was two or so I was curious to know how the mail left the mailbox. I mean, it never occurred to me that somebody came and picked it up. I always thought the mail was moved in the kind of vacuum tubes they had in department stores in those days. So I would investigate things like that. Of the people I liked and remember in Rochester, one was a very eccentric doctor, probably the only man in town with a beard. He really lived like an eccentric. He was a collector; I mean, he never got rid of anything. His house looked like a junk pile. He always drove an old Ford station wagon and he always drove in second gear. Very slow. I don't remember much except that the only friends I had were guys from the other side of the tracks, so to speak—guys who looked like they were either inbred or had been exposed to a lot of scurvy. Which could have been the case in the 1930s in Rochester—people probably didn't know apples from oranges, or something. The town wasn't really a place where I got on well; no one got my humor.

JS: What about your family, what were they doing as you were growing up?

JC: I don't know what they were doing, because they never told me. They never had too much love for one another. My father was mostly drunk. He was either asleep in the house or he was off to the "store"—what they called the store, which was the saloon. When he got to the store he would talk to these rumguts, people who would sit against the wall, tipped back in their chairs, nursing a beer all day. Or he'd play cards. I wasn't allowed in there very often. Of course, I did steal the rubber money. He sold rubbers there. This was before they were a chic item for drugstores to sell, I guess. I figured I could steal that money and no one would complain about it. For some reason, I understood that much, although I didn't understand what the rubbers were for. When I started smoking, when I was ten, my friends and I would walk along the railroad tracks to look for long butts, but then it occurred to me that I could just go to the store, to the saloon, and take the cigarettes from there.

JS: When did you move to Chicago?

JC: Whenever they took me there. I was three or four when we moved to Chicago. My grandmother sort of ran the house, and my mother and my Aunt Jane went out to work. My mother and father were divorced around 1930, 1931, for which he was required to pay her three dollars a month for each child. So he had to pay something like six dollars a month in alimony. Try doing that today.

JS: So Grandma ran the household. She must have been a strong influence on you; you often quote her.

JC: Well, Grandma had a lot of things to say in those days. "My God, Effie," she used to say, "That's enough to scare the green paint out of you!" My mother and my Aunt Jane were waitresses at the World's Fair in Chicago in 1933 or 1934. I went to local grammar schools there. There's nothing memorable. My frequent trips on the railroad, going back to Rochester to see if my father was ready to say anything to me, produced almost no response at all, except that evidently I constantly needed a haircut. Which, as I remember it, was about all he ever said to me.

A series of tape-recorded interviews with John Chamberlain took place in June 1981 in Sarasota, Florida; in January 1983 in Sarasota; in February 1984 in New York; in December 1984 in Sarasota; and in June 1985 in New York. The original transcripts have been combined and edited to follow a chronology of the artist's life and the development of his work.

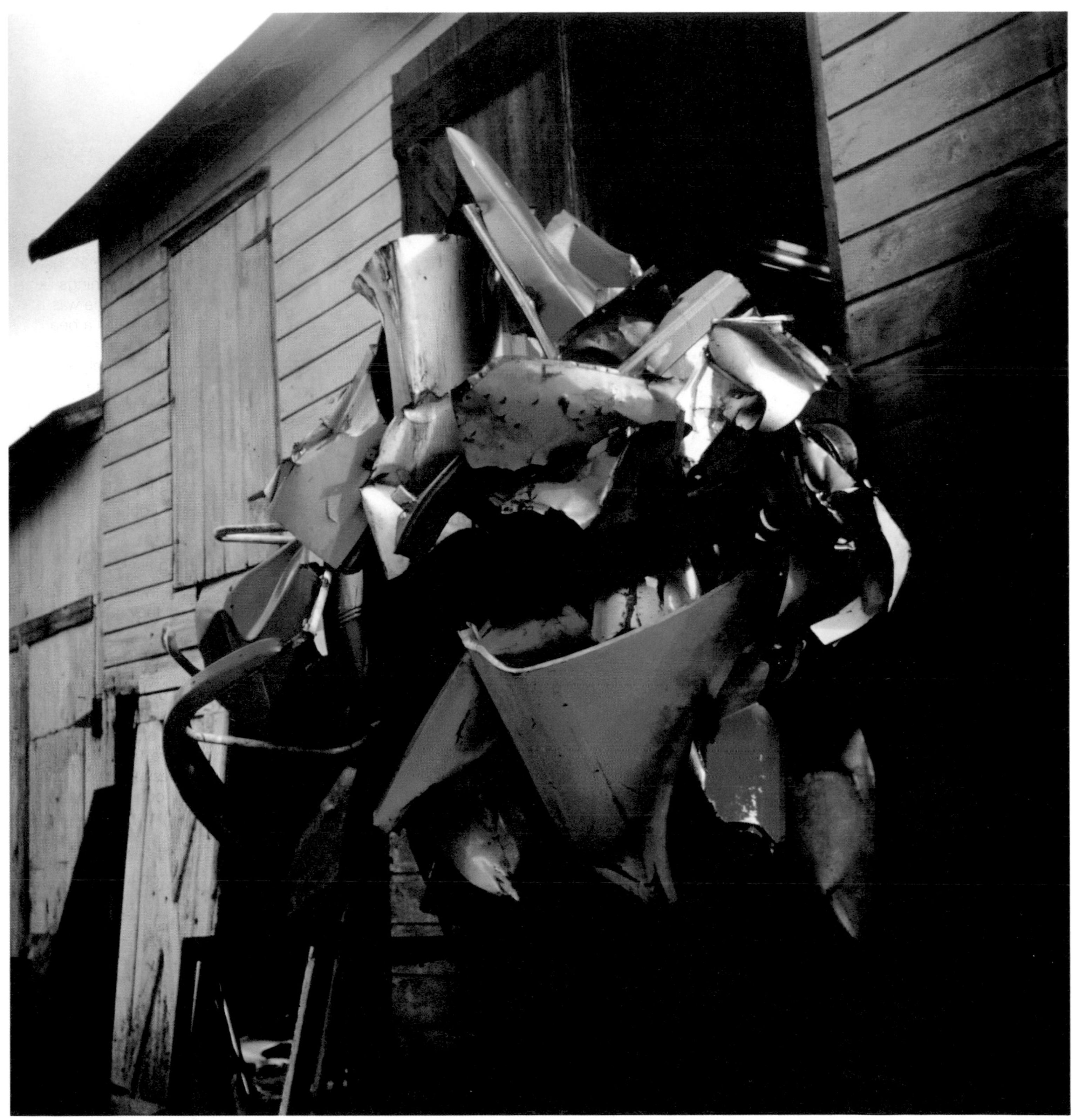

White Thumb, 1960–61 (cat. no. 98)

JS: You were very young when you went into the navy.

JC: I didn't make it in high school; nothing was interesting there. I was interested in music, but I never practiced enough. Actually, what I wanted to do was to get out into the night life. But I did join the navy, in order not to go to jail. As it turned out, it was another kind of jail. They had to whip you into shape; you had to do what they said. I joined in September 1943. I was sixteen. Another fellow and I had left Chicago. We had hitchhiked all the way to Arizona, trying to get to California. But we couldn't get any farther than Arizona. Or, rather, as a matter of fact, we did get to California—Blythe, California, where we got put in the tank one night for vagrancy. I remember that we had gone into a couple of places, asking if we could work for our breakfast, since we had no money, and they had all said no. Then we found the last place in town. We thought, "If we hear the same song from them, we'll still be hungry." So we just went in and ate. Both of us ate all we could eat; the bill came to eighty-five cents. We said, "Well, we ain't got no money." We told our story. The guy says, "If you'd asked, I would have given you something to do, and you could've had breakfast." So that's how we came to spend the night in the tank; the next day they told us to get out of town. So we had to go back to Phoenix. When we got back to Phoenix I saw the sign that says "Join the Navy." Well, I was not going back to Chicago, that's for damn sure, and sure enough I joined the navy, and I got to California. They sent me to San Diego.

JS: Why were you going to California in the first place?

JC: Oh, to seek our fortunes and be movie stars. Turns out, they already had a bunch. I was in the navy for about three years. I was on a small aircraft carrier for most of that time, in the Pacific and in the Mediterranean. We made two round trips in the Atlantic, and two round trips in the Pacific. I was in four different "battles"—the last two were even somewhat close. On the U.S.S. *Tulagi*, CVE-72. I wonder where it is now.

JS: What's memorable about those years?

JC: Oh, not a hell of a lot. It was just more finding out that this wasn't what I found interesting.

JS: Were you thinking about art at that time?

JC: I didn't understand about art until 1948. Up until 1947 or 1948, I thought art was something that you bought in a furniture store. When I got out of the service, I figured I had to get a job doing something, and hairdressing came by.

JS: How did you ever discover that you had a flair for hairdressing?

JC: I don't know. Maybe it just struck me as something that I could do, or it was convenient, right there—something like that. The government supplied education funds for veterans and I was very interested in getting into a certain music school. There was a long wait, and there was no wait at beauty school. Hairdressing was very easy to understand, and I understood it very quickly. I was good at it, except that I was terribly unsociable.

JS: And you worked in beauty shops?

JC: Yes. I could do the job easily, but I wasn't very successful at it. I was sort of ahead of my time, in a sense. Like, if we had a *Vogue* magazine lying around, and somebody saw a hairdo in it, I was the one who could figure out how to do it. When I took my state board tests, I passed the marcelling test with a cold iron.

JS: How?

JC: I had a lady with naturally wavy hair. The inspector didn't notice that the iron was cold. It was that kind of thing that made me figure I didn't belong there. Or when I cut the hair. The examiner said, "Cut this person's hair. I want to watch you do it," and then she turned away. When she turned around again the hair was all cut, but she still said, "When are you going to cut the hair?" I told her to look on the floor. I mean, she didn't know by looking at it whether the hair was cut or not. So if those things can happen, that's not the place you want to be. It was a good job, though, because there was always a need for people who could cut hair, and I could always get work.

JS: How did you go from beauty school to the Art Institute of Chicago?

JC: After I learned hairdressing, I had some more time due me on the Veterans Administration G.I. Bill. Sid Simon was a makeup artist in Chicago, and he started a little makeup school; there were four students. Now, this was before television, you have to understand. This was 1947. There were no jobs for makeup artists, but it was a very interesting class. I went for a year and a half to his classes in makeup, grotesque makeups, mask-making . . . latex had just been invented, and it was a material that was available, so we made molds of our own faces. We'd make grotesque masks on our faces, and then peel off the latex and end up with these very light things that we could put on. After that was over, I took a job teaching hairdressing and makeup in a modeling school. I'd have a morning class or an afternoon class or an evening class, but in between those I'd have two or three hours off, when I'd doodle or try to draw something. *And I couldn't figure it out*. I wasn't figuring it out for myself. Eventually, I met Lucretia Melcher, who had a little studio in a place in Chicago, not far from where I worked. I started going to her art classes. She showed me books and put me through a series of little tests. She thought I was very talented. I remember her saying, "Very good colors," and all that kind of thing. Well, I got very involved in it. I would go home and look at the pictures in the books and I couldn't believe how marvelous they were. I remember thinking, "Where are these people? This is terrific!" Even in bad reproductions you could see the excellence and the high standards involved in this particular occupation. And that's how I decided that finally I'd found my occupation. Art was equivalent to the standard I was looking for, which was why I had rejected everything else, why I had been resistant to everything prior to this.

When I got into the Art Institute of Chicago—this was after another year or two—it was there that I discovered how much art had been going on, and how important it was to the process of finding things out in the world. It was a place where you exercised your faculties far beyond what was demanded of you in regular life. For that reason, I felt very much at home there. I often knew what things were when other people did not know. It was difficult for me to convey my perceptions to others—how I saw such a little thing like a Giacometti sculpture take up so much room it could virtually measure the huge room that it was in. The scale of it! It reminded me of when I was little and stole little ceramic cats from the dime store, because I liked their scale. So one day, when I saw all these little brown clay bodies standing on platforms in the sculpture class, I was astounded. The same model had been used but each person had made his version a little different—just a little bit larger, a little bit fatter, a little bit skinnier—it was so charming, so staggering, and I knew that this was where I wanted to be. I believed it. And then I had to work it out, which I felt was what the job meant. Perhaps art gets done because it's your occupation. It's a very difficult one, as I've come to find out.

JS: At this point, in 1951 or 1952, you had not yet begun making sculpture.

JC: When I found out about sculpture I got very interested in it. When the first year of art school was over, I just continued going there for the summer, and then I went another half-year before I was invited to leave.

JS: Why was that?

JC: Well, somebody was very dumb about something, and I felt I'd had enough. I'd become very interested in the history of art, and I was especially excited about an area in India where they carve columns of people all huddled together naked. There was something fascinating about the spirit of it, so I wrote a paper about it. At that time, a few things hadn't occurred to me. I got a low grade on the paper, much lower than I should have gotten. Their response to it was, "We didn't want that," that it wasn't needed. I asked the heads of the art-history department about it and they blushed; they both got red-faced. It occurred to me years later that they thought I was talking about sex. But I was talking about *fit*, how it all fit together. No one went anywhere in that part of India in those years, no one left town; there was no transportation. So their spirits and whatever they felt life was about had to be contained right there. They carved their art in that spirit, and it showed when you looked at it. But all the art-history department wanted me to do was to analyze its line, color, texture. I said, "Shit, you can do that to *anything!*" Since they took such a bad attitude, I decided I didn't want to be around those people. That's why I left.

JS: And that's the origin of your one-line response, when asked about your sculpture, "It's all in the fit"?

JC: Oh, I don't know. That developed much later, although you can piece all these elements together. Then I went to the University of Illinois for about six weeks. They had a sculpture class, so I went to it. In the sculpture class, there was an active/passive, or equal-opposition, test, where everybody did the same thing. Everyone would make a piece with two hunks of clay, and then they'd polish it for two weeks. Then somebody would come in and tell them whether they'd got the point or not. Whereas, if you did a crab holding an egg, they weren't sure whether you got the point, or how to grade you on it. So I wasn't sure whether you were supposed to make it look like Henry Moore or whether you were supposed to make it look like active/passive.

JS: So art school didn't meet your standards either?

JC: Art school is all right. At that time, the function of art school was to show you the different materials available and how history has shown they're used, in a social setting. If they'd just say some of these things, you'd get through school. I left there because I felt they were inadequate. I felt they weren't teaching the history of art; they could have been teaching the history of what your desk looks like.

JS: In other words, you had no important or influential teachers at that time.

JC: The only time I ever started getting interested in anything, or where I became interesting to anyone else, was when I went to Black Mountain College.

JS: How was Black Mountain College introduced to you?

JC: I learned about Black Mountain from Jerry van de Wiele, a friend of mine from Chicago. He's probably the person I have known the longest who I can still possibly find in New York. Black Mountain was a nice place, very country, mountainy, just east of Asheville, North Carolina—Tom Wolfe's old hometown. Joel Oppenheimer was there, Stefan Wolpe was there; I took a little music course with him. Charles Olson was there, and Robert Duncan; Robert Creeley came for a while, a guy named Wes Huss, who was interested in theater. Actually, Wes liked to sit around and watch everything else go on, as though it were theater. Joseph Fiore, Dan Rice, and Tom Field were artists there.

People came with their families; there were about five students and fifteen teachers. It was in 1955, the final year of Black Mountain College. The school sort of dribbled down to zero after that, and it was time for everybody to split, it was time to make the next move. The attitude of people who went there was that of graduate students, interested in the information and the knowledge that they were acquiring, and having to deal with it on a daily basis. You could start anywhere at any time. You could study everything or you could study nothing. There were some funny work schedules, but they never lasted. Black Mountain had its life. It went through a lot of changes, a lot of different regimes. At its most crowded it had ninety students.

JS: What was your first important impression at Black Mountain College?

JC: It was an essay by Ernest Fenollosa, who had taught English in China in around 1900. He wrote an essay discussing the ideogram as a unit of poetry, in the sense that it said exactly what it said. That's why the ideogram became important. It didn't mean different things to different people, depending on how they felt at the moment; it meant what it meant. It has occurred to me that the cliché is the ideogram of the United States, because the cliché means what it means, and it means the same to the Poles or the Italians or the French or the Germans or the English in the United States. When people came to this country, they brought their own syntax, to which they attached English words, so no one understood anyone else. But when somebody said, "I second the motion," or, "It's too hot to handle," those kinds of things meant the same thing to everyone. That's how the language of the United States came to be based on cliché and slogan, because everyone could understand it.

JS: Would you say that the greatest influence on your work or on your thinking about your work came initially from the poets at Black Mountain?

JC: Absolutely. Not only that, it's still so. At Black Mountain College, everybody read books. You had to read about the Old West, you had to read anything D. H. Lawrence wrote, and Ezra Pound and William Carlos Williams, and detective stories by Dashiell Hammett and Raymond Chandler. All of those were popular. I read these things and when I saw a word I liked, I'd isolate it, I'd write it down. So I had this collection of words that I liked to look at. It didn't matter what they meant, I liked the way they looked. I would look at these words and I would put them together and come up with an image that was unlike anything you could achieve if you didn't do it this way. I remember one line I wrote in which I put together two words: *blonde day*. I'd never thought of a day being blonde. I still haven't, but I liked the way that the connection functioned, and it's a very good example of how I work. I still process stuff in the same way. There is material to be seen around you every day. But one day something—some one thing—pops out at you, and you pick it up, and you take it over, and you put it somewhere else, and it *fits*, it's just the right thing at the right moment. You can do the same thing with words or with metal. I guess that's part of my definition of art. Art is a peculiar madness in which you use other means of communication, means that are recognizable to other people, to say something that they haven't yet heard, or haven't perceived, or had repressed. I get the feeling that I didn't repress what I should have. If I had, I would be a saloon keeper today. But I was constantly dissatisfied; I didn't follow suit when I was told, "You've got to do this, because that's what's required." I walked away. It was very easy. I had a great sense that out there somewhere, there must be some place that I could be, goddammit.

JS: And you found that first at Black Mountain?

JC: Yes, I found it when I went to Black Mountain. Curiously, it's only recently that I've noticed that I'm still making sculpture in the way that I made the poems. I didn't get the point of quite a few of these stories I'm telling you until years later. When I went to Black Mountain, I found that there were other people who spoke with tension, trying to find out what they didn't know. Everybody in those other places had been happy with what they knew. They weren't curious about what they didn't know. Probably the key activity in the occupation of art is to find out what you don't know. To start someplace that's curious to you and delve into it in a common way and come out with an uncommon satisfaction, an uncommon piece of knowledge—that is very satisfying to your nervous system.

JS: I've read some of your poetry. It's intimate, sweet, humorous, passionate. How did you feel about your poetry at the time, and how do you feel about it now? Did you ever want it read or was it only for you?

JC: I'm certain it's all very personal. I don't think I have a body of work, so I couldn't consider myself a poet in the true sense, like Robert Creeley. Creeley is a real poet. Whether it's on a postcard or in the phrasing of sentences, he works with words. He has his own manners and attitudes in that regard. He understands my foam sculpture, but that doesn't make him a sculptor. From having the foam sculpture around, did he understand the wadding technique,

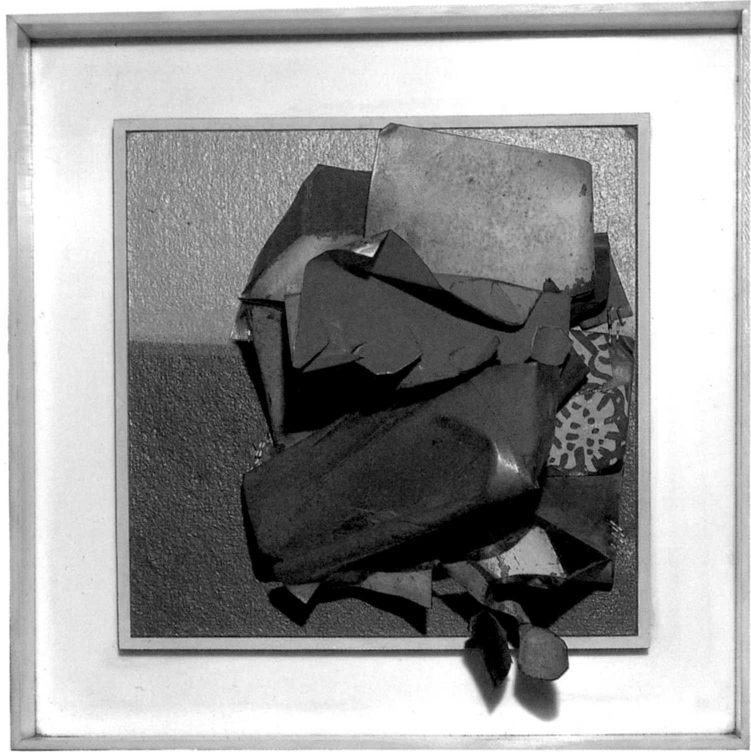

Untitled 1962
Painted tin on Masonite,
13½ × 12 × 7 in. (34 × 30.5 × 18 cm).
Collection Oliver and Jessica Murray, London.

or the compression? Not necessarily. But when he washed the dishes, when he squeezed the sponge and one end of it popped out of the end of his fist, it looked like the sculpture, and he saw that. It was because of the one that he could see the other. He could get an added perception. It's daily life. That's where I get the idea that everybody makes sculpture every day, whether in the way they wad up a newspaper or the way they throw the towel over the rack or the way they wad up the toilet paper. That's all very personal and very exact, and in some sense very skillful on their part, but it is discarded as useless information. But it's not useless. Those little things, like blowing up a paper bag and hitting it so it pops—take it one little step further and do it in slow motion and explore what the resistance of the air in the bag is, and you make something. To me that is very interesting. If there is a body of work demonstrating all these things that come together, that's useful in art history, as a record of the accumulation and development of knowledge in this occupation.

JS: Everyone agrees that no one can crush a pack of cigarettes the way you do, though, John. People are always saving your crushed packs.

JC: They should crush them the way *they* do. I don't crush them the way they do and they don't crush them the way I do.

JS: So your poetry taught you how to put your sculptures together?

JC: The sculptures that I made at Black Mountain were strongly influenced by David Smith. The first piece of Smith's that I saw was at the Art Institute of Chicago. I liked it a lot because it wasn't representing something else, or it didn't seem so to me, and it was a very strange-looking thing; I liked it because it was strange and because I hadn't seen anything like that before. It was nice to be around. The pieces *Clytie* and *Calliope*, *Clytie* especially, look similar to it. In the development of both of those pieces, I found myself working with a certain spontaneity. I was trying to attach the top part of *Clytie* to the lower half, but when I put it in the right place, it connected up in three different places, so *it* told *me* how to put it together. I think in this particular area, in the way I've gone about this, I've led a charmed life. Smith was quite good, I felt, but as I got to know his work better and better, the pieces got smaller to me, and then I started disagreeing with his attitude about a lot of things, and then I thought the work was very flat, but I still liked it a lot. Besides, he looked like my father and we were born about sixty miles apart. He came from Indiana also. That apprenticeship, however, was very good and it was useful for a time.

JS: Some of the early works that you made in New York were small collages of ripped paper, tin, fabric—whatever materials seemed to be at hand. There are quite a few of them.

JC: I saw Al Leslie use a staple gun for his collages and I thought, "Oh, that's the perfect answer," and then all of a sudden collages became very easy, because I could work fast and they would stay where I put them. I had gotten all screwed up by the process of gluing something down, somehow; it interrupted the impetus and they always came out different; it wasn't really tight. They weren't spontaneous because I always had to be lifting them up and gluing them. By screwing around with something that was terribly unimportant, except that it made the materials stay in one place, you lost it. Or I lost it. With stapling, it was boom, boom, boom, boom. And if you didn't want it there later, you'd just rip it off, or rip half of it off . . . use the staple as a barrier to pull against. Then I got to the point where I could hide the staples, or very few would show.

JS: Your first show in New York, in 1958, was with Joseph Fiore at Davida Gallery on Fifth Avenue.

JC: Yes. Everybody from the Cedar Bar attended. It was just a little room, at about Twenty-ninth and Fifth Avenue. I didn't sell anything from that show. The first thing I ever sold, I guess, was *Stiele*, which Howard Lipman bought. I think my share of it was $365. I went right

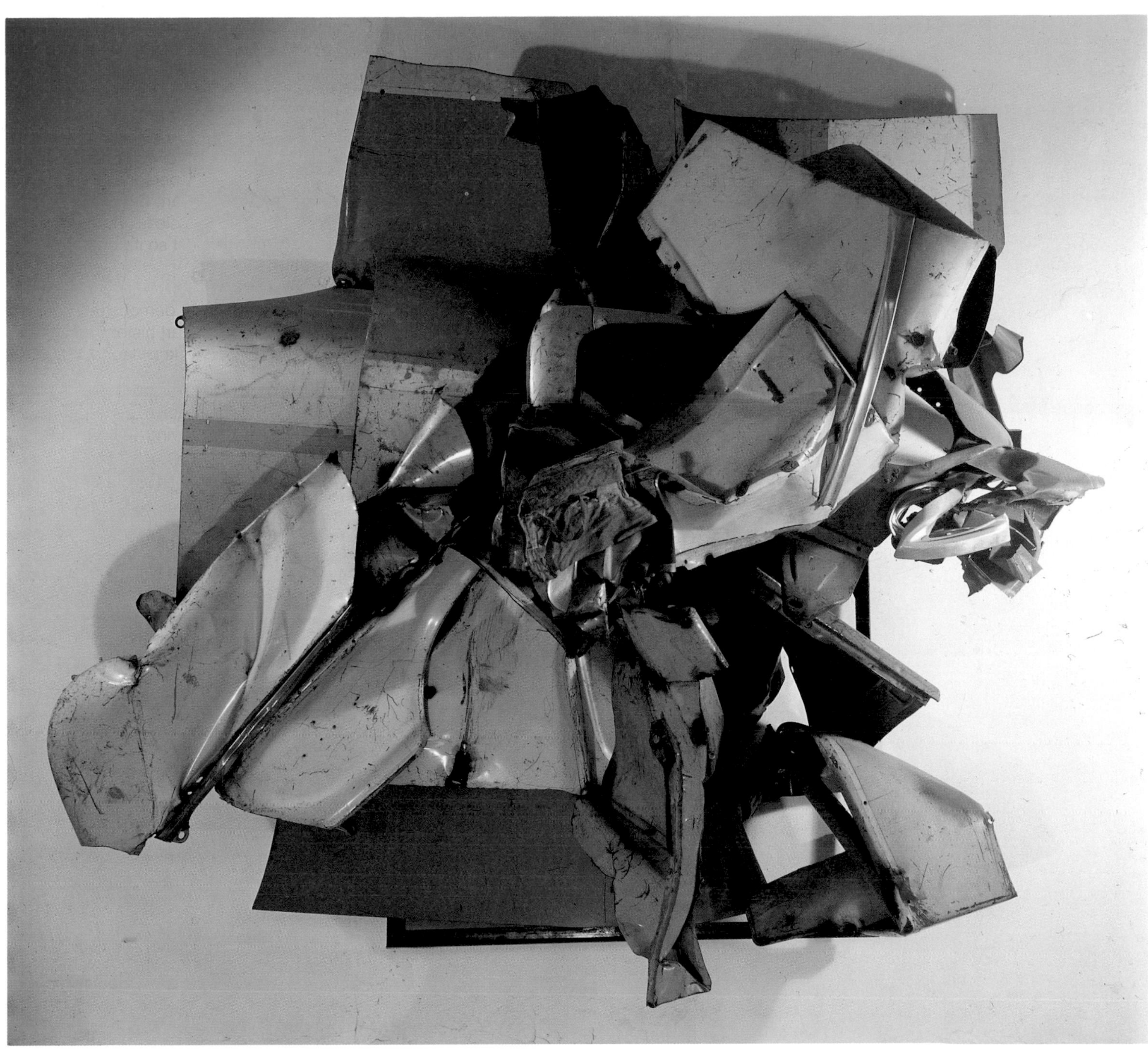

Mr. Press, 1961 (cat. no. 83)

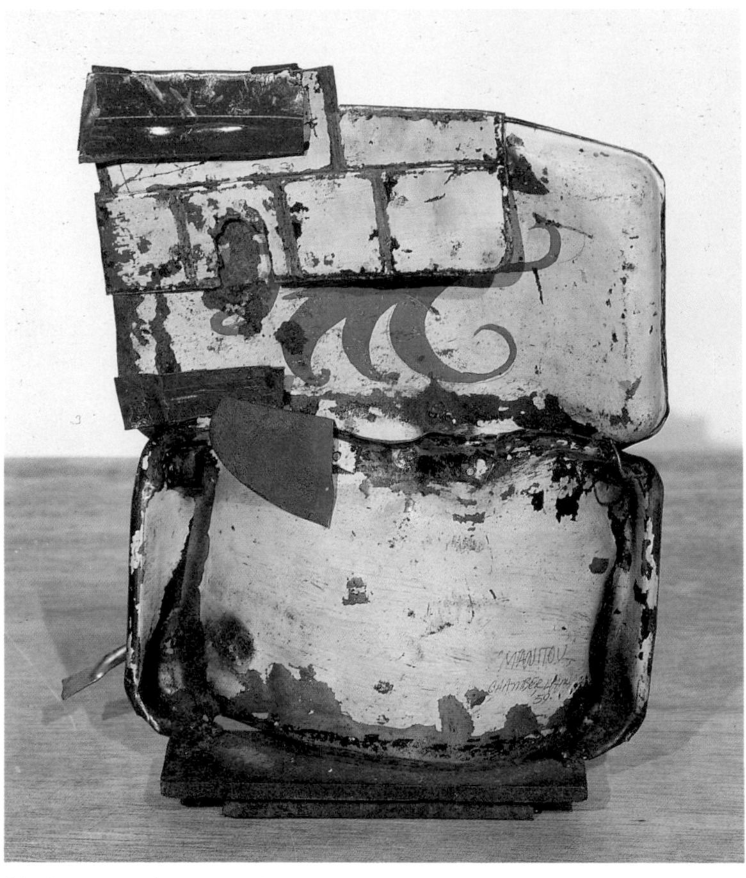

Manitou, 1959 (cat. no. 30)

out and gave it to some guy who was a landlord. He let me in, and the minute he found out I had children, he booted me out. We had moved from Larry Rivers's place in the country to what is known as SoHo now. Actually, the first time I showed was in the Mars Gallery. That's where Richard Bellamy found out what I was doing, and he and Ivan Karp invited me to have a show at the Hansa Gallery. I was not a member of the cooperative, I was just invited. They liked the work—it was something they hadn't seen before. They knew that there was a force involved that was going to have to be seen. But you should quiz them about what they remember or how they remember what went on, because their memories are better than mine, since I proceeded from the time I was about thirty to drink a lot. Those were days when drinking was heroic. At the Cedar Bar, if you didn't drink you were sort of left out. Besides, I was very shy and couldn't speak well; drinking opened me up, and although I didn't speak a lot, at least I opened up enough to listen. I was scared to death and had never met such people in my life, never known that they existed. When I came to New York City, the electricity of the attitudes of all the people around—it was enough to shock anybody half to death. Then I took certain attitudes that were not necessarily correct, but a lot of it had to do with learning how to support my family and take care of things and still be an artist.

JS: This was the heyday of Abstract Expressionism and the Cedar Bar was the center. You are often compared to the painters Franz Kline and Willem de Kooning, because of your use of color and concern for light and surface. How do you feel about being labeled an Abstract Expressionist sculptor?

JC: I'm sure that Abstract Expressionism is where I was intuitively in tune, whether or not I was conscious at the time of what the influence was—or am even now. For instance, it has just lately occurred to me that the comparison of my color to de Kooning's color has a lot to do with the fact that Detroit puts a lot of white in the color that they put in the paint that they mix for putting on cars.

With Franz Kline, it was power. Franz always spoke well, and I always listened to him. Not that I remember a hell of a lot, right now, of what he said, but there was a way that he said things, and he was complete in saying things—his way of talking always amazed me. One time after he had made a little money, he bought a Thunderbird and drove off to Provincetown. In Provincetown he met up with Charles Olson. This story is very nifty for me because they were two of my teachers. They were sitting in the car—and you can imagine Charles, who's six foot eight and 285 pounds, sitting in this little Thunderbird with Franz, who's probably about five foot nine or ten, and they're sitting there, not going anywhere, and the conclusion is: "Well, Charles, I guess there's no place to go." Which I thought was a very crucial line. I don't remember how I even got hold of that story.

JS: This was before the first colored steel sculptures were shown in New York.

JC: When I began making colored sculpture, I had a show with Martha Jackson. It was a two-man show with Alfred Leslie, where he was all over the gallery and I had a little room upstairs. I used to go up there every now and then and sit around and see who would come in. Women would come to the doorway and look in and then recede. I thought that was kind of peculiar. It seemed to me that they were somewhat frightened to go in, or to walk around the sculptures or something. That was kind of interesting.

I was interviewed there by Robert Trout. He kept asking me these silly questions, which we are just now getting around to answering here, twenty-five years later. Everyone always wanted to know what it meant. You know, "What Does It Mean, Jelly Bean?" At that time, I wasn't sure what it meant either, except that it was agreeable to me, but I didn't know "what it meant"; I didn't know any more "what it meant" than Trout did. I thought, why should I tell him what it means? Even if I knew, I could only know what I thought it meant, and if he couldn't figure out "what it meant," then it didn't mean anything to him. This was difficult to say then, I guess. All these things I can say to you now, though I couldn't have said them then.

JS: What prompted you to begin using colored steel?

JC: The early colored sculptures came about when I ran out of the material I'd been working with before, iron rod. For about six months I did some drawings and things like that. I was looking for another material. I was looking for the next way to go. This was in 1957 or 1958. Then, all of a sudden, it occurred to me one day that all this material was just lying all over the place. I saw the material as other people's idea of waste. *Shortstop* was made at Larry Rivers's house, and only years later did it occur to me that I had taken the material from an antique car of his—it was material from a 1929 Ford. So it was an antique, it wasn't throw-away junk. It was years later that I figured out that what I had done was a little presumptuous: to use material of his that very likely had some value to him. Nevertheless I took a fender. I didn't want to use it as a fender, so I drove over it a few times to rearrange its shape, which was the beginning of what I now know as *process*.

In the early sculptures I used anything made of steel that had color on it. There were metal benches, metal signs, sand pails, lunch boxes, stuff like that. For instance, there is a sculpture, *Zaar*, that was titled after a permanent wave. It was made from a green metal bench with a red stripe on the side of the seat. I used a variety of parts. Body shops would cut parts away, and I would choose what I wanted from whatever was in their scrap pile. I remember one junk dealer in Rockland County who had a pile of scrap that seemed like it would never end. As soon as I took some of it away to do something with it, he became concerned that he wasn't getting his due.

I wasn't interested in the car parts *per se*, I was interested in either the color or the shape or the amount. I didn't want engine parts, I didn't want wheels, upholstery, glass, oil, tires, rubber, lining, what somebody'd left in the car when they dumped it, dashboards, steering wheels, shafts, rear ends, muffler systems, transmissions, fly wheels, none of that. Just the sheet metal. It already had a coat of paint on it, and some of it was formed. You choose the material at a time when that's the material you want to use, and then you develop your processes so that when you put things together it gives you a sense of satisfaction.

It never occurred to me that sculpture shouldn't be colored.

JS: Early on, people reacted to your material as violent. You've always said that you appreciated Claes Oldenburg's observation that he understood the sculptures as soft.

JC: I don't know why people think that my work is about violence. Oldenburg got it and they didn't. He understood that there is a softness in the steel material, especially in the steel that covers a car. Suppose I were to respond to people by saying that my sculpture *is* violent, that all they are getting out of one of my sculptures is a reaction to a car crash. Have they ever been in a crash? Do they know what violence really is? If they do, how can the sculpture be violent? It's a selection of material that's processed in another way.

JS: The observation was once made by another artist that changes in Chamberlain sculptures are due to changes in models of automobiles. *Miss Lucy Pink* is a sculpture that could not be made in 1983. It is twenty-one years old; do you think it looks twenty-one years old?

JC: It does look twenty-one years old, but not for the reason you mention. Construction has gotten denser, since then; I put things together differently now; the material is processed differently. I think that I selected those materials at that time for that particular piece because they were pink, all different shades of pink, very close, and not because they came from one automobile. *Miss Lucy Pink* has a sort of a front and a back. I look at the piece every now and then and sometimes it reminds me of somebody who's putting on a good front, but you take a look around the back and her ass is hanging out. That doesn't happen in my sculpture any longer. Now, even in cases where a piece is supposed to be up against the wall, and is

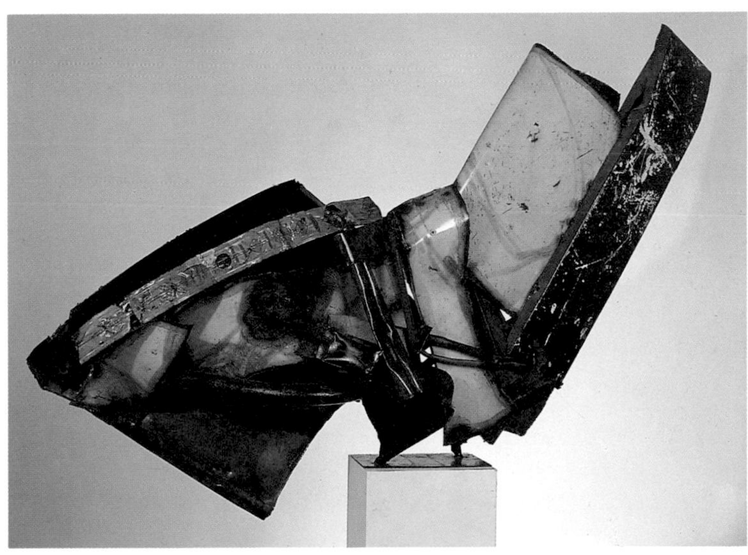

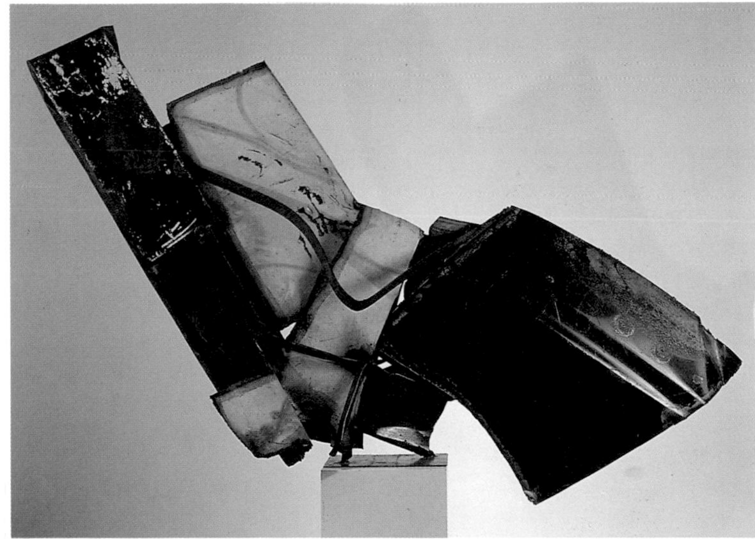

Zaar, 1959 (cat. no. 37, two views)

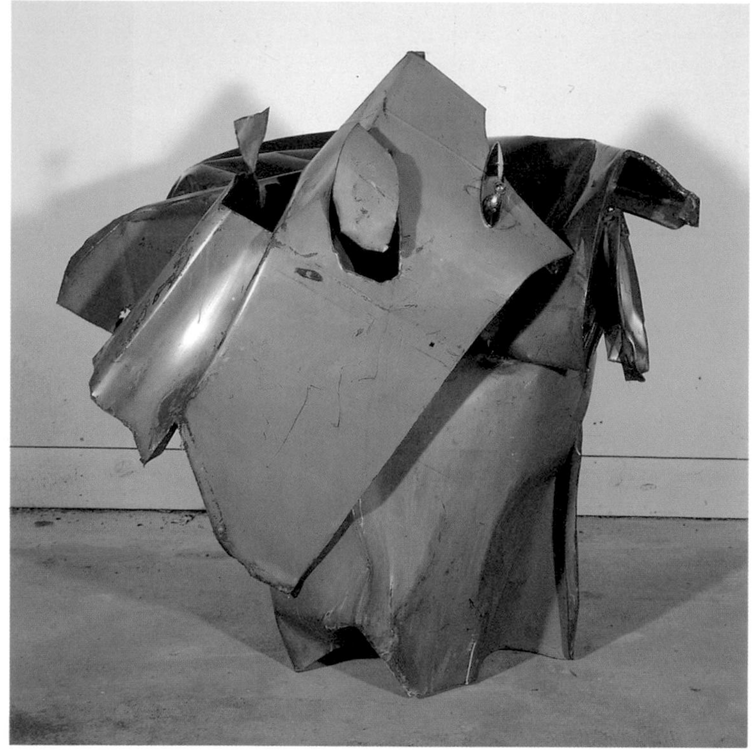

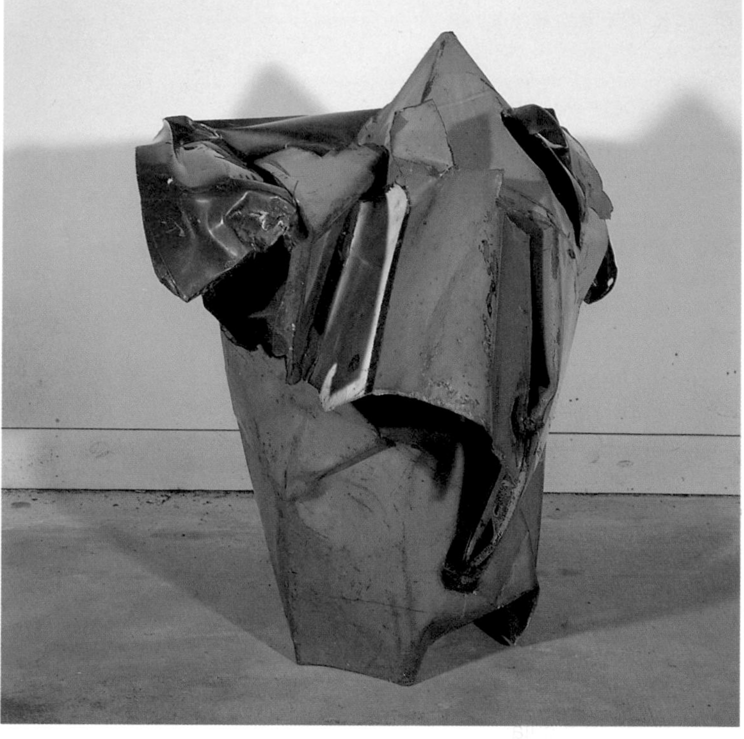

Miss Lucy Pink, 1962 (cat. no. 121, two views)

made that way, I'll still continue working on the back; sculptures with unfinished backs do not happen any longer. Some of the earlier works that were made against a wall and stayed there could possibly be talked about in that manner, as lacking completeness, but they were done that way and that's the way they were left. They were finished at the time, and I don't really remake pieces—if you did that then all of your work would culminate in your attitude of a single year. When you do lots of paintings, or sculptures, or whatever, you leave the old ones alone, because that's where they were in 1963, or in 1974. That's the way you thought and acted and responded in, say, 1980. You can't work on something you made in 1962 in 1983.

JS: How else do you think the work has evolved over the years? What about the changes in your use of paint? The added paint or deliberate removal of paint is very sophisticated now.

JC: Sometimes material accumulates in the studio and I think it looks all right, nice sizes, but say the color's terrible. Say I have three boxes of paint of various colors. It doesn't matter what colors they are, I just open them up at random, shake up the paint, and throw it at the metal. So then they're painted. Well, say the paint job is a little bit corny, for the moment. I'll tell you how I solved this once. I had just come back from the hobby shop, where I'd gotten a bunch of little candy colors, the kind used for painting models. I started spraying them onto the metal pieces, and it perked up the color immediately, by the addition of just a tad of green or a tad of blue. A tad being a small amount. It's a glaze; you put a green glaze over a dull green and it hypes it, or blue glaze changes the blue underneath, yellow gives it a little amber. Or you use it in a graffiti manner, or as though you were writing a foreign language that you didn't really know, so you write as if it were a penmanship exercise rather than communication. That's the way I paint. My graffiti, or what's referred to as graffiti in my work, expresses my thoughts about how painting comes about.

JS: The paint is always applied to individual pieces of sheet metal at random. It isn't applied in a decorative manner after a sculpture is resolved in its fit.

JC: That's right. Say you take one word that's on a page. You like this word; the word looks nice to you. Maybe you don't even care what the word means. But you like the word. You can conjugate the word. If the word is "beauty," it can become "beautiful." Then it can become "beauteous," can't it? Or "beautification." You can play around with it, add to it, or if you want you can take the word apart. You can play with the letters in the word, making anagrams. There's also a way of taking the syllables apart, rearranging the syllables. What I do is not unlike this.

JS: But that has to do with the way you put your sculptures together, each component already having its shape and color. I think it is very important to realize that any paint you apply or any way that you add something to the material happens before you arrange the parts. The paint is never the icing on the cake.

JC: That's not always true, nothing's always true. One time, I was tired of the paint on a piece. I didn't know what to do, so I thought, "Let's do something I've never done." That's always a way to kick off and start something. I said, "Let's sandblast the paint off, maybe the metal will shine." Well, in this case it didn't shine, it became a dull gray. It looked yawn, so instead of blasting off all of the rest of it, I had my assistant blast following certain lines. When you're sandblasting, sand comes out like paint from a spray gun, only when it hits the surface it takes the paint off of it, rather than adding something. I watched this guy do it, sort of directing from a distance, because I didn't want to get near such a thing. I could tell when he was in a hurry and when he wasn't in a hurry, because the line would get wider, or it would get more dense. Whatever he did was fine. At this moment in 1984 there are lots of parts at the studio that have not been processed at all that I could paint repeatedly, in layers, and then sandblast in a similar manner. Then, along the edges of the sandblasting, a multicolored line would appear. It's much the same process as when I made irregular surfaces for paintings and then painted on a lot of colors and then sanded them down so that the underpainting showed through as a line. You can see this in some of the paintings I did in 1970, like *Morgansplit*. The material from a body shop, which is usually resin and aluminum powder, is a very good compound for filling in steel and body-shop repairs. I scrawled this stuff on a flat fiberboard panel to make an irregular surface that looked very much like the ground viewed from an airplane. Like a geographic surface. I'd paint that with maybe thirty colors, or I'd change the color every third spraying. I'd spray and let it dry, and what was left over I'd change by adding something else, and spray that, then sand it, to see what I'd gotten. When you start out there is one color on top, and the top color will also be a lowest color; wherever there is a depression in the surface, that will still be there. So you sand down, and it becomes another surface, but a lot of the buried color—the fourteenth coat, the eighteenth coat, the twenty-second coat—will show up as lines.

JS: Then this is similar in process to the 1963–65 metal-flake paintings?

JC: The format was similar, except that there the paint was mostly clear, and I had to build up an accumulation to arrive at one color. What we are talking about now is the accumulation of lots of colors. The accumulation is then reduced, so only parts of each color come through.

JS: In the *Rock and Roller* series, an important element was that you often forgot which colors were underneath, so that the final contrast of colors was in a random relation, unplanned.

JC: "Random" has a lot to do with people's idea of what they think it's supposed to be. Suppose that all colors are terrific—then how do you choose? You have to choose in what they refer to as "a random manner." Nothing is really all that random, because you always invent new ways of deciding things. The way you decide things this year is not the way you'll decide things next year. There won't necessarily be a great difference, but there'll be a slight movement to one side or the other.

JS: In these particular paintings, the *Rock and Rollers*, what did you see as a departure from the earlier paintings? How did you decide to make these?

JC: I just thought it was a good idea at the time. Something triggered an urge, or I thought, "Let's do something new this year," or I had the paint and I had the spray equipment around, and I didn't have anything else, or I thought I was going to do one thing and I ended up doing another. You start doing something based on what you know, and it leads you into what you don't know. That is one of the main reasons that I use different materials, whether it's sponge rubber or melted Plexiglas or paper bags. I can take a material I'm not necessarily known for or familiar with (and I believe that common materials are the best materials) and rearrange it in a way that's compatible with my particular madness, but that I hadn't seen before. For instance, my work with paper bags started with me blowing up and popping a bag, as everybody has done. Except that then I felt that the air resistance inside the bag was very crucial and was something I didn't know about. I started making the sculptures. Then I felt someone might look at these bags, these little paper sculptures, and think someone had merely wadded them up and forgotten to throw them away. How was I going to retain the delicacy of the paper and the delicacy of the little watercolors I put on them? So I dripped clear plastic resin down in the creases, and I thought that was one of the most marvelous pieces of engineering I'd seen for a long time. That's how it accumulates: you find out something that you didn't know by doing these things and the dumber they seem, the more you get out of them.

JS: By pouring the resin you were trying to contain the twist, or the moment?

JC: I poured it down the creases, so it didn't really show, but it made the bag a little heavier and also made it a little stronger. And it was no longer something someone had forgotten to throw away.

JS: Would you say that the paper-bag sculptures isolate the primary issues of the larger sculptures? Wadding, getting to the cracks, pointing to the internal life?

JC: I only brought them up because I felt I was using a common material in my particular, uncommon way. What's uncommon here is the artfulness. Artfulness has to do with taking a common thing and making an uncommon item. That's where I exercise my skills or my

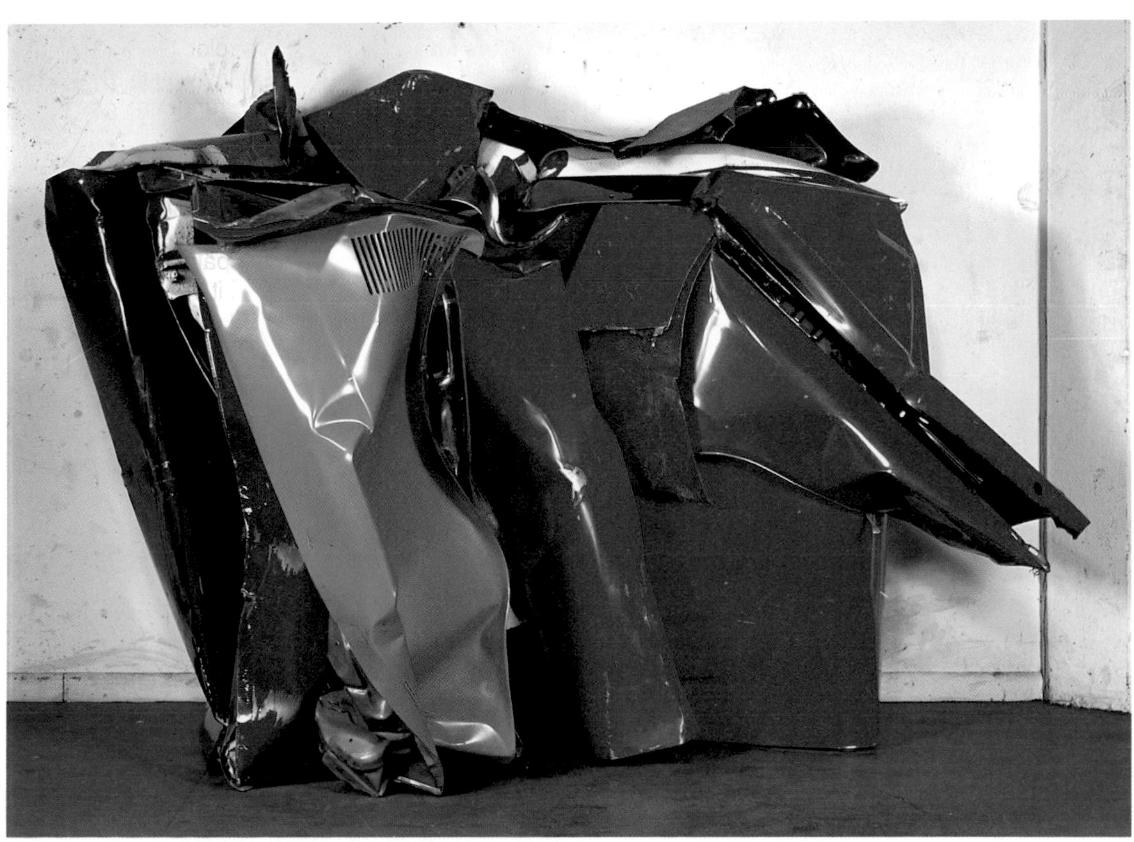

Three-Cornered Desire, 1979 (cat. no. 620)

madness or whatever. It's the difference between just making a product, copying something you happen to like, and going into an idea deeply and using a very common material to bring out a knowledge that has not yet been revealed. It's new information or new knowledge. The perception of this knowledge will produce a certain wisdom. This is in the high tradition of what art is about, or what I feel it is about. How I feel about it changes from minute to half second sometimes.

I'm somewhat proud of having taken a certain amount of time off from working in the way that I was accustomed to, with the materials I was familiar with, and instead doing things in a manner that was not customary as far as what my work looked like. But if you really look at these pieces, you'll see that they still look like my work. Using car metal is fine, but the sculptures are not car crashes and they're not violent. Perhaps there was a violence in me that produced these things that then became much more serene and soft. Perhaps I wasn't happy with a certain softness at a given time. Perhaps they appear violent to people, but I prefer not to think about that as much as I think about the poetics and the processes. I prefer to think about how art occurs by approaching an idea with an interest that then disappears into what's emerging next, something unknown. What I don't know is what I'm after. Whether it's 1957 or 1987.

JS: Back to the paintings, from 1963 to 1965. Was there any conscious adherence to, or involvement with, the minimal art of that time?

JC: As far as a minimal phase, it wasn't so minimal. Each of the paintings contains about one hundred coats of paint. Art is not minimal only because there is not a great deal of garbage involved in it. I was interested in an accumulation of layers of paint, an accumulation to make color. I was interested in taking a can full of clear glaze and dumping a teaspoon of color into it and then painting and painting, maybe changing the color a little bit or not changing it at all, but painting and painting it. The paint dried almost immediately. It took fifty coats before I got a color. In the metal-flake paintings, the image of nine squares came from a template I found somewhere that I liked because it had the number nine (a square-root number) and it was square and it had a particular fascination for me which I probably still don't know all the components of. I used it to let these squares try to ride in the middle of the painting. By "middle," I mean between the upper surface and the surface of the support. I'm not sure that I accomplished that. Are these squares riding within the paint? I wanted to make them complementary to the main color, as I saw it. I used the base color up to that moment, as an undercoat for the colors of the squares. I think I made about fifty of these paintings. At different times I worked on about twelve at a time. Some were made in Topanga Canyon, some in Embudo, New Mexico, some in New York. I still have the template and I know exactly where it is. And whether or not I found out enough about them is something else, but for the most part it's an experiment that could go on.

I made eight larger paintings, each forty-eight inches square, using a similar idea. I once counted five components in those paintings: there was the field, there were two painted bars and then two chrome bars that stood up. But if you counted everything going all the way across, you could count up to thirty: thirty different changes, thirty different notations—how the light struck, how the light changed the field or changed the painted bar, then the bar itself and the reflection, and so on. You take five parts and make interchanges that multiply by six—although you have to add light as a sixth component, I guess.

JS: During this time you had moved out of New York again, to California.

JC: In 1963 [my wife] Elaine and the children and I moved to Topanga Canyon, where we had this beautiful little house on the bluff, overlooking the Pacific, with marvelous trees and a little yard and a little garage where I had my studio. We lived there in peace. That's where I had one of Warhol's *100 Campbell's Soup Cans* paintings and an aluminum Frank Stella painting from 1959 or so. A guy came to the house one day when we were about to go out, and wanted to rent it for a while. The man and I got into a forty-five-minute discussion, except that he hardly said anything. I rambled on at him because he had said he didn't like the Warhol painting. I went through repetition and print-making techniques and common object, blah blah blah, and he said, No, that wasn't it, no, that wasn't it, and no, that wasn't it, and finally I said, "Well, the only thing I can think of is that you don't like Campbell's soup," and he said, "Yeah, that's it." That was the house that neither wives nor children took away from me, but Ronald Reagan and the state of California. They wanted the land back. If your house happened to be on the land, tough. That was the place where *Madam Moon* and some of the first painted sculptures were done, as well as some of the small paintings in acrylic lacquer.

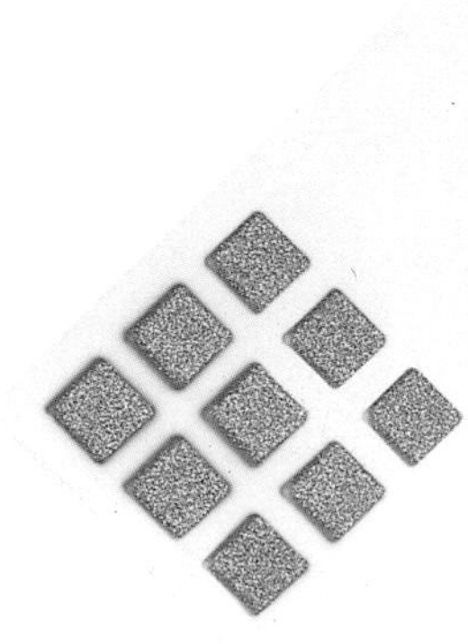

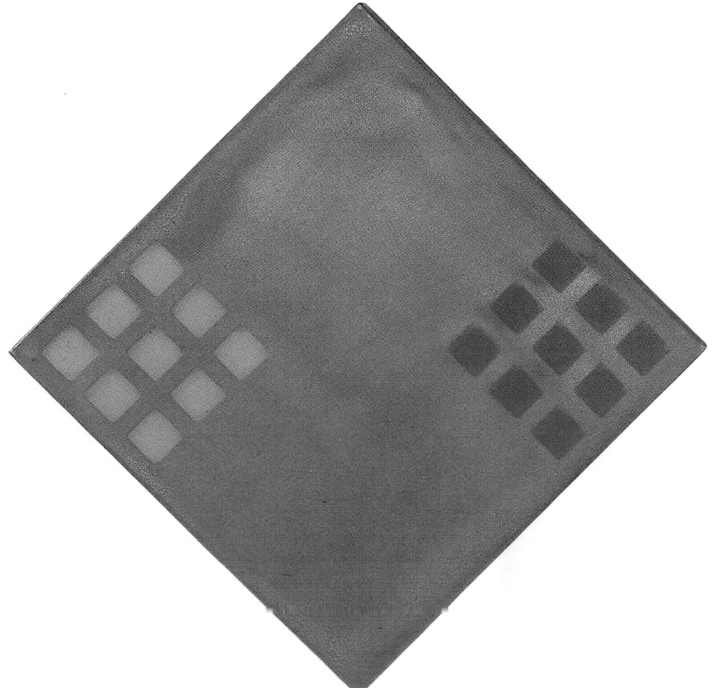

JS: John, you hardly ever make drawings and if you do they are independent of the sculptures. There was one exception to this in 1966, when you made a series of drawings based on a french curve.

JC: In 1966 I made a series of sculptures in New Mexico that I thought was the biggest flop I'd ever done. I started doing drawings with a french curve. Out of the french-curve drawings, which I thought were terribly successful, I tried to make sculptures that resembled the drawings of the french curve—the attitude or the sense or the vision of them. Then, as I remember, I spent all my money working with materials, and the sculptures were some of the worst sculptures I'd ever done in my life. I used fireplace screening and rod for the forms. Then the forms were plastic-coated and covered, and then I painted them and glossied them and added bits of chrome and things like that. It was as if I were making a product instead of a sculpture. On the other hand, I did learn that my particular way of making sculpture first and the drawing second turns out always to be a good idea for me.

JS: But directly after these sculptures you came up with the terrific idea of tying foam and making instant sculptures.

JC: Later that same year I spent a couple of months out at Virginia Dwan's beach house in Malibu, and one day toward the end of September, or in October somewhere, a month before a show was scheduled at her gallery, I made something like thirty small sketches, each of them three, four, five, maybe six inches in any given direction, of squeezed, tied sponge—small pieces that became very indicative of a way to go. It had to do with a certain treatment of a material that from my point of view was engaging. I wanted to do a sculpture that was quick, in a different material from what I'd used before, and instant sculpture was the result. When I showed these works to the gallery, the show was postponed a month. Even later, everyone thought I was very frivolous when I made the foam sculptures; everyone thought that they were too easy. On the other hand, I was terribly impressed with the idea that I could make a sculpture in five minutes, and I felt good about the fact that no one had ever made such a sculpture.

As it turned out, later I went out and did them, but larger. Bought some foam rubber and some knives, and cut up the foam and squeezed it and tied it with lassos. A couple of people came and helped. The idea was that a certain amount of foam was taken, and as the lasso went around the midsection, someone pulled at the lasso while I folded and tucked. When it was all squeezed as far as I wanted it squeezed, either the sculpture made it or it didn't make it. It could simply be untied, and something else could be done, or another piece could be added—there were various immediate solutions and combinations. I felt they were a huge success artistically.

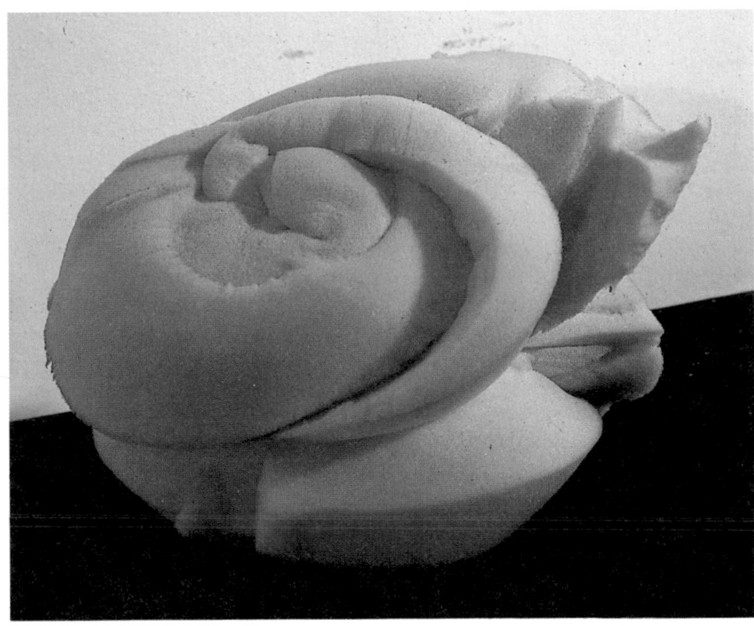

Untitled, 1979 (cat. no. 627)

Opposite left:
Raindrops 1965
Auto lacquer and metal-flake on Masonite,
17×17 in. (43×43 cm).
Collection Thordis Moeller, New York, New York.

Opposite right:
Four Seasons 1964
Auto lacquer and metal-flake on Masonite,
17×17 in. (43×43 cm).
Collection Thordis Moeller, New York, New York.

Below left:
Righteous Brothers 1965
Auto lacquer and metal-flake on Formica,
12×12 in. (30.5×30.5 cm).
Collection Thordis Moeller, New York, New York.

Below right:
Ray Charles 1963
Auto lacquer and metal-flake on Masonite,
12×12 in. (30.5×30.5 cm).
Collection Thordis Moeller, New York, New York.

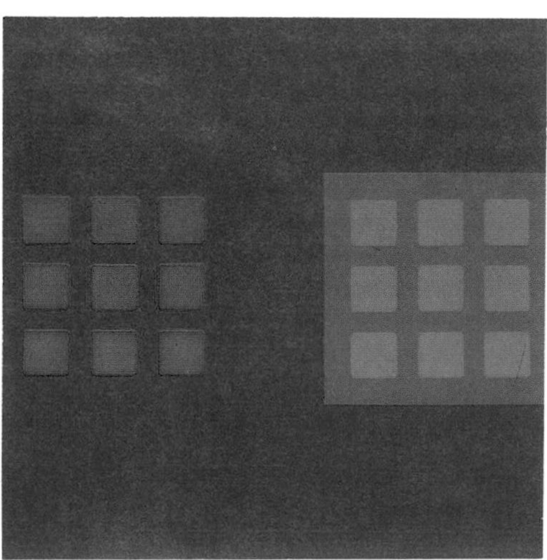

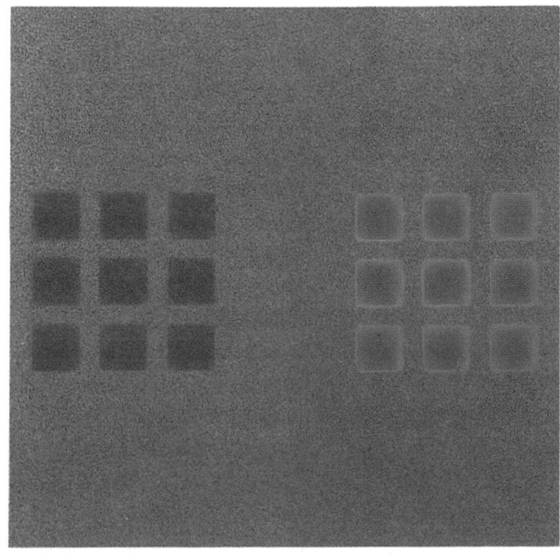

JS: And you continued the foam pieces when you returned to New York. Friends remember the studio you shared with Neil Williams being filled to the ceiling with foam.

JC: In the second series of foam sculptures the combinations of the foam itself became a little more complicated, so that instead of just one piece, there were two and three pieces, and some were inserted in the middle, so that the squeeze produced another kind of effect. As the cinching got tighter, or if the pieces were larger, we'd need two lassos (since the lasso itself would not stretch or shift) so that we could make one end of the foam or one part of it tighter than another. Another lasso would go somewhere else and you'd end up pulling on both as you tightened, to get a full-circle band around the foam.

JS: The foam pieces are very fragile and very vulnerable, which perhaps explains why there was such a reluctance to appreciate them at first.

JC: The nature of the material is such that light, air, oxygen, and so forth tend to disintegrate it. The only factor in this that people might shudder at in terms of maintenance is the fact that it deteriorates faster than cell tissue. The material evokes a relativity, so that humans reject it if it deteriorates faster than they do. That's how I look at it, anyway.

By the way, urethane foam is a plastic product and it's measured by the size of the cell; this is exactly how it's referred to by the manufacturers. I usually use the middle-resistance foam for the couches, which is to say, the formula for the cell that's between the extremities, between a very soft foam and Styrofoam.

I started the couches in about 1969, when I was living in a penthouse on Twenty-third and Madison, about the same time I was making what's become known as the *Penthouse* series. It was during this time that I cut one of the pieces of foam that had been in the Dwan show in order to make something to sit on. I cut it in two and ended up with two pieces that were somewhat at a slant; put together, they looked like a piece of the beach. This was my first couch. Later I made seats and buckets and depressions where you could jump in and jump out, roll in and roll out.

JS: You were very sure about the success of the couches from the beginning.

JC: At first I thought that the couches were so great that I was sure I would become an instant millionaire. I have not discovered one person who dislikes them. People have kept the couches for years, they're constantly being used and people go right through them. I've felt that some of them could have been more important to the space that they were in, but others were exquisite in their locations. The couch that I did for the Guggenheim for my show in 1971 was a very good example. I had always felt that the rotunda in the Guggenheim was a very difficult place to put a work of art, and I had always secretly wanted to do something that exercised the entire space of the rotunda. That couch did. It was twenty-five feet long, approximately seven feet wide and very low to the floor—I imagine about thirty inches—and was of the softest material I could buy. It was right in the middle of the rotunda and when anyone just flopped in it they were horizontal and their gaze went to the top. It was sort of like an inverted T square, where the crossbar of the T was the bottom and your gaze or your view ran to the top. There were two television sets, one at either end, with videotapes of friends of mine playing music at Larry Rivers's house. The two television sets became somewhat like earphones or bookends. The televisions themselves were horizontal. The couch was horizontal. At that point, the televisions were just one more unit to capture you in the couch itself. Then, because of the nature of your posture in it, which was horizontal, any time you opened your eyes you were looking straight at the ceiling, or to the top of the rotunda. People fell asleep in it. The other marvelous thing was that they cut their initials into it (this was before I insisted that the couches be covered).

The couch that was at Westkunst, *American Barge*, is nearly forty feet long, twelve feet wide, and four feet high. It also has two television sets, one at each end. There is a fifty-minute tape of American commercials, of which twelve are fake. The twelve are "Saturday Night Live" commercials for products that do not exist, but poke fun at those that do. The tapes for the television should always be something with no beginning and no end, like a shot of a fireplace, or weather patterns for a certain area in a given month, or commercials in America in 1979.

JS: Do you consider the couches and barges furniture or sculpture?

JC: I think they are sculpture because I think they do more for you than furniture does.

JS: The couches are made specifically to relate to their locations or, in some cases, to an individual, the owner of a couch.

JC: In less public places each couch is a very special commission for a very special person. I need to be in the place where it's going to be for a little bit of time in order to decide quite thoroughly what to do. I investigate the egress and entrance so that I can order the right blocks of foam. The blocks are glued and tied together and then they are carved out. To make a couch in a specific place I have to include the individual's particular requirements, such as whether its height is right for his or her manner of living. People are usually astounded at how marvelous they are.

The couches are pieces of furniture that excite a particular kind of attitude about posture, and create multiple seating arrangements at the sixth-grade level. I feel that's like the old picket fence or gate you had when you were a child; when you grow up and look at it again, you can't believe the scale. That's how scale becomes known, that's the kind of thing scale is about. The couches have to be large. They're also catchalls, whether for you or your friends, your money, dumping your pockets, magazines, newspapers, clothing, sheets, blankets, pillows.

JS: You spent most of 1968 making films. It seems to me that you make films the same way you make sculpture. You accumulate material, choose bits from it, and collage or fit parts together—and in the outcome color is always an important element. What was your motivation for working with film?

JC: The sculpture has to do with moving industrial materials around and processing them. In the movies, the process involved collaborating with people, which is very difficult. In *The Secret Life of Hernando Cortez* the cast was just friends of mine who were fooling around with notions of conquest. Andy Warhol was making some of these dumb movies also.

JS: From 1967 to 1969 you began the galvanized-steel pieces. I believe *Norma Jean Rising* was the first one.

JC: The galvanized sculptures began with fabricated boxes; they were something like forty-two inches high, eighteen inches deep, maybe twenty-eight inches wide. They had the same proportions as the cigarette packs I'd been crushing when I sat around in bars, drinking a lot and making sculpture out of cigarette packs as we emptied them. This was another instance when the "drawings" were made first, but in this case they weren't drawings on paper: I used small boxes. It was very much like taking small pieces of foam and tying them. I had the galvanized boxes built in Manhattan. I found a compactor that I could use on White Street, and I took the boxes there and crushed them and popped them and then took them back to my studio. I had a studio on Thirteenth and First Avenue then. The only thing I can remember there was that the elevator operator who saw the boxes go in straight and come out somewhat smashed said they looked a hell of a lot more interesting going out than they had coming in. So I felt that perhaps I might be on the right track. As one American to another.

JS: Were the boxes closed on all sides?

JC: No, they were open on one side.

JS: And the boxes were all exactly the same size?

JC: I don't remember, but I think that's probably true. When the pieces went together, there were sets of two, three, or four of these boxes, rather than single boxes.

JS: How did you arrive at the decision to use this material.

JC: I was tired of using automobile material, because the only response I ever got was that I was making automobile crashes and that I used the automobile as some symbolic bullshit about our society. All of a sudden sculpture was the only thing that was supposed not to have color in our society. The fact that all this material had color had made it very interesting to me. But the more interested I got in it, the more everyone kept insisting it was car crashes. Since nobody got it, I grew bored with the whole idea and thought I would do something that had no color in it.

JS: So it was a conscious decision to abandon color. This material was also a lot thinner, a lot more malleable.

JC: It had to do with wadding something up, without color, and without being a goddamn car crash. It seems no one can get free of the car-crash syndrome. For twenty-five years I've been using colored metal to make sculpture, and all they can think of is, "What the hell car did that come from?" Who gives a shit what car it came from?

JS: A bit later you made a piece out of a discarded Donald Judd sculpture, or you used rejected sculptures by Judd as scrap for your pieces.

JC: Judd had some pieces made of stainless steel. They were large boxes that had been damaged by the usual idiots transporting things around and Donald, as you know, is very particular about these things. They have to be just so, otherwise they're not his. I hired a big truck and made my way up to Great Barrington, Massachusetts, where Micky Ruskin had a small ranch, or farm. I dumped them there, and tried to use the truck to run over them a few times, but that didn't work. Nothing happened. I didn't get all that excited about it, nothing really came of them. I don't even know where they are anymore. But nothing really happened.

JS: But there exist a few pieces made of stainless steel. *Tippecanoe* is stainless and galvanized steel.

JC: Is it? If you say so.

JS: Well, it must certainly be made from one of those Judd boxes.

JC: Let's say yes, because I'm sure that it will make a big difference to somebody if we say yes.

JS: In fact, somewhere there's reference to one sculpture with stainless-steel parts that was outside the Guggenheim during your retrospective in 1971.

JC: No, the piece that was outside was a black-and-white piece that might have had stainless in it, but as far as I remember, it was a piece called *N.D.W.* That's Neil Williams's initials. His middle name is D.

JS: The next group of works to appear are the Plexiglas pieces. Where were these made and what were the circumstances necessary to make them?

JC: They were just an extension of the galvanized boxes. I made them in California, in East Los Angeles. I can't quite remember who made the boxes, but I do remember renting a large oven, a walk-in oven. The temperature had to be about 295 degrees. Then they were melted and I had to go in at that heat and take them out. The idea of it was that they would melt and collapse on themselves, and you had to play with them at that moment. When you took them out of the oven, into a lower temperature, they would stiffen. After that they'd have to go back in the oven at a lower temperature, in this case 160 degrees, where they'd have to sit for twelve hours to anneal. Then they were transported back to the studio, which was actually back to Larry Bell's place, or someplace in Venice, close by there. As I remember, they were unsatisfactory. I wanted them shot or coated in Larry Bell's vacuum coater. Well, as it turns out, they needed to be superclean, and they were difficult to clean because of their irregular shapes. Although Larry did shoot them, he wasn't terribly interested and so we only shot them once instead of three or four times. I think

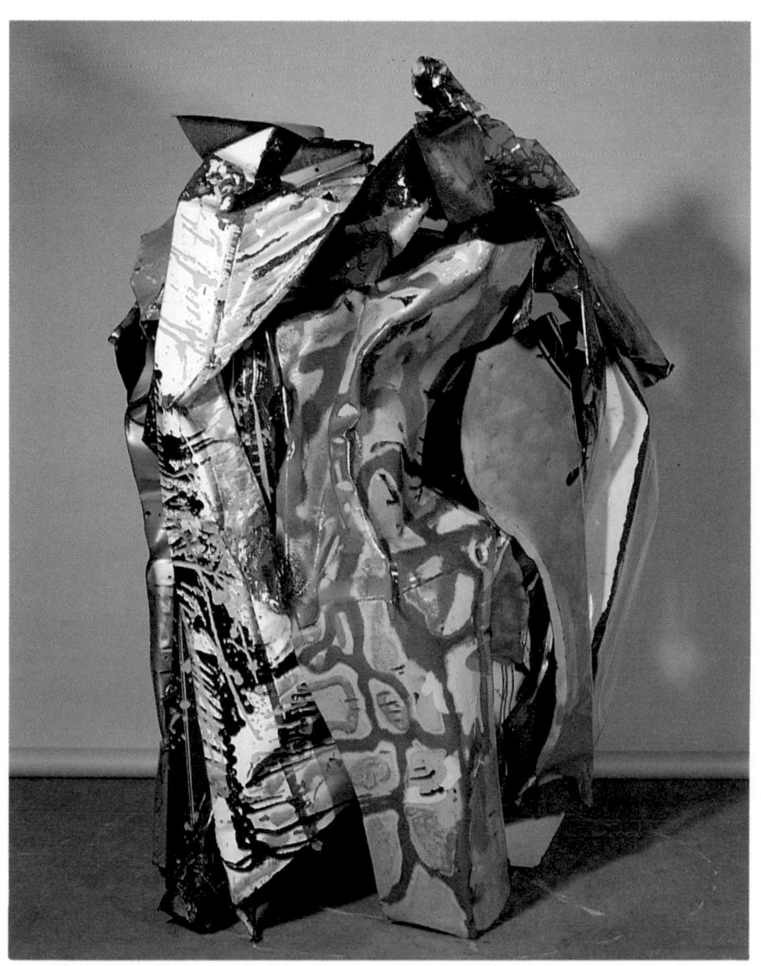

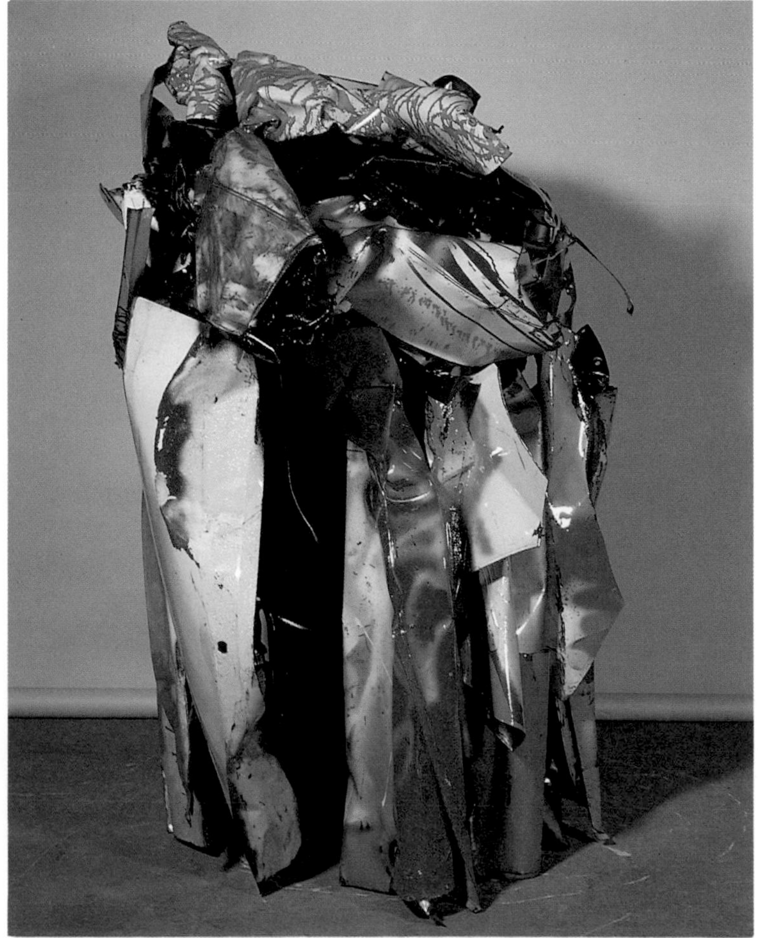

Bent Tynes, 1983 (cat. no. 714, two views)

the coating was quartz and aluminum. They were very expensive to make and there was no real market for them, nobody wanted them. They were too large, actually; that was one of the things I found out. If I'd had the money to go ahead, I probably would have made them much smaller, so that they would have been easier to handle. We would have probably seen the same thing, and would have got a better run for our money on the second run. Actually, it would have been the third run, after we had gotten the bugs out of the second run; the third run would probably have been fairly good sculpture. But this is hindsight. Few of the pieces exist anymore, though there are several examples that show what a good idea it was. It didn't go far enough as a body of work. Nothing makes it unless it's a body of work.

JS: You began with about thirty boxes, each corresponding in dimensions to a pack of Lucky Strikes. This was the same way you started with the galvanized-steel pieces, correct?

JC: Yeah, but that's just a starting point. I was working in exotic materials that have just arrived in the last fifty years. I did not let the material transcend my madness, but let my madness work around the exoticism of the material, the medium.

JS: And you continued this foray into other materials with the aluminum-foil sculptures of 1972–73.

JC: In 1972, 1973, and part of 1974, perhaps, I tried stapling large sheets of heavy-gauge aluminum foil together to make huge bags. Then I would pull them in and wad them. It was an extension of the paper-bag series, but these were much larger, and of a different material. In order to make them harden and stay where I finally put them, I would make two bags, one inside the other, laminated with a resin. In other words, I had to make the sculpture between the time that we got the resin in and the bags made, and the time that the resin set. So I had something like thirty minutes to make a sculpture. Since the bags measured anywhere from twenty to thirty to forty feet in length, they could be considered quickies. I made the last foil sculptures while I was in Eugene, Oregon, in 1974. By the way, all of these methods, whether paper, glass, or foam, are wadding techniques that were peculiar to the materials themselves. They were peculiar to my peculiar madness about scale and the manipulation of these different materials, and they're all quite successful, although commercially they were not successful. There was not really a large enough body of work of any of them, but there was enough to indicate that a large body of work would be valuable. It's necessary for me to explain how I feel about that.

There are two exceptions to my seven-year sabbatical from working with colored steel. At the end of 1969 I went to Chicago for a month with the specific idea of making black-and-chrome sculpture. When I got there, it seemed as though they'd just had an enema of white metal parts, it seemed as though they must have had large sales of kitchen products—refrigerators and washing machines and dryers; the parts seemed to litter the highway even—they were just everywhere I went. It seemed I had to switch to white-and-chrome. Which I did. So much for the anticipation. I did ten or twelve sculptures in that month. I thought some of them were quite successful, and all were sold; two were even stolen. Then, in 1972 I went to Amarillo, Texas, for six months. I made something like twelve pieces there in six months, very large; I think they still exist.

JS: What then made you decide in 1974 to return to colored-steel auto-body parts?

JC: I resumed work with colored steel when my friend David Budd said I owned that material. And in a way I felt that I did. I was convinced that it was a very good idea for me to go back to it, and coming back to New York to live, I was ready for it. Nobody else seemed to be using the material, and it had been piling up again in all the body shops.

JS: I'd like you to talk about how you make the sculptures, because most people don't know what "it's all in the fit" means. Many people don't know that in your sculpture, each separate part of each

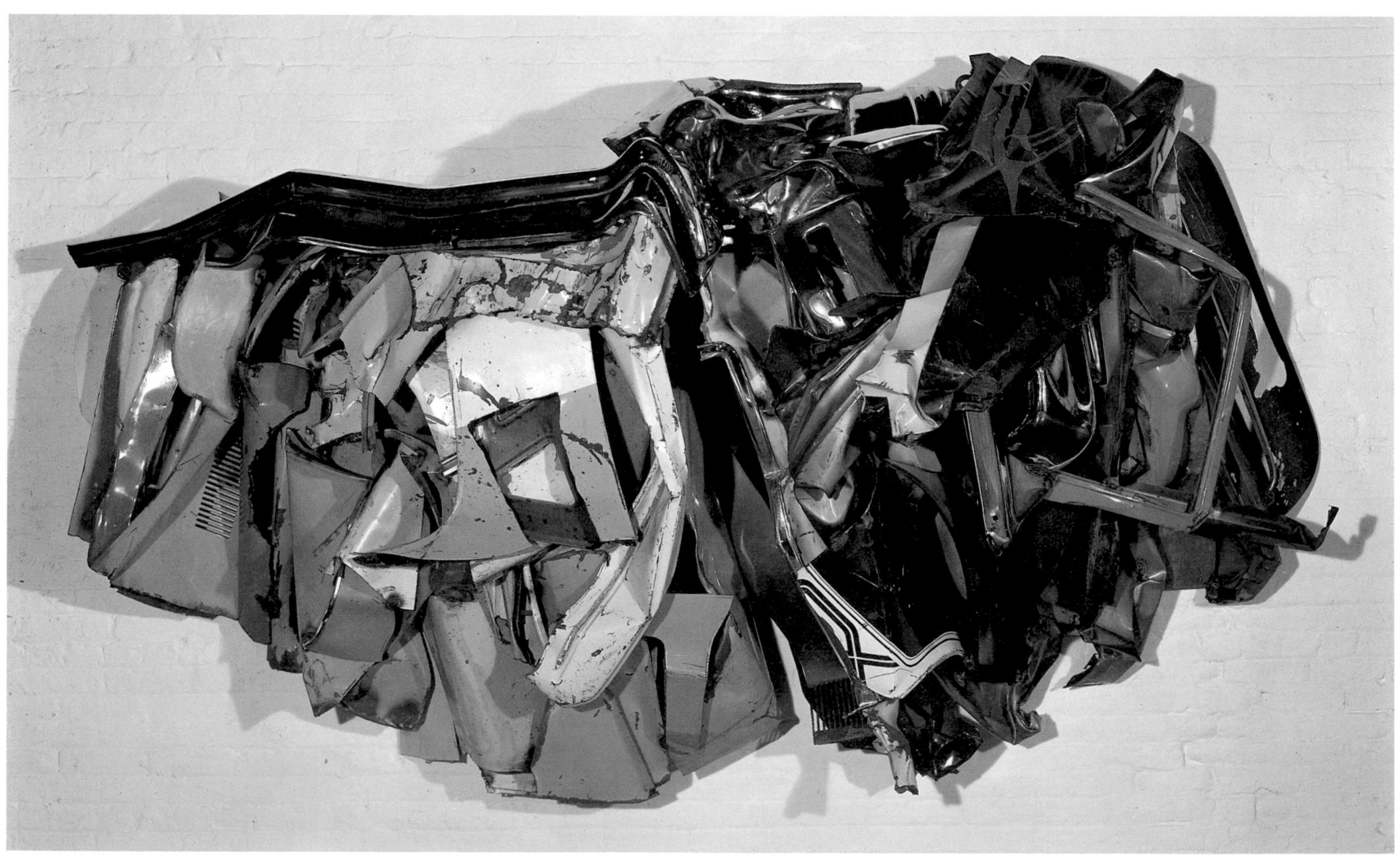

White Thumb Four, 1978 (cat. no. 591)

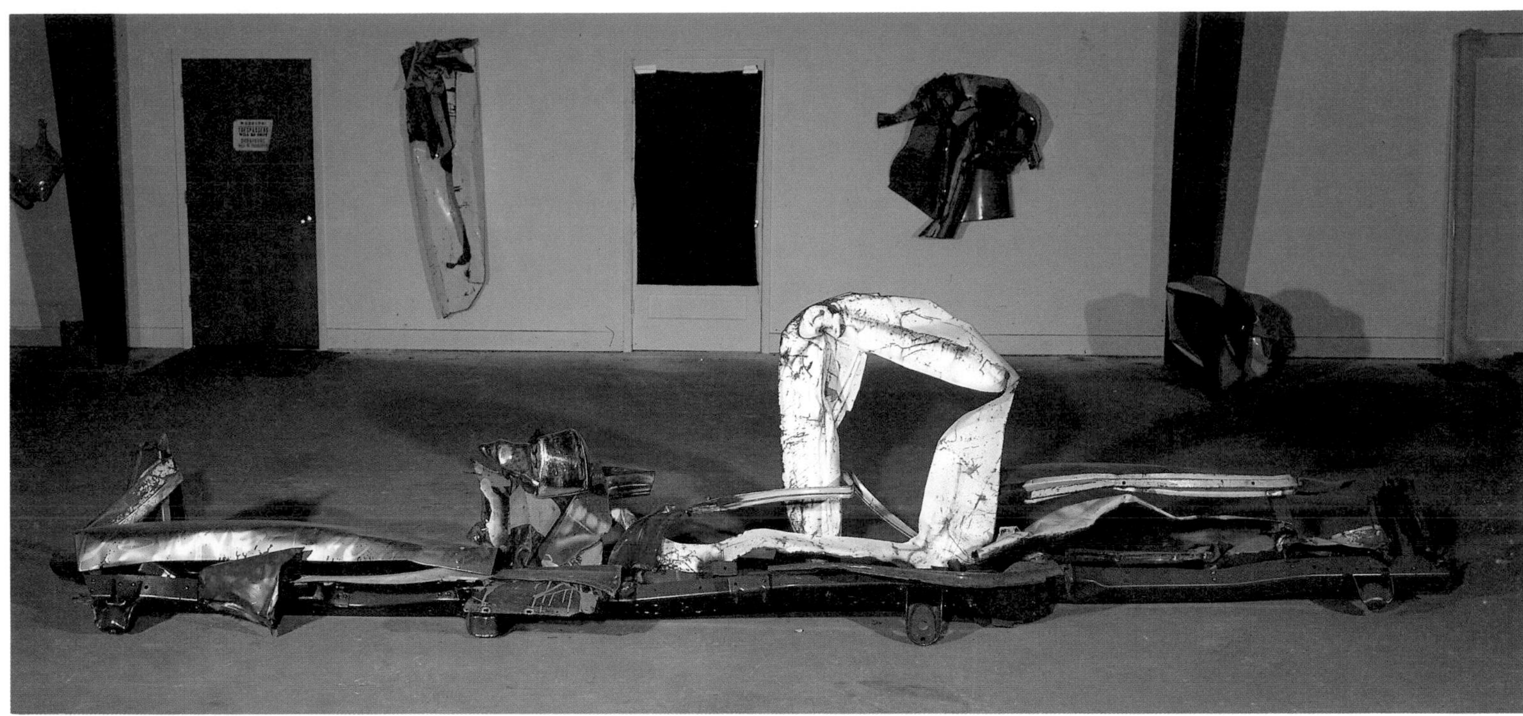

Gondola Charles Olson, 1982 (cat. no. 671)

element fits together with the rest in a certain way; each part is held together by the other parts. The welding is not necessary to hold the pieces together; it is done when the piece is finished, as a reinforcement.

JC: The welds are necessary, otherwise you couldn't move the sculptures. However, that doesn't mean that the parts don't fit together. They do, but in order to keep the thing together in one place, you have to weld it. Welding also makes it one piece of steel. I'm a collagist. A collagist fits things together. It's not difficult to understand.

JS: What's important about the method is that in your work none of the pieces are added as extra little lines or extra bits of color for effect. Each part has to fit. If it fits it stays; if it doesn't it goes.

JC: OK.

JS: The large wall pieces that you were making in 1960 and 1961, such as *Mr. Press* and *Spiro*—those started with a framework.

JC: I didn't know much about what I was doing then. I didn't want to lift something in order to put a framework behind it. Those were the early times: I couldn't weld well, and the frame was a guide, or a help. I still do it in a sense, but only to add strength, only because when it goes out into a public space it has to be strong and put together well. It has to hold up and be more than what it appears to be to most people, which is a piece of junk. The people who handle it, who actually put it up and on the walls or take it down, or put it back in its box, or send it somewhere and open the box up and take it out—it has to survive the acts and attitudes of these people. But all I knew in 1960–61 was that this kind of metal fit together in a certain way that was interesting to me. What we're talking about can be talked about in terms of the couches too. How do you get all that foam into a big space through a little door? You're talking about logistics. I had to figure this out over a long period of time. One factor is that these parts are each made separately, and each part is different from every other, none are the same—or at least I haven't seen any. Not that they can't be, but I haven't seen it happen. I've seen parts that are similar, but I haven't seen any that are exactly the same. So it's not like messing around with the same material all the time. Each part is different, and each part can fit to some place convenient to itself. In other words, if you have two parts and they fit together, not only do they become much stronger because of their union, but they tend to develop certain lines in relation to each other that suggest a marriage. I didn't figure all this out until much later.

JS: Most of the early wall pieces were actually begun on the floor, not on the wall.

JC: That just had to do with gravity. When I discovered that they could be built directly on the wall—that's when the fit really fit. The units were much more fitted then, and had a higher density.

JS: Other than the frames behind those early wall pieces, the only free-standing sculptures I can think of that have an armature underneath are *Luftschloss* and *Deliquescence*, the sculpture commissioned by the U.S. government for Detroit.

JC: That's just because of their size. I thought it'd be prudent to do that. I start in a lot of different ways. A start is a start. I mean, armatures aren't important. I stick something in if I need structure. It's usually a hidden quotient. I don't start with the armature and add the parts, or cover the armature with the parts. The Detroit piece started with an armature because I'd figured out what I wanted to do, then I figured I'd better make the armature so that the parts fit on properly, because they're awfully heavy, and could get to be too heavy; and it had to come apart for shipping in any case.

JS: In accumulating the parts that you needed for the armature for the Detroit piece, you began the *Gondolas*.

JC: That's right, you were there. Someone working for me was cutting up pieces of channel steel for something else. They looked so nifty the way they were that it reminded me of some other direction. See? That's what I mean: if you ignore an input as strong as that, then you've got no business in this business. That's what you've got to do; you've got to say, "OK, I see that. Well, that shifts everything," and go down that road. That's how an artist has to work. The *Gondolas* were marvelous for several different reasons. First, I left a studio with a very low ceiling to get one with a high ceiling and then ended up making three-foot-high sculptures. Another factor is that at the time I was making very elaborate sculptures, and I would put one together without welding it, and it had fifty parts that weren't welded, and I wouldn't know how to start. When you get to a point where so much goes in and nothing makes any difference, then you're overloaded.

You're making the same decisions over and over again in the same place. Then you go over to a *Gondola*, where you only need to put on a couple of things, and it's very low to the ground; you pick something up and you saunter over and you drop it, and any place it falls is OK. When you go from one intensity to another, you're still making the same decision, but by going about it in a different way, or changing the material or the process, you can make it seem like a fresh idea again. Of course, it's still the same old decision-making, but it's fresh. I figure, since the *Gondolas* are hard to photograph, they must be all right.

JS: One of the strongest elements of your sculpture is stance and attitude.

JC: Well, that's just what *I* said. I could have been lying.

JS: Were you?

JC: I'm not certain. Only time will tell.

JS: How direct is the relation between your attitude at the time you're making a sculpture and the attitude that the sculpture takes? Or how relevant is your attitude?

JC: Well, it's all relevant. Let me just say this once and for all. See, I go out and collect all this shit. Then I bring it in. What I do next is based on what I collect. For example, the last thing that came into the studio was van tops, right off the van, so they're all flat. What's the next thing to do? I'll tell you as soon as I do it. All right. Based on that, the next thing we do, we wad it up in some way, or we make tubes out of it. It's just flat sheet steel. It happened to come off a van, but essentially, it's sheet steel coated with a blue or green or white color—which is what they paint vans. So suppose we roll these sheets up. You can see from the last half-year's works that a lot of these things were rolled up. Because I had piles and piles of stuff that I wasn't using for anything, and I had this guy who gets paid a hundred dollars a day and I had to figure out something for him to do. So I said, "Roll all this stuff up," and I showed him how I wanted him to do it. And he did it. I was just trying to figure out how to keep the guy out of my hair. Every time he gets done with a job he comes in and wants to know what to do next. Then he started laying these tubes out. It looked pretty good—I've still got a mess of them, I've got a floorful that won't quit. So I got started that way. So I sort through the pieces and find two that go together, and I put them together, which I then refer to as a section. I can do this for a long time, because I don't have anything else to do with them. So, I could put twos together for a long time. Nothing happens with them until later on. Then say I get drunk, I come in and throw things around, I wake up the next morning and say, "Who did this last night?" Then I take half of it apart, and the other half's not bad. I couldn't have done it sober. Anyway, so it goes on. And sometimes all of a sudden I hit a couple things that look pretty good, though parts don't look like anything. It doesn't matter if I'm assembling them against the wall, or on the floor, or standing up in the middle of the room. Things go together. If a piece is up against the wall a lot less is going together than if it's standing out in the middle of the room. Depending on how you're doing it, or what material you have, you have to go with this process. There's no formula. Then you get to the point where you think, "This looks dumber than three rocks." So you have to figure out what to do about it; you have to make a radical move. Sometimes big parts that are just parts, just sections, can be put up against something and used as a shield. When a sculpture is overdone, it looks as though it goes on for ever and ever and doesn't do much, as though there's too much stuff that you don't need. Nothing happens, there's just a lot of material there. You know a sculpture clicks when—well, I always get the feeling that I just run on intuition and use that as a general mediator among emotion and sexuality and drive. (We have to leave out intelligence, because I really don't exercise too much of that.) All of a sudden, at some point, there's nothing else to do. It's quite nice. I've had it with little sculptures and with big ones. When a sculpture is nearly done, you can put things on and you take them off and it doesn't make any difference. You don't miss an element here or there. Stopping is the key; you have to know when to stop. If I feel so glad that a sculpture is here, and I don't care who did it, then I figure it's a good piece.

JS: Let's speak for a moment about the stance of a piece. Is it something that has to do with the way you work on a given piece, or is it more reasonable to say that all of a sudden you notice a certain stance in the work?

JC: It's a combination of both.

JS: At Vestry Street, your studio between 1974 and 1980, it seemed that you used all of the wall space available until finally you started making standing and leaning pieces. I wonder how those pieces came about, because the early ones look as if you were too tired to put them up on the wall, or too tired to bring them out from the wall, or your assistant wasn't there, or something.

JC: These started as pictures on the wall, and as the pictures developed, they sort of went this way and that way, and then they came down and hit the floor, and then they came up. That's natural progression. You do it as it goes. You can't do the same thing all the time because that's what you already know. The idea is to find out what you don't know. There's plenty in that category, you know; I mean, you're not really going to get to the bottom of that barrel. So what you end up doing is screwing around with your barrel.

JS: You use up studios completely; you become finished with them and shed them and it seems that five or six years is about the longest time you've spent in one place.

JC: It's called the seven-year itch.

JS: John, for the last show you had at Castelli, in 1982, you made a number of sculptures to go into that space before you knew whether the exhibition was going to be in the big gallery or the small one, so you weren't addressing any space in particular and as it ended up there was one sculpture that practically brushed the ceiling.

JC: There were three that did. David Budd and I talked about that and I said, "Listen, Dave, that was the length of the piece of metal, I didn't shorten it or anything. It was just intuitive." He said, "Well, they won't believe that; you have to tell them it was planned." He felt that the public would never believe a sculpture's relation to its site was accidental. The couch *American Barge* fit in the museum in Eindhoven in the same accidental way. They had this room; I didn't pace it off, I sort of walked around in it. They were wondering what to put in it, and I said, "Put the couch in it." They said, "Would it fit?" And I said, "Sure." Then I almost blanched, thinking, Oh geez, I've done it now. To move that thing is no easy job. And as you know, it did fit—just.

JS: The same thing occurred when we took the same couch to the Palacio Cristal in Madrid. The space was a central rectangle surrounded by three semicircles, and the couch fit exactly in the rectangle. We relied on intuition; and of course it worked.

I think that happens so frequently because the work really does have to do with human scale. It has to do with your size, first of all, the way that many wall pieces have similar dimensions because of your reach. And as you say about the couches, the seating addresses a sixth-grade mentality—that's really human scale.

JC: If you say something like "mentality" or "sixth-grade mentality" to the public they'll get pissed off at you because they don't hear anymore. You have to be careful how you speak to the public. That's the reason I'm doing this interview for the public. If you want to know what a sculpture does when it goes out to the public, you should ask the public, because through the public you'll find out a lot more about the thing than you would by asking me. All you get out of me is the same old trash you get out of all artists. Just because they've done a work of art doesn't mean anything. No, they just have the dumbness or curiosity to do it. It's their own unique madness. Doesn't mean they know all about it. They just didn't get their madness stepped on when they were growing up.

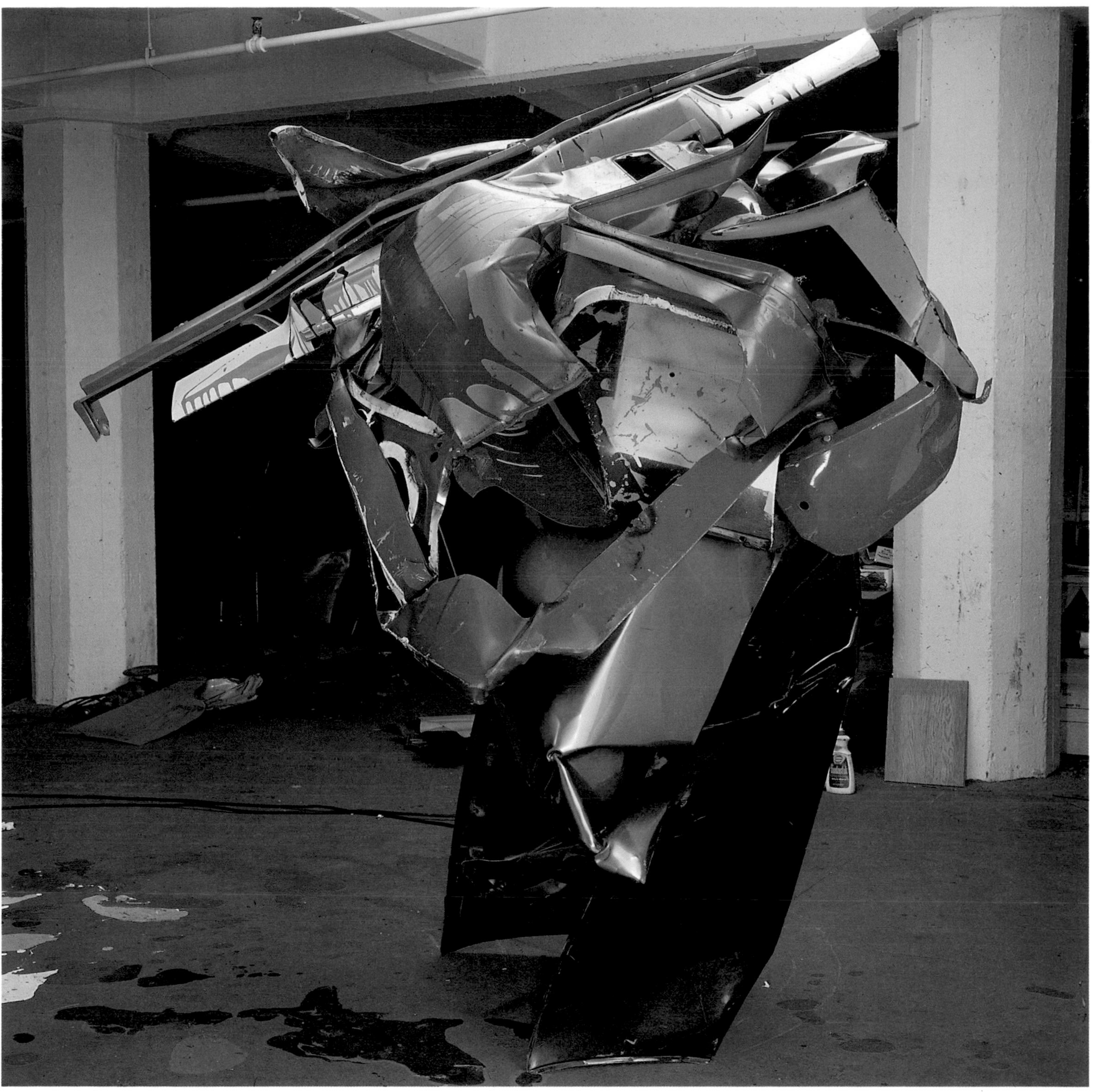

Rooster Starfoot, 1976 (cat. no. 542)

It is the risk of obtaining unprecedented information, even within a given madness, that is the key to art. Art is never boring and never presumptuous, and it doesn't deal in a state of fear. There are no crowbars. It's based on the sharing of a madness that you do not think peculiar at all. Where others suppress it, you have unleashed it, and you do it in such a way that you establish a liaison between your madness and other people. The socially redeeming factor is absolutely evident. Many times, when I've seen an artist's work, my reaction has been, "Oh, so you think so too!" The artist had revealed his madness to me and it was something I might have suppressed. I was relieved to know that someone refused to suppress it, and was astute enough, at some point, to make an object that revealed it to someone else. That is a very high point, a point of one of the greatest feelings of love. Without fear or crowbars. Art is one of the great gifts. It ranks right up there with gardening and sex.

Art has a lot to do with feeling. I'm sorry to be so blunt.

Color in the Round and Then Some: John Chamberlain's Work, 1954–1985

Klaus Kertess

For some thirty years, John Chamberlain has cajoled, crushed, melted, and embraced the detritus of American consumerism to create, casually and forcefully, sculptures whose provocative beauty is as visually brilliant as it is formally intelligent. Employing means as ordinary as his materials, he has reinvented casting and modeling and liberated them from expressive, technical, and aesthetic restraints. Moving out of both the Cubist-Constructivist gridlock and the Surrealist symbolism that together threatened to trap so much sculpture of the 1950s, Chamberlain found a way to add the dimension of volume to the urgent spontaneity and procedural clarity so crucial to the Abstract Expressionist painters. Engaging chance and intuition, he transgressed lavishly the prohibition of color in sculpture, employing hues that ranged from the virginal to the lurid as major protagonists of sculptural structure.

Chamberlain's visual excess is matched by his verbal reticence; he has little desire to dogmatize. The programmatic is foreign to his being; the conjunctions of drift and invention are his way. Like his peers Robert Rauschenberg and Jasper Johns, Chamberlain has had almost no institutional art training. Regularity and regimentation are alien to his personality and work; he enrolled in the School of the Art Institute of Chicago in 1951 and left the next year to try the University of Illinois—that lasted six weeks.

If school did little to relieve Chamberlain's aggravated placelessness, art-history classes and the impressive holdings of the Art Institute opened his eyes to his options. Chinese bronzes, Paul Cézanne, Georges Seurat, and Alberto Giacometti all took their places in his memory; he wrote a paper on the sculpture of India, which made a lasting impression on him. The sculpture of David Smith and the paintings of Franz Kline and Willem de Kooning, however, were what engaged Chamberlain most viscerally. They had a newness, an abstract otherness, openness, and strength that he found he wanted to achieve for himself. With his preference for the physical and his acute awareness of the configural possibilities of the routine movements of the hands, sculpture would seem to have been the natural winner in Chamberlain's vote for a vocation, but painting, nonetheless, provided the inspiration. The rambling vastness of de Kooning's major early painting *Excavation* (1950) and the procedural clarity and force of Kline's surging swathes of paint would somehow have to be integrated into a three-dimensional form. Smith's sculpture propelled the potential.

In the mid-1950s, when Chamberlain began to objectify his ambitions, sculpture lagged far behind painting in terms of the sense of radicalism so crucial to modernism. In the late 1940s painting had achieved a breakthrough to an abstract, nonnarrative and noncompositional imagery, whose overall homogeneity galvanized the flatness of the picture plane and the physicality of paint into a unity that turned the making of the painting into the subject of the painting. This leap of vision eluded the sculptors of the same generation. The spontaneity and incorporation of chance procedures so vital to Jackson Pollock, de Kooning, and Kline, seemed incompatible with the relatively slow, cumbersome, and deliberate methods necessary to the manipulation of sculptural materials. Sculptors contemporary with de Kooning and Pollock, such as Herbert Ferber, David Hare, Seymour Lipton, and Smith, continued to amalgamate Cubist-Constructivist drawing-in-space with the atavistic anthropomorphism of Surrealism. Many of these sculptors did achieve an expansion of scale and a more emphatic exploitation of the industrial materials and techniques first introduced to sculpture by Pablo Picasso and Julio Gonzalez, as well as by the Constructivists, in the early decades of the twentieth century. (Uncast and nonprecious metals and welding were still new to art history in the 1920s—to say nothing of materials like plastic.) Ferber extended Surrealist imagery into monu-mythic spatial drawing; Frederick Kiesler transformed Giacometti's space cage *The Palace at Four AM* (1932–33) into environmental configurations that engulfed the viewer in cosmic confinement; Lipton's biomechanical forms began to call more attention to the sculptural procedures of cutting and welding.

While sculptors strove for raw beauty and directness, too often they were constrained by premeditated compositions and fussy surfaces more suitable to the barnacled artifacts of some prehistoric grotto than to totems of contemporaneity. It was Alexander Calder and Smith who proved to be the most consistently successful fabricators of sculpture in the American grain. A stay in Paris (1926–33) and the encouragement of Marcel Duchamp and Joan Miró catalyzed Calder's early and cogent synthesis of the biomorphic and the mechanical; he cut the flat planes of Constructivism into shapes derived from Miró and Jean Arp. He suspended, balanced, and dispersed these shapes in what might be the same breezes that waft through American folk-art weathervanes and whirligigs. The mobiles, started in the early 1930s, were soon (1937) joined by stabiles, whose simple cut and bolted structure merged the primal imagery of Surrealism with industrial construction techniques.

The success of Calder's modernity is relatively isolated, whereas Smith's achievement has had far more wide-ranging repercussions. Smith, more than anyone else, is responsible for making welded construction the center of American sculpture from the forties through the early sixties. In the thirties and early forties he rapidly assimilated European modernism, and was strongly influenced by the open, linear constructions of Picasso and Gonzalez, as well as by Giacometti's Surrealist sculpture of the thirties. His beginnings as a painter marked most of his sculpture with a strong pictorial frontality. He had already started welding in the twenties, and made his first welded-steel piece in 1933. Like so many other sculptors, Smith fabricated flocks of skeletal, mythic, frequently birdlike presences, but with an elegant economy and directness that gave his drawing-in-space a stately velocity, a resilient clarity of configuration, and an imposing scale unsurpassed by his peers. By the late forties, Smith began to relinquish apocalyptic expressiveness in favor of a cooler formalism; while retaining residual figuration, his work became far more abstract. In 1951 he began a series of some twenty sculptures incorporating discarded farming tools (the *Agricola* series) that brought a new monumentality and unity to Cubist collage, as well as a raw but poetic insistence on the vernacular. In *Agricola IX* (1952), he perched his long-favored device of a horizon line on a base and welded to it a series of wrenchlike mechanical rods that reach out from the horizontal like branches in winter's bareness. Here Chamberlain's art finds its beginnings.

Encouraged by his friend Joseph Gotto to try his hand at welding, Chamberlain began to assimilate Smith's linear, monumental matter-of-factness of the early fifties. His first successful sculptures were

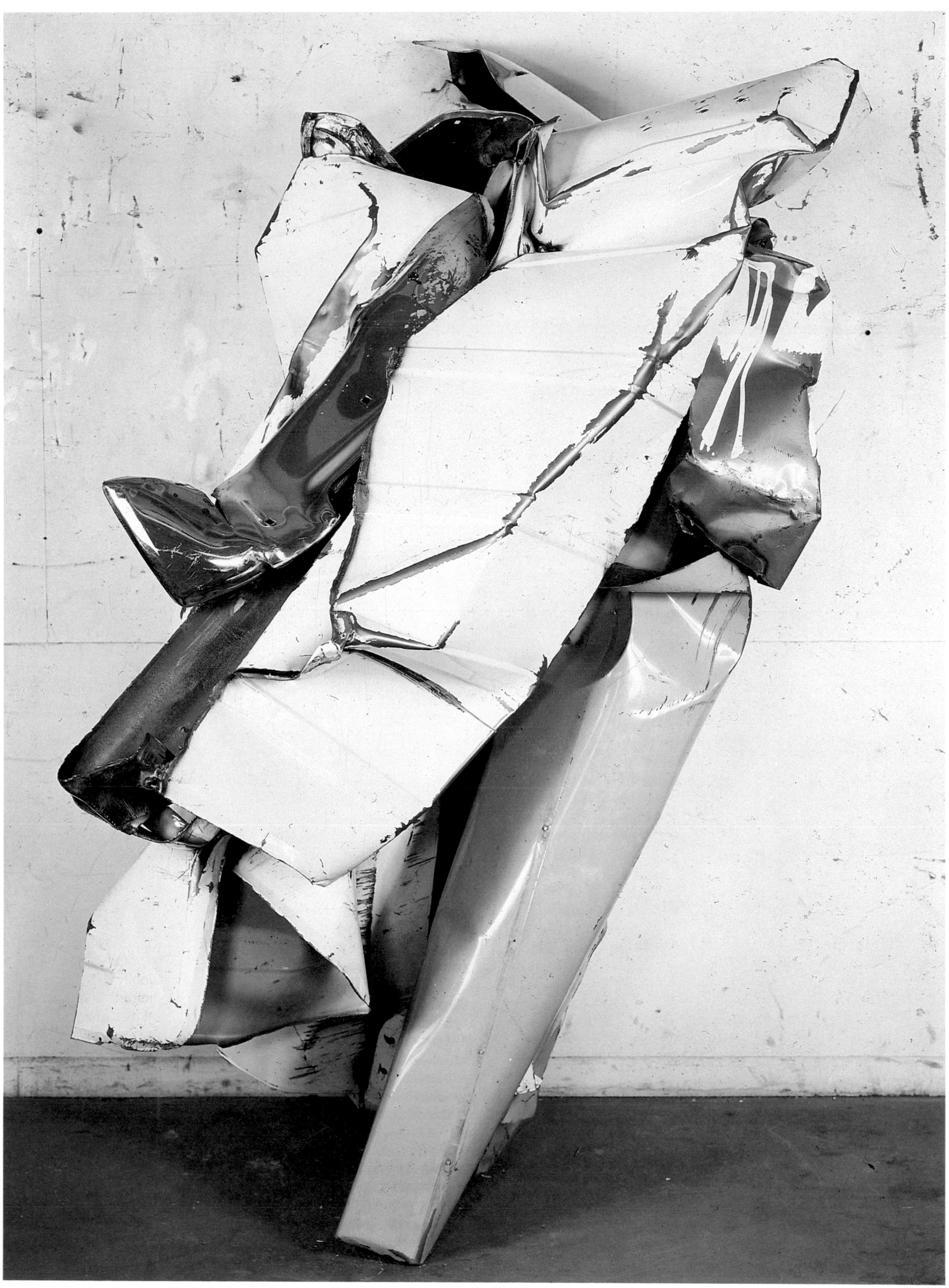

The Hot Lady from Bristol, 1979 (cat. no. 619)

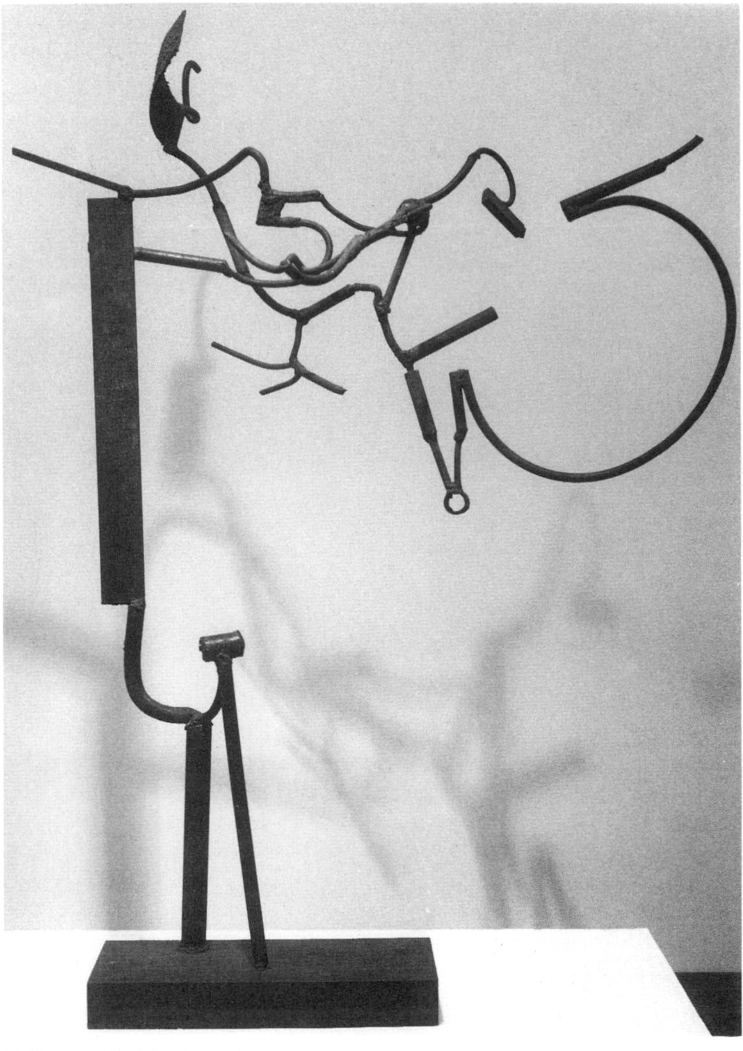

Calliope, 1954 (cat. no. 1)

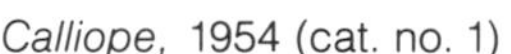

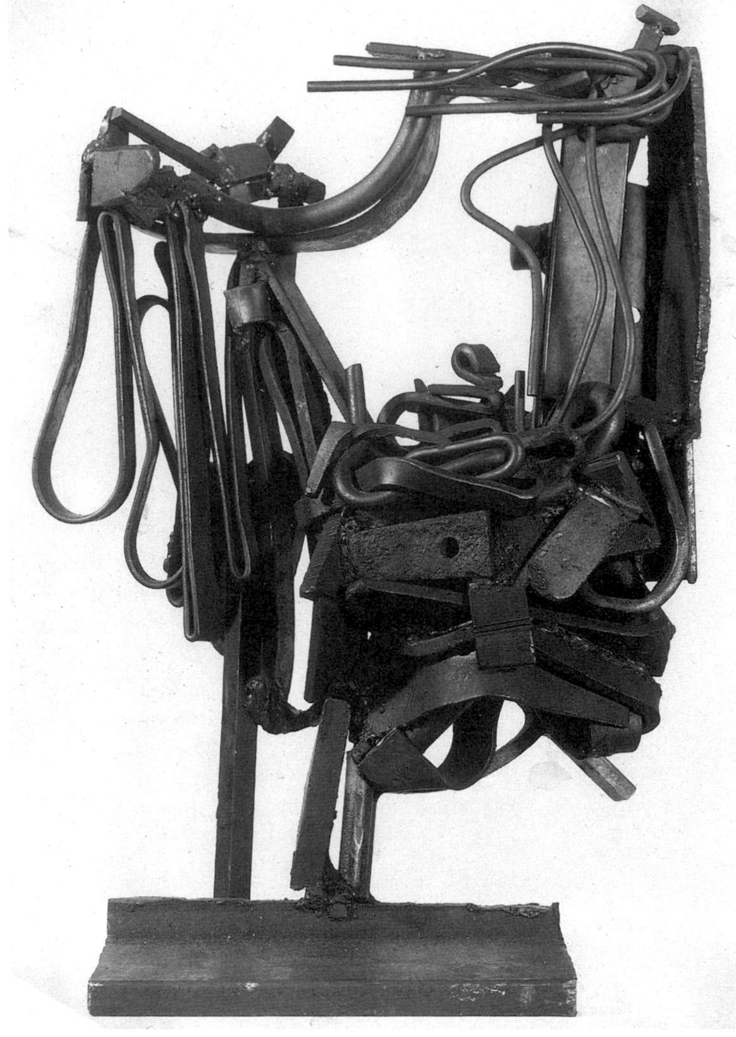

Cord, 1957 (cat. no. 13)

completed in 1954, and drew heavily on the vocabulary of Smith's *Agricolas*. *Calliope* (1954) incorporates mechanical parts but they are more specifically automotive or mechanical than Smith's agricultural tools: a wrench similar in configuration to the rods of *Agricola IX* is joined by a jumper cable with its alligator plug. The sculpture radiates out into a linear, frontal pictorialism similar to Smith's but purged of any residual narrative, landscape, or figurative allusions. *Calliope* is staunchly vertical, rising from its base in a bipedal configuration, but it cantilevers out to one side in a long, multisectioned, fractured horizontal that curves back in on itself. Linear bands of cut and welded metal, responding to and working against an implied pictorial plane, are the components of Chamberlain's work until and through most of 1957 (e.g., *Interiors* of 1955, with its flattened jungle-gymlike structure). These works are less totemic and composed-looking than Smith's; they tend to ramble and shamble, and they revel in a decidedly urban scruffiness. Smith's works, even his later, magnificent stainless-steel *Cubi* series, are more compatible with a rural environment. If Chamberlain's early works do not fully achieve Smith's scale and clarity, their casual composition and confidence, as well as their inclination to roll into roundness, begin to stake out the territory that he very soon claimed completely for his own.

Too ambitious to remain a mere appendage of Smith, Chamberlain still needed other nourishment and stimulation to give fuller definition to his early growth. He decided to risk further study and in 1955 left Chicago for one of the remotest but most vital outposts of the avant garde—Black Mountain College in North Carolina. Rigorous and radical thought was the norm at Black Mountain, as was the freedom to tinker and drift so crucial to many a creative act. Chamberlain arrived at a time when poets and writers were the school's dominant force; Josef Albers no longer taught painting there and Rauschenberg and John Cage had already left to provoke the eyes and ears of New York. But in the poet Charles Olson's teaching, Chamberlain found the final catalyst for his sculpture; and in the poet Robert Creeley he found a vital peer and friend for life.

Olson's verse, like Pollock's paint, strove for an overall vitality. In his critical writings, he propounded "composition by field," and stressed the "obedience of [the poet's] ear to the syllables." "Structure derived from the circumstances of its making" was paramount. Olson sought an open poetry, an "energy discharge" fueled by active verbs, spontaneously twisted tenses, chance associations, simplicity, and directness—a kind of energized American pragmatism grown from Ezra Pound and William Carlos Williams. His verse makes verbal what Chamberlain wished to make visual.

Encouraged by Olson's emphasis on direct procedures, and fully sympathetic to his antipathy to the interference of the conceptual, Chamberlain began to make spontaneously calligraphic pen-and-ink drawings and abbreviated word-collages of nonsense—emphasizing the junction and disjunction of sounds more than Freudian word association. The poetics of structure were becoming sensate. Chamberlain's drawn and written word-play is at least as significant as the Smith-influenced sculptures he continued to construct at Black Mountain. The word collages presage the melodious non sequiturs that he often still uses in the titles of his sculptures to create verbal parallels to his images.

In 1957, as almost any ambitious artist of the time would have done, Chamberlain moved to New York. He now began to feel increasingly confined by Smith's flatness, and started to strive for

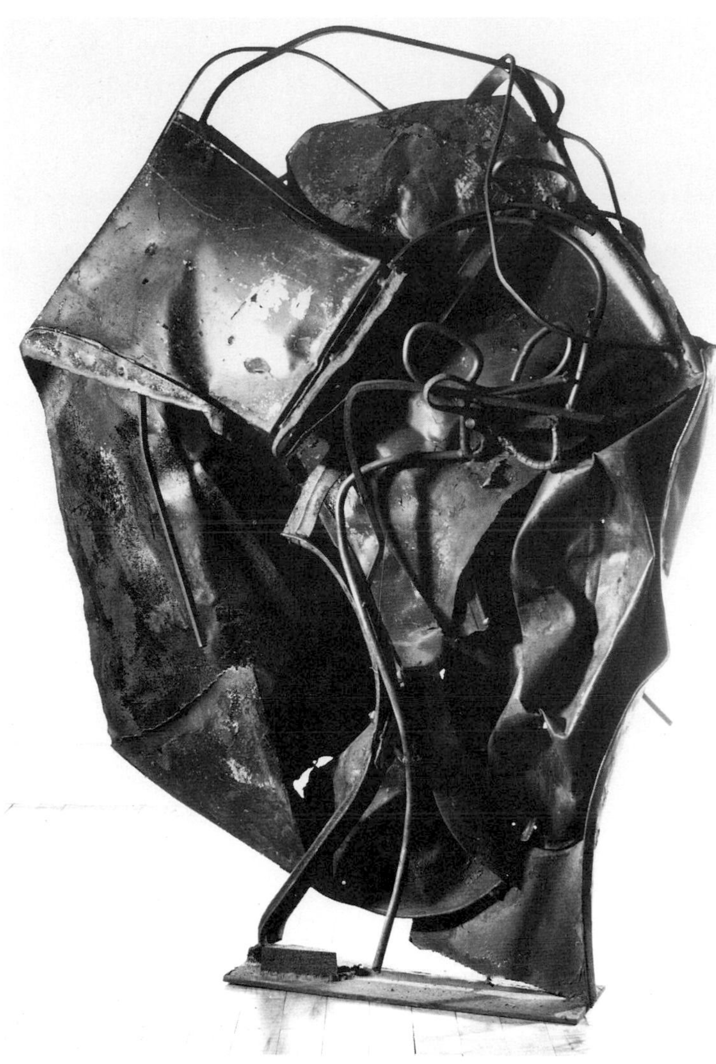

Shortstop, 1957 (cat. no. 15)

more roundness. Thicker metal rods and flat bands were loosely urged to bunch and crunch into configurations with a will to volume; in *Cord* (1957), he made the metal droop like folds of drapery. Still, linearity prevailed, and linearity could not fully satisfy his new hunger for volume. Nor could compositions of cut planes of metal fulfill his desire for spontaneity and the visual clarity of procedures. How to proceed while avoiding the toilsome vagaries of conventional composition?

While visiting Larry Rivers in Southampton at this time, Chamberlain found himself without materials. Looking around for something to work with, he discovered the perfect container for his will—an old Ford. He stripped the car of its front fenders, crushed them a bit, and fitted them into an embrace wrapped with stringy steel. Finding the embrace not fully consummated, he drove over the piece once or twice and called it *Shortstop* (1957). In this work, for the first time, folds, wrinkles, and rounded planes envelop and swell into volumes that replace the frontal linearity of welded vectors of time in space. Literally and figuratively retaining the tracks of its making, a readily apparent crushedness, the configuration refuses to resolve in a discrete shape. *Shortstop* folds in on itself in a constant flow of force and forming.

Far more than just another new wrinkle on assemblage, *Shortstop* and subsequent works completely reinvented modeling, casting, and volume—altering Marcel Duchamp's notion of the ready-made, and using the car as both medium and tool. In them, Chamberlain incorporated euphoric spontaneity, destruction, and chance and gave body to modernism's developing belief that the subject of art be its own making. These very strategies were then made to breathe new life into the volume modernism had deflated, and to revive the techniques of modeling and casting modernism had declared obsolete.

In the first decade of this century, Elie Nadelman and Constantin Brancusi's radical simplifications of volume, form, and carving, as well as Henri Matisse's boldly distorted modeling, had all given new hope to the then relatively moribund means of sculpture; at around the same time, Picasso had summarily collapsed and compressed these techniques into planar, fragmented flatness. In his *Still Life with Chair Caning* of 1912, he had incorporated a piece of real rope as a frame and printed oilcloth to simulate the chair-caning of the title, thus claiming some of sculpture's three-dimensionality for painting and profoundly disturbing traditional notions of painting (just as the facility of the hand itself was soon to be rendered virtually superfluous by assembly-line production). His constructed cardboard *Guitar*, also of 1912, extended the uniquely modernist medium of collage into greater three-dimensionality and completely redefined sculpture as it had been practiced since prehistory. From Cubism and Constructivism on, sculpture's central, unified core was increasingly dissolved into open, planar, linear constructs. In America, the retrograde dominance of direct carving and traditionalist respect for form and volume held on until the forties, when Smith and the welders took over.

Chamberlain's revival of volume in sculpture contains echoes of early modernism, but also some radical innovations. His works do not compose and enclose discrete forms as did the prior works of Nadelman and Gaston Lachaise; Chamberlain's volumes blossom in fluctuating, bruised, dented, and amorphous roundness. He eschews preorganized composition in favor of the casual or randomly compatible fit and juncture of individually created components. The volumes of each sculpture are seamless in energy but not in surface. Ragged edges, open gaps, and the undisguised independence of the clustered, separate parts throw the surfaces into continuous movement. These frenetic junctions and junctures for the first time give sculptural volume to the gestural spontaneity of Abstract Expressionism and provide a clear index of the artist's investigations, manipulations, stops, and starts as he strives for volume. However, Chamberlain's materials and procedures are consciously employed to lower the intensity of Abstract Expressionist heat. The organic fervor of his sculptures' crushed and crushing roundness is offset by the mechanical coolness of the steel and the partially prefabricated modeling and casting. Like Jasper Johns and Rauschenberg, Chamberlain immobilizes the mythic existentialism of the late forties and early fifties with vernacular constructs of collage.

Chamberlain has not only revived volume but activated and swathed it in coats of many colors. The color, too, is mostly ready-made: he simply takes advantage of the existing color of each individual car fragment he uses. His palette thus ranges from ragged rust to the wilder shades of Detroit delirium, with a middle range of the pastels softened with white so favored both by car manufacturers and (as it happens) by de Kooning. The individual parts of each sculpture are chosen for their roundness and color. Because the parts are already colored before they are assembled, rather than painted after the configuration is completed, he sidesteps the constricted, composed, decorative quality that color often lends to sculpture. Color is automatically integrated into the structure to give clear visual evidence of each part's interaction with the others. Color maps and defines the stages, phases, and procedures of forming a sculpture—very much the way Johns's colored bunches of brushstrokes are employed in such paintings as *False Start* (1959) and *Map* (1961). The shiny lacquer of car enamel punctuates the membranelike thinness of the steel surfaces and facilitates the glide of the eye over and around them. Last, but hardly least, the pure optical pleasure of polychrome must be reckoned with; one of Chamberlain's principal strengths is his ability to unite pleasure with intelligence. Applied color has been largely absent from Western sculpture since the early Renaissance and was programmatically prohibited by twentieth-century modernism's dictum of truth to materials. Chamberlain's use of prefabricated materials and colors at once conforms to the tenets of modernism and releases him from modernism's monochromatic restraints to indulge in greater visual variety.

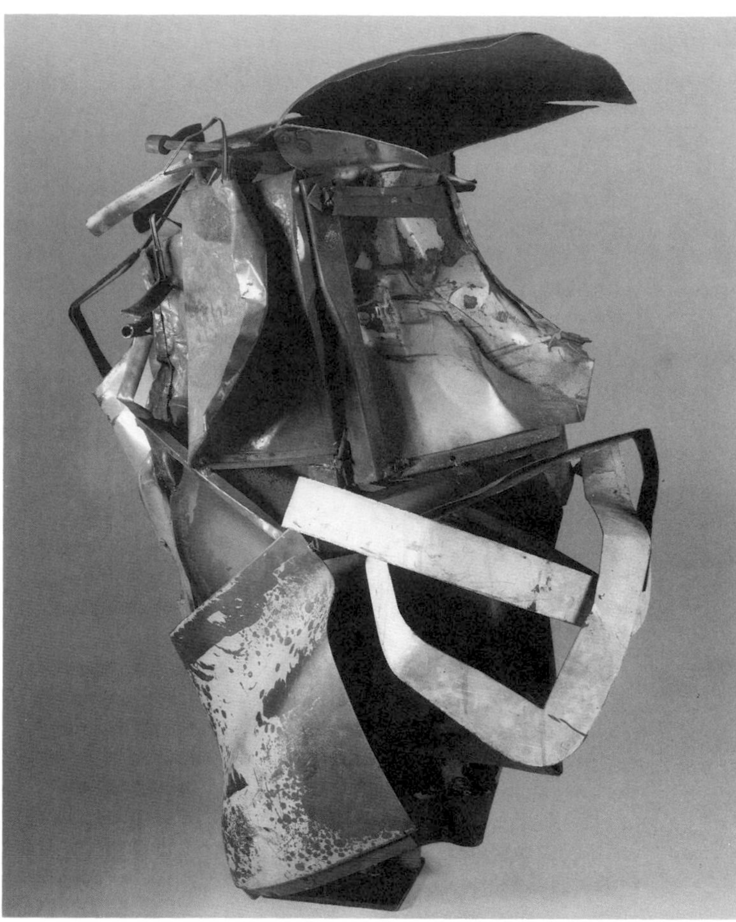

Johnny Bird, 1959 (cat. no. 29)

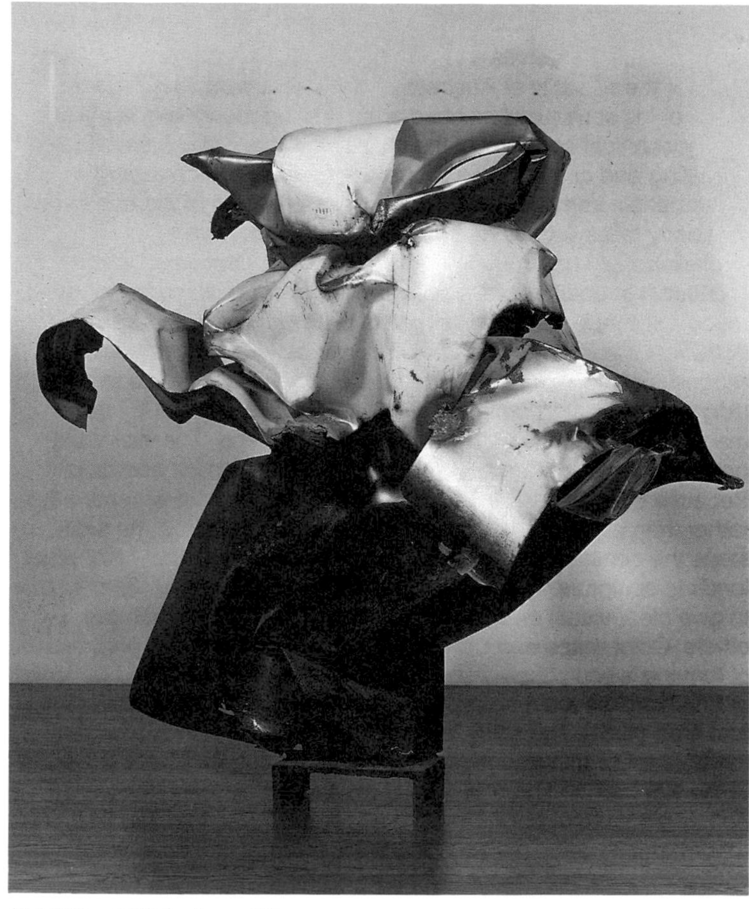

H.A.W.K., 1959 (cat. no. 27)

Shortstop and other formative steel pieces still pay token homage to early modernist works, while twisting the planar flatness that dominates them and relying heavily on the rich tones of rust and corrosion. By 1959, Chamberlain's work had acquired the full voluminousness and complex chroma that were unique to his sculpture through 1967, and have been again from 1974 to the present. *Johnny Bird* (1959) rises up in a predominantly vertical configuration; sharp edges and cuts and the protruding angularity of flat, twisted bands push the piece into a confrontational rawness that is reinforced by the corroded and torched opacity of some of the color—a scratchy and scorched red, faded and speckled gray, dirty white, and muted military blue. The compacted volumes of *H.A.W.K.* (1959) billow more willingly into a smoother, rounder marriage of color and shape; a fractured, irregular Z, half dark, shiny blue, half acid yellow, is topped with a blob of glistening mint green. Both sculptures pay only the slightest attention to the bird images of their titles. Like much of Chamberlain's work from this time, they are bunched and stacked into torsolike configurations. But the constant shifts and breaks in contour prevent the resolution of any anthropomorphic gestalt, or any gestalt at all. There is more surface roundness than is necessary to close a volume in a finite form; the metal surrounds and structures a constantly shifting space and volume. The concrete reading of form is frustrated, though we are aware of ambiguous sexual references in the mounting, plugging, and hugging that take place among the individual components. The multiple junctures, cracks, crevices, and phallic protrusions frequently approach the orgiastic; but the orgy is purely abstract. The coldness and hardness of steel, often menacing in its sharpness, repel touch and arrest arousal.

Although Chamberlain has always been willing to employ anything steel and painted in his work (a bench, signs, sand pails, a lunch box, kitchen appliances, oil drums, etc.), his signature source of material is automotive. And clearly the *motive* of his *auto* is erotics—the erotics of art. Given Chamberlain's desire for a simple, common medium and methods that minimize the obstacles to making that may impede access to the acts of art, the ready-made volume, modeling, casting, shape, and color of car parts are certainly suitable for his intentions. He has offhandedly stated that car parts are simply an available material, as marble was in Michelangelo's time. A culture geared to consumerism and planned obsolescence quite naturally incorporates its detritus in its art, as artists have done since Picasso and Duchamp. While Chamberlain has no inclination toward the literary symbolism of Duchamp's and Francis Picabia's biomechanical images, the irony of deconstructing America's number-one consumer icon must appeal to him. In the fifties the cult of the car was at its peak; cars and highways easily took precedence over nature in popular interest. The car had become an extension of the body and played an active role in bourgeois fantasy life. Cars looked like aerodynamic desire then; now they look like aerodynamic discretion. They were enthusiastically anthropomorphized (a convertible was an exotic mistress; a coupé a wife). The car was both trusted steed and knight's shining armor. The incredulity that Chamberlain's work still often provokes is at least partially due to the grip consumerism has on our culture. If there is irony in Chamberlain's attack on America's pride, it is powerfully visual: the irony of a finished product turned into an indeterminate, abstract state of energy—an art that visibly and viscerally incorporates the acts of destruction necessary to the act of creation. The initial violence of a car crash implicit in the sculptures dissolves in the forcefulness of Chamberlain's art.

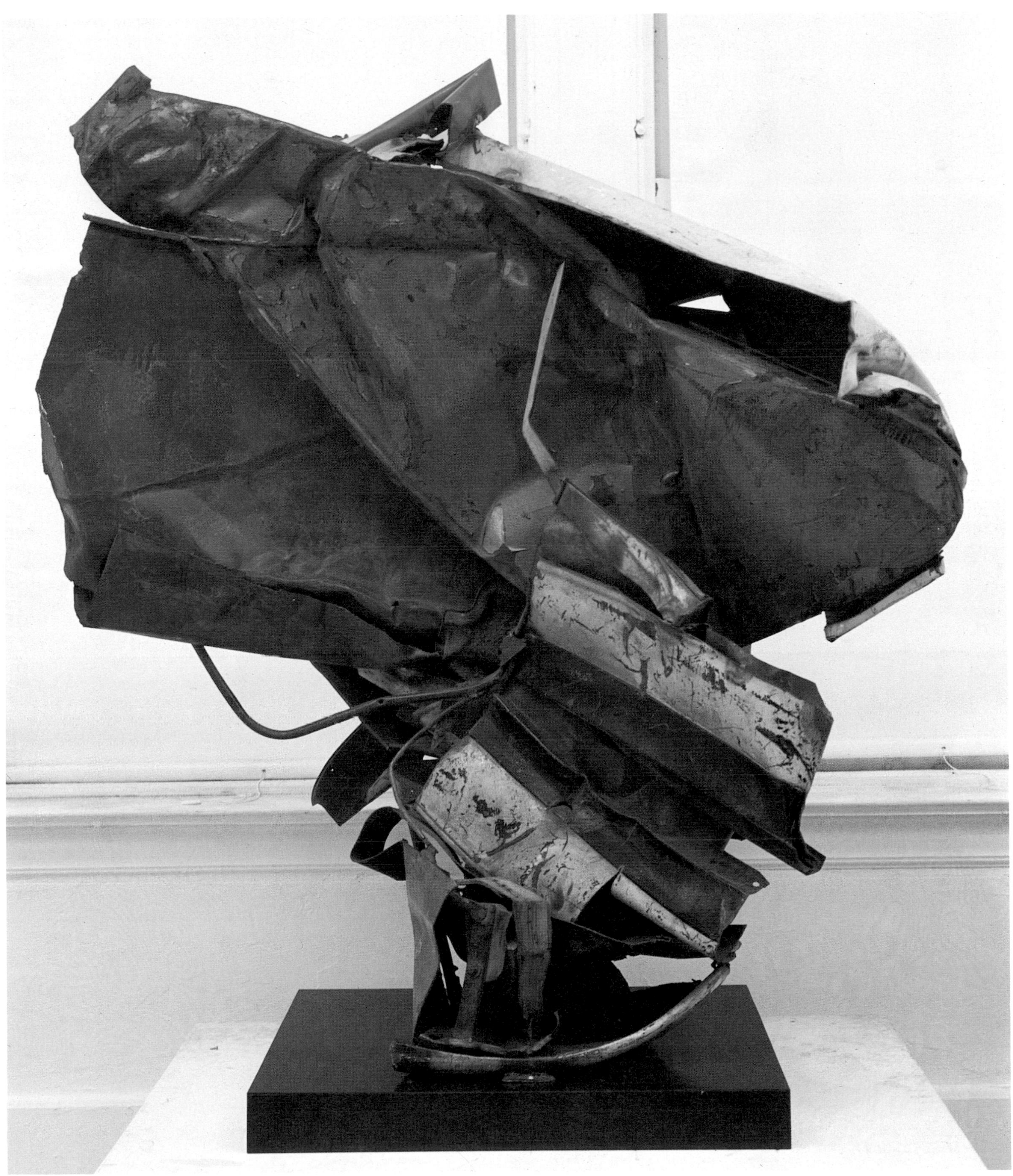

Hatband, 1960 (cat. no. 48)

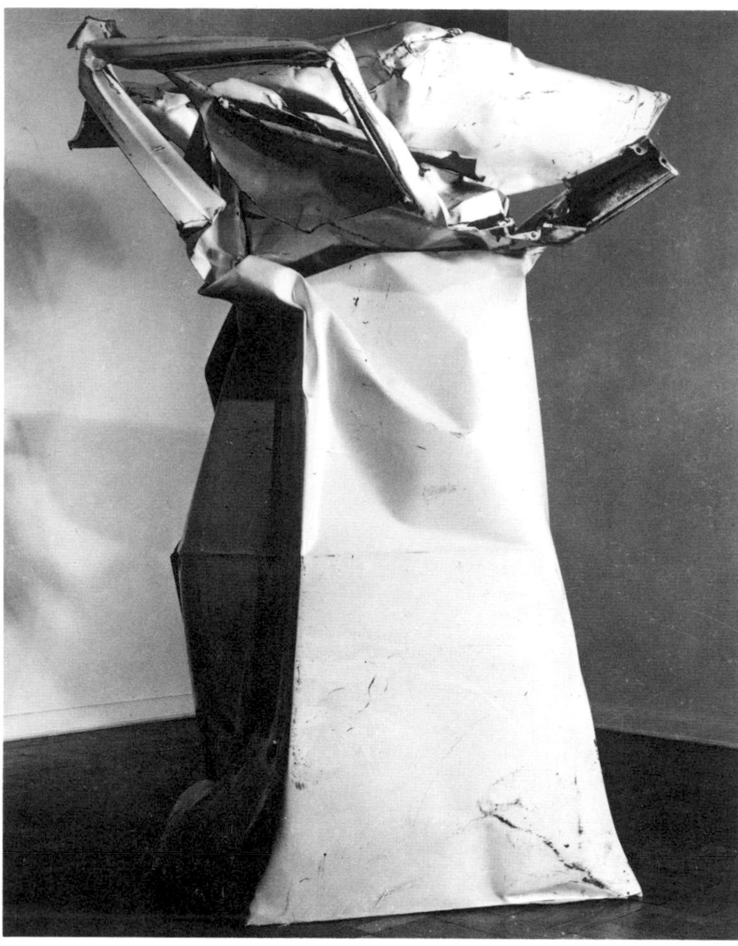

Velvet White, 1962 (cat. no. 132)

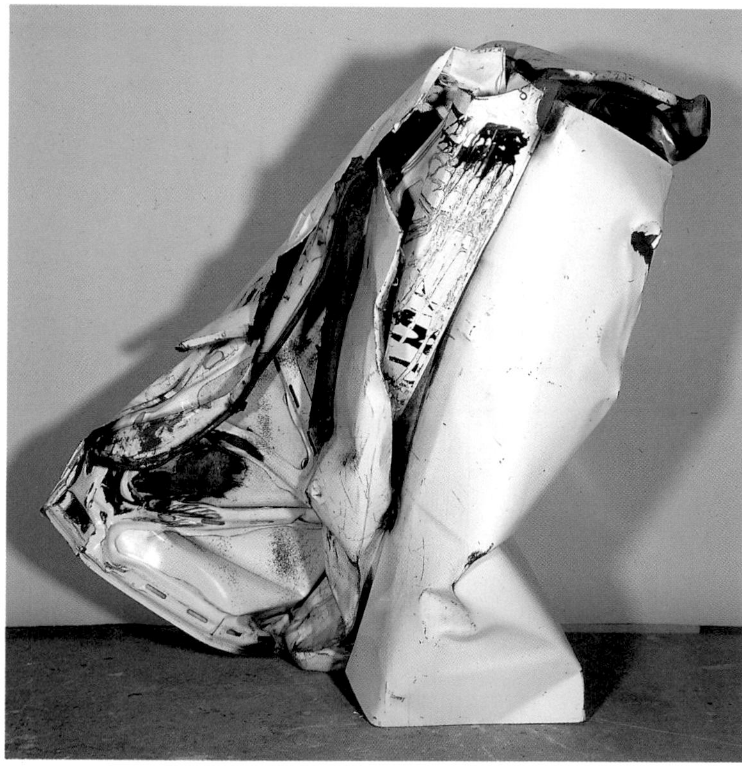

French Lace, 1982 (cat. no. 690)

Chamberlain is of a generation that produced a veritable avalanche of the vernacular. In the mid-fifties numberless artists seem to have moved their studios to junkyards and thrift shops. If the majority of the sculpture made then has deservedly sunk back into the obsolescence from which it was extruded (Jason Seley's bumper sculptures, Richard Stankiewicz's Smith-derived, industrialized totems, and César's compacted cars being among the more deserving survivors), painting was generally more successful in squeezing new juices from junk and cliché. Rauschenberg's combine paintings, filled with nostalgic debris, and Johns's painted and collaged flags and targets, like Chamberlain's sculpture, neutralized Abstract Expressionist concerns and extended them into the realm of the poetics of the ordinary. Chamberlain, unlike Johns, Rauschenberg, and the Pop artists, remained resolutely abstract, avoiding all direct social and political commentary and satire. His matter-of-fact, intuitive abstraction is most closely related to Cy Twombly's elegant, graffitilike painterliness.

Among sculptors, the older Reuben Nakian and Chamberlain's contemporary Mark di Suvero were the only others to attempt the extension of Pollock's, Kline's, and de Kooning's painterly procedures into the third dimension. Strongly influenced by de Kooning, Nakian employed thin coats of wet plaster over cloth attached to an armature of steel pipes or wire mesh. All was then cast in bronze to create rippling compositions of curved, organic slabs. In a series of large-scale sculptures done between 1955 and 1958, he welded curved and diagonal steel plates onto a complex arrangement of metal pipes. As impressive and imposing in scale as these seemingly malleable slabs are, they still adhere to Cubist-Constructivist planar compositional constructs. Chamberlain's noncompositional directness escapes the constraints of Nakian's similarly intended sculpture, as it does those of di Suvero. Di Suvero's work of the early sixties incorporates discarded construction materials in forceful, energetic formations directly related to Kline's boldly stroked paintings. The weight of the materials and the slowness and deliberation required for their engineering rule out the manifest speed, spontaneity, and clarity achieved by Chamberlain. This is not to belittle di Suvero; the muscular, flexible monumentality he began to achieve fully in the early seventies with his I-beam constructions makes him, as much as Anthony Caro, the major heir to Smith's legacy.

In his use of color, too, Chamberlain is singular. Calder had already employed color in the late thirties, in his mobiles and stabiles, but he limited himself to the primaries—red, yellow, and blue—as well as black and white in his mobiles, and to a single color for each of his stabiles. Not particularly interested in color as such, Calder used it mainly to lighten the weight of the metal and, as economically as possible, to punctuate the individuality of each shape. Smith occasionally employed a Cubist-derived polychrome in the forties, and in the fifties sporadically applied a single color to a work, after completion of the welding, to lighten the material as Calder had done, and to give unity to its underlying pictorialism. In the late fifties and early sixties, he experimented again with polychrome on steel, but was not able to achieve the kind of resolution he had attained in his earlier stainless-steel pieces. The color seems arbitrary and becomes fussy when the outside edges of a shape are painted a different color from its interior. In the sixties Caro regularly applied a single color to each work, after completion, not only to achieve antigravitational lightness but also to link together welded components that were widely dispersed in space. Again, color itself was secondary and frequently seemed arbitrary. Jules Olitski's later (1968), brief foray into sculpture is closer to Chamberlain's intentions of spreading colors over glossy volumes. His ground-hugging, volumetric curved forms are coated with speckles of pigment suspended and dispersed in transparent medium. The color is politely lavish, but the composition of the forms is too imposing to dissolve sufficiently in the light of the transparent solution and free the flow of the color.

Chamberlain had also started two groups of paintings that suspend pigment in a clear solution. In the first *Embudo* series, of 1963, a found template (a square divided into nine squares) was laid on a twelve-by-twelve-inch piece of formica, which was then coated with as many as one hundred layers of almost clear auto lacquer holding metal-flake pigment in suspension. In the second series of paintings, of 1964, each forty-eight inches square, he employed the same technique with a different configuration (two L shapes, each framed on one side with a flat, protruding metal band). Experimenting with the effects of light on color and its fugitive nontactility, Chamberlain wanted to see how many layers of near-colorless glaze were necessary to make a color congeal and rise to the surface. The template-derived image floated somewhere between the bottom surface of the formica and the top of the last layer of paint. These investigations of surface transparency and density are less compositionally contrived than Olitski's sculpture; still, they lack the full fragrance and exhilaration of Chamberlain's sculpture. As Olitski's intentions are better realized in painting, so Chamberlain's are better realized in sculpture.

The only sculptor in the late fifties as intent upon color as Chamberlain was George Sugarman. Perhaps emboldened by Chamberlain's slightly earlier success with color, Sugarman made his first polychrome sculpture in 1959 after having made a series of engagingly awkward cubistic sculptures in wood. Rambling elements crawl across the floor or sprout up in a discontinuous vertical to form a variegated, abstract composition out of forms that frequently refer to nature. Each form is soaked with paint of a bright, matte hue, taken from a palette similar to Stuart Davis's. Because Sugarman's color soaks into the wood and is matte, it emphasizes the mass and form of the material as it extends into space, whereas Chamberlain sought a more immaterial flow. The boldness and unity-in-variety achieved by Sugarman's color (and form) provide more tension and punch than does Smith's or Caro's color; but, like them, he has maintained the inherently conservative compositional strategies already long rejected by painting. Chamberlain alone in the fifties achieved a noncompositional radicality for sculpture that could successfully incorporate color.

Chamberlain continued to make volumetric accumulations of painted steel at full force through 1966, gaining greater confidence in his use of scale and visual complexity. In 1960, he made his first wall piece, *Essex*; paradoxically, the invasion of painting's place purged his sculpture of the residual pictorial respect for the planar still evident in some of his first car-part sculptures. *Essex* heaves and swells out like the crumbling breastplate of some embattled science-fiction monster (Rodan meets Rodin), crackling and hissing with the ferocious humor of breaking and making. The increased size of this piece (it is some nine feet in height) permits a greater visual sense of speed and a dizzying multiplicity of colored shapes—round swellings, bends, cracks, wrinkles, and fissures. A mutual attraction of edges and volumes prevents eruption into chaos; the precarious leftward tilt is barely held in tense check by two restraining verticals. *Mr. Press* (1961) is more self-composed in its monumentality; it is made up of fewer and larger sections that shift and bend toward a billowing rectangularity. The inhaling swell is anchored by a multisectioned diagonal of off-whites that occasionally secretes a pale, shiny blue and drips with a cascade of yellow-orange. Broad, irregular rectangular blades of red push out from underneath, at the top and the bottom. As in so many of Chamberlain's pieces, this chromatic monumentality seems to have happened by chance.

Like the new wall pieces, the fully three-dimensional work gained an abundance of presence. The appendages and table bases that had propped up earlier sculptures were now eliminated; the works assume their own stances and poses—frequently precariously. Chamberlain's growing control of scale now allowed him to evoke monumental power in a small work (*Scotch Spur* of 1961 is but eight inches high) as readily as in a large one. The liberated stance could range in attitude from menacing to mellow, while the colors unfolded in a panoply that started with torrid cacophony and ended with mute monochrome. Pieces of predominantly one color, generally an unwashed white, also made their first appearance at this time. *Velvet*

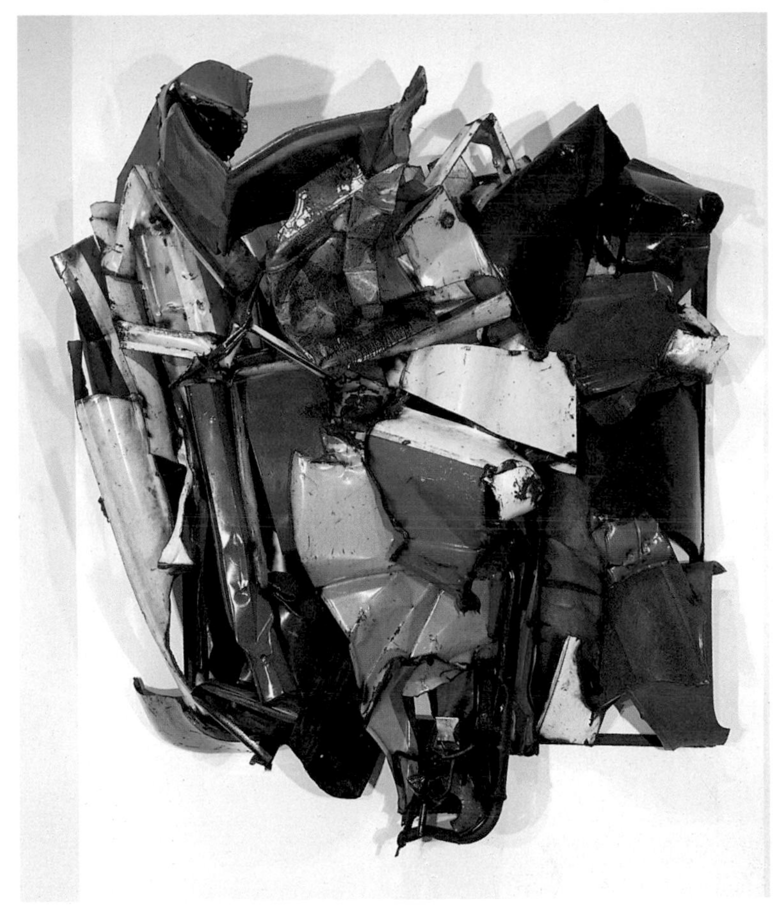

Essex, 1960 (cat. no. 45)

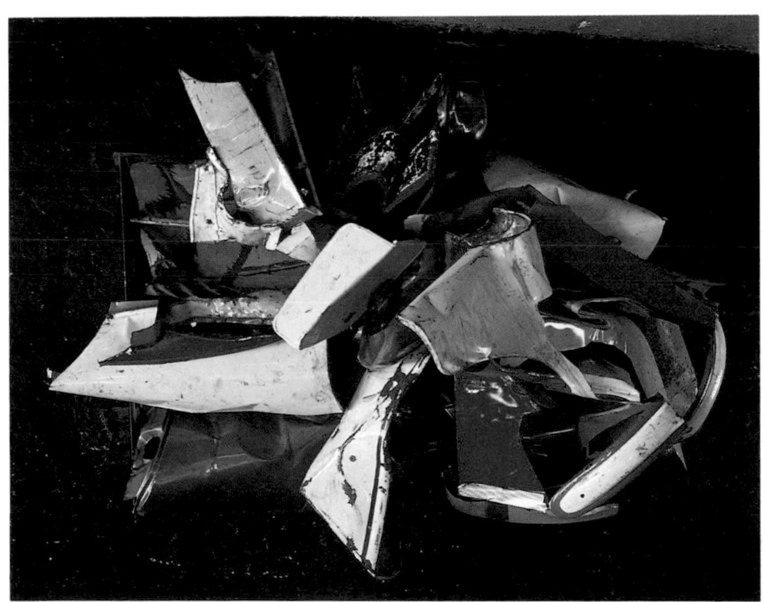

Dolores James, 1962 (cat. no. 111)

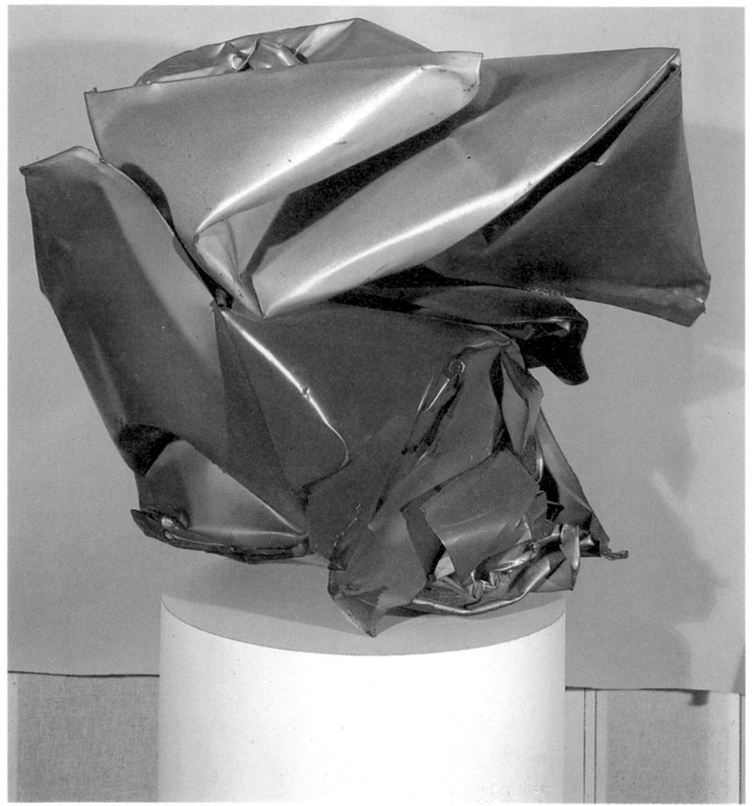

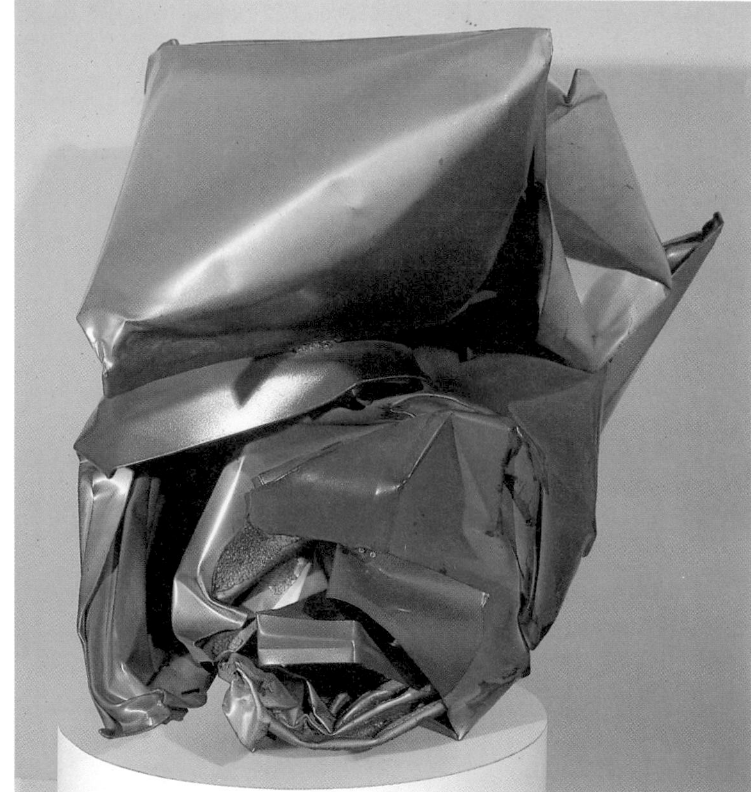

CA-D'ORO, 1964 (cat. no. 183, four views)

White (1962) is a dented, tapering vertical box topped with a flustered torsolike shape; in its gawky, tarnished beauty it stands like a battered but determined bride.

Chamberlain's sculpture, with its fractured and convoluted volumes, is totally three-dimensional. There is no front or back, no favored view inclining toward the static or planar. The viewer's eye is taken on an alluring trip over a rolling and cascading topography such as had not been seen since the extravagances of the baroque. Photographs of two different views of one work quite often seem to be of two completely different sculptures. A relatively small piece such as *CA-D'ORO* (1964), thirty-four inches high, expands, contracts, constricts, and expels in a constantly changing and revolving multiplicity of actions and colored volumes. One view presents a pale silver-lilac boxlike container capped with a peaked golden umbel shape. This configuration begins to break up as the viewer moves around it, until it bursts open to reveal a flatulent gable sheltering a wrinkled blue cone with an orifice enveloping red folds. Unnatural acts have turned the container into the contained—optically sumptuous, tactilely repellent.

By the early 1960s Chamberlain had become a regular at junkyards and body shops. Sometimes he actually worked in junkyards, but more often he chose and collected pieces to pile up in his studio. Individual pieces were selected for their color and roundness, sometimes to be cut up and reshaped, in the studio, and occasionally even to be touched up or painted over with fresh auto lacquer. Each piece was treated as an individual entity before it was returned to the pile on the floor. Chamberlain used a variety of tools: a slicer, a steel-cutting chisel, an acetylene torch, a bandsaw, a grinder, a truck, and a compactor. Each tool had a different impact on the metal; the rough edges left by a saw were as pleasing to the artist as the burn marks of the torch. After a gestation period, Chamberlain began to assemble some of these worked pieces into a configuration that maximized the volumes and the colors into a unique presence and attitude. Seeking what he regularly refers to as "fit," or "sexual fit," Chamberlain joined piece to piece, forming a puzzle whose final configuration would not be known until it was completed. Almost all of the car-part sculptures are self-supporting—the pieces hold together without welding—but were spot-welded after completion, so that they could be safely transported and maintained outside the studio. Sheet steel is relatively soft and malleable and readily receives and retains the acts performed upon it. Chamberlain has an intuitive sense that sheet steel gives about the same resistance as a human body does, and he has acted upon the metal accordingly. Just as his process joins chance and intuition with the prefabricated and the ready-made, it also unites the industrial and the organic. The procedures that follow the initial choice of ready-made parts are openly visible and engage the viewer's eye.

Chamberlain's use of individual prefabricated parts cohering in an overall, noncompositional, purely visual unity relates his aims more to the sculptors and painters of the sixties than to those of the fifties. Donald Judd, Carle Andre, and Dan Flavin all used prefabricated or made-to-order industrial parts in homogeneous, unified configurations. Like Chamberlain's, their works present themselves as non-imagistic, abstract facts. Like Chamberlain's sculpture, Flavin's ready-made fluorescent lights and Judd's fabricated boxes actively incorporate industrial color, but with far greater restraint. Their geometry is not manipulated and composed but, rather, based on repetition or on simple mathematical and geometrical progressions—virtual ready-mades. (In the sixties, Judd became one of Chamberlain's strongest supporters, both as a critic and as a collector.) The related intentions of Judd, Andre, Sol LeWitt, Flavin, and Robert Morris fully restored sculpture to the forefront of modernism. Chamberlain's is a more isolated achievement, as different from the Minimalists as it is similar. His nonimagistic uniformity relies heavily on intuition and the pulse of passion, whereas theirs is grounded in regimented, pragmatic regularity—they have rules; he plays. He remains the pagan friend of the monastic order.

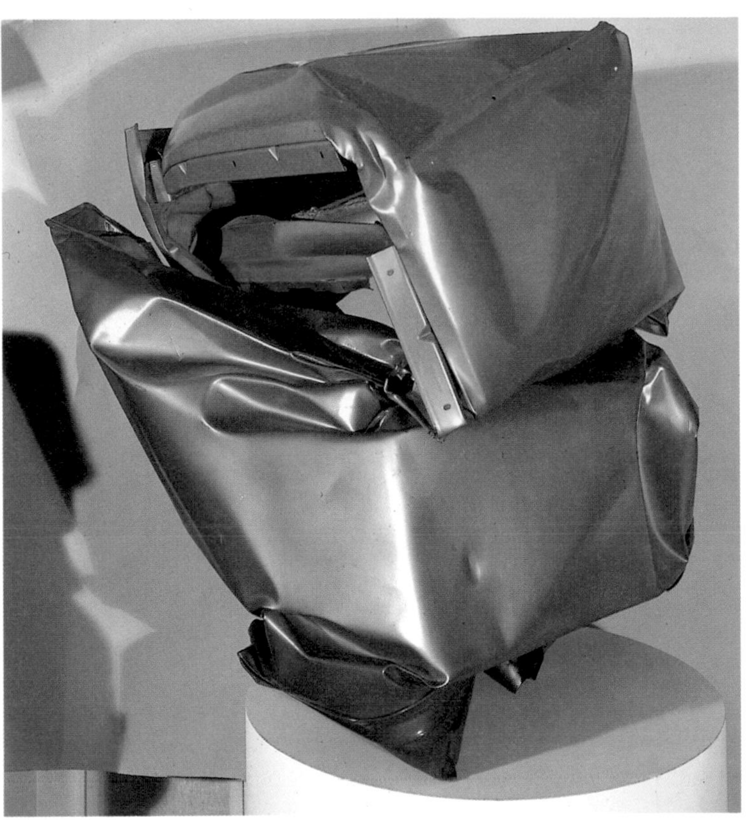

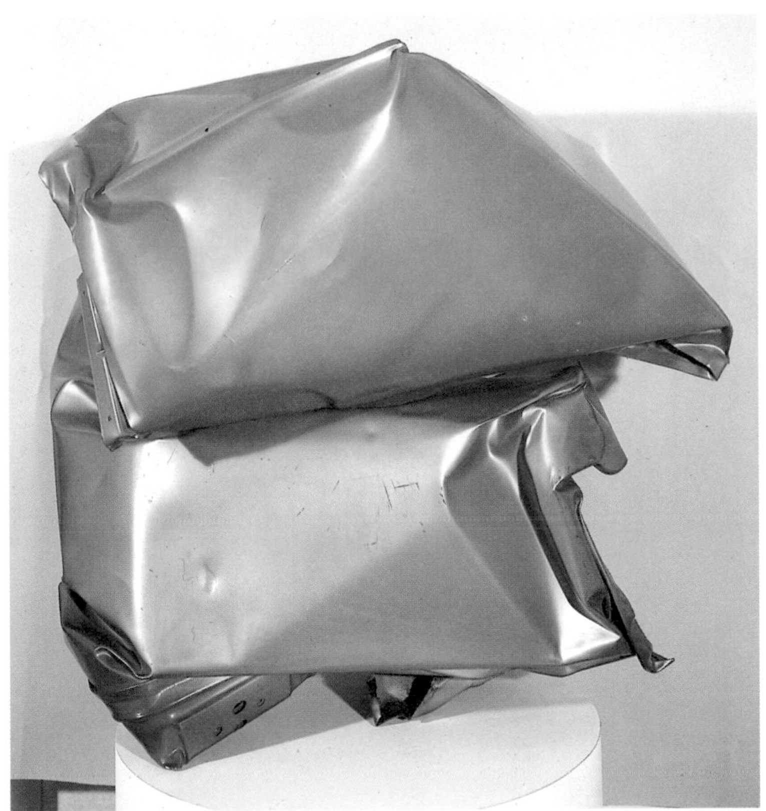

Chamberlain's rangy intuitive sense is not without its pitfalls, but it has kept him open to new risks and opportunities, whether in his studio or in a bar. By the mid-sixties, he had become a ranking member of the art scene; but his acceptance was primarily among fellow artists and the immediate inner circle of the art world. Deserved critical and commercial success still eluded him. Partially, perhaps, because he wished to overcome his reputation as a fender bender and partially because he was ready to try something new, Chamberlain started working with other media and techniques. By 1967, he had decided to stop working with painted steel; with the exception of two series of sculptures, he maintained this resolve until 1974.

In 1966, Chamberlain tried his hand at constructed (rather than fitted), preconceived forms, making small fiber glass sculptures based on french-curve drawings. These look like sleek winged and finned Hollywood appliances of unknown function. They are only slightly better and more concise than much of the stuff that was being produced then; Chamberlain was the first to admit their inconsequence.

On the other hand, a series of foam pieces, started in 1966, initiated several successful groups of works, all more or less based on Chamberlain's observation of the commonplace movements of the hands: wadding tissues and toilet paper, popping paper bags, crumpling empty cigarette packs. The foam pieces started simply, with the squeeze of a sponge—quick, ordinary, and easy. While in Malibu in 1966, Chamberlain made some thirty small (three-to-six-inch) sketches using squeezed and tied sponges. Later that year he switched to larger pieces of urethane foam, which was denser and more resistant and encouraged more buoyant and complex configurations (see *I-Chiang*, 1966). After being squeezed and tied with a rope, the foam was bounced into a writhing donut form—now like a volcanic crater, now like an epic-sized vagina. The simplicity of the form, the uninflected, porous smoothness of the surface, and the generosity of the curves all give these pieces a monumentality belied by their size. A second series, begun in 1967, was made with

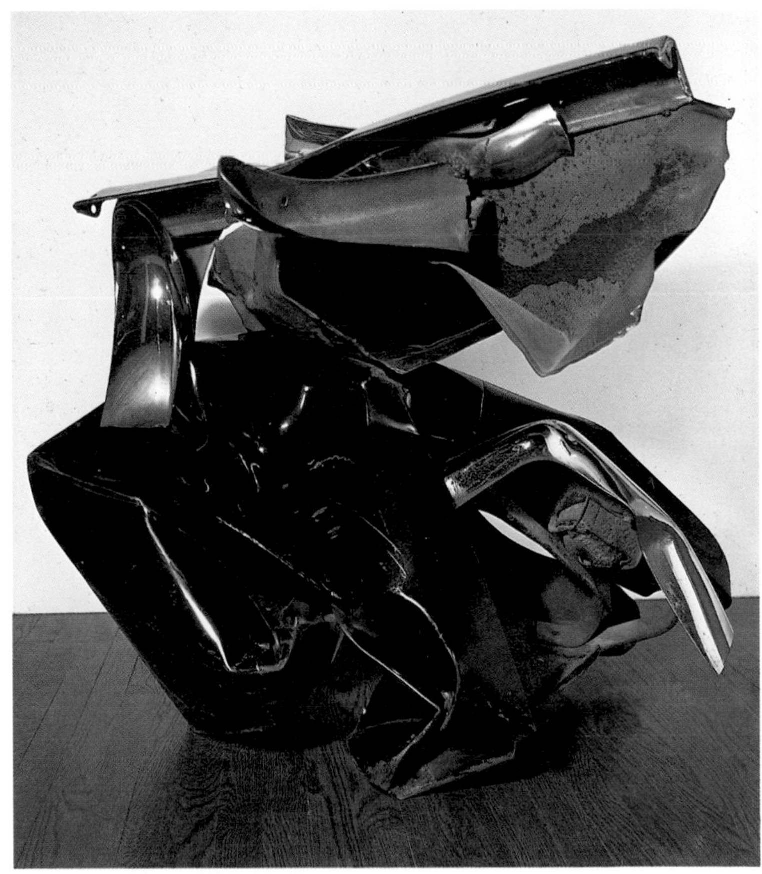

Marilyn Monroe, 1963 (cat. no. 160)

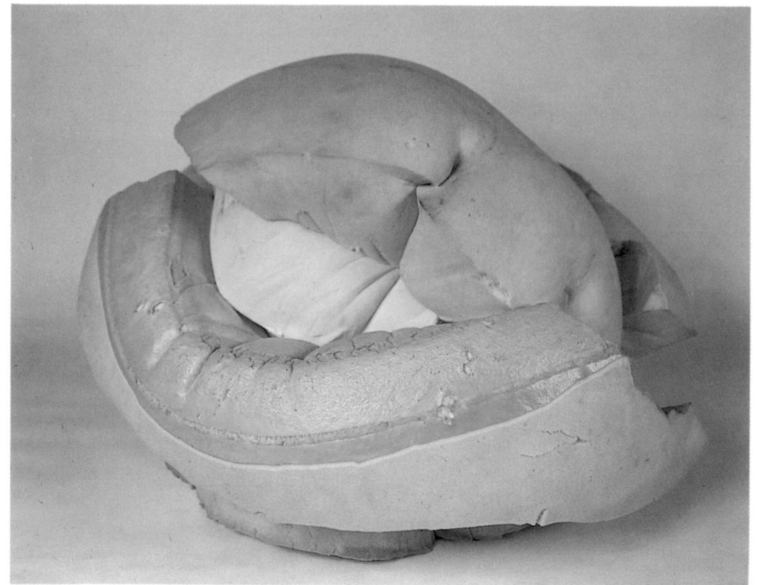

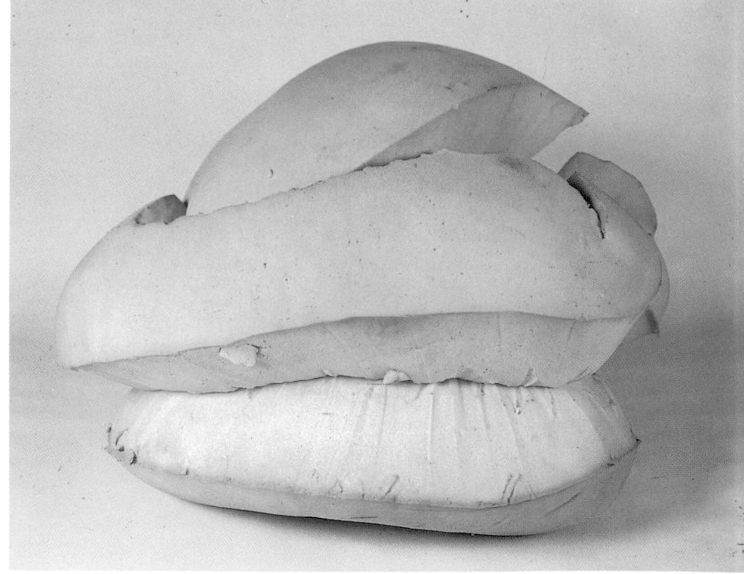

Shan, 1967 (cat. no. 315, two views).

larger pieces of foam and sometimes bound with two ropes. In 1970 another smaller series was begun, followed by a fourth in 1972, sparingly dappled with a confetti of watercolor.

Urethane foam is Chamberlain's marble—porous and tactile but cheap, and softly and directly responsive to the bare hands. These, and to a lesser degree the subsequent paper pieces, are the only tactile sculptures made by Chamberlain thus far. Their smooth, sensuous surfaces and bulging forms immediately suggest hands kneading—and needing—surrogate flesh. In them, Chamberlain reveals a respect for the dictates and nature of the material (no ready-made shapes are employed) and finds in its transformation the direct logic of the work. Thus, his emphasis on structure and construction, based on close attention to the nature of the material, becomes the subject of the work, predating by at least a year Morris's swathes of gray felt, cut and draped by gravity, started in 1967.

In the late sixties, Morris, together with such artists as Richard Serra, Eva Hesse, Alan Saret, Barry Le Va, and Lynda Benglis, propounded a sculpture of malleable and often mutable materials in which the actions of the artist and of gravity were made visible and interactive. They became known as "Process" artists, reacting against and succeeding Minimalism. Although Chamberlain's painted-steel pieces are not so exclusively concerned with the dictates of material and gravity, their spontaneous, visible unfolding of process claims for him the role of preeminent precursor of this extraordinary generation of sculptors. His urethane pieces give him a senior place in this group. Like Chamberlain, most of them sought to reactivate some of the tenets of Abstract Expressionism; Benglis, with her multilayered, poured liquid urethane-foam pieces and Saret, with his bodily choreographed folds, furls, and swirls of chicken wire, share Chamberlain's desire for an open, organic voluminousness. Morris, the self-styled spokesman for this group (as he had earlier been for the Minimalists), completely ignored Chamberlain in his manifestos, published as articles in *Artforum* ("Anti-Form," volume 6, April 1968, pp. 33–35, and "Notes on Sculpture, Part IV: Beyond Objects," volume 7, April 1969, pp. 50–55). While Morris bowed to the Abstract Expressionists and wrote of sculpture's need for chance and indeterminacy, he called Claes Oldenburg the movement's precursor (despite having elsewhere denigrated the finiteness of all figurative and Minimal sculpture). Oldenburg's soft sculptures (first done in 1962) are certainly responsive to gravity and less finite than the versions in hard materials; however, his primary interest was in a finite, concrete form totally antithetical to the tenets of Process art. Was Chamberlain too close for comfort? Did he suffer from his disinterest in self-promotion? Curators joined Morris in his blind spot; Chamberlain was not included in either of the two major museum exhibitions that first documented this group ("When Attitudes Become Form," at the Kunsthalle Bern, and "Anti-Illusion: Procedures? Materials," at the Whitney Museum in New York, both in 1969). Two years later, Chamberlain was given a major retrospective at the Guggenheim Museum, but has never until now been seen in the context of the Process art movement.

Chamberlain is not one to doodle on tablecloths or napkins, but he is not averse to exercising his visual acuity at a bar. Many a fellow drinker, in the late sixties, left Max's Kansas City gingerly holding one of Chamberlain's crumpled, empty cigarette packs. These sketches became the loose models for two series of galvanized-steel and aluminum pieces done between 1967 and 1969. The first series was done with unpainted metal boxes whose dimensions were proportionate to cigarette packages, but now the compactor did the wadding. These pieces acknowledge the whole they were derived from: they collapse and fold into themselves with less clamor and more upright dignity than do the multisectioned, painted-steel pieces. The bends, dents, and wrinkles motivate the smooth, silvery softness of the surfaces into a discreetly luxuriant play of rippling light and shadow. The galvanized pieces are related, in their relative self-containment, to some of the all-white painted works. There is more than a little humor and criticism implicit in Chamberlain's deformation and re-formation of a form and an industrial material identified so completely with the rigors of Minimalism (several of these sculptures were made from slightly damaged boxes initially produced for Judd).

What industrial metal was to New York, plastic was to Los Angeles. In 1970 Chamberlain started the California version of his wadded boxes, using Plexiglas. He rented a walk-in oven in East Los Angeles, and in it brought Plexiglas boxes to the melting point, then stepped in quickly to encourage the flow of their curves as the boxes returned to a liquid state. After annealing in the oven at a lower temperature, each piece was brought to Larry Bell's studio to be vacuum-coated with a slithering, transparent rainbow of quartz and aluminum. The extreme heat of the oven and the difficulty in using Bell's machine to coat so irregular a surface impeded the full development of these works; but by reducing the plastic material to its original liquidity and then manipulating it, Chamberlain was able to draw more from its ungiving, antiseptic vulgarity than was evident in the countless art-souvenirs so often fabricated by one plastician or another. The cascading play of waves of light; lyric, rippling edges; and volumes rolling in and out of transparency pull an exotic, living presence from an almost entirely lifeless source. These works are like the mutant flora and fauna of some post-nuclear reverie.

Two other contemporary groups of works return to more mundane means. In the *Penthouse* sculptures of 1969, Chamberlain, sharply aware of the unique resistance of a given material, turned his energies to the air resistance encountered when a paper bag was blown up and popped. These crushed-paper pieces speak plainly and modestly and have strong affinities with drawing. They are often delicately stained with watercolor, and their fragile paper forms are preserved with clear resin, randomly dripped in some of the crumpled crevices. Turning in 1972 to the aluminum foil that might have wrapped the sandwiches in the paper bags, Chamberlain next made meteorlike wads, ranging in size from softball to boulder. For each piece he stapled together two sheets of heavy foil, then crinkled them up and heightened the gleam of the endless wrinkles and facets with auto lacquer. A final coat of clear resin proved not fully successful in preserving the shapes of these fragile painted pieces. While they are not completely compelling, they did serve to encourage a new, more responsible freedom with paint later on.

Chamberlain also made a foray into furniture design, using urethane foam for one of its intended purposes—though certainly not in an expected form. Starting in 1970, he united huge sections of foam and scooped out a number of shallow depressions for seating—making environmental couches geared to the spaces for which they were intended (they are large—up to forty feet in length). The couches comfortingly dwarf the user, embracing him in velvety sensuosity. Like the other foam sculptures, they too have proved sadly perishable, but delicious nonetheless.

Chamberlain broke his abstinence from ready-made painted steel twice between 1967 and 1974. While in Chicago in 1969, he proved unable to resist the countless objects of white-and-chrome steel (mainly kitchen appliances and cabinets) he kept encountering. Large sculptures like *Nanoweap* and *Coconino* are ragged, raucous, and far more confrontational than Chamberlain's other white works. In *Nanoweap* a stranded drawer and still-recognizable cabinet dance through a kitchen worker's burlesque nightmare. A second series, done in 1972 in Amarillo, is no less confrontational but more resolutely abstract and once again rumbles with the rhythmic polyphony of color. In 1974, Chamberlain fully returned his attention and intentions to painted steel.

Undeniably, some of the work Chamberlain completed between 1967 and 1974 is best regarded as high-risk exploration and experimentation. Not many artists are so willing repeatedly to start the learning process all over again, at the height of their early maturity. That Chamberlain's risks often proved fruitful is borne out by the success of his work since 1974. The urethane and galvanized-steel sculptures must be considered important milestones in his ongoing development, and in the development of sculpture in America.

In 1974 the procedures remained essentially the same as before, but the painted works Chamberlain showed then bristle with an exhilarating new freedom. A new group of wall pieces was made up of smoother, more simply compacted components bunched together in a strong vertical or diagonal thrust. This sleeker surface purged the work of its last similarities to Abstract Expressionist painting facture and speeded up the flight of the color across the metal membrane. In the past Chamberlain had occasionally added to or modified the preexisting color of a component; now he took the liberty of applying his own paint: multicolored splatters and drips, bursting with the euphoria of mark-making. This joyous, garish paint both mirrors and mocks the uniform overall polychrome of the work and makes emphatically clear the independent prefabrication of each component shape. The gravitational pull of the splattered paint on a shape punctuates its roundness with ups and downs, often turned on a different axis when that shape is finally integrated into the whole. What is painted both reinforces and contradicts what is volume. We see a more literally painted, Disneyesque Abstract Expressionism replace some of the physical dents and creases of the earlier, more sculptural Abstract Expressionism, only to then see the paint in its turn become sculptural volume. Sculptures like *Coke Ennyday* (1977) know why they are laughing.

Chamberlain continued to experiment boldly with color and paint. In 1977, he began to coat some of his shapes with spray-painted graffiti, with subway speed and trashy color. More recently, he has by chance hit upon a form of negative painting. Drawing with a

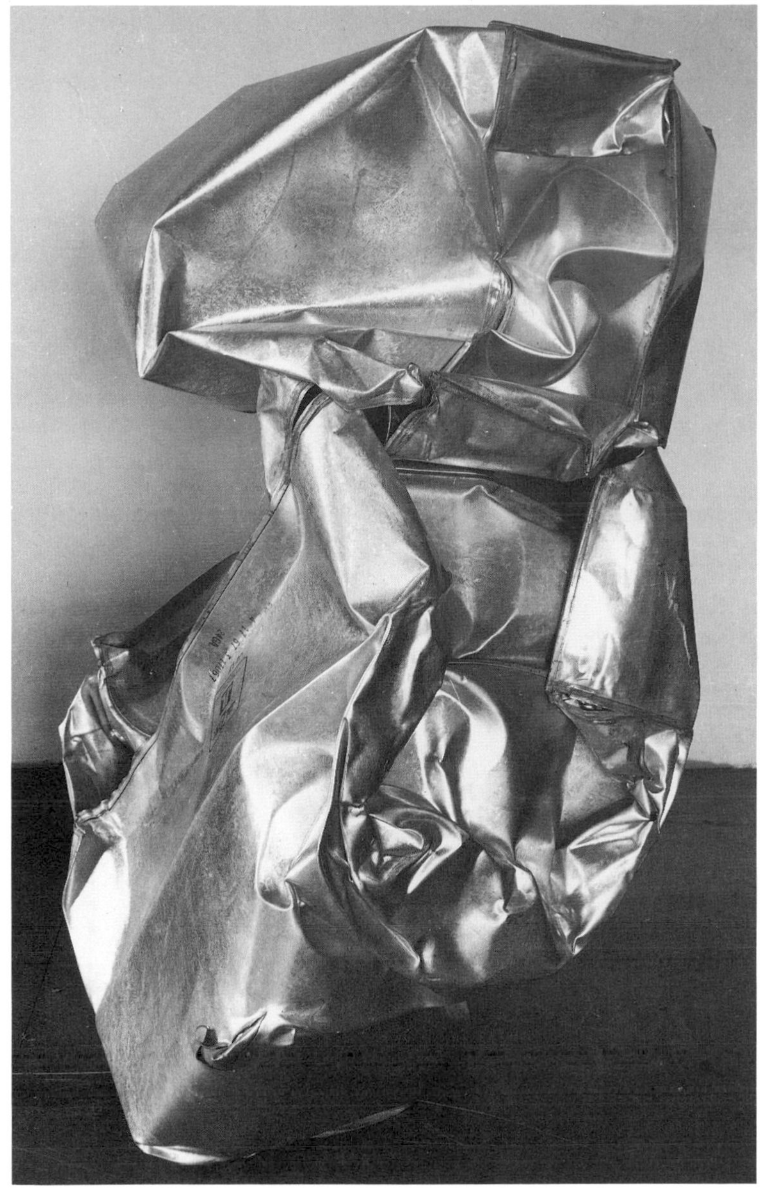

Norma Jean Rising, 1967 (cat. no. 291)

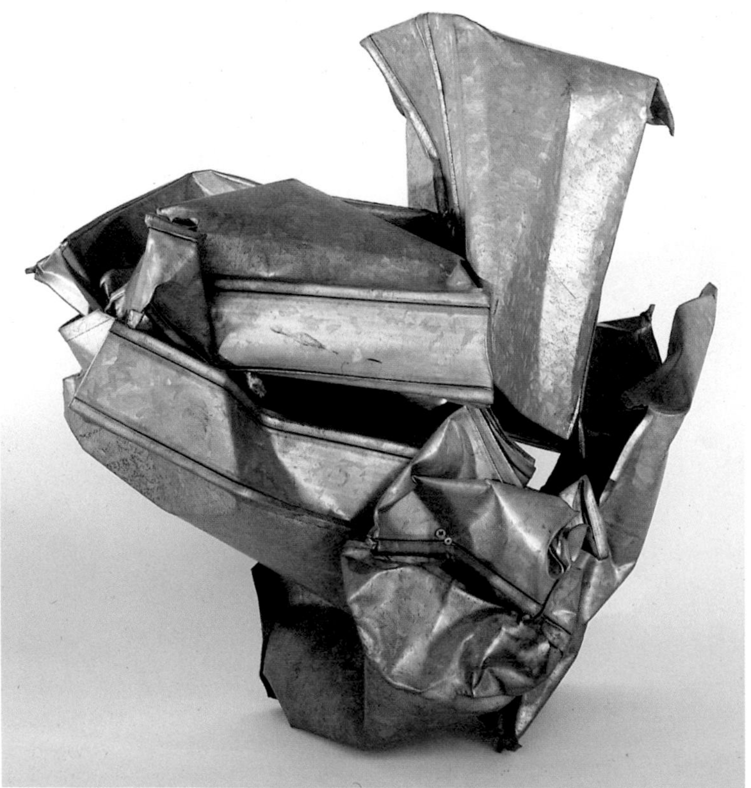

Malaprop, 1969 (cat. no. 352)

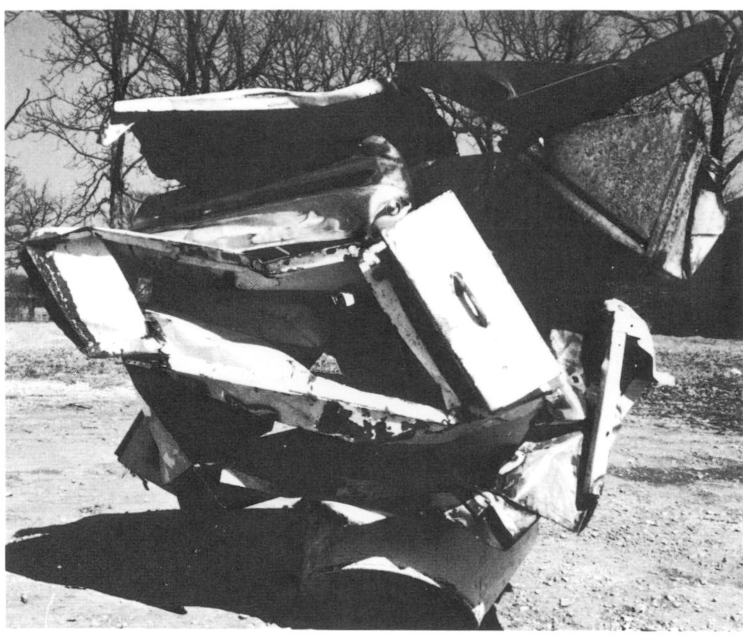

Nanoweap, 1969 (cat. no. 345)

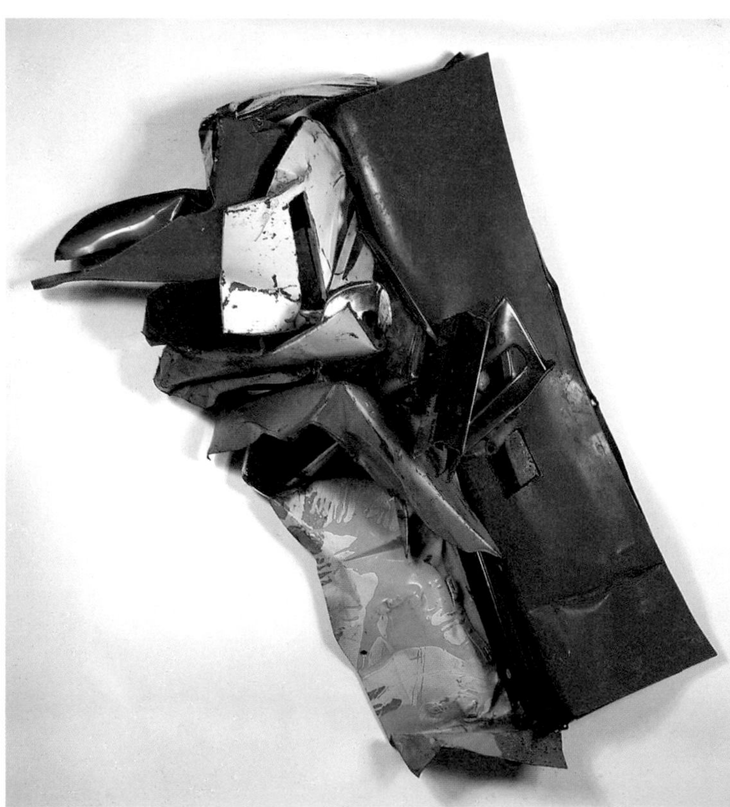

Daddy-O-Springs, 1975 (cat. no. 511)

sandblaster, he etches a giraffe-skin or camouflage pattern into a surface, mocking and making a design out of the shapes of the compactor's bruises.

The vertical and diagonal torsion seen in the wall pieces is even more active in the sculptures in the round and those that are free-standing but placed against a wall (most often in a horizontal formation dominated by four or more vertical volumes). Here too, the individual components are less compacted and more simply rolled; but they are more densely packed into huddles of wild disparity. The multiplicity of roundness and juncture is more confident. *Luftschloss* (1979) hazardously leans and rises to over twelve feet. From one view, it is dominated by an orange-red shape tipping into and almost over a purer red accumulation topped with white. Another view restores balance with the counter-movement of a billowing white flying buttress. The reduced compaction and contraction of the shapes and their new, relatively insistent verticality insinuate anthropomorphic figuration; but still, any attempt to read a closed gestalt in these works is frustrated and dissolved as soon as the eye starts on its rolling ride.

Since 1981 Chamberlain has increasingly pushed his configurations into upwardly cascading verticals and ground-hugging horizontals. The *Gondola* series, begun in 1981 in Osprey, Florida, and dedicated to his favorite writers (Hart Crane, Charles Olson, Herman Melville, Robert Creeley, etc.), utilizes chassis forms as armatures and piles them with loosely dispersed packages of painted steel—floats in a carnival of celebration, bearing gifts to kindred spirits. In a recent vertical sculpture such as *Wongkong Melong* (1982), an aquatic blue, phallic diagonal rises out of a vaginal base in one view, only to become a mere backdrop in another for a rumpled fan shape that flowers out of a rich, red giraffe-patterned mound. In *The Arch of Lumps* (1983), a more insistent vertical opens out of a giraffe-patterned cocoon to peel and soar into twelve feet of unfolding bliss. These sculptures have an unceasing visual richness of variegated roundness and color.

Like the paintings of Twombly, Johns, and Frank Stella, Chamberlain's sculpture has remained on the cutting edge of contemporary art through several later generations of painters and sculptors. Stella's push toward three-dimensional roundness, pulsing color, and use of an Abstract Expressionist, painterly agitation began with his *Indian Bird* wall-relief series in 1977; his work has continued to acquire ever greater spatial complexity and has surely developed with an eye on Chamberlain's works—one of which Stella owns. Unlike Chamberlain, Stella, even at his wildest, always maintains obsessive control (the french curve, for example, is more compatible with his procedures than with Chamberlain's). The generation of artists that has matured in the last ten years has placed renewed emphasis on expressiveness of surface and subject, while cooling them off with a variety of undermining strategies; their means and ends are often similar to Chamberlain's, if not directly influenced by him. Julian Schnabel's flashy intuitiveness, especially in his broken-crockery paintings; Cora Cohen's bristling, squeezed-from-the-tube strokes, partially wiped out and blurred on the edge of figuration—these, among others, are responding to Chamberlain's innovations. Artists with a renewed interest in sculpture's presence and volume have emerged: Mel Kendrick's organic, neo-Cubist figurations; John Newman's organically sensuous industrialized volumes; Bill Woodrow's Chamberlain-gone-to-prep-school accumulations. Chamberlain continues to provoke.

John Chamberlain is the first artist in post–World War II America to rehabilitate sculpture's volume and to achieve for it a potent presence and the radicality of painting. His ability to make roundness into color and color into roundness, pushing the two into an overall unity, is without equal. His sculptures invite and desire endless adjectives, but none of them can stick. His configurations are in a referential state, but their constant re-forming slips out of the adjectival grip; ultimately they transcend the language of analysis and description. The ravishing opticality must be its own pleasure and reward.

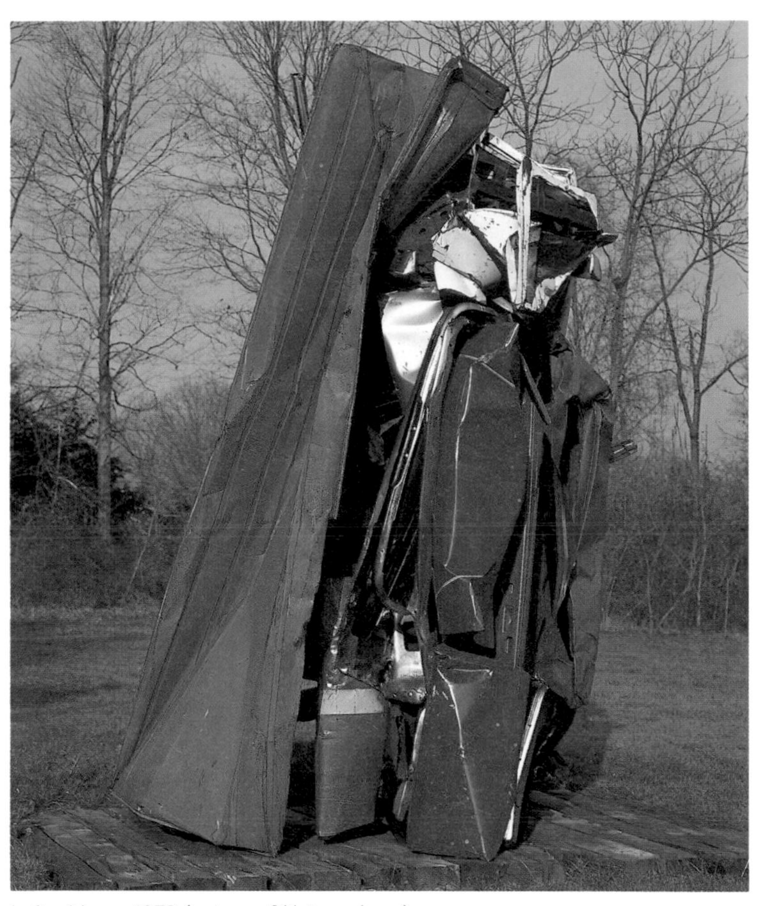
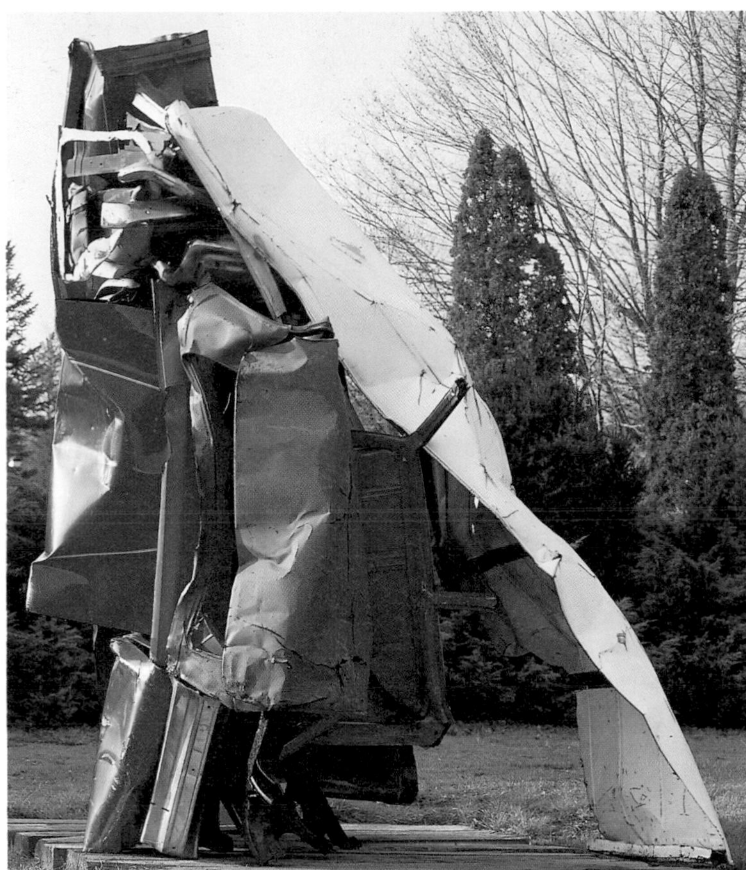

Luftschloss, 1979 (cat. no. 611, two views)

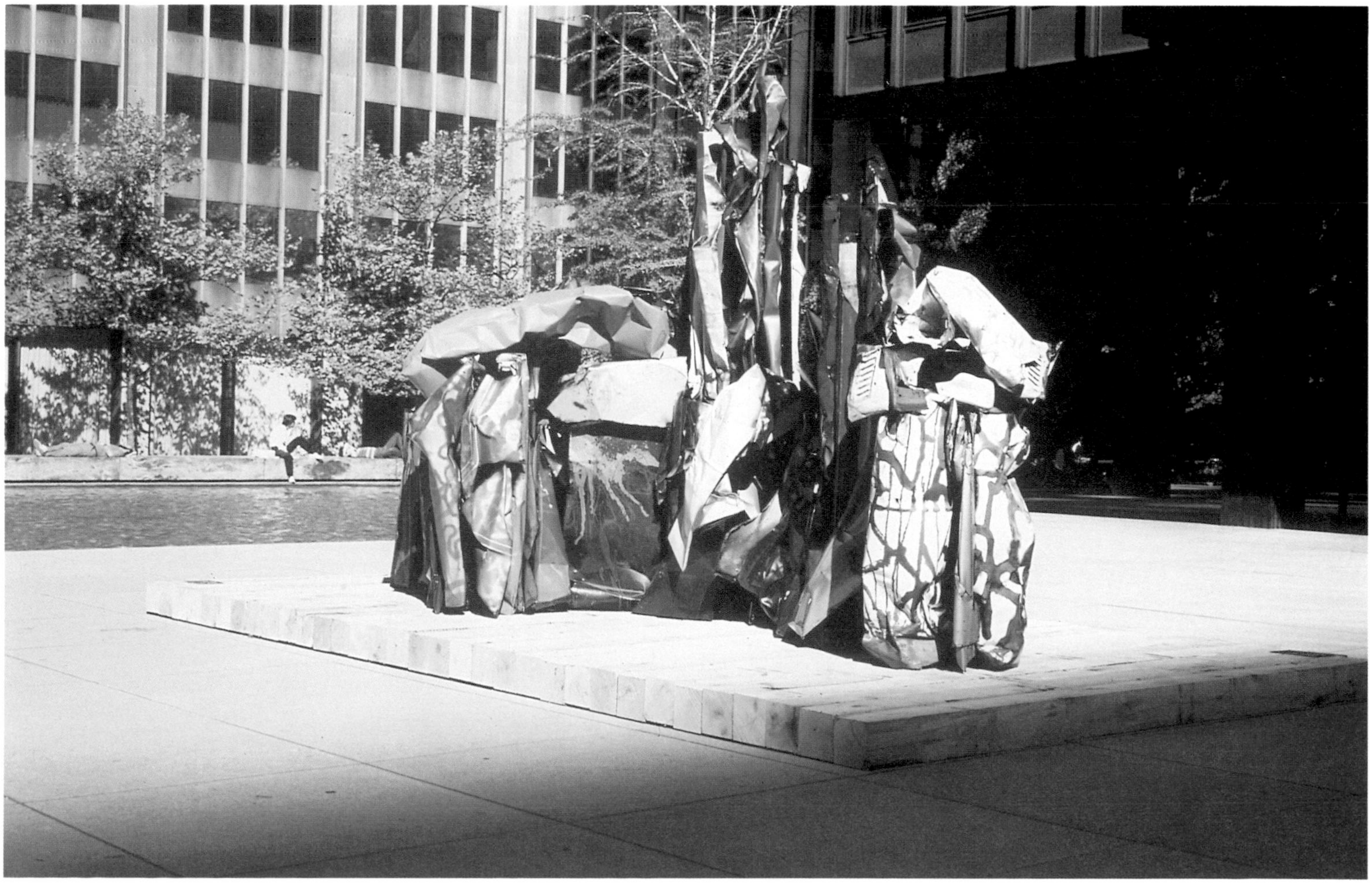

American Tableau, 1984 (cat. no. 762)

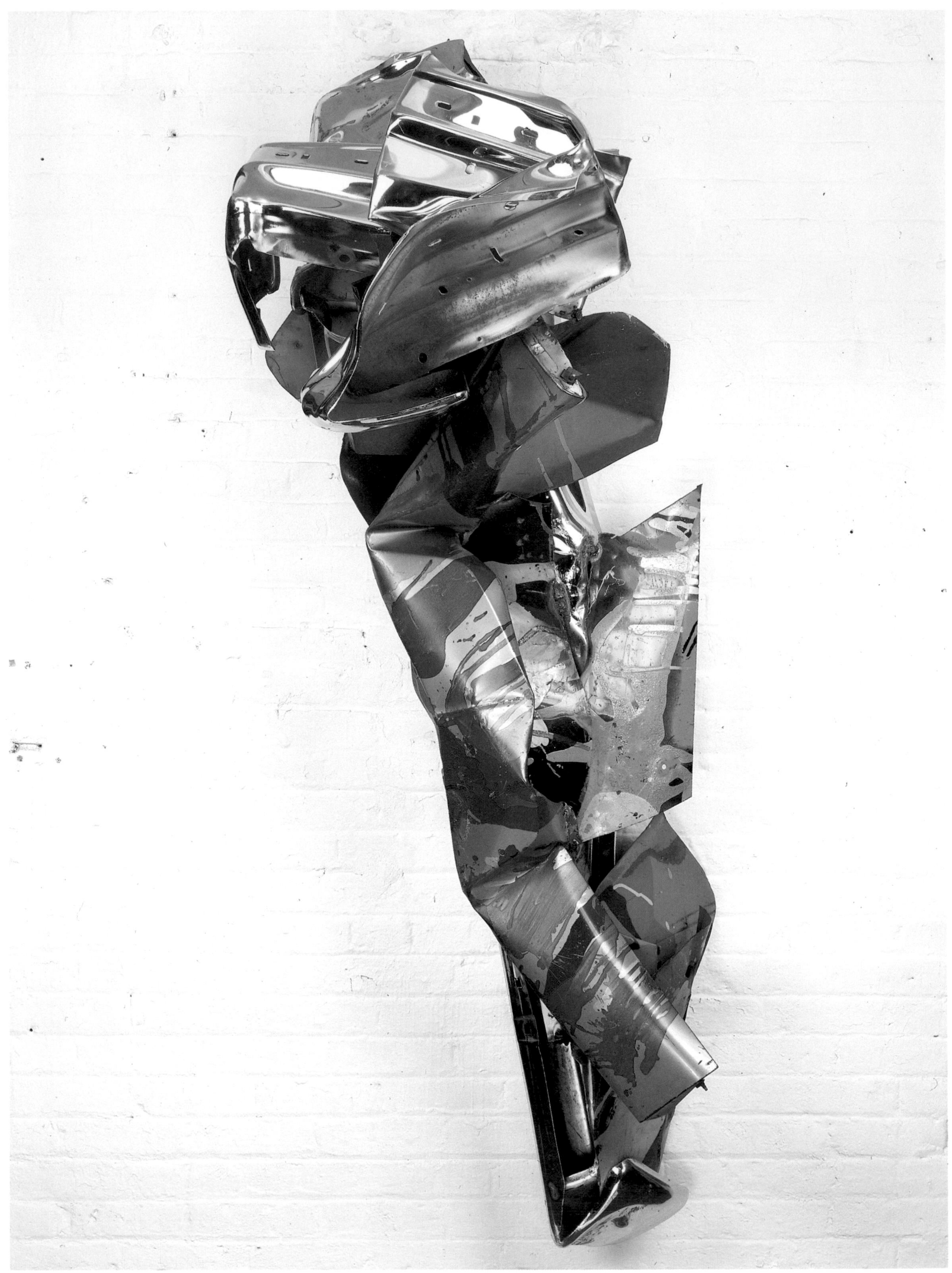

Coke Ennyday, 1977 (cat. no. 557)

Catalogue Raisonné of the Sculpture

Notes on the Organization of the Catalogue Raisonné

The catalogue raisonné represents the known body of John Chamberlain's sculpture between 1954 and 1985. It is according to Chamberlain's wishes that every sculpture, regardless of size, is recorded in this volume. The catalogue raisonné therefore includes major as well as minor works, occasional experimentations in new materials, and, in fact, every sculpture acknowledged by Chamberlain. Exception is made for small, so-called *sketches*, objects regarded by Chamberlain as studies, which are mentioned throughout but not individually recorded. Sculptures known to have been destroyed and those recently declared by the artist to be destroyed because of damage or neglect are recorded as well.

A number of small, abstract paintings made throughout the 1950s, a significant number of collages and reliefs of painted paper and metal, which embody a sizable portion of Chamberlain's output in the years between 1960 and 1963, and the auto-lacquer and metal-flake paintings of 1963 through 1965, which play an important role in Chamberlain's oeuvre, are not included here. All deserve to be acknowledged in another volume.

Necessary factual information is provided, but because the body of work speaks for itself, this has been limited. Introductions and notations to the sculptures have strictly to do with their physical nature, history, and present state; there are no statements of speculation or interpretation. I have chosen to omit rather than include any information that cannot be supported by written record or informed testimony.

I have had the great advantage of being able to consult with the artist, and I am very grateful to him for his collaboration. On many occasions, however, even his participation was not sufficient to solve the mysteries that a catalogue raisonné brings to light. All appropriate efforts have been made to seek information and record the history of each sculpture. In many instances it has not been possible to determine the present location of a sculpture or to trace it back to its origin. Some sculptures have been given away by the artist with no record; others have been lost through the years. For some of these latter, photographic documentation has been provided. As well, a few individuals have not cooperated in the research, and have withheld information. For these reasons, a supplement may at some time be necessary, in order to absorb the new information that the catalogue raisonné will generate. In the meantime, this volume is complete, to the best of my knowledge, as of December 1985.

Brief introductions precede special sections or groups of sculptures that need further explanation. These segments summarize relevant information that is not found in the catalogue entries.

Catalogue number

The sculptures are numbered chronologically by year, and alphabetically by title within each year. Exception is made for the urethane-foam couches, which are grouped chronologically at the end of 1985, and for several other series of works, such as the *Tonks*, which appear grouped at the end of their respective years. Chronological sequence within each year is known only infrequently, and has not been adhered to.

Title

The title of each work has been determined by accurate record or by John Chamberlain. In cases where the title has been changed over the course of years or has been confused with another title, the title presently preferred by the artist is used and the matter is discussed in the notes. In some cases where the artist himself has retitled a work at a later date, both titles are recorded: the original first, followed by a slash, followed by the more recent title. Example: *Tiny Piece #4/Scotch Spur*. The same format is used for a work that has been significantly altered by the artist. Example: *Swannanoa/Swannanoa II*.

In most cases, an untitled work was meant to be titled at a later date. Many untitled works have been recorded as such in gallery registries and exhibition catalogues. In recent years, Chamberlain has tried to retitle the untitled works he has come across, and in such cases the new title is listed and the matter is discussed in the notes. Other works that are listed as untitled are quite possibly works that have lost their titles over the years and that, for one reason or another, have not been positively identified.

Date

A positive date is stated as such and has been determined by record or by the artist. A questionable date is preceded by "circa," and has been determined by me or by the artist. Example: *c. 1960*.

In cases where a sculpture has been made over a period of years and acknowledged as such by the artist, the date will read with a dash between the first and final years, and the work is catalogued in the year of its completion. Example: 1960–62. In cases where a sculpture was restored by the artist and acknowledged as such, it is listed with a slash between the two dates and included in the year of its original creation. Example: *1959/1972*.

Dimensions

Dimensions are given in inches to the nearest half-inch and in centimeters to the nearest half-centimeter. Height precedes width, which precedes depth. In cases where only two dimensions are known, height precedes width. In cases where a work is mounted on a base that was made by the artist and acknowledged as such, the base is included in the dimensions. No dimensions were made by sight; all were either taken from verified records or from the artist's or owner's measurements.

Collection

The collection is listed as specified by the owner, with location and, where possible, date of acquisition. If the sculpture was acquired directly from the artist, whether by gift, purchase, or exchange, this fact is also noted. An owner requesting anonymity is listed as "private collection." Works that could not be located but that are known to have existed are listed as "present location unknown."

Provenance

The history of a work's previous ownership is listed in chronological sequence from earliest to latest, with location and date of acquisition, when known. Dealers and galleries are listed in the provenance only when directly involved in the transfer of a work.

Exhibitions

Exhibitions in which each work appeared are listed chronologically, from earliest to latest, and mentioned first by institution and location. This information is followed by the title of the exhibition, which is followed by catalogue information: catalogue number, page mentioned, page illustrated; a color illustration is specified. In the case of an unpaginated catalogue or a catalogue with no numbered objects, the title of the exhibition is followed by the word "listed." Finally, the exhibition dates are listed. Itineraries of traveling exhibitions are listed after the originating institution.

References

References include commentaries or reproductions in books and periodicals, and significant mentions in newspapers or magazines, and are listed in chronological order, from earliest to latest. Catalogues listed in the exhibitions list are not repeated in the reference list. References are listed by author, title of publication or title of article and title of publication, place of publication, publisher, date of publication or volume and issue number of periodical, page number, and illustration or plate number.

Notes

The notes record any information pertinent to the history or physical nature of the work that is not recorded in the preceding information. These may include the existence and location of a signature and date. In cases where there is a title or inscription, or an unusual signature, a full transcription is provided. Example: "#48 Cham '70." The notes also provide circumstances of destroyed works.

Reproductions

The best available reproductions have been selected; in some cases no photographic records exist.

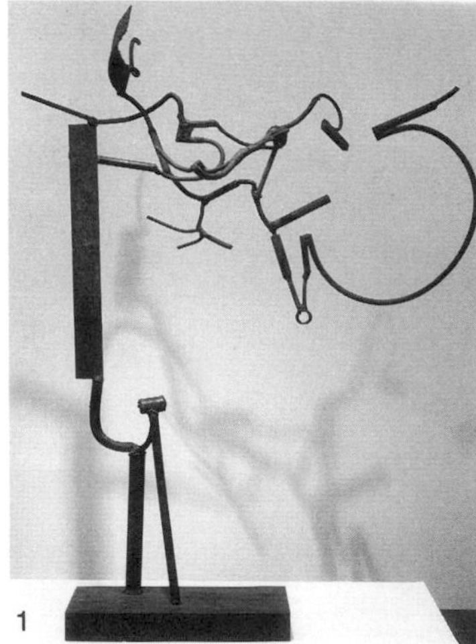
1

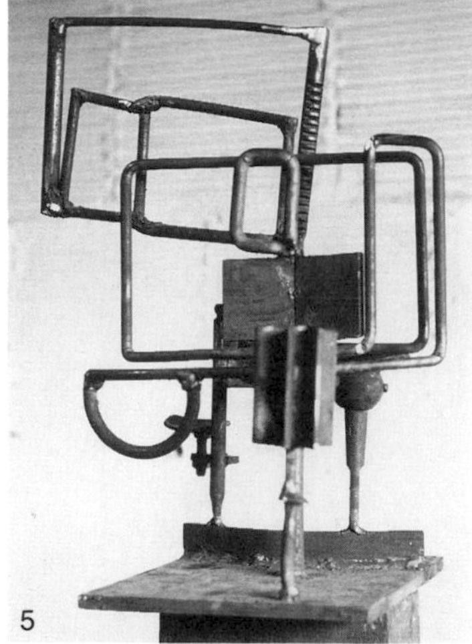
5

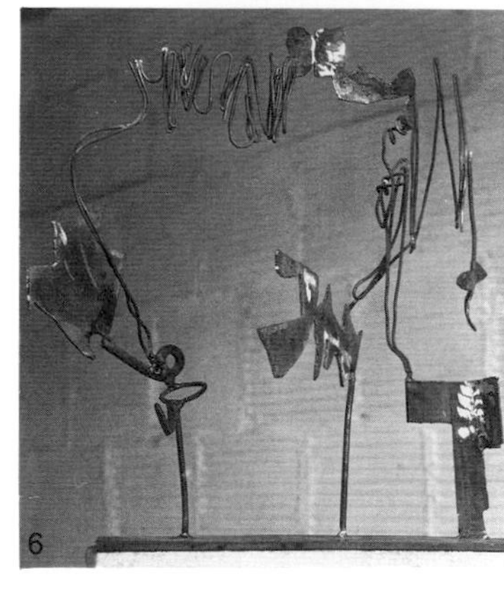
6

2

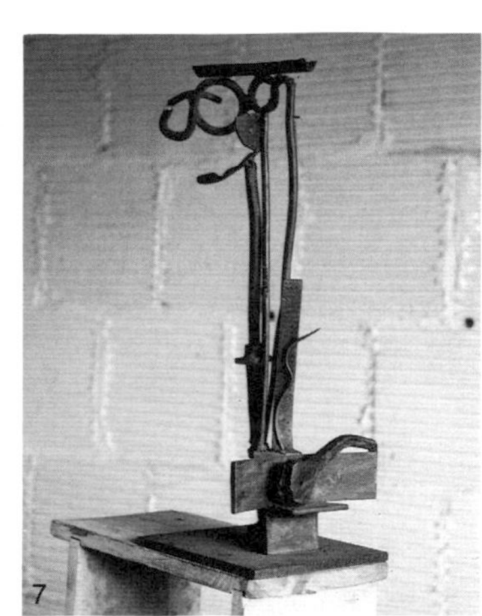
7

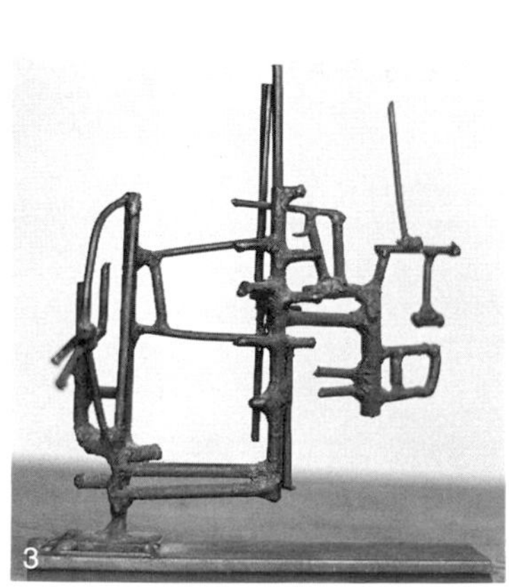
3

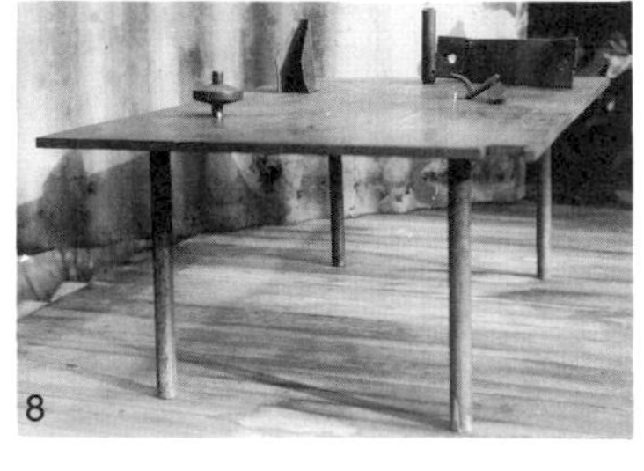
8

1

Calliope 1954
Steel
52 × 37 × 24 in.
(132 × 94 × 61 cm)

Collection
Collection of the artist, on extended loan to Weatherspoon Art Gallery, University of North Carolina at Greensboro, North Carolina, 1968.

Notes
See *Clytie*, cat. no. 2.

2

Clytie 1954
Steel
66 × 19½ × 13 in.
(167.5 × 49.5 × 33 cm).

Collection
Collection of the artist, Sarasota, Florida.

Notes
Clytie and *Calliope* (see cat. no. 1) were made simultaneously in Chicago. They are considered by Chamberlain to be his first successful sculptures.

Clytie was stolen from the artist's studio in Sarasota, Florida, in 1985.

3

Untitled 1954
Steel
9 × 8 × 3 in. (22.9 × 20 × 7.6 cm).

Collection
Joel Oppenheimer, New York, New York, 1956; acquired directly from the artist.

Notes
The sculpture was made while Chamberlain was an art student in Chicago and is his first sculpture made from steel rods. At present it is missing a piece; as seen in this photograph, a second rabbit ear on the top right has been lost.

4

Untitled c. 1954
Steel
28½ × 31 × 7½ in.
(72.5 × 79 × 19 cm).

Collection
Darlene Valentine, Santa Monica, California, 1966; acquired directly from the artist.

Notes
At present a portion of the sculpture is missing; there is no photograph of the sculpture in its original state.

The following group of sculptures (cat. nos. 5–10) was made at Black Mountain College, in North Carolina.

5

Interiors 1955
Steel
16 × 13 × 9 in.
(40.5 × 33 × 23 cm).

Collection
Hilda Wolpe, New York, New York, 1955; acquired directly from the artist.

Notes
The sculpture has suffered rust damage as the result of a fire.

6

Untitled 1955
Steel
Dimensions unknown.

Collection
Present location unknown.

7

Untitled 1955
Steel
Dimensions unknown.

Collection
Present location unknown.

8

Untitled c. 1955
Steel
Dimensions unknown.

Collection
Present location unknown.

9

Untitled c. 1955
Steel
Dimensions unknown.

Collection
Present location unknown.

Notes
According to Chamberlain, the sculpture may have been destroyed.

10

Untitled c. 1955
Steel
Dimensions unknown.

Collection
Present location unknown.

Notes
According to Chamberlain, the sculpture may have been destroyed.

11

G.G. 1956
Steel
77 × 24 × 23 in.
(195.5 × 61 × 58.5 cm).

Collection
Robert Natkin and Judith Dolnick, Redding, Connecticut; acquired directly from the artist.

12

Ballantine 1957
Painted steel
18 × 48 × 10 in.
(45.5 × 122 × 25.5 cm).

Collection
Allan Stone, New York, New York, 1963.

Provenance
Martha Jackson Gallery, New York, New York, 1958.

References
Diane Waldman, *John Chamberlain: A Retrospective Exhibition* (New York: The Solomon R. Guggenheim Foundation, 1971), illus. p. 23.

Notes
The sculpture has been painted with a black rust-resistant coating by the owner.

13

Cord 1957
Steel
16 × 12 × 10 in.
(40.5 × 30.5 × 25.5 cm).

Collection
Allan Stone, New York, New York, 1960.

Provenance
Martha Jackson Gallery, New York, New York, 1958.

Exhibitions
The Solomon R. Guggenheim Museum, New York, New York. *John Chamberlain: A Retrospective Exhibition*, cat. no. 3, illus. p. 22. December 23, 1971–February 20, 1972.

Whitney Museum of American Art, New York, New York. *The Third Dimension*, illus. cover and p. 63. December 6, 1984–March 3, 1985. Traveled to Fort Worth Art Museum, Fort Worth, Texas. May 12–July 21, 1985; The Cleveland Museum of Art, Cleveland, Ohio. August 21–October 17, 1985; Newport Harbor Art Museum, Newport Beach, California. November 7, 1985–January 5, 1986.

References
Elizabeth C. Baker, "The Chamberlain Crunch," *Art News*, vol. 70, no. 10 (February 1972), illus. p. 28.

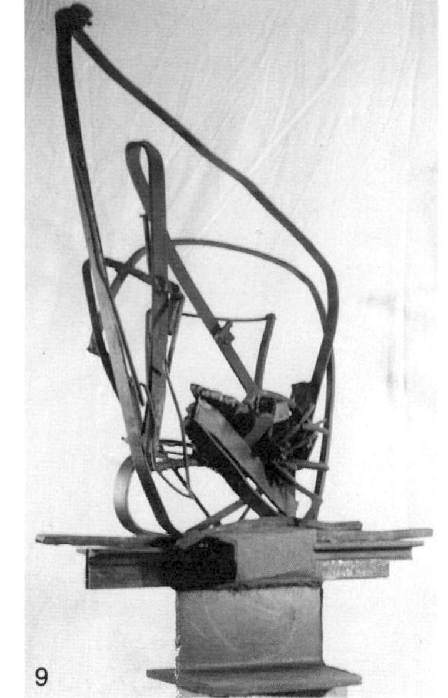
9

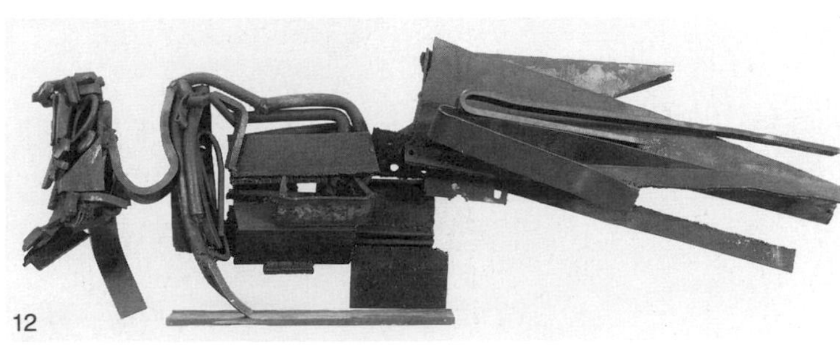
12

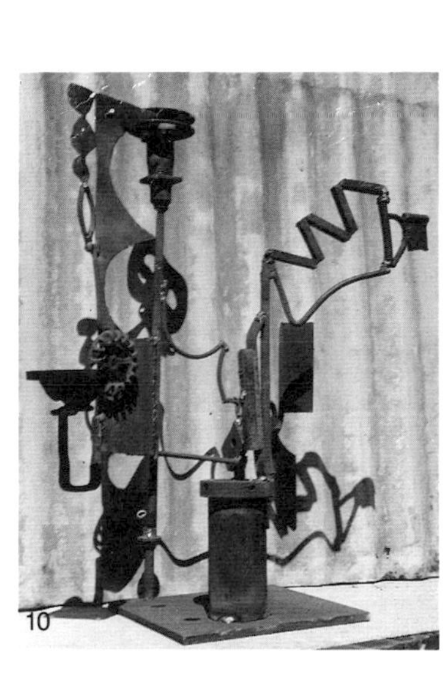
10

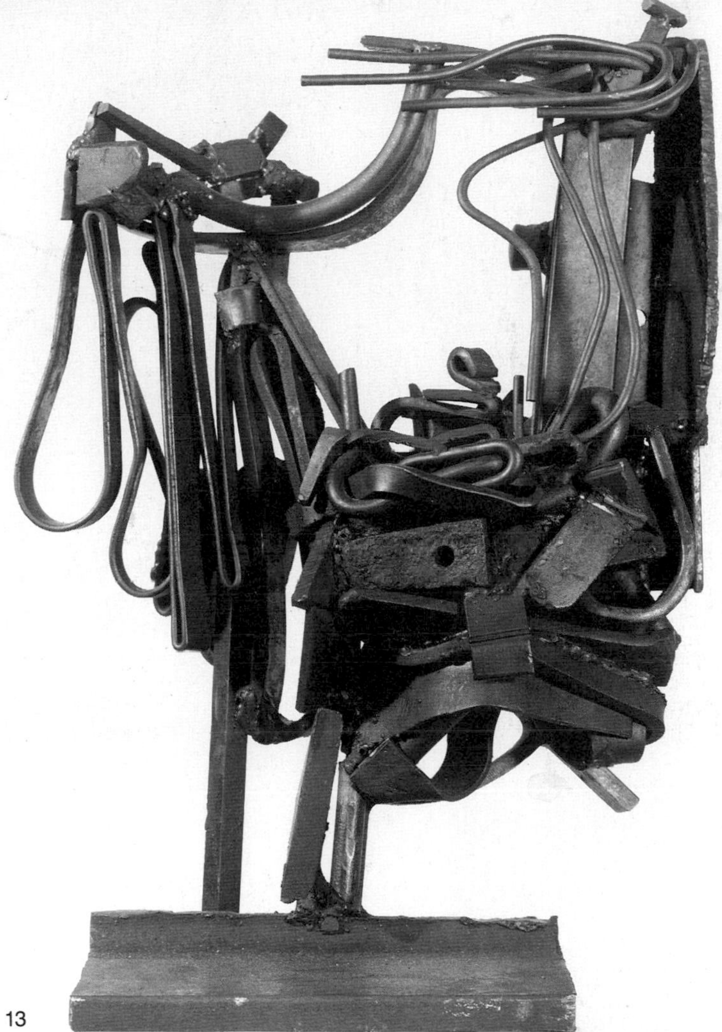
13

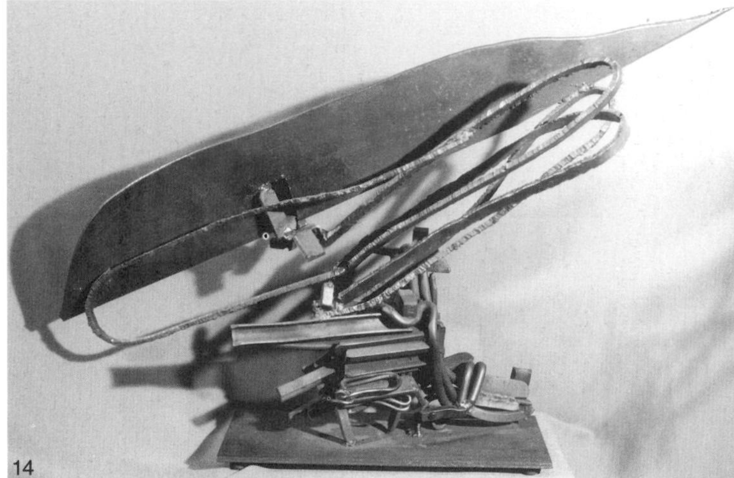
14

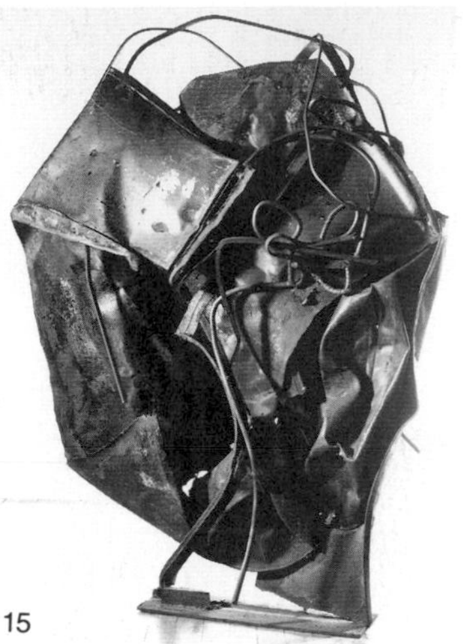
15

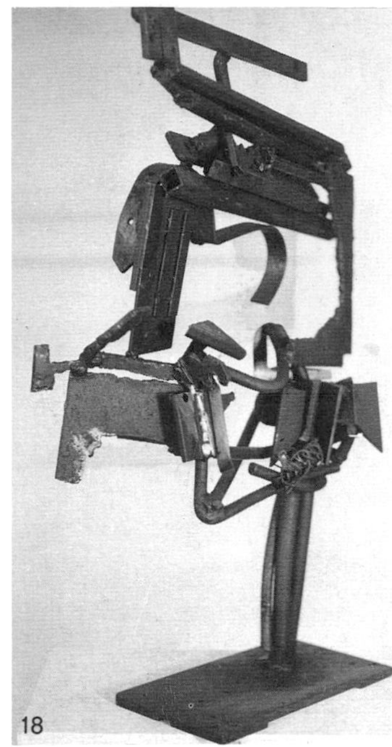
18

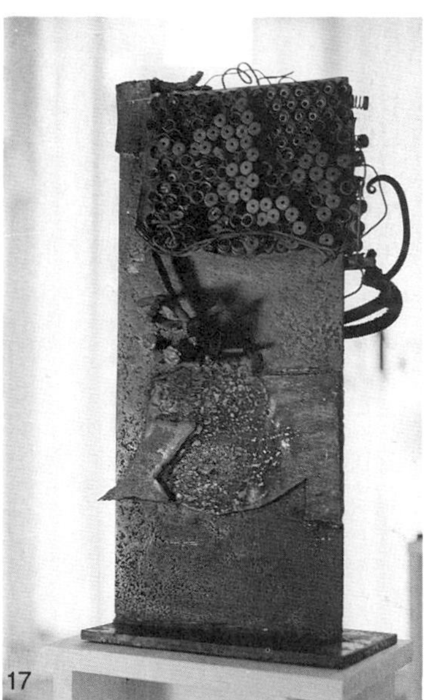
17

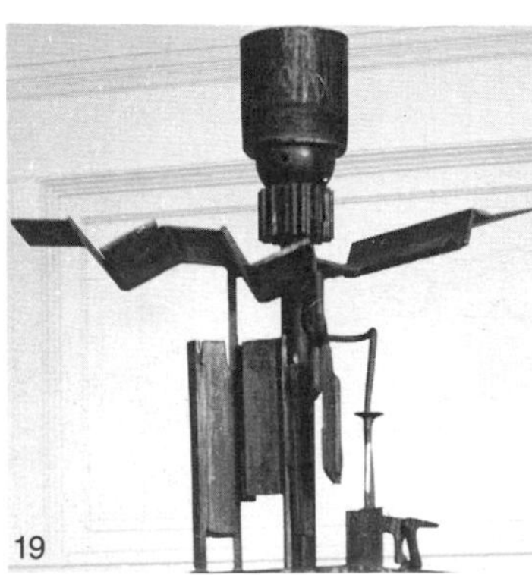
19

14

Projectile D.S.N.Y. 1957

Steel

23 × 38 × 22½ in.
(58.5 × 96.5 × 57 cm).

Collection

American Broadcasting Companies, Inc., New York, New York, 1967.

Provenance

Martha Jackson Gallery, New York, New York, 1958; Allan Stone Gallery, New York, New York, 1963.

Exhibitions

The Solomon R. Guggenheim Museum, New York, New York. *John Chamberlain: A Retrospective Exhibition*, cat. no. 2, illus. p. 22. December 23, 1971–February 20, 1972.

15

Shortstop 1957

Painted and chromium-plated steel and iron

58 × 44 × 18 in.
(147.5 × 112 × 45.5 cm)

Collection

Dia Art Foundation, New York, New York, 1980.

Provenance

Richard Bellamy, New York, New York; Ed Cauduro, Portland, Oregon; Lone Star Foundation, New York, New York, 1978.

Exhibitions

Hansa Gallery, New York, New York. *Group Show*. 1958.

The Cleveland Museum of Art, Cleveland, Ohio. *Sculpture by John Chamberlain*, listed. January 3–29, 1967.

The Solomon R. Guggenheim Museum, New York, New York. *John Chamberlain: A Retrospective Exhibition*, cat. no. 4, pp. 6, 7, illus. p. 24. December 23, 1971–February 20, 1972.

Portland Art Museum, Portland, Oregon. *Sixties to Seventy-Two: American Art from the Collection of Ed Cauduro*, cat. no. 16. September 29–October 29, 1972.

The Art Galleries, University of California, Santa Barbara. *7 + 5: Sculptors in the 1950s*, cat. no. 5, p. 25, illus. p. 27. January 6–February 15, 1976. Traveled to Phoenix Art Museum, Phoenix, Arizona. March 5–April 11, 1976.

References

Phyllis Tuchman, "An Interview with John Chamberlain," *Artforum*, vol. 10, no. 6 (February 1972), illus. p. 40.

Edward B. Henning, "An Important Sculpture by John Chamberlain," *The Bulletin of the Cleveland Museum of Art*, vol. 60, no. 8 (October 1973), p. 246.

Wayne Anderson, *American Sculpture in Process: 1930–1970* (Boston: New York Graphic Society, 1975), p. 127.

Matthew Baigell, *Dictionary of American Art* (New York: Harper and Row, 1979), p. 64.

Notes

Shortstop is the sculpture that marks Chamberlain's departure from the exclusive use of steel rods as material. It is the first piece made from automobile body parts. The two bumpers that have been fitted together and wrapped with iron rods were originally part of a 1929 Ford that Chamberlain had found at Larry Rivers' property on Long Island.

16

Untitled 1957

Steel

26 × 19½ × 6½ in.
(66 × 49.5 × 16.5 cm).

Collection

Paul R. Campagna, Chicago, Illinois, 1957.

Provenance

Wells Street Gallery, Chicago, Illinois.

Exhibitions

Wells Street Gallery, Chicago, Illinois. *John Chamberlain*. 1957.

Museum of Contemporary Art, Chicago, Illinois. *Alternative Spaces: A History in Chicago*. June 23–August 19, 1984.

The following three sculptures (cat. nos. 17–19) were made in New York when John Chamberlain returned from Black Mountain College in 1957.

17

Stiele c. 1957

Steel

Dimensions unknown.

Collection

Present location unknown.

Provenance

Davida Gallery, New York, New York, 1958; Howard and Jean Lipman, New York, New York, 1958.

18

Untitled c. 1957

Steel

Dimensions unknown.

Collection

Present location unknown.

19

Untitled c. 1957
Steel
Dimensions unknown.

Collection
Present location unknown.

Notes
According to Chamberlain, this sculpture may have been destroyed.

20

Construction 1958
Steel
22 in. high (56 cm).

Collection
Present location unknown.

Provenance
Leo Castelli Gallery, New York, New York; Robert and Ethel Scull, New York, New York.

21

Nutcracker 1958
Painted steel
50 × 50 × 30 in.
(127 × 127 × 76 cm)

Collection
Allan Stone, New York, New York, 1963.

Provenance
Martha Jackson Gallery, New York, New York, 1960.

Exhibitions
Martha Jackson Gallery, New York, New York. *New Forms—New Media I*. June 6–24, 1960.

Martha Jackson Gallery, New York, New York. *New Forms—New Media II*, cat. no. 14, illus. September 8–24, 1960.

The Cleveland Museum of Art, Cleveland, Ohio. *Sculpture by John Chamberlain*, listed. January 3–29, 1967.

The Solomon R. Guggenheim Museum, New York, New York. *John Chamberlain: A Retrospective Exhibition*, cat. no. 6, illus. p. 25. December 23, 1971–February 20, 1972.

References
John D. Morse, "He Returns to Dada," *Art in America*, vol. 48, no. 3 (October 1960), illus. p. 76.

Emily Genauer, "Art and the Artist," *New York Post*, January 8, 1972, illus.

22

Rochester 1958
Steel
47 × 77 × 9 in.
(119.5 × 195.5 × 23 cm).

Collection
Collection of the artist, Sarasota, Florida.

Exhibitions
Museum of Modern Art, New York, New York. *Recent Sculpture USA*. May 13–August 16, 1959. Traveled to The Denver Art Museum, Denver, Colorado. October 12–November 22, 1959; The Tucson Fine Arts Association, Tucson, Arizona. December 5, 1959–January 10, 1960; The Los Angeles County Museum of Art, Los Angeles, California. February 22–April 3, 1960; The City Art Museum of Saint Louis, Saint Louis, Missouri. May 3–June 12, 1960; The Museum of Fine Arts, Boston, Massachusetts. September 14–October 16, 1960.

23

Waumandie Gate 1958
Steel and brass
85 × 29½ × 14 in.
(216 × 75 × 35.5 cm).

Collection
Hirshhorn Museum and Sculpture Garden, Smithsonian Institution, Washington, D.C., 1980, The Martha Jackson Memorial Collection; gift of Mr. and Mrs. David K. Anderson.

Provenance
Martha Jackson Gallery, New York, New York, 1959; David Anderson Gallery, New York, New York, 1969.

Exhibitions
Martha Jackson Gallery, New York, New York. *The Enormous Room*. January 2–23, 1959.

References
Diane Waldman, *John Chamberlain: A Retrospective Exhibition* (New York: The Solomon R. Guggenheim Foundation, 1971), illus. p. 26.

University of Maryland Art Gallery, College Park, Maryland, *The Private Collection of Martha Jackson* (Mount Vernon, New York: A. Colish, 1973), illus. p. 8.

Notes
Waumandie Gate was originally made as a gate for the home of Martha Jackson.

While in the possession of David Anderson, *Waumandie Gate* was coated with a Rustoleum primer paint that destroyed the original rusted finish. Upon discovering this, Chamberlain refused to allow the work to be shown at the Guggenheim retrospective exhibition in 1971. It was donated to the Hirshhorn in this state. In 1983, following the artist's instructions, the conservator at the Hirshhorn had the sculpture sandblasted and given a polyurethane coating.

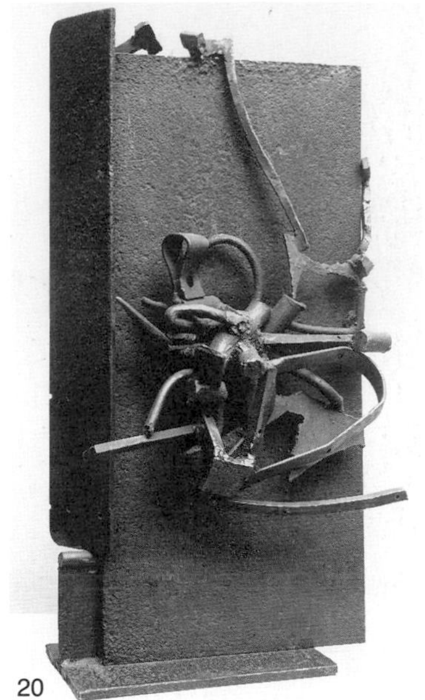
20

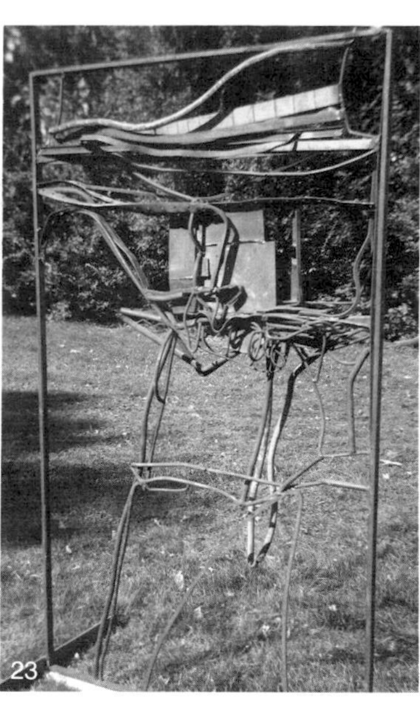
23

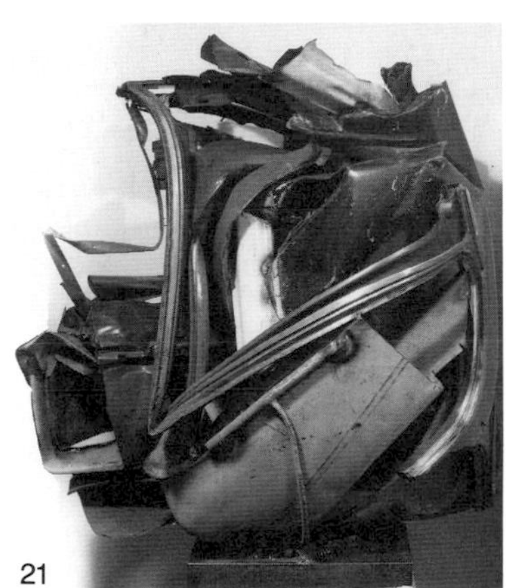
21

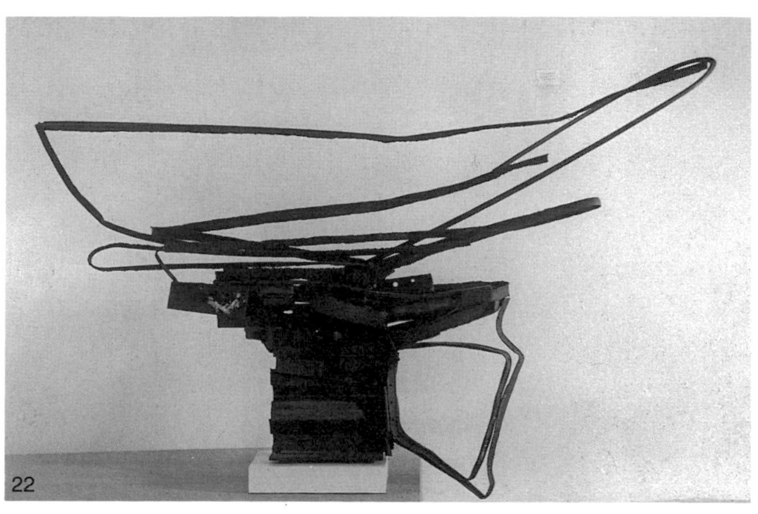
22

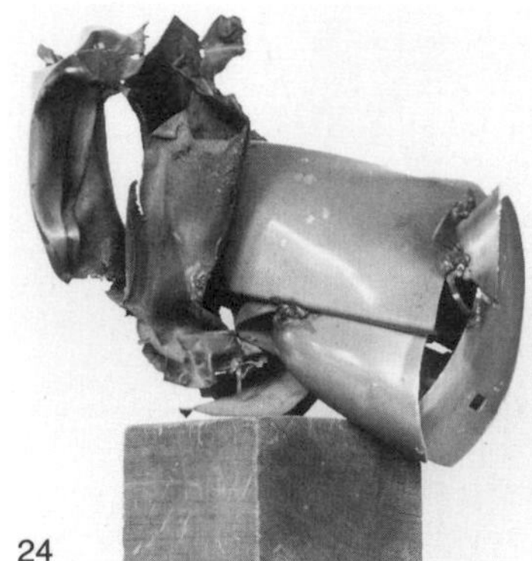
24

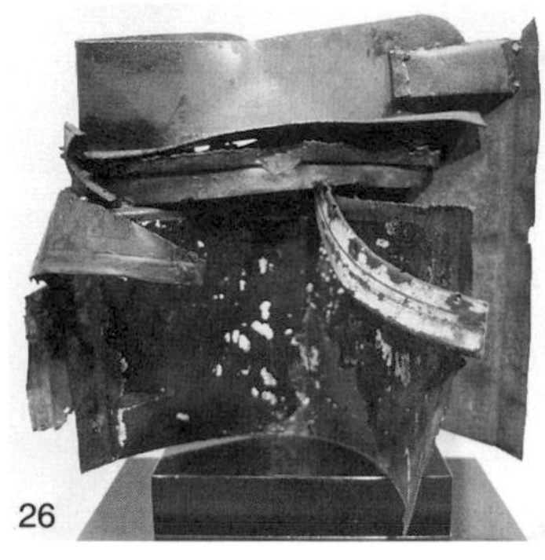
26

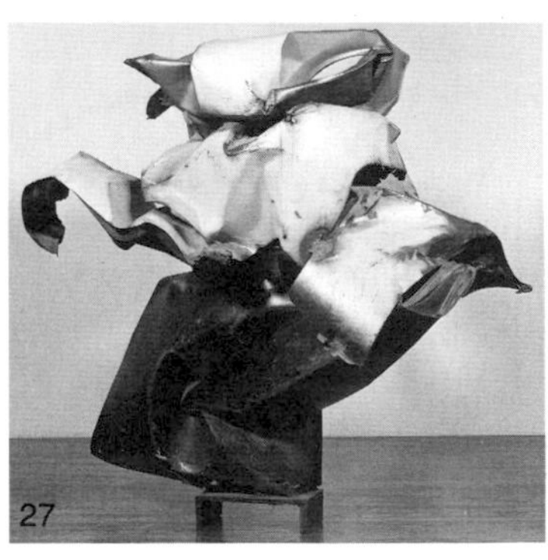
27

24

Untitled 1958

Painted metal with wood base

11 × 12 × 12 in.

(28 × 30.5 × 30.5 cm).

Collection

Joshua Aronson, New York, New York.

Provenance

Allan Stone, New York, New York, 1967; Adam and Judith Aronson, Saint Louis, Missouri.

25

Untitled c. 1958

Painted steel

40 × 38 × 14 in.

(101.5 × 96.5 × 35.5 cm).

Collection

Neumann Family Collection, New York, New York, 1959.

Provenance

Hansa Gallery, New York, New York, 1958.

Exhibitions

The Solomon R. Guggenheim Museum, New York, New York. *John Chamberlain: A Retrospective Exhibition* (see notes). December 23, 1971–February 20, 1972.

Notes

The sculpture has been incorrectly referred to as *Redwing* since the early sixties (see cat. no. 56). It was exhibited at the Guggenheim retrospective exhibition, but was listed as *Redwing* and a photograph of *Redwing* was reproduced in the catalogue. *Redwing* was not exhibited at the Guggenheim.

26

Arcadia 1959

Painted steel

14 × 13½ × 10 in.

(35.5 × 35 × 25.5 cm).

Collection

Olga Hirshhorn, Naples, Florida, 1980.

Provenance

Martha Jackson Gallery, New York, New York, 1960; Donald Peters, New York, New York, 1960; G. David Thompson, Pittsburgh, Pennsylvania; Joseph H. Hirshhorn, New York, New York, 1966.

Exhibitions

Parke-Bernet Galleries, Inc., New York, New York. *Modern Sculptures from Various Owners: An Important Group of Contemporary Works from the Collection Formed by the Late G. David Thompson*, cat. no. 28, illus. p. 29. May 19, 1966.

Bruce Museum, Greenwich, Connecticut. *A Collector's Eye: The Olga Hirshhorn Collection*, cat. no. 16. Organized by the Smithsonian Institution Traveling Exhibition Service. March 28–April 26, 1981. Traveled to Fine Arts Center, Nashville, Tennessee. May 16–August 16, 1981; Florida International University, Miami, Florida. September 5–October 4, 1981; Art Museum of Southern Texas, Corpus Christi, Texas. October 24, 1981–January 10, 1982; Meadows Museum of Art, Shreveport, Louisiana. January 30–February 28, 1982; Smith College Museum of Art, Northampton, Massachusetts. March 20–April 19, 1982; Iowa State University, Ames, Iowa. May 8–June 6, 1982; Oak Ridge Community Art Center, Oak Ridge, Indiana. June 26–July 25, 1982; Evansville Museum of Art, Evansville, Indiana. August 14–September 12, 1982; Mansfield Art Center, Mansfield, Ohio. October 2–31, 1982; Santa Fe Community College, Gainesville, Florida. November 20–December 19, 1982; Arapahoe Community College, Littleton, Colorado. January 8–February 5, 1983; Colorado Springs Fine Arts Center, Colorado Springs, Colorado. February 26–March 27, 1983; Duke University, Durham, North Carolina. April 16–June 1983; Western College Center for the Arts, Grand Junction, Colorado. July 6–August 10, 1983; Tacoma Art Museum, Tacoma, Washington. September 10–October 9, 1983; Southeast Arkansas Art Center, Pine Bluff, Arkansas. October 29–December 4, 1983; University of Alabama Art Gallery, Birmingham, Alabama. December 17, 1983–January 15, 1984; Bradley Gallery, Naples, Florida. February 4, 1984–March 4, 1984; Muskegon Museum of Art, Muskegon, Michigan. May 12–June 10, 1984; San Jose Museum of Art, San Jose, California. June 30–July 29, 1984; Laumeier International Sculpture Park, Saint Louis, Missouri. August 18–September 16, 1984; Skidmore College, Saratoga Springs, New York. October 6–November 4, 1984.

27

H.A.W.K. 1959

Painted steel

60 × 60 × 60 in.

(152.5 × 152.5 × 152.5 cm).

Collection

Philip Johnson, New Canaan, Connecticut, 1981.

Provenance

Mr. and Mrs. Allan Stone, Purchase, New York; The Mayor Gallery, London; Peder Bonnier, New York, New York; Leo Castelli Gallery, New York, New York, 1981.

Exhibitions

The Solomon R. Guggenheim Museum, New York, New York. *John Chamberlain: A Retrospective Exhibition*, cat. no. 8, illus. p. 28. December 23, 1971–February 20, 1972.

The Mayor Gallery, London. *John Chamberlain: An Exhibition of Sculpture: 1959–1962*, cat. no. 4, illus. June 27–August 12, 1977.

28

Hawthorne c. 1959

Painted steel

16 × 21½ × 11 in.

(40.5 × 55 × 28 cm).

Collection

Richard Brown Baker, New York, New York, 1960.

Provenance

Martha Jackson Gallery, New York, New York, 1960.

Exhibitions

Martha Jackson Gallery, New York, New York. *John Chamberlain*. January 5–30, 1960.

Staten Island Museum, Staten Island, New York. *Contemporary Americans Selected from the Richard Brown Baker Collection*. February 21–April 17, 1960.

Martha Jackson Gallery, New York, New York. *John Chamberlain: Sculpture*. November 22–December 17, 1960.

Walker Art Center, Minneapolis, Minnesota. *Eighty Works from the Richard Brown Baker Collection*. March 12–April 16, 1961.

Jewett Art Center of Wellesley College, Wellesley, Massachusetts. *The Richard Brown Baker Collection of Contemporary Art*. May 5–26, 1963.

The Aldrich Museum of Contemporary Art, Ridgefield, Connecticut. *Art of the Fifties and Sixties: Selections from the Richard Brown Baker Collection*, illus. April 25–July 5, 1965.

Museum of Art, Science and Industry, Bridgeport, Connecticut. *The Machine in Art*. October 15, 1965–January 30, 1966.

The Newark Museum, Newark, New Jersey. *Trends in Painting and Sculpture*. January 25–March 1967.

Museum of Art, Rhode Island School of Design, Providence, Rhode Island. *Small Works: Selections from the Richard Brown Baker Collection of Contemporary Art*. April 5–May 6, 1973.

29

Johnny Bird 1959

Painted steel
59 × 53 × 45½ in.
(150 × 134.5 × 115.5 cm).

Collection
Sydney and Frances Lewis, Richmond, Virginia, 1970.

Provenance
Martha Jackson Gallery, New York, New York, 1960.

Exhibitions
Andrew Dickson White Museum of Art, Cornell University, Ithaca, New York. *Fourteenth Festival of Contemporary Art*. February 11, 1960.

Martha Jackson Gallery, New York, New York. *John Chamberlain: Sculpture*. November 22–December 17, 1960.

Parke-Bernet, New York, New York. *Important Contemporary Paintings and Sculpture*, cat. no. 40, illus. November 18, 1970.

The Solomon R. Guggenheim Museum, New York, New York. *John Chamberlain: A Retrospective Exhibition*, cat. no. 11, color illus. p. 39. December 23, 1971–February 20, 1972.

Richmond Public Library, Richmond, Virginia. *Selections from the Sydney and Frances Lewis Collection*. February–April 1978.

Whitney Museum of American Art, New York, New York. *The Third Dimension*, color illus. p. 52. December 6, 1984–March 3, 1985. Traveled to Fort Worth Art Museum, Fort Worth, Texas. May 12–July 21, 1985; The Cleveland Museum of Art, Cleveland, Ohio. August 21–October 17, 1985; Newport Harbor Art Museum, Newport Beach, California. November 7, 1985–January 5, 1986.

References
Barbara Butler, "Movie Stars and Other Members of the Cast," *Art International*, vol. 4, no. 2/3 (February/March 1960), illus. p. 52.

Wayne Anderson, "American Sculpture: The Situation in the Fifties," *Artforum*, vol. 5, no. 10 (Summer 1967), illus. p. 67.

Phaidon Dictionary of Twentieth-Century Art (Oxford: Phaidon, and New York: Dutton, 1973), p. 67.

Benjamin H. D. Buchloh, ed., *Carl Andre—Hollis Frampton/Twelve Dialogues 1962–1963* (Halifax: Press of the Nova Scotia College of Art and Design, and New York: New York University Press, 1980), illus. p. 15.

30

Manitou 1959

Painted steel
13 × 13 × 3 in.
(33 × 33 × 7.5 cm).

Collection
Dia Art Foundation, New York, New York, 1980.

Provenance
Martha Jackson Gallery, New York, New York, 1960; The Mayor Gallery, London, 1977; Peder Bonnier, New York, New York; Lone Star Foundation, New York, New York, 1979.

Exhibitions
Martha Jackson Gallery, New York, New York. *John Chamberlain: Sculpture*. November 22–December 17, 1960.

Martha Jackson Gallery, New York, New York. *Sculpture International*. November 23–December 29, 1962.

Dwan Gallery, Los Angeles, California. *John Chamberlain*. November 29, 1966–January 7, 1967.

The Solomon R. Guggenheim Museum, New York, New York. *John Chamberlain: A Retrospective Exhibition*, cat. no. 7, illus. p. 27. December 23, 1971–February 20, 1972.

Zabriskie Gallery, New York, New York. *Welded Sculpture*. September 7–October 7, 1976.

The Mayor Gallery, London. *John Chamberlain: An Exhibition of Sculpture: 1959–1962*, cat. no. 1, illus. June 27–August 12, 1977.

Grace Borgenicht Gallery and Terry Dintenfass Gallery, New York, New York. *Twenty Galleries/Twenty Years*, illus. p. 16. January 9–February 4, 1982.

Notes
The Manitou was a powerful nature spirit of the Algonquian Indians, who lived in the area around Rochester, Indiana, the artist's birthplace.

The sculpture was made from a lunch box; the painted symbol is a part of the original object and was not painted by the artist.

The piece is signed in pen: *Manitou/Chamberlain '59*.

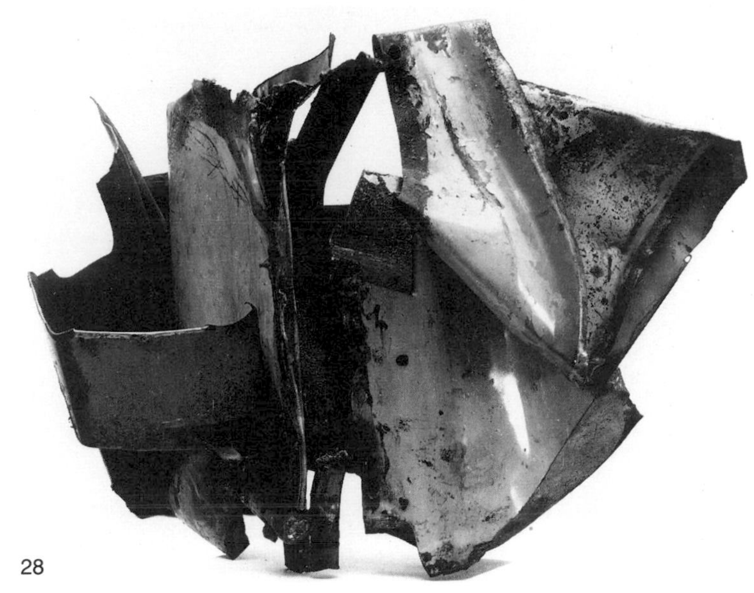

28

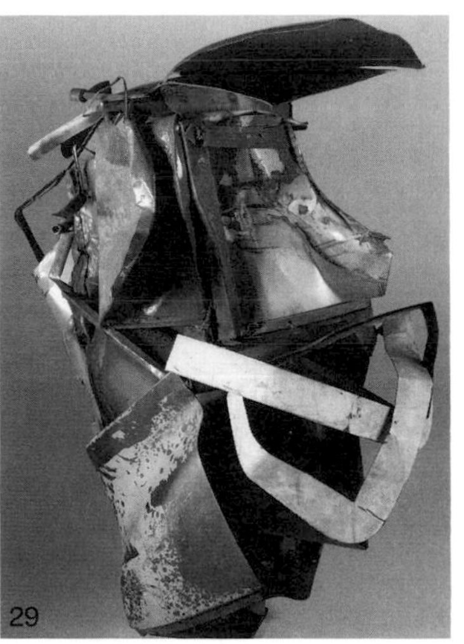

29

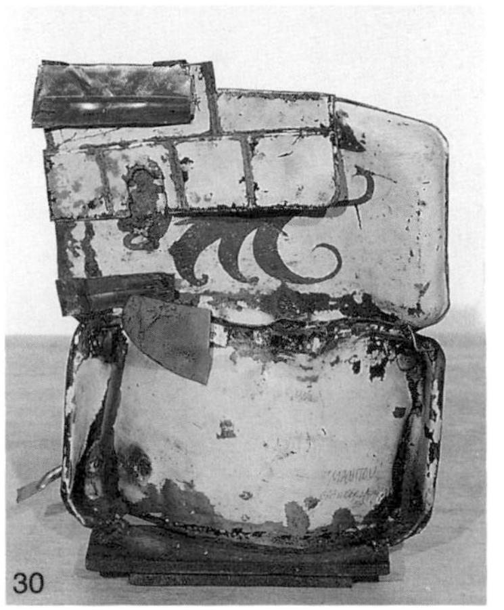

30

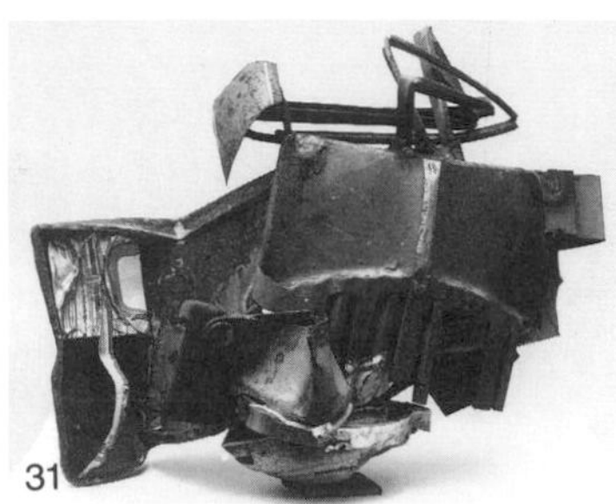
31

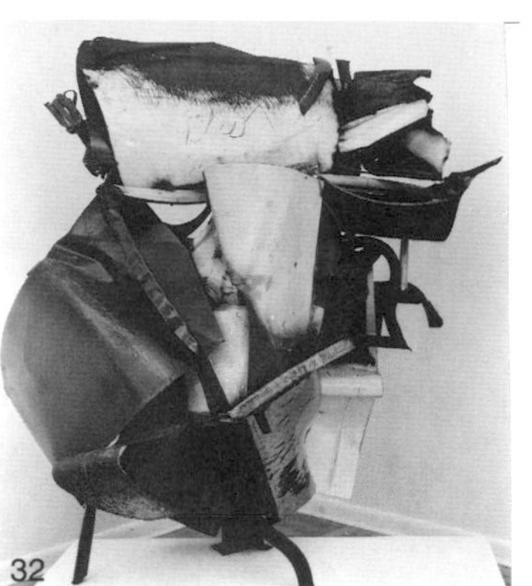
32

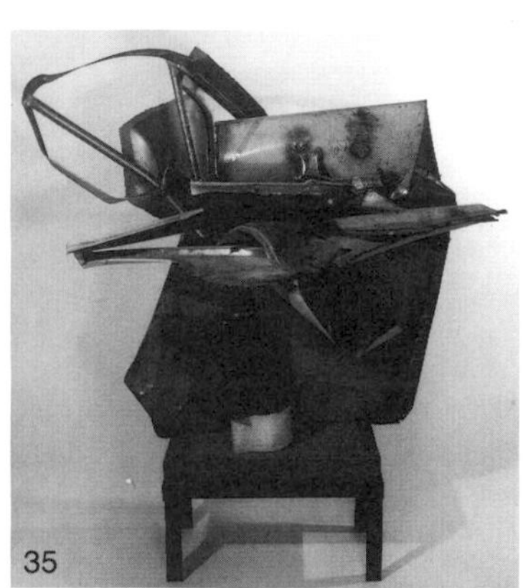
35

31

S 1959

Painted steel
17½ × 21½ × 13 in.
(44.5 × 55 × 33 cm).

Collection

Hirshhorn Museum and Sculpture Garden, Smithsonian Institution, Washington, D.C., 1966.

Provenance

Martha Jackson Gallery, New York, New York, 1960; Donald Peters, New York, New York, 1960; Harold Diamond, New York, New York; Joseph H. Hirshhorn, New York, New York, 1963.

Exhibitions

Martha Jackson Gallery, New York, New York. *John Chamberlain: Sculpture*. November 22–December 17, 1960.

References

Dore Ashton, "Art: Two Abstractionists," *New York Times*, January 6, 1960, illus.

32

Summer Sequence 1959

Painted steel
69 in. high (175 cm).

Provenance

Leo Castelli Gallery, New York, New York, 1959; Martha Jackson Gallery, New York, New York, 1960.

Exhibitions

Leo Castelli Gallery, New York, New York. *Work in Three Dimensions*. October 20–November 7, 1959.

Martha Jackson Gallery, New York, New York. *John Chamberlain: Sculpture*. November 22–December 17, 1960.

References

Dore Ashton, "John Chamberlain at the Martha Jackson Gallery," *Arts and Architecture*, vol. 77, no. 3 (March 1960), illus. p. 11.

Notes

The records of the Martha Jackson Gallery indicate that the work was returned to the artist in 1960. However, there is a note on an inventory card that the work may have been destroyed; the artist remembers that the sculpture was destroyed after the exhibition.

33

Swannanoa/Swannanoa II 1959 / 74

Painted and chromium-plated steel
45½ × 66 × 25½ in.
(115.5 × 167.5 × 65 cm).

Collection

Dia Art Foundation, New York, New York, 1980.

Provenance

Martha Jackson Gallery, New York, New York, 1960; The Mayor Gallery, London, 1977; Peder Bonnier, New York, New York; Lone Star Foundation, New York, New York, 1979.

Exhibitions

Martha Jackson Gallery, New York, New York. *John Chamberlain*. January 5–30, 1960.

Andrew Dickson White Museum of Art, Cornell University, Ithaca, New York. *Fourteenth Festival of Contemporary Art*. February 11, 1960.

Museu de Arte Moderna, São Paulo, Brazil. *VI Bienal do Museu de Arte Moderna, São Paolo*. September–December 1961.

Dwan Gallery, Los Angeles, California. *John Chamberlain*. November 29, 1966–January 7, 1967.

Seibu Department Store, Tokyo. *Martha Jackson Gallery Collection*, illus. September 17–30, 1971.

The Solomon R. Guggenheim Museum, New York, New York. *John Chamberlain: A Retrospective Exhibition*, cat. no. 10, illus. p. 30. December 23, 1971–February 20, 1972.

The University of Maryland Art Gallery, College Park, Maryland. *The Private Collection of Martha Jackson*, cat. no. 85, illus. p. 35. June 22–September 3, 1973. Traveled to The Finch College Museum of Art, New York, New York. October 16–25, 1973; The Albright-Knox Art Gallery, Buffalo, New York. January 8–February 10, 1973.

Rockland Center for the Arts and Rockland Community College, West Nyack, New York. *Works from the Martha Jackson Gallery Collection*. November 2–December 2, 1974. Traveled to University Art Gallery, State University of New York, Albany, New York. February 23–March 23, 1975; Koehler Cultural Center, San Antonio College, San Antonio, Texas. May 1–30, 1975.

The Art Galleries, University of California, Santa Barbara. *7 + 5: Sculptors in the 1950s*, cat. no. 6, illus. p. 28. January 6–February 15, 1976. Traveled to Phoenix Art Museum, Phoenix, Arizona. March 5–April 11, 1976.

Zabriskie Gallery, New York, New York. *Welded Sculpture*. September 7–October 7, 1976.

The Mayor Gallery, London. *John Chamberlain: An Exhibition of Sculpture: 1959–1962*, cat. no. 5, illus. June 27–August 12, 1977.

The John and Mable Ringling Museum of Art, Sarasota, Florida. *International Florida Artists Exhibition*, listed. February 26–April 26, 1981.

References

D[onald] J[udd], "In the Galleries," *Arts*, vol. 34, no. 5 (February 1960), illus. p. 57.

Irving H. Sandler, *The New York School: The Painters and Sculptors of the Fifties* (New York: Harper and Row, 1978), fig. no. 116, illus. p. 156.

Notes

The sculpture was restored by Chamberlain in New Mexico in 1974. The original dimensions of the work were 45½ × 64½ × 35 in. (115.5 × 164 × 89 cm).

The photograph is of the sculpture in its present state.

34

Waller 1959

Painted steel
29 × 49 × 23 in.
(73.5 × 124.5 × 58.5 cm).

Collection

Mr. and Mrs. Ronald K. Greenberg, Saint Louis, Missouri; acquired directly from the artist.

Exhibitions

Martha Jackson Gallery, New York, New York. *John Chamberlain: Sculpture*. November 22–December 17, 1960.

The University Art Museum, Albuquerque, New Mexico. *Faculty Artists at UNM 1960–1970*, illus. December 7, 1970–January 3, 1971.

Brooks Memorial Art Gallery, Memphis, Tennessee. *American Masters of the Sixties and Seventies*, cat. no. 8, illus. December 9–28, 1978.

Notes

Mr. and Mrs. Ronald K. Greenberg were under the impression that this work was *Swannanoa*, a similar work of the same year. See cat. no. 33.

35

Wellsroot 1959

Painted steel
40 × 42 × 29 in.
(101.5 × 106.5 × 73.5 cm).

Collection

Dia Art Foundation, New York, New York, 1980.

Provenance

Martha Jackson Gallery, New York, New York, 1960; The Mayor Gallery, London, 1977; Peder Bonnier, New York, New York; Lone Star Foundation, New York, New York, 1979.

Exhibitions

Martha Jackson Gallery, New York, New York. *John Chamberlain: Sculpture*. November 22–December 17, 1960.

Martha Jackson Gallery, New York, New York. *Sculpture International*. November 23–December 29, 1962.

The Mayor Gallery, London. *John Chamberlain: An Exhibition of Sculpture: 1959–1962*, cat. no. 3, illus. June 27–August 12, 1977.

References

Documenta 7 / Kassel, vol. 1, (Kassel, West Germany: D + V Paul Dierichs, 1982), illus. p. 35.

Notes

The sculpture is signed. The dimensions do not include the base.

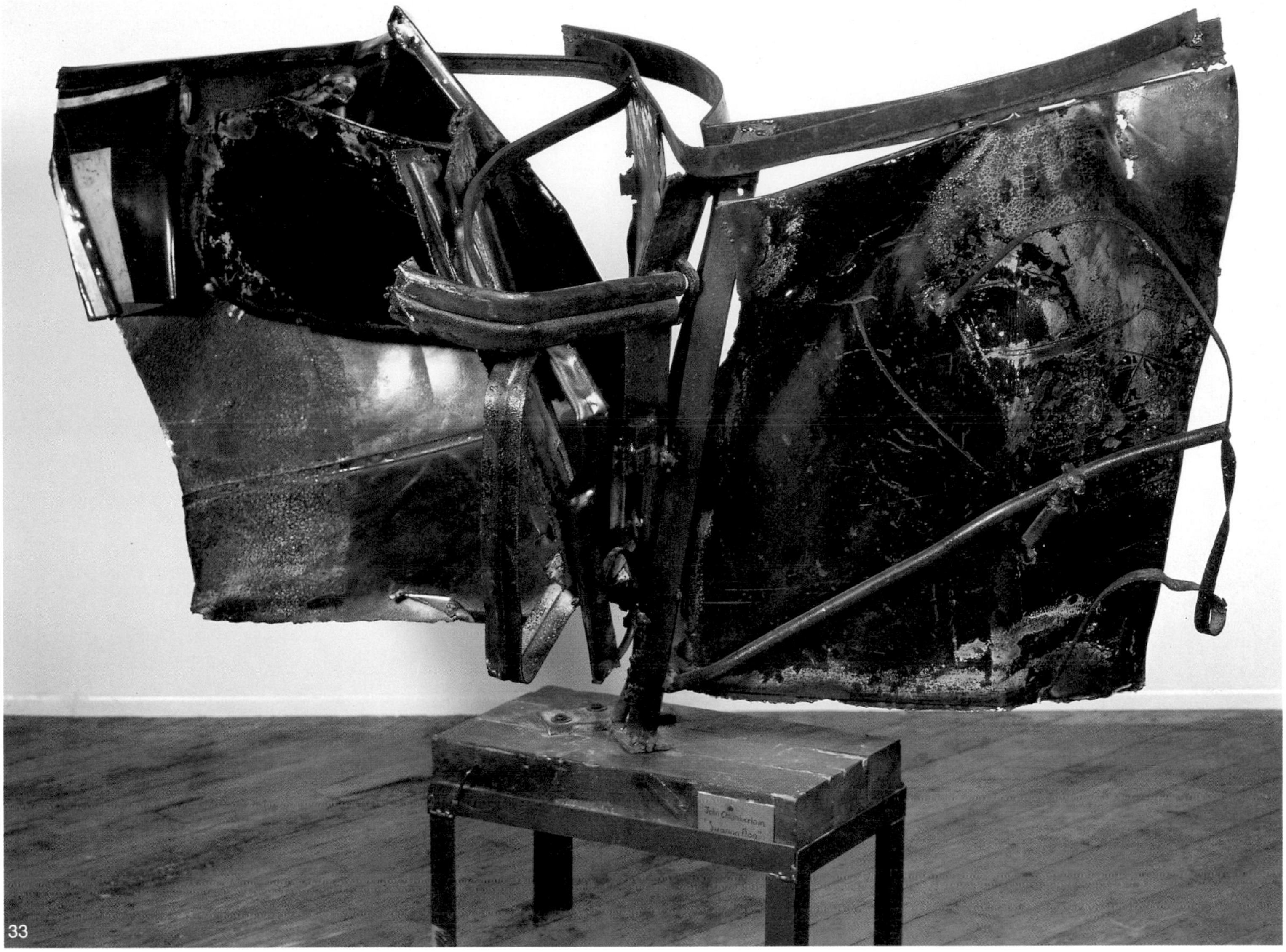

33

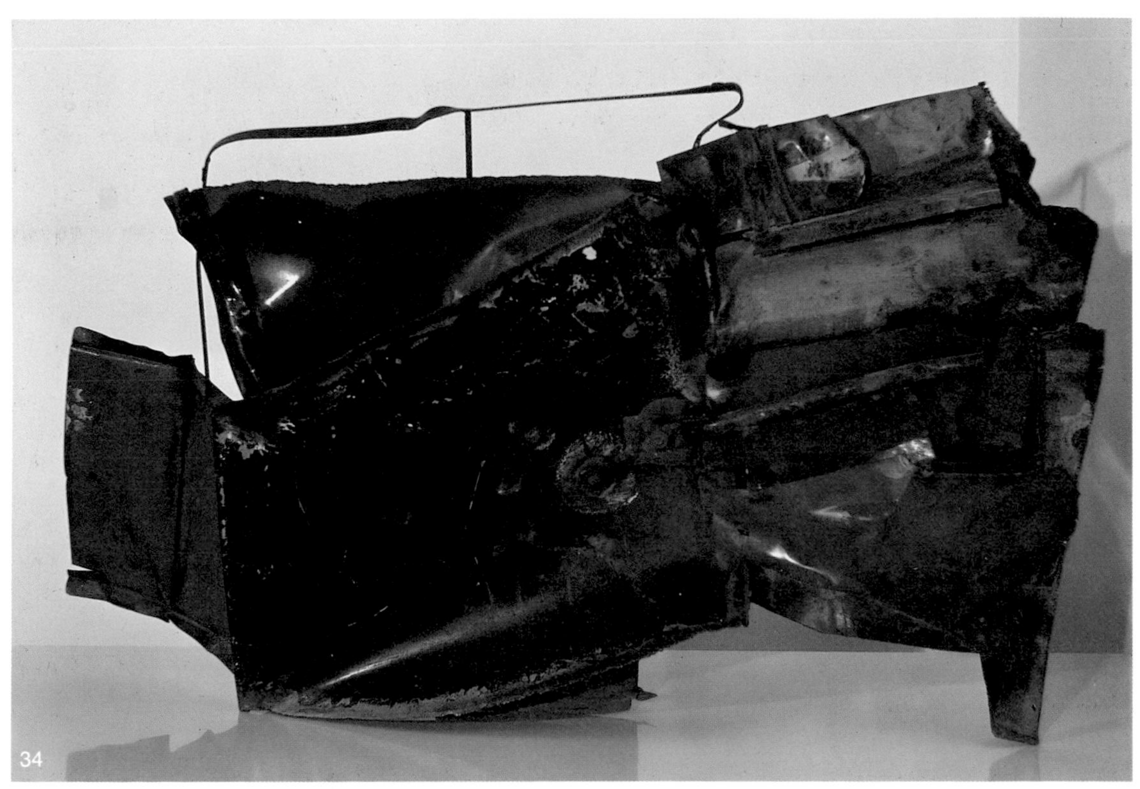

34

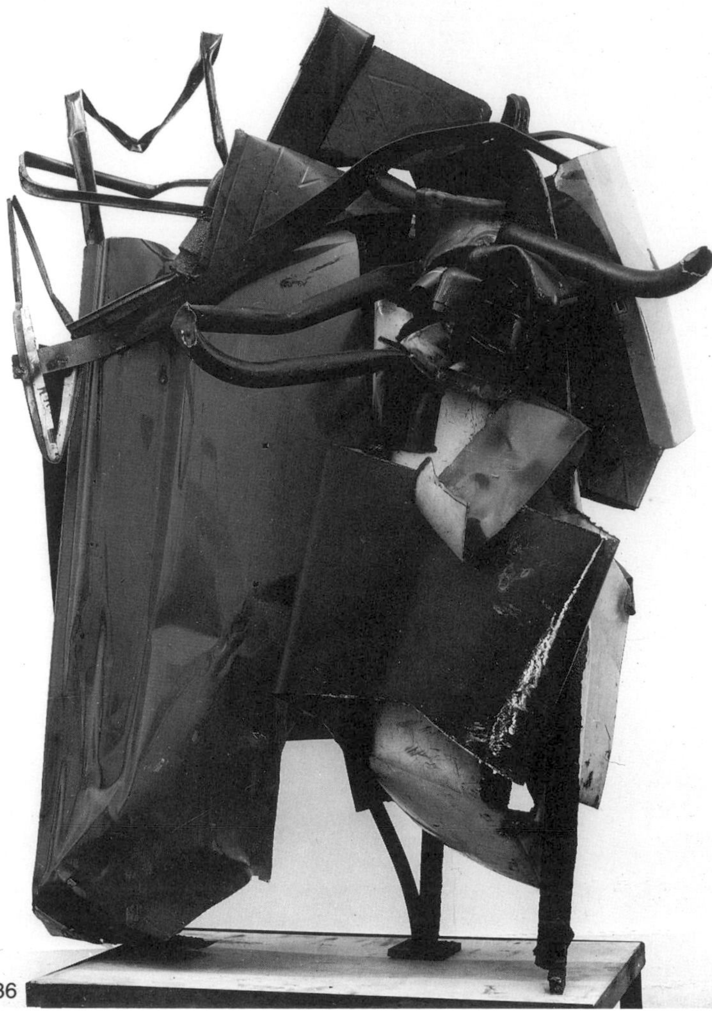

36

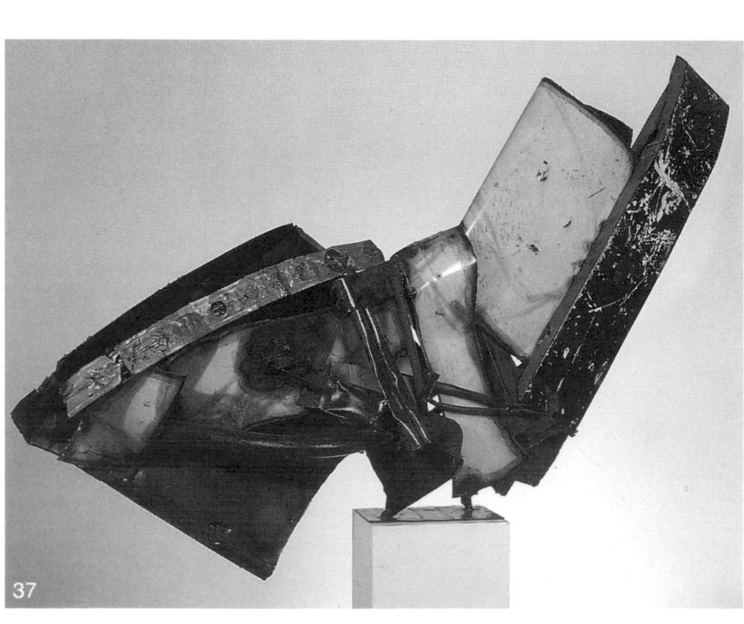

37

36

Wildroot 1959

Painted steel

69 × 52½ × 35½ in.
(175 × 133 × 90 cm).

Collection

Museum für Moderne Kunst, Frankfurt.

Provenance

Martha Jackson Gallery, New York, New York, 1960; Leon Kraushaar, Lawrence, New York; Karl Ströher, Darmstadt.

Exhibitions

Martha Jackson Gallery, New York, New York. *John Chamberlain: Sculpture*. November 22–December 17, 1960

Museum of Art, Carnegie Institute, Pittsburgh, Pennsylvania. *1961 Pittsburgh International Exhibition of Contemporary Paintings and Sculpture*, cat. no. 63, illus. October 27, 1961–January 7, 1962.

Dwan Gallery, Los Angeles, California. *John Chamberlain*. November 29, 1966–January 7, 1967.

Galerie-Verein München, Neue Pinakothek, Haus der Kunst, Munich. *Sammlung 1968 Karl Ströher*, cat. no. 43, color illus. June 14–August 9, 1968. Traveled to Kunstverein in Hamburg. August 24–October 6, 1968.

Deutsche Gesellschaft für Bildende Kunst e.V. (Kunstverein Berlin) and Nationalgalerie der Staatlichen Museen Preussischer Kulturbesitz, Neue Nationalgalerie Berlin. *Sammlung 1968 Karl Ströher*, cat. no. 17, color illus. March 1–April 14, 1969. Traveled to Städtische Kunsthalle, Düsseldorf. April 25–June 17, 1969; Kunsthalle Bern. July 12–August 17 and August 23–September 28, 1969.

Deutsches Architekturmuseum, Frankfurt. *Bilder für Frankfurt*, cat. no. 10, color illus. p. 37. February 8–April 14, 1985.

The Solomon R. Guggenheim Museum, New York, New York. *John Chamberlain: A Retrospective Exhibition*, cat. no. 9, illus. p. 29. December 23, 1971–February 20, 1972.

References

I[rving] H. S[andler], "Reviews and Previews," *Art News*, vol. 58, no. 9 (January 1960), illus. p. 18.

John Canaday, "Gargoyles for the Machine Age," *Horizon*, vol. 3, no. 4 (March 1961), illus. p. 112.

William Rubin, "The International Style: Notes on the Pittsburgh Triennial," *Art International*, vol. 5, no. 9 (November 1961), illus. p. 34.

Barbara Rose, "How to Look at John Chamberlain's Sculpture," *Art International*, vol. 7, no. 10 (January 1964), illus. p. 37.

Art International, vol. 8, no. 3 (April 1964), illus. back cover.

K. Jürgen-Fischer, "Die NEW Yorker Szene," *Kunstwerk*, vol. 19 (April/June 1966), illus. p. 34.

Phyllis Tuchman, "American Art in Germany: The History of a Phenomenon," *Artforum*, vol. 9, no. 3 (November 1970), illus. p. 58.

Bildnerische Ausdrucksformen 1960–1970: Sammlung Karl Ströher (Darmstadt: Hessisches Landesmuseum, 1970), color illus. p. 95.

Sam Hunter and John Jacobus, *American Art of the Twentieth Century* (New York: Abrams, 1972), illus. no. 597, p. 324.

Peter Selz, *Art in Our Times: A Pictorial History 1890–1980* (New York: Abrams, 1981), illus. no. 1071, p. 396.

Notes

The sculpture was restored by the artist at the time of the Guggenheim exhibition.

37

Zaar 1959

Steel

49 × 72 × 17 in.
(124.5 × 183 × 43 cm).

Collection

Mr. and Mrs. Raymond Nasher, Dallas, Texas, 1985.

Provenance

Leo Castelli Gallery, New York, New York; Robert and Ethel Scull, New York, New York, 1959; Dayton's Gallery 12, Minneapolis, Minnesota, and James Corcoran Gallery, Los Angeles, California, 1973; Joyce and Ted Ashley, New York, New York, 1978.

Exhibitions

Museum of Modern Art, New York, New York. *The Art of Assemblage*. October 4–November 12, 1961. (Not exhibited in New York.) Traveled to Dallas Museum of Contemporary Arts, Dallas, Texas. January 9–February 11, 1962; San Francisco Museum of Modern Art, San Francisco, California. March 5–April 15, 1962.

Sotheby Parke-Bernet, Inc., New York, New York. *A Selection of Fifty Works from the Collection of Robert C. Scull*, cat. no. 2, color illus. October 18, 1973.

Dallas Museum of Fine Arts and Southern Methodist University, Dallas, Texas. *poets of the cities new york and san francisco 1950–1965*, cat. no. 6, illus. no. 33, p. 105. November 20–December 29, 1974. Traveled to San Francisco Museum of Modern Art, San Francisco, California. January 31–March 23, 1975; Wadsworth Atheneum, Hartford, Connecticut. April 23–June 1, 1975.

References

"From Exhibitions Here and There," *Art International*, vol. 4, no. 1 (January 1960), illus. p. 67.

Gregoire Mueller, "Points of View: A Taped Conversation with Robert C. Scull," *Arts*, vol. 45, no. 2 (November 1970), illus. p. 39.

38

Untitled 1958–59

Painted steel

6 × 6 × 6 in. (15 × 15 × 15 cm).

Collection

Dolores James Muller, New York, New York, 1959; acquired directly from the artist.

Notes

According to the owner, the sculpture is in a state of disrepair. There is no photograph available of the sculpture in its original state.

39

Untitled c. 1958–59

Painted metal

32½ × 26½ × 24 in.
(82.5 × 67.5 × 61 cm).

Collection

The Cleveland Museum of Art, Cleveland, Ohio, 1973; Andrew R. and Martha Holden Jennings Fund.

Provenance

Allan Stone Gallery, New York, New York.

Exhibitions

The Cleveland Museum of Art, Cleveland, Ohio. *The Year in Review for 1973*. January 30–March 17, 1974.

The Butler Institute of American Art, Youngstown, Ohio. *John Chamberlain: Sculpture and Work on Paper*, cat. no. 1. May 1–29, 1983.

References

Edward B. Henning, "An Important Sculpture by John Chamberlain," *The Bulletin of the Cleveland Museum of Art*, vol. 60, no. 8 (October 1973), illus. p. 242.

"The Year in Review for 1973," *The Bulletin of the Cleveland Museum of Art* (February 1974), cat. no. 141, illus. p. 77.

40

AAP 1960

Painted steel

25 × 33 × 23 in.
(63.5 × 84 × 58.5 cm).

Collection

Mr. and Mrs. Radoslav L. Sutnar, Los Angeles, California, 1970.

Provenance

Leo Castelli Gallery, New York, New York, 1961; Allan Stone, New York, New York.

Exhibitions

Allen Memorial Art Museum, Oberlin College, Oberlin, Ohio. *Three Young Americans*. April 28–May 28, 1961.

Leo Castelli Gallery, New York, New York. *Group Show*. June 6–30, 1964.

References

Forbes Whiteside, "Three Young Americans," *Allen Memorial Art Museum Bulletin*, vol. 19, no. 1 (Fall 1961), pp. 52–57.

Notes

AAP was called *AC-DC* while in the *Three Young Americans* exhibition at the Allen Memorial Art Museum, and has frequently been referred to as such since that time; there is no record of another sculpture titled *AC-DC*.

41

April 1960

Painted tin with wood base

16 × 20 × 10 in.
(40.5 × 50.5 × 25.5 cm).

Collection

Robert H. Halff, Beverly Hills, California, 1961.

Provenance

Martha Jackson Gallery, New York, New York, 1960.

Exhibitions

Martha Jackson Gallery, New York, New York. *New Forms—New Media I*. June 6–24, 1960.

The Stable Gallery, New York, New York. *New Sculpture Group*. September 27–October 15, 1960.

The Art Galleries, University of California, Santa Barbara. *John Chamberlain/Alan Saret—Contemporary Sculpture*. March 27–April 29, 1984.

42

Baythrom 1960

Painted steel

13½ × 17 in. (34.5 × 43 cm).

Collection

Present location unknown.

Provenance

Martha Jackson Gallery, New York, New York, 1960.

Notes

According to records of the Martha Jackson Gallery, the sculpture was returned to the artist.

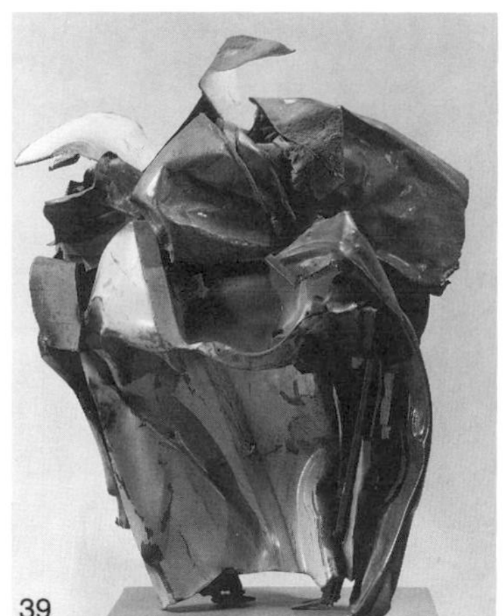

39

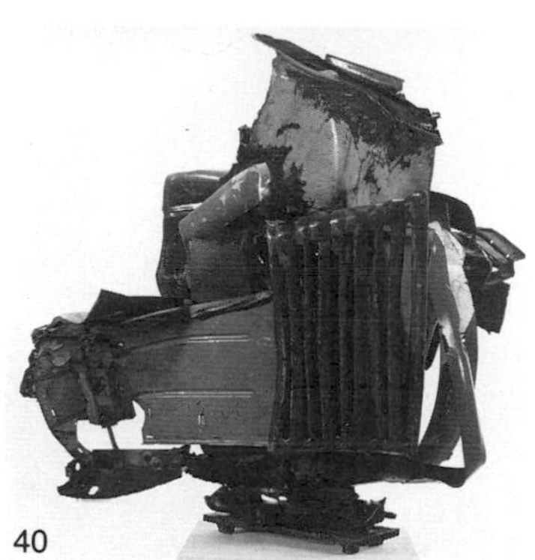

40

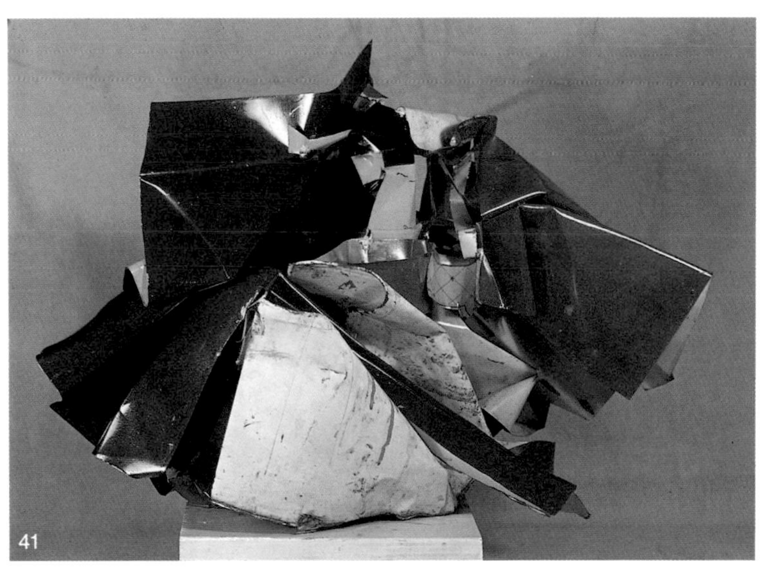

41

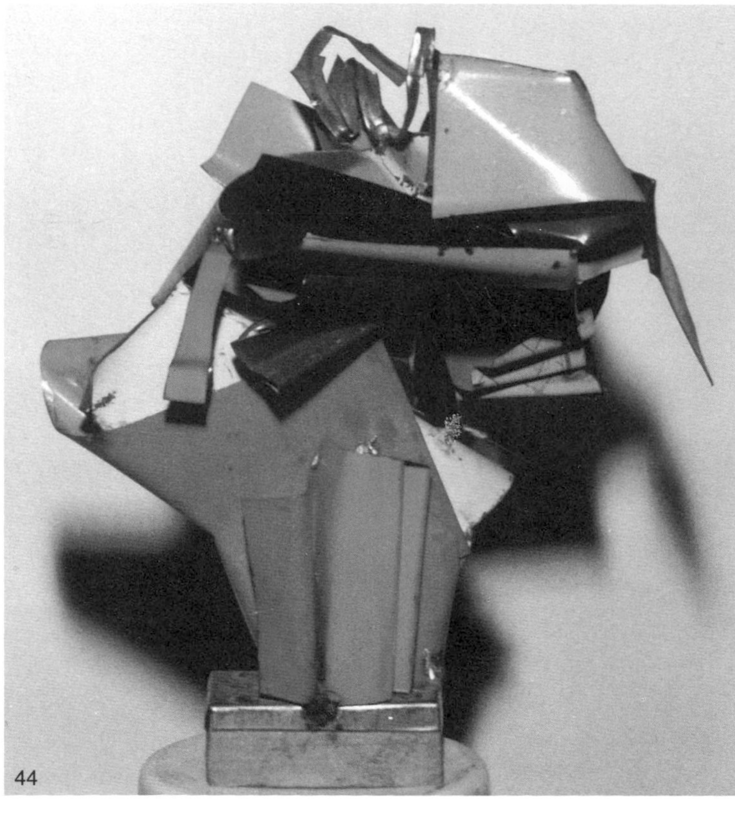
44

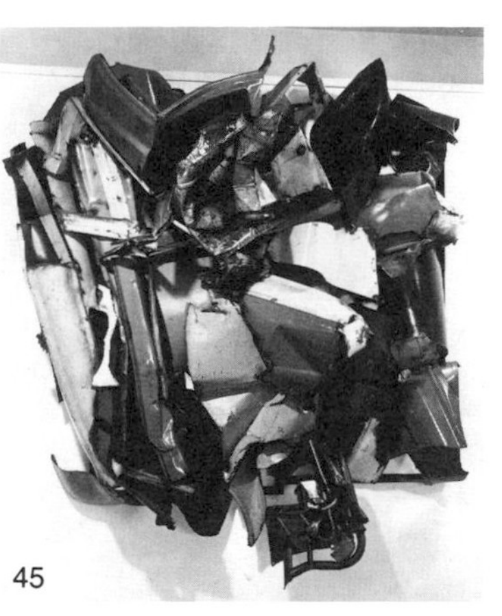
45

43

Bouquet 1960

Painted tin
16 × 13 × 13 in.
(40.5 × 33 × 33 cm).

Collection

Martin Z. Margulies, Coconut Grove, Florida, 1983.

Provenance

Leo Castelli Gallery, New York, New York; Kay Hillman, New York, New York, 1960; Martha Jackson Gallery, New York, New York, 1961; Mr. and Mrs. Robert B. Mayer, Chicago, Illinois, 1962; Gordon Locksley, Minneapolis, Minnesota, 1972; Dr. Stacy Roback; Larry Gagosian Gallery, Los Angeles, California.

Exhibitions

Sotheby Parke-Bernet, Inc., New York, New York. *Contemporary Paintings*, cat. no. 3426, illus. October 26, 1972.

Notes

The sculpture has been referred to as "Untitled, 1962" while in Mr. Margulies' possession.

44

E.D. 1960

Painted tin with wood base
7¾ × 6½ × 5 in.
(19.5 × 16.5 × 13 cm).

Collection

Mr. and Mrs. Alvin S. Lane, Riverdale, New York, 1960.

Provenance

Martha Jackson Gallery, New York, New York, 1960.

45

Essex 1960

Painted and chromium-plated steel
108 × 80 × 43 in.
(274 × 203 × 109 cm).

Collection

Museum of Modern Art, New York, New York, 1961; gift of Mr. and Mrs. Robert C. Scull and purchase fund.

Provenance

Leo Castelli Gallery, New York, New York, 1961; Robert and Ethel Scull, New York, New York, 1961.

Exhibitions

Leo Castelli Gallery, New York, New York. *Sculpture and Relief*. May 23–June 1961.

Museum of Modern Art, New York, New York. *The Museum of Modern Art, New York/Painting and Sculpture Acquisitions/January 1, 1961, through December 31, 1961*, p. 58.

Museum of Modern Art, New York, New York. *The Art of Assemblage*, cat. no. 33, illus. p. 138. October 4–November 12, 1961. Traveled to Dallas Museum of Contemporary Arts, Dallas, Texas. January 9–February 11, 1962; San Francisco Museum of Modern Art, San Francisco, California. March 5–April 15, 1962.

Museum of Modern Art, New York, New York. *The 1960s: Painting and Sculpture from the Museum Collection*. June 28–September 24, 1967.

Museum of Modern Art, New York, New York. *Younger Abstract Expressionists of the Fifties*. April 26–July 26, 1971.

The Solomon R. Guggenheim Museum, New York, New York. *John Chamberlain: A Retrospective Exhibition*, cat. no. 20, illus. p. 36. December 23, 1971–February 20, 1972.

Internationale Ausstellung Köln 1981, organized by the Museum der Stadt Köln, Cologne. *Westkunst—Contemporary Art since 1939*, cat. no. 702, illus. p. 269. May 30–August 16, 1981.

The John and Mable Ringling Museum of Art, Sarasota, Florida. *John Chamberlain Reliefs 1960–1982*, color illus. p. 21. January 28–March 27, 1983.

References

Fred W. McDarrah and Thomas B. Hess, *The Artist's World* (New York: Dutton, 1961), illus.

Vivien Raynor, "The Art of Assemblage," *Arts*, vol. 36, no. 2 (November 1961), illus. p. 19.

Ralph Caplan, "Cars as Collage," *Canadian Art*, vol. 19, no. 1 (January/February 1962), illus. p. 25.

Donald Judd, "Chamberlain—Another View," *Art International*, vol. 7, no. 10 (January 1964), pp. 38–39. Reprinted in *Donald Judd—Complete Writings 1959–1975* (Halifax: Press of the Nova Scotia College of Art and Design, and New York: New York University Press, 1975), pp. 108–10; and in *Chamberlain* (Bern: Kunsthalle Bern and Van Abbemuseum, Eindhoven, Netherlands, 1979).

Sidney Tillim, "Scale and the Future of Modernism," *Artforum*, vol. 6, no. 2 (October 1967), illus. p. 16.

Hilton Kramer, "Serving a Period Taste," *New York Times*, January 2, 1972, illus. p. 17.

Gary Indiana, "John Chamberlain's Irregular Set," *Art in America*, vol. 71, no. 10 (November 1983), p. 212.

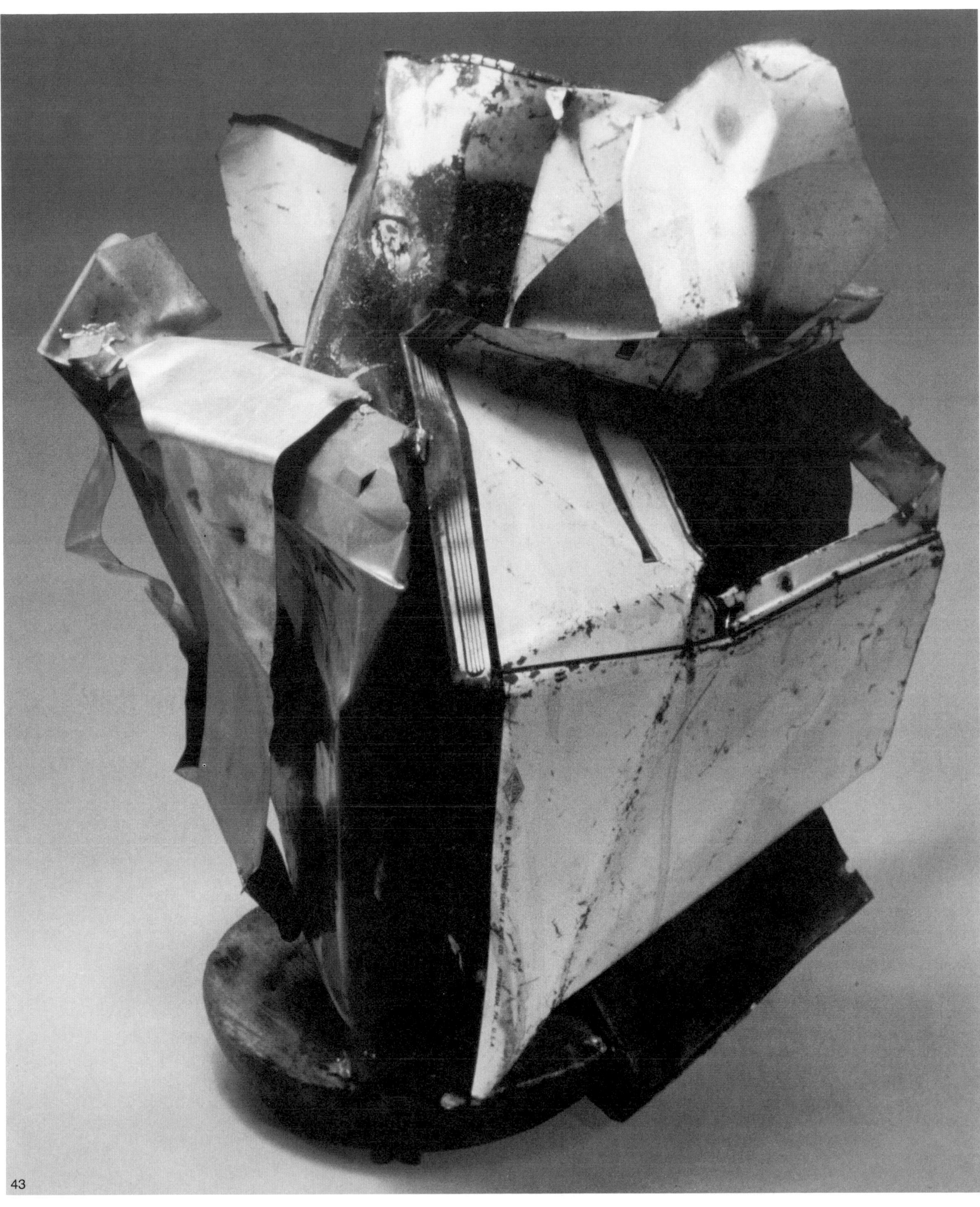

43

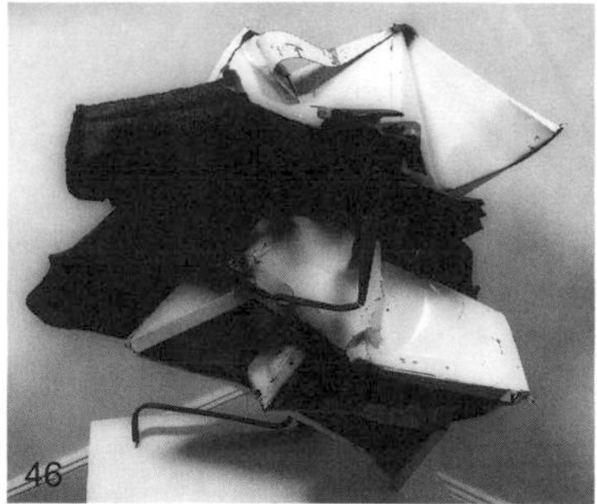
46

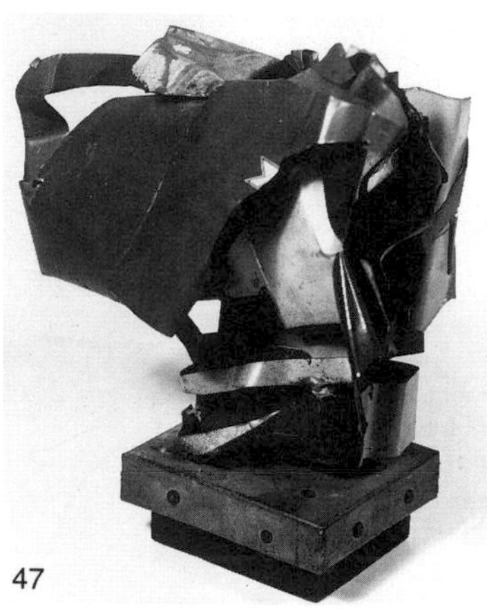
47

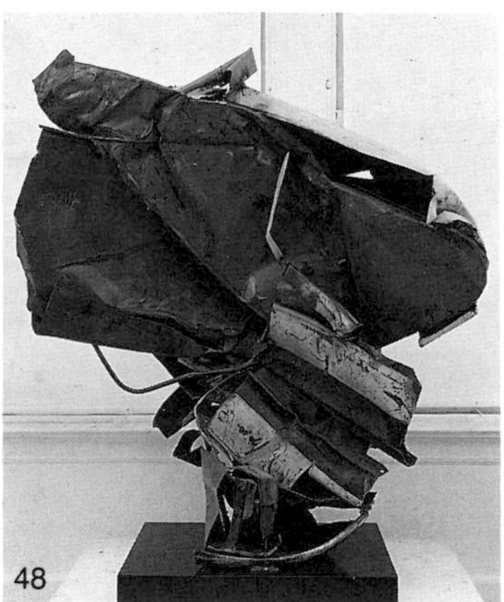
48

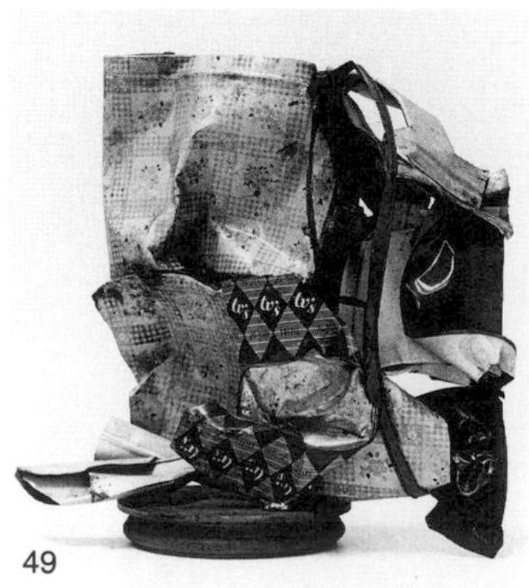
49

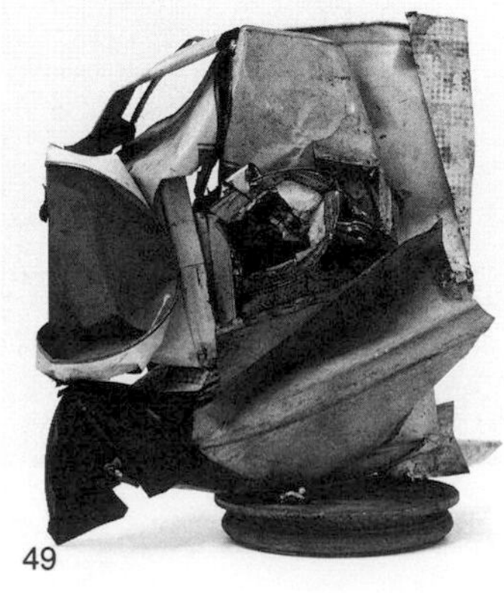
49

46

Falconer-Fitten 1960

Painted steel
32 × 42 × 34 in.
(81.5 × 106.5 × 86.5 cm).

Collection
Private collection, London, 1978.

Provenance
William Dorr, New York, New York; Allan Stone, New York, New York; The Mayor Gallery, London.

Exhibitions
The Solomon R. Guggenheim Museum, New York, New York. *John Chamberlain: A Retrospective Exhibition*, cat. no. 18, illus. p. 34. December 23, 1971–February 20, 1972.

The Fitzwilliam Museum, Cambridge. *Jubilation: American Art during the Reign of Elizabeth II*, cat. no. 6. May 10–June 18, 1977.

The Mayor Gallery, London. *John Chamberlain: An Exhibition of Sculpture: 1959–1962*, cat. no. 6, illus. June 27–August 12, 1977.

References
Donald Judd, "Chamberlain—Another View," *Art International*, vol. 7, no. 10 (January 1964), pp. 38–39. Reprinted in *Donald Judd—Complete Writings 1959–1975* (Halifax: Press of the Nova Scotia College of Art and Design, and New York: New York University Press, 1975), pp. 108–10; and in *Chamberlain* (Bern: Kunsthalle Bern and Van Abbemuseum, Eindhoven, Netherlands, 1979).

47

G.V.D.W. 1960

Painted tin
7 × 7 × 8 in.
(17.5 × 17.5 × 20 cm).

Collection
Private collection, Illinois, 1975.

Provenance
Martha Jackson Gallery, New York, New York, 1960; The Mayor Gallery, London.

Exhibitions
Seibu Department Store, Tokyo. *Martha Jackson Gallery Collection*, cat. no. 18, illus. pl. 18. September 17–30, 1971.

48

Hatband 1960

Painted and chromium-plated steel and iron
60 × 53 × 36 in.
(152.5 × 134.5 × 91.5 cm).

Collection
Allan Stone, New York, New York.

Provenance
Leo Castelli Gallery, New York, New York; Mr. and Mrs. Stanley Poler, New York, New York, 1968.

Exhibitions
Museu de Arte Moderna, São Paulo, Brazil. *VI Bienal do Museu de Arte Moderna, São Paulo*, cat. no. 85, illus. September–December 1961. Listed incorrectly as *Mr. Blue*.

The Cleveland Museum of Art, Cleveland, Ohio. *Sculpture by John Chamberlain*, listed. January 3–29, 1967.

The Solomon R. Guggenheim Museum, New York, New York. *John Chamberlain: A Retrospective Exhibition*, cat. no. 19, illus. p. 37. December 23, 1971–February 20, 1972.

Notes
Hatband has been known as *Green Lantern* while in the possession of Allan Stone; there is no record of another sculpture entitled *Green Lantern*.

49

Homer 1960

Painted tin with wood base
16 × 13½ × 11 in.
(40.5 × 34.5 × 28 cm).

Collection
Robert Rauschenberg, New York, New York.

Provenance
Leo Castelli Gallery, New York, New York.

Notes
The sculpture is signed on the underside: *"Homer" Chamberlain '60.*

50

Hudson 1960

Painted and chromium-plated steel
27 × 27 × 12 in.
(68.5 × 68.5 × 30.5 cm).

Collection
Mr. and Mrs. Allan Stone, Purchase, New York.

Provenance
Leo Castelli Gallery, New York, New York.

Exhibitions
The Solomon R. Guggenheim Museum, New York, New York. *John Chamberlain: A Retrospective Exhibition*, cat. no. 16, illus. p. 31. December 23, 1971–February 20, 1972.

Notes
The sculpture is signed and titled by the artist: *Hudson/Chamberlain.*

51

Jo-So 1960

Painted steel with wood base
26 × 21 × 26 in.
(66 × 53.5 × 66 cm).

Collection

David K. Anderson, New York, New York.

Provenance

Martha Jackson Gallery, New York, New York, 1960.

Exhibitions

Allen Memorial Art Museum, Oberlin College, Oberlin, Ohio. *Three Young Americans*. April 28–May 28, 1961.

The Solomon R. Guggenheim Museum, New York, New York. *John Chamberlain: A Retrospective Exhibition*, cat. no. 14, illus. p. 30. December 23, 1971–February 20, 1972.

References

"American Sculpture in Paris," *Art in America*, vol. 48, no. 3 (1960), illus. p. 97.

Françoise Choay, "Lettre de Paris," *Art International*, vol. 4, no. 5 (December 1960), illus. p. 36.

Forbes Whiteside, "Three Young Americans," *Allen Memorial Art Museum Bulletin*, vol. 19, no. 1 (Fall 1961), pp. 52–57.

52

Longclove 1960

Steel
16½ × 21 × 16 in.
(42 × 53.5 × 41 cm).

Collection

Mr. and Mrs. Lewis G. Pollock, Lexington, Massachusetts, 1960.

Provenance

Leo Castelli Gallery, New York, New York.

Exhibitions

Boston Public Garden, Boston, Massachusetts. *Boston Arts Festival*. 1960.

Boston University Art Gallery, Boston, Massachusetts. *Six Sculptors*. March 30–April 25, 1963.

Institute of Contemporary Art, Boston, Massachusetts. *Collectors Collect Contemporary: A Selection from Boston Collections*. June 22–September 4, 1977.

53

Ma Perkins 1960

Painted steel
11 × 12 × 12 in.
(28 × 30.5 × 30.5 cm).

Collection

Present location unknown.

Provenance

Leo Castelli Gallery, New York, New York; Martha Jackson Gallery, New York, New York, 1961; Dilexi Gallery, San Francisco, California, 1966.

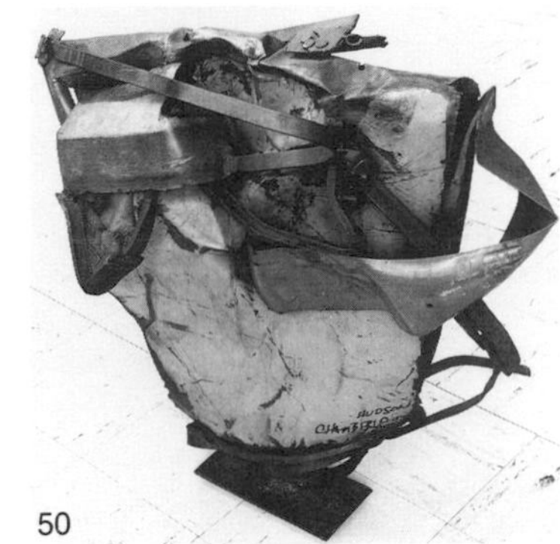

50

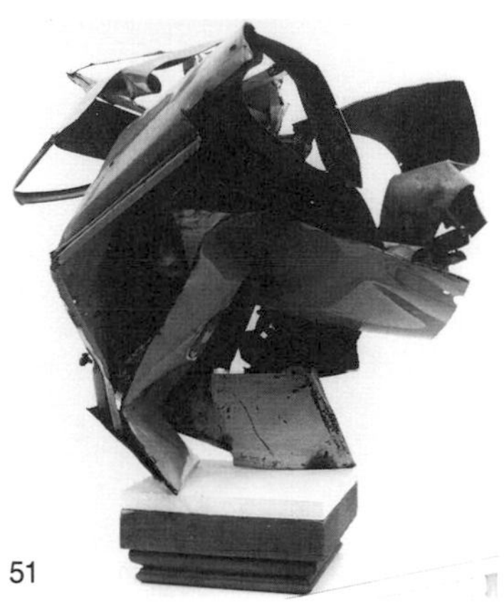

51

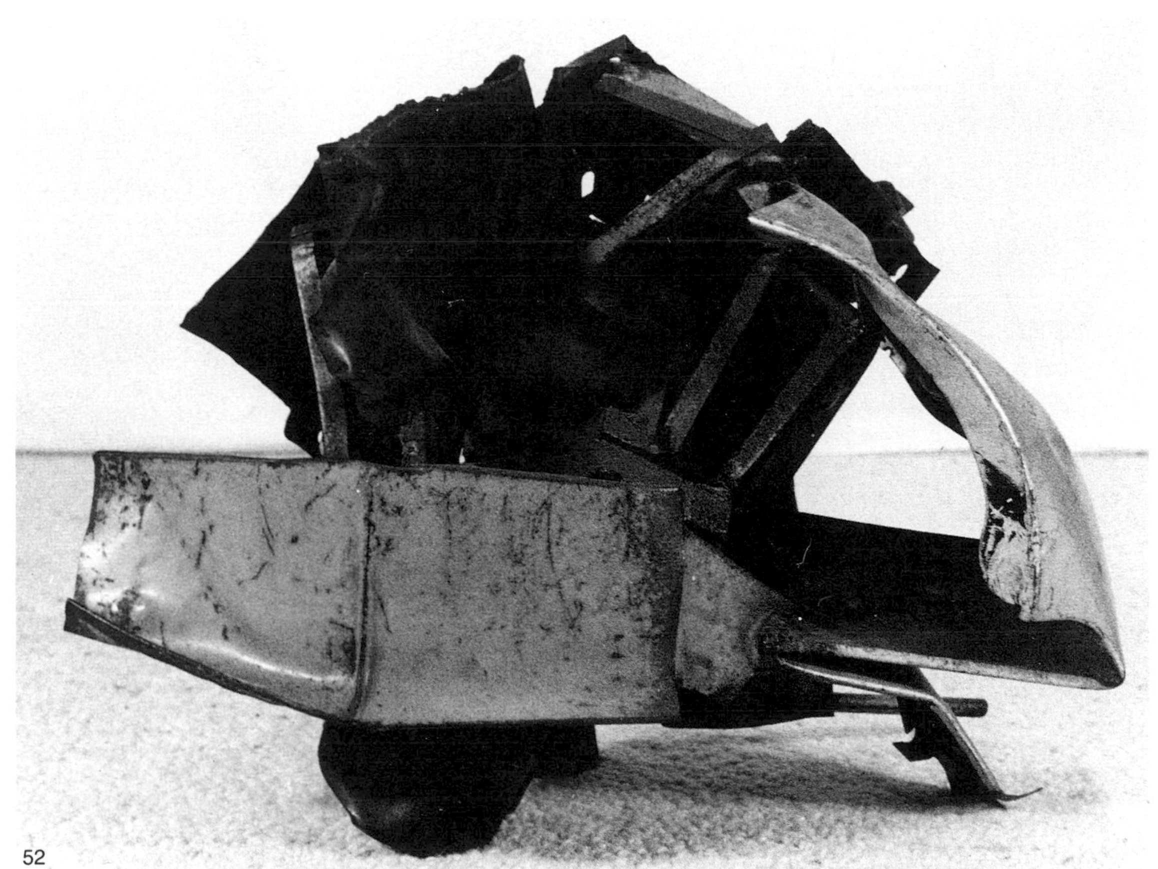

52

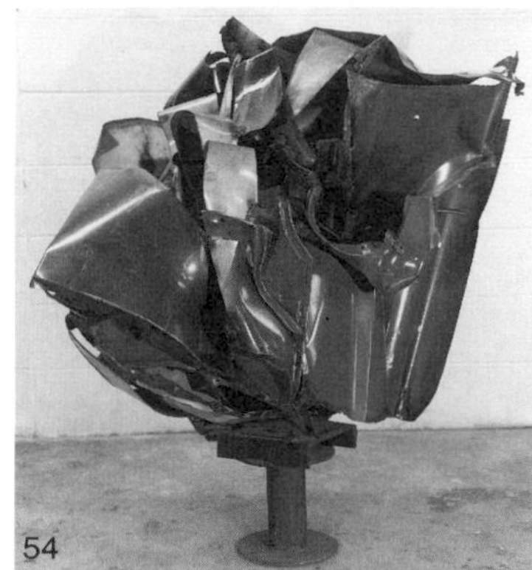
54

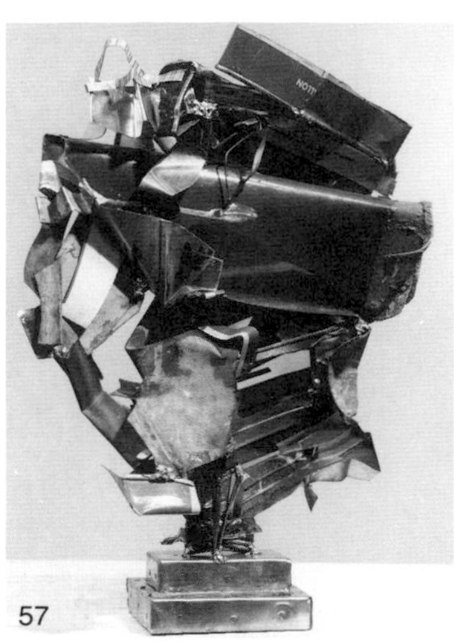
57

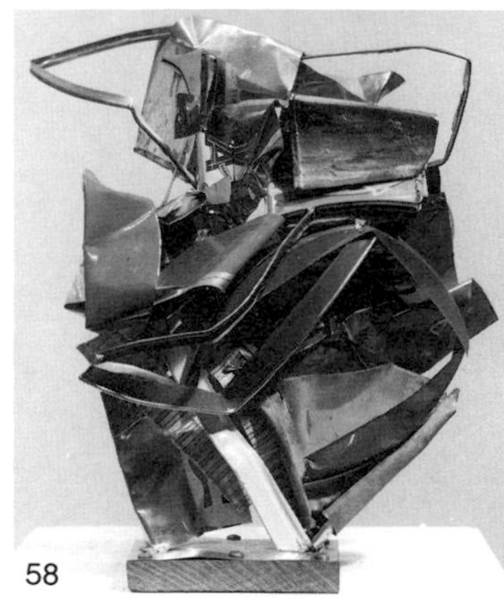
58

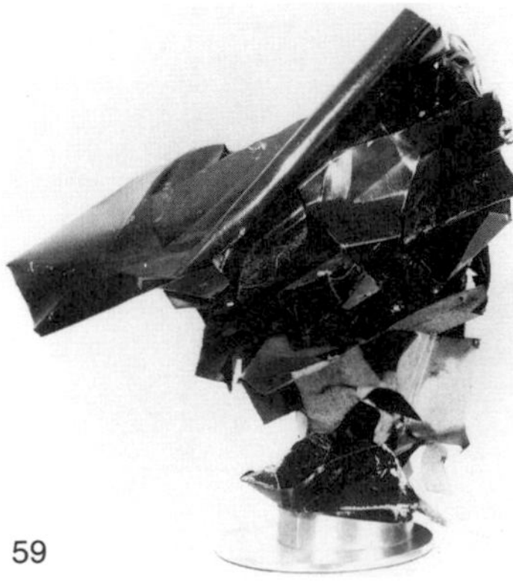
59

54

Maz 1960

Painted steel
48 × 40 × 36 in.
(122 × 101.5 × 91.5 cm).

Collection
Vanderbilt Art Collection, Vanderbilt University, Nashville, Tennessee, 1979.

Provenance
Leo Castelli Gallery, New York, New York; Robert and Ethel Scull, New York, New York, 1960; Leo Castelli Gallery, New York, New York, 1961; Fine Arts Museum, George Peabody College for Teachers, Nashville, Tennessee, 1965.

Exhibitions
Museum of Modern Art, New York, New York, organized a circulating exhibition, *Assemblages*, not exhibited in New York. Traveled to Andrew Dickson White Museum of Art, Cornell University, Ithaca, New York. January 31–February 21, 1963; Montreal Museum of Fine Arts, Montreal. March 7–28, 1963; Hackley Art Gallery, Muskegon, Michigan. April 12–May 3, 1963; Indiana University at Bloomington, Indiana. May 10–31, 1963; Isaac Delgado Museum of Art, New Orleans, Louisiana. September 1–22, 1963; Tucson Art Center, Tucson, Arizona. October 2–23, 1963; Washington University Gallery of Art, Saint Louis, Missouri. November 4–25, 1963; San Francisco State College, San Francisco, California. January 16–February 6, 1964; University of Oregon, Eugene, Oregon. February 21–March 14, 1964; University of South Florida, Tampa, Florida. May 7–28, 1964; Detroit Institute of Arts, Detroit, Michigan. June 12–July 3, 1964.

The Solomon R. Guggenheim Museum, New York, New York. *John Chamberlain: A Retrospective Exhibition*, cat. no. 17, illus. p. 32. December 23, 1971–February 20, 1972.

Vanderbilt Art Gallery, Nashville, Tennessee. *Sculpture from the Vanderbilt Art Collection*. Summer 1982.

Notes
The sculpture was purchased by Robert and Ethel Scull from the Leo Castelli Gallery in 1960. It was donated to and accepted by the Museum of Modern Art in January 1961, but the gift was canceled in December 1961 and the sculpture was returned to the Castelli Gallery in partial exchange for *Essex* (cat. no. 45).

The dimensions include the steel base.

55

Pullo 1960

Painted tin
19 × 17 × 16 in.
(48 × 43 × 40.5 cm).

Collection
A. James Speyer, Chicago, Illinois, 1961.

Provenance
Martha Jackson Gallery, New York, New York, 1960.

56

Redwing 1960

Painted steel
41 × 32 × 14 in.
(104 × 81.5 × 35.5 cm).

Collection
Mr. and Mrs. Edmond Ruben, Minneapolis, Minnesota, 1982.

Provenance
Martha Jackson Gallery, New York, New York, 1960; Charlotte Bell and J. Boyer Bell, New York, New York; Barbara Divver Fine Art, New York, New York; Anita Friedman Fine Arts, New York, New York; Adler Gallery, Beverly Hills, California.

Exhibitions
Martha Jackson Gallery, New York, New York. *John Chamberlain: Sculpture*. November 22–December 17, 1960.

References
D[onald] J[udd], "In the Galleries," *Arts*, vol. 34, no. 5 (February 1960), illus. p. 57.

Diane Waldman, *John Chamberlain: A Retrospective Exhibition* (New York: The Solomon R. Guggenheim Foundation, 1971), illus. p. 31. See notes.

Notes
Redwing is reproduced in the Guggenheim catalogue and is entered as cat. no. 15, but the sculpture was not exhibited. An untitled sculpture dated c. 1958 has been confused with *Redwing* since the early sixties, and although similarities exist between the two sculptures, they clearly have very different histories (see cat. no. 25).

57

S.K. 1960

Painted tin
14½ × 11 in. (37 × 28 cm).

Collection
Present location unknown.

Provenance
Martha Jackson Gallery, New York, New York, 1961.

References
Irving H. Sandler, "Ash Can Revisited: A New York Letter," *Art International*, vol. 4, no. 8 (October 1960), illus. p. 29.

Notes
The records of the Martha Jackson Gallery indicate that the sculpture was returned to the artist in 1961. However, it is noted on the back of a photograph from the gallery files that the work was destroyed.

58

T.C. 1960

Painted tin and wood
15 in. high (38 cm).

Collection
Present location unknown.

Provenance
Martha Jackson Gallery, New York, New York, 1960; Mr. and Mrs. Thomas Petschek, Scarsdale, New York.

59

Valentine 1960

Painted and chromium-plated steel
20 × 18 × 13 in.
(51 × 45.5 × 33 cm).

Collection
Present location unknown.

Provenance
Martha Jackson Gallery, New York, New York, 1960; Stephen Paine, Boston, Massachusetts, 1961; Allan Stone Gallery, New York, New York, 1970; The Mayor Gallery, London; Mr. and Mrs. Lewis Manilow, Chicago, Illinois; B. C. Holland & Co., Chicago, Illinois.

Exhibitions
The Stable Gallery, New York, New York. *New Sculpture Group*. September 27–October 15, 1960.

Boston University Art Gallery, Boston, Massachusetts. *Six Sculptors*. March 30–April 25, 1963.

The Mayor Gallery, London. *John Chamberlain: An Exhibition of Sculpture: 1959–1962*, cat. no. 2, illus., incorrectly listed as "Untitled, 1960." June 27–August 12, 1977.

Christie, Manson & Woods International, Inc., New York, New York. *Contemporary Art*, cat. no. 62, illus. November 13, 1980.

60

Untitled 1960

Painted steel
20 × 13 in. (51 × 33 cm).

Collection
Present location unknown.

Provenance
Martha Jackson Gallery, New York, New York; William Dorr, New York, New York, 1961.

61

Untitled 1960

Painted steel

16½ × 25 × 19 in.
(42 × 63.5 × 48 cm).

Collection

Mr. and Mrs. John Rosenkrans, Jr., San Francisco, California, 1982.

Provenance

Leo Castelli Gallery, New York, New York; Ann Uribe, London; Leo Castelli Gallery, New York, New York; Hanson Fuller Goldeen Gallery, San Francisco, California, 1981.

62

Untitled 1960

Painted tin with wood base

18 × 14½ × 10½ in.
(46 × 37 × 27 cm).

Collection

Pat and Phil Hack, Phoenix, Arizona, 1968.

Provenance

Jorge Fick, Santa Fe, New Mexico.

Exhibitions

Phoenix Art Museum, Phoenix, Arizona. *The Nuclear Age: Tradition and Transition*. September–October 1983.

62a

Untitled 1960

Painted tin

10 × 9 × 5½ in.
(25.5 × 23 × 14 cm).

Collection

Mr. and Mrs. Robert L. Shapiro, San Diego, California.

Provenance

Adler Gallery, Beverly Hills, California; Dr. Nathan Alpers, Los Angeles, California.

Notes

This sculpture came to light while this catalogue raisonné was in press.

63

Untitled c. 1960

Painted tin

Dimensions unavailable.

Collection

J. Boyer Bell, New York, New York.

Provenance

Charlotte Waring, New York, New York, 1961.

Notes

According to the owner, the sculpture is in need of restoration and therefore no dimensions are available. There is no photograph available of the sculpture in its original state.

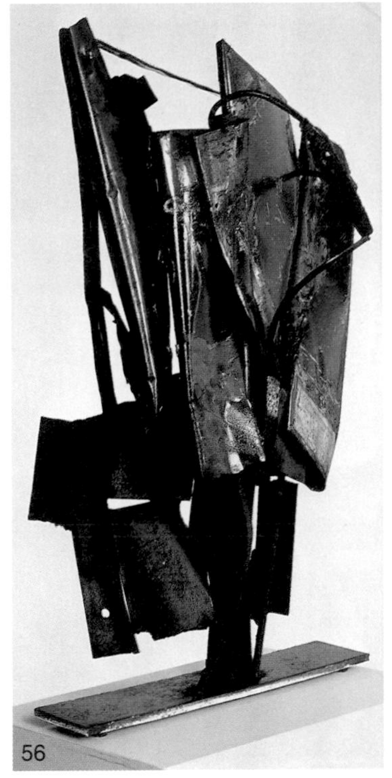

56

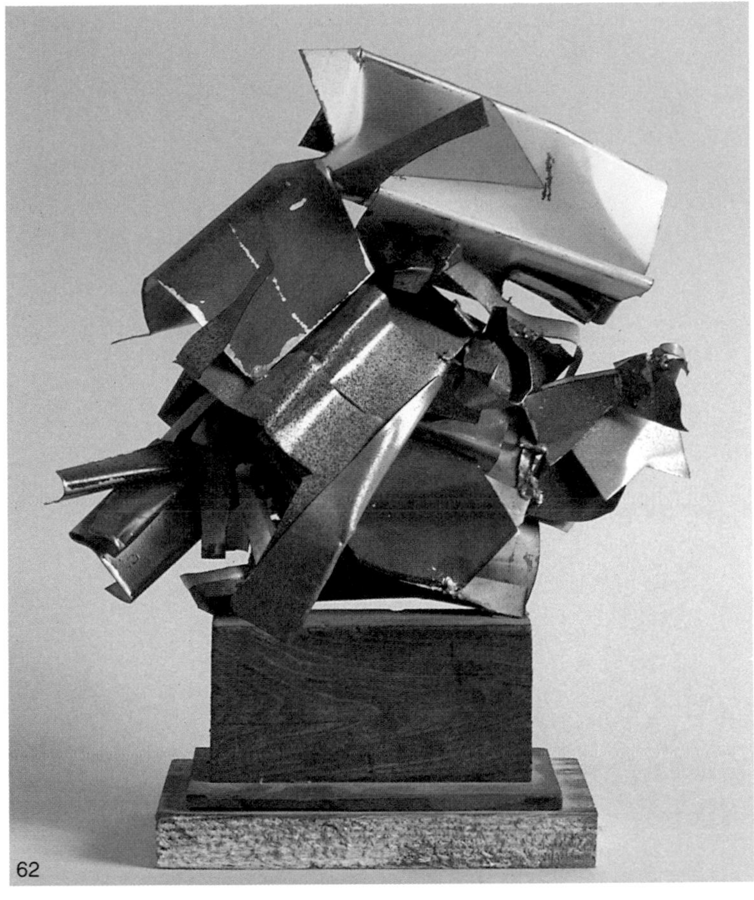

62

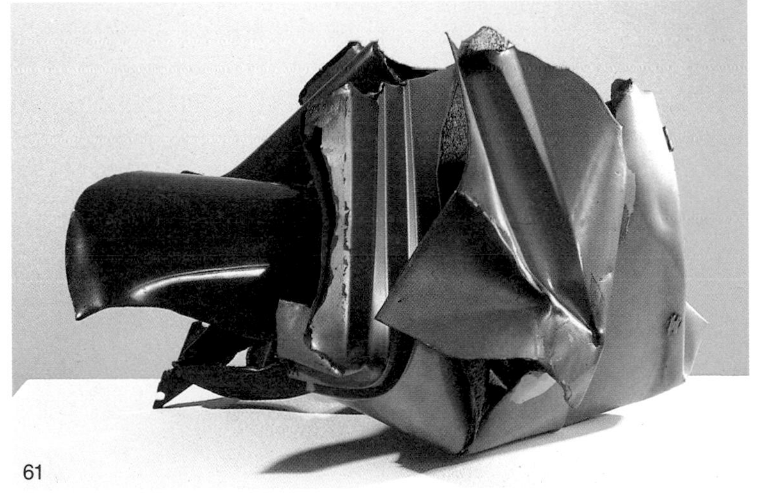

61

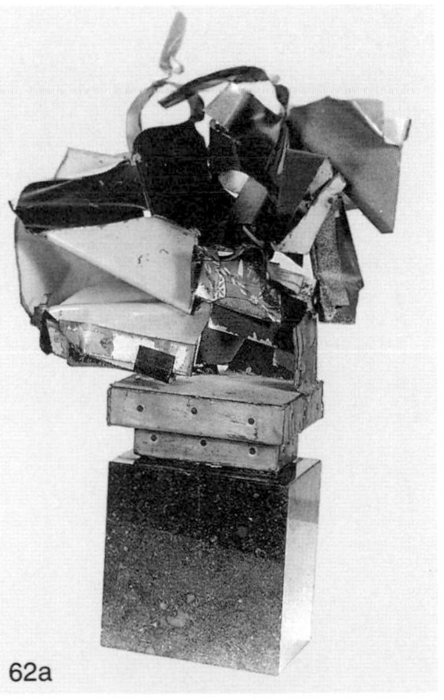

62a

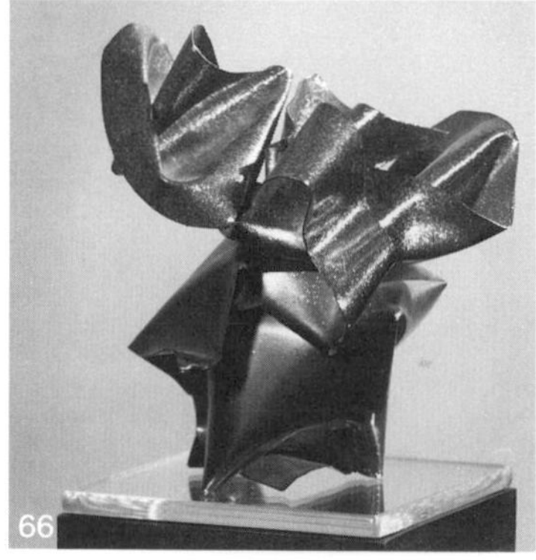
66

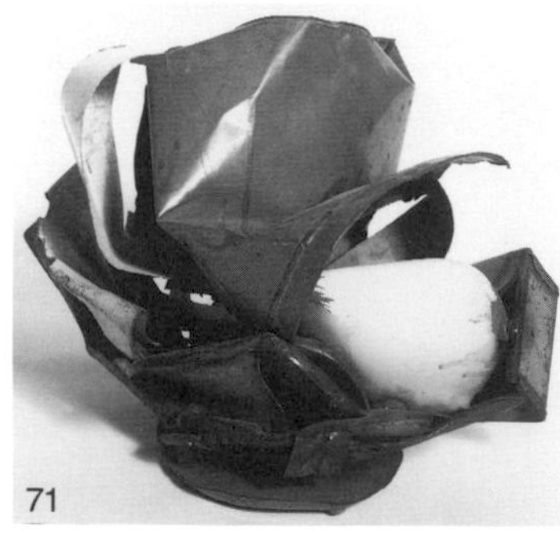
71

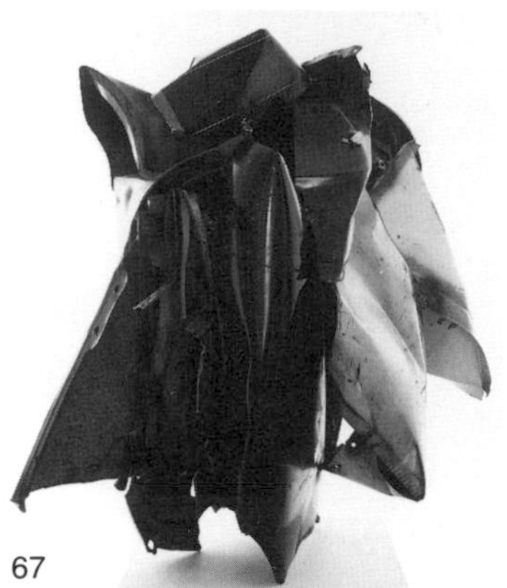
67

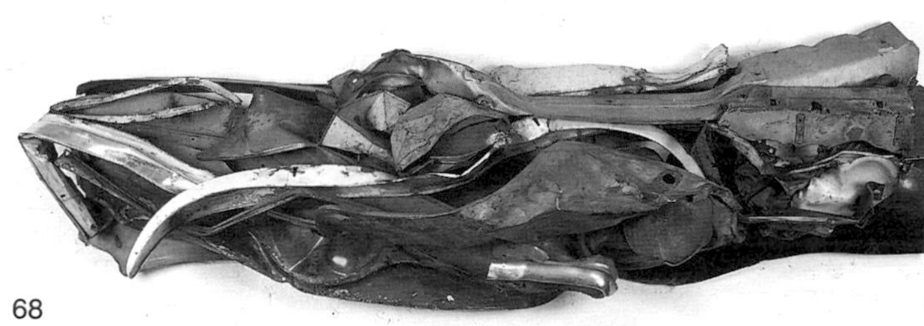
68

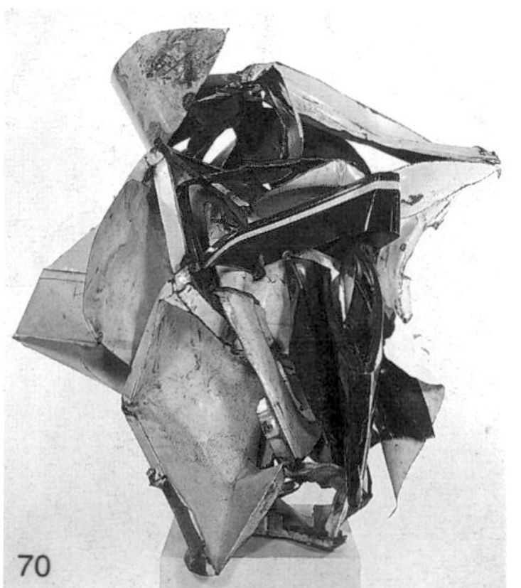
70

64

Untitled 1960
Steel
22½ × 24 in. (57 × 61 cm).

Collection
Present location unknown.

Exhibitions
Allen Memorial Art Museum, Oberlin College, Oberlin, Ohio. *Three Young Americans*. April 28–May 28, 1961.

References
Forbes Whiteside, "Three Young Americans," *Allen Memorial Art Museum Bulletin*, vol. 19, no. 1 (Fall 1961), pp. 52–57.

65

Untitled 1960
Steel
60 × 60 in. (152.5 × 152.5 cm).

Collection
Present location unknown.

Exhibitions
Allen Memorial Art Museum, Oberlin College, Oberlin, Ohio. *Three Young Americans*. April 28–May 28, 1961.

References
Forbes Whiteside, "Three Young Americans," *Allen Memorial Art Museum Bulletin*, vol. 19, no. 1 (Fall 1961), pp. 52–57.

66

Untitled 1960
Painted tin
5½ × 4½ × 3½ in.
(14 × 11.5 × 9 cm).

Collection
Frederick Weisman Company Collection, Los Angeles, California, 1963.

Provenance
Mr. and Mrs. Abe Adler, Los Angeles, California; Dwan Gallery, Los Angeles, California.

67

Bad Axe 1961
Painted steel
33 × 29 × 26 in.
(84 × 73.5 × 66 cm).

Collection
Present location unknown.

Provenance
Leo Castelli Gallery, New York, New York; Galerie Rive Droite, Paris.

68

Bijou 1961
Painted and chromium-plated steel
36 × 72 × 24 in.
(91.5 × 183 × 61 cm).

Collection
Private collection, New York, New York, 1971.

Provenance
Elaine Chamberlain, New York, New York; Richard Bellamy, New York, New York; Heiner Friedrich GmbH, Cologne.

Exhibitions
Pasadena Art Museum, Pasadena, California. *New American Sculpture*, cat. no. 8. February 11–March 7, 1964.

Dwan Gallery, Los Angeles, California. *John Chamberlain*. November 29, 1966–January 7, 1967.

Heiner Friedrich GmbH, Cologne. *Group Exhibition*. September 3–25, 1971.

The Solomon R. Guggenheim Museum, New York, New York. *John Chamberlain: A Retrospective Exhibition*, cat. no. 32, illus. p. 41. December 23, 1971–February 20, 1972.

The John and Mable Ringling Museum of Art, Sarasota, Florida. *John Chamberlain Reliefs 1960–1982*, color illus. p. 25. January 28–March 27, 1983.

Dia Art Foundation, New York, New York. *John Chamberlain Sculpture: An Extended Exhibition*. September 22, 1983–February 23, 1985.

69

Bullwinkle 1961
Painted and chromium-plated steel
48 × 47 × 32 in.
(122 × 119.5 × 81.5 cm).

Collection
Allan Stone, New York, New York, 1967.

Provenance
James Goodman Gallery, New York, New York, 1962.

Exhibitions
Institute of Contemporary Art, Philadelphia, Pennsylvania. *The Atmosphere of 'Sixty-Four*. April 17–June 1, 1964.

70

Captain O'Hay 1961
Painted steel
45 × 38 × 36 in.
(114 × 96.5 × 91.5 cm).

Collection
Doris and Charles Saatchi, London.

Provenance
Hanford Yang, New York, New York, 1961; Leo Castelli Gallery, New York, New York; Locksley/Shea Gallery, Minneapolis, Minnesota.

Exhibitions
Leo Castelli Gallery, New York, New York. *Sculpture and Relief*. May 23–June 1961.

Boston University Art Gallery, Boston, Massachusetts. *Six Sculptors*. March 30–April 25, 1963.

The Aldrich Museum of Contemporary Art, Ridgefield, Connecticut. *Selections from the Collection of Hanford Yang.* September 29–December 22, 1968.

References

Diane Waldman, *John Chamberlain: A Retrospective Exhibition* (New York: The Solomon R. Guggenheim Foundation, 1971), cat. no. 26, illus. p. 44.

71

Clyde 1961

Welded and painted steel
14 × 15 × 15 in.
(35.5 × 38 × 38 cm).

Collection

Walker Art Center, Minneapolis, Minnesota; gift of Fred Mueller, 1970.

Provenance

Leo Castelli Gallery, New York, New York; Fred Mueller, New York, New York.

72

Davis 1961

Painted steel and wood
20 × 17½ × 12 in.
(51 × 44.5 × 30.5 cm).

Collection

Hirshhorn Museum and Sculpture Garden, Smithsonian Institution, Washington, D.C., 1966.

Provenance

Leo Castelli Gallery, New York, New York; H.C.E. Gallery, Provincetown, Massachusetts, 1961; Joseph H. Hirshhorn, New York, New York, 1961.

Exhibitions

The Solomon R. Guggenheim Museum, New York, New York. *Modern Sculpture from the Joseph H. Hirshhorn Collection*, cat. no. 56, p. 193. October 3, 1962–January 6, 1963.

The Jewish Museum, New York, New York. *Recent American Sculpture*, cat. no. 14, listed as "Untitled, 1960." October 15–November 29, 1964.

References

Newsweek (October 15, 1962), illus. p. 110.

Daniel Robbins, "Modern Sculpture from the Joseph H. Hirshhorn Collection," *Apollo*, vol. 76, no. 9 (November 1962), p. 721, incorrectly referred to as "Untitled, 1960."

Herbert Read, *A Concise History of Modern Sculpture* (New York: Praeger, 1964), p. 270, pl. 335.

Robert Goldwater, *What Is Modern Sculpture?* (New York: Museum of Modern Art, 1969), p. 142, illus. p. 99.

Edward Lucie-Smith, *Late Modern: The Visual Arts since 1945* (New York: Praeger, 1969), p. 22, no. 192.

Notes

In 1964, as a result of correspondence between Mr. Hirshhorn and the Jewish Museum, *Davis*, 1961, came to be known as "Untitled, 1960." The error occurred when, in response to the Jewish Museum's request for *Davis*, Mr. Hirshhorn offered the sculpture as Untitled, 1960. It was exhibited with the incorrect title and date.

73

Fantail 1961

Painted steel
70 × 75 × 60 in.
(178 × 190.5 × 152.5 cm).

Collection

National Museum of American Art, Smithsonian Institution, Washington, D.C.; on loan from Jasper Johns.

Provenance

Leo Castelli Gallery, New York, New York; Jasper Johns, New York, New York.

Exhibitions

The Jewish Museum, New York, New York. *Recent American Sculpture*, cat. no. 15. October 15–November 29, 1964.

The Metropolitan Museum of Art, New York, New York. *New York Painting and Sculpture: 1940–1970*, cat. no. 24, illus. p. 124. October 18, 1969–February 1, 1970.

The Solomon R. Guggenheim Museum, New York, New York. *John Chamberlain: A Retrospective Exhibition*, cat. no. 30, illus. p. 53. December 23, 1971–February 20, 1972.

National Collection of Fine Arts, Smithsonian Institution, Washington, D.C. *Sculpture: American Directions, 1945–1975.* October 3–November 30, 1975.

References

Dore Ashton, "Art," *Arts and Architecture*, vol. 79, no. 3 (March 1962), illus. p. 7.

Max Kozloff, "New York Letter," *Art International*, vol. 6, no. 2 (March 1962), illus. p. 57.

Phyllis Tuchman, "An Interview with John Chamberlain," *Artforum*, vol. 10, no. 6 (February 1972), illus. p. 40.

74

Gerard 1961

Painted and chromium-plated steel
22 × 19 × 14½ in.
(56 × 48.5 × 37 cm).

Collection

Private collection, Boston, Massachusetts, 1966.

Provenance

Leo Castelli Gallery, New York, New York; Noah Goldowsky, New York, New York.

Exhibitions

The Art Galleries, University of California, Santa Barbara. *7 + 5: Sculptors in the 1950s*, cat. no. 7. January 6–February 15, 1976. Traveled to Phoenix Art Museum, Phoenix, Arizona. March 5–April 11, 1976.

75

Ginger 1961

Painted and chromium-plated steel
37 × 25 × 22 in.
(94 × 63.5 × 56 cm).

Collection

Present location unknown.

Provenance

Leo Castelli Gallery, New York, New York; Dilexi Gallery, San Francisco, California, 1963.

Exhibitions

Dilexi Gallery, San Francisco, California. *John Chamberlain.* 1963.

References

J[ohn] C[oplans], "Reviews: John Chamberlain, Dilexi Gallery," *Artforum*, vol. 1, no. 9 (March 1963), illus. p. 10.

Darby Bannard, "Cubism, Abstract Expressionism, David Smith," *Artforum*, vol. 6, no. 8 (April 1968), illus. p. 31.

76

Huzzy 1961

Painted and chromium-plated steel
54 × 33 × 21 in.
(137 × 84 × 53.5 cm).

Collection

The Nelson-Atkins Museum of Art, Kansas City, Missouri, 1964; gift of Mrs. Charles F. Buckwalter in memory of Charles F. Buckwalter.

Provenance

Mr. and Mrs. Charles F. Buckwalter, Kansas City, Missouri, 1961.

Exhibitions

The Cleveland Museum of Art, Cleveland, Ohio. *Sculpture by John Chamberlain*, listed. January 3–29, 1967.

The Solomon R. Guggenheim Museum, New York, New York. *John Chamberlain: A Retrospective Exhibition*, cat. no. 28, illus. p. 50. December 23, 1971–February 20, 1972.

The John and Mable Ringling Museum of Art, Sarasota, Florida. *John Chamberlain Reliefs 1960–1982*, color illus. p. 23. January 28–March 27, 1983.

References

Pierre Restany, "The New Realism," *Art in America*, vol. 51, no. 1 (February 1963), illus. p. 104.

Donald Judd, "Kansas City Report," *Arts*, vol. 38, no. 3 (December 1963), illus. p. 26.

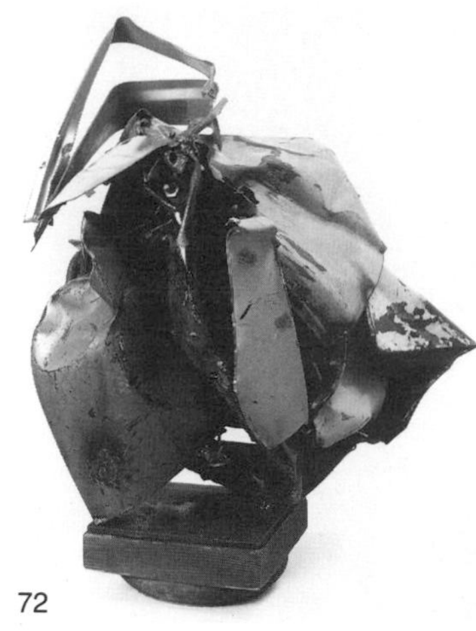
72

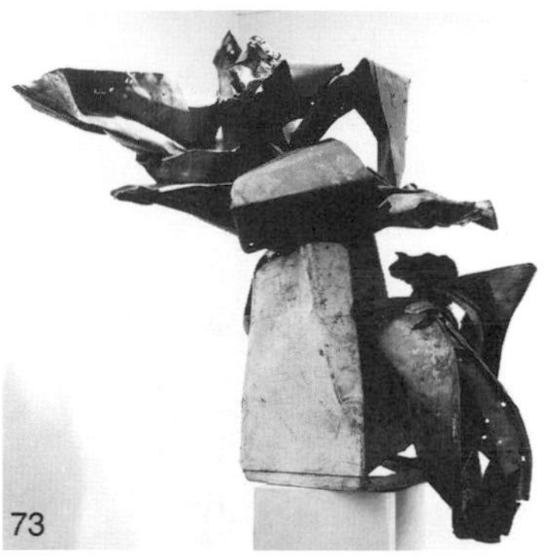
73

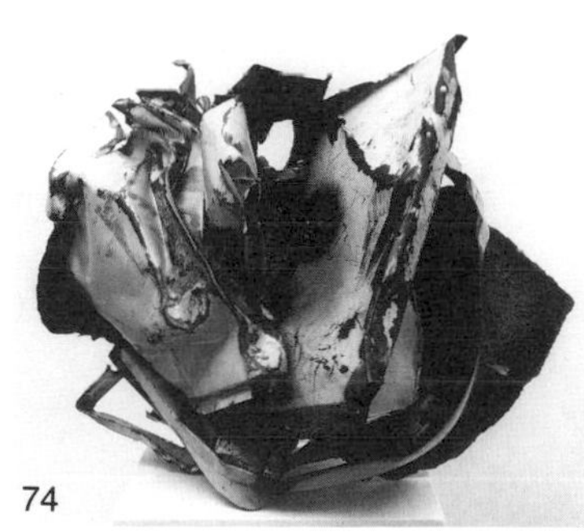
74

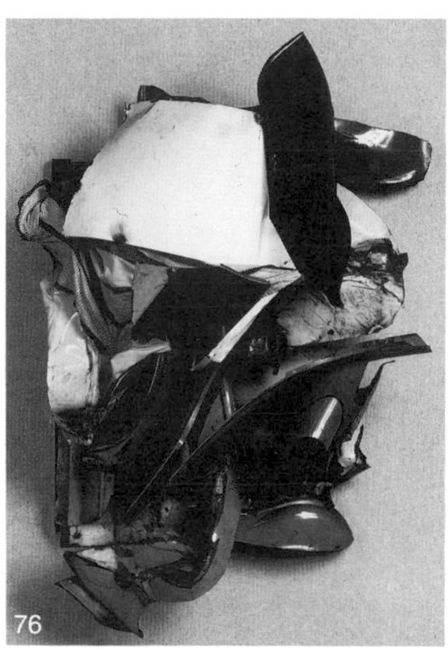
76

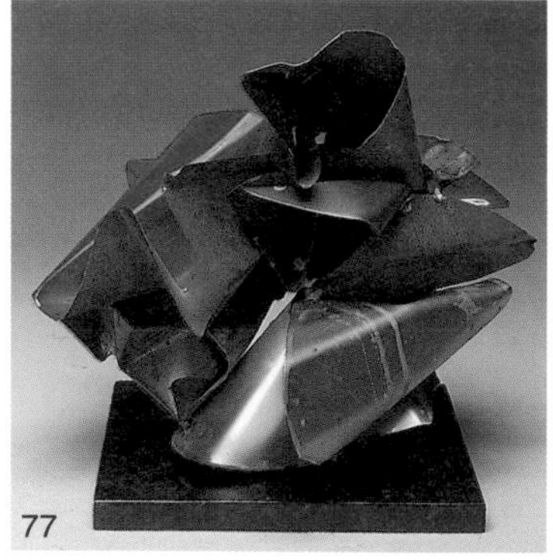
77

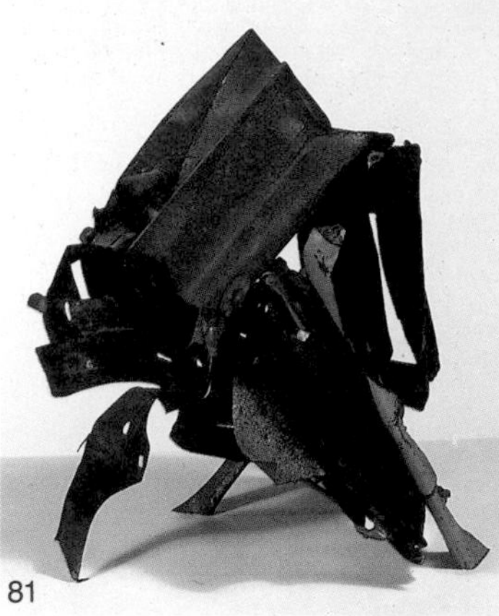
81

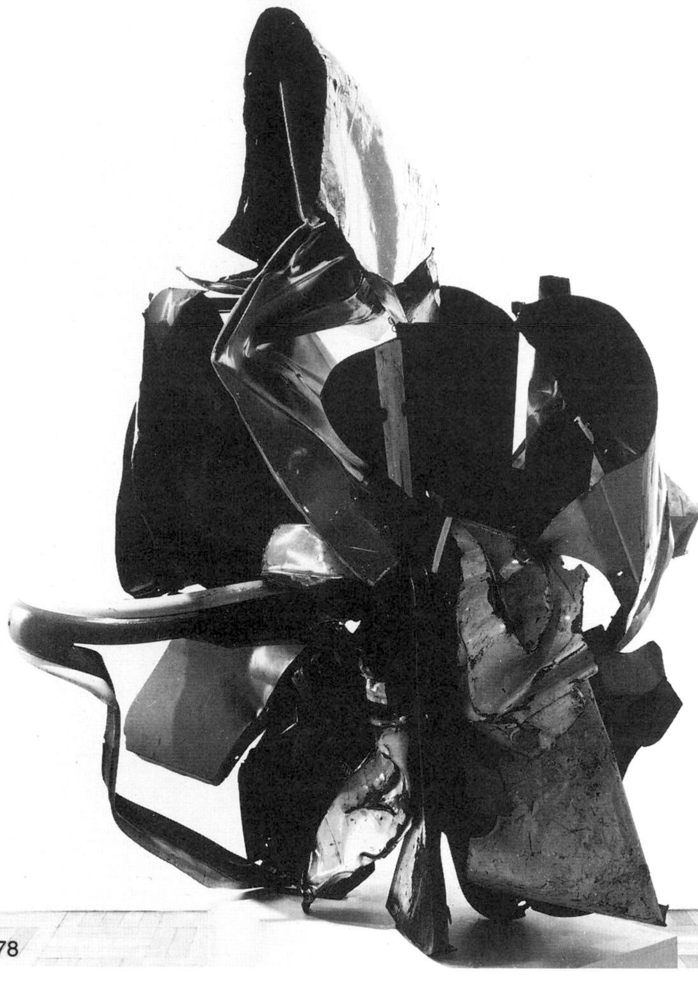
78

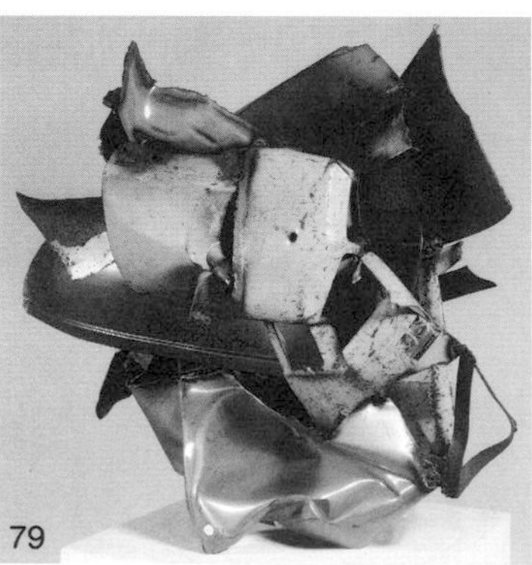
79

Donald Judd, "Chamberlain—Another View," *Art International*, vol. 7, no. 10 (January 1964), p. 39. Reprinted in *Donald Judd—Complete Writings 1959–1975* (Halifax: Press of the Nova Scotia College of Art and Design, and New York: New York University Press, 1975), pp. 108–10; and in *Chamberlain* (Bern: Kunsthalle Bern and Van Abbemuseum, Eindhoven, Netherlands, 1979).

Metro International 1964 Directory of Contemporary Art (Milan: Editoriale Metro, 1964), illus. pp. 76–77.

Nelson Gallery—Atkins Museum Handbook, vol. 1 (fifth edition, 1973), illus. p. 213.

77

Ignaatz 1961

Painted tin

10½ × 11 × 8 in.
(26.5 × 28 × 20.5 cm).

Collection

Judge and Mrs. Peter B. Spivak, Grosse Pointe, Michigan, 1965; acquired directly from the artist.

Notes

The sculpture is signed *Chamberlain '61*. It was titled by the artist in 1982.

78

Jackpot 1961

Painted and chromium-plated steel with gilt cardboard

60 × 52 × 46 in.
(152.5 × 132 × 117 cm).

Collection

Whitney Museum of American Art, New York, New York, 1975; gift of Andy Warhol.

Provenance

Andy Warhol, New York, New York.

Exhibitions

Leo Castelli Gallery, New York, New York. *An Exhibition in Progress*. September–October 14, 1961.

The Solomon R. Guggenheim Museum, New York, New York. *John Chamberlain: A Retrospective Exhibition*, cat. no. 27, illus. p. 45. December 23, 1971–February 20, 1972.

Whitney Museum of American Art, Downtown Branch, New York, New York. *Auto Icons*, cat. no. 2, p. 5. March 7–April 11, 1979.

Whitney Museum of American Art, Fairfield County, Connecticut. *Autoscape: The Automobile in the American Landscape*, cat. March 30–May 30, 1984.

References

N[atalie] E[dgar], "John Chamberlain," *Art News*, vol. 60, no. 10 (February 1962), illus. p. 15.

79

Kroll 1961

Painted steel

26 × 34 × 24 in.
(66 × 86.5 × 61 cm).

Collection

The Albright-Knox Art Gallery, Buffalo, New York, 1961; gift of Seymour H. Knox.

Provenance

Leo Castelli Gallery, New York, New York.

Exhibitions

The Albright-Knox Art Gallery, Buffalo, New York. *Mixed Media and Pop Art*, cat. no. 7. November 19–December 15, 1963.

Colgate University, Hamilton, New York. *Festival of the Creative Arts*. October 9–25, 1964.

State University of New York at Buffalo, New York. *Spring Art Festival*. April 4–10, 1965.

The Solomon R. Guggenheim Museum, New York, New York. *John Chamberlain: A Retrospective Exhibition*, cat. no. 21, p. 3, illus. p. 52. December 23, 1971–February 20, 1972.

The Albright-Knox Art Gallery, Buffalo, New York. *Recent American Painting and Sculpture in the Albright-Knox Art Gallery*, catalogue. November 17–December 31, 1972.

References

The Art Quarterly, vol. 24, no. 3 (Autumn 1961), p. 318.

Benjamin Townsend, "Albright-Knox Buffalo: Work in Progress," *Art News*, vol. 65, no. 9 (January 1967), illus. p. 30.

The 1969 Compton Yearbook (F. E. Compton Co., 1969), illus. p. 43.

Charlotte Buell, *Contemporary Art—Exploring Its Roots and Development* (Worcester, Massachusetts: Davis Publications, 1972), illus. p. 48.

Notes

The sculpture is signed and dated: *Chamberlain '61*.

80

Max 1961

Painted steel

24 × 33 × 29 in.
(61 × 84 × 73.5 cm).

Notes

The Leo Castelli Gallery records indicate that this sculpture was destroyed and that no photograph of the work exists.

81

Maza 1961

Painted tin

5 × 4½ × 4½ in.
(12.5 × 11.5 × 11.5 cm).

Collection

James Mayor, London, 1975.

Provenance

Martha Jackson Gallery, New York, New York, 1961.

82

Mr. Blue 1961

Painted and chromium-plated steel
84 in. high (213.5 cm).

Exhibitions

Museu de Arte Moderna, São Paulo, Brazil. *VI Bienal do Museu de Arte Moderna, São Paolo*. September–December 1961.

References

Jean Lipman and Richard Marshall, *Art about Art* (New York: Dutton, 1978), pp. 142 and 149, illus. of George Segal's *John Chamberlain Working*. Published in association with Whitney Museum of American Art exhibition, July 19–September 24, 1978.

Barbara Rose, *American Art since 1900: A Critical History* (New York: Praeger, 1967), fig. II–29, illus. p. 262.

Artforum, vol. 10, no. 6 (February 1972), color illus. cover.

Elizabeth C. Baker, "The Chamberlain Crunch," *Art News*, vol. 70, no. 10 (February 1972), color illus. p. 29.

Notes

Mr. Blue was given to George Segal to be used as part of a portrait sculpture of John Chamberlain by Segal. It was destroyed when Segal incorporated parts of it into his sculpture *John Chamberlain Working*, 1965–67 (Collection of the Museum of Modern Art, New York; promised gift of Carroll Janis and Conrad Janis). *Mr. Blue* is unrecognizable in the Segal sculpture; only remnants of the original Chamberlain sculpture were used and Chamberlain's color has been obliterated by an aluminum paint.

The sculpture was altered by the artist in 1969.

83

Mr. Press 1961

Painted and chromium-plated steel and fabric
95 × 90 × 50 in.
(241.5 × 228.5 × 127 cm).

Collection

Donald Judd, Marfa, Texas.

Provenance

Leo Castelli Gallery, New York, New York.

Exhibitions

The Jewish Museum, New York, New York. *Recent American Sculpture*, cat. no. 16. October 15–November 29, 1964.

Leo Castelli Warehouse, New York, New York. *John Chamberlain: Recent Sculpture*. February 2–22, 1969.

References

Donald Judd, "Chamberlain—Another View," Art International, vol. 7, no. 10 (January 1964), p. 39. Reprinted in *Donald Judd—Complete Writings 1959–1975* (Halifax: Press of the Nova Scotia College of Art and Design, and New York: New York University Press, 1975), pp. 108–10; and in *Chamberlain* (Bern: Kunsthalle Bern and Van Abbemuseum, Eindhoven, Netherlands, 1979), illus. p. 12.

84

Oteen 1961

Painted steel
24½ × 36 × 26½ in.
(62 × 91.5 × 67.5 cm).

Collection

Present location unknown.

Provenance

Leo Castelli Gallery, New York, New York; Florence and Brooks Barron, Detroit, Michigan, 1961; O. K. Harris Works of Art, New York, New York.

Exhibitions

The Solomon R. Guggenheim Museum, New York, New York. *John Chamberlain: A Retrospective Exhibition*, cat. no. 24, illus. p. 51. December 23, 1971–February 20, 1972.

85

Relief 1961

Painted and chromium-plated steel
26½ × 24½ × 10½ in.
(67.5 × 62 × 26.5 cm).

Collection

Present location unknown.

Notes

The only evidence of the existence of this sculpture is that it was entered into the Castelli registry in 1961.

86

Score 1961

Painted and chromium-plated steel
72 × 72 × 23 in.
(183 × 183 × 58.5 cm).

Collection

Neumann Family Collection, New York, New York, 1960; acquired directly from the artist.

Exhibitions

The Solomon R. Guggenheim Museum, New York, New York. *John Chamberlain: A Retrospective Exhibition*, cat. no. 29, illus. p. 47. December 23, 1971–February 20, 1972.

References

Marjorie Welish, "Chamberlain at the Guggenheim," *Arts*, vol. 46, no. 4 (February 1972), illus. p. 55.

XXe Siècle, no. 41 (December 1973), illus. p. 146.

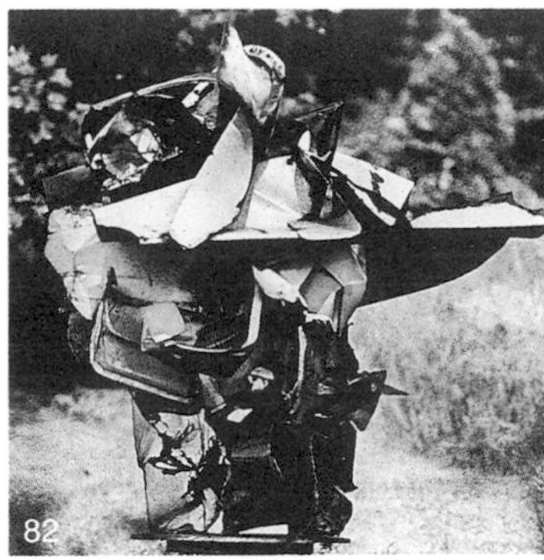
82

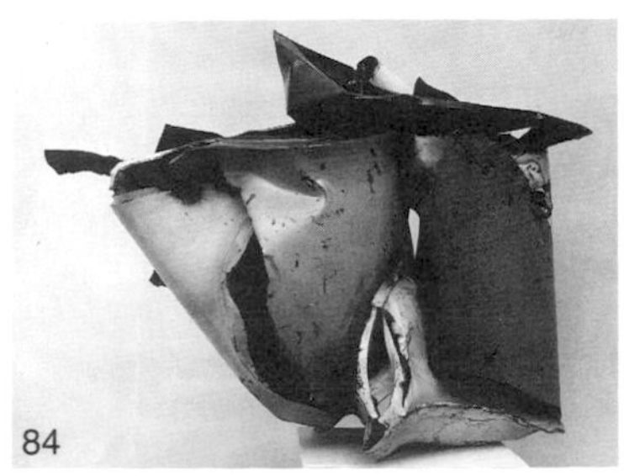
84

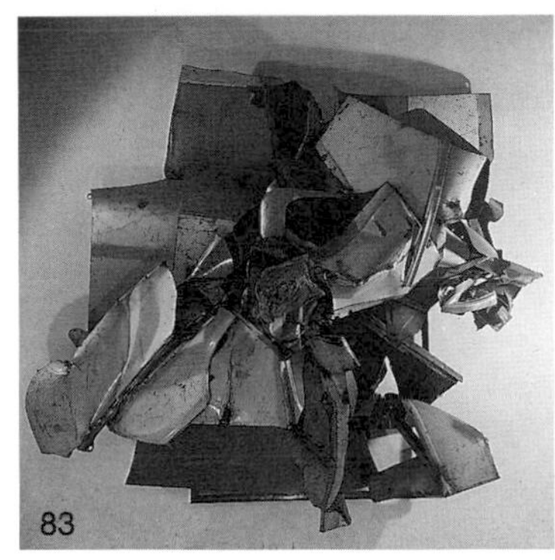
83

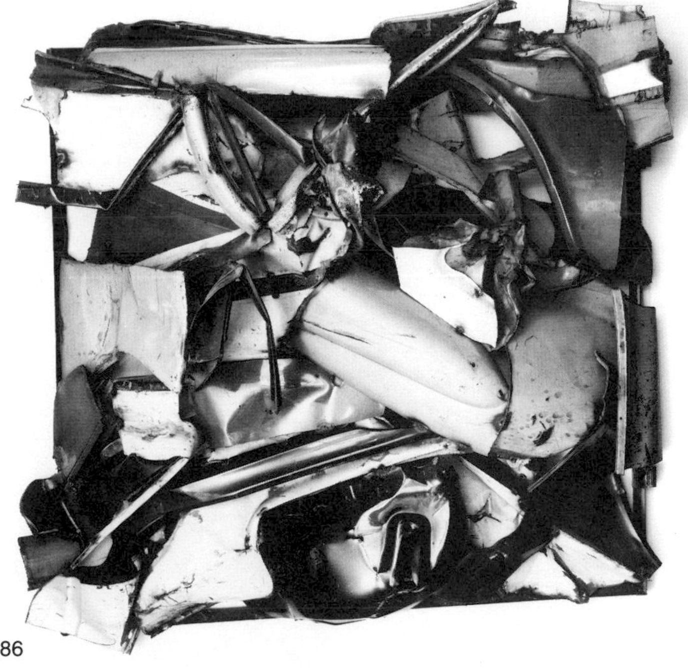
86

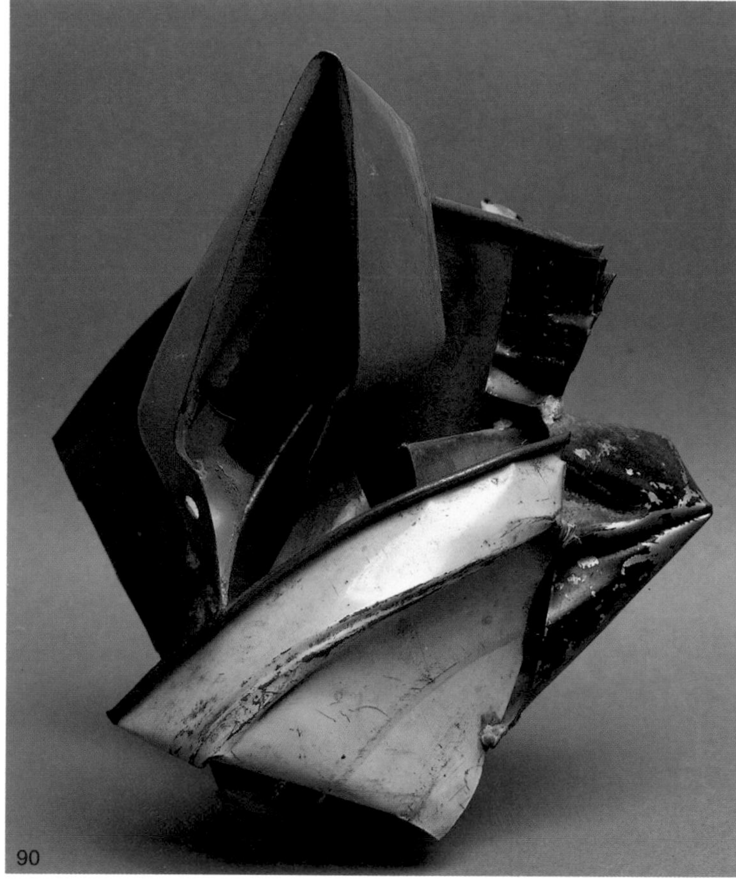
90

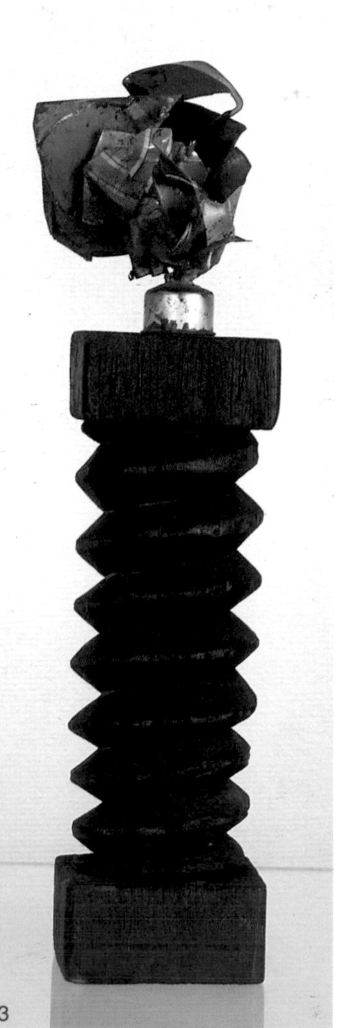
93

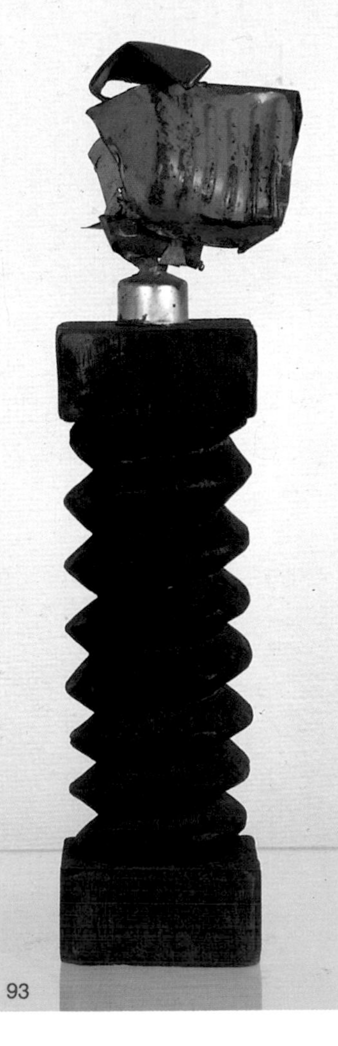
93

87

Tiny Piece #1 1961
Painted tin
6½ in. high (16.5 cm).

Collection
Present location unknown.

Provenance
Leo Castelli Gallery, New York, New York; Campbell Wylly, New York, New York.

88

Tiny Piece #2 1961
Painted tin
6½ in. high (16.5 cm).

Collection
Present location unknown.

Provenance
Leo Castelli Gallery, New York, New York; Campbell Wylly, New York, New York.

89

Tiny Piece #3 1961
Painted tin
6½ in. high (16.5 cm).

Collection
Mr. and Mrs. Armand P. Bartos, New York, New York.

Provenance
Leo Castelli Gallery, New York, New York; Priscilla Morgan, New York, New York.

90

Tiny Piece #4/Scotch Spur 1961
Painted tin
8 × 7 × 6½ in.
(20.5 × 18 × 16.5 cm).

Collection
Mme Marcel Duchamp, Villiers-sous-Grez, France.

Provenance
Leo Castelli Gallery, New York, New York; Marcel Duchamp, New York, New York.

Exhibitions
Cordier and Ekstrom Gallery, New York, New York; organized by Marcel Duchamp for the American Chess Foundation. *Hommage à Caissa*. February 7, 1966.

The Solomon R. Guggenheim Museum, New York, New York. *John Chamberlain: A Retrospective Exhibition*, cat. no. 25. December 23, 1971–February 20, 1972.

Notes
The sculpture was retitled *Scotch Spur* by the artist in 1983 when he met Mme Duchamp in Sarasota, Florida.

91

Tiny Piece #5 1961
Painted tin
5 in. high (12.5 cm).

Provenance
Leo Castelli Gallery, New York, New York; Mr. and Mrs. Michael Sundell, New York, New York.

Notes
According to Mr. and Mrs. Sundell, the sculpture was accidentally destroyed.

92

Tiny Piece #6 1961
Painted steel and glass (ink bottle)
7½ in. high (19 cm).

Collection
Present location unknown.

Provenance
Ed Meneely, New York, New York; O. K. Harris Works of Art, New York, New York, 1980.

93

Tiny Piece #7 1961
Painted tin
5½ × 4 in. (14 × 10 cm).

Collection
Present location unknown.

Provenance
Gordon Locksley, Minneapolis, Minnesota, 1969.

94

Untitled 1961
Painted tin
5 × 4 × 3 in. (12.5 × 10 × 7.5 cm).

Collection
Allan Stone, New York, New York.

Provenance
Leo Castelli Gallery, New York, New York.

Notes
The sculpture is possibly one of the unlocated works from the *Tiny Piece* series (see cat. nos. 87–93).

95

H. and S. Roth 1961
Painted tin
5½ × 5 × 4½ in.
(14 × 12.5 × 11.5 cm).

Collection
Dia Art Foundation, New York, New York, 1982.

Provenance
Henry and Sylvia Roth, Garnerville, New York.

Notes
The sculpture was titled by the artist in 1982. It is possible that it is part of the *Tiny Piece* series (see cat. nos. 87–93).

96

Tonk 1961
Painted steel
36 × 25 × 25 in.
(91.5 × 63.5 × 63.5 cm).

Collection
Present location unknown.

Provenance
Leo Castelli Gallery, New York, New York; Jonathan Streep, New York, New York, 1961.

Exhibitions
Leo Castelli Gallery, New York, New York. *Sculpture and Relief*. May 23–June 1961.

97

Ioy 1961
Painted steel and plastic
53½ × 38½ × 30½ in.
(136 × 98 × 77.5 cm).

Collection
The Art Institute of Chicago, Chicago, Illinois, 1969; gift of Mr. William Hokin.

Provenance
Dwan Gallery, Los Angeles, California; Lo Giudice Gallery, Chicago, Illinois, 1967; William J. Hokin, Chicago, Illinois, 1969.

Exhibitions
Los Angeles County Museum of Art, Los Angeles, California. *American Sculpture of the Sixties*. April 28–June 25, 1967.

Museum of Contemporary Art, Chicago, Illinois. *Selections from the William J. Hokin Collection*, illus. April 20–June 16, 1985.

98

White Thumb 1960–61
Painted and chromium-plated steel
84 × 84 in. (213.4 × 213.4 cm).

Provenance
Leo Castelli Gallery, New York, New York, 1962.

Exhibitions
The Art Institute of Chicago, Chicago, Illinois. *Sixty-Fifth Annual American Exhibition: Some Directions in Contemporary Painting and Sculpture*, cat. no. 14, illus. January 15–February 18, 1962.

References
Kevin Power, "Robert Creeley on Art and Poetry," *The Niagara Magazine*, no. 9 (Fall 1978).

Notes
According to the artist, the sculpture was destroyed. A sculpture based on *White Thumb* was completed in 1978. (See *White Thumb Four*, cat. no. 591.)

"I remember one beautiful moment with Chamberlain. We were at his house, and he was then living in New City, like the whole house was just beautifully abstract. It was a crazy old farmhouse that they were variously remodelling. There was a small barn, and a garage adjacent, which he used as a working place. He was working down on the floor of this garage-barn, and he'd been trying to put together this large piece, and so he had all this metal all over the place. He hasn't welded it yet. It's just been put together, and we're now up on this grid looking down on this kind of small space. John says maybe it should be this way or that way, and there we are just looking at it, when John suddenly moves in this beautiful gesture and just jumps right down into it. He's kicking and hauling the jagged pieces of metal around, and at the same time he's looking up and saying—'How does it look now?' So there's this incredible moment for me when Chamberlain was there *in* his sculpture. I love this quality of his work." (From Kevin Power, "Robert Creeley on Art and Poetry," *The Niagara Magazine*.)

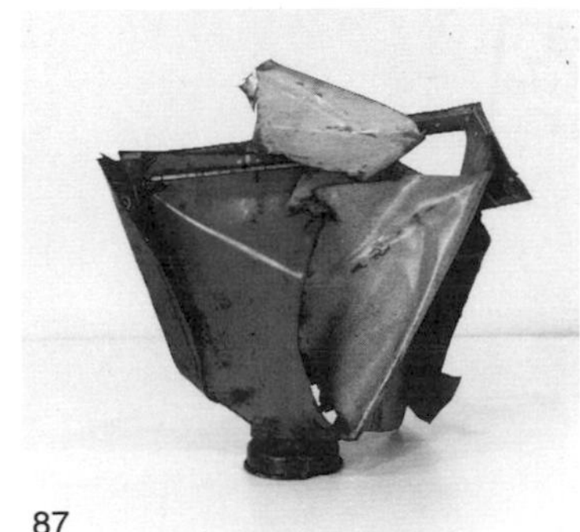
87

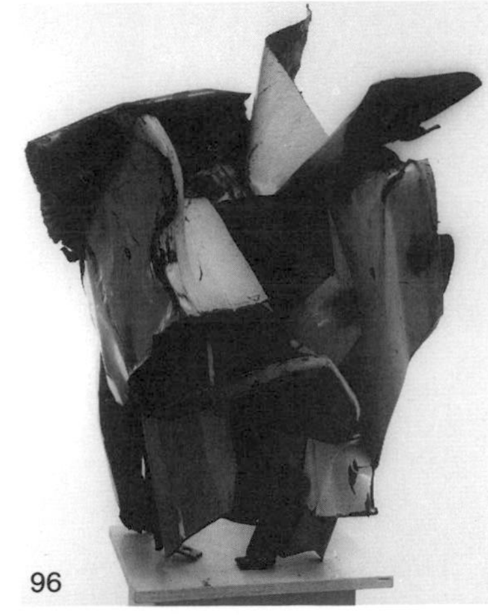
96

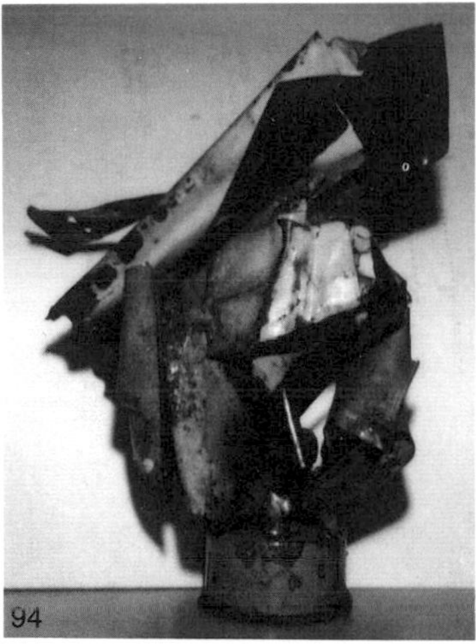
94

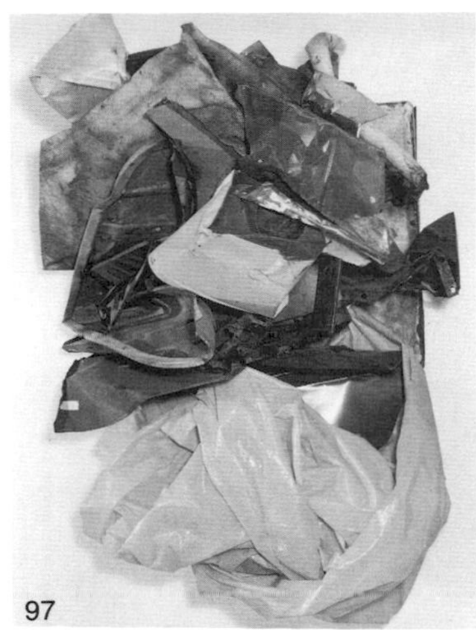
97

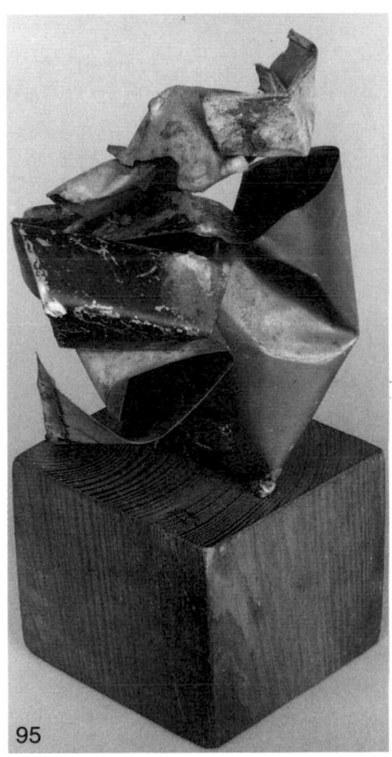
95

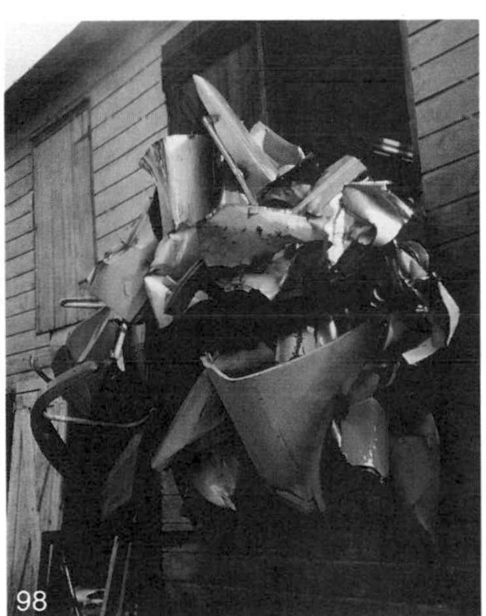
98

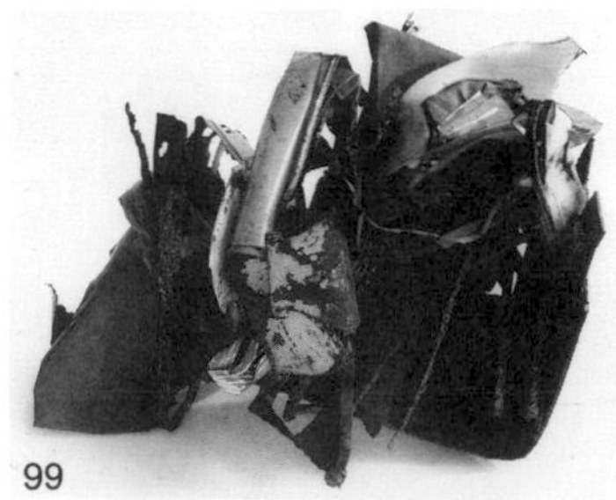
99

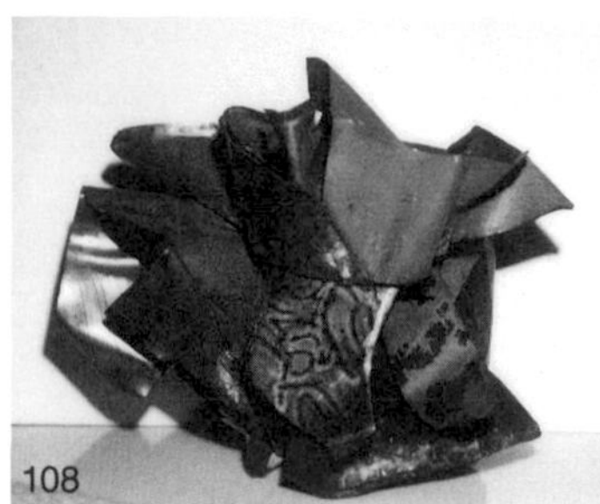
108

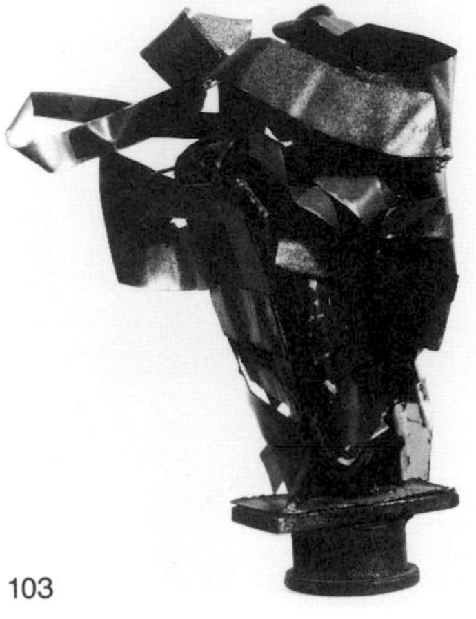
103

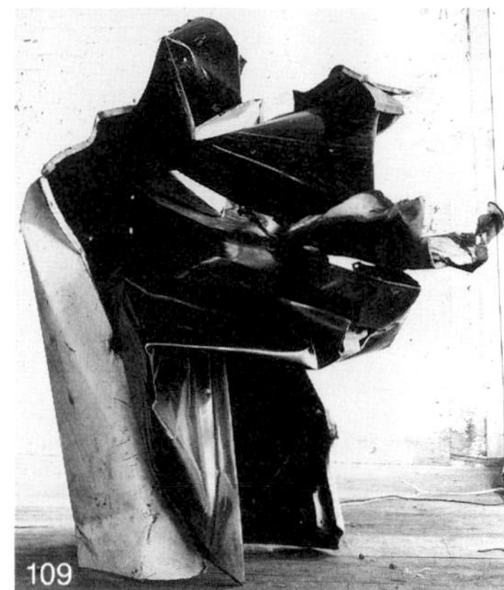
109

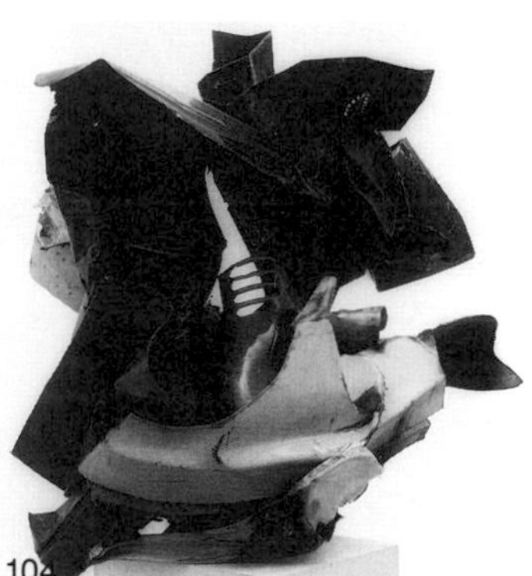
104

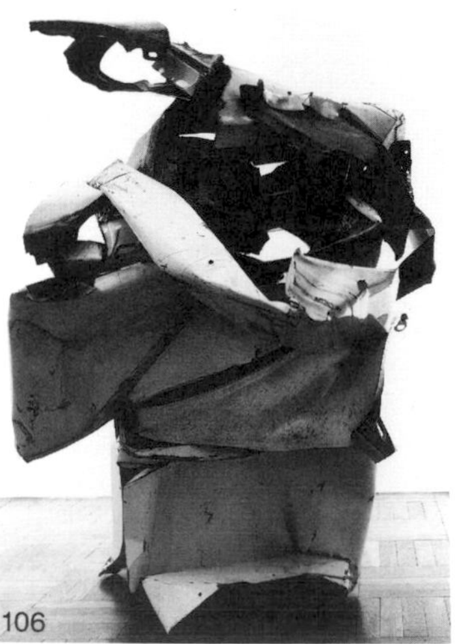
106

99

Wuzza 1961
Painted steel and fabric
21 × 16 × 16 in.
(53.5 × 40.5 × 40.5 cm).

Collection
Present location unknown.

Provenance
Leo Castelli Gallery, New York, New York; Dr. Arthur Carr, New York, New York.

100

Untitled 1961
Painted and chromium-plated steel
33 × 33 × 24 in.
(84 × 84 × 61 cm).

Collection
Colombe and Leonard Rosenberg, New York, New York, 1985.

Provenance
Tadasuke Kuwayama, New York, New York, 1961.

101

Untitled 1961
Painted metal
19 × 13 × 4 in. (48 × 33 × 10 cm).

Collection
Mr. and Mrs. Arthur Formichelli, Berkeley, California, 1967.

Provenance
Leo Castelli Gallery, New York, New York; Mr. and Mrs. John Bransten, San Francisco, California.

Notes
The sculpture has also been known as *Piece on Grey Pedestal*.

The sculpture was donated by the Branstens to the San Francisco Art Institute in 1967 for auction, where it was acquired by Mr. and Mrs. Formichelli.

102

Amoco 1962
Painted tin
8½ × 9 × 7 in.
(21.5 × 23 × 18 cm).

Collection
Present location unknown.

Provenance
Leo Castelli Gallery, New York, New York; Felix Landau, New York, New York.

103

Angus 1962
Painted tin and steel
9 × 7 × 5½ in. (23 × 18 × 14 cm).

Collection
Allan Stone, New York, New York, 1963.

Provenance
Leo Castelli Gallery, New York, New York.

104

Arch Brown 1962
Painted steel
37 × 38 × 29 in.
(94 × 96.5 × 73.5 cm).

Collection
Mr. and Mrs. Burton Tremaine, Meriden, Connecticut, 1962.

Provenance
Leo Castelli Gallery, New York, New York.

Exhibitions
Cordier and Ekstrom Gallery, New York, New York. *Seven Decades 1895–1965*; organized by the Public Education Association. April 26–May 21, 1966.

The Solomon R. Guggenheim Museum, New York, New York. *John Chamberlain: A Retrospective Exhibition*, cat. no. 41, illus. p. 56. December 23, 1971–February 20, 1972.

References
Nan R. Piene, "New York: Gallery Notes," *Art in America*, vol. 54, no. 3 (May/June 1966), illus. p. 109.

105

Belvo Violet 1962
Painted steel with unit of pressed-metal ceiling
50 × 50 × 30 in.
(127 × 127 × 76 cm).

Collection
Frank Stella, New York, New York; acquired directly from the artist.

Exhibitions
Leo Castelli Gallery, New York, New York. *Group Show*. April 7–21, 1962.

The Solomon R. Guggenheim Museum, New York, New York. *John Chamberlain: A Retrospective Exhibition*, cat. no. 39. December 23, 1971–February 20, 1972.

The John and Mable Ringling Museum of Art, Sarasota, Florida. *John Chamberlain Reliefs 1960–1982*, color illus. p. 27. January 28–March 27, 1983.

References
Noel Frackman, "Tracking Frank Stella's Circuit Series," *Arts*, vol. 56, no. 8 (April 1982), color illus. p. 135.

106

Big E 1962

Painted and chromium-plated steel
60 × 59 × 48 in.
(153 × 150 × 122 cm).

Collection

Ed Cauduro, Portland, Oregon.

Provenance

Elaine Chamberlain, New York, New York; Richard Bellamy, New York, New York.

Exhibitions

The Institute of Contemporary Art, Philadelphia, Pennsylvania. *The Atmosphere of 'Sixty-Four*. April 17–June 1, 1964.

The Institute of Contemporary Art, Boston, Massachusetts. *The Biennale Eight*, cat. no. 1. June 20–July 26, 1964.

Seattle Art Museum, Seattle, Washington. *American Art 1948–1973*, cat. no. 12, illus. p. 23, listed as "Untitled, 1962." August 22–October 14, 1973.

Washington State University, Pullman, Washington. *Two Decades 1957–1977: American Sculpture in Northwest Collections*. October 7–November 18, 1977.

Seattle Art Museum, Seattle, Washington. *American Sculpture: Three Decades*, cat. no. 5. November 15, 1984–January 27, 1985.

References

Rosalind E. Krauss, "Boston Letter," *Art International*, vol. 8, no. 1 (February 1964), illus. p. 33.

History of World Art. Vol. 38, *Postwar Art* (Tokyo, Kadokawa Publishing), illus. no. 86.

107

Black Cocktail 1962

Painted tin
7 × 9 × 6 in. (18 × 23 × 15 cm).

Collection

Present location unknown.

Provenance

Leo Castelli Gallery, New York, New York; Gerald Fisher, New York, New York.

108

Cities Service 1962

Painted tin
6 × 7 × 5½ in. (15 × 18 × 14 cm).

Collection

Mr. and Mrs. Allan Stone, Purchase, New York.

Provenance

Leo Castelli Gallery, New York, New York.

109

Coo Wha Zee 1962

Painted steel
72 × 60 × 50 in.
(183 × 152 × 127 cm).

Collection

Detroit Institute of Arts, Detroit, Michigan, 1965; gift of Florence and Brooks Barron.

Provenance

Florence and Brooks Barron, Detroit, Michigan.

Exhibitions

Leo Castelli Gallery, New York, New York. *John Chamberlain and Frank Stella*. October 16–November 7, 1962.

Battersea Park, London. *Sculpture in the Open Air*; organized by the Museum of Modern Art, New York, New York, cat. no. 11, illus. May 29–September 28, 1963.

The Solomon R. Guggenheim Museum, New York, New York. *John Chamberlain: A Retrospective Exhibition*, cat. no. 45, illus. p. 57. December 23, 1971–February 20, 1972.

References

Colette Roberts, "Lettre de New York," *Aujourd'hui*, vol. 7, no. 39 (November 1962), illus. p. 50, incorrectly identified as *Baby Jane*, 1962.

Frederick J. Cummings and Charles H. Elam, eds., *The Detroit Institute of Arts Illustrated Handbook* (Detroit: Wayne State University Press, 1971), illus. p. 185.

110

Doc 1962

Painted steel
25 × 29 × 25 in.
(63.5 × 73.5 × 63.5 cm).

Collection

Present location unknown.

Notes

The only evidence of the existence of this sculpture is that it was entered into the Castelli registry in 1962.

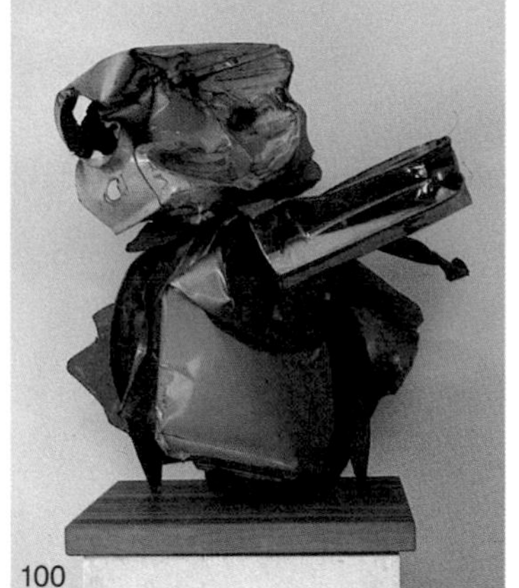
100

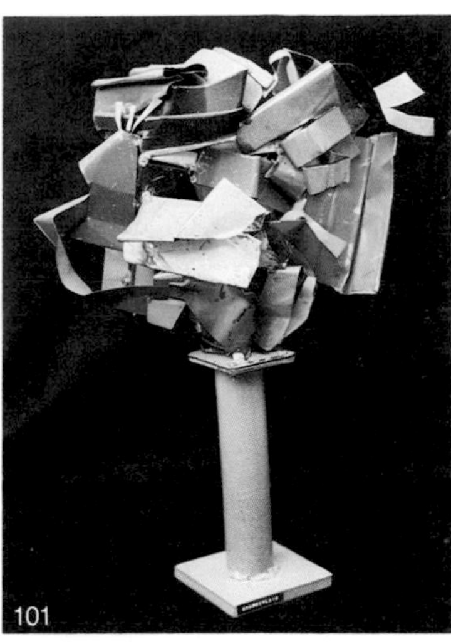
101

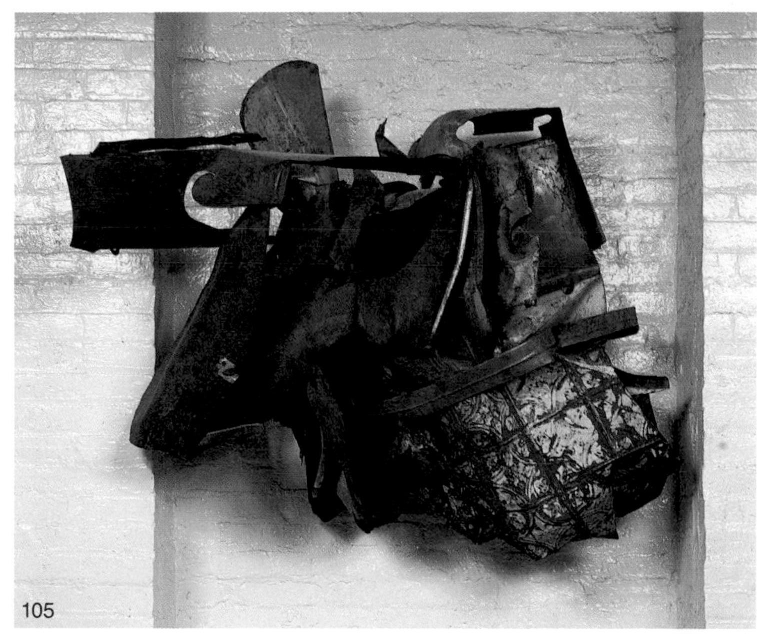
105

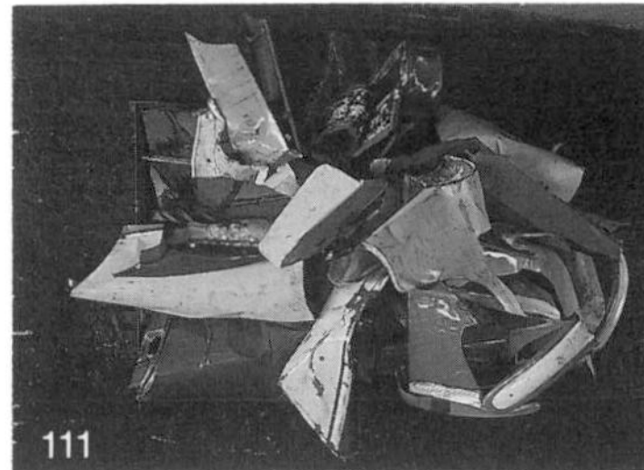
111

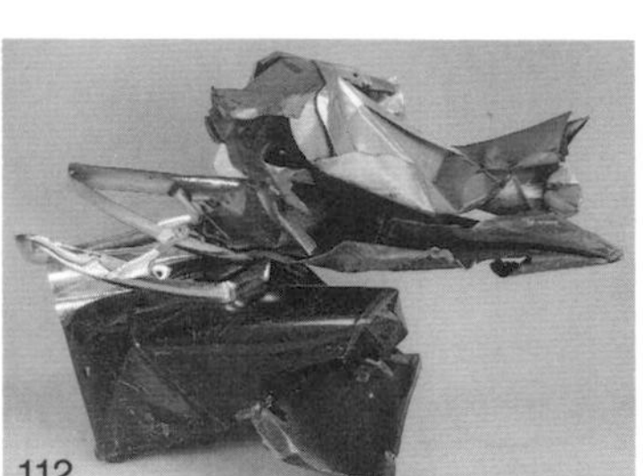
112

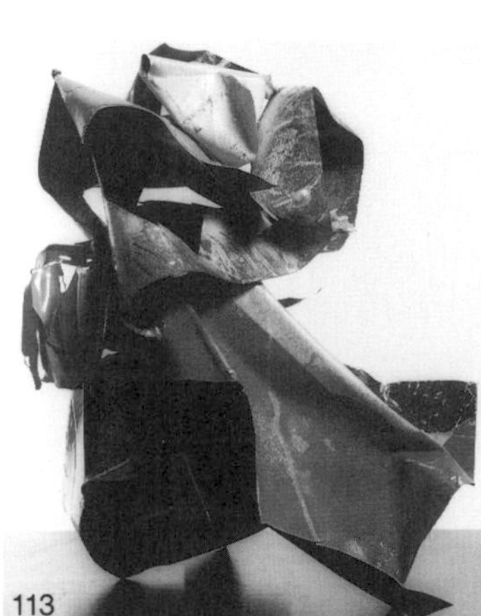
113

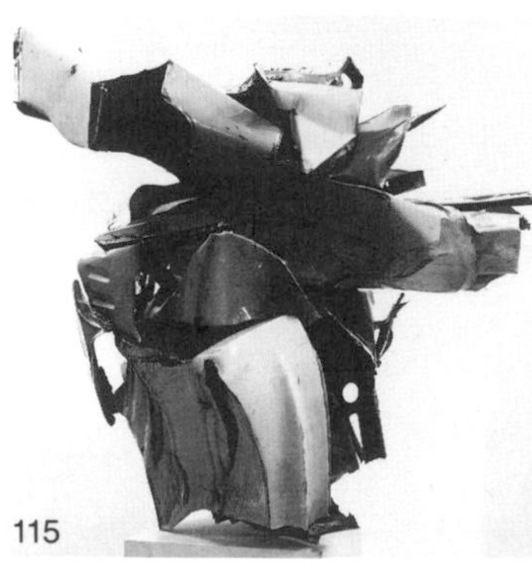
115

111

Dolores James 1962

Painted and chromium-plated steel
76 × 97 × 39 in.
(193 × 246 × 99 cm).

Collection
The Solomon R. Guggenheim Museum, New York, New York, 1970.

Provenance
Leo Castelli Gallery, New York, New York.

Exhibitions
The Jewish Museum, New York, New York. *Recent American Sculpture*, cat. no. 17. October 15–November 29, 1964.

Leo Castelli Warehouse, New York, New York. *John Chamberlain: Recent Sculpture*. February 2–22, 1969.

The Metropolitan Museum of Art, New York, New York. *New York Painting and Sculpture: 1940–1970*, cat. no. 26, color illus. p. 68. October 18, 1969–February 1, 1970.

The Solomon R. Guggenheim Museum, New York, New York. *Selections from the Museum Collection and Recent Acquisitions, 1971*. June 11–September 12, 1971.

The Solomon R. Guggenheim Museum, New York, New York. *John Chamberlain: A Retrospective Exhibition*, cat. no. 47, color illus. December 23, 1971–February 20, 1972.

The Solomon R. Guggenheim Museum, New York, New York. *Collection: American Sculpture*. January 24–April 16, 1978.

The Solomon R. Guggenheim Museum, New York, New York. *Collection: Art in America after World War II*. January 18–February 25, 1979.

The Solomon R. Guggenheim Museum, New York, New York. *Collection Exhibition*. May 23–August 17, 1980.

The Solomon R. Guggenheim Museum, New York, New York. *The New York School: Four Decades, Guggenheim Collection and Major Loans*. July 1–August 29, 1982.

The John and Mable Ringling Museum of Art, Sarasota, Florida. *John Chamberlain Reliefs 1960–1982*, color illus. p. 8. January 28–March 27, 1983.

The Solomon R. Guggenheim Museum, New York, New York. *Transformations in Sculpture: Four Decades of American and European Art*, cat. no. 53, color illus. November 22, 1985–February 16, 1986.

References
Elizabeth C. Baker, "The Secret Life of John Chamberlain," *Art News*, vol. 68, no. 2 (April 1969), illus. p. 51.

Emily Wasserman, "Review: New York," *Artforum*, vol. 7, no. 8 (April 1969), illus. p. 73.

Phyllis Tuchman, "An Interview with John Chamberlain," *Artforum*, vol. 10, no. 6 (February 1972), p. 39.

John Wilmerding, *American Art* (New York: Pelican, 1976), pp. 211–12, illus. pl. 265.

Edward Lucie-Smith, *Art Now: From Abstract Expressionism to Superrealism* (New York: Morrow, 1977), p. 184, color illus. pl. 143.

Vivian Endicott Barnett, *Handbook: The Guggenheim Museum Collection, 1900–1980* (New York: The Solomon R. Guggenheim Museum, 1980), illus. p. 483.

Carter Ratcliff, "The 'Art' of Chic," *Saturday Review*, vol. 8, no. 4 (April 1981), illus. p. 15.

Dietrich Mahlow, *100 Jahre Metallplastik*, vol. 2 (Frankfurt: Metallgesellschaft AG, 1981), cat. no. 189, illus. p. 171.

Noel Frackman, "Tracking Frank Stella's Circuit Series," *Arts*, vol. 56, no. 8 (April 1982), illus. p. 137.

112

Du Lang 1962

Painted and chromium-plated steel
36 × 55 × 29 in.
(91.5 × 139.5 × 73.5 cm).

Collection
Private collection, New York, New York, 1981.

Provenance
Alfred Ordover, New York, New York; Michael Bennet, New York, New York.

Exhibitions
Christie, Manson & Woods International, Inc., New York, New York. *Contemporary Art*, cat. no. 45, illus. p. 95. May 13, 1981.

113

El Reno 1962

Painted steel
11 × 9 × 8 in. (28 × 23 × 20 cm).

Collection
Mr. and Mrs. Alvin S. Lane, Riverdale, New York, 1962.

Provenance
Leo Castelli Gallery, New York, New York.

Exhibitions
The Solomon R. Guggenheim Museum, New York, New York. *John Chamberlain: A Retrospective Exhibition*, cat. no. 35, illus. p. 60. December 23, 1971–February 20, 1972.

References
Donald Judd, "Chamberlain—Another View," *Art International*, vol. 7, no. 10 (January 1964), pp. 38–39. Reprinted in *Donald Judd—Complete Writings 1959–1975* (Halifax: Press of the Nova Scotia College of Art and Design, and New York: New York University Press, 1975), pp. 108–10; and in *Chamberlain* (Bern: Kunsthalle Bern and Van Abbemuseum, Eindhoven, Netherlands, 1979).

Metro International 1964 Directory of Contemporary Art (Milan: Editoriale Metro, 1964), illus. pp. 76–77.

114

Esso 1962

Painted tin
6 × 8 × 7 in. (15 × 20.5 × 18 cm).

Collection
Present location unknown.

Provenance
Leo Castelli Gallery, New York, New York; Felix Landau, New York, New York.

115

Ezra-Jack 1962

Painted and chromium-plated steel
36 × 38 × 26 in.
(91.5 × 96.5 × 66 cm).

Collection
Present location unknown.

Provenance
Leo Castelli Gallery, New York, New York; O. K. Harris Works of Art, New York, New York.

Exhibitions
Leo Castelli Gallery, New York, New York. *Summer Group Show*. June 30–August 28, 1970.

116

Hidden Face 1962

Painted and chromium–plated steel
41 × 50 × 33½ in.
(104 × 127 × 85 cm).

Collection
Dia Art Foundation, New York, New York, 1980.

Provenance
Locksley/Shea Gallery, Minneapolis, Minnesota; Lone Star Foundation, New York, 1978.

Notes
The sculpture was titled by the artist in 1982.

117

Hollywood John 1962

Painted and chromium-plated steel
64 × 60 × 43 in.
(162.5 × 152.5 × 109.5 cm).

Collection
Donald Judd, Marfa, Texas.

Provenance
Leo Castelli Gallery, New York, New York.

Exhibitions

Boston University Art Gallery, Boston, Massachusetts. *Six Sculptors*. March 30–April 25, 1963.

Leo Castelli Gallery, New York, New York. *Group Show*. February 18–March 12, 1964.

The Art Institute of Chicago, Chicago, Illinois. *Twenty-Fourth Annual Exhibition by the Society for Contemporary American Art*, cat. no. 9. May 8–30, 1964.

The Solomon R. Guggenheim Museum, New York, New York. *John Chamberlain: A Retrospective Exhibition*, cat. no. 46, illus. p. 54. December 23, 1971–February 20, 1972.

118

Jim 1962

Painted and chromium-plated steel
31 × 32 × 28 in.
(78.5 × 81.5 × 71 cm).

Collection

Howard and Jean Lipman, New York, New York, 1962.

Provenance

Leo Castelli Gallery, New York, New York.

119

Laro 1962

Painted and chromium-plated steel
28 × 35 × 30 in.
(71 × 89 × 76 cm).

Collection

Present location unknown.

Provenance

Leo Castelli Gallery, New York, New York; Alfred Ordover, New York, New York, 1962.

120

Marina Marina 1962

Painted and chromium-plated steel
54 × 69 × 43 in.
(137 × 175.5 × 109 cm).

Collection

Present location unknown.

Provenance

Leo Castelli Gallery, New York, New York; Dilexi Gallery, San Francisco, California, 1963.

Exhibitions

Dilexi Gallery, San Francisco, California. *John Chamberlain*. 1963.

References

J[ohn] C[oplans], "Reviews: John Chamberlain, Dilexi Gallery," *Artforum*, vol. 1, no. 9 (March 1963), illus. p. 11. Reprinted in Amy Baker Sandback, ed., *Looking Critically: Twenty-one Years of Artforum Magazine* (Ann Arbor: UMI Research Press, 1984), illus. p. 275.

121

Miss Lucy Pink 1962

Painted and chromium-plated steel
47 × 42 × 39 in.
(119.5 × 106.5 × 99 cm).

Collection

Collection of the artist, Sarasota, Florida.

Exhibitions

Leo Castelli Gallery, New York, New York. *Group Show*. September 22–October 13, 1962.

Pasadena Art Museum, Pasadena, California. *New American Sculpture*, cat. no. 7, illus. February 11–March 7, 1964.

Leo Castelli Warehouse, New York, New York. *John Chamberlain: Recent Sculpture*. February 2–22, 1969.

The Solomon R. Guggenheim Museum, New York, New York. *John Chamberlain: A Retrospective Exhibition*, cat. no. 42, illus. p. 38. December 23, 1971–February 20, 1972.

References

Michael Fried, "New York Letter," *Art International*, vol. 6, no. 8 (October 1962), illus. p. 75.

Donald Judd, "Chamberlain—Another View," *Art International*, vol. 7, no. 10 (January 1964), illus. p. 38. Reprinted in *Donald Judd—Complete Writings 1959–1975*. (Halifax: Press of the Nova Scotia College of Art and Design, and New York: New York University Press, 1975), pp. 108–10; and in *Chamberlain* (Bern: Kunsthalle Bern and Van Abbemuseum, Eindhoven, Netherlands, 1979).

Art News, vol. 70, no. 10 (February 1972), color illus. cover.

122

M. Junior Love 1962

Painted metal
20 × 20 × 14 in.
(51 × 51 × 35.5 cm).

Collection

Mr. and Mrs. Allan Stone, Purchase, New York, 1975.

Provenance

Leo Castelli Gallery, New York, New York; Ferus Gallery, Los Angeles, California; Edwin Janss, Thousand Oaks, California, 1963; James Corcoran Gallery, Los Angeles, California, 1974; Leo Castelli Gallery, New York, New York; Stephen Mazoh, New York, New York.

123

Mozo 1962

Painted and chromium-plated steel
42 × 50 × 30 in.
(106.5 × 127 × 76 cm).

Collection

Present location unknown.

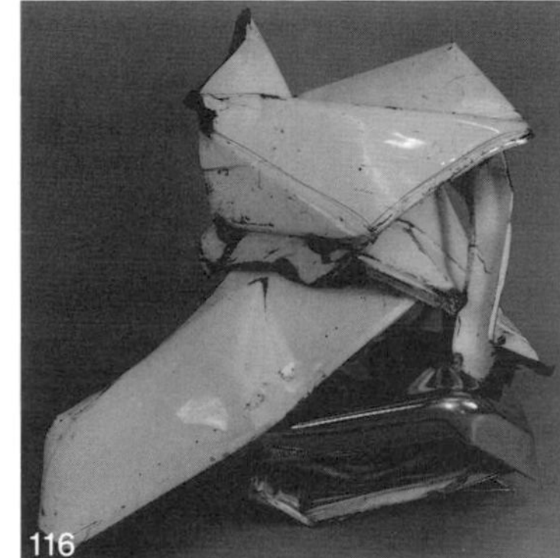

116

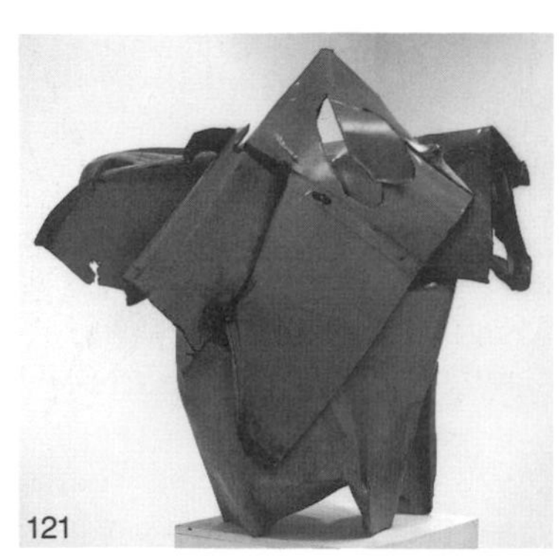

121

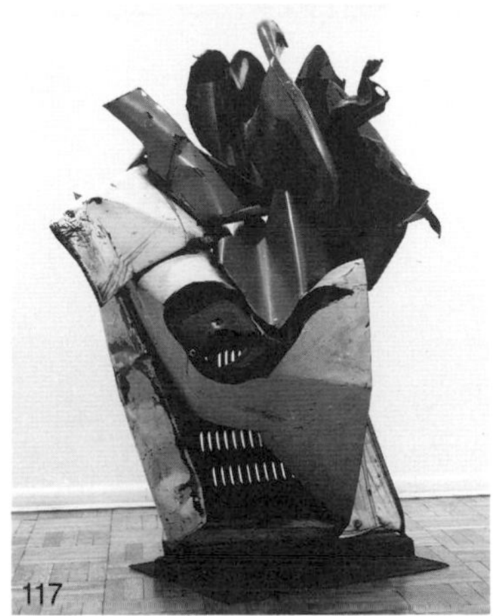

117

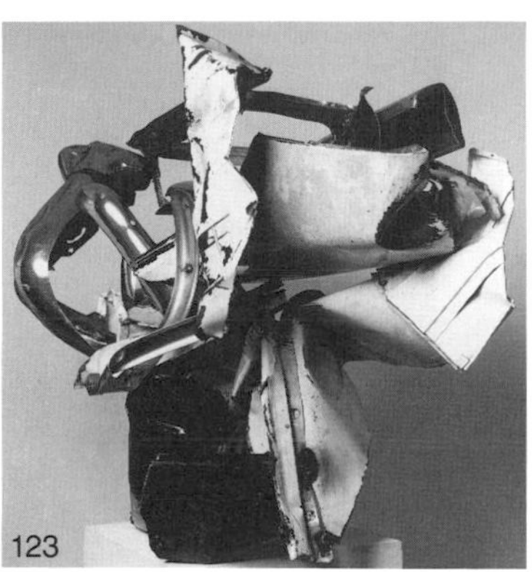

123

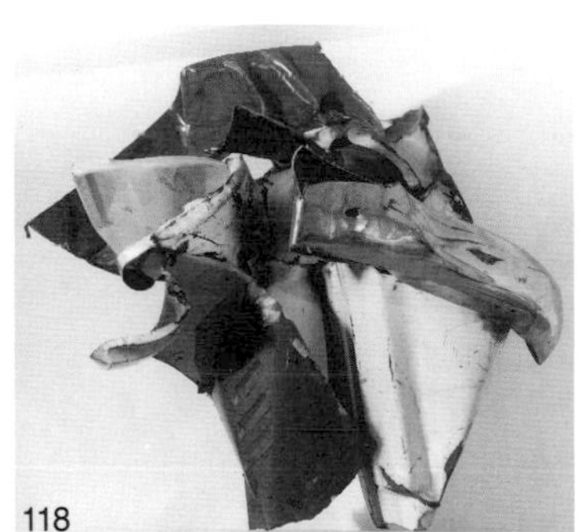

118

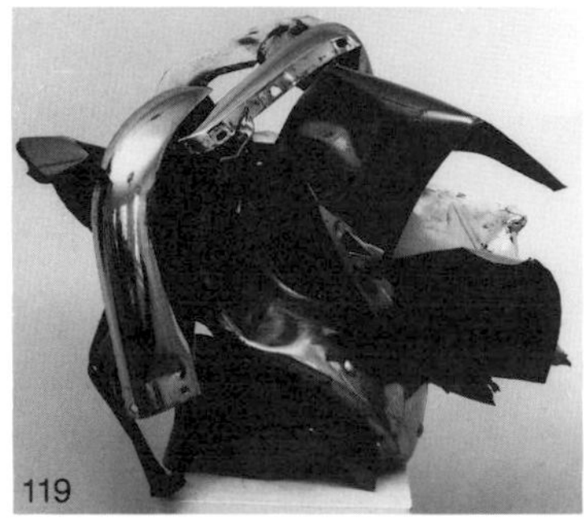

119

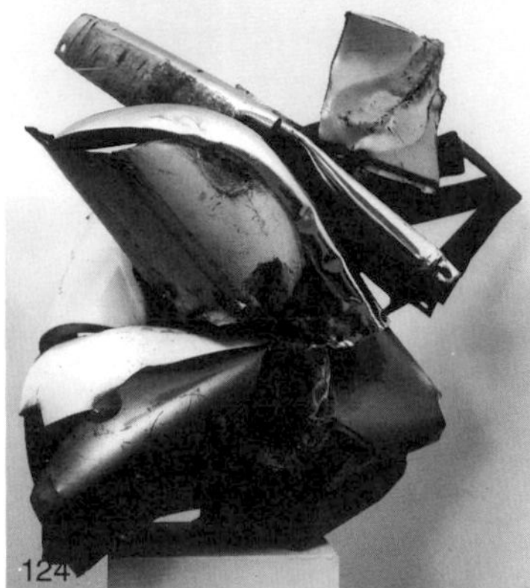
124

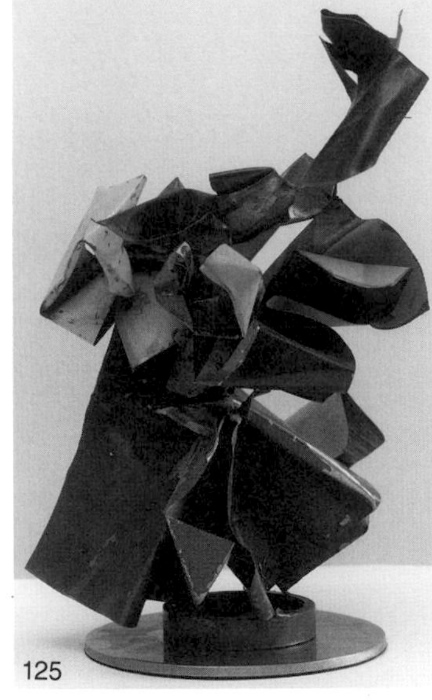
125

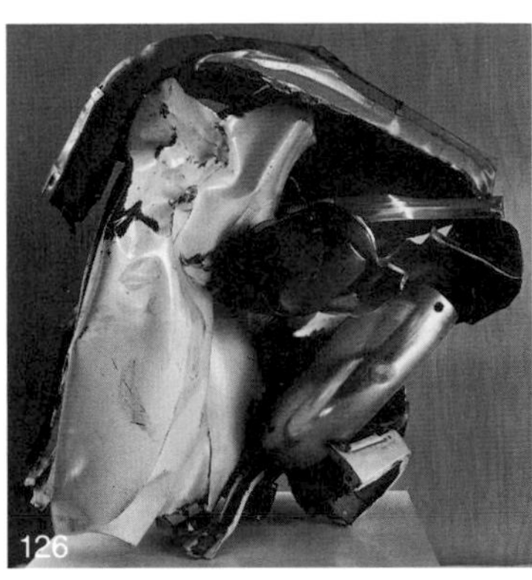
126

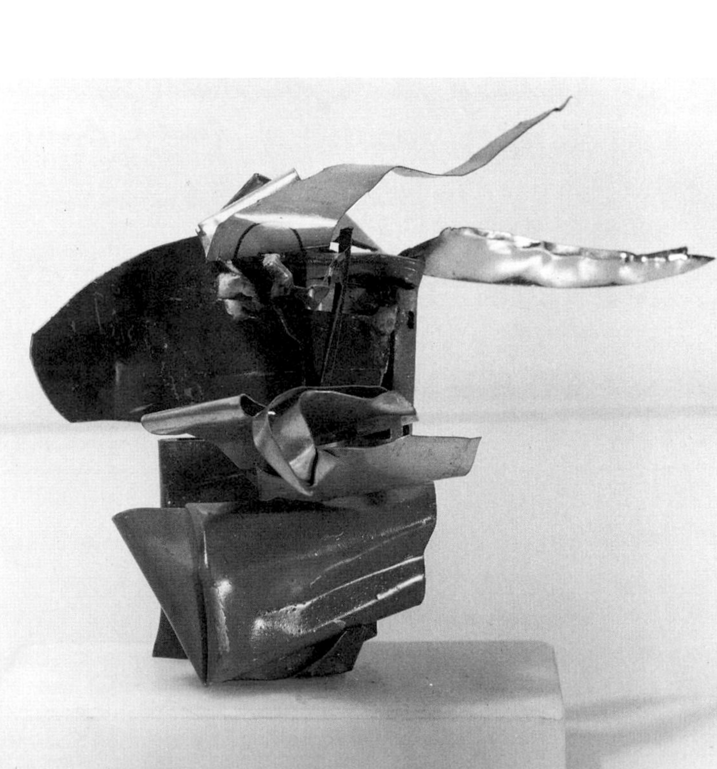
128

Provenance

Leo Castelli Gallery, New York, New York, 1971.

Exhibitions

Galerie Ileana Sonnabend, Paris. *John Chamberlain*, illus. April 8–May 4, 1964.

The Cleveland Museum of Art, Cleveland, Ohio. *Sculpture by John Chamberlain*, listed. January 3–29, 1967.

References

Diane Waldman, *John Chamberlain: A Retrospective Exhibition* (New York: The Solomon R. Guggenheim Foundation, 1971), illus. p. 63.

124

Nehoc 1962

Painted steel
33 × 22 × 27 in.
(84 × 56 × 68.5 cm).

Collection

Mr. and Mrs. Alvin S. Lane, Riverdale, New York.

Provenance

Pace Gallery, Boston, Massachusetts.

125

Plymouth 1962

Painted steel
9 × 8½ × 5 in.
(23 × 21.5 × 12.5 cm).

Collection

Holly and Horace Solomon, New York, New York, 1964.

Provenance

Martha Jackson Gallery, New York, New York, 1962; Allan Stone Gallery, New York, New York, 1963.

126

Rayvredd 1962

Painted and chromium-plated steel
34 × 34 × 38 in.
(86.5 × 86.5 × 96.5 cm).

Collection

Robert H. Halff, Beverly Hills, California, 1967.

Provenance

Dwan Gallery, Los Angeles, California; Mr. and Mrs. Abe Adler, Los Angeles, California.

Exhibitions

Dwan Gallery, Los Angeles, California. *My Country 'Tis of Thee*, illus. p. 2. November 18–December 15, 1962.

University of California at Los Angeles Art Galleries, Dickson Art Center, Los Angeles. *Twentieth Century Sculpture from Southern California Collections*, illus. p. 54. April 1972.

Museum of Contemporary Art, Los Angeles, California. *Automobile and Culture*, illus. p. 142. July 21, 1984–January 6, 1985.

127

Shell Oil 1962

Painted tin
7 × 7½ × 8 in.
(17.5 × 19 × 20.5 cm).

Collection

Present location unknown.

Provenance

Leo Castelli Gallery, New York, New York; Martha Jackson Gallery, New York, New York, 1962; Willie Schniewind, West Germany, 1962.

128

Sinclair 1962

Painted steel
4½ × 6½ × 4½ in.
(11.5 × 16.5 × 11.5 cm).

Collection

Mr. and Mrs. Burton Tremaine, Meriden, Connecticut, 1962.

Provenance

Leo Castelli Gallery, New York, New York.

Exhibitions

The Solomon R. Guggenheim Museum, New York, New York. *John Chamberlain: A Retrospective Exhibition*, cat. no. 37, illus. p. 59. December 23, 1971–February 20, 1972.

129

Spiro 1962

Painted and chromium-plated steel
29 × 36 × 26 in.
(73.5 × 91.5 × 66 cm).

Collection

Edmund Pillsbury, Fort Worth, Texas, 1975.

Provenance

Florence and Brooks Barron, Detroit, Michigan; O. K. Harris Works of Art, New York, New York; Bykert Gallery, New York, New York, 1974.

Exhibitions

The Solomon R. Guggenheim Museum, New York, New York. *John Chamberlain: A Retrospective Exhibition*, cat. no. 40, illus. p. 62. December 23, 1971–February 20, 1972.

130

Sunoco 1962

Painted tin
8 × 9 × 8 in.
(20.5 × 23 × 20.5 cm).

Collection

Present location unknown.

Provenance

Leo Castelli Gallery, New York, New York; Mrs. Dorothy Wick, New York, New York.

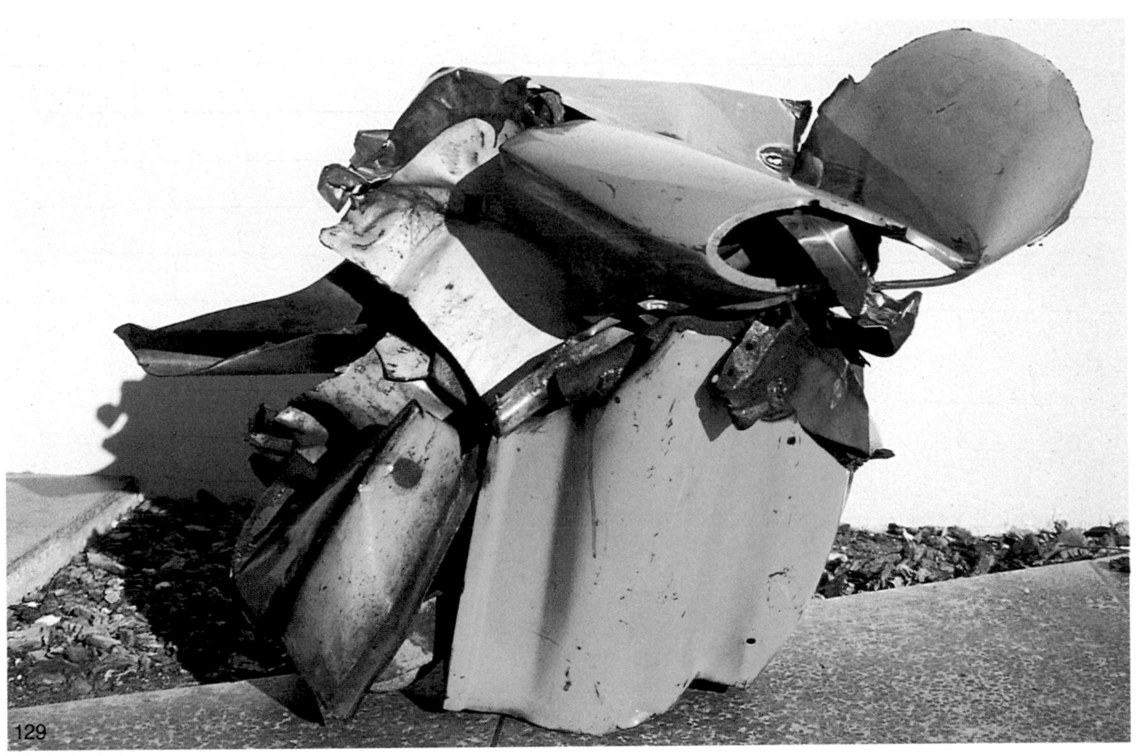

129

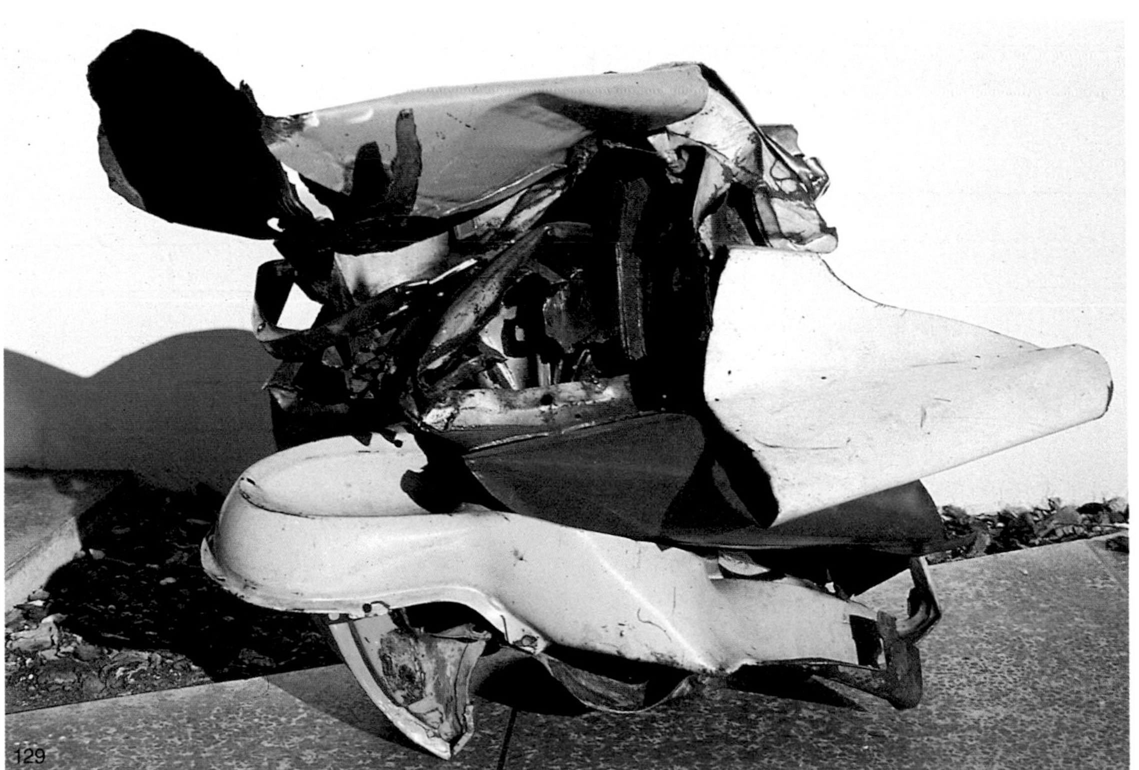

129

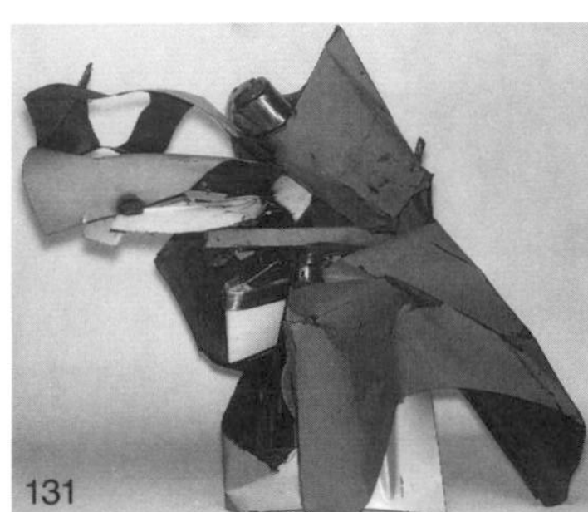
131

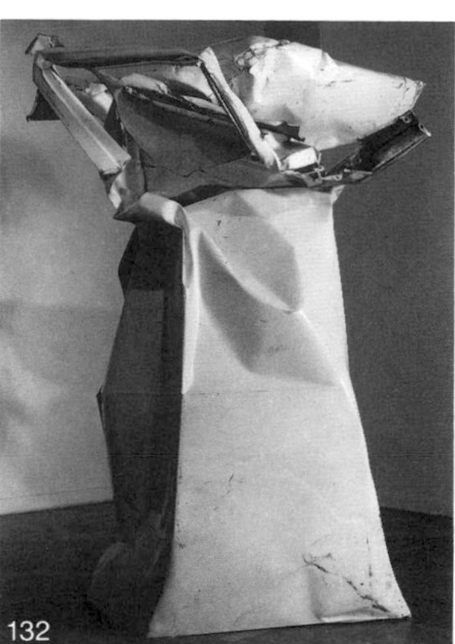
132

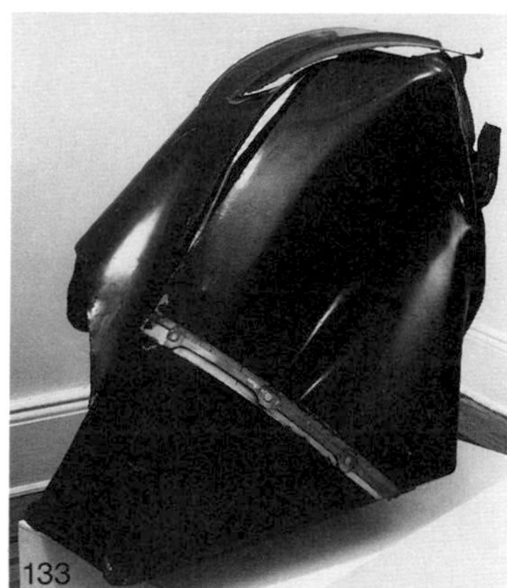
133

131

Sweet William 1962

Painted and chromium-plated steel
69 × 46 × 62 in.
(175 × 117 × 157.5 cm).

Collection

Los Angeles County Museum of Art, Los Angeles, California, 1963; gift of Mr. and Mrs. Abe Adler, in memory of Mrs. Esther Steif Rosen through the Contemporary Art Council.

Provenance

Mr. and Mrs. Abe Adler, Los Angeles, California.

Exhibitions

Los Angeles Country Museum of Art, Los Angeles, California. *American Sculpture of the Sixties*, cat. no. 21. April 28–June 25, 1967. Traveled to Philadelphia Museum of Art, Philadelphia, Pennsylvania. September 15–November 5, 1967.

The Solomon R. Guggenheim Museum, New York, New York. *John Chamberlain: A Retrospective Exhibition*, cat. no. 43, illus. p. 58. December 23, 1971–February 20, 1972.

Dallas Museum of Fine Arts and Southern Methodist University, Dallas, Texas. *poets of the cities new york and san francisco 1950–1965*, cat. no. 7, illus. no. 70, p. 142. November 20–December 29, 1974.

The Art Galleries, University of California, Santa Barbara. *John Chamberlain/Alan Saret—Contemporary Sculpture*. March 27–April 29, 1984.

References

Henry J. Seldis, "West Coast Milestone," *Art in America*, vol. 53, no. 2 (April 1965), color illus. p. 109.

Max Kozloff, "Modern Art and the Virtues of Decadence," *Studio*, vol. 174, no. 894 (November 1967), illus. p. 195.

Kurt von Meier, "Violence, Art and the American Way," *Artscanada*, vol. 25, no. 116–17 (April 1968), p. 24.

Jack Selleck, *Contrast* (Worcester, Massachusetts: Davis Publications, 1975), p. 29.

132

Velvet White 1962

Painted and chromium-plated steel
81½ × 61 × 54½ in.
(207 × 155 × 138.5 cm)

Collection

Whitney Museum of American Art, New York, New York, 1970; gift of the Albert A. List family.

Provenance

Mr. and Mrs. Albert A. List, New York, New York.

Exhibitions

Leo Castelli Gallery, New York, New York. *John Chamberlain and Frank Stella*. October 16–November 7, 1962.

The Jewish Museum, New York, New York. *Recent American Sculpture*, cat. no. 18, illus. October 15–November 29, 1964.

Museum of Modern Art, New York, New York. *Modern Sculpture: USA*. Opened May 26, 1965; traveled through 1966 to Musée Rodin, Paris. *Etats-Unis sculptures de XXe siècle*, cat. no. 4, illus.; Hochschule für Bildende Kunste, Berlin. *Amerikanische Plastik USA 20. Jahrhundert*, cat. no. 56, illus.; Staatliche Kunsthalle Baden-Baden, Baden-Baden. *Amerikanische Plastik USA 20. Jahrhundert*, cat. no. 56, illus.

Whitney Museum of American Art, New York, New York. *Art of the United States: 1670–1966*, cat. no. 306, p. 155. September 28–October 27, 1966.

The Metropolitan Museum of Art, New York, New York. *New York Painting and Sculpture: 1940–1970*, cat. no. 25, p. 42, illus. p. 125. October 18, 1969–February 1, 1970.

The Solomon R. Guggenheim Museum, New York, New York. *John Chamberlain: A Retrospective Exhibition*, cat. no. 44, illus. p. 55. December 23, 1971–February 20, 1972.

Whitney Museum of American Art, New York, New York. *Selections from the Permanent Collection*. November 28, 1973–February 4, 1974.

Whitney Museum of American Art, New York, New York. *Two Hundred Years of American Sculpture*, pp. 187 and 192, color illus. pl. 51. March 16–September 26, 1976.

Whitney Museum of American Art, Downtown Branch, New York, New York. *Pop Plus*, illus. in brochure. June 20–August 15, 1977.

Whitney Museum of American Art, New York, New York. *American Art 1950 to the Present*. May 3–September 12, 1978.

Whitney Museum of American Art, Downtown Branch, New York, New York. *Auto Icons*, cat. no. 1, illus. p. 3. March 7–April 11, 1979.

Whitney Museum of American Art, New York, New York. *Twentieth-Century American Art: Highlights of the Permanent Collection*. From October 28, 1981.

References

New School Art Center Series, "American Private Collections" (1965), entry no. 21, p. 7, illus. p. 44.

Rosalind E. Krauss, *Passages in Modern Sculpture* (New York: Viking, 1977), pp. 181–83, illus. p. 183.

133

Yorikke 1962

Painted and chromium-plated steel
25 × 36 × 23 in.
(63.5 × 91.5 × 58.5 cm).

Collection

Jorge Fick, Santa Fe, New Mexico, 1966; acquired directly from the artist.

134

Young Wing 1962

Painted copper
8 × 6½ × 5 in.
(20.5 × 16.5 × 12.5 cm).

Collection

Alf Young, New York, New York, 1976; acquired directly from the artist.

Notes

The sculpture was titled by the artist in 1976. It was originally entered in the Castelli registry as "Untitled."

135

Untitled 1962

Painted tin
7 × 6½ × 5 in.
(18 × 16.5 × 12.5 cm).

Collection

Present location unknown.

Provenance

Leo Castelli Gallery, New York, New York; Kay Hillman, New York, New York.

136

Untitled 1962

Painted tin
10 × 9 × 8 in.
(25.5 × 23 × 20.5 cm).

Collection

Present location unknown.

Provenance

Leo Castelli Gallery, New York, New York; Miss Landau, New York, New York.

137

Untitled 1962
Painted tin and copper
9 in. high (23 cm).

Collection
Present location unknown.

Provenance
Leo Castelli Gallery, New York, New York; Mr. Ellison, New York, New York.

Notes
The Castelli registry notes that the sculpture is copper, with white and black paint.

138

Untitled 1962
Painted tin
9 × 8½ × 7½ in.
(23 × 21.5 × 19 cm).

Collection
Present location unknown.

Provenance
Leo Castelli Gallery, New York, New York; Martha Jackson Gallery, New York, New York.

139

Untitled 1962
Painted tin
7½ × 7½ × 6½ in.
(19 × 19 × 16.5 cm).

Collection
A. Alfred Taubman, Bloomfield Hills, Michigan.

Provenance
Leo Castelli Gallery, New York, New York.

140

Untitled 1962
Painted steel
11 × 8½ × 8 in.
(28 × 21.5 × 20.5 cm).

Provenance
Leo Castelli Gallery, New York, New York; Mr. and Mrs. Burton Tremaine, Meriden, Connecticut.

Notes
According to Mr. and Mrs. Tremaine, the sculpture was destroyed.

141

Untitled c. 1962
Painted steel
7 × 4½ × 4 in.
(18 × 11.5 × 10 cm).

Collection
Victoria Sorrentino, Stanford, California, 1962; acquired directly from the artist.

Notes
It is possible that this is one of the missing *Tiny Pieces*. See cat. nos. 87–93.

142

Untitled c. 1962
Painted tin and wood
13½ × 8 × 5 in.
(34 × 20 × 12.5 cm).

Collection
Mr. and Mrs. Robert Shapiro, San Diego, California.

Provenance
Adler Gallery, Beverly Hills, California.

Exhibitions
La Jolla Museum of Contemporary Art, La Jolla, California. *San Diego Collects*. January 10–February 24, 1975.

143

Untitled 1962
Painted steel
8½ × 12 × 8 in.
(21.5 × 30.5 × 20.5 cm),
on 3 in. (7.5 cm) wood base.

Collection
Dorothy and Herbert Vogel, New York, New York, 1962; acquired directly from the artist.

Exhibitions
The Solomon R. Guggenheim Museum, New York, New York. *John Chamberlain: A Retrospective Exhibition*, cat. no. 34, illus. p. 62. December 23, 1971–February 20, 1972.

Institute of Contemporary Art, Philadelphia, Pennsylvania. *Painting, Drawing and Sculpture of the Sixties and Seventies from the Dorothy and Herbert Vogel Collection*. October 7–November 18, 1975. Traveled to Contemporary Arts Center, Cincinnati, Ohio. December 17, 1975–February 15, 1976.

144

Untitled 1962
Painted steel
57 × 57 × 25 in.
(145 × 145 × 63.5 cm).

Collection
A. James Speyer, Chicago, Illinois, 1967.

Provenance
Leo Castelli Gallery, New York, New York.

Exhibitions
The Art Institute of Chicago, Chicago, Illinois. *Sculpture: A Generation of Innovation*. June 23–August 27, 1967.

145

Untitled 1962
Painted tin
8½ × 8 × 7 in.
(21.5 × 20.5 × 18 cm).

Collection
Rena Bransten, San Francisco, California.

Provenance
Leo Castelli Gallery, New York, New York.

Notes
The sculpture is in a state of disrepair.

146

Untitled 1962
Painted steel
27 × 26 in. (68.5 × 66 cm).

Collection
Mr. and Mrs. Gifford Phillips, New York, New York.

Provenance
Henry Geldzahler, New York, New York; Irving Blum Gallery, Los Angeles, California, 1965.

Exhibitions
The Art Galleries, University of California, Santa Barbara. *7 + 5: Sculptors in the 1950s*, cat. no. 9, illus. p. 31. January 6–February 15, 1976. Traveled to Phoenix Art Museum, Phoenix, Arizona. March 5–April 11, 1976.

147

Untitled c. 1962
Painted tin
8 × 8 × 7 in.
(20.5 × 20.5 × 18 cm).

Collection
Allan Stone, New York, New York.

Provenance
Mr. and Mrs. Abe Adler, Los Angeles, California.

Notes
This sculpture may be one of the 1962 sculptures catalogued above as unlocated.

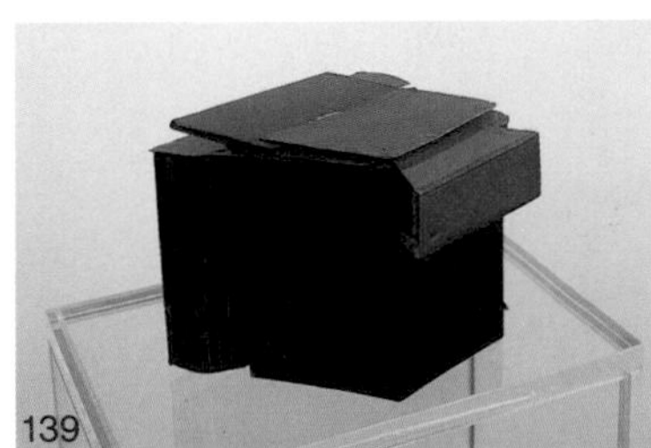
139

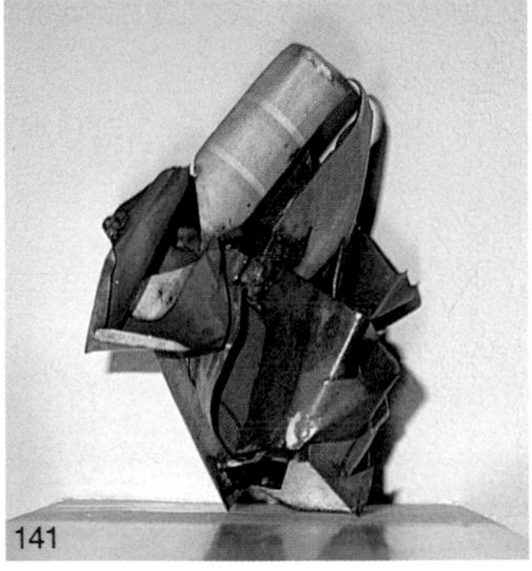
141

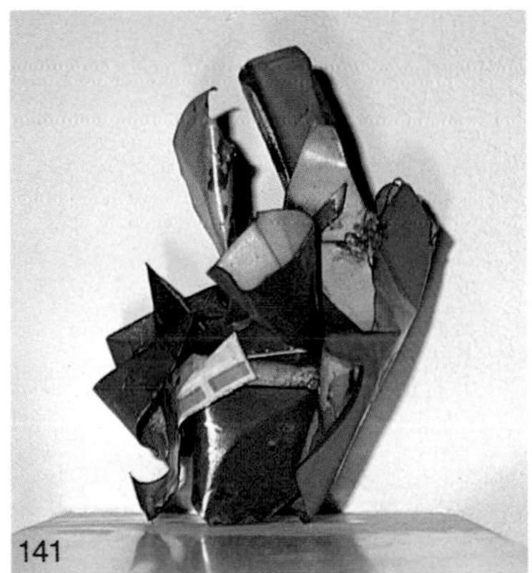
141

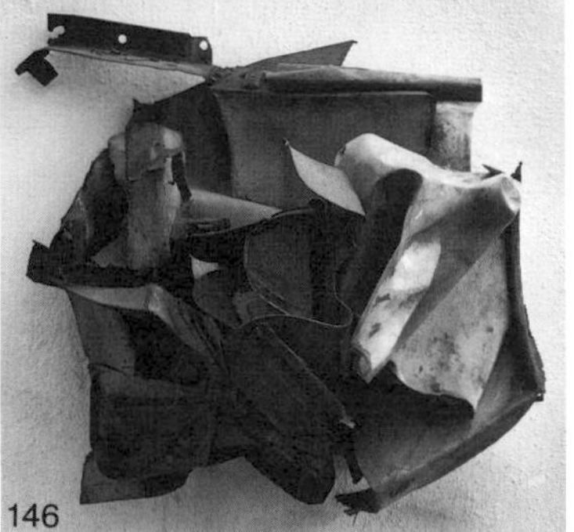
146

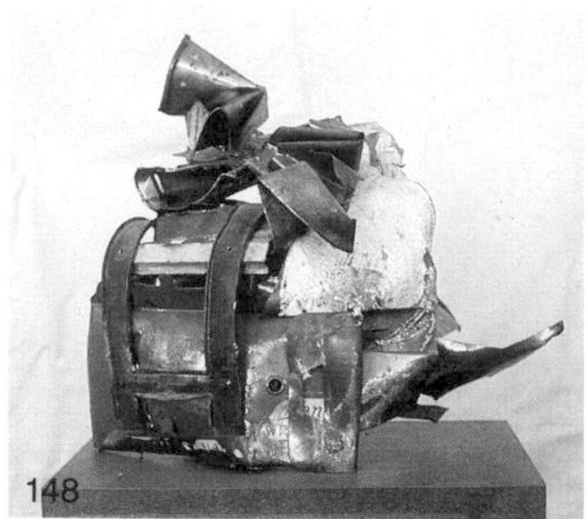
148

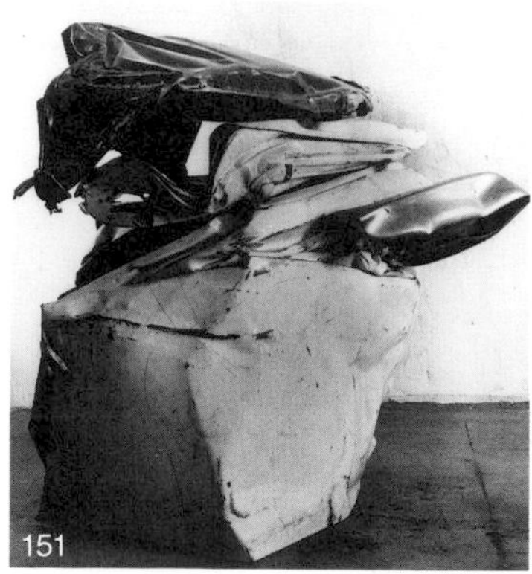
151

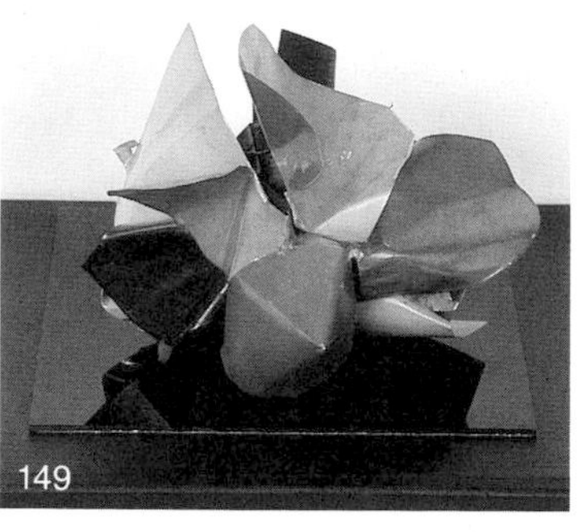
149

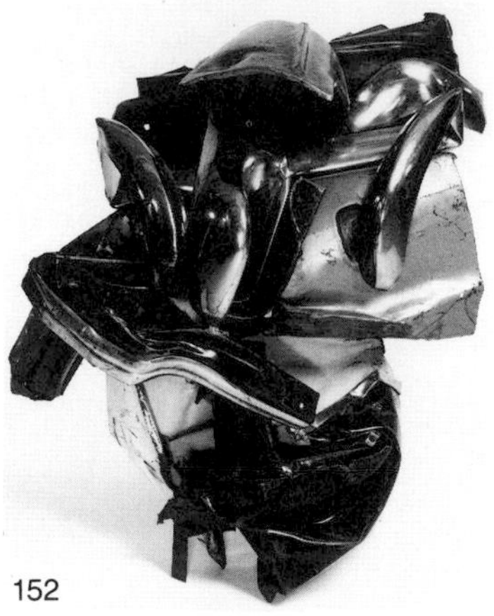
152

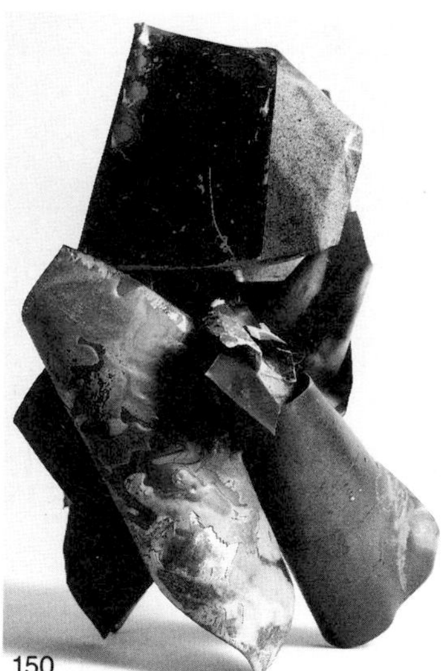
150

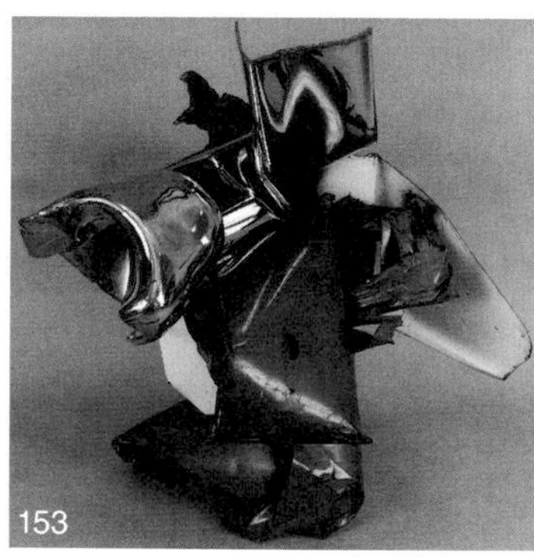
153

148

Untitled c. 1962
Painted tin
10½ × 13½ × 8 in.
(26.5 × 34.5 × 20.5 cm).

Collection
Allan Stone, New York, New York.

Notes
This sculpture may be one of the 1962 sculptures catalogued above as unlocated.

149

Untitled c. 1962.
Painted tin
9 × 10½ × 9 in.
(23 × 26.5 × 23 cm).

Collection
Thordis Moeller, New York, New York.

Provenance
Leon Kraushaar, Lawrence, New York.

150

Untitled c. 1962
Painted tin and paper
8½ × 7 in. (21.5 × 18 cm).

Collection
Private collection, Boston, Massachusetts, 1962.

Provenance
Allan Stone Gallery, New York, New York.

Exhibitions
The Art Galleries, University of California, Santa Barbara. *7 + 5: Sculptors in the 1950s*, cat. no. 8, illus. p. 30. January 6–February 15, 1976. Traveled to Phoenix Art Museum, Phoenix, Arizona. March 5–April 11, 1976.

Notes
This sculpture may be one of the 1962 sculptures catalogued above as unlocated.

151

Buckshutam 1963
Painted and chromium-plated steel
47½ × 45 × 45 in.
(120.5 × 114.5 × 114.5 cm).

Collection
Donald Judd, Marfa, Texas.

Provenance
Leo Castelli Gallery, New York, New York.

Exhibitions
The Solomon R. Guggenheim Museum, New York, New York. *John Chamberlain: A Retrospective Exhibition*, cat. no. 49, illus. p. 68. December 23, 1971–February 20, 1972.

152

Butternut 1963
Welded metal
41 × 26 × 40 in.
(104 × 66 × 101.5 cm).

Collection
Virginia Museum of Fine Arts, Richmond, Virginia, 1972.

Provenance
Leo Castelli Gallery, New York, New York; Galerie Ileana Sonnabend, Paris; Philippe Dotrement, Brussels; Leo Castelli Gallery, New York, New York; O. K. Harris Works of Art, New York, New York; Sydney and Frances Lewis, Richmond, Virginia.

Exhibitions
Musée des Beaux-Arts, Lausanne. *Ier Salon international de galeries-pilotes*. June 20–September 22, 1963.

Galerie Ileana Sonnabend, Paris. *John Chamberlain*, illus. April 8–May 4, 1964.

Leo Castelli Gallery, New York, New York. *Summer Group Exhibition*. June 17–September 6, 1972.

Alexandria Chapter of the Virginia Museum, Alexandria, Virginia. February 1973.

Virginia Museum of Fine Arts, Richmond, Virginia. *Contemporary Art Acquisitions from Sydney and Frances Lewis*. January 16–March 4, 1979.

References
"Ier Salon international de galeries-pilotes," *Art International*, vol. 7, no. 6 (January 1963), illus. p. 26.

Kunstwerk, no. 17 (August 1963), p. 70.

Rebecca Massie, *The Lewis Contemporary Art Fund Collection* (Richmond: Virginia Museum, 1980), pp. 10 and 22, illus. p. 22.

153

Candy Andy 1963
Painted and chromium-plated steel
37 × 31½ × 27 in.
(94 × 80 × 68.5 cm).

Collection
Dia Art Foundation, New York, New York, 1980.

Provenance
Mario Yrisarry, New York, New York; Lone Star Foundation, New York, New York, 1977.

Notes
The sculpture has been incorrectly referred to as *Indiana*, 1961, while in the possession of all of the above owners. There is no record of another sculpture titled *Indiana*.

154

Che-Che 1963

Painted steel
51 × 51 × 26 in.
(130 × 130 × 66 cm).

Collection

Städtisches Museum Abteiberg, Mönchengladbach, West Germany, 1980.

Provenance

Leo Castelli Gallery, New York, New York; Galerie Ileana Sonnabend, Paris; Galerie Rudolf Zwirner, Cologne.

Exhibitions

Galerie Ileana Sonnabend, Paris. *John Chamberlain*, illus. April 8–May 4, 1964.

Leo Castelli Gallery, New York, New York. *Summer Group Show*. June 23–September 22, 1973.

Christie, Manson & Woods, Ltd., London. *Contemporary Art*, cat. no. 131, illus. p. 55. December 2, 1975.

Galerien Maximilianstrasse, Munich. *Zum Thema Skulptur*, illus. 1979.

References

Diane Waldman, *John Chamberlain: A Retrospective Exhibition* (New York: The Solomon R. Guggenheim Foundation, 1971), illus. p. 67.

"Christie's Contemporary Art," *Apollo* (November 1975), illus. p. 37.

Sabine Kimpel, *Bestandskatalog II Städtisches Museum Abteiberg Mönchengladbach* (Mönchengladbach, 1980), illus. p. 50.

155

Dandy Dan-D 1963

Painted steel
42 × 47 × 19½ in.
(106.5 × 119.5 × 49.5 cm).

Collection

Kaiser Wilhelm Museum, Krefeld, West Germany, 1967.

Provenance

Mr. and Mrs. Michael Sonnabend, New York, New York; Galerie Rudolf Zwirner, Cologne.

Exhibitions

Galerie Ileana Sonnabend, Paris. *John Chamberlain*, illus. April 8–May 4, 1964.

Kunstmuseum Winterthur, Switzerland. *Experiment Sammlung I: Une collection imaginaire*, cat. no. 56, illus. p. 41. April 1–May 27, 1984.

References

Nicolas Calas and Elena Calas, *Icons and Images of the Sixties* (New York: Dutton, 1971), illus. p. 52.

156

De La Nuit 1963

Painted and chromium-plated steel
54 × 42 × 38 in.
(137 × 107 × 97 cm).

Collection

Herbert F. Johnson Museum of Art, Cornell University, Ithaca, New York, 1975.

Provenance

Michael Ruskin, New York, New York; Seymour C. Kaback, Kaback Enterprises, New York, New York, 1974.

Exhibitions

Michael C. Rockefeller Arts Center, Fredonia, New York. *Wreck*, cat. no. 6, illus. 1972. Traveled to The Canton Art Institute, Canton, Ohio. *Wreck*. 1974; The C. W. Post College Art Gallery, Greenvale, New York. *Wreck: A Tragic-Romantic American Theme*. 1975.

References

"Acquisitions/Sculpture: 1800 to the Present," *Art Journal*, vol. 35, no. 3 (Spring 1976), illus.

157

Fancy 1963

Painted and chromium-plated steel
54 × 49 × 30 in.
(137 × 124.5 × 76 cm).

Collection

The Chrysler Museum, Norfolk, Virginia, 1971; gift of Walter P. Chrysler, Jr.

Provenance

Ben Birillo, New York, New York, 1961; Walter P. Chrysler, Jr., Norfolk, Virginia.

Exhibitions

The Chrysler Museum, Norfolk, Virginia. *Three Hundred Years of American Art at the Chrysler Museum*, illus. p. 235. March 1–July 4, 1976.

References

Selections from the Permanent Collection (Norfolk, Virginia: The Chrysler Museum, 1982), illus. p. 116.

158

Hunkpapa 1963

Painted steel
44 × 50 × 14 in.
(112 × 127 × 35.5 cm).

Collection

Present location unknown.

Provenance

Leo Castelli Gallery, New York, New York.

Exhibitions

The Cleveland Museum of Art, Cleveland, Ohio. *Sculpture by John Chamberlain*. January 3–29, 1967.

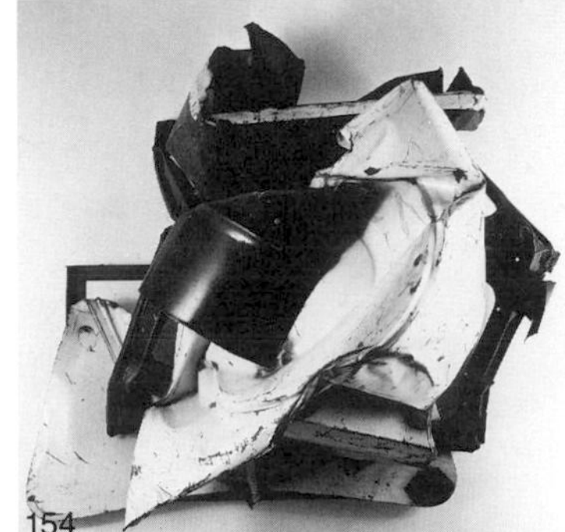

154

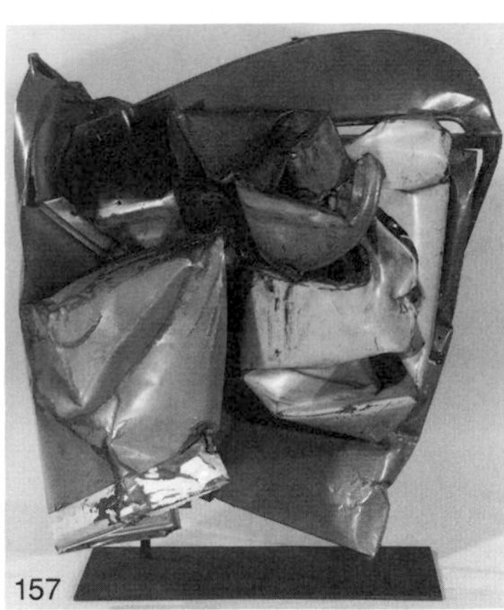

157

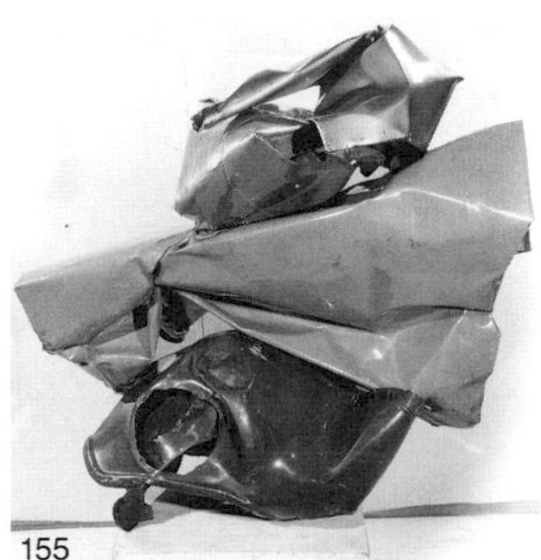

155

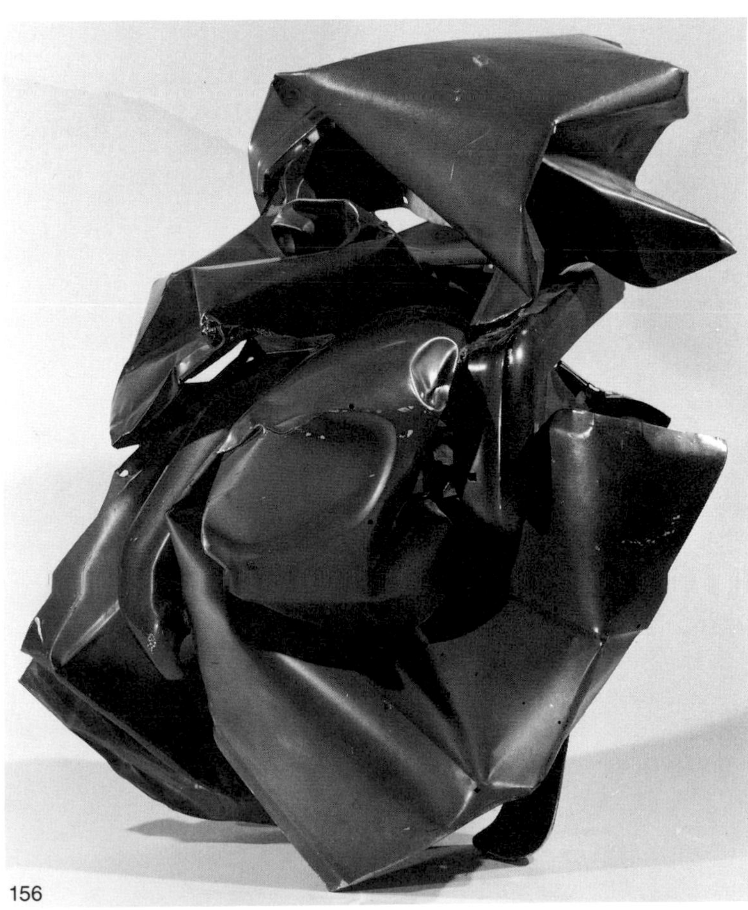

156

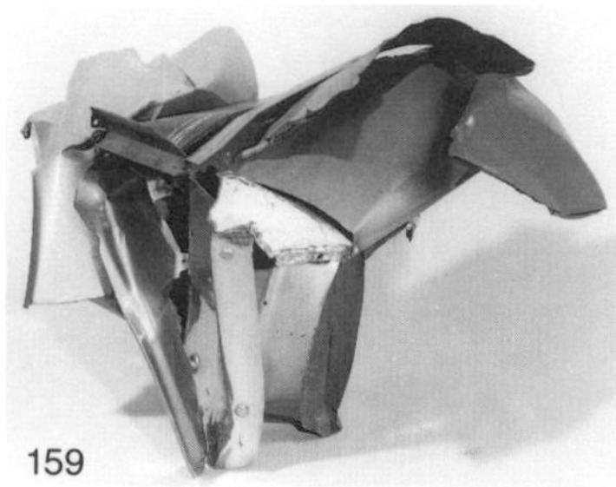
159

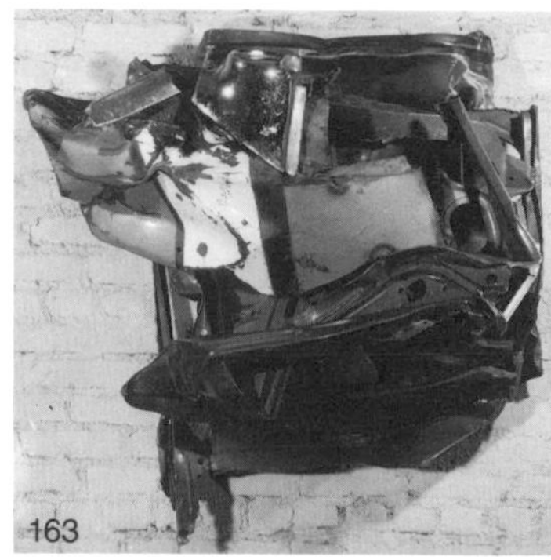
163

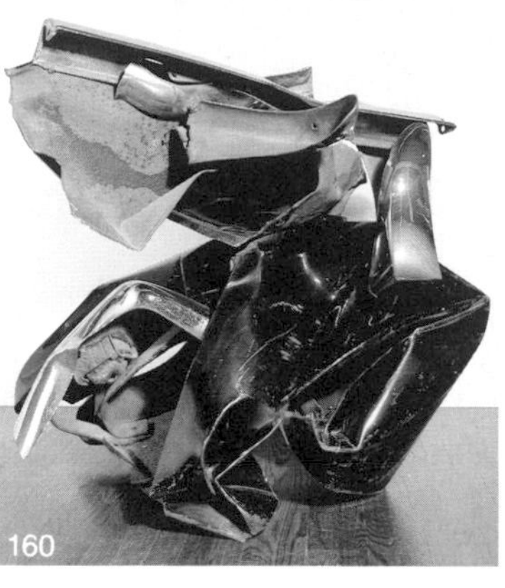
160

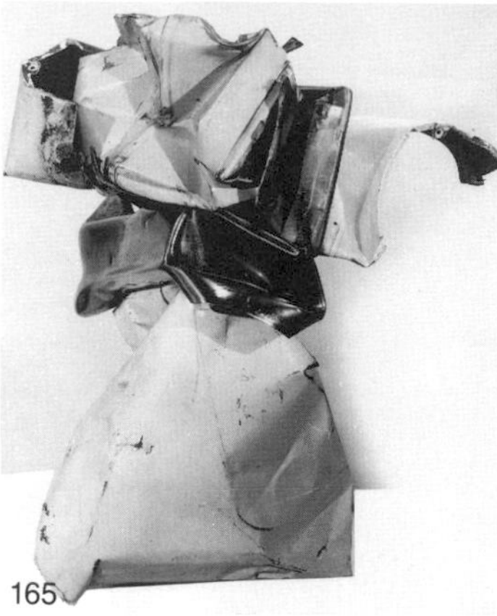
165

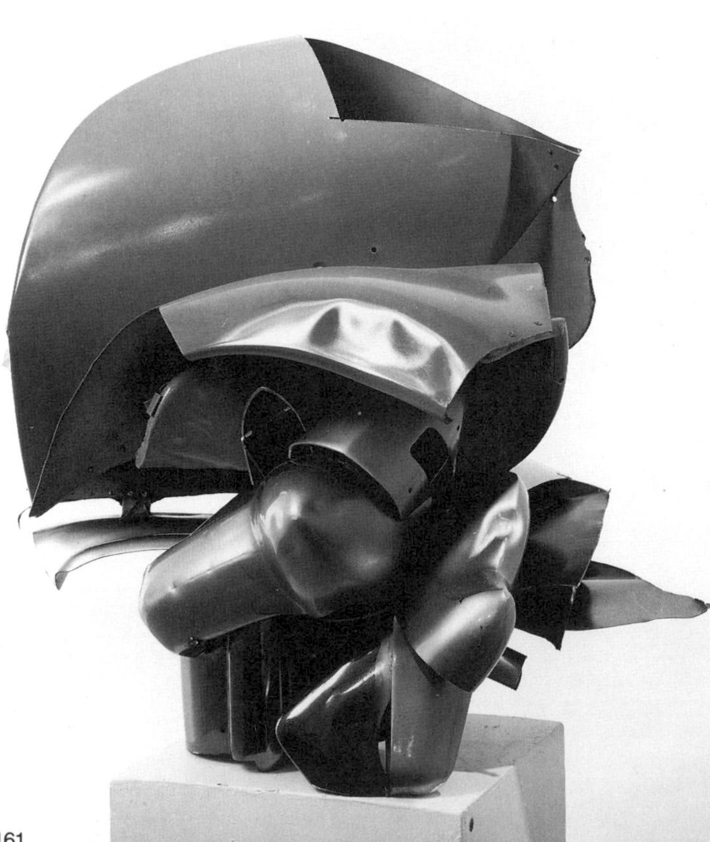
161

159

Kora 1963
Painted steel
34½ × 55½ × 41½ in.
(87.5 × 141 × 105.5 cm).

Collection
The Tate Gallery, London, 1968; presented by Mrs. Martha Jackson through the American Federation of Arts.

Provenance
Martha Jackson Gallery, New York, New York, 1963.

Exhibitions
Martha Jackson Gallery, New York, New York. *Garden Sculpture*. May 14, 1963.

References
Catalogue of the Tate Gallery's Collection of Modern Art (London: Tate Gallery, 1981), cat. no. T.1094, illus. p. 115.

160

Marilyn Monroe 1963
Painted and chromium-plated steel
36 × 45 × 38 in.
(91.5 × 114 × 96.5 cm).

Collection
Private collection, Illinois, 1976.

Provenance
Neil Williams, New York, New York; David Brown and Jason Croy, New York, New York; Dan Grossman, New York, New York; Leo Castelli Gallery, New York, New York; The Mayor Gallery, London.

Notes
Institute of Contemporary Art, Philadelphia, Pennsylvania. *The Atmosphere of 'Sixty-Four*. April 17–June 1, 1964.

Notes
The sculpture was originally untitled; it was titled *Marilyn Monroe* by the artist in 1975.

161

Mr. Moto 1963
Painted and chromium-plated steel
29½ × 32 × 23 in.
(75 × 81.5 × 58.5 cm).

Collection
Robert A. Rowan, Pasadena, California, 1964.

Provenance
Leo Castelli Gallery, New York, New York.

Exhibitions
Pasadena Art Museum, Pasadena, California. *New American Sculpture*, cat. no. 9, illus. February 11–March 7, 1964.

Leo Castelli Gallery, New York, New York. *John Chamberlain*. April 11–30, 1964.

University of California, Irvine. *A Selection from the Collection of Mr. and Mrs. Robert Rowan*. May 2–21, 1967. Traveled to San Francisco Museum of Modern Art, San Francisco, California. June 2–July 2, 1967.

162

Ozark City 1963
Painted steel
50 × 55 × 38 in.
(127 × 139.5 × 96.5 cm).

Collection
Present location unknown.

Notes
The only evidence of the existence of this sculpture is that it was entered in the Castelli registry in 1963.

163

Ruby-Ruby 1963
Painted and chromium-plated steel
35 × 37 × 29 in.
(89 × 94 × 73.5 cm).

Collection
Private collection, Bethesda, Maryland, 1974.

Provenance
Leo Castelli Gallery, New York, New York; Allan Stone, New York, New York.

Exhibitions
Robert Fraser Gallery, London. *John Chamberlain and Richard Stankiewicz*. 1963.

Galerie Ileana Sonnabend, Paris. *John Chamberlain*, illus. April 8–May 4, 1964.

Leo Castelli Gallery, New York, New York. *Summer Group Exhibition*. June 17–September 6, 1972.

References
Diane Waldman, *John Chamberlain: A Retrospective Exhibition* (New York: The Solomon R. Guggenheim Foundation, 1971), illus. p. 69.

164

Silverheels 1963
Painted and chromium-plated steel
46 × 41 × 36 in.
(117 × 104 × 91.5 cm).

Collection
Mrs. Antoinette Castelli, New York, New York, 1963.

Provenance
Neil Williams, New York, New York.

Exhibitions

Washington Gallery of Modern Art, Washington, D.C. *Sculptors of Our Time*. September 17–October 31, 1963.

Gulbenkian Foundation, Tate Gallery, London. *Painting and Sculpture of a Decade*. March–August 1964.

Institute of Contemporary Art, Philadelphia, Pennsylvania. *The Highway*. January 14–February 25, 1970. Traveled to Institute for the Arts, Rice University, Houston, Texas. March 12–May 18, 1970; The Akron Art Institute, Akron, Ohio. June 5–July 26, 1970.

Emily Lowe Gallery, Hofstra University, Hempstead, New York. *Art around the Automobile*. June 20–August 26, 1971.

The Corcoran Gallery of Art, Washington, D.C. *Wilderness*, cat. no. 52. October 1–November 14, 1971.

The Solomon R. Guggenheim Museum, New York, New York. *John Chamberlain: A Retrospective Exhibition*, cat. no. 50, illus. p. 66. December 23, 1971–February 20, 1972.

Leo Castelli Gallery, New York, New York. *Benefit Exhibition for the Committee to Save Venice*. October 18–November 10, 1973.

References

William Fleming, *Art and Ideas* (New York: Holt, Rinehart and Winston, 1968), pl. 517, illus. p. 454.

165

Trixie Dee 1963

Painted and chromium-plated steel
53 × 54½ × 30 in.
(135 × 138 × 76 cm).

Collection

Museum Moderner Kunst Wien, Vienna, 1978; formerly Sammlung Hahn.

Provenance

Galerie Ileana Sonnabend, Paris; Professor Wolfgang Hahn, Cologne.

Exhibitions

Galerie Ileana Sonnabend, Paris. *John Chamberlain*, illus. April 8–May 4, 1964.

XXXII Esposizione biennale internazionale d'arte, Venice. June 20–October 15, 1964.

Städtische Kunsthalle Düsseldorf. *Kunst des 20. Jahrhunderts aus rheinisch-westfälischem Privatbesitz*, cat. no. 52, illus. no. 122. 1967.

Wallraf-Richartz-Museum, Cologne. *Sammlung Hahn: Zeitgenössische Kunst*, cat. no. 35, illus. no. 10. May 3–July 7, 1968.

Württembergischer Kunstverein, Stuttgart. *Eisen- und Stahlplastik 1930–1970*. 1970.

Palais des Beaux-Arts, Brussels. *Metamorphose des Dinges*. 1971. Traveled to Museum Boymans-van Beuningen, Rotterdam. 1971; Nationalgalerie Berlin. 1971; Palazzo Reale, Milan. 1972; Kunsthalle Basel. 1972; Musée des Arts Decoratifs, Paris. 1972.

Museum Moderner Kunst Wien, Vienna. *Faszination des Objekts*, illus. pl. II, p. 75. November 27, 1980–August 11, 1981. Traveled to Stadthaus Klagenfurt, Austria. September 30–November 10, 1981.

References

"Mit der Pop Kiste Leben" (interview of E. Weiss with W. Hahn), *Köln: Vierteljahresschrift für die Freunde der Stadt*, no. 3 (September 1968), illus.

Philippe Sers, "Prendre l'objet pour sujet," *Connaissance des arts*, no. 242 (April 1972), color illus. p. 106.

Karin Thomas, *DuMont's kleines Sachwörterbuch zur Kunst des 20. Jahrhunderts* (Cologne, 1973), illus. pl. 92, p. 152.

W. Rotzler, *Objekt-Kunst: Von Duchamp bis zur Gegenwart* (Cologne, 1975), illus. pl. 97, pp. 155 ff.

Sammlung Hahn (Vienna: Museum Moderner Kunst Wien, 1979), cat. no. 34, illus.

Eva Maria Triska, "Pop-Art," *Kunst der letzten 30 Jahre* (Vienna: Museum Moderner Kunst Wien, 1979).

Dieter Ronte, *Museum moderner Kunst Wien* (Brunswick, West Germany, 1982), illus. pl. 71, p. 72.

166

Untitled c. 1963

Painted and chromium-plated steel
22 × 23 × 22 in.
(56 × 58.5 × 56 cm).

Collection

Gilbert and Lila Silverman, Detroit, Michigan, 1978.

Exhibitions

Christie, Manson & Woods International, Inc., New York, New York. *Contemporary Art*, cat. no. 30. November 13, 1978.

Michigan Artrain, Michigan. *Michigan Collects*. 1980.

Cranbrook Academy of Art Museum, Bloomfield Hills, Michigan. *The Gilbert and Lila Silverman Collection*, cat. no. 58. September 20–November 1, 1981.

Notes

The provenance of this sculpture is unknown; it is likely that it is one of the works listed in this catalogue as unlocated.

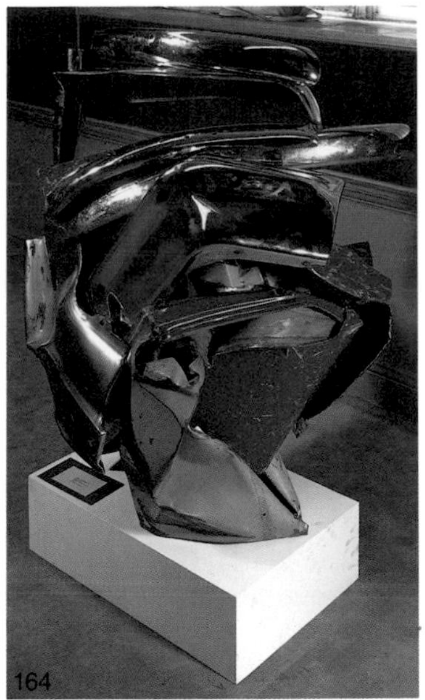

164

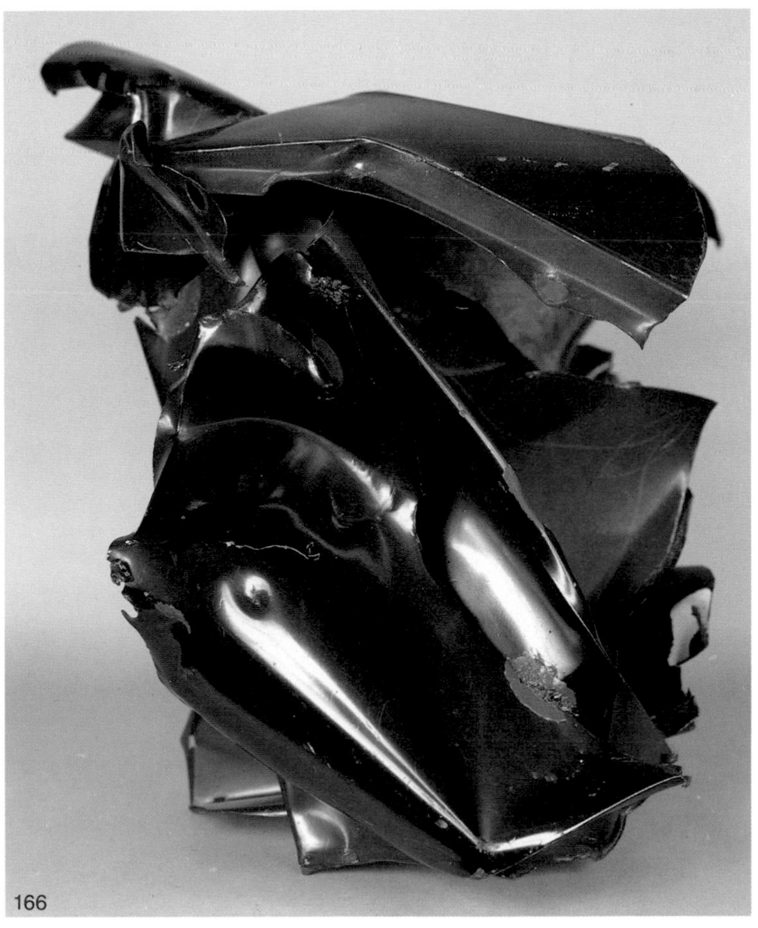

166

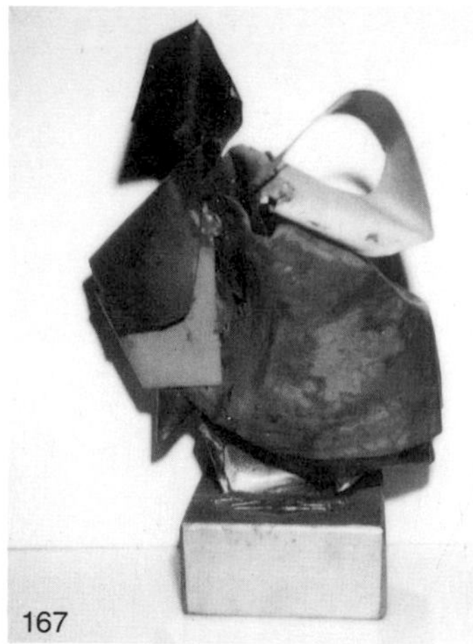
167

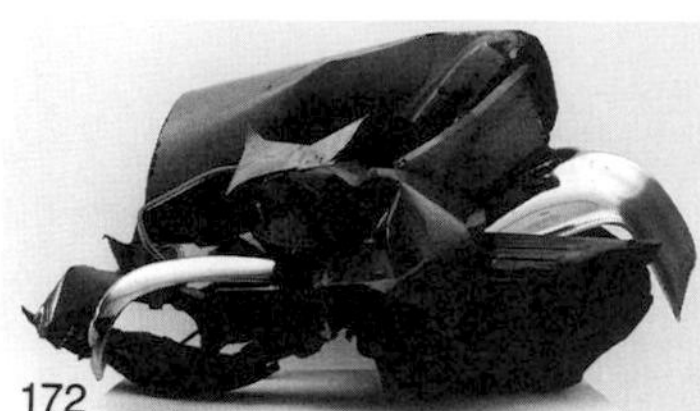
172

167

Untitled 1963

Painted steel and wood
8 × 5 × 4½ in.
(20.5 × 12.5 × 11.5 cm).

Collection

Allan Stone, New York, New York.

Provenance

Leo Castelli Gallery, New York, New York; Donald Beckerman, New York, New York, 1963.

168

Untitled 1963

Painted and chromium-plated steel
31 × 37½ × 28 in.
(79 × 95 × 71 cm).

Collection

Whitney Museum of American Art, New York, New York, 1966; purchased with funds from the Howard and Jean Lipman Foundation, Inc., and exchange.

Provenance

Leo Castelli Gallery, New York, New York; Pace Gallery, Boston, Massachusetts; Pace Gallery, New York, New York.

Exhibitions

Leo Castelli Gallery, New York, New York. *Group Show*. April 2–25, 1963.

Institute of Contemporary Art, Boston, Massachusetts. *The Biennale Eight*, cat. no. 2, incorrectly listed as "Untitled, 1962." June 20–July 26, 1964.

The Jewish Museum, New York, New York. *Recent American Sculpture*, cat. no. 19. October 15–November 29, 1964.

Whitney Museum of American Art, New York, New York. *Contemporary American Sculpture: Selection 1*, illus. p. 26. April 5–May 15, 1966. Traveled to Everson Museum of Art, Syracuse, New York. December 13, 1967–January 21, 1968; Albany Institute of History and Art, Albany, New York. February 14–March 17, 1968; Andrew Dickson White Museum of Art, Cornell University, Ithaca, New York. April 10–May 12, 1968; The Memorial Art Gallery of the University of Rochester, Rochester, New York. July 31–September 1, 1968; Munson-Williams-Proctor Institute, Utica, New York. September 25–October 27, 1968; Vassar College Art Gallery, Poughkeepsie, New York. November 20–December 22, 1968; Arnot Art Gallery, Elmira, New York. January 15–February 16, 1969.

Fort Worth Art Museum, Fort Worth, Texas. *Contemporary American Sculpture* (organized by the Whitney Museum of American Art, New York, New York), illus. p. 15. August 19–September 14, 1969. Traveled to Isaac Delgado Museum of Art, New Orleans, Louisiana. September 27–October 26, 1969; The High Museum of Art, Atlanta, Georgia. January 5–February 1, 1970.

The Society of the Four Arts, Palm Beach, Florida. *Contemporary American Sculpture*, cat. no. 8. March 9–April 7, 1974.

Whitney Museum of American Art, Downtown Branch, New York, New York. *Sculpture of the Sixties*, listed. March 13–April 16, 1975.

Whitney Museum of American Art, New York, New York. *Permanent Collection: Thirty Years of American Art 1945–1975*. January 29–May 1, 1977.

Whitney Museum of American Art, New York, New York. *American Sculpture: Gifts of Howard and Jean Lipman*, listed. April 15–June 15, 1980.

Museum of Contemporary Art, Los Angeles, California. *The First Show: Painting and Sculpture from Eight Collections 1940–1980*, illus. p. 200. November 20–February 19, 1984.

169

(While this catalogue raisonné was in press, it was learned that the sculpture previously catalogued as number 169 and catalogue number 66 are actually one and the same piece.)

170

Untitled 1963

Painted and chromium-plated steel
22 × 20 × 18 in.
(55.5 × 50 × 45.5 cm).

Collection

Museum für Moderne Kunst, Frankfurt.

Provenance

Leo Castelli Gallery, New York, New York; Leon Kraushaar, Lawrence, New York; Karl Ströher, Darmstadt, 1968.

Exhibitions

Galerie-Verein München, Neue Pinakothek, Haus der Kunst, Munich. *Sammlung 1968 Karl Ströher*, cat. no. 41, illus. June 14–August 9, 1968. Traveled to Kunstverein, Hamburg. August 24–October 6, 1968.

Deutsche Gesellschaft für Bildende Kunst e.V. (Kunstverein Berlin) and Nationalgalerie der Staatlichen Museen Preussischer Kulturbesitz, Neue Nationalgalerie Berlin. *Sammlung 1968 Karl Ströher*, cat. no. 16, illus. March 1–April 14, 1969. Traveled to Städtische Kunsthalle, Düsseldorf. April 25–June 17, 1969; Kunsthalle Bern. July 12–August 17 and August 23–September 29, 1969.

Deutsches Architekturmuseum, Frankfurt. *Bilder für Frankfurt*, cat. no. 11, illus. p. 167. February 8–April 14, 1985.

References

Bildnerische Ausdrucksformen 1960–1970: Sammlung Karl Ströher, (Darmstadt: Hessisches Landesmuseum, 1970), color illus. p. 96.

171

Untitled 1963

Painted and chromium-plated steel
25 × 38 × 28 in.
(63.5 × 96.5 × 71 cm).

Collection

George S. Elliott, Chicago, Illinois, 1985.

Provenance

Leon Kraushaar, Lawrence, New York; Karl Ströher, Darmstadt; Thordis Moeller, New York, New York, 1967; Marian Goodman Gallery, New York, New York, 1985.

Notes

The sculpture was restored by the artist in 1983. The original dimensions were 27½ × 23½ × 23½ in. (70 × 60 × 60 cm).

The photograph is of the sculpture's original state.

172

Untitled 1963

Painted and chromium-plated steel
36 × 50 × 53 in.
(91.5 × 127 × 134.5 cm).

Collection

The David and Alfred Smart Gallery, The University of Chicago, Chicago, Illinois, 1972; gift of Mr. and Mrs. Richard L. Selle.

Provenance

Leo Castelli Gallery, New York, New York; Mr. and Mrs. Richard L. Selle, Chicago, Illinois.

173

Untitled 1963

Painted tin and wood
7 × 6 × 4 in. (18 × 15.5 × 10 cm).

Collection

Private collection, Munich, 1963.

Provenance

Leo Castelli Gallery, New York, New York.

Notes

The sculpture is one of the *Playskool* series of 1963. These pieces incorporated children's building blocks as bases (see also cat. no. 174).

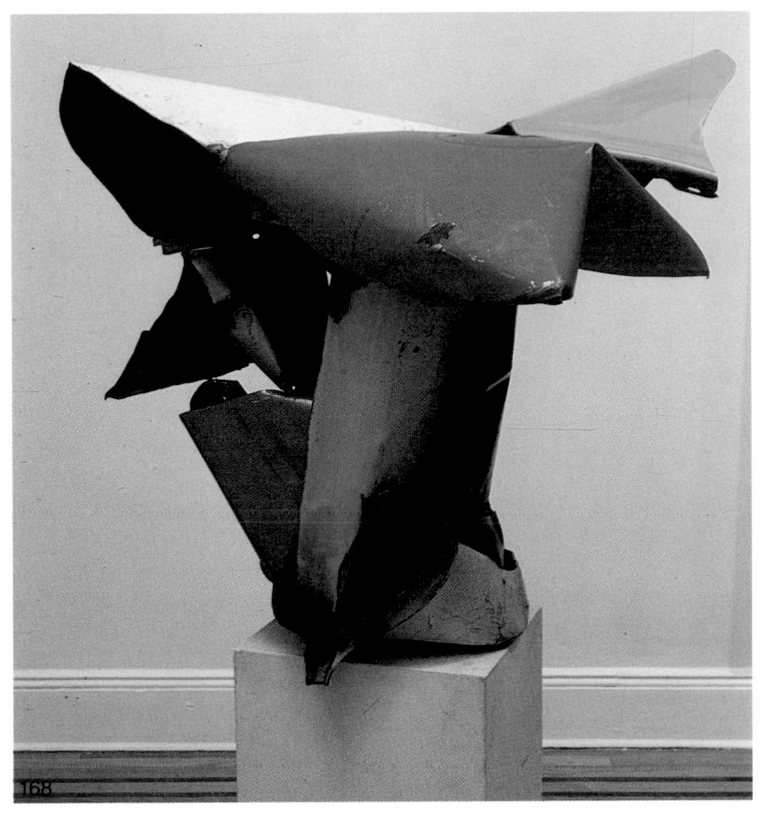
168

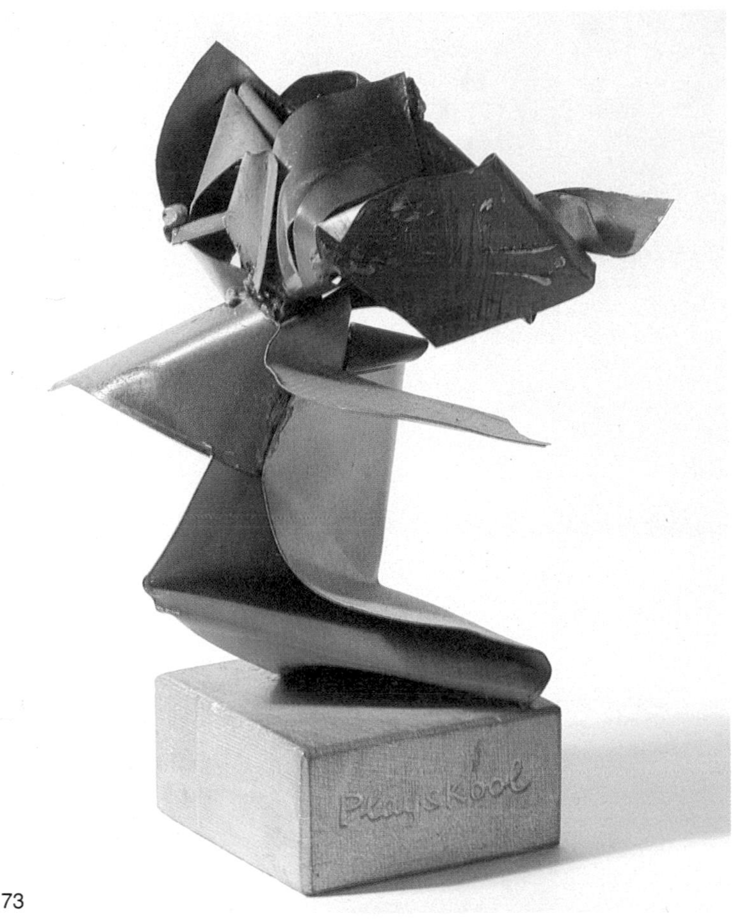

173

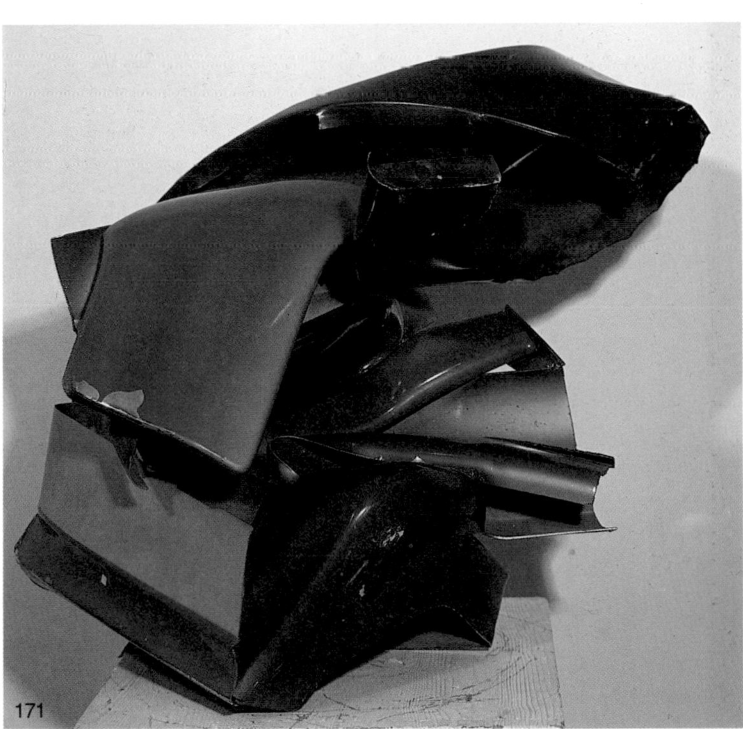
171

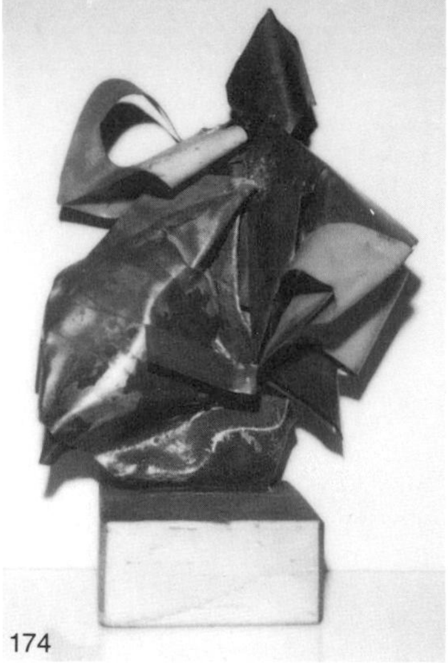
174

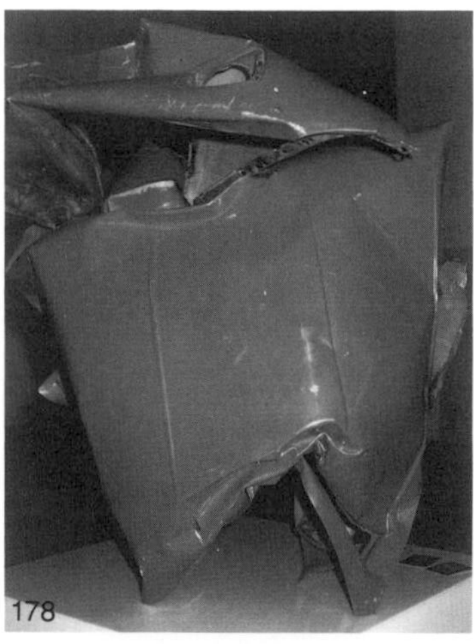
178

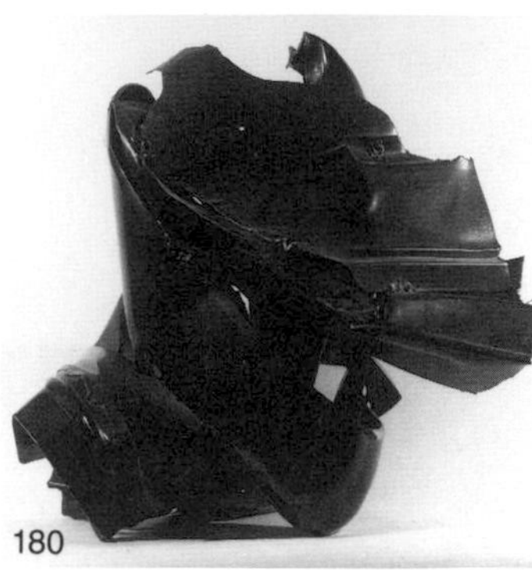
180

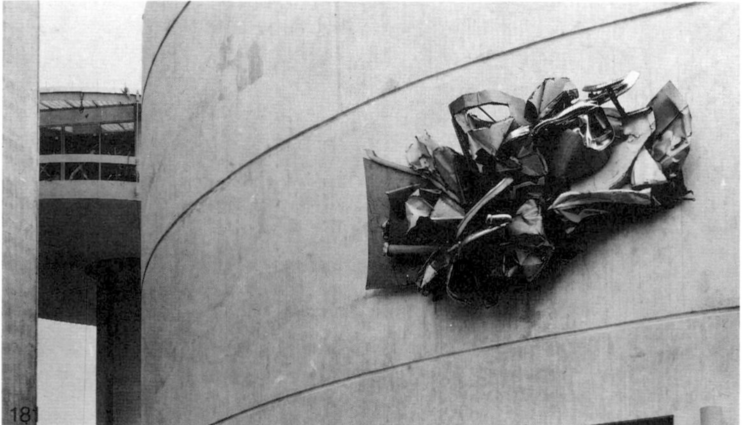
181

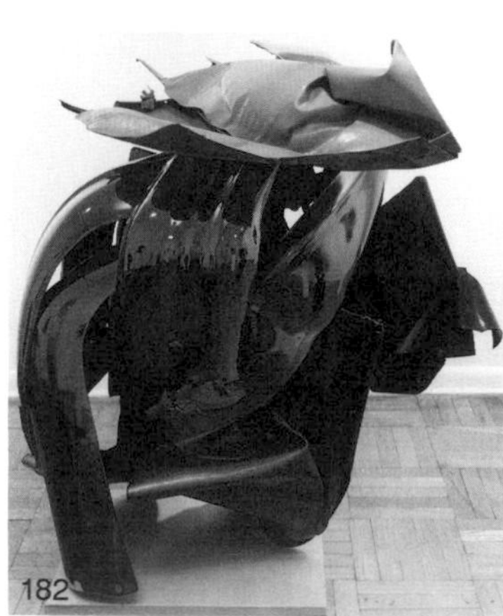
182

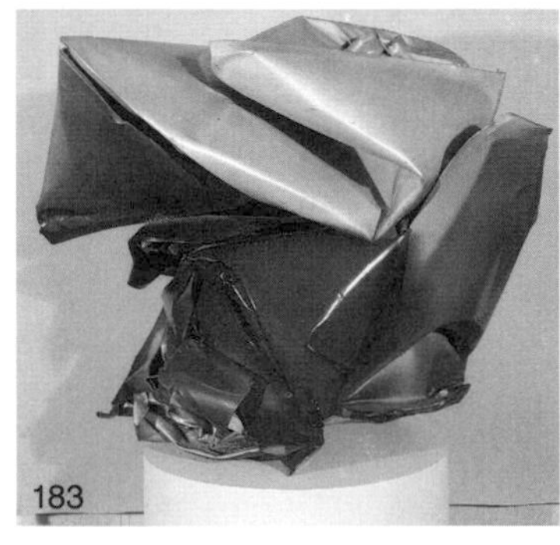
183

174

Untitled 1963

Painted tin and wood
4 × 5 × 5½ in.
(10 × 12.5 × 14 cm).

Collection
Present location unknown.

Provenance
Leo Castelli Gallery, New York, New York; private collection, West Germany, 1963.

Notes
The sculpture is one of the *Playskool* series of 1963. These pieces incorporated children's building blocks as bases (see also cat. no. 173).

175

Untitled 1963

Painted tin and wood
7½ × 6 × 4½ in.
(19 × 15 × 11.5 cm).

Collection
Private collection, Boston, Massachusetts, 1983; acquired directly from the artist.

Notes
According to the artist, the sculpture was made in 1963 from two damaged works, both of which were untitled 1963 sculptures. It is not known which two sculptures were used.

176

Untitled 1963

Painted steel
20 in. high (51 cm).

Collection
Present location unknown.

Provenance
Leo Castelli Gallery, New York, New York; The Mayor Gallery, London; Quireba Foundation, London; Leo Castelli Gallery, New York, New York.

177

Untitled 1963

Painted and chromium-plated steel
47 × 47 × 40 in.
(119.5 × 119.5 × 101.5 cm).

Collection
Present location unknown.

Provenance
Dwan Gallery, Los Angeles, California; Lo Giudice Gallery, Chicago, Illinois, 1968.

Notes
The Castelli registry describes the sculpture as white, chrome, and red.

178

J.J.J.J. c. 1963

Painted steel
51 × 50 × 48 in.
(129.5 × 127 × 122 cm).

Collection
Present location unknown.

Notes
The sculpture is listed in the Castelli registry as dating from 1970–71. Still, it appears to be a 1963 sculpture and it is quite likely that it may be cat. no. 177. It is likely that it was titled by the artist in 1970–71, because in those years he titled several pieces with the initials of friends' names.

179

Untitled c. 1963

Painted and chromium-plated steel
72 × 48 × 42 in.
(183 × 122 × 106.5 cm).

Collection
Private collection, Bethesda, Maryland.

Provenance
Allan Stone, New York, New York.

180

Untitled c. 1963

Painted steel
22½ × 22½ × 22 in.
(57 × 57 × 56 cm).

Collection
Hirshhorn Museum and Sculpture Garden, Smithsonian Institution, Washington, D.C., 1972.

Provenance
Murray Hill Antiques, New York, New York; Joseph H. Hirshhorn, New York, New York, 1967.

References
George Heard Hamilton, *Nineteenth- and Twentieth-Century Art* (New York: Abrams, 1970), illus. pl. 356, p. 387.

181

Untitled 1963–64

Painted and chromium-plated steel
Dimensions unknown.

Collection
Present location unknown.

References
Philip Johnson, "Young Artists at the Fair and at Lincoln Center," *Art in America*, vol. 52, no. 4 (August 1964), color illus. p. 117.

Notes
The sculpture was rented through the Leo Castelli Gallery to the New York State Pavilion at the World's Fair in Flushing, New York, in 1964. It was lost and never returned to the gallery.

182

Bags Down/Bags Down II 1964/73

Painted and chromium-plated steel
37 × 29 × 29 in.
(94 × 73.5 × 73.5 cm).

Collection
Present location unknown.

Provenance
Leo Castelli Gallery, New York, New York; Lo Giudice Gallery, Chicago, Illinois; Hugh Hefner, Lake Geneva, Wisconsin; Leo Castelli Gallery, New York, New York, 1973; Bo Alveryd, Kävlinge, Sweden.

Exhibitions
Pasadena Art Museum, Pasadena, California. *New American Sculpture*, cat. no. 10. February 11–March 7, 1964.

Leo Castelli Gallery, New York, New York. *John Chamberlain*. April 11–30, 1964.

Notes
Bags Down was sold to Hugh Hefner and installed at the Playboy Mansion in Lake Geneva, Wisconsin, where it was destroyed. *Bags Down II* was made from parts of the destroyed sculpture in 1973.

The dimensions of the original sculpture were 37 × 36 × 40 in. (94 × 91.5 × 101.5 cm). The original sculpture is reproduced here.

183

CA-D'ORO 1964

Painted steel
34 × 37 × 32 in.
(86.5 × 94 × 81.5 cm).

Collection
Irving and Natalie Forman, Chicago, Illinois, 1966.

Provenance
Leo Castelli Gallery, New York, New York.

Exhibitions
Leo Castelli Gallery, New York, New York. *John Chamberlain*. April 11–30, 1964.

184

Colonel Splendid 1964

Painted and chromium-plated steel
25 × 26 × 22 in.
(63.5 × 66 × 56 cm).

Collection
Mr. and Mrs. Michael Sonnabend, New York, New York.

Provenance
Leo Castelli Gallery, New York, New York.

Exhibitions
Leo Castelli Gallery, New York, New York. *John Chamberlain*. April 11–30, 1964.

References
"Venice: The Biennale XXXII," *Arts*, vol. 38, no. 9 (May/June 1964), illus. p. 77.

185

Dogstarman (for Stan Brakhage) 1964

Painted steel
16 × 28 × 18 in.
(40.5 × 71 × 45.5 cm).

Collection
Solomon and Co., New York, New York, 1977.

Provenance
Leo Castelli Gallery, New York, New York; Mr. and Mrs. Arthur Mones, New York, New York.

Exhibitions
Leo Castelli Gallery, New York, New York. *John Chamberlain*. April 11–30, 1964.

The Jewish Museum, New York, New York. *Recent American Sculpture*, cat. no. 20. October 15–November 29, 1964.

Leo Castelli Warehouse, New York, New York. *John Chamberlain: Recent Sculpture*. February 2–22, 1969.

The Solomon R. Guggenheim Museum, New York, New York. *John Chamberlain: A Retrospective Exhibition*, cat. no. 58, illus. p. 69. December 23, 1971–February 20, 1972.

186

Emperor Hudson 1964

Painted and chromium-plated steel
28 × 32 × 24 in.
(71 × 81 × 61 cm).

Collection
Judy and Jim Newman, San Francisco, California, 1967.

Provenance
Leo Castelli Gallery, New York, New York.

Exhibitions
Leo Castelli Gallery, New York, New York. *John Chamberlain*. April 11–30, 1964.

Institute of Contemporary Art, Boston, Massachusetts. *The Biennale Eight*. June 20–July 26, 1964.

The Cleveland Museum of Art, Cleveland, Ohio. *Sculpture by John Chamberlain*, listed. January 3–29, 1967.

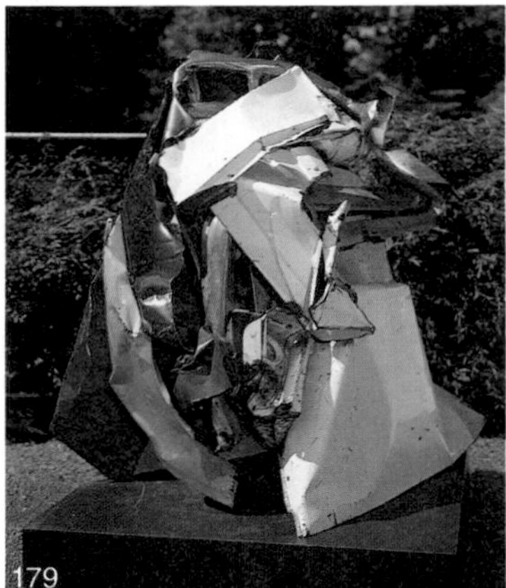
179

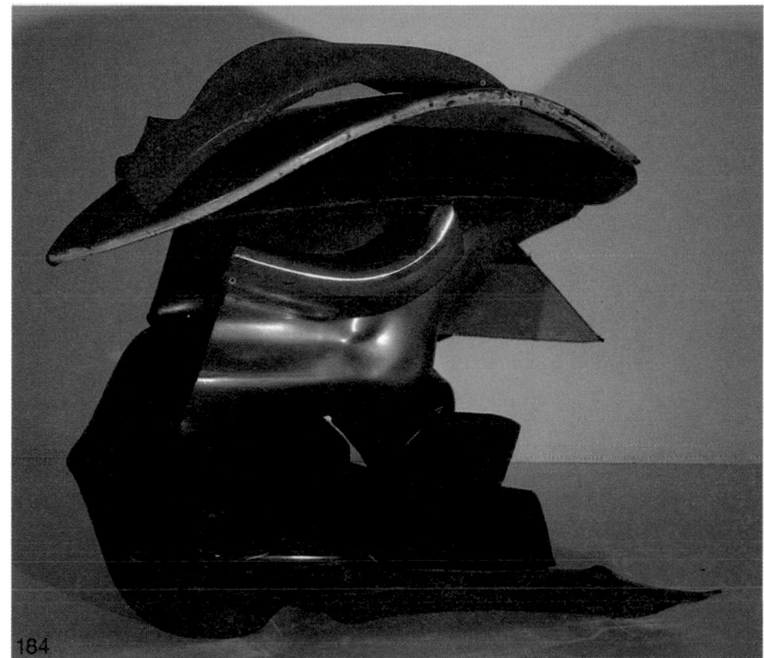
184

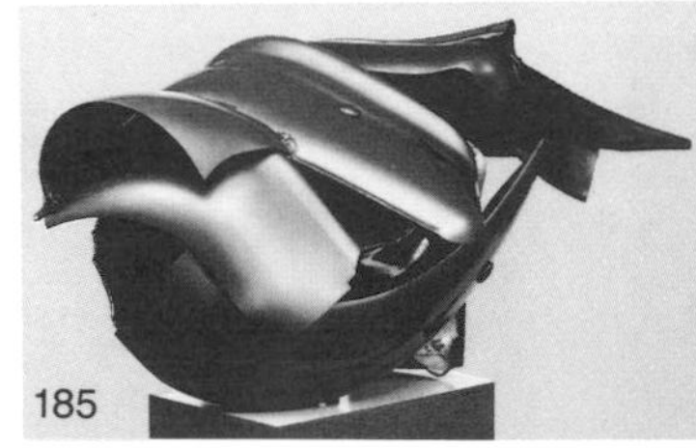
185

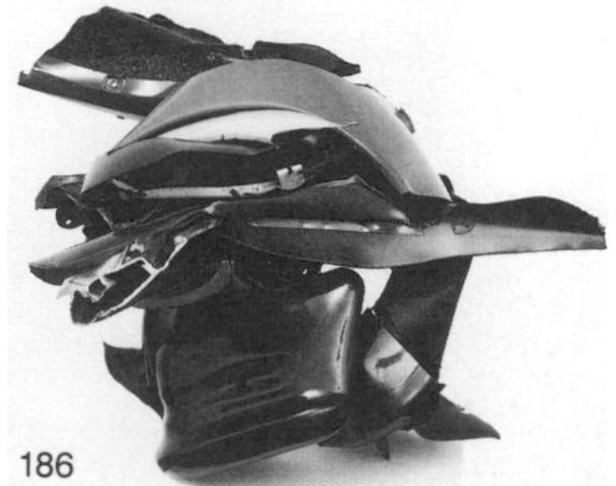
186

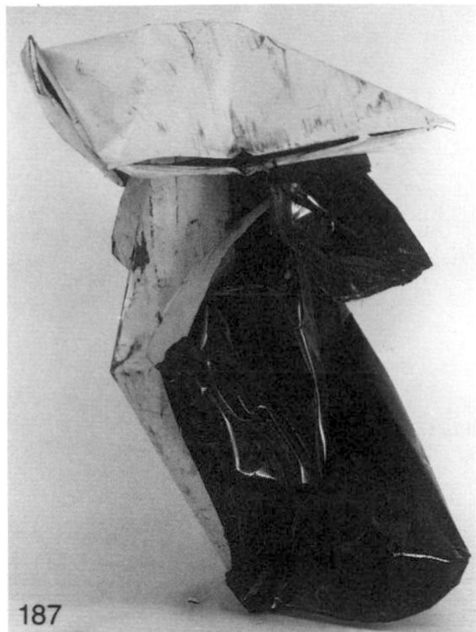
187

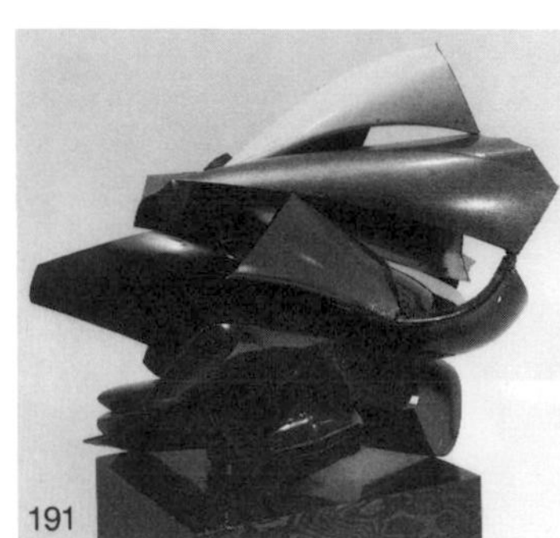
191

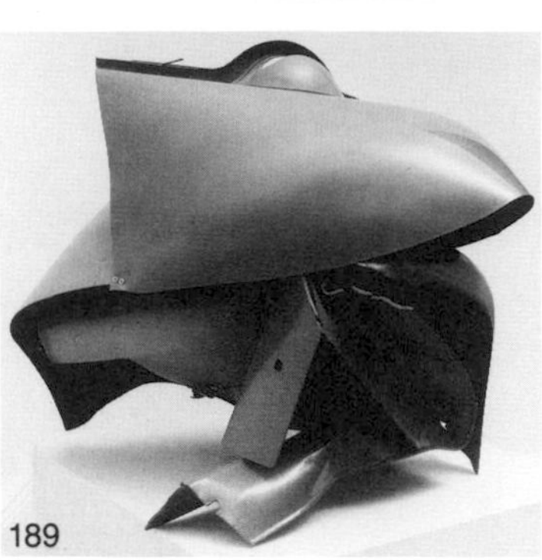
189

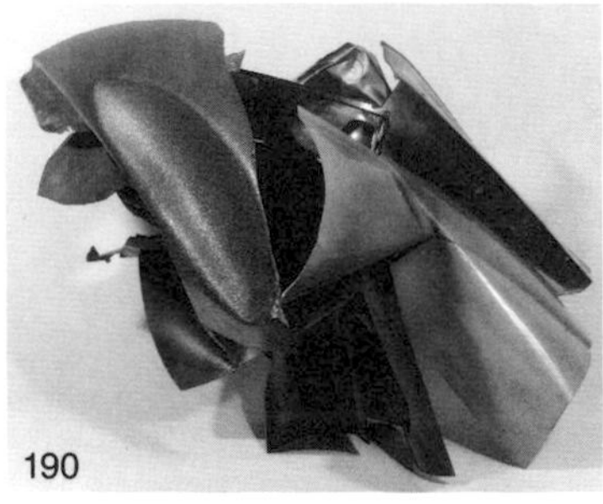
190

187

Exciter/(White Shadow) 1964

Painted and chromium-plated steel
72 × 36 × 36 in.
(183 × 91.5 × 91.5 cm).

Collection

Museum Ludwig, Cologne, 1976.

Provenance

Leo Castelli Gallery, New York, New York; Jonathan Streep, New York, New York; Leo Castelli Gallery, New York, New York; Leon Kraushaar, Lawrence, New York; Karl Ströher, Darmstadt; Irene and Peter Ludwig, Aachen; Sammlung Ludwig, Cologne, 1969.

Exhibitions

Galerie-Verein München, Neue Pinakothek, Haus der Kunst, Munich. *Sammlung 1968 Karl Ströher*, cat. no. 42, illus. June 14–August 9, 1968. Traveled to Kunstverein, Hamburg. August 24–October 6, 1968.

Museum der Stadt Köln, Cologne. *Westkunst*, cat. no. 703, illus. p. 461. May 30–August 16, 1981.

References

H. Keller, "Sechsmal aktuelle Kunst—Sechs Fragezeichen," *Westermanns Monatshefte* (April 1970), pp. 18–24, color illus. p. 21.

H. Lützeler, "Kunst und Literatur um 1960. Dreistücke aus der Sammlung Ludwig," *Festschrift für Gert von der Osten* (Cologne, 1970), pp. 243–56, illus. p. 247.

Rainer Budde and Evelyn Weiss, *Katalog der Bildwerke und Objekte, Neuzugänge seit 1965 im Wallraf-Richartz-Museum mit Teilen der Sammlung Ludwig* (Cologne: Wallraf-Richartz-Museum, 1973), p. 20, illus.

Karl Ruhrberg, "Museum Ludwig Köln," *Du*, no. 1 (1979), illus. p. 73.

Notes

The sculpture has been referred to as *White Shadow* since it entered the Ludwig collection. The origin of this title is unknown; the sculpture was never titled *White Shadow* by the artist. There is no record of another sculpture titled *White Shadow*.

188

Madam Moon 1964

Painted and chromium-plated steel
19 × 29 × 21 in.
(48.5 × 73.5 × 53.5 cm).

Collection

Robert A. Rowan, Pasadena, California, 1964.

Provenance

Leo Castelli Gallery, New York, New York.

Exhibitions

Pasadena Art Museum, Pasadena, California. *New American Sculpture*, cat. no. 11. February 11–March 7, 1964.

Leo Castelli Gallery, New York, New York. *John Chamberlain*. April 11–30, 1964.

XXXII Esposizione biennale internazionale d'arte, Venice. June 20–October 15, 1964.

The Cleveland Museum of Art, Cleveland, Ohio. *Sculpture by John Chamberlain*, listed. January 3–29, 1967.

University of California, Irvine. *A Selection from the Collection of Mr. and Mrs. Robert Rowan*. May 2–21, 1967. Traveled to San Francisco Museum of Modern Art, San Francisco, California. June 2–July 2, 1967.

The Solomon R. Guggenheim Museum, New York, New York. *John Chamberlain: A Retrospective Exhibition*, cat. no. 57, illus. p. 71. December 23, 1971–February 20, 1972.

References

Sam Hunter et al., *New Art around the World: Painting and Sculpture* (New York: Abrams, 1966), p. 465, illus. pl. 39.

Barbara Rose, "On Chamberlain's Interview," *Artforum*, vol. 10, no. 6 (February 1972), illus. p. 45.

189

Ma Green 1964

Painted and chromium-plated steel
20 × 24 × 20 in.
(51 × 61 × 51 cm).

Collection

Present location unknown.

Provenance

Leo Castelli Gallery, New York, New York; William Zierler, Inc., New York, New York.

Exhibitions

Herron Museum of Art, Indianapolis, Indiana. *Painting and Sculpture Today*, cat. no. 8, illus. January 1–31, 1965.

Sotheby Parke-Bernet, Inc., New York, New York. *Contemporary Art*, cat. no. 246, illus. October 21, 1976.

190

Miss Remember Ford 1964
Painted steel
27 × 34 × 26½ in.
(68.5 × 86.5 × 67.5 cm).

Collection
Abrams Family Collection, New York, New York, 1980.

Provenance
Leo Castelli Gallery, New York, New York; Mr. and Mrs. Thomas Petschek, Scarsdale, New York, 1964.

Exhibitions
Sotheby & Co., London. *Sale of Contemporary Art 1945–1974*, cat. no. 11, color illus., incorrectly listed as "Untitled, 1961." April 3, 1974.

Christie, Manson & Woods International, Inc., New York, New York. *Contemporary Art*, cat. no. 40, color illus. May 16, 1980.

Notes
The sculpture has frequently been misdated as 1961.

191

Red Ryder 1964
Painted and chromium-plated steel
22 × 26 × 19 in.
(56 × 66 × 48 cm).

Collection
Present location unknown.

Provenance
Leo Castelli Gallery, New York, New York; Susan Morse Hilles, New York, New York.

Exhibitions
Leo Castelli Gallery, New York, New York. *John Chamberlain*. April 11–30, 1964.

The Aldrich Museum of Contemporary Art, Ridgefield, Connecticut. *Selections from the Collection of Susan Morse Hilles*. September 17–December 3, 1967.

192

Shadow Smart 1964
Painted and chromium-plated steel
26 × 29 × 28 in.
(66 × 73.5 × 71 cm).

Collection
J. W. Froehlich GmbH., Stuttgart.

Provenance
Leo Castelli Gallery, New York, New York; Leon Kraushaar, Lawrence, New York; Six Friedrich, Munich.

193

Slauson 1964
Painted and chromium-plated steel
20 × 24 × 22 in.
(51 × 61 × 56 cm).

Collection
William J. Hokin, Chicago, Illinois, 1968.

Provenance
Leo Castelli Gallery, New York, New York; Dwan Gallery, Los Angeles, California; Lo Giudice Gallery, Chicago, Illinois.

Exhibitions
Dwan Gallery, Los Angeles, California. *Group Exhibition*. December 29, 1963–January 3, 1964.

Pasadena Art Museum, Pasadena, California. *New American Sculpture*, cat. no. 8, illus. February 11–March 7, 1964.

Leo Castelli Gallery, New York, New York. *John Chamberlain*. April 11–30, 1964.

XXXII Esposizione biennale internazionale d'arte, Venice. June 20–October 15, 1964.

University of California at Los Angeles Art Galleries, Los Angeles. *Virginia Dwan Kondratief Collection*. September–October 1965.

A Go Go Films, Allied Artists, Los Angeles, California. *Group Exhibition*. November–December 1966.

Long Beach State College, Long Beach, California. *Group Exhibition*. January–February 1967.

Art Rental Gallery, Los Angeles County Museum of Art, Los Angeles, California. April–June 1967.

References
John Coplans, "Higgins/Price/Chamberlain/Bontecou/Westermann," *Artforum*, vol. 2, no. 10 (April 1964), illus. p. 39.

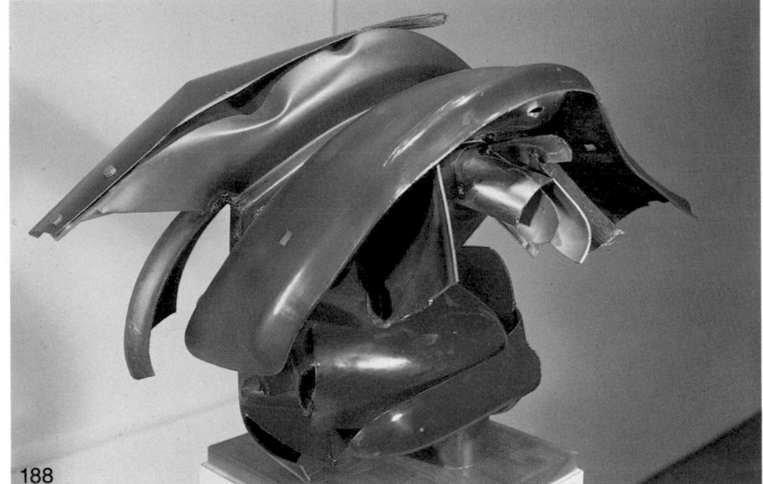
188

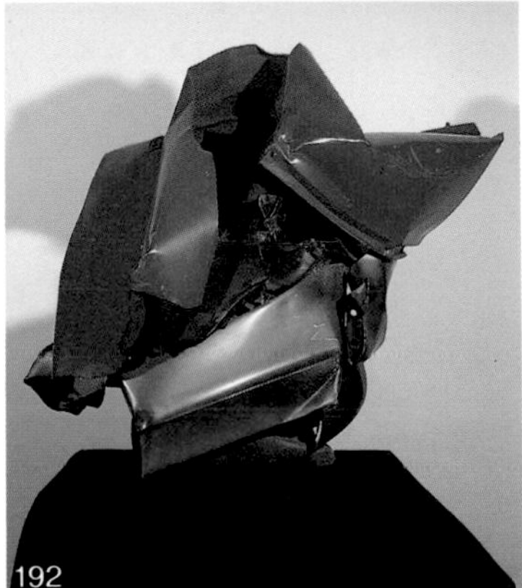
192

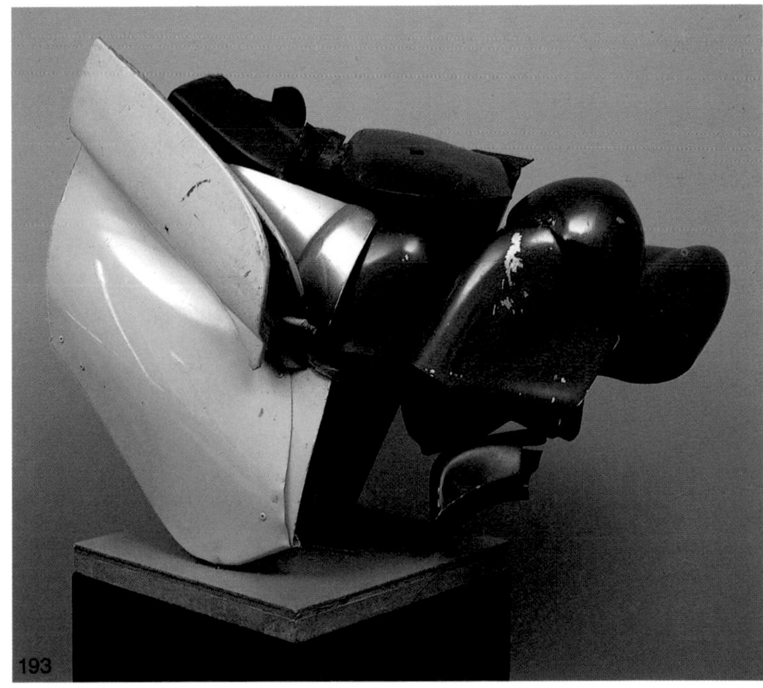
193

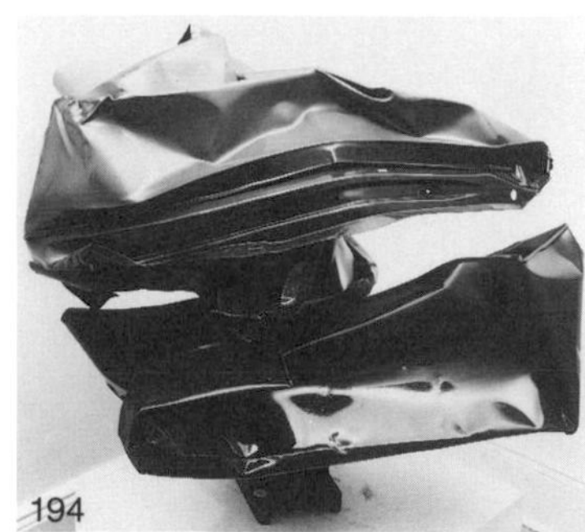
194

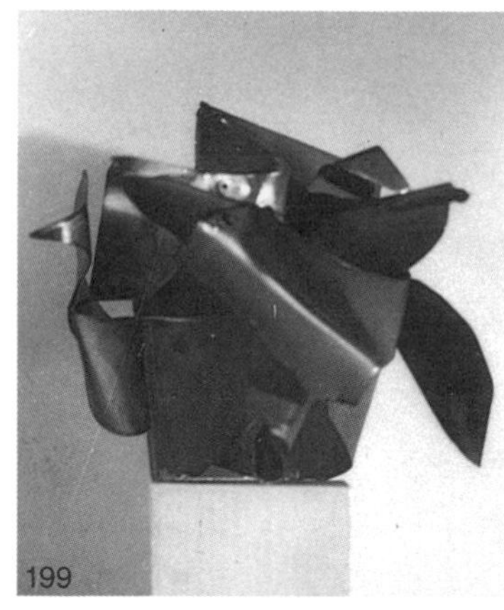
199

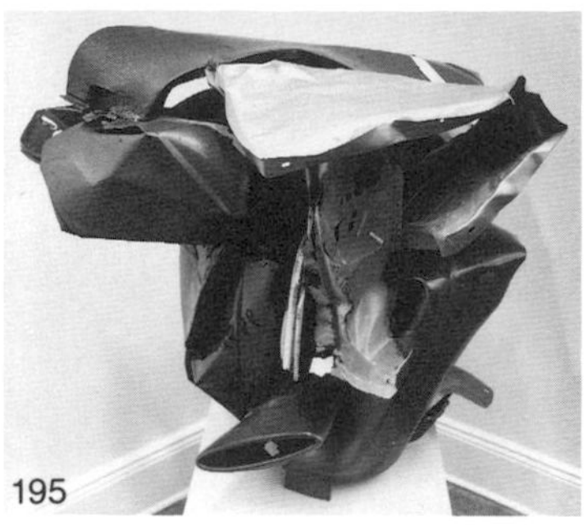
195

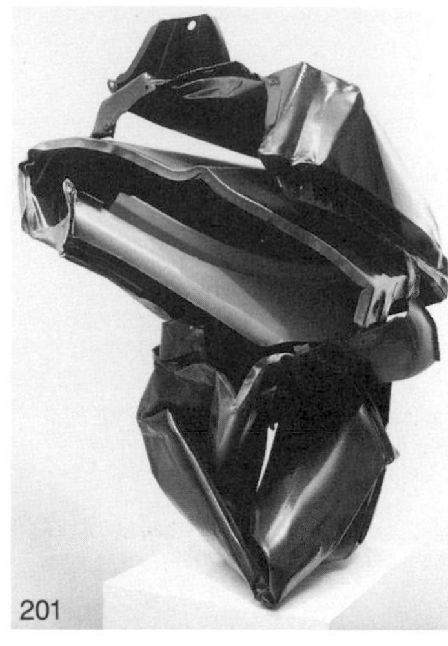
201

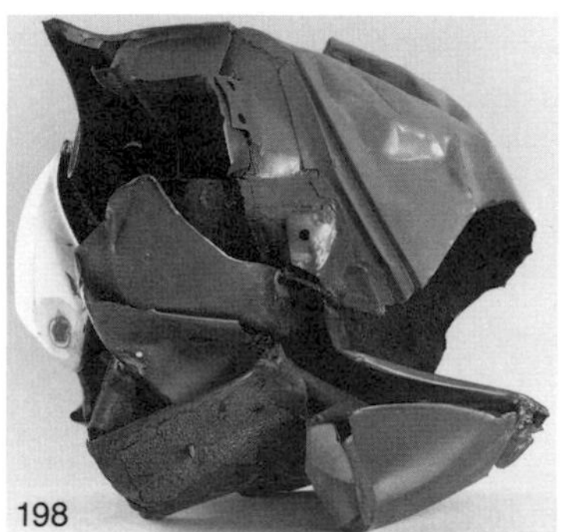
198

194

Spike 1964
Painted and chromium-plated steel
28 × 31 × 24 in.
(71 × 78.5 × 61 cm).

Collection
Holly and Horace Solomon, New York, New York, 1969.

Provenance
Leo Castelli Gallery, New York, New York.

195

Sugar Tit 1964
Painted and chromium-plated steel
36 × 38 × 26 in.
(91.5 × 96.5 × 66 cm).

Collection
Marilyn and Ivan Karp, New York, New York, 1966.

Provenance
Leo Castelli Gallery, New York, New York.

Exhibitions
Leo Castelli Gallery, New York, New York. *John Chamberlain*. April 11–30, 1964.

The Solomon R. Guggenheim Museum, New York, New York. *John Chamberlain: A Retrospective Exhibition*, cat. no. 59, illus. p. 70. December 23, 1971–February 20, 1972.

196

Summer Romance 1964
Painted tin
7 × 6 × 6 in. (18 × 15 × 15 cm).

Collection
William J. Hokin, Chicago, Illinois, 1978.

Provenance
Leo Castelli Gallery, New York, New York; Edwin Janss, Thousand Oaks, California, 1964; James Corcoran Gallery, Los Angeles, California, 1974; Stephen Mazoh, New York, New York; The Mayor Gallery, London.

Exhibitions
Museum of Contemporary Art, Chicago, Illinois. *Fourth Benefit Auction*, cat. no. 47A. December 1, 1978.

Notes
The sculpture was listed as "Untitled, 1964" in the Castelli registry.

197

Untitled 1964
Painted tin
8 × 7 × 6 in. (20.5 × 18 × 15 cm).

Collection
Present location unknown.

Provenance
Leo Castelli Gallery, New York, New York; Mr. and Mrs. Taft Schreiber, New York, New York.

198

Untitled c. 1964
Painted steel
19 × 26 × 23 in.
(48 × 66 × 58.5 cm).

Collection
Menil Collection, Houston, Texas, 1979.

Provenance
Bianchini Gallery, New York, New York.

Exhibitions
Christie, Manson & Woods International, Inc., New York, New York. *Contemporary Art*, cat. no. 44. May 18, 1979.

199

Untitled 1964
Painted steel
6½ × 7½ × 5 in.
(16.5 × 19 × 12.5 cm).

Collection
Linda Rosenkrantz Finch, New York, New York, 1964.

Provenance
Peter Marks Works of Art, New York, New York.

200

Untitled 1964
Painted steel
42 × 24 × 24 in.
(106.5 × 61 × 61 cm).

Collection
Private collection, New York, New York, 1979.

Provenance
O. K. Harris Works of Art, New York, New York, 1978; James Corcoran Gallery, Los Angeles, California.

201

Untitled 1964
Painted and chromium-plated steel
36 × 30 × 24 in.
(91.5 × 76 × 61 cm).

Collection
Edmund Pillsbury, Fort Worth, Texas, 1974.

Provenance
Leo Castelli Gallery, New York, New York; Ben Birillo, New York, New York; Leo Castelli Gallery, New York, New York; Allan Stone, New York, New York.

202

Untitled 1964
Painted steel
8 × 5 × 6 in.
(20.5 × 12.5 × 15 cm).

Collection
Private collection, New York, New York, 1964.

Provenance
Leo Castelli Gallery, New York, New York.

203

Bluevein 1965
Painted tin
11 × 9 × 8½ in.
(28 × 23 × 21.5 cm).

Collection
Allan Stone, New York, New York, 1965.

Provenance
Leo Castelli Gallery, New York, New York.

Notes
The sculpture has been referred to as "Untitled" in all records.

204

Boydille 1965
Fiber glass
42 × 51 × 42 in.
(106.5 × 129.5 × 106.5 cm).

Collection
Present location unknown.

Exhibitions
The Los Angeles County Museum of Art, Los Angeles, California. *American Sculpture of the Sixties*, cat. no. 23. April 28–June 25, 1967. Traveled to Philadelphia Museum of Art, Philadelphia, Pennsylvania. September 15–November 15, 1967.

Notes
The sculpture may be related to the group of seven sculptures made in 1966 in New Mexico (cat. nos. 227–233).

205

Bunyan 1965
Painted and chromium-plated steel
14½ × 25 × 26 in.
(37 × 63.5 × 66 cm).

Collection
Mr. and Mrs. Miles Q. Fiterman, Minneapolis, Minnesota.

Provenance
Leo Castelli Gallery, New York, New York; Noah Goldowsky, New York, New York; Leo Castelli Gallery, New York, New York; Lo Giudice Gallery, Chicago, Illinois; Dayton's Gallery 12, Minneapolis, Minnesota.

Notes
The sculpture was originally listed as "Untitled" in the Castelli registry; it was later titled by the artist. It was also at one time misdated 1962.

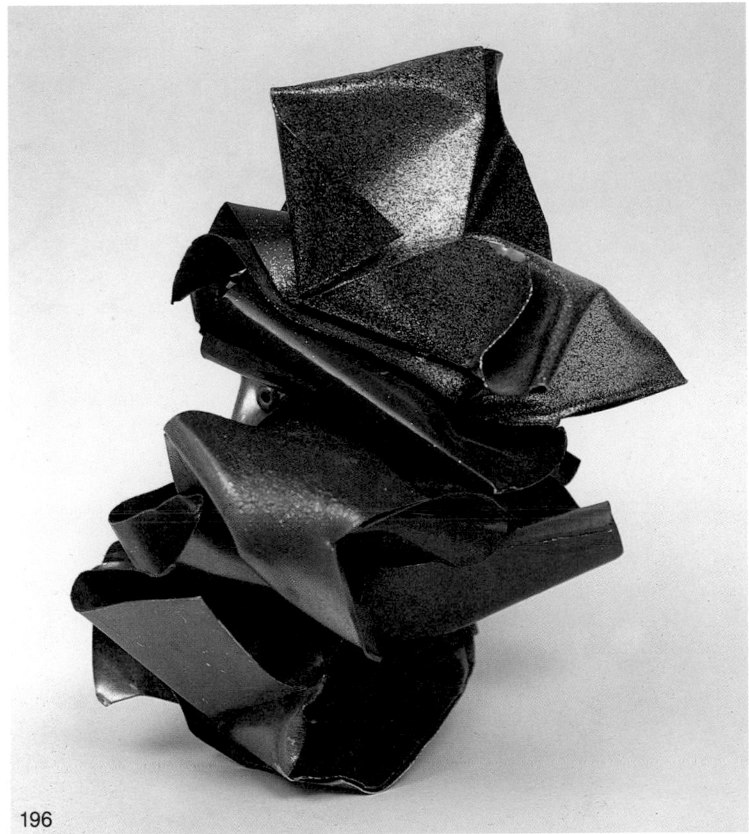
196

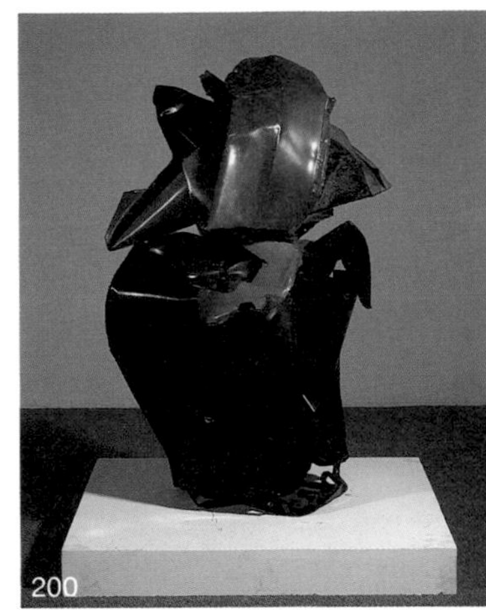
200

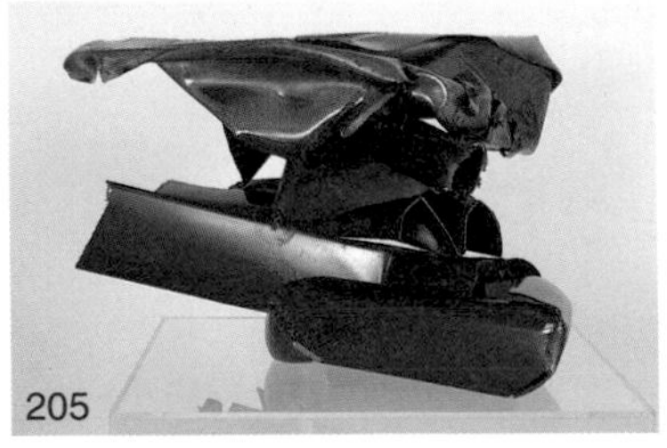
205

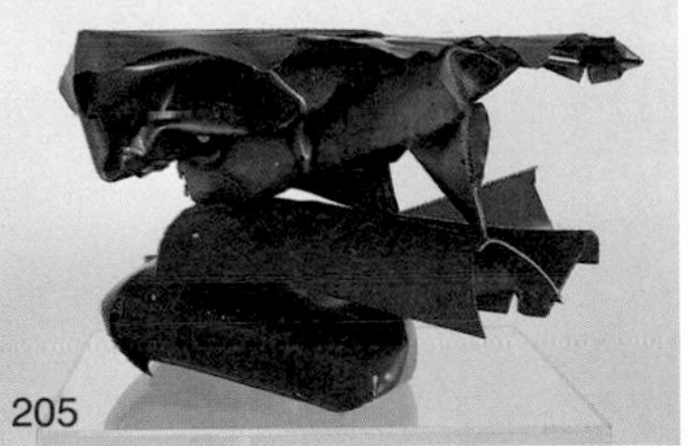
205

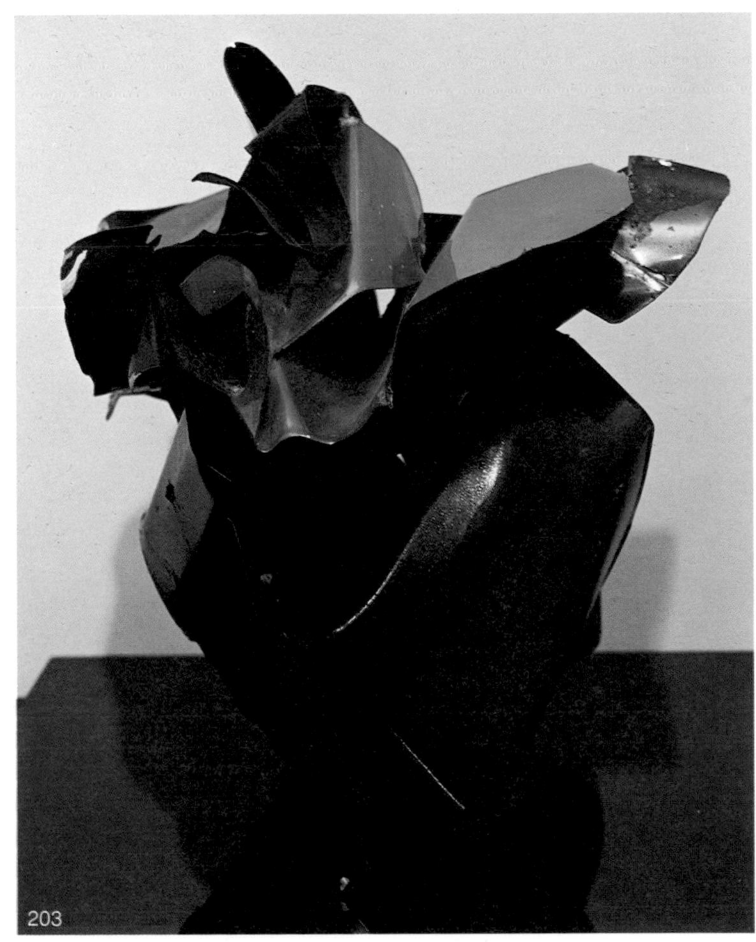
203

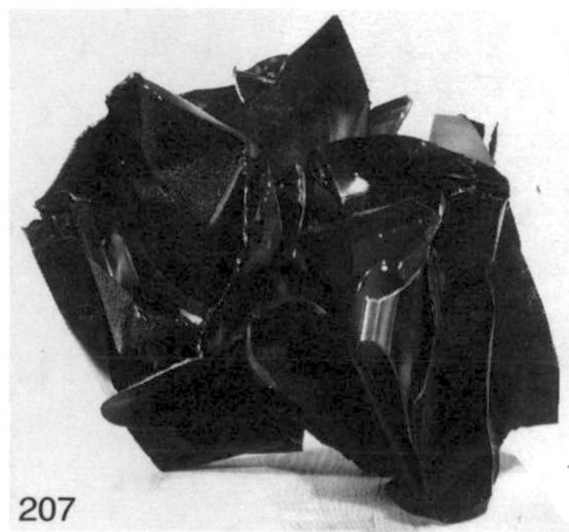
207

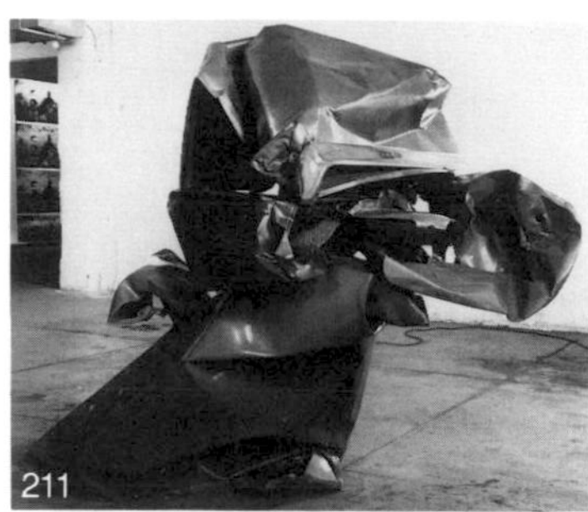
211

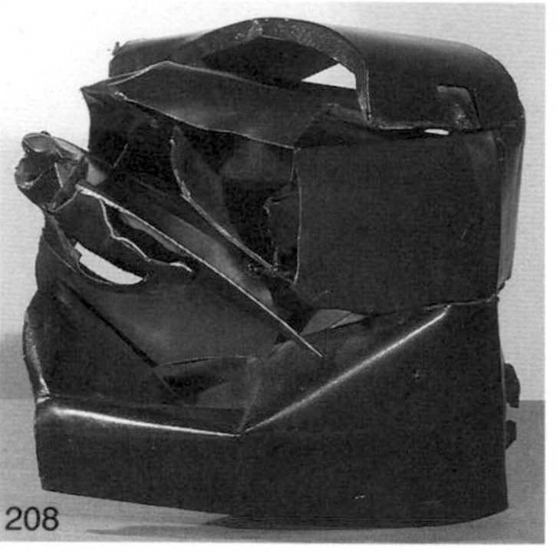
208

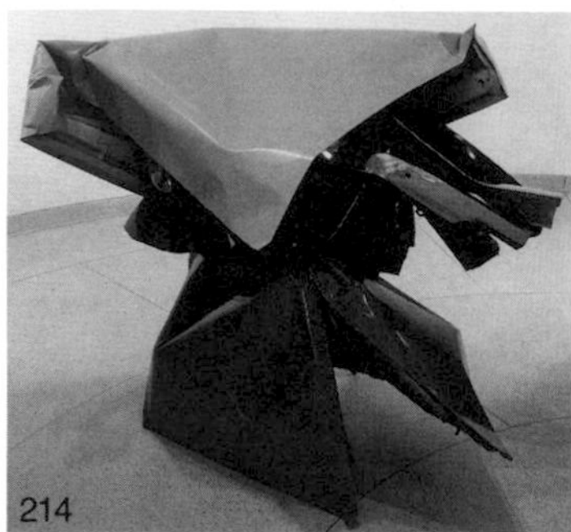
214

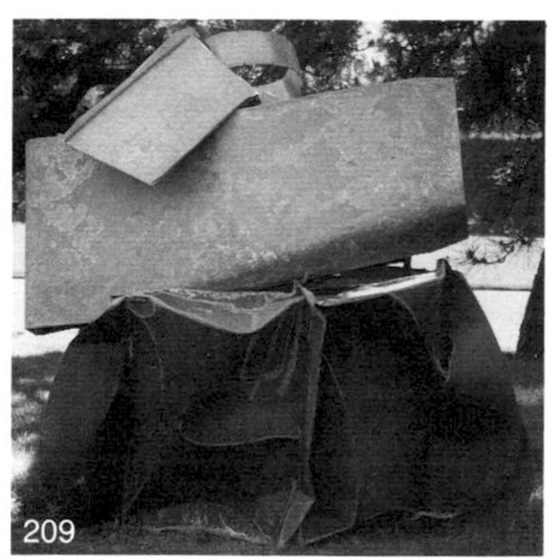
209

206

Famous Flames 1965
Painted metal
19 × 25 × 16 in.
(48 × 63.5 × 40.5 cm).

Collection
Private collection, New York, New York.

Provenance
Leo Castelli Gallery, New York, New York.

Exhibitions
American Embassy in Mexico City. *Art in Embassies*, organized by the Museum of Modern Art, New York, New York. August 1965.

207

Homer Jack 1965
Painted and chromium-plated steel
19 × 19 × 19 in.
(48 × 48 × 48 cm).

Collection
Frederic Roberts, Lawrence, New York, 1966.

Provenance
Leo Castelli Gallery, New York, New York.

Exhibitions
The Solomon R. Guggenheim Museum, New York, New York. *John Chamberlain: A Retrospective Exhibition*, cat. no. 71, illus. p. 75. December 23, 1971–February 20, 1972.

208

It Ain't Cheap 1965
Painted steel
18 × 20½ × 19 in.
(46 × 52 × 48 cm).

Collection
Dia Art Foundation, New York, New York, 1980.

Provenance
William Zierler, Inc., New York, New York; Lone Star Foundation, New York, New York, 1979.

Exhibitions
Sotheby Parke-Bernet, Inc., New York, New York. *Important Contemporary Paintings, Drawings and Sculpture*, cat. no. 870, illus., listed as "Untitled." November 8, 1979.

Notes
The sculpture was titled by the artist in 1980.

209

Koma/(Koma II) 1965/68
Painted and chromium-plated steel
61 × 53 × 25 in.
(155 × 134.5 × 63.5 cm).

Collection
Dorothy and Roy Lichtenstein, Southampton, New York.

Provenance
Leo Castelli Gallery, New York, New York; Jack H. Klein, New York, New York.

Exhibitions
Institute of Contemporary Art, Philadelphia, Pennsylvania. *Seven Sculptors*. December 1, 1965–January 17, 1966.

Leo Castelli Warehouse, New York, New York. *John Chamberlain: Recent Sculpture*. February 2–22, 1969.

Notes
The sculpture was remade by the artist in 1968.

210

Madison 1965
Painted steel
20 × 26 × 16 in.
(51 × 66 × 40.5 cm).

Collection
Robert and Suzanne Pannier, Brugge, Belgium, 1978.

Provenance
Mr. and Mrs. Abe Adler, Los Angeles, California.

211

Mustang Sally McBright 1965
Painted and chromium-plated steel
56 × 63 × 44 in.
(142.5 × 160 × 111.5 cm).

Collection
Martin Z. Margulies, Coconut Grove, Florida, 1981.

Provenance
Leo Castelli Gallery, New York, New York, 1965; Mr. and Mrs. Robert B. Mayer, Chicago, Illinois, 1965; Robert B. Mayer Memorial Loan Collection of the Museum of Contemporary Art, Chicago, Illinois, 1975–80; O. K. Harris Works of Art, New York, New York, 1981.

Exhibitions
Museum of Contemporary Art, Chicago, Illinois. *Selections from the Collection of Mr. and Mrs. Robert B. Mayer*, cat. no. 13. July 13–September 8, 1968.

212

Richmond Ruckus Again 1965
Painted and chromium-plated steel
36 × 45 × 30 in.
(91.5 × 114.5 × 76 cm).

Collection
Present location unknown.

Provenance
Leo Castelli Gallery, New York, New York; Selma Milgram, Lawrence, New York; Hineni Organization, New York, New York.

Exhibitions

Sotheby Parke-Bernet, Inc., New York, New York. *Contemporary Paintings, Drawings and Sculpture*, cat. no. 50, incorrectly listed as *Fender*. November 9–10, 1983.

213

Stevie Wonder 1965

Painted tin
8½ × 10 × 9 in.
(21.5 × 25.5 × 23 cm).

Collection
Present location unknown.

Notes
The only evidence of the existence of this sculpture is that it was entered in the Castelli registry in 1965.

214

Tomahawk Nolan 1965

Painted and chromium-plated steel
44 × 52 × 36 in.
(112 × 132 × 91.5 cm).

Collection
Museum of Modern Art, New York, New York; gift of Philip Johnson, 1971.

Provenance
Leo Castelli Gallery, New York, New York; Philip Johnson, New Canaan, Connecticut, 1965.

Exhibitions
Leo Castelli Gallery, New York, New York. *Ten Years*. February 4–26, 1967.

Philadelphia Museum of Art, Philadelphia, Pennsylvania. *American Art since 1945*, a loan exhibition from the Museum of Modern Art, New York, New York, listed. September 15–October 22, 1972.

Worcester Art Museum, Worcester, Massachusetts. *American Art since 1945*, from the collection of the Museum of Modern Art, New York, New York, illus. p. 48. October 20–November 30, 1975. Traveled to Toledo Museum of Art, Toledo, Ohio. January 10–February 22, 1976; The Denver Art Museum, Denver, Colorado. March 22–May 2, 1976; Fine Arts Gallery of San Diego, San Diego, California. May 31–July 11, 1976; Dallas Museum of Fine Arts, Dallas, Texas. August 19–October 3, 1976; Joslyn Art Museum, Omaha, Nebraska. October 25–December 5, 1976; Greenville County Museum, Greenville, South Carolina. January 8–February 20, 1977; Virginia Museum of Fine Arts, Richmond, Virginia. March 14–April 17, 1977; The Bronx Museum of the Arts, Bronx, New York. May 9–June 30, 1977.

Museum of Modern Art, New York, New York. *Contemporary Sculpture: Selections from the Collection of the Museum of Modern Art*, cat. no. 19, illus. May 18–August 7, 1979.

La Jolla Museum of Contemporary Art, La Jolla, California. *Castelli and His Artists*. April 23–June 6, 1982. Traveled to Aspen Center for Visual Arts, Aspen, Colorado. June 17–August 7, 1982; Leo Castelli Gallery, New York, New York. September 11–October 9, 1982; Portland Center for the Visual Arts, Portland, Oregon. October 22–December 3, 1982; Laguna Gloria Art Museum, Austin, Texas. December 17, 1982–February 13, 1983.

References
Marco Dezzi Bardeschi, "From Johnson to John Soane," *Domus*, no. 631 (September 1982), pp. 44–48, color illus. pp. 44, 48.

215

Untitled 1965

Painted tin
7 × 11 × 8 in. (18 × 28 × 20.5 cm).

Collection
Allan Stone, New York, New York, 1965.

Provenance
Leo Castelli Gallery, New York, New York.

216

Untitled 1965

Painted tin
10 × 8 × 9 in.
(25.5 × 20.5 × 22 cm).

Collection
Irving and Natalie Forman, Chicago, Illinois, 1965.

Provenance
Leo Castelli Gallery, New York, New York.

217

Untitled 1965

Painted and chromium-plated steel
17 × 23 × 16 in.
(43 × 58.5 × 40.5 cm).

Collection
Present location unknown.

Provenance
Leo Castelli Gallery, New York, New York; Norman Diekman, New York, New York.

218

Untitled 1965

Painted tin
9 × 11 × 7 in. (23 × 28 × 18 cm).

Collection
Present location unknown.

Notes
The only evidence of the existence of this sculpture is that it was entered in the Castelli registry in 1965.

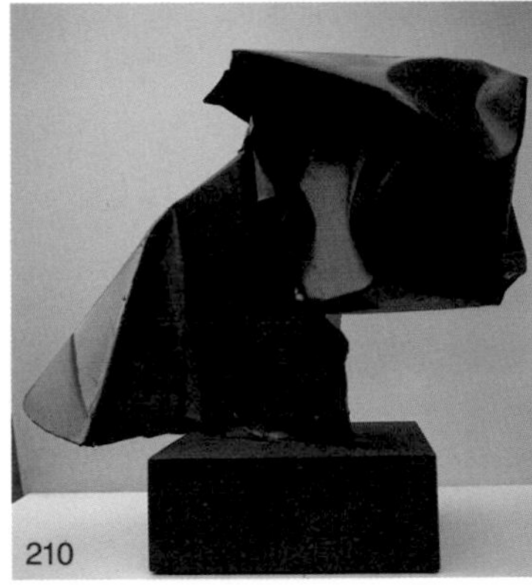
210

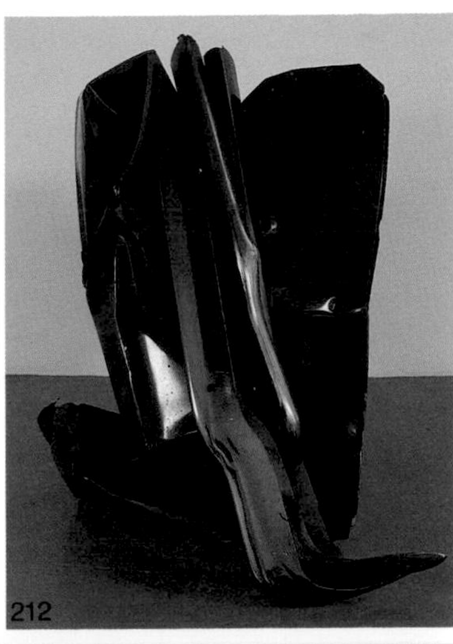
212

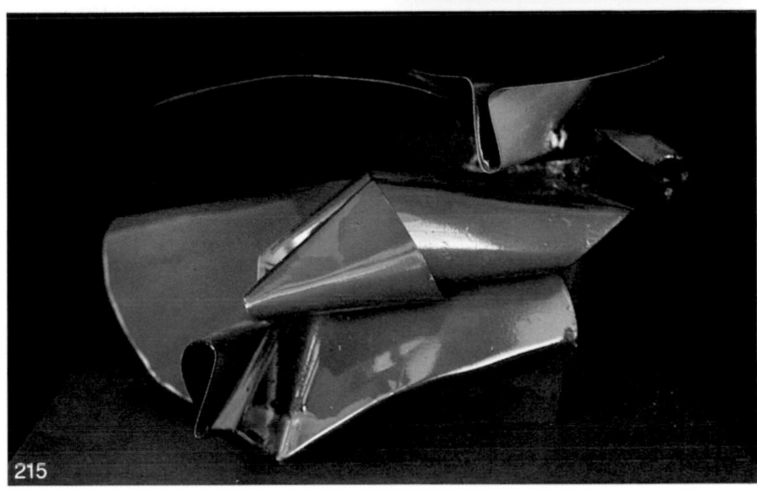
215

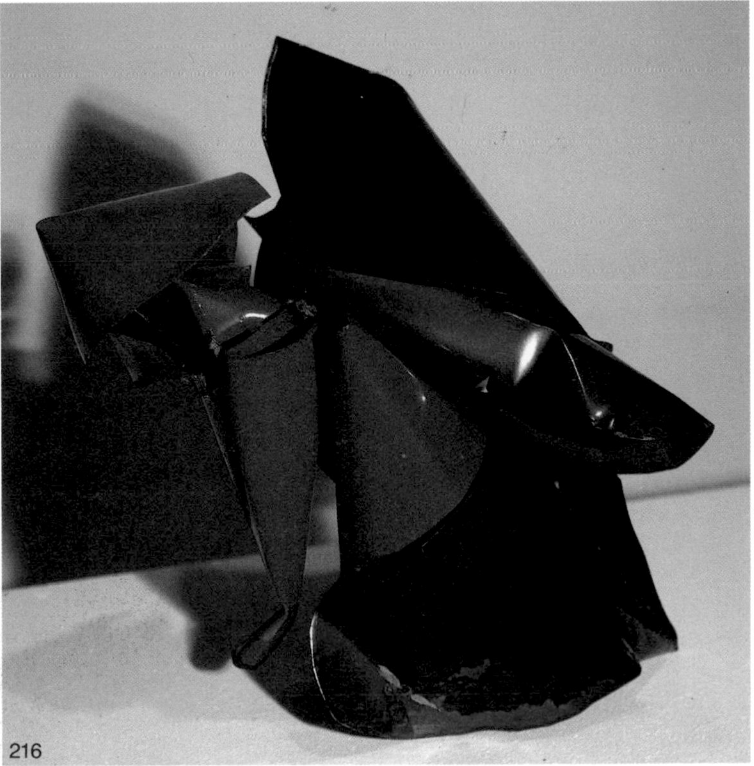
216

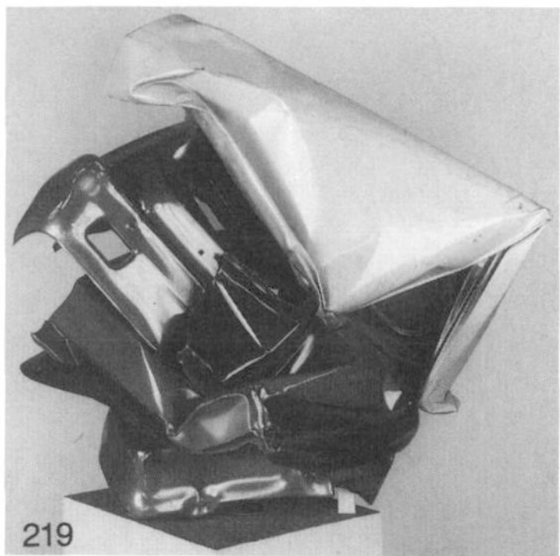
219

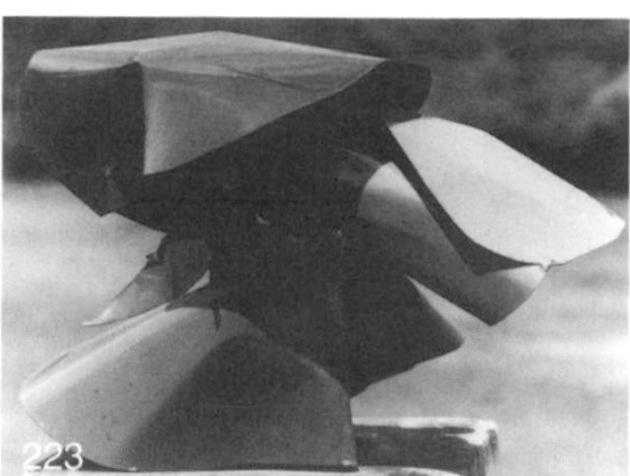
223

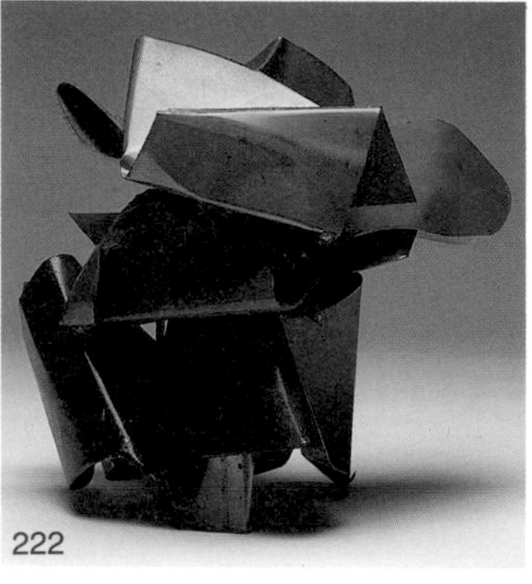
222

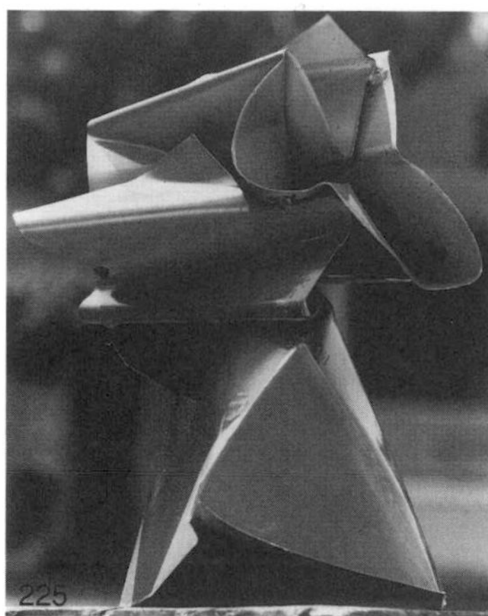
225

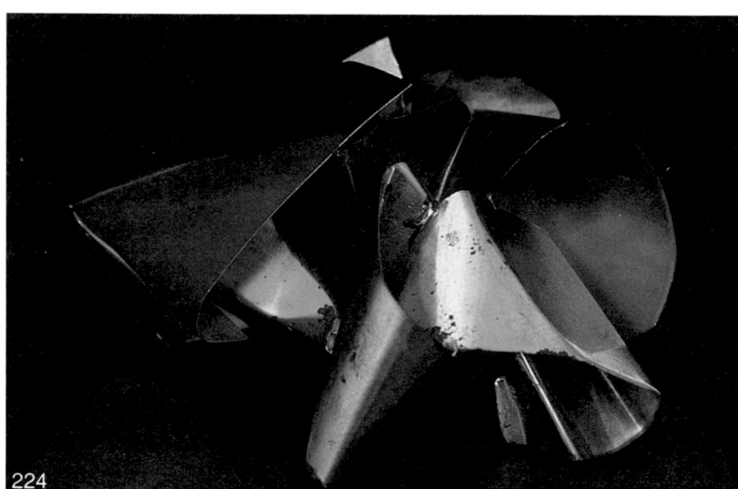
224

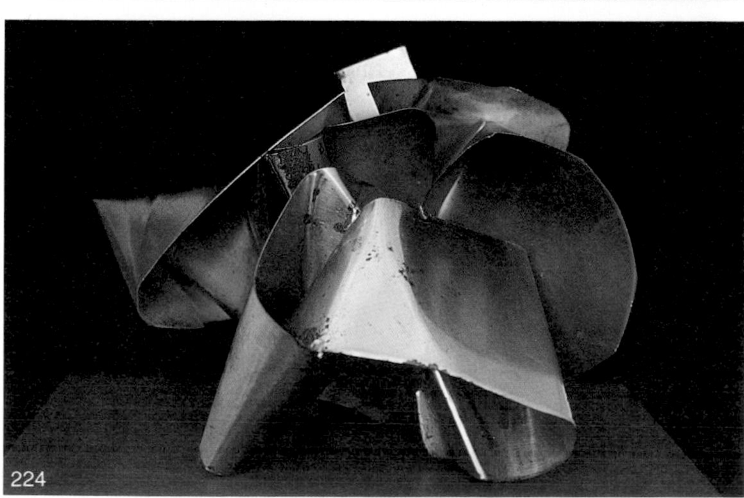
224

219

Untitled 1965
Painted and chromium-plated steel
58 × 57 × 46 in.
(147.5 × 145 × 117 cm).

Collection
Galleria Nazionale d'Arte Moderna e Contemporanea, Rome, 1968.

Provenance
Leo Castelli Gallery, New York, New York.

Exhibitions
The Art Institute of Chicago, Chicago, Illinois. *Sculpture: A Generation of Innovation*, illus. June 23–August 27, 1967.

XXXIV Esposizione biennale internazionale d'arte, Venice. June–October 1968.

220

Untitled 1965
Painted steel
8½ × 11½ × 8 in.
(21.5 × 29 × 20.5 cm).

Collection
Richard L. Ackerman, Jr., Brookline, Massachusetts, 1965.

Provenance
Leo Castelli Gallery, New York, New York.

221

Untitled 1965
Painted tin
8 × 10 × 8½ in.
(20.5 × 25.5 × 21.5 cm).

Collection
Present location unknown.

Provenance
Leo Castelli Gallery, New York, New York; Aaron Copland, Peekskill, New York, 1967.

Exhibitions
Leo Castelli Gallery, New York, New York. *Ten Years*. February 4–26, 1967.

222

Untitled 1965
Painted tin
9½ × 10 × 9 in.
(24 × 25.5 × 23 cm).

Collection
Councilman Joel Wachs, Los Angeles, California, 1976.

Provenance
Leo Castelli Gallery, New York, New York; Mrs. Joseph Pollock, Beverly Hills, California, 1965; Margo Leavin Gallery, Los Angeles, California, 1976.

223

Untitled 1965
Painted tin
9 × 15 × 8 in. (23 × 38 × 20 cm).

Collection
Private collection, Bethesda, Maryland, 1971.

Provenance
Leo Castelli Gallery, New York, New York; Allan Stone, New York, New York.

224

Untitled 1965
Painted tin
9½ × 9½ × 7 in.
(24 × 24 × 18 cm).

Collection
Private collection, Bethesda, Maryland, 1971.

Provenance
Leo Castelli Gallery, New York, New York; Allan Stone, New York, New York.

225

Untitled 1965
Painted tin
7½ × 11 × 7 in.
(19 × 28 × 17.5 cm).

Collection
Private collection, Bethesda, Maryland, 1971.

Provenance
Leo Castelli Gallery, New York, New York; Allan Stone, New York, New York.

226

Untitled c. 1965
Painted steel
33 × 32 × 28 in.
(84 × 81.5 × 71 cm).

Collection
Dorothy and Roy Lichtenstein, Southampton, New York.

Seven sculptures (cat. nos. 227–233) were made in Santa Fe, New Mexico, in 1966, based on a series of french-curve drawings. The sculptures are very unusual in Chamberlain's oeuvre and are the only instance in which he began an idea for sculptures with drawings. He translated the drawings into three-dimensional objects by creating forms of steel rod and wire mesh, which were then coated with fiber glass and painted with acrylic lacquer. In some instances, the lacquer was sanded down in order to reveal the surface underneath.

The sculptures are regarded by Chamberlain as an experimental process, rather than as a series of finished works. Two sculptures from this period, nos. 227 and 229, are known to be extant.

227

Cat-Bird Seat 1966

Painted and flocked fiber glass with brass on steel structure
41 × 60 × 35 in.
(104 × 152.5 × 89 cm).

Collection
Virginia Dwan, New York, New York.

Exhibitions
Dwan Gallery, Los Angeles, California. *Group Exhibition*. May 10–28, 1966.

228

Fluff 1966

Painted and flocked fiber glass on steel structure
22 × 31 × 33 in.
(56 × 78.5 × 84 cm).

Collection
Present location unknown.

229

Nanny 1966

Painted and flocked fiber glass with chromium-plated steel on steel structure
44 × 48 × 56 in.
(112 × 122 × 142 cm).

Collection
Virginia Dwan, New York, New York.

Exhibitions
Dwan Gallery, Los Angeles, California. *Group Exhibition*. May 10–28, 1966.

230

Nix-Nox 1966

Painted fiber glass on steel structure
41 × 31 × 44 in.
(104 × 78.5 × 112 cm).

Collection
Present location unknown.

Provenance
William Katz, New York, New York; Leo Castelli Gallery, New York, New York.

231

No-Nix-Nox 1966

Painted and flocked fiber glass with chromium-plated steel on steel structure
30 × 40 × 42½ in.
(76 × 101.5 × 108 cm).

Collection
Present location unknown.

232

No-Nix-Nox-Now 1966

Painted and flocked fiber glass on steel structure
31 × 34 × 32 in.
(78.5 × 86.5 × 81 cm).

Collection
Present location unknown.

233

Stella-By-Starlite 1966

Painted and flocked fiber glass on steel structure
23 × 15½ × 17 in.
(58.5 × 39.5 × 43 cm).

Collection
Present location unknown.

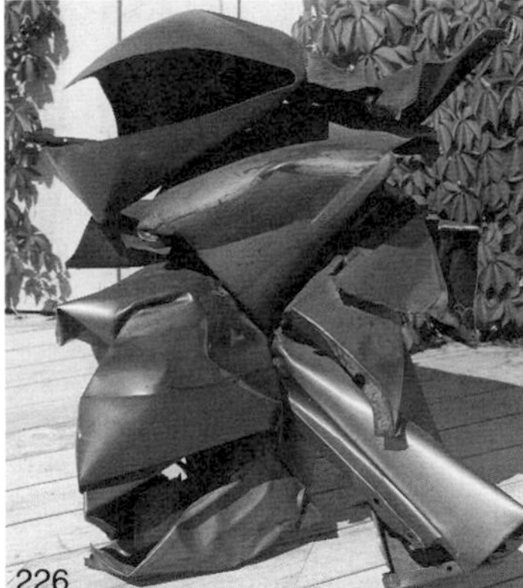
226

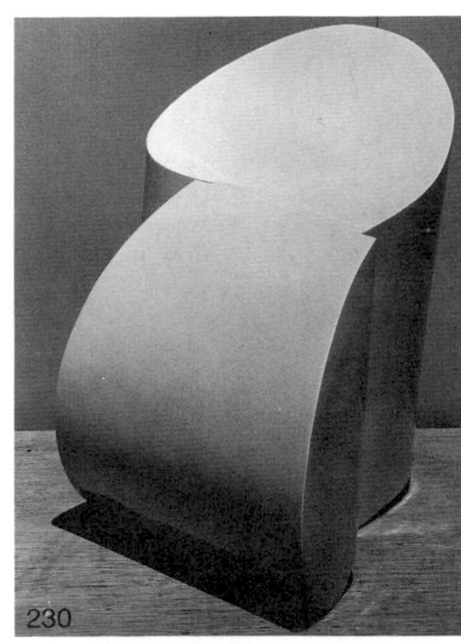
230

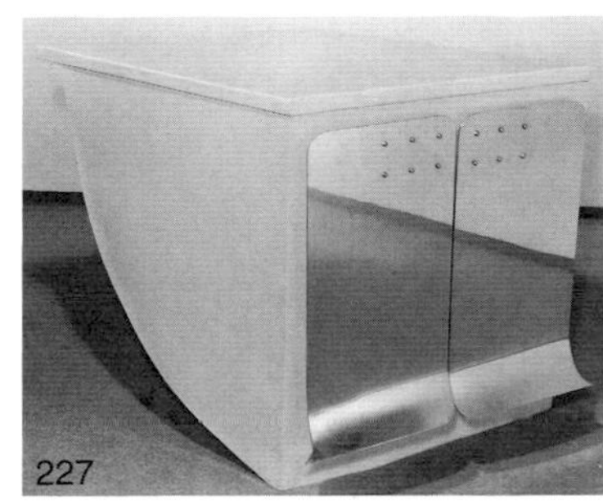
227

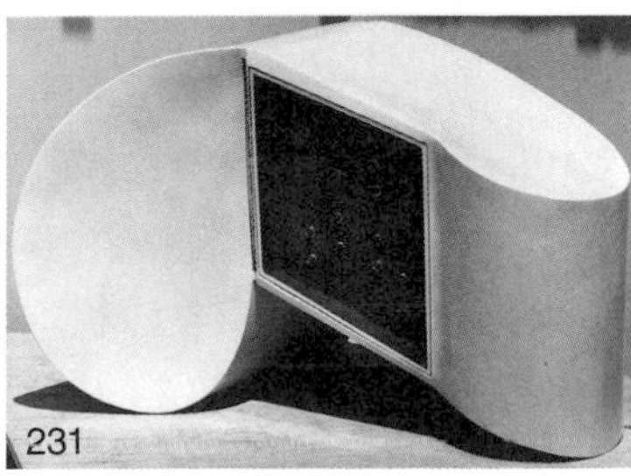
231

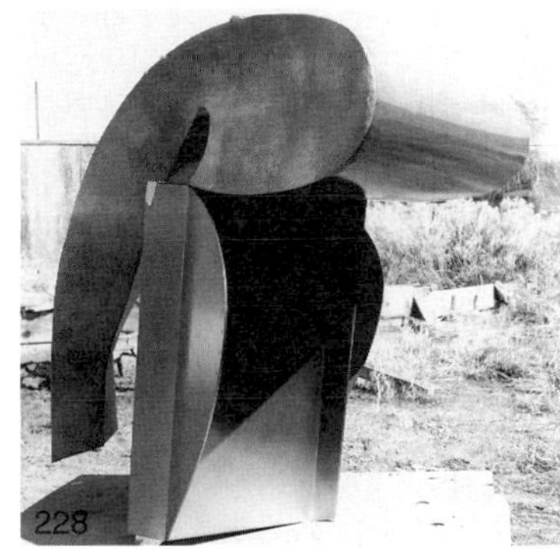
228

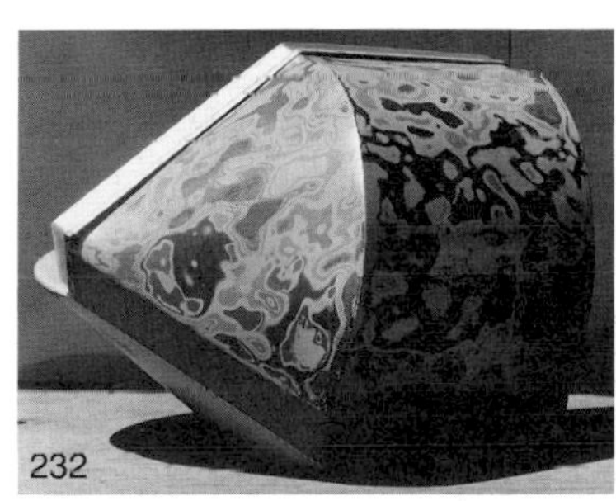
232

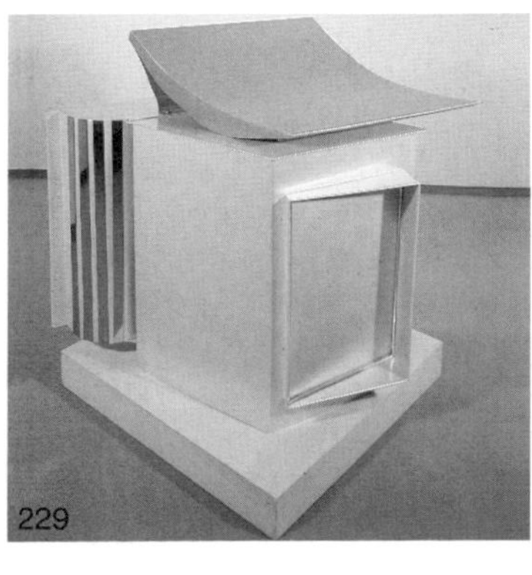
229

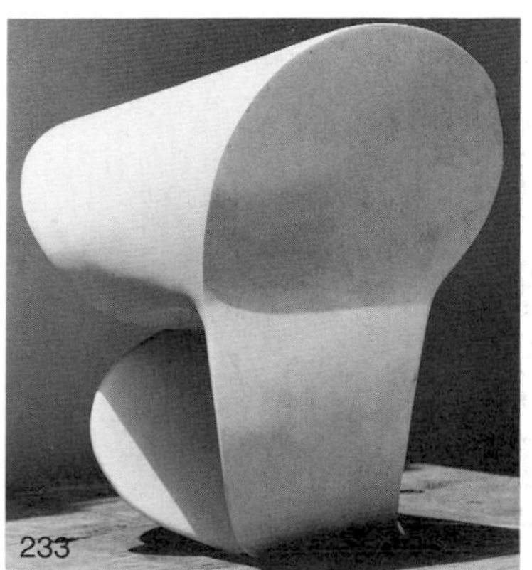
233

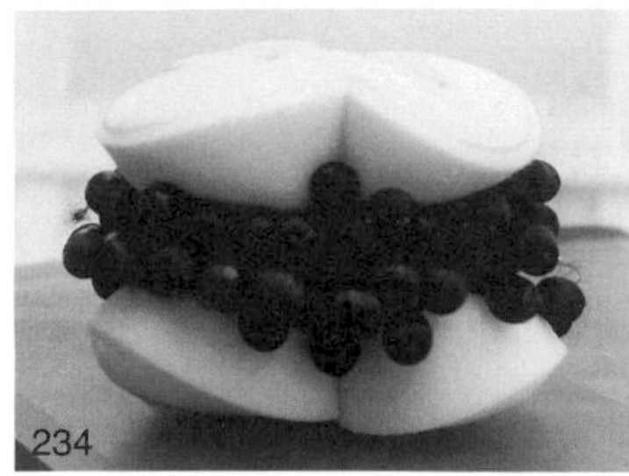
234

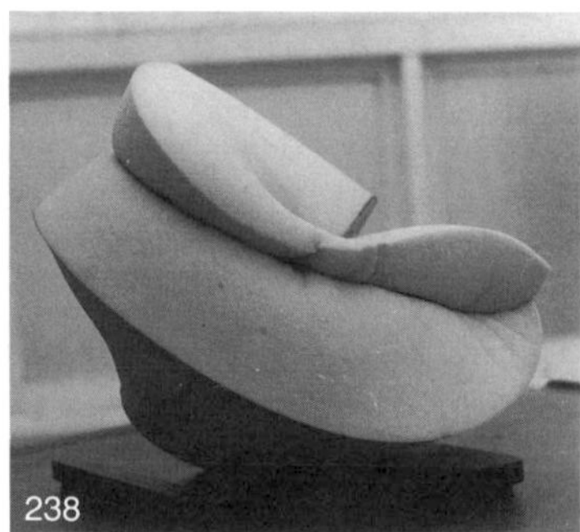
238

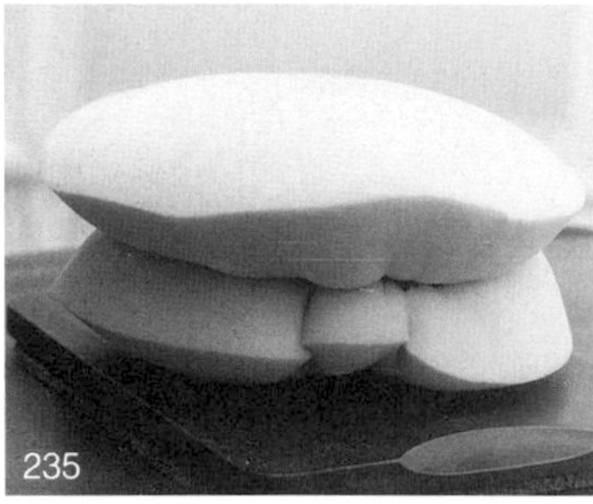
235

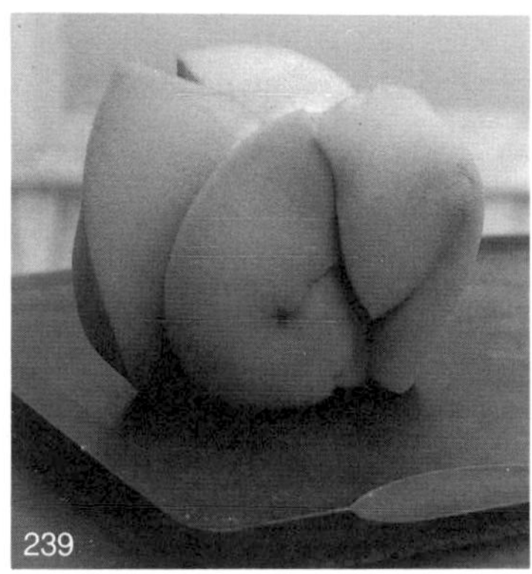
239

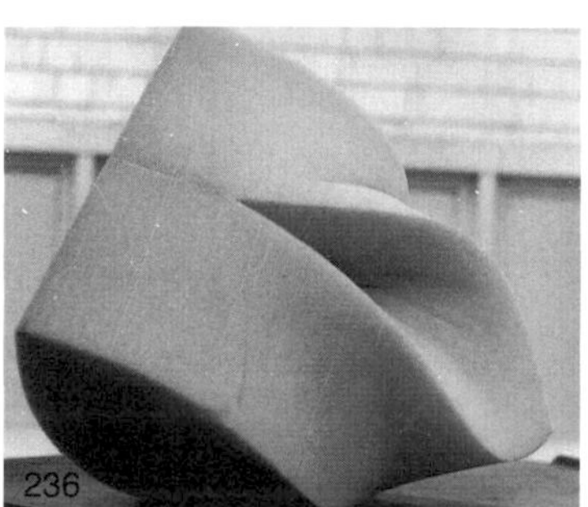
236

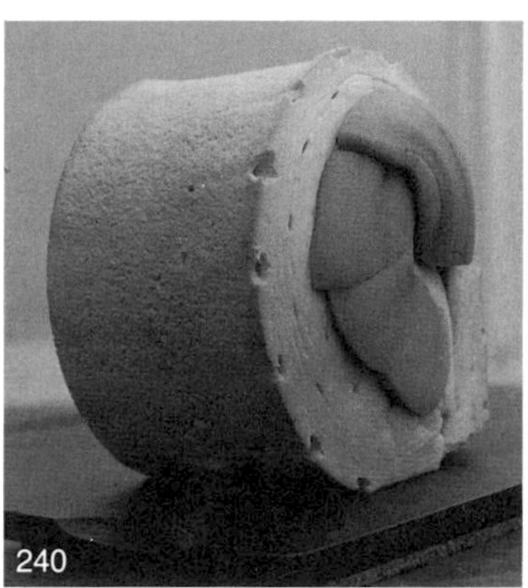
240

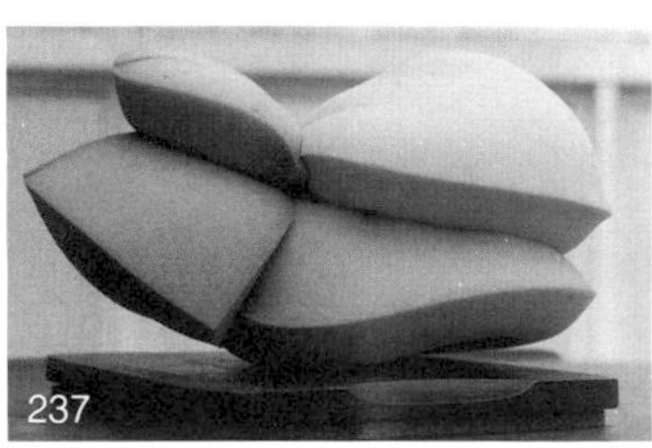
237

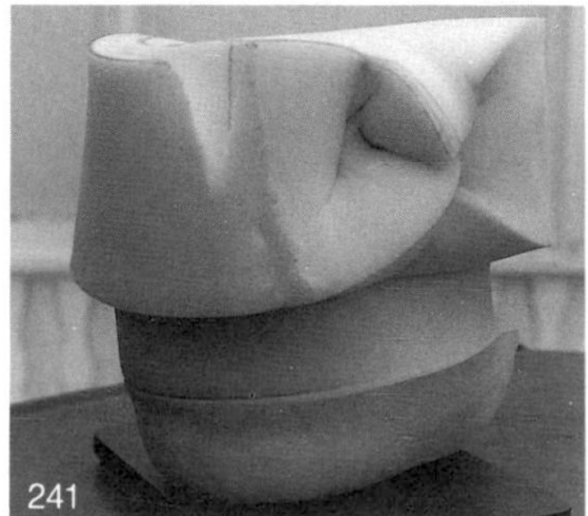
241

In 1966, in Malibu, California, Chamberlain began what was to become a major interest in working with urethane foam. His first urethane sculptures (cat. nos. 234–243) were a group of untitled sketches, made of squeezed sponge less than six inches in each dimension. The development led to a group of larger squeezed and tied sculptures of urethane foam, some of which Chamberlain titled after regions in China and some of which which were exhibited at the Dwan Gallery in 1966.

Because of the vulnerability of the material to light and air, the sculptures have had a tendency to disintegrate if not properly maintained. For this reason, reproductions of the foam works appear in the catalogue raisonné only if the sculpture was photographed in its original state or in a well-preserved state.

234

Untitled 1966

Urethane foam, cloth, and wood
4 × 7½ × 6½ in.
(10 × 19 × 16.5 cm).

Collection

Private collection, New York, New York, 1984; acquired directly from the artist.

Notes

This unique sculpture is tied with black drapery trim.

235

Untitled 1966

Urethane foam and cord
Dimensions unknown.

Notes

The sculpture was identified in 1984 as having been destroyed.

236

Untitled 1966

Urethane foam and cord
Dimensions unknown.

Collection

Present location unknown.

237

Untitled 1966

Urethane foam and cord
Dimensions unknown.

Collection

Present location unknown.

238

Untitled 1966

Urethane foam and cord
Dimensions unknown.

Collection

Present location unknown.

239

Untitled 1966

Urethane foam and cord
Dimensions unknown.

Collection

Present location unknown.

240

Untitled 1966

Urethane foam and cord
Dimensions unknown.

Collection

Present location unknown.

241

Untitled 1966

Urethane foam and cord
Dimensions unknown.

Collection

Present location unknown.

242

Untitled 1966

Urethane foam and cord
Dimensions unknown.

Collection

Present location unknown.

243

Untitled 1966

Urethane foam and cord
8 × 4½ × 4 in. (20 × 11 × 10 cm).

Collection

Annina Nosei, New York, New York, 1966.

Provenance

Dwan Gallery, Los Angeles, California.

244

Changsha 1966

Urethane foam and cord
18 × 32 × 27 in.
(45.5 × 81.5 × 68.5 cm).

Collection

Present location unknown.

Provenance

Michael Ruskin, New York, New York.

Exhibitions

Dwan Gallery, Los Angeles, California. *John Chamberlain.* November 29, 1966–January 7, 1967.

Notes

The sculpture is also known as *No. 45.*

245

Chefoo 1966
Urethane foam
15½ × 29½ × 24 in.
(39 × 75 × 61 cm).

Collection
Present location unknown.

Exhibitions
Dwan Gallery, Los Angeles, California. *John Chamberlain*. November 29, 1966–January 7, 1967.

Notes
The sculpture is also known as *No. 56*.

246

Chingkanshan 1966
Urethane foam and cord
31½ × 84 × 72 in.
(80 × 213.5 × 183 cm).

Collection
Present location unknown.

Exhibitions
Dwan Gallery, Los Angeles, California. *John Chamberlain*. November 29, 1966–January 7, 1967.

References
Philip Leider, "A New Medium for John Chamberlain," *Artforum*, vol. 5, no. 6 (February 1967), illus. p. 49.

Notes
The sculpture is also known as *No. 59*.
It is very likely that *Chingkanshan* was the sculpture that Chamberlain sliced in half in 1967 in order to create his first couch. (See *Judd's Couch*, 1967, cat. appendix, no. I.)

247

Fukien 1966
Urethane foam and cord
12 × 19 × 15½ in.
(30.5 × 48 × 39.5 cm).

Collection
Present location unknown.

Exhibitions
Dwan Gallery, Los Angeles, California. *John Chamberlain*. November 29, 1966–January 7, 1967.

Notes
The sculpture is also known as *No. 27*.

248

I-Chiang 1966
Urethane foam and cord
15½ × 25 × 19 in.
(39 × 63.5 × 48 cm).

Collection
Collection of the artist, Sarasota, Florida.

Exhibitions
Leo Castelli Gallery, New York, New York. *John Chamberlain*. April 17–May 8, 1971.

References
Nicolas Calas and Elena Calas, *Icons and Images of the Sixties* (New York: Dutton, 1971), illus. p. 52.

249

Kian 1966
Urethane foam and cord
13½ × 24 × 21 in.
(34 × 61 × 53.5 cm).

Collection
Present location unknown.

Exhibitions
Dwan Gallery, Los Angeles, California. *John Chamberlain*. November 29, 1966–January 7, 1967.

Notes
The sculpture is also known as *No. 30*.

250

Kiangsi 1966
Urethane foam and cord
14 × 27 × 26½ in.
(35.5 × 68.5 × 67.5 cm).

Collection
Present location unknown.

Exhibitions
Dwan Gallery, Los Angeles, California. *John Chamberlain*. November 29, 1966–January 7, 1967.

Notes
The sculpture is also known as *No. 42*.

251

Liu Ting 1966
Urethane foam and cord
17 × 22 × 24½ in.
(43 × 56 × 62 cm).

Collection
Present location unknown.

Exhibitions
Dwan Gallery, Los Angeles, California. *John Chamberlain*. November 29, 1966–January 7, 1967.

Notes
The sculpture is also known as *No. 50*.

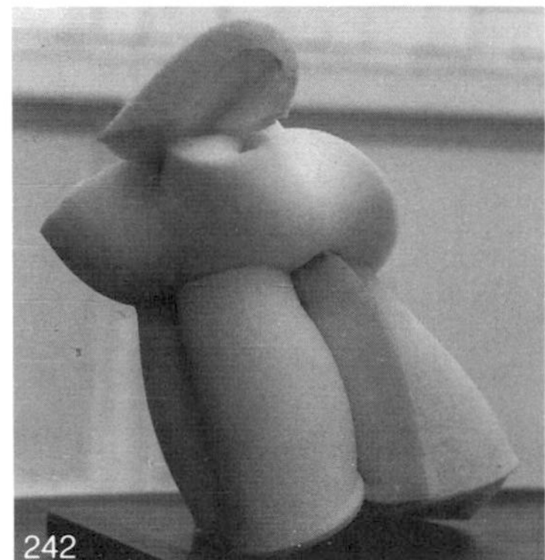
242

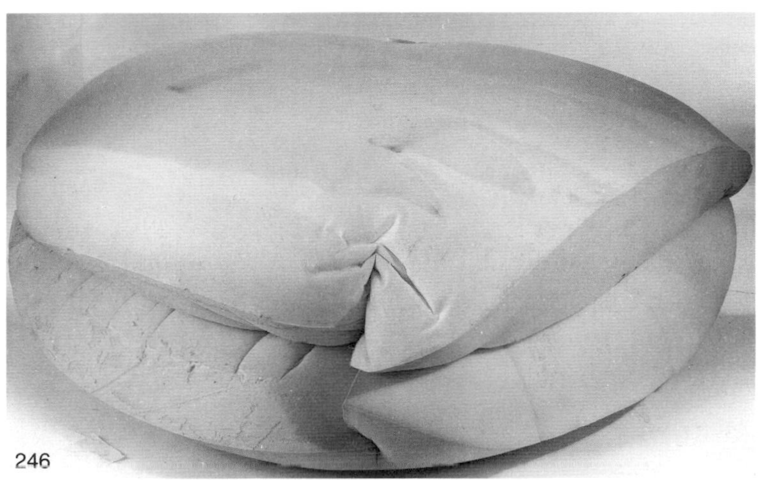
246

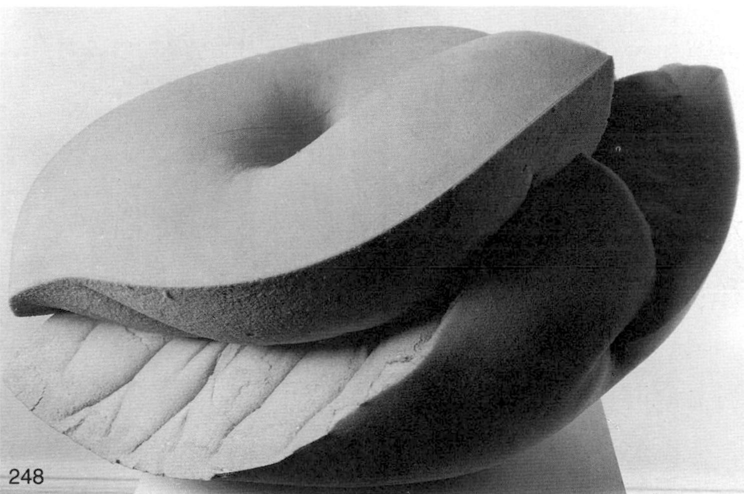
248

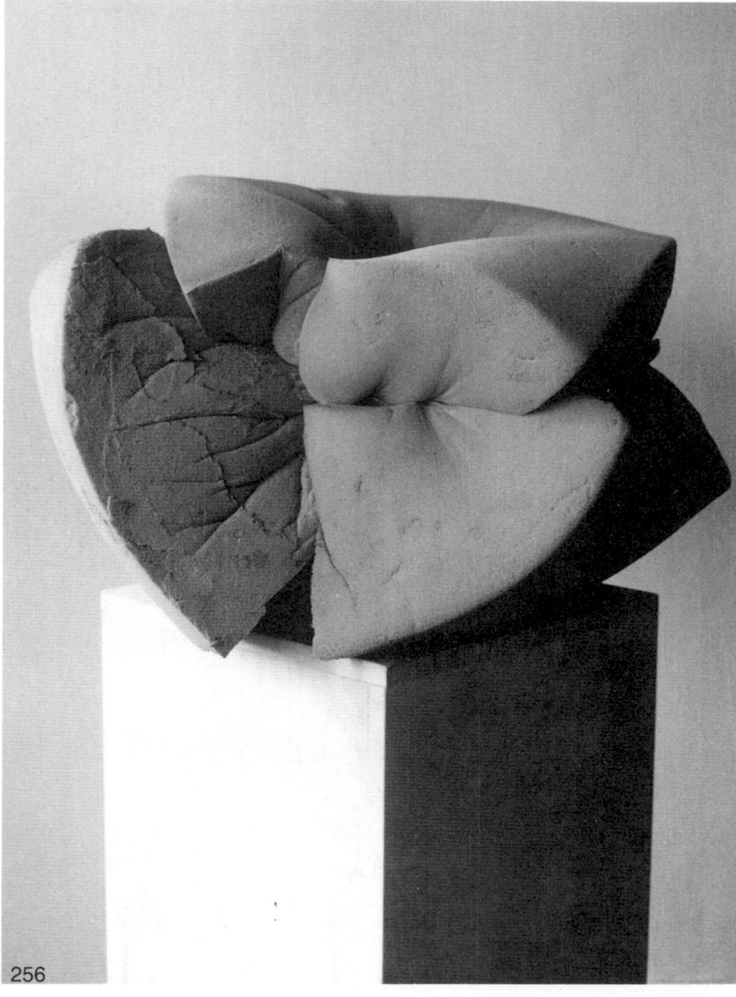

256

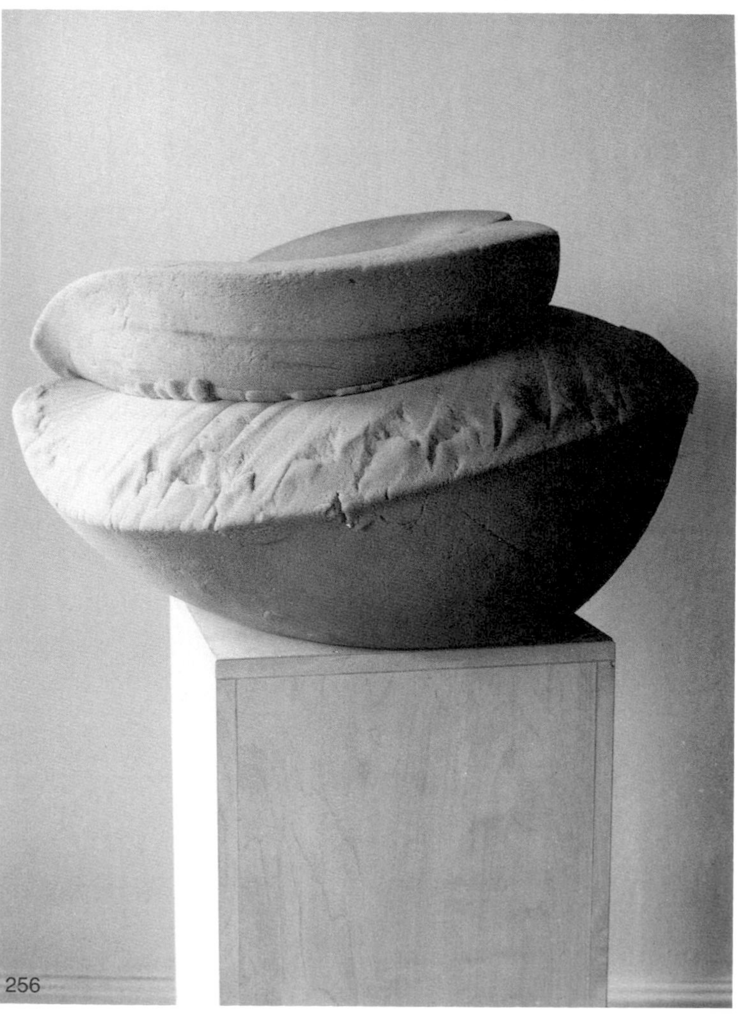

256

252

Lo An 1966

Urethane foam and cord
17 × 26 × 29 in.
(43 × 66 × 73.5 cm).

Collection

Richard Bellamy, New York, New York, 1968.

Exhibitions

Dwan Gallery, Los Angeles, California *John Chamberlain*. November 29, 1966–January 7, 1967.

The Solomon R. Guggenheim Museum, New York, New York. *John Chamberlain: A Retrospective Exhibition*, cat. no. 73, listed as "Untitled *(No. 33)*." December 23, 1971–February 20, 1972.

Notes

The sculpture is signed by the artist on the underside: *#33, Chamberlain '66*. A second sculpture was given the same title; see cat. no. 253.

253

Lo An 1966

Urethane foam and cord
12 × 18 × 18 in.
(30.5 × 45.5 × 45.5 cm).

Collection

Jerald Ordover, New York, New York, 1966; acquired directly from the artist.

Notes

The sculpture is signed by the artist on the underside: *#33, Chamberlain 1966*. A second sculpture was given the same title; see cat. no. 252.

254

Lolos 1966

Urethane foam and cord
15 × 26 × 28½ in.
(38 × 66 × 72 cm).

Collection

Present location unknown.

Exhibitions

Dwan Gallery, Los Angeles, California. *John Chamberlain*. November 29, 1966–January 7, 1967.

Notes

The sculpture is also known as *No. 52*.

255

Lo Man 1966

Urethane foam and cord
32 × 66 × 53½ in.
(81 × 167.5 × 136 cm).

Collection

Present location unknown.

Exhibitions

Dwan Gallery, Los Angeles, California. *John Chamberlain*. November 29, 1966–January 7, 1967.

References

Philip Leider, "A New Medium for John Chamberlain," *Artforum*, vol. 5, no. 6 (February 1967), illus. p. 49.

Notes

The sculpture is also known as *No. 58*.

256

Ma An-Shan 1966

Urethane foam and cord
15 × 24½ × 23 in.
(38 × 62 × 58 cm).

Collection

Gachnang Collections, Bern, 1979.

Provenance

Galerie Quatre Mouvement, Paris; Michael Werner, Cologne.

Exhibitions

Dwan Gallery, Los Angeles, California. *John Chamberlain*. November 29, 1966–January 7, 1967.

References

Diane Waldman, *John Chamberlain: A Retrospective Exhibition* (New York: The Solomon R. Guggenheim Foundation, 1971), illus. p. 13.

Notes

The sculpture is also known as *No. 51*. It is signed and dated by the artist on the underside: *Chamberlain '66 51*.

257

Mannabend Ra 1966

Urethane foam and cord
27½ × 52 × 48 in.
(70 × 132 × 122 cm).

Collection

The Solomon R. Guggenheim Museum, New York, New York, 1975.

Provenance

Dwan Gallery, Los Angeles, California; Leo Castelli Gallery, New York, New York.

Exhibitions

Dwan Gallery, Los Angeles, California. *John Chamberlain*. November 29, 1966–January 7, 1967.

The Solomon R. Guggenheim Museum, New York, New York. *Recent Acquisitions*. February 4–27, 1977.

References

Philip Leider, "A New Medium for John Chamberlain," *Artforum*, vol. 5, no. 6 (February 1967), illus. pp. 48–49.

Phyllis Tuchman, "An Interview with John Chamberlain," *Artforum*, vol. 10, no. 6 (February 1972), illus. p. 41.

Notes

The sculpture is also known as *No. 57*.

258

Nanchang 1966

Urethane foam and cord
17½ × 38 × 30 in.
(44.5 × 96.5 × 76 cm).

Collection

Present location unknown.

Provenance

Richard Carpenter, Los Angeles, 1967.

Exhibitions

Dwan Gallery, Los Angeles, California. *John Chamberlain*. November 29, 1966–January 7, 1967.

Notes

The sculpture is also known as *No. 43*.

259

Nanfeng 1966

Urethane foam and cord
12 × 24½ × 21½ in.
(30.5 × 62 × 54.5 cm).

Collection

Richard Artschwager, Charlotteville, New York, 1972; acquired directly from the artist.

Exhibitions

Dwan Gallery, Los Angeles, California. *John Chamberlain*. November 29, 1966–January 7, 1967.

The Solomon R. Guggenheim Museum, New York, New York. *John Chamberlain: A Retrospective Exhibition*, cat. no. 74, listed as "Untitled *(No. 34)*." December 23, 1971–February 20, 1972.

Notes

The sculpture is also known as *No. 34*. It is signed, dated, and numbered on the underside.

260

Ning Tu 1966

Urethane foam
13½ × 21 × 18 in.
(34 × 53.5 × 45.5 cm).

Collection

Present location unknown.

Notes

The sculpture is also known as *No. 28*.

261

Pa An 1966

Urethane foam and cord
16 × 25 × 24 in.
(40.5 × 63.5 × 61 cm).

Collection

Present location unknown.

Notes

The sculpture is also known as *No. 46*.

262

Pao An 1966

Urethane foam and cord
14½ × 28½ × 27½ in.
(37 × 72.5 × 70 cm).

Collection

Present location unknown.

Notes

The sculpture is also known as *No. 49*.

263

Shensi 1966

Urethane foam and cord
15 × 22½ × 23 in.
(38 × 57 × 58.5 cm).

Collection

Present location unknown.

References

Philip Leider, "A New Medium for John Chamberlain," *Artforum*, vol. 5, no. 6 (February 1967), illus. p. 49.

Notes

The sculpture is also known as *No. 53*.

264

Sian 1966

Urethane foam and cord
17 × 32½ × 28 in.
(43 × 82.5 × 71 cm).

Collection

Present location unknown.

Exhibitions

Dwan Gallery, Los Angeles, California. *John Chamberlain*. November 29, 1966–January 7, 1967.

Notes

The sculpture is also known as *No. 54*.

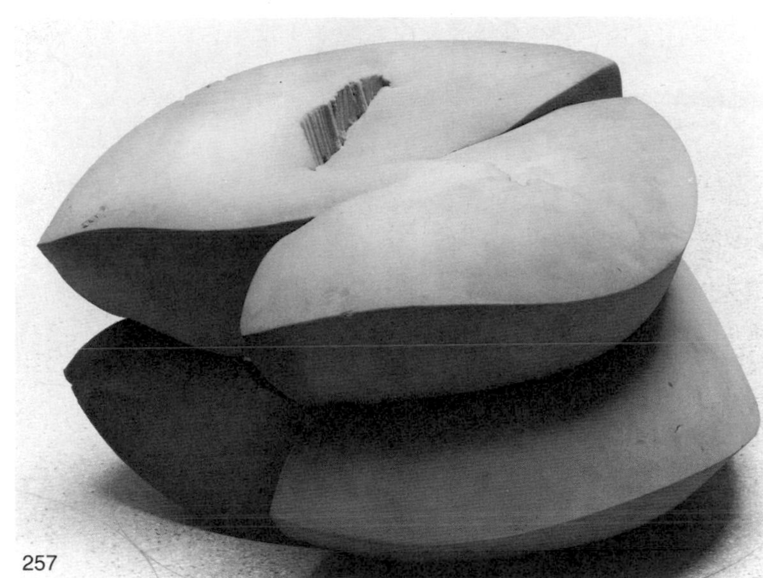

257

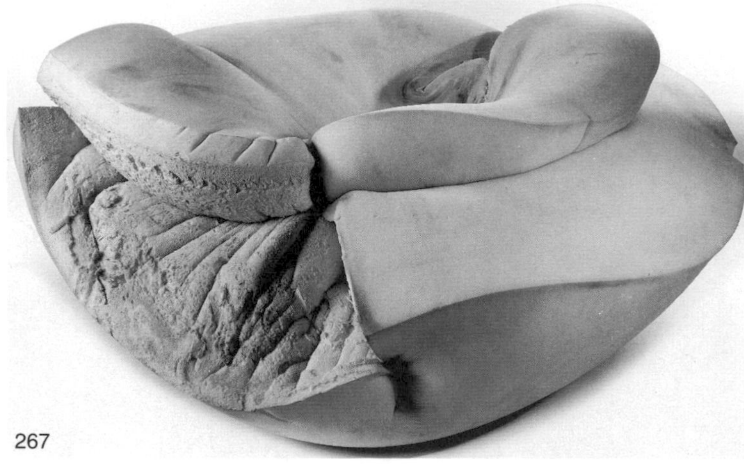
267

265

Sining 1966
Urethane foam and cord
26 × 31 × 31 in.
(66 × 78.5 × 78.5 cm).

Collection
Present location unknown.

Exhibitions
Dwan Gallery, Los Angeles, California. *John Chamberlain*. November 29, 1966–January 7, 1967.

Notes
The sculpture is also known as *No. 47*.

266

Szechuan 1966
Urethane foam and cord
14 × 24 × 26 in.
(35.5 × 61 × 66 cm).

Collection
Robbin Cullinen, New York, New York; acquired directly from the artist.

Exhibitions
Dwan Gallery, Los Angeles, California. *John Chamberlain*. November 29, 1966–January 7, 1967

Notes
The sculpture is also known as *No. 38*.

267

Taiping 1966
Urethane foam and cord
77 × 73 × 33 in.
(195.5 × 185.5 × 84 cm).

Collection
Present location unknown.

Exhibitions
Dwan Gallery, Los Angeles, California. *John Chamberlain*. November 29, 1966–January 7, 1967.

Notes
The sculpture is also known as *No. 60*.

268

Ta Tung 1966
Urethane foam and cord
42 × 50 × 50 in.
(106.5 × 127 × 127 cm).

Collection
Present location unknown.

Exhibitions
The Los Angeles County Museum of Art, Los Angeles, California. *American Sculpture of the Sixties*, cat. no. 24. April 28–June 25, 1967. Traveled to Philadelphia Museum of Art, Philadelphia, Pennsylvania. September 15–November 5, 1967.

Dwan Gallery, Los Angeles, California. *John Chamberlain*. November 29, 1966–January 7, 1967.

269

Toupi 1966
Urethane foam and cord
13 × 21 × 20 in.
(33 × 53.5 × 51 cm).

Collection
Present location unknown.

Exhibitions
Dwan Gallery, Los Angeles, California. *John Chamberlain*. November 29, 1966–January 7, 1967.

Notes
The sculpture is also known as *No. 29*.

270

Tungku 1966
Urethane foam and cord
15 × 26 × 22 in.
(38 × 66 × 56 cm).

Collection
Present location unknown.

Exhibitions
Dwan Gallery, Los Angeles, California. *John Chamberlain*. November 29, 1966–January 7, 1967.

Notes
The sculpture is also known as *No. 36*.

271

Whampoa 1966
Urethane foam and cord
19½ × 32½ × 32 in.
(49.5 × 82.5 × 81 cm).

Collection
Present location unknown.

Exhibitions
Dwan Gallery, Los Angeles, California. *John Chamberlain*. November 29, 1966–January 7, 1967.

Notes
The sculpture is also known as *No. 55*.

272

Yin Yang 1966
Urethane foam and cord
16 × 22 × 22 in.
(40.5 × 56 × 56 cm).

Collection
Present location unknown.

Provenance
Dwan Gallery, Los Angeles, California; Noah Goldowsky and Richard Bellamy, New York, New York.

Exhibitions
Dwan Gallery, Los Angeles, California. *John Chamberlain*. November 29, 1966–January 7, 1967.

The Solomon R. Guggenheim Museum, New York, New York. *John Chamberlain: A Retrospective Exhibition*, cat. no. 72, listed as "Untitled *(No. 26)*." December 23, 1971–February 20, 1972.

Notes
The sculpture is also known as *No. 26*.

273

Yungfeng 1966
Urethane foam and cord
13½ × 23 × 25 in.
(34 × 58.5 × 63.5 cm).

Collection
Present location unknown.

Exhibitions
Dwan Gallery, Los Angeles, California. *John Chamberlain*. November 29, 1966–January 7, 1967.

Notes
The sculpture is also known as *No. 37*.

274

Yunnan 1966
Urethane foam and cord
18½ × 26 × 26 in.
(47 × 66 × 66 cm).

Collection
Present location unknown.

Exhibitions
Dwan Gallery, Los Angeles, California. *John Chamberlain*. November 29, 1966–January 7, 1967.

Notes
The sculpture is also known as *No. 44*.

275

Yutu 1966
Urethane foam and cord
14 × 24 × 21½ in.
(35.5 × 61 × 54.5 cm).

Collection
Present location unknown.

Exhibitions
Dwan Gallery, Los Angeles, California. *John Chamberlain*. November 29, 1966–January 7, 1967.

Notes
The sculpture is also known as *No. 35*.

276

Untitled 1966
Urethane foam and cord
10 × 17 × 14 in.
(25.5 × 43 × 35.5 cm).

Collection
Present location unknown.

Exhibitions
Pomona College Art Department, Claremont, California. March–April 1967.

Notes
The sculpture is also known as *No. 63*.

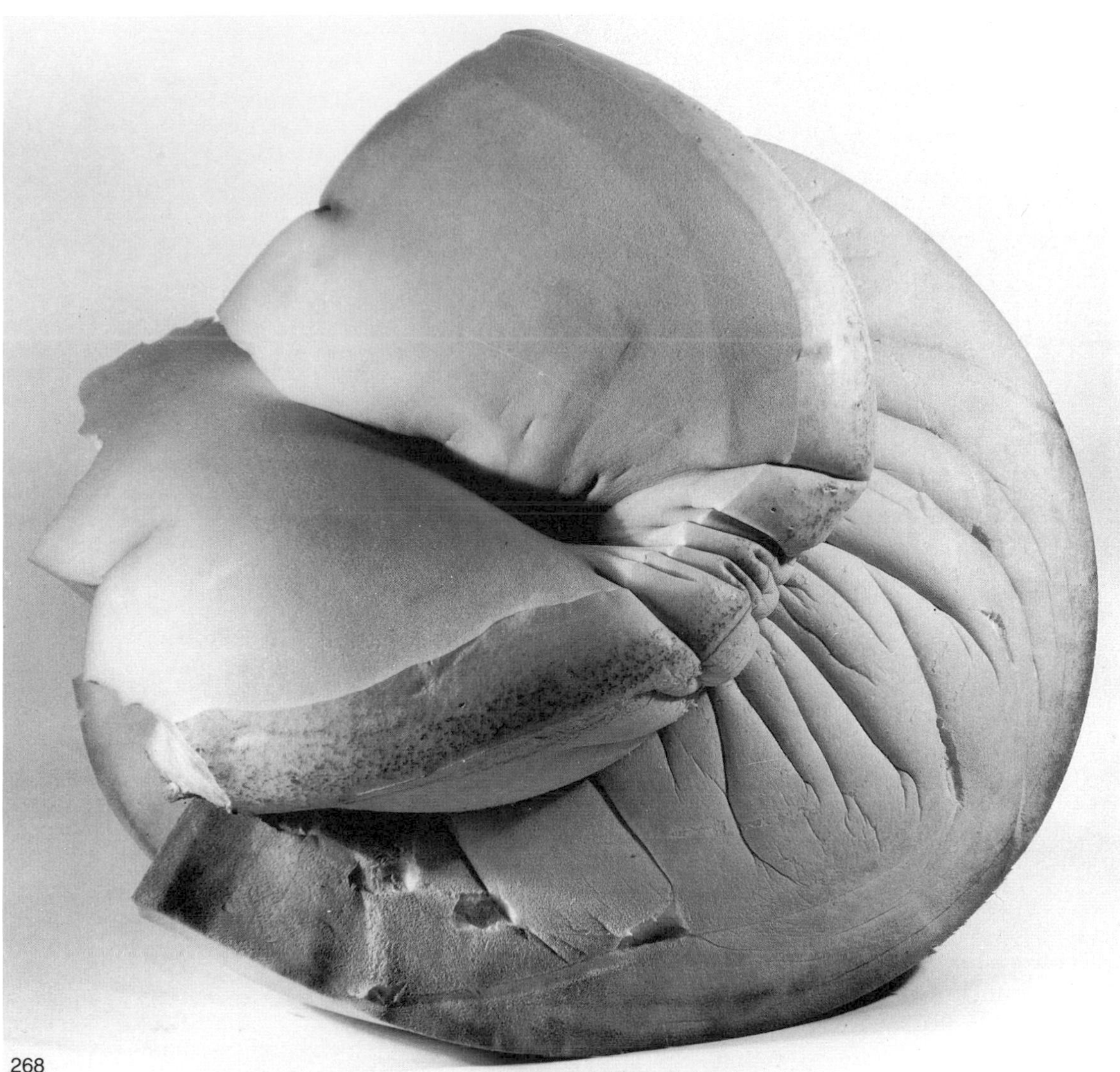

268

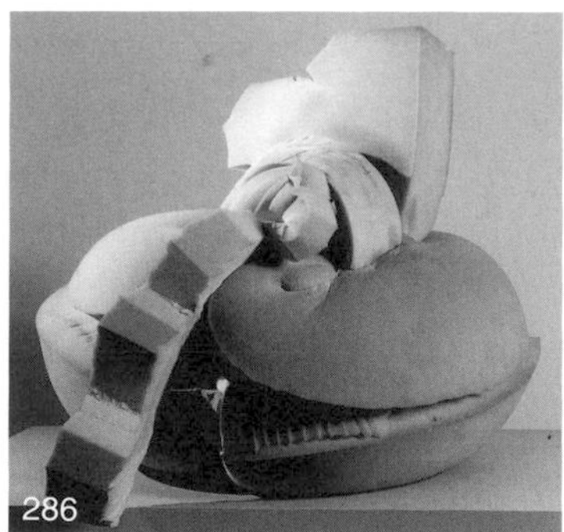
286

277

Untitled 1966
Urethane foam and cord
8 × 16 × 14½ in.
(20.5 × 40.5 × 37 cm).

Collection
Present location unknown.

Provenance
Dwan Gallery, Los Angeles, California, 1966; Tony Gould, Los Angeles, California.

Exhibitions
Dwan Gallery, Los Angeles, California. *John Chamberlain*. November 29, 1966–January 7, 1967.

Notes
The sculpture is also known as *No. 25*. It is signed on a label on the underside: *#25 Chamberlain '66*.

278

Ju 1966
Urethane foam and cord
C. 12 × 12 in. (30.5 × 30.5 cm).

Collection
Mr. and Mrs. Robert Creeley, Buffalo, New York; acquired directly from the artist.

Notes
Ju may be one of the previously unidentified sculptures from the Dwan Gallery exhibition. It was probably titled by the artist at a later date.

279

Untitled 1966
Painted urethane foam
9½ × 11 × 5½ in.
(24 × 28 × 14 cm).

Collection
Mr. and Mrs. Miles Q. Fiterman, Minneapolis, Minnesota.

Provenance
John C. Stoller, Minneapolis, Minnesota.

Notes
The sculpture is signed and dated on the underside.

280

Untitled 1966
Urethane foam and cord
7½ × 14 × 12½ in.
(19 × 35.5 × 32 cm).

Collection
Museum of Modern Art, New York, New York, 1973; gift of Mr. and Mrs. Richard L. Selle.

Provenance
Richard Bellamy, New York, New York; Mr. and Mrs. Richard L. Selle, New York, New York.

Notes
The sculpture is signed and dated on the underside.

281

Untitled 1966
Urethane foam
5 × 9½ × 9½ in.
(12.5 × 24 × 24 cm).

Collection
Florence and Brooks Barron, Detroit, Michigan, 1966; acquired directly from the artist.

282

Untitled 1966
Urethane foam and cord
30 × 34 × 30 in.
(76 × 86.5 × 76 cm).

Collection
Florence and Brooks Barron, Detroit, Michigan, 1966; acquired directly from the artist.

283

Untitled 1966
Urethane foam and cord
6½ × 10 × 11 in.
(16.5 × 25.5 × 28 cm).

Collection
Joel Oppenheimer, New York, New York, 1966; acquired directly from the artist.

Notes
The sculpture is signed on the underside: *#8 Chamberlain '66*.

284

Untitled 1966
Urethane foam
6 × 9 × 9 in. (15 × 23 × 23 cm).

Collection
Dorothy and Herbert Vogel, New York, New York.

Provenance
A. Aladar Marberger, New York, New York, 1974.

Exhibitions
Sotheby Parke-Bernet, Inc., New York, New York. *Important Postwar and Contemporary Art*, cat. no. 651. May 5, 1974.

285

Untitled 1966
Urethane foam and cord
15 × 27 × 27 in.
(38 × 68.5 × 68.5 cm).

Collection
Mr. and Mrs. Michael Sonnabend, New York, New York.

Notes
The sculpture is also known as *No. 48*.

286

Untitled 1966
Urethane foam
30½ × 35½ × 40 in.
(77.5 × 90 × 101.5 cm).

Collection
Neuberger Museum, State University of New York at Purchase, New York, 1982; promised gift of Mr. and Mrs. Robert Creeley.

Provenance
Mr. and Mrs. Robert Creeley, Buffalo, New York.

287

Untitled 1966
Urethane foam and cord
9½ × 13½ × 12 in.
(24 × 34.5 × 30.5 cm).

Collection
Collection of the artist, Sarasota, Florida.

Notes
The sculpture is also known as *No. 17*. It is signed on the underside: *#17, Chamberlain '66*.

288

Untitled 1966
Urethane foam and cord
12 × 14 in. (30.5 × 35.5 cm).

Collection
Holly and Horace Solomon, New York, New York, 1970.

Provenance
Richard Bellamy, New York, New York.

Notes
The sculpture is also known as *No. 19*.

289

Untitled 1966
Urethane foam and cord
8 × 14 × 14 in.
(20.5 × 35.5 × 35.5 cm).

Collection
Alf Young, New York, New York, 1967; acquired directly from the artist.

Notes
The sculpture is also known as *No. 72*.

290

Untitled 1966
Urethane foam and cord
25 × 11 × 8 in.
(63.5 × 28 × 20 cm).

Collection
Present location unknown.

Provenance
Mr. and Mrs. Max Weinstein, Seattle, Washington.

Exhibitions
Western Washington University, Bellingham, Washington. *Contemporary Sculpture from Northwest Colections*, illus. March 2–19, 1971.

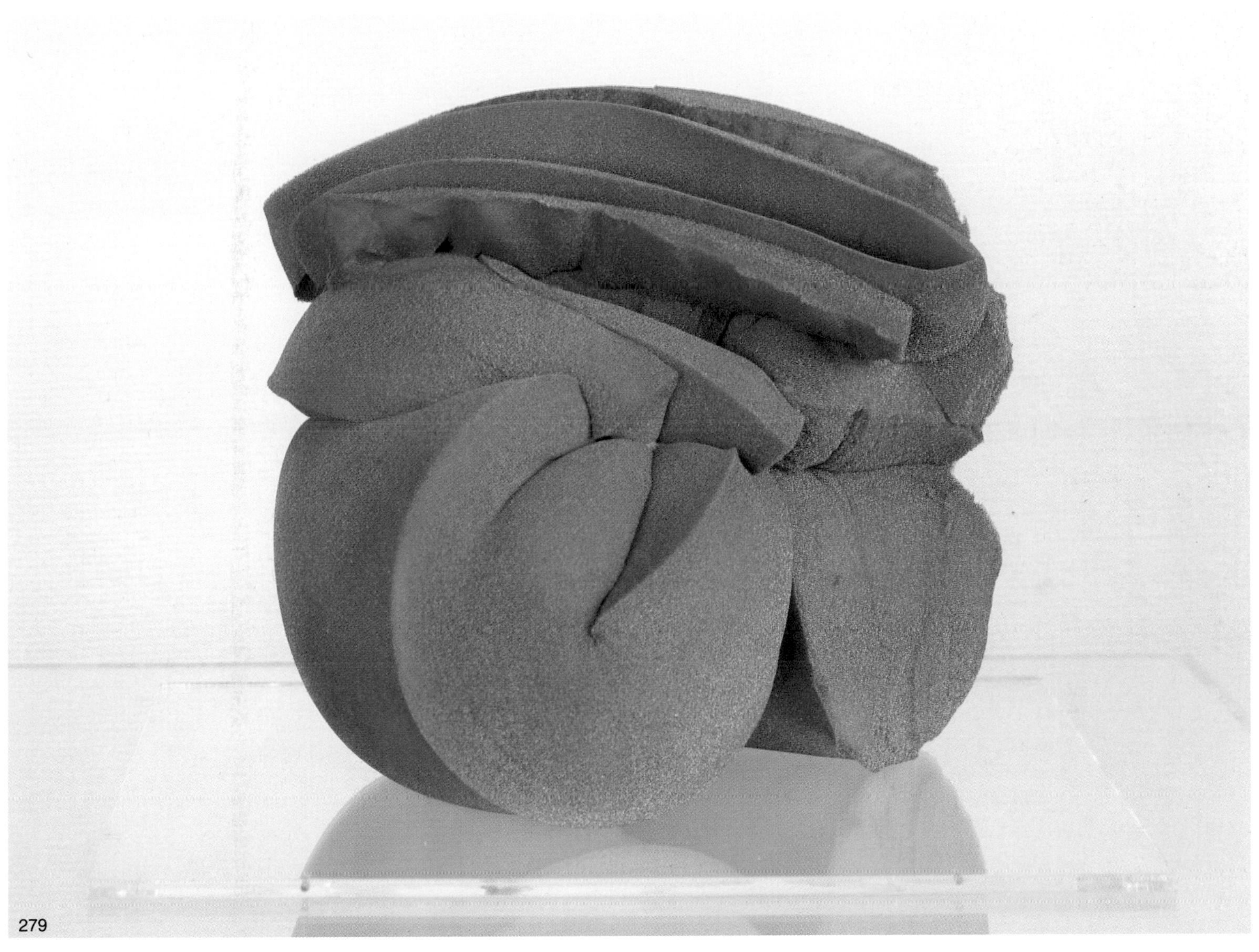

279

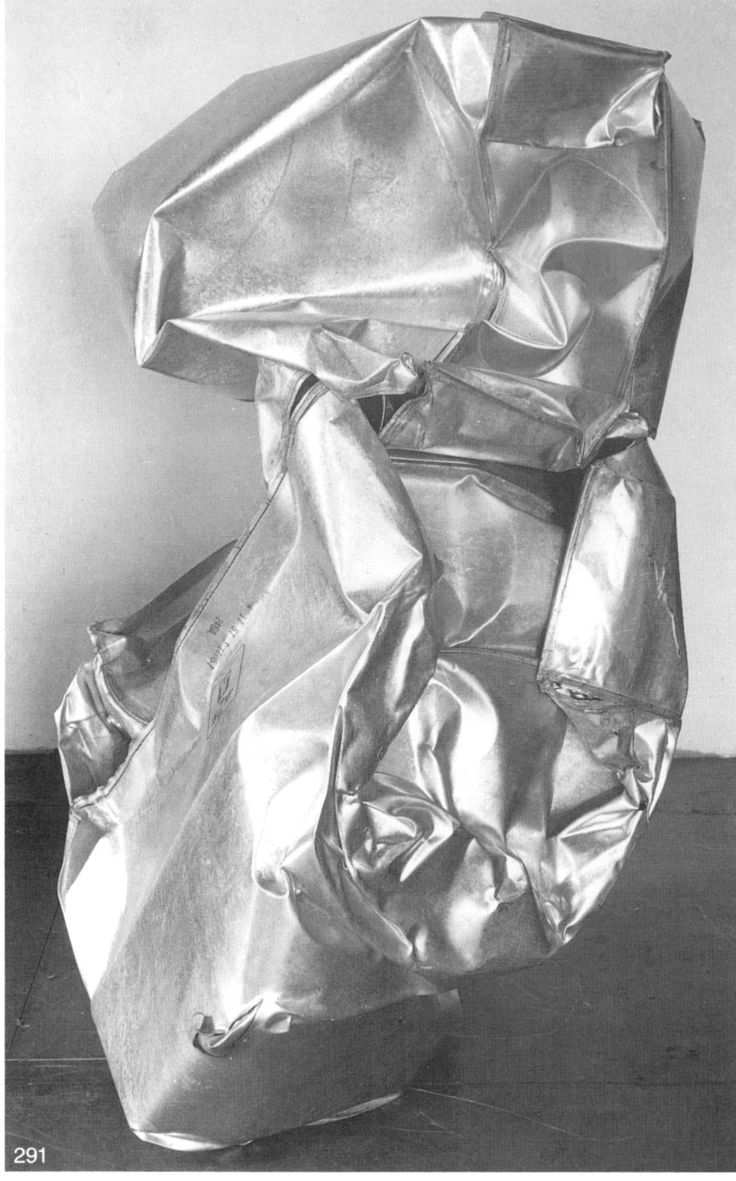
291

The galvanized-steel sculptures were made in New York City between 1967 and 1969 as the result of a decision by Chamberlain to abandon the use of colored steel. Galvanized-steel boxes were fabricated in dimensions approximately 42 × 28 × 18 in. (106.5 × 71 × 45.5 cm), handled by Chamberlain in a compactor on White Street, and finished in his studio. These pieces are variously titled after constellations and British porcelain-toilet manufacturers.

291

Norma Jean Rising/Norma Jean Risen 1967/81

Painted galvanized steel
65½ × 44½ × 39½ in.
(166 × 113 × 100.5 cm).

Collection

Dia Art Foundation, New York, New York, 1984.

Provenance

Mr. and Mrs. Richard L. Selle, New York, New York, 1967.

Exhibitions

Sidney Janis Gallery, New York, New York. *Homage to Marilyn Monroe*, cat. no. 10, illus. December 6–30, 1967.

Leo Castelli Warehouse, New York, New York. *John Chamberlain: Recent Sculpture*. February 2–22, 1969.

The Solomon R. Guggenheim Museum, New York, New York. *John Chamberlain: A Retrospective Exhibition*, cat. no. 83, color illus. p. 33, December 23, 1971–February 20, 1972.

References

Lawrence Alloway, "Marilyn as Subject Matter," *Arts*, vol. 42, no. 3 (September/October 1967), p. 30.

Elizabeth C. Baker, "The Chamberlain Crunch," *Art News*, vol. 70, no. 10 (February 1972), color illus. p. 30.

Notes

The sculpture, the first in the series of galvanized pieces, was remade and painted by the artist in 1981 and retitled *Norma Jean Risen*.

The dimensions of the original sculpture were 66 × 38 × 38 in. (167.5 × 96.5 × 96.5 cm).

The photograph is of the sculpture in its original state.

292

Alouette 1967

Galvanized steel
20½ × 18 × 14 in.
(52 × 45.5 × 35.5 cm).

Collection

Susan and Terry Grody, West Hartford, Connecticut, 1968.

Provenance

Leo Castelli Gallery, New York, New York.

293

Angel Beyond Opio 1967

Galvanized steel
82 × 48 × 48 in.
(208.5 × 122 × 122 cm).

Exhibitions

Leo Castelli Warehouse, New York, New York. *John Chamberlain: Recent Sculpture*. February 2–22, 1969.

References

Elizabeth C. Baker, "The Secret Life of John Chamberlain," *Art News*, vol. 68, no. 2 (April 1969), illus.

Diane Waldman, *John Chamberlain: A Retrospective Exhibition* (New York: The Solomon R. Guggenheim Foundation, 1971), illus. p. 81.

Notes

According to the artist, the sculpture was destroyed in the winter of 1970–71, while in the possession of the Lo Giudice Gallery, New York, New York.

294

Brophill Lowdown 1967

Galvanized steel
60 × 56 × 50 in.
(152.5 × 142 × 127 cm).

Collection

Collection of the artist, Sarasota, Florida.

Exhibitions

Whitney Museum of American Art, New York, New York. *1968 Annual Contemporary American Sculpture*. December 17, 1968–February 9, 1969.

Leo Castelli Gallery, New York, New York. *Summer Group Exhibition*. June 21–July 31, 1969.

Notes

The sculpture has been disassembled.

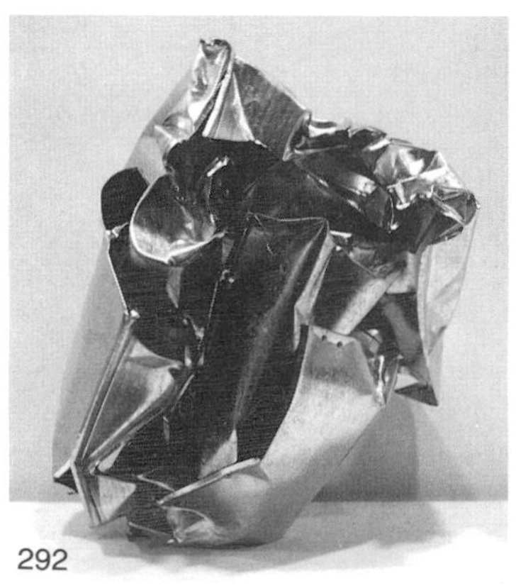
292

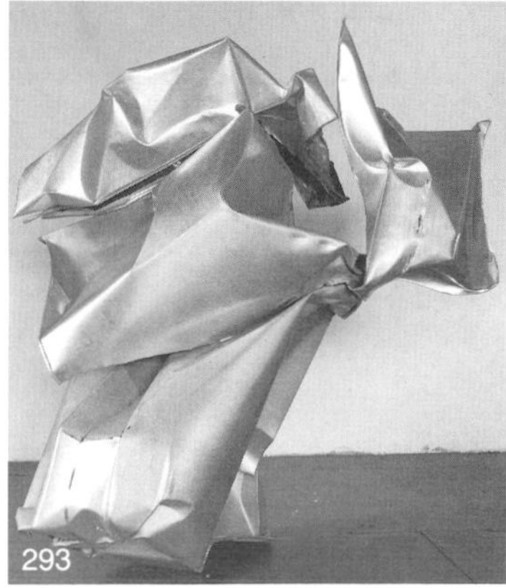
293

295

Coma Berenices—North of Virgo 1967

Galvanized steel
67½ × 77 × 60 in.
(171 × 195.5 × 152.5 cm).

Exhibitions

Leo Castelli Warehouse, New York, New York. *John Chamberlain: Recent Sculpture*. February 2–22, 1969.

Dayton's Gallery 12, Minneapolis, Minnesota. *Castelli at Dayton's*, illus. April 19–May 17, 1969.

Indianapolis Museum of Art, Indianapolis, Indiana. *Painting and Sculpture Today—1970*, p. 114, illus. April 21–June 1, 1970.

The Contemporary Arts Center, Cincinnati, Ohio. *Monumental Art*, illus. September 13–November 1, 1970.

Lo Giudice Gallery, New York, New York. *Group Exhibition*. 1970.

The Solomon R. Guggenheim Museum, New York, New York. *John Chamberlain: A Retrospective Exhibition*, cat. no. 85, illus. p. 80. December 23, 1971–February 20, 1972.

References

Elizabeth C. Baker, "The Secret Life of John Chamberlain," *Art News*, vol. 68, no. 2 (April 1969), illus.

Notes

According to the artist, the sculpture was destroyed by a vandal while in the possession of the Lo Giudice Gallery, New York, New York, in 1972.

296

Crissum-Kiss 1967

Galvanized steel
21 × 18 × 15 in.
(53.5 × 45.5 × 38 cm).

Collection

Sidney and Selma Milgram, Lawrence, New York.

Provenance

Leo Castelli Gallery, New York, New York.

Exhibitions

American Embassy in Budapest. *Art in Embassies*, organized by the Museum of Modern Art, New York, New York. 1968.

297

Lilith New Moon 1967

Galvanized steel
82 × 80 × 48 in.
(208.5 × 203 × 122 cm).

Exhibitions

San Antonio Fair, San Antonio, Texas. *Sculpture, Murals and Fountains at HemisFair 1968*, cat. no. 25, illus. 1968.

Leo Castelli Warehouse, New York, New York. *John Chamberlain: Recent Sculpture*. February 2–22, 1969.

School of Fine and Applied Arts Gallery, Boston, Massachusetts. *American Artists of the Nineteen Sixties*, illus. p. 18. February 6–March 14, 1970.

References

Peter Schjeldahl, "The Vicissitudes of Sculpture," *New York Times*, February 9, 1969, illus.

Elizabeth C. Baker, "The Secret Life of John Chamberlain," *Art News*, vol. 68, no. 2 (April 1969), illus.

Diane Waldman, *John Chamberlain: A Retrospective Exhibition* (New York: The Solomon R. Guggenheim Foundation, 1971), illus. p. 79.

Notes

According to the artist, the sculpture was destroyed in the winter of 1970–71, while in the possession of the Lo Giudice Gallery, New York, New York.

298

Papagayo 1967

Galvanized steel
72 × 44 × 46 in.
(183 × 111.5 × 117 cm).

Collection

Andy Warhol, New York, New York, 1967; acquired directly from the artist.

Exhibitions

The Solomon R. Guggenheim Museum, New York, New York. *John Chamberlain: A Retrospective Exhibition*, cat. no. 82. December 23, 1971–February 20, 1972.

299

Royal Ventor 1967

Galvanized steel, steel, and aluminum
61½ × 57 × 46½ in.
(156 × 145 × 118 cm).

Collection

Dia Art Foundation, New York, New York, 1980.

Provenance

Alfred Ordover, New York, New York; O. K. Harris Works of Art, New York, New York; Lone Star Foundation, New York, New York, 1977.

Exhibitions

Leo Castelli Warehouse, New York, New York. *John Chamberlain: Recent Sculpture*. February 2–22, 1969.

References

Elizabeth C. Baker, "The Secret Life of John Chamberlain," *Art News*, vol. 68, no. 2 (April 1969), illus.

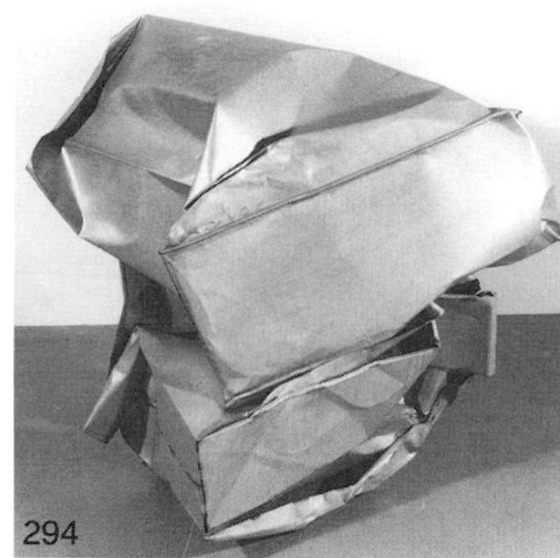
294

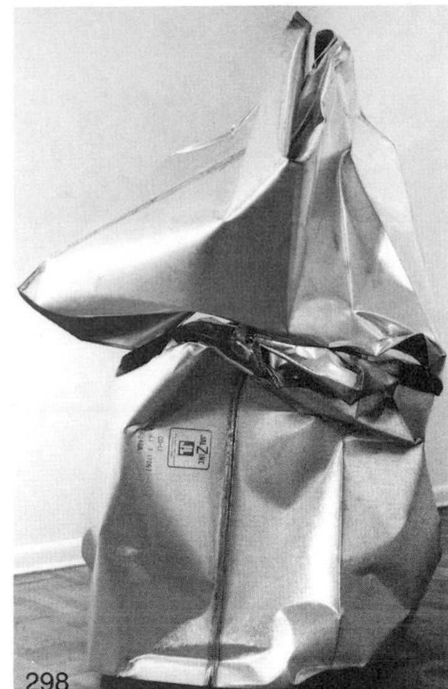
298

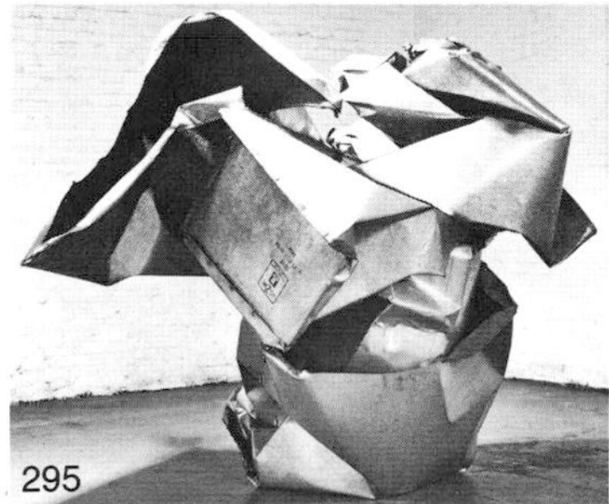
295

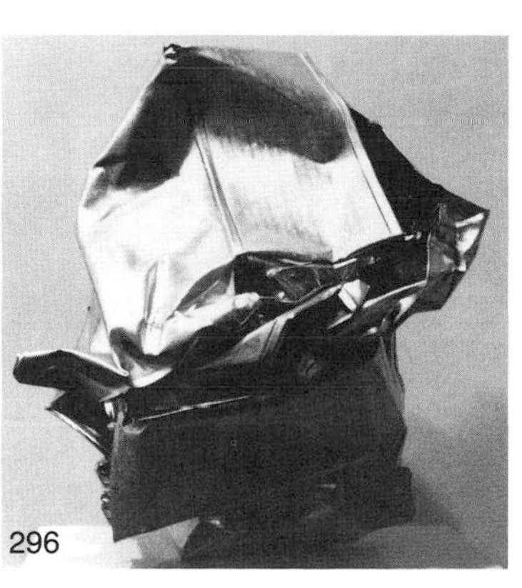
296

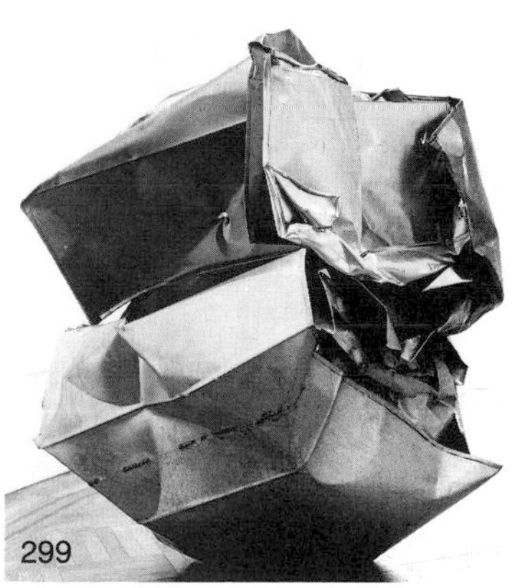
299

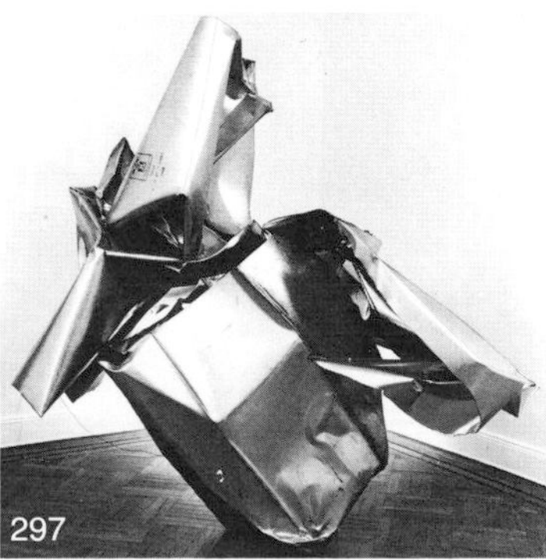
297

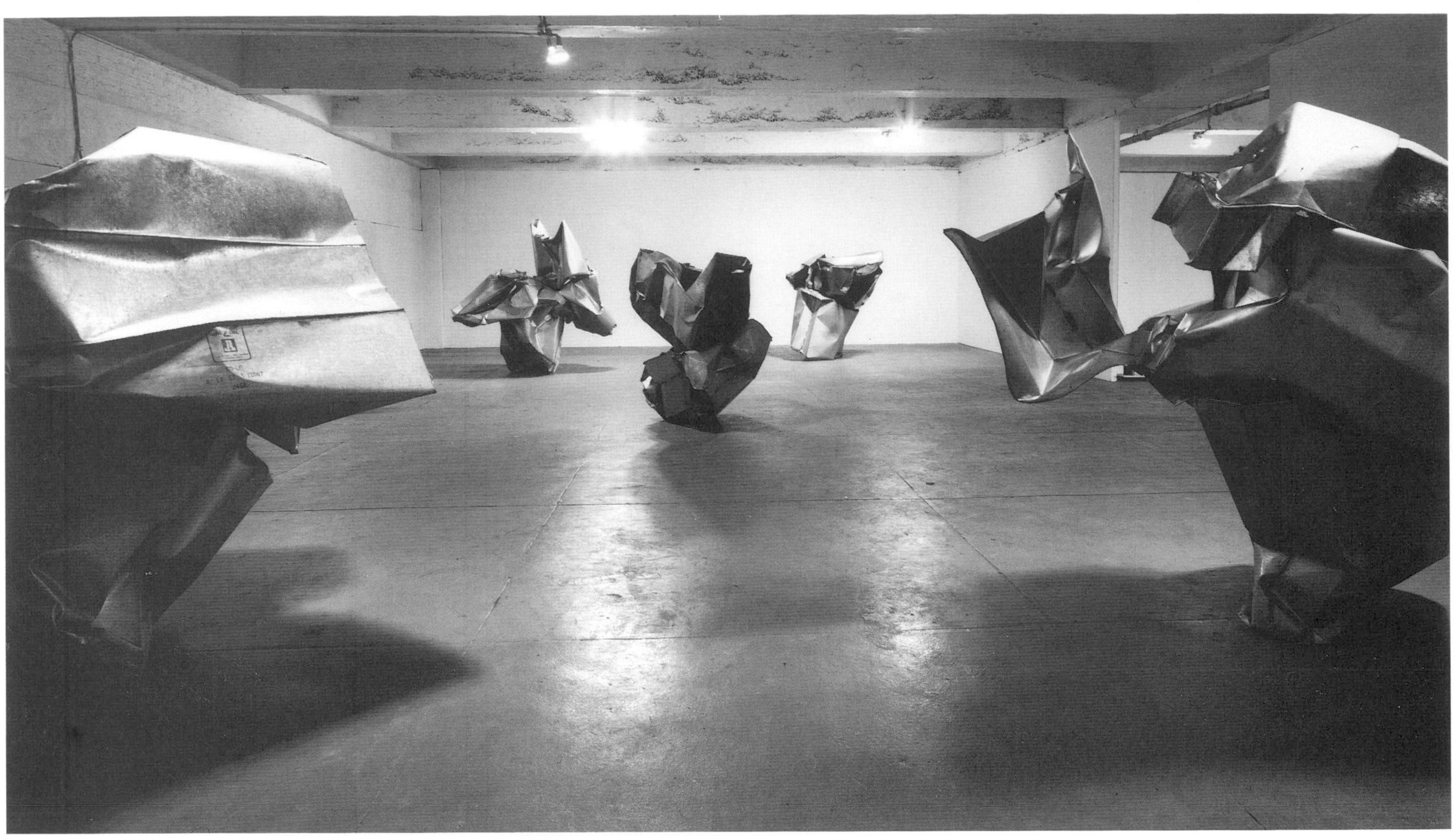

View of the installation at the Leo Castelli Warehouse exhibition *John Chamberlain: Recent Sculpture*, February 2–22, 1969. From left to right: *Coma Berenices— North of Virgo* (cat. no. 295), *Lilith New Moon* (cat. no. 297), *Royal Ventor* (299), *Ultrafull Private* (cat. no. 303), and *Angel Beyond Opio* (cat. no. 293).

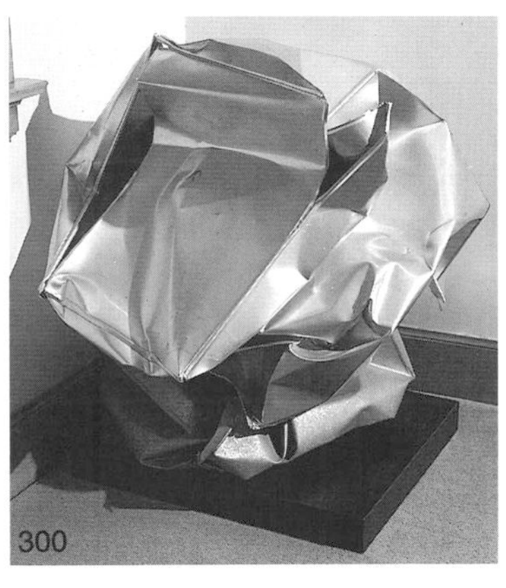

300

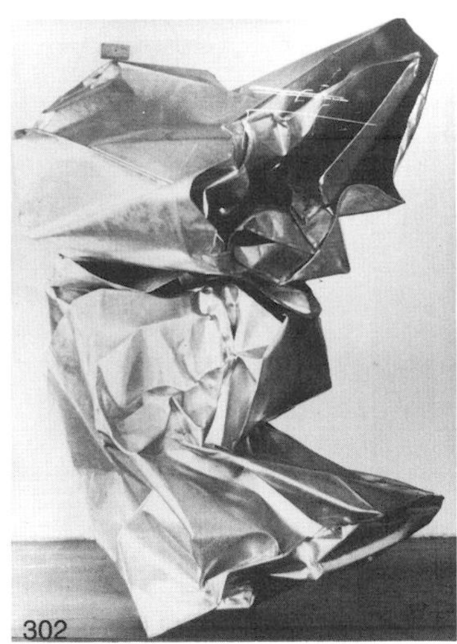

302

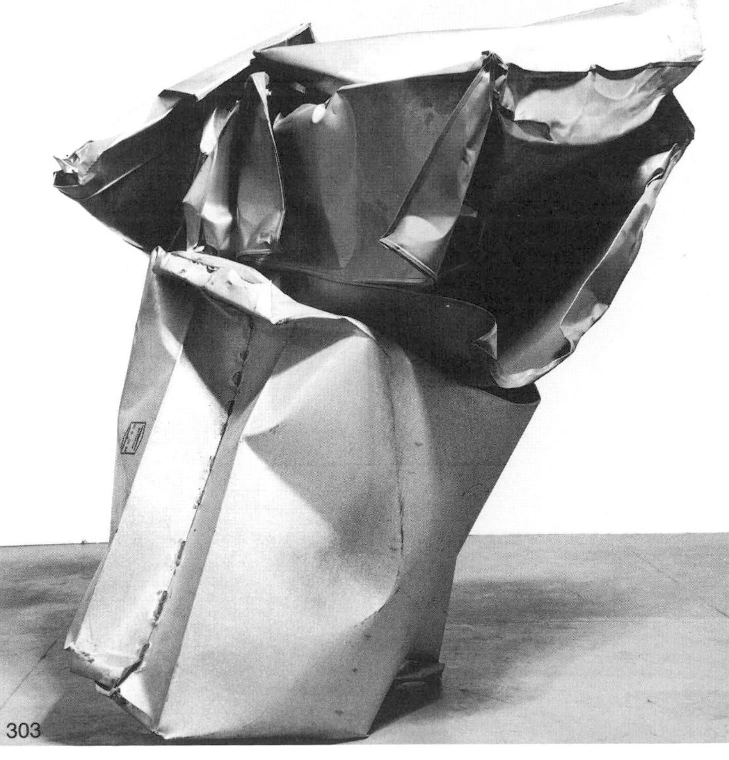

303

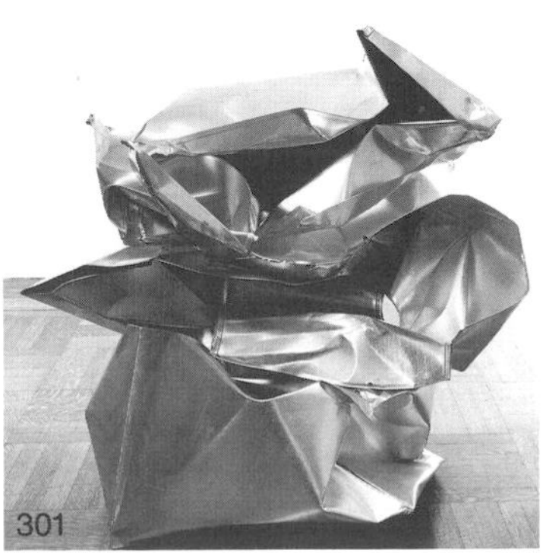

301

300

Tintinnabulary 1967
Galvanized steel
38 × 33 × 31 in.
(96.5 × 84 × 78.5 cm).

Collection
Roger Davidson, Toronto, Canada, 1967.

Provenance
Leo Castelli Gallery, New York, New York.

301

Tippecanoe 1967
Galvanized and stainless steel
40 × 42 × 36 in.
(101.5 × 106.5 × 91.5 cm).

Collection
David Whitney, New York, New York, 1967.

Provenance
Leo Castelli Gallery, New York, New York, 1967.

Exhibitions
Leo Castelli Gallery, New York, New York. *Summer Group Exhibition*. June 21–July 31, 1969.

References
Sam Hunter and John Jacobus, *American Art of the Twentieth Century* (New York: Abrams, 1972), p. 364.

302

Ultima Thule 1967
Galvanized steel
64 × 44 × 36 in.
(162.5 × 111.5 × 91.5 cm).

Collection
Sam Wagstaff, New York, New York; on loan to Wadsworth Atheneum, Hartford, Connecticut, 1972.

Provenance
Sam Wagstaff, New York, New York.

Exhibitions
The Solomon R. Guggenheim Museum, New York, New York. *John Chamberlain: A Retrospective Exhibition*, cat. no. 84. December 23, 1971–February 20, 1972.

References
Phyllis Tuchman, "An Interview with John Chamberlain," *Artforum*, vol. 10, no. 6 (February 1972), color illus. p. 38.

303

Ultrafull Private 1967
Galvanized steel
66½ × 57½ × 54½ in.
(169 × 146 × 138.5 cm).

Collection
Dia Art Foundation, New York, New York, 1980.

Provenance
David White, New York, New York, 1967; Annina Nosei, New York, New York, 1968; Lone Star Foundation, New York, New York, 1978.

Exhibitions
Leo Castelli Warehouse, New York, New York. *John Chamberlain: Recent Sculpture*. February 2–22, 1969.

304

Ultra Yahoo 1967
Galvanized steel
60 × 60 × 60 in.
(152.5 × 152.5 × 152.5 cm).

Collection
Neil Williams, Sagaponack, New York, 1982.

Provenance
Michael Ruskin, New York, New York, 1967.

Exhibitions
Anne Plumb Gallery, New York, New York. *Silver*. November 23–December 21, 1985.

Notes
The sculpture was displayed at Max's Kansas City, a New York nightspot, for several years.

305

Untitled 1967
Galvanized steel
19 × 21 × 18½ in.
(48 × 53.5 × 47 cm).

Collection
Noel and Dick Frackman, Scarsdale, New York, 1982.

Provenance
Leo Castelli Gallery, New York, New York; Anita Friedman Fine Arts, New York, New York; Solomon and Co., New York, New York; Allan Stone Gallery, New York, New York.

306

Untitled 1967
Galvanized steel
15 × 16 × 17½ in.
(38 × 40.5 × 44.5 cm).

Collection
Joe D'Urso, New York, New York.

Provenance
Lo Giudice Gallery, New York, New York; David Boyce, New York, New York; Leo Castelli Gallery, New York, New York.

307

Untitled c. 1967
Galvanized steel
28½ × 36 × 27½ in.
(72.5 × 91.5 × 70 cm).

Collection
Cy Twombly, Rome.

Provenance
Leo Castelli Gallery, New York, New York.

Exhibitions
The Denver Art Museum, Denver, Colorado. *An American Report on the Sixties*. October 24–December 7, 1969.

308

Untitled 1967
Galvanized steel
26½ × 22½ × 16½ in.
(67 × 57 × 42 cm).

Collection
Robert A. M. Stern, New York, New York.

Provenance
Leo Castelli Gallery, New York, New York.

309

Untitled 1967
Galvanized steel
25½ × 17 × 20½ in.
(64.5 × 43 × 52 cm).

Collection
Private collection, New York, New York, 1968.

Provenance
Leo Castelli Gallery, New York, New York.

310

Untitled c. 1967
Painted, chromium-plated, and stainless steel
54 × 65 × 53 in.
(137 × 165 × 134.5 cm).

Collection
Allan Stone, New York, New York.

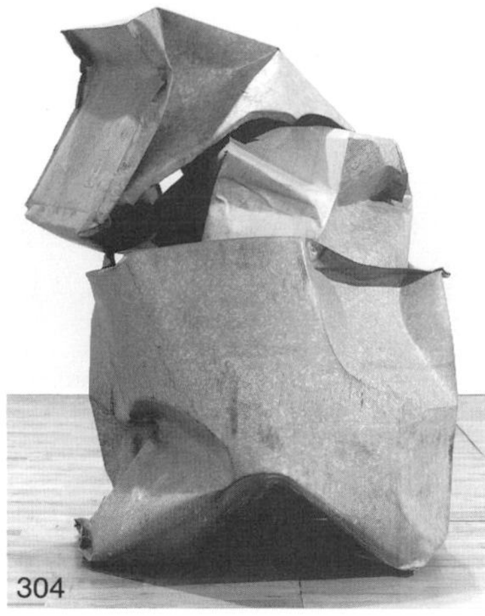
304

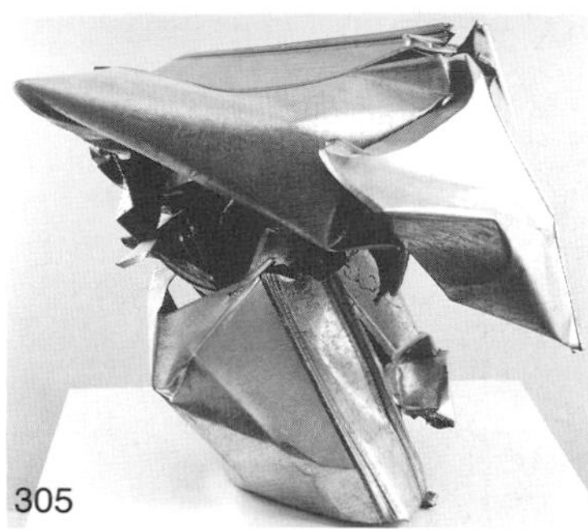
305

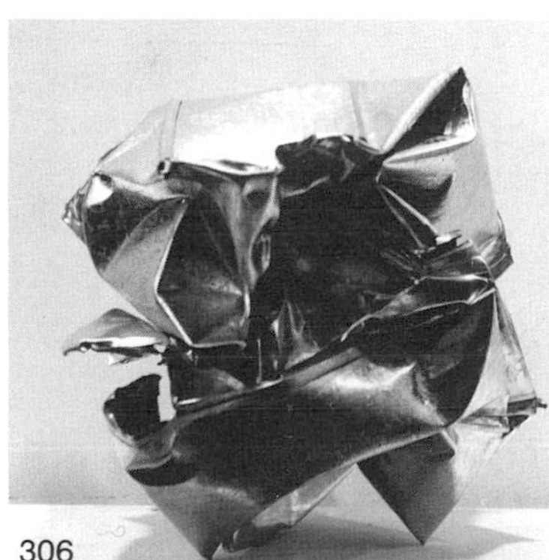
306

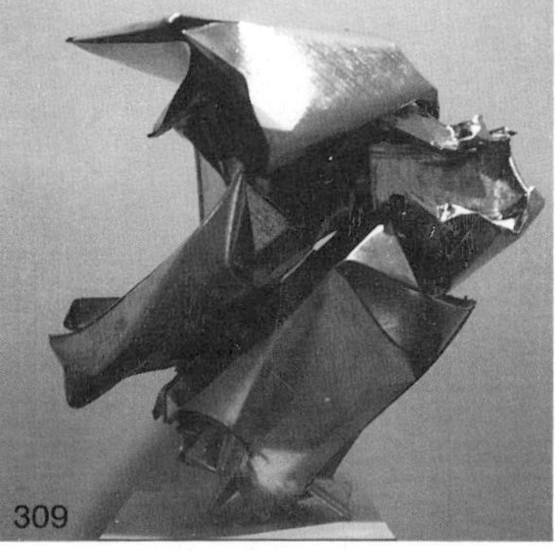
309

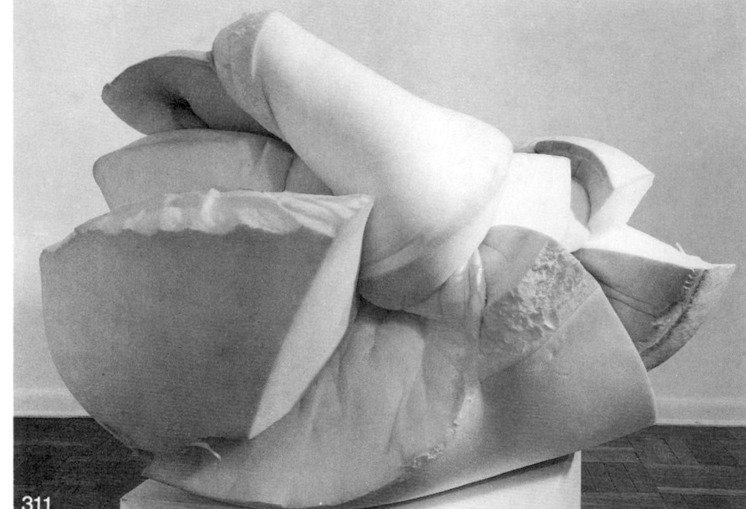
311

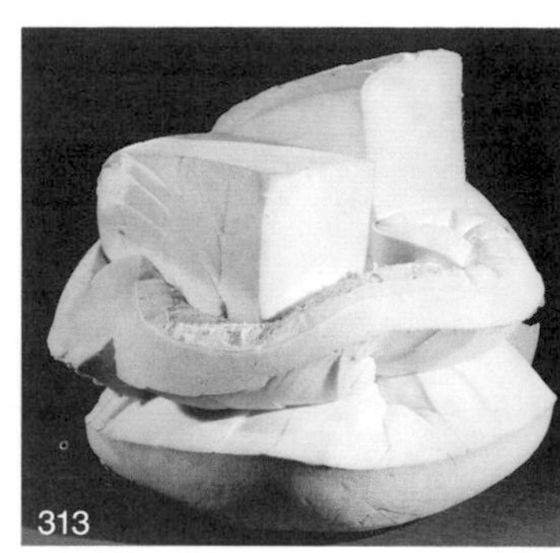
313

311

Heng 1967

Urethane foam and cord
54 × 54 × 36 in.
(137 × 137 × 91.5 cm).

Collection
Present location unknown.

Provenance
Michael Ruskin, New York, New York.

Exhibitions
New Jersey State Museum, Trenton, New Jersey. *Soft Art*. March 1–April 27, 1969.

References
Ralph Pomeroy, "Soft Objects at the New Jersey State Museum," *Arts*, vol. 43, no. 5 (March 1969), illus. p. 47.

Sam Hunter and John Jacobus, *American Art of the Twentieth Century* (New York: Abrams, 1972), illus. no. 802, p. 425.

312

Hua 1967

Urethane foam and cord
32 × 33 × 33 in.
(81.5 × 84 × 84 cm).

Provenance
Mr. and Mrs. Jared Sable, Toronto.

Exhibitions
York University, Toronto. *American Art of the Sixties in Toronto Private Collections*. May–June 1969.

The Solomon R. Guggenheim Museum, New York, New York. *John Chamberlain: A Retrospective Exhibition*, cat. no. 76, illus. p. 76. December 23, 1971–February 20, 1972.

References
Jeremy Adamson, "American Art of the Sixties in Toronto Private Collections," *Artscanada*, vol. 26, no. 134–35 (August 1969), illus. p. 41.

Notes
The sculpture was destroyed while in the possession of the Sables.

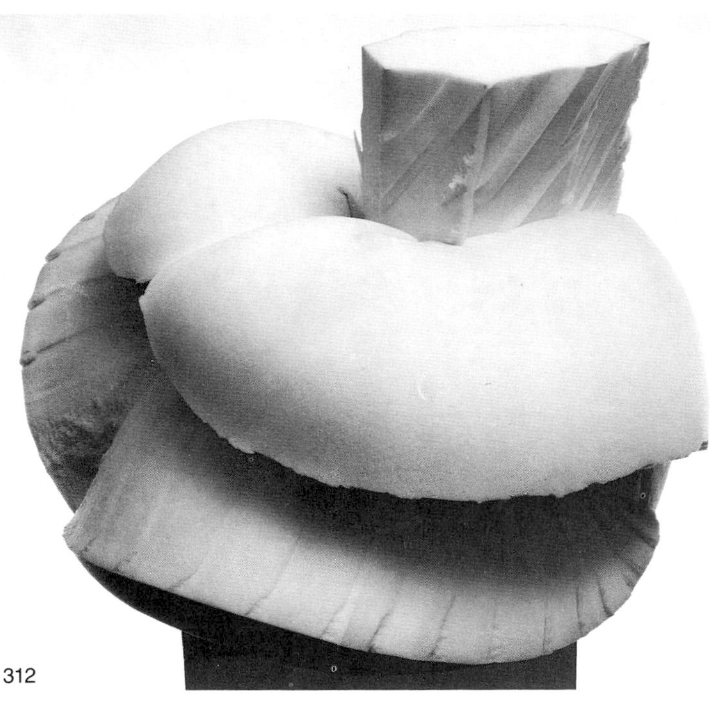
312

313

Koko-Nor II 1967

Urethane foam and cord
39 × 50 × 48 in.
(99 × 127 × 122 cm).

Collection
Tate Gallery, London, 1968; presented by Alan Power.

Provenance
Alan Power, London, 1967.

Exhibitions
The Solomon R. Guggenheim Museum, New York, New York. *John Chamberlain: A Retrospective Exhibition*, cat. no. 77, listed as "Untitled," with incorrect dimensions. December 23, 1971–February 20, 1972.

References

Ronald Alley, *Recent American Art* (London: Tate Gallery, 1969), illus. pl. 26.

Catalogue of the Tate Gallery's Collection of Modern Art (London: Tate Gallery, 1981), cat. no. T.1089, illus. p. 116.

314

Lop Nor 1967

Urethane foam and cord
37 × 51 × 50 in.
(94 × 129.5 × 127 cm).

Collection

Dia Art Foundation, New York, New York, 1980.

Provenance

Lone Star Foundation, New York, New York, 1977.

Exhibitions

Roberson Center for the Arts and Sciences, Binghamton, New York. *New Media: New Methods* (organized by the Museum of Modern Art, New York, New York). March 16–April 13, 1969. Travelled to Montclair Art Museum, Montclair, New Jersey. May 4–25, 1969; University of South Florida, Tampa, Florida. July 28–August 21, 1969; George Thomas Hunter Gallery, Chattanooga, Tennessee. September 7–28, 1969; Krannert Art Museum, University of Illinois, Champaign, Illinois. October 12–November 9, 1969; Dulin Gallery of Art, Knoxville, Tennessee. December 1–22, 1969; Des Moines Art Center, Des Moines, Iowa. January 16–February 8, 1970; The Memorial Art Gallery of the University of Rochester, Rochester, New York. March 6–29, 1970; Arkansas Arts Center, Little Rock, Arkansas. May 17–June 14, 1970; Edmonton Art Gallery, Edmonton, Canada. July 13–August 16, 1970.

The Solomon R. Guggenheim Museum, New York, New York. *John Chamberlain: A Retrospective Exhibition*, cat. no. 81. December 23, 1971–February 20, 1972.

Notes

The sculpture is titled, signed, and dated on the underside.

315

Shan 1967

Urethane foam
42 × 45 × 34 in.
(106.5 × 114.5 × 86.5 cm).

Collection

Gilbert and Lila Silverman, Detroit, Michigan, 1973.

Provenance

Robert and Ethel Scull, New York, New York.

Exhibitions

Leo Castelli Gallery, New York, New York. *New Work*. April 1967.

Sotheby Parke-Bernet, Inc., New York, New York. *A Selection of Fifty Works from the Collection of Robert C. Scull*, cat. no. 3, illus. October 18, 1973.

Cranbrook Academy of Art Museum, Bloomfield Hills, Michigan. *The Gilbert and Lila Silverman Collection*, p. 58. September 20–November 1, 1981.

316

Strawberry Mush 1967

Urethane foam
24 × 48 × 48 in.
(61 × 122 × 122 cm).

Collection

Jim Jacobs, New York, New York; acquired directly from the artist.

Exhibitions

The Solomon R. Guggenheim Museum, New York, New York. *John Chamberlain: A Retrospective Exhibition*, cat. no. 78, illus. p. 78. December 23, 1971–February 20, 1972.

Notes

The sculpture is in a state of disrepair.

317

Tung Ting Hu 1967

Urethane foam
37½ × 54 × 52 in.
(95 × 137 × 132 cm).

References

Edward F. Fry, "Sculpture of the Sixties," *Art in America*, vol. 55, no. 5 (September/October 1967), color illus. p. 26.

Edward F. Fry, "The Issue of Innovation," *Art News*, vol. 66, no. 6 (October 1967), color illus. p. 40.

James R. Mellow, "The 1967 Guggenheim International," *Art International*, vol. 11, no. 10 (December 1967), illus. p. 53.

Diane Waldman, *John Chamberlain: A Retrospective Exhibition* (New York: The Solomon R. Guggenheim Foundation, 1971), color illus. p. 43.

Elizabeth C. Baker, "The Chamberlain Crunch," *Art News*, vol. 70, no. 10 (February 1972), color illus. p. 31.

Notes

The sculpture has been destroyed.

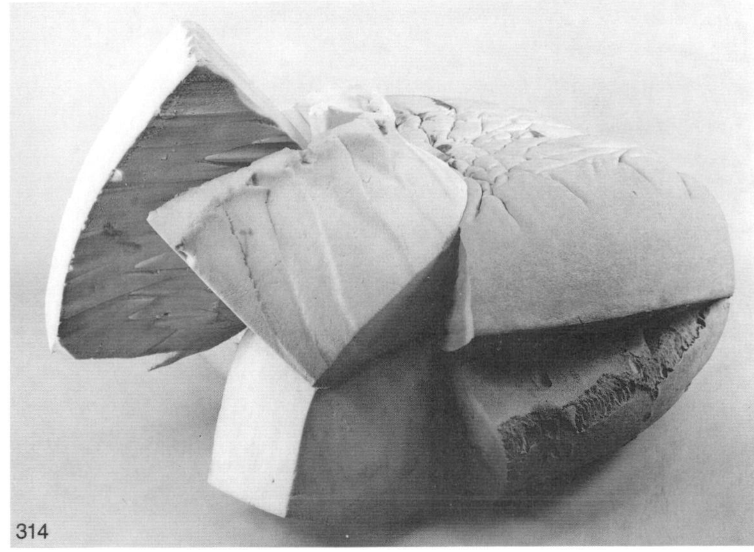
314

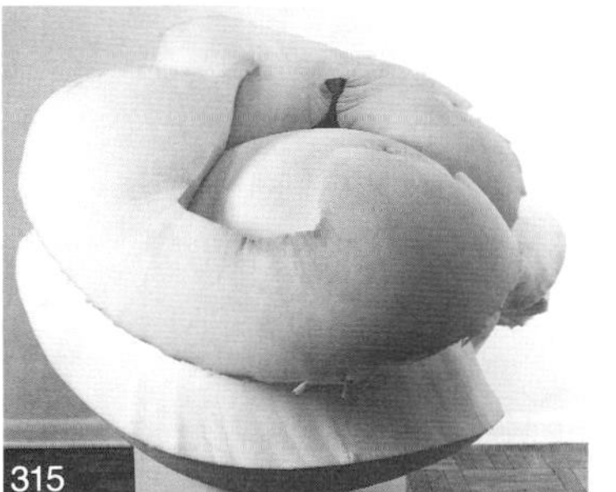
315

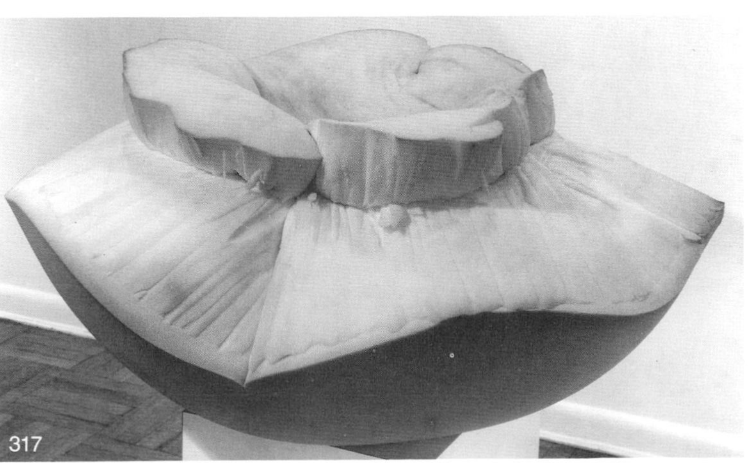
317

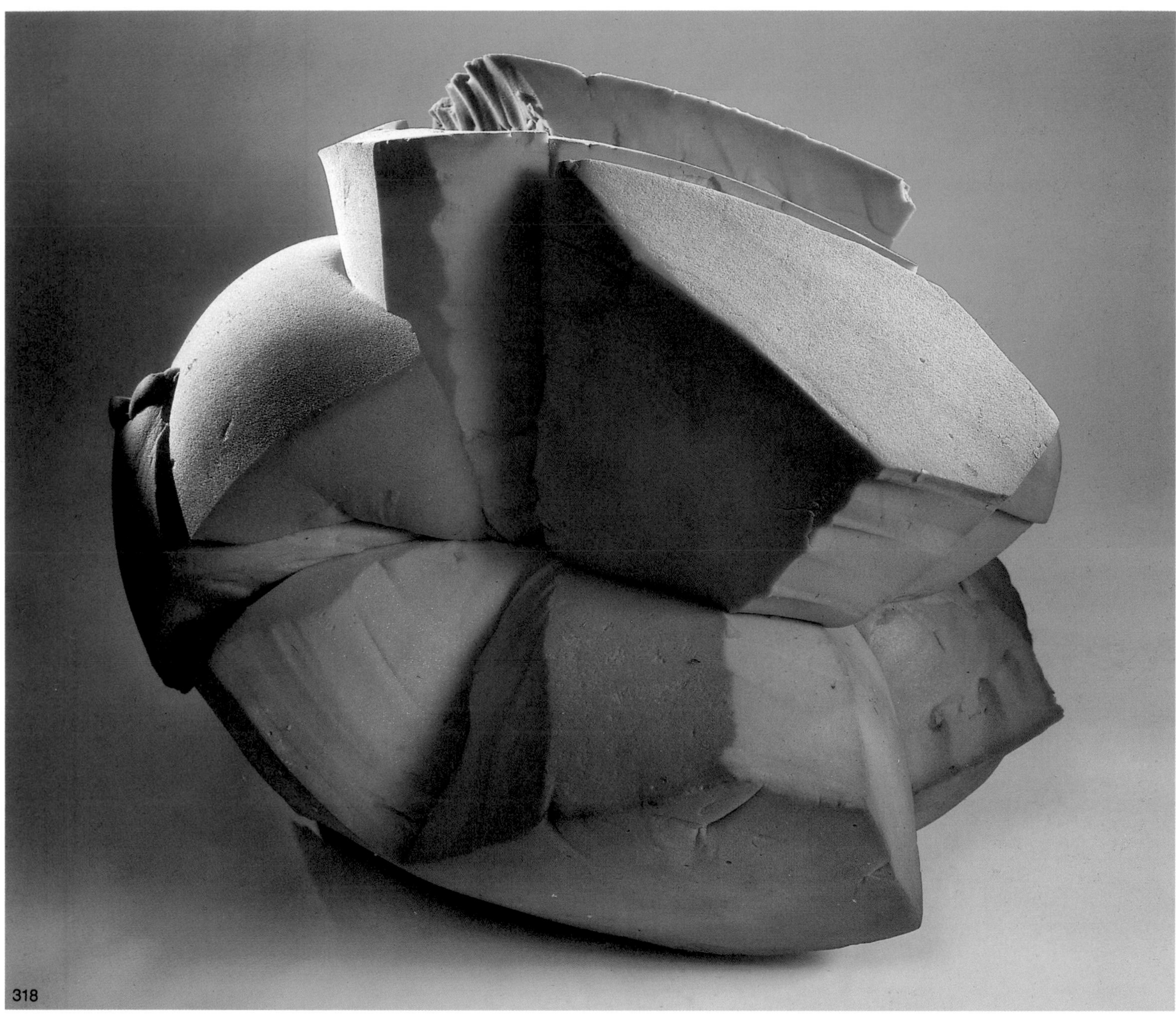

318

318

Untitled 1967
Urethane foam and cord
32 × 42 × 40 in.
(81.5 × 106.5 × 101.5 cm).

Collection
Dia Art Foundation, New York, New York, 1980.

Provenance
Lone Star Foundation, New York, New York, 1977.

Exhibitions
The Solomon R. Guggenheim Museum, New York, New York. *John Chamberlain: A Retrospective Exhibition*, cat. no. 80, illus. p. 77, incorrectly listed as *Soopad*. December 23, 1971–February 20, 1972.

Notes
The sculpture is signed and dated on the underside.

319

Untitled 1967
Urethane foam and cord
24 × 36 × 41 in.
(61 × 91.5 × 104 cm).

Collection
Present location unknown.

Notes
The only evidence of the existence of this sculpture is that it was entered in the Castelli registry in 1967.

320

Untitled 1967
Urethane foam and cord
27 × 40 × 40 in.
(68.5 × 101.5 × 101.5 cm).

Notes
The Castelli registry lists the sculpture as destroyed.

321

Untitled 1967
Urethane foam and cord
8 × 12 × 12 in.
(20 × 30.5 × 30.5 cm).

Collection
Weatherspoon Art Gallery, University of North Carolina at Greensboro, North Carolina, 1976.

Provenance
Raydon Gallery, New York, New York, 1976.

Notes
The sculpture is signed and dated on the underside.

322

Untitled 1967
Urethane foam
14 × 14 × 12 in.
(35.5 × 35.5 × 30.5 cm).

Collection
Christophe de Menil, New York, New York.

Provenance
Leo Castelli Gallery, New York, New York.

323

Untitled 1967
Urethane foam and cord
Dimensions unknown.

Collection
Cy Twombly, Rome.

Provenance
Leo Castelli Gallery, New York, New York.

Exhibitions
Leo Castelli Warehouse, New York, New York. *John Chamberlain: Recent Sculpture*. February 2–22, 1969.

324

Untitled 1967
Urethane foam and cord
5 × 8½ × 8½ in.
(12.5 × 21.5 × 21.5 cm).

Collection
Freide and Rubin Gorewitz, West Nyack, New York, 1967; acquired directly from the artist.

Notes
The sculpture is signed and dated on the underside.

325

Untitled 1967
Urethane foam and cord
10 × 13 × 13 in.
(25.5 × 33 × 33 cm).

Collection
Present location unknown.

Provenance
Leo Castelli Gallery, New York, New York; Nicola del Roscia, Rome; Galleria Giuseppe Marino, Rome.

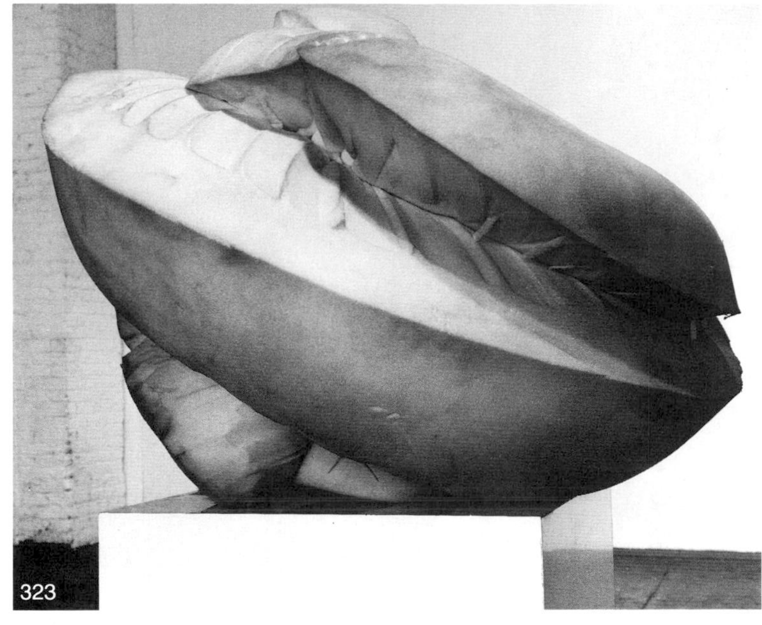
323

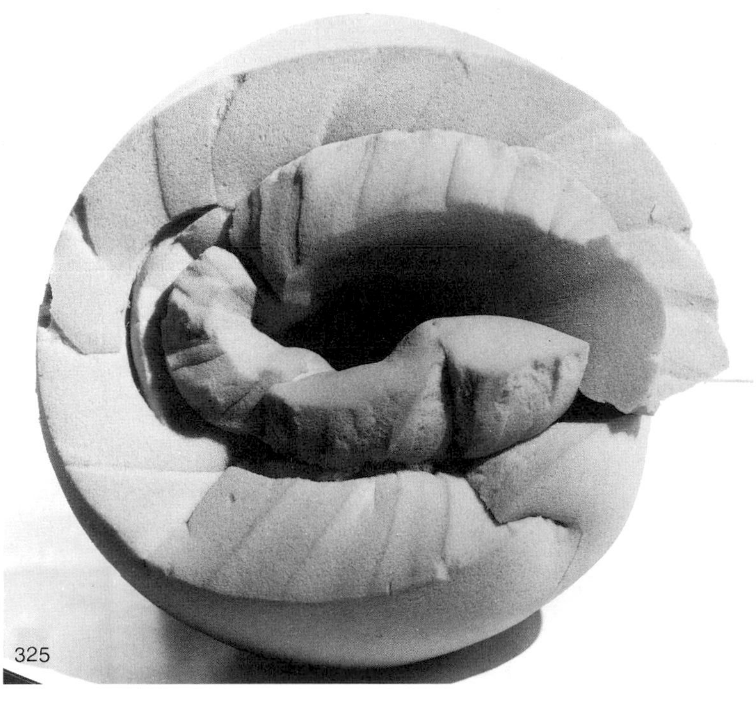
325

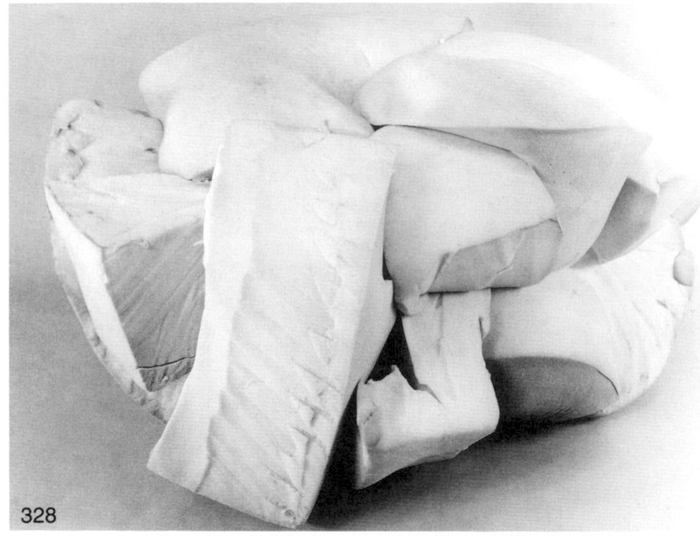
328

326

Untitled 1967

Urethane foam and cord
27 × 47 × 42 in.
(68.5 × 119.5 × 106.5 cm).

Collection

Private collection, New York, New York; acquired directly from the artist.

327

Untitled 1967

Urethane foam and cord
12 × 16 × 14 in.
(30.5 × 40.5 × 35.5 cm).

Collection

Thordis Moeller, New York, New York.

Provenance

Leon Kraushaar, Lawrence, New York; Heiner Friedrich GmbH, Cologne.

Notes

The sculpture is signed and dated on the underside.

Ten urethane foam sculptures (cat. nos. 328–337) were made in 1967 and sent to West Germany to be exhibited at the Galerie Rudolf Zwirner, Cologne, from October 10 to November 9, and at the Galerie Heiner Friedrich, Munich, in November and December.

Two of the sculptures are known to have been accidentally destroyed in the early seventies in Cologne, but it is not known which of the unlocated pieces they are.

328

Badshan 1967

Urethane foam and cord
26½ × 47½ × 46 in.
(67.5 × 120.5 × 117 cm).

Collection

Private collection, New York, New York.

Provenance

Leo Castelli Gallery, New York, New York; Galerie Rudolf Zwirner, Cologne; Galerie Heiner Friedrich, Munich; private collection, New York, New York.

Exhibitions

Galerie Rudolf Zwirner, Cologne. *John Chamberlain*. October 10–November 9, 1967.

Galerie Heiner Friedrich, Munich. *John Chamberlain USA Skulpturen*. November–December 1967.

Notes

The sculpture is signed and dated on the underside.

329

Cooldot 1967

Urethane foam and cord
43 × 60 × 46 in.
(109 × 152.5 × 117 cm).

Collection

Present location unknown.

Provenance

Leo Castelli Gallery, New York, New York; Galerie Rudolf Zwirner, Cologne; Galerie Heiner Friedrich, Munich.

Exhibitions

Galerie Rudolf Zwirner, Cologne. *John Chamberlain*. October 10–November 9, 1967.

Galerie Heiner Friedrich, Munich. *John Chamberlain USA Skulpturen*. November–December 1967.

Notes

The sculpture is signed and dated on the underside.

330

Daftlok 1967

Urethane foam and cord
34 × 42 × 38 in.
(86.5 × 106.5 × 96.5 cm).

Collection

Present location unknown.

Provenance

Leo Castelli Gallery, New York, New York; Galerie Rudolf Zwirner, Cologne; Galerie Heiner Friedrich, Munich.

Exhibitions

Galerie Rudolf Zwirner, Cologne. *John Chamberlain*. October 10–November 9, 1967.

Galerie Heiner Friedrich, Munich. *John Chamberlain USA Skulpturen*. November–December 1967.

Notes

The sculpture is signed on the underside.

331

Fandurt 1967

Urethane foam and cord
32 × 50 × 48 in.
(81.5 × 127 × 122 cm).

Collection

Present location unknown.

Provenance

Leo Castelli Gallery, New York, New York; Galerie Rudolf Zwirner, Cologne; Galerie Heiner Friedrich, Munich.

Exhibitions

Galerie Rudolf Zwirner, Cologne. *John Chamberlain*. October 10–November 9, 1967.

Galerie Heiner Friedrich, Munich. *John Chamberlain USA Skulpturen*. November–December 1967.

Notes

The sculpture is signed on the underside.

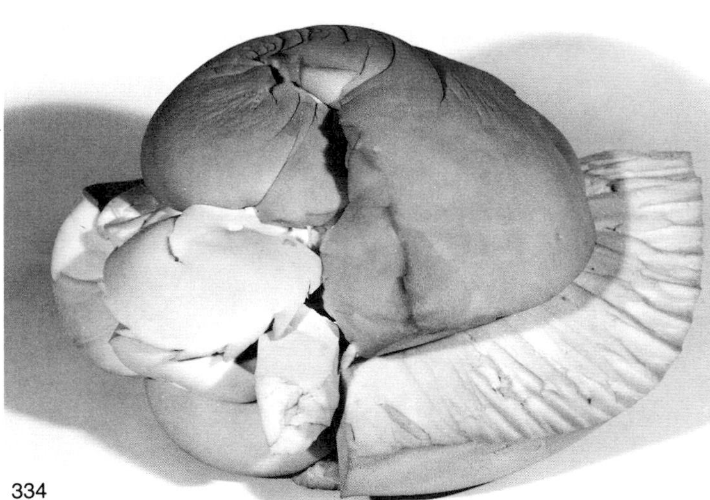
334

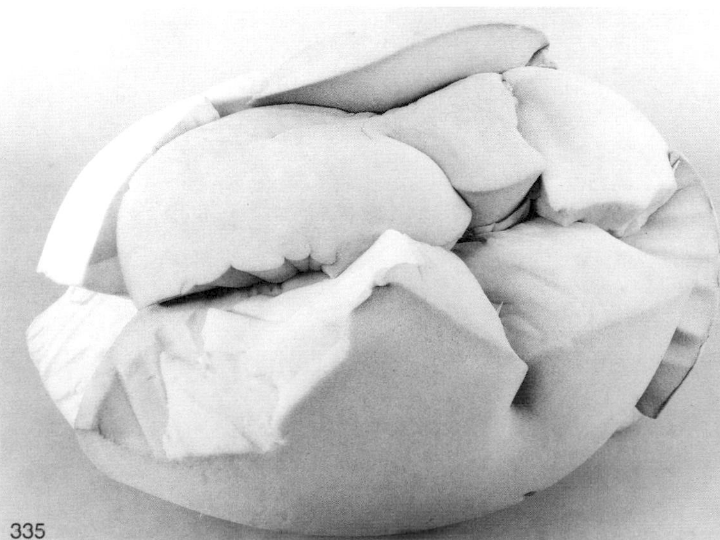
335

332

Funburn 1967
Urethane foam and cord
40 × 66 × 62 in.
(102 × 167.5 × 157.5 cm).

Collection
Museum für Moderne Kunst, Frankfurt.

Provenance
Leo Castelli Gallery, New York, New York; Galerie Rudolf Zwirner, Cologne; Galerie Heiner Friedrich, Munich; Karl Ströher, Darmstadt, 1969.

Exhibitions
Galerie Rudolf Zwirner, Cologne. *John Chamberlain*. October 10–November 9, 1967.

Galerie Heiner Friedrich, Munich. *John Chamberlain USA Skulpturen*. November–December 1967.

Deutsche Gesellschaft für Bildende Kunst e.V. (Kunstverein Berlin) and Nationalgalerie der Staatlichen Museen Preussischer Kulturbesitz, Neue Nationalgalerie Berlin. *Sammlung 1968 Karl Ströher*, cat. no. 18, illus. March 1–April 14, 1969. Traveled to Städtische Kunsthalle Düsseldorf. April 25–June 17, 1969; Kunsthalle Bern. July 12–August 17 and August 23–September 28, 1969.

Deutsches Architekturmuseum, Frankfurt. *Bilder für Frankfurt*, cat. no. 12, illus. p. 168. February 8–April 14, 1985.

References
J. Roh, "Ausstellungen," *Kunstwerk*, no. 21 (December 1967/January 1968), illus. p. 76.

Bildnerische Ausdrucksformen 1960–1970: Sammlung Karl Ströher, (Darmstadt: Hessisches Landesmuseum, 1970), color illus. p. 97.

Notes
The sculpture is signed and dated on the underside.

333

Kootan 1967
Urethane foam and cord
25 × 33 × 32½ in.
(63 × 84 × 82.5 cm).

Collection
Museum Moderner Kunst Wien, Vienna, 1978.

Provenance
Leo Castelli Gallery, New York, New York; Galerie Rudolf Zwirner, Cologne; Professor Wolfgang Hahn, Cologne.

Exhibitions
Galerie Rudolf Zwirner, Cologne. *John Chamberlain*. October 10–November 9, 1967.

Wallraf-Richartz-Museum, Cologne. *Sammlung Hahn: Zeitgenössische Kunst*, cat. no. 36. May 3–July 7, 1968.

The Solomon R. Guggenheim Museum, New York, New York. *John Chamberlain: A Retrospective Exhibition*, cat. no. 75, illus. p. 76. December 23, 1971–February 20, 1972.

Notes
The sculpture is signed and dated on the underside.

334

Lapnor 1967
Urethane foam and cord
30 × 54 × 47 in.
(76 × 137 × 119.5 cm).

Collection
Present location unknown.

Provenance
Leo Castelli Gallery, New York, New York; Galerie Rudolf Zwirner, Cologne; Galerie Heiner Friedrich, Munich.

Exhibitions
Galerie Rudolf Zwirner, Cologne. *John Chamberlain*. October 10–November 9, 1967.

Galerie Heiner Friedrich, Munich. *John Chamberlain USA Skulpturen*. November–December 1967.

Notes
The sculpture is signed and dated on the underside.

335

Latback 1967
Urethane foam and cord
21 × 31 × 29 in.
(53.5 × 78.5 × 73.5 cm).

Collection
Private collection, New York, New York.

Provenance
Leo Castelli Gallery, New York, New York; Galerie Rudolf Zwirner, Cologne; Galerie Heiner Friedrich, Munich.

Exhibitions
Galerie Rudolf Zwirner, Cologne. *John Chamberlain*. October 10–November 9, 1967.

Galerie Heiner Friedrich, Munich. *John Chamberlain USA Skulpturen*. November–December 1967.

Notes
The sculpture is signed and dated on the underside.

336

Puswah 1967
Urethane foam and cord
27 × 41 × 38 in.
(68.5 × 104 × 96.5 cm).

Collection
Six Friedrich, Munich, 1967.

Provenance
Leo Castelli Gallery, New York, New York; Galerie Rudolf Zwirner, Cologne; Galerie Heiner Friedrich, Munich.

Exhibitions
Galerie Rudolf Zwirner, Cologne. *John Chamberlain*. October 10–November 9, 1967.

Galerie Heiner Friedrich, Munich. *John Chamberlain USA Skulpturen*. November–December 1967.

Notes
The sculpture is signed on the underside.

337

Soopad 1967
Urethane foam and cord
34 × 44 × 33 in.
(86.5 × 112 × 84 cm).

Collection
Present location unknown.

Provenance
Leo Castelli Gallery, New York, New York; Galerie Rudolf Zwirner, Cologne; Galerie Heiner Friedrich, Munich.

Exhibitions
Galerie Rudolf Zwirner, Cologne. *John Chamberlain*. October 10–November 9, 1967.

Galerie Heiner Friedrich, Munich. *John Chamberlain USA Skulpturen*. November–December 1967

Notes
The sculpture is signed on the underside.

A sculpture exhibited in the Guggenheim retrospective as cat. no. 80 is incorrectly titled *Soopad* (see cat. no. 318); *Soopad* was not actually exhibited.

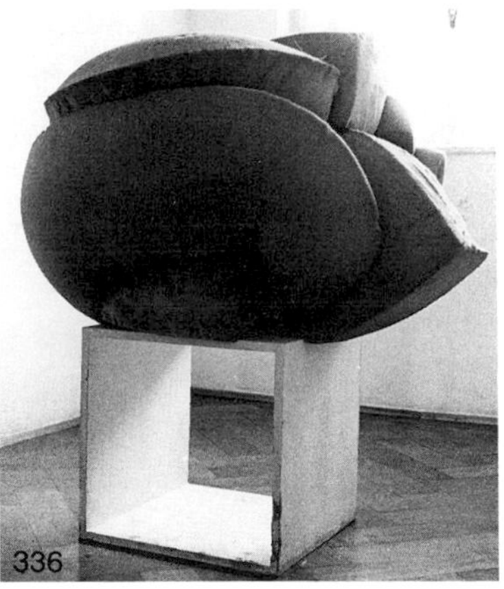
336

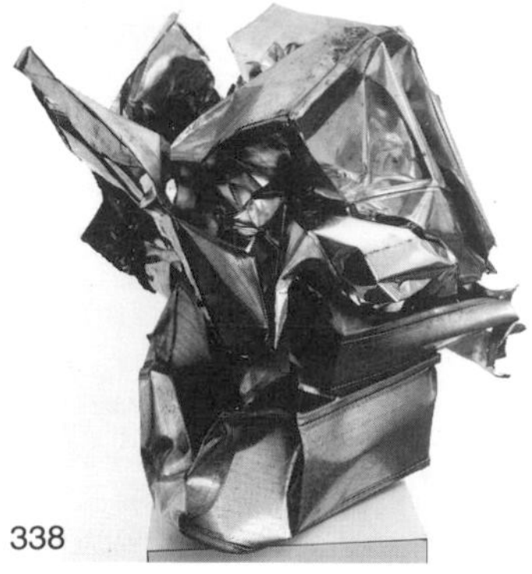
338

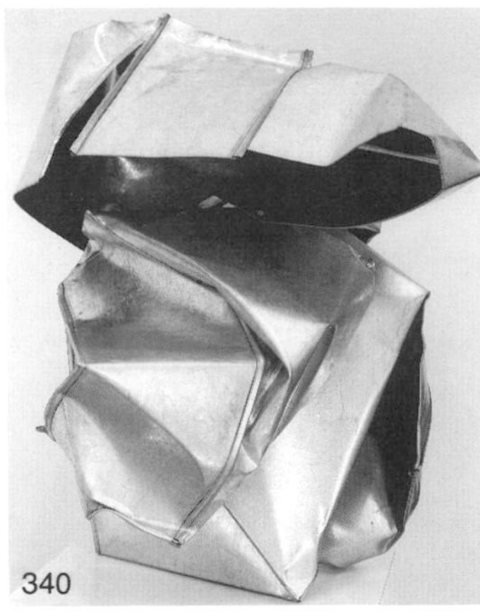
340

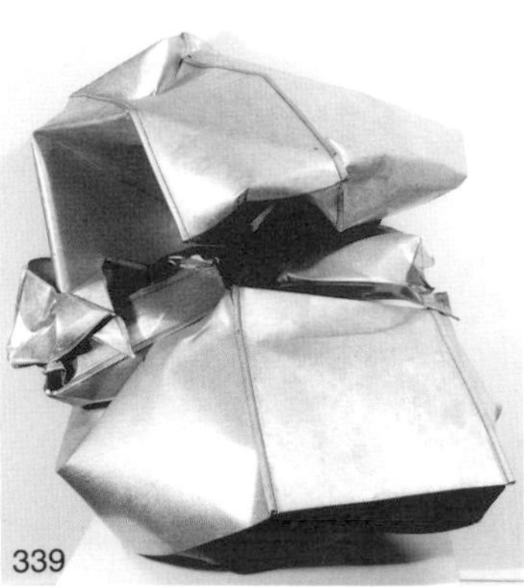
339

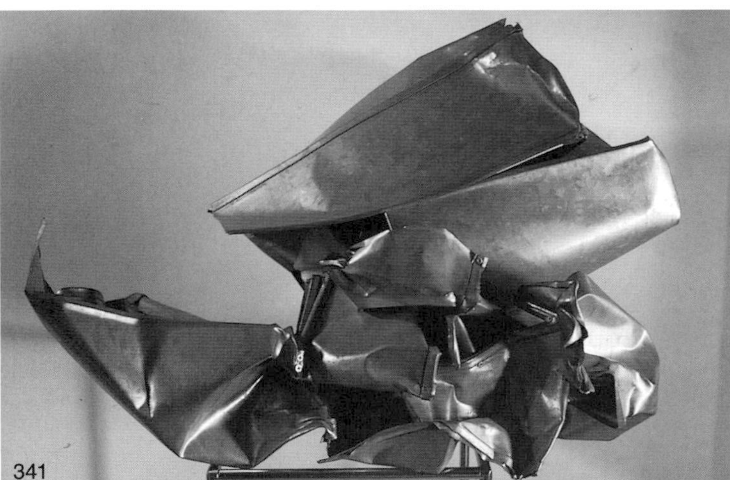
341

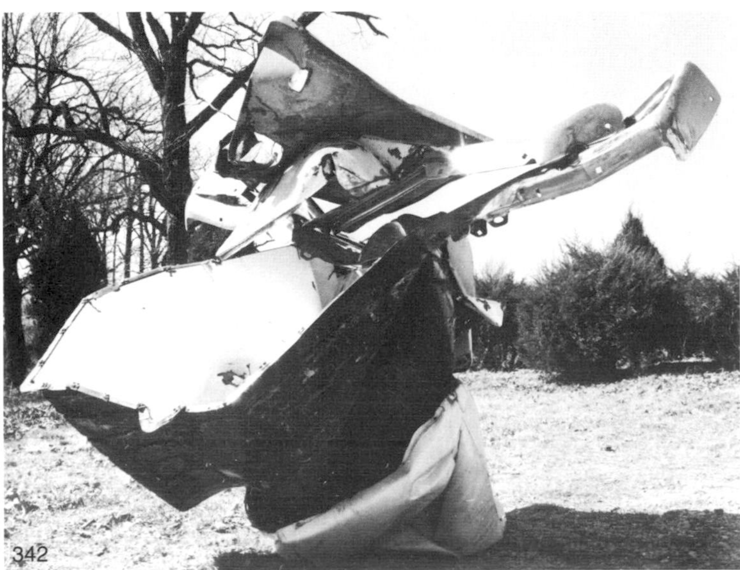
342

338

Knightsbridge Slug 1968
Galvanized steel
22½ × 24 × 19 in.
(57 × 61 × 48 cm).

Collection
William M. Speiller, Philadelphia, Pennsylvania, 1968.

Provenance
Leo Castelli Gallery, New York, New York.

Exhibitions
The Solomon R. Guggenheim Museum, New York, New York. *John Chamberlain: A Retrospective Exhibition*, cat. no. 86, illus. p. 82. December 23, 1971–February 20, 1972.

339

Slow Christmas 1968
Galvanized steel and vinyl
32 × 34 × 32 in.
(81.5 × 86.5 × 81.5 cm).

Collection
Present location unknown.

Provenance
Mrs. Leon Kraushaar, Lawrence, New York.

340

Untitled 1968
Galvanized steel
36 × 37 × 34 in.
(91.5 × 94 × 86.5 cm).

Collection
Present location unknown.

Provenance
Leo Castelli Gallery, New York, New York; Cy Twombly, Rome.

341

Untitled 1968
Galvanized steel
20½ × 28 × 15½ in.
(52 × 71 × 39.5 cm).

Collection
Mr. and Mrs. Harris K. Weston, Cincinnati, Ohio, 1968.

Provenance
Leo Castelli Gallery, New York, New York.

Exhibitions
Cincinnati Art Museum, Cincinnati, Ohio. *Small Sculptures from Cincinnati Collections*, cat. no. 40. November 5–December 6, 1970.

In May 1969 Chamberlain flew to Chicago, intending to make a series of black-and-chrome sculptures for his upcoming exhibition at the Lo Giudice Gallery. While driving into town from the airport, however, he witnessed such an abundance of discarded washing machines, refrigerators, stoves, and so forth, that a new choice became obvious. The following nine white-and-chrome sculptures (cat. nos. 342–350) were made at the Manilow residence in Park Forest South, Illinois, in May 1969.

342

Coconino 1969
Painted and chromium-plated steel
58½ × 77 × 60½ in.
(148.5 × 195.5 × 153.5 cm).

Provenance
Mr. and Mrs. Lewis Manilow, Chicago, Illinois.

Exhibitions
Lo Giudice Gallery, Chicago, Illinois. *Hard and Soft: Recent Sculpture*. 1970.

The Solomon R. Guggenheim Museum, New York, New York. *John Chamberlain: A Retrospective Exhibition*, cat. no. 89, illus. p. 84. December 23, 1971–February 20, 1972.

References
Michael Andre and Erika Rothenberg, eds., *The Poets' Encyclopedia*, vol. IV, no. IV/vol. V (New York: Unmuzzled Ox Editions, 1979), illus. p. 179, referred to as *Coco Wino*.

Notes
Coconino and *Vulcan Rapid*, cat. no. 348, disappeared from the courtyard of the Walter Kelly Gallery in Chicago in 1973. It is believed that both sculptures were taken for scrap metal, and therefore destroyed.

343

Diamond Lee 1969
Painted and chromium-plated steel
59 × 57 × 45 in.
(150 × 145 × 114.5 cm).

Collection
Private collection, New York, New York.

Provenance
Lo Giudice Gallery, Chicago, Illinois; O. K. Harris Works of Art, New York, New York.

Exhibitions
Lo Giudice Gallery, Chicago, Illinois. *Hard and Soft: Recent Sculpture*. 1970.

344

Iron Stone 1969

Painted and chromium-plated steel
40 × 48½ × 44 in.
(101.5 × 123 × 111.5 cm).

Collection

Francesco Pellizzi, New York, New York, 1978.

Provenance

Lo Giudice Gallery, Chicago, Illinois; Walter Kelly Gallery, Chicago, Illinois; Mr. and Mrs. Abe Adler, Los Angeles, California, 1976; Larry Gagosian Gallery, Los Angeles, California; Annina Nosei, New York, New York.

Exhibitions

Lo Giudice Gallery, Chicago, Illinois. *Hard and Soft: Recent Sculpture.* 1970.

The Solomon R. Guggenheim Museum, New York, New York. *John Chamberlain: A Retrospective Exhibition*, cat. no. 90, illus. p. 86. December 23, 1971–February 20, 1972.

Walter Kelly Gallery, Chicago, Illinois. *John Chamberlain*. December 1974–January 1975.

345

Nanoweap 1969

Painted steel
55 × 60 × 42 in.
(139.5 × 152 × 107 cm).

Collection

Menil Collection, Houston, Texas, 1974.

Provenance

Lo Giudice Gallery, Chicago, Illinois; Walter Kelly Gallery, Chicago, Illinois; Mr. and Mrs. Lewis Manilow, Chicago, Illinois.

Exhibitions

Lo Giudice Gallery, Chicago, Illinois. *Hard and Soft: Recent Sculpture.* 1970.

Sotheby Parke-Bernet, Inc., New York, New York. *Important Postwar and Contemporary Art*, cat. no. 583, illus. October 24–25, 1974.

Notes

The sculpture was referred to as "Untitled, 1969" in the Sotheby Parke-Bernet catalogue in 1974.

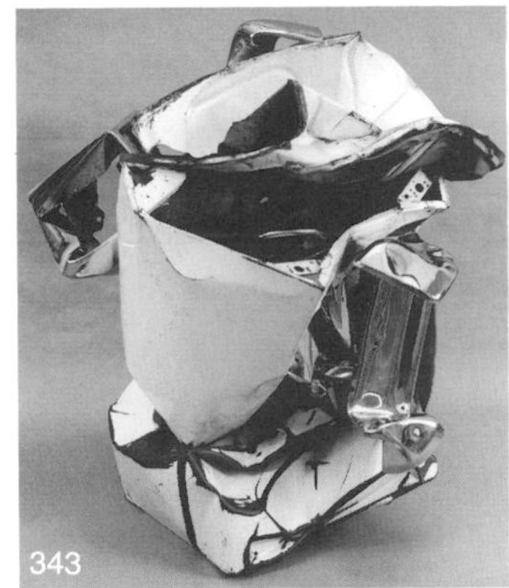
343

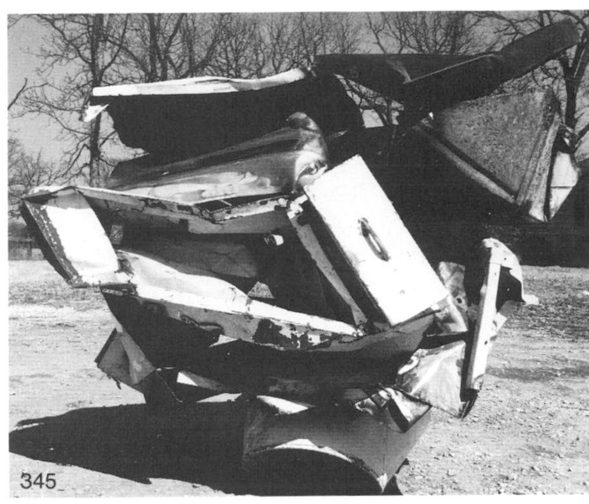
345

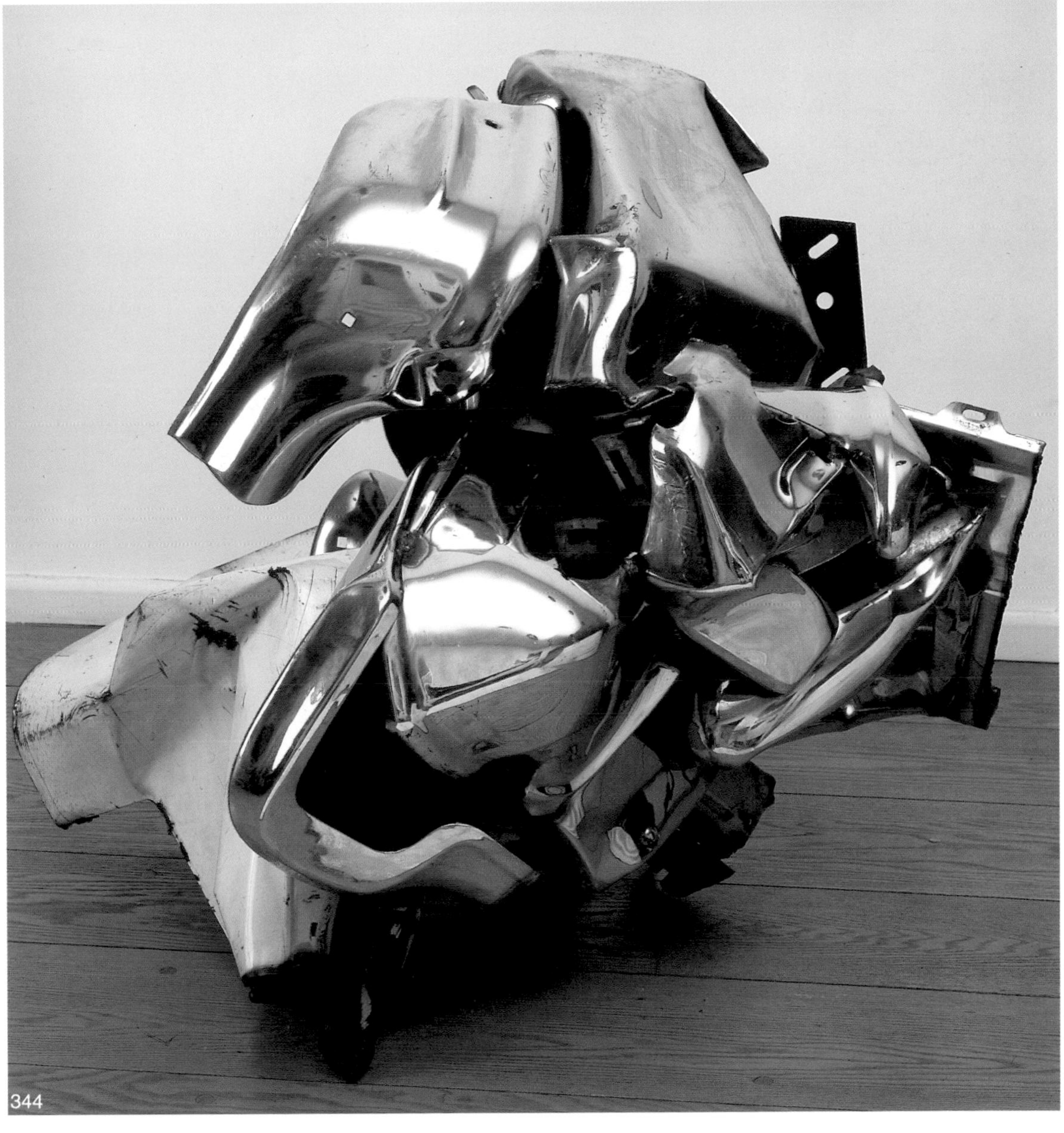
344

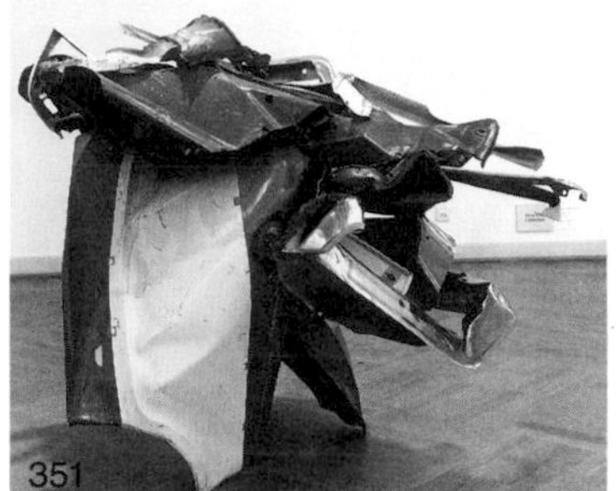
351

346

Parashont Wash 1969

Painted and chromium-plated steel
63 × 85 × 60 in.
(160 × 216 × 152.5 cm).

Collection
Present location unknown.

Provenance
Lo Giudice Gallery, Chicago, Illinois.

Exhibitions
Lo Giudice Gallery, Chicago, Illinois. *Hard and Soft: Recent Sculpture*. 1970.

347

Toroweap 1969

Painted and chromium-plated steel
29 × 40 × 32 in.
(73.5 × 101.5 × 81.5 cm).

Collection
Silverman Collection, Santa Fe, New Mexico.

Provenance
Lo Giudice Gallery, Chicago, Illinois; Walter Kelly Gallery, Chicago, Illinois.

Exhibitions
Lo Giudice Gallery, Chicago, Illinois. *Hard and Soft: Recent Sculpture*. 1970.

348

Vulcan Rapid 1969

Painted and chromium-plated steel
Dimensions unknown.

Provenance
Lo Giudice Gallery, Chicago, Illinois; Silverman Collection, Santa Fe, New Mexico; Walter Kelly Gallery, Chicago, Illinois.

Exhibitions
Lo Giudice Gallery, Chicago, Illinois. *Hard and Soft: Recent Sculpture*. 1970.

Notes
The sculpture is believed to have been destroyed; see cat. no. 342.

349

Whitmore Wash 1969

Painted and chromium-plated steel
52 × 49 × 40 in.
(132 × 124.5 × 101.5 cm).

Collection
Present location unknown.

Provenance
Lo Giudice Gallery, Chicago, Illinois.

Exhibitions
Indianapolis Museum of Art, Indianapolis, Indiana. *Painting and Sculpture Today—1969*, cat. no. 33. 1969.

Lo Giudice Gallery, Chicago, Illinois. *Hard and Soft: Recent Sculpture*. 1970.

The Solomon R. Guggenheim Museum, New York, New York. *John Chamberlain: A Retrospective Exhibition*, cat. no. 87, illus. p. 83. December 23, 1971–February 20, 1972.

350

Yampa 1969

Painted and chromium-plated steel
44 × 56 × 49 in.
(112 × 142 × 124.5 cm).

Collection
Present location unknown.

Provenance
Lo Giudice Gallery, Chicago, Illinois.

Exhibitions
Lo Giudice Gallery, Chicago, Illinois. *Hard and Soft: Recent Sculpture*. 1970.

351

M.A.A.B. c. 1969

Painted and chromium-plated steel
50 × 78 × 50 in.
(127 × 198 × 127 cm).

Collection
Moderna Museet, Stockholm, 1973; acquired directly from the artist.

Exhibitions
The Solomon R. Guggenheim Museum, New York, New York. *John Chamberlain: A Retrospective Exhibition*, cat. no. 105. December 23, 1971–February 20, 1972.

Leo Castelli Gallery, New York, New York. *New York Collection for Stockholm*. October 27–28, 1972.

Moderna Museet, Stockholm. *New York Collection for Stockholm*, color illus. October 27–December 2, 1973.

352

Malaprop 1969

Galvanized steel
24 × 23½ × 12½ in.
(61 × 59.5 × 31.5 cm).

Collection
Dia Art Foundation, New York, New York, 1980.

Provenance
Leo Castelli Gallery, New York, New York; Alfred Ordover, New York, New York; O. K. Harris Works of Art, New York, New York; Ed Cauduro, Portland, Oregon, 1972; O. K. Harris Works of Art, New York, New York; Lone Star Foundation, New York, New York, 1978.

Exhibitions
Portland Art Museum, Portland, Oregon. *Sixties to Seventy-Two: American Art from the Collection of Ed Cauduro*, cat. no. 17, illus., listed as "Untitled." September 29–October 29, 1972.

Notes
Originally untitled, the sculpture was titled by the artist in 1982.

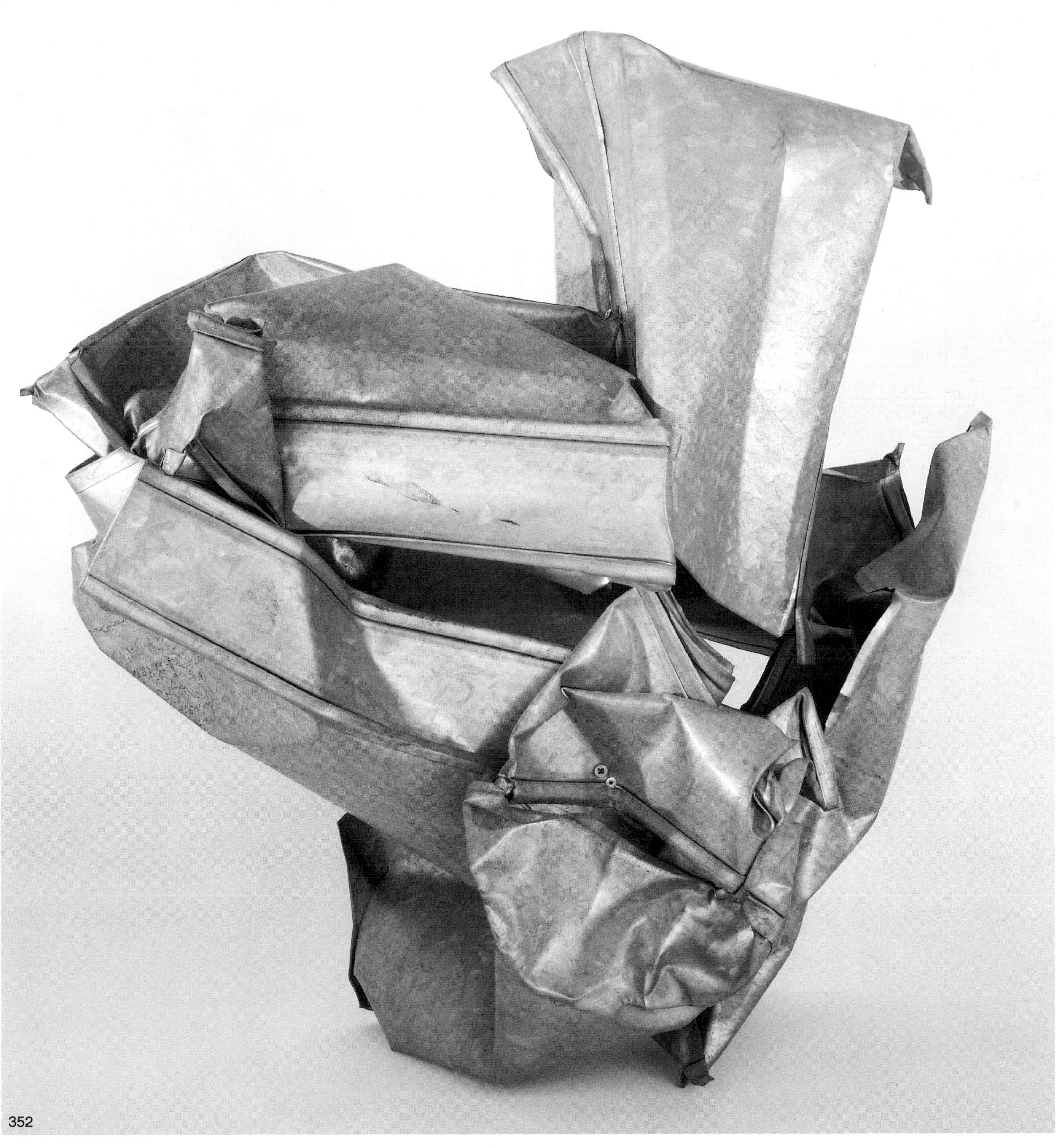

352

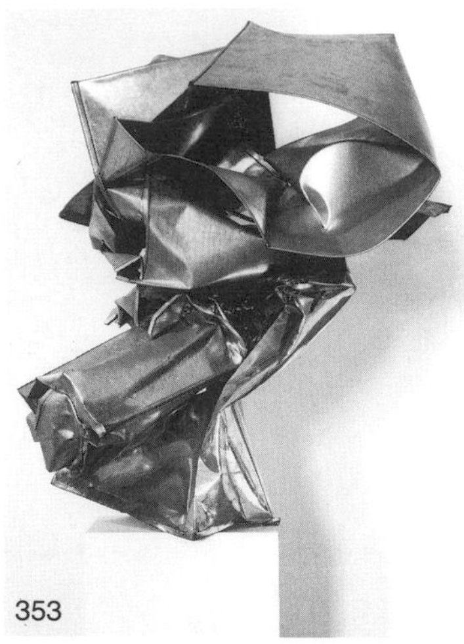
353

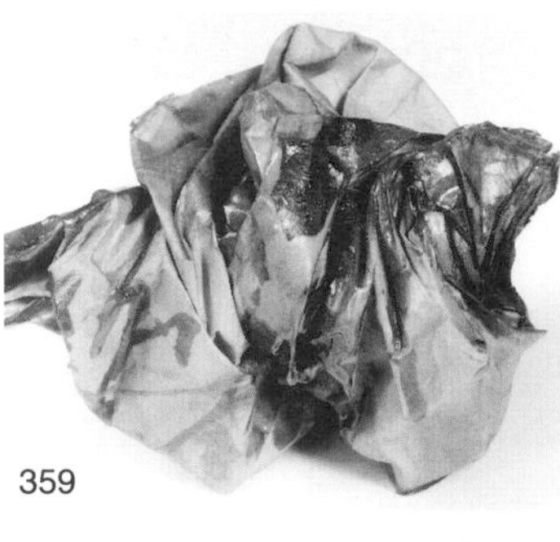
359

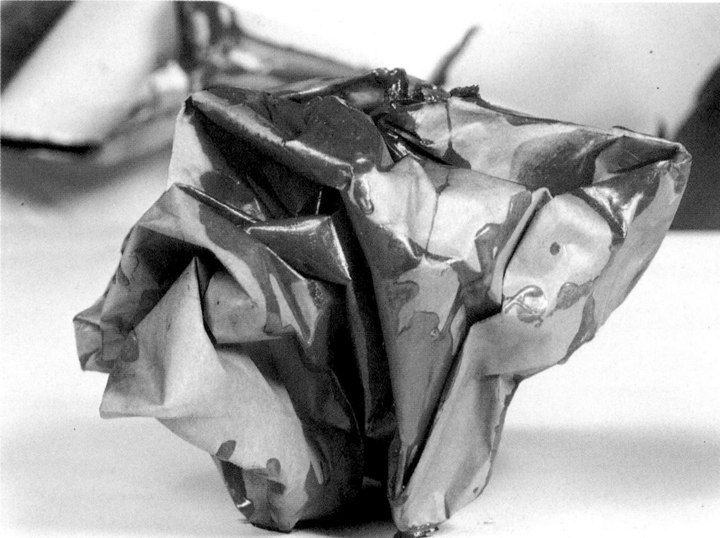
357

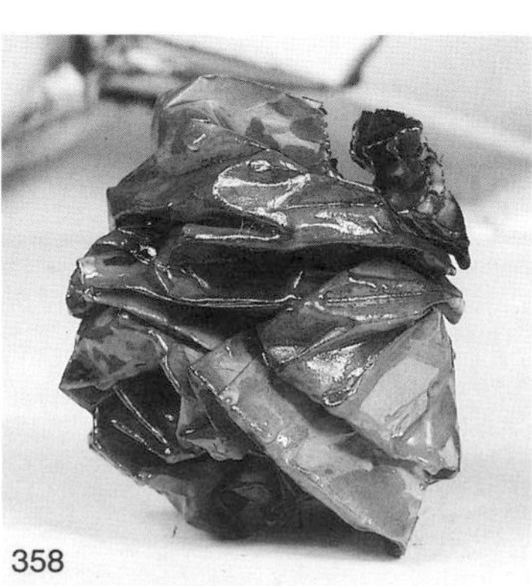
358

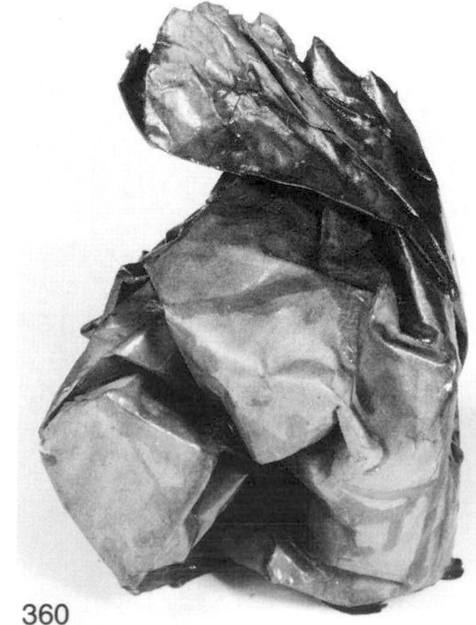
360

353

Untitled 1969
Galvanized steel
33 × 34 × 29 in.
(84 × 86.5 × 73.5 cm).

Collection
Elizabeth C. Baker, New York, New York.

Provenance
Leo Castelli Gallery, New York, New York.

Exhibitions
Leo Castelli Warehouse, New York, New York. *John Chamberlain: Recent Sculpture*. February 2–22, 1969.

The Solomon R. Guggenheim Museum, New York, New York. *John Chamberlain: A Retrospective Exhibition*, cat. no. 88, illus. p. 85. December 23, 1971–February 20, 1972.

354

Untitled c. 1969
Urethane foam and cord
14 × 15 × 15 in.
(35.5 × 38 × 38 cm).

Collection
Stanley Marsh III, Amarillo, Texas, 1974; acquired directly from the artist.

355

Untitled c. 1969
Urethane foam, cord, and paint
9 × 13 × 13 in. (23 × 33 × 33 cm).

Collection
Richard Bellamy, New York, New York, 1969; acquired directly from the artist.

356

Untitled c. 1969
Urethane foam and cord
6 × 16 × 15 in.
(15 × 40.5 × 38 cm).

Collection
Charlotte Bellamy, New York, New York, 1969; acquired directly from the artist.

The following sculptures (cat. nos. 357–370) are known as the *Penthouse* series. The original nine were made in Chamberlain's penthouse apartment on Park Avenue South in New York City in 1969. The sculptures were untitled until 1981, when the artist named the paper-bag sculptures as a group the *Penthouse* series.

357

Penthouse #44 1969
Paper, resin, and watercolor
6 × 6 × 6 in. (15 × 15 × 15 cm).

Collection
Present location unknown.

358

Penthouse #45 1969
Paper, resin, and watercolor
6 × 6 × 6 in. (15 × 15 × 15 cm).

Collection
Present location unknown.

359

Penthouse #46 1969
Paper, resin, and watercolor
5 × 7 × 4½ in.
(12.5 × 18 × 11.5 cm).

Collection
Dia Art Foundation, New York, New York, 1980.

Provenance
Lone Star Foundation, New York, New York, 1977.

360

Penthouse #47 1969
Paper, resin, and watercolor
6½ × 5½ × 4½ in.
(16.5 × 14 × 11.5 cm).

Collection
Dia Art Foundation, New York, New York, 1980.

Provenance
Lone Star Foundation, New York, New York, 1977.

361

Penthouse #48 1969
Paper, resin, and watercolor
5½ × 7 × 6½ in.
(14 × 18 × 16.5 cm).

Collection
Dia Art Foundation, New York, New York, 1980.

Provenance
Lone Star Foundation, New York, New York, 1977.

362

Penthouse #49 1969
Paper, resin, and watercolor
5 × 7½ × 6 in.
(12.5 × 19 × 15 cm).

Collection
Dia Art Foundation, New York, New York, 1980.

Provenance
Lone Star Foundation, New York, New York, 1977.

363

Penthouse #50 1969
Paper, resin, and watercolor
5 × 6½ × 4½ in.
(12.5 × 16.5 × 11.5 cm).

Collection
Dia Art Foundation, New York, New York, 1980.

Provenance
Lone Star Foundation, New York, New York, 1977.

364

Penthouse #69 1969
Paper, resin, and watercolor
8 × 8 × 7 in.
(20.5 × 20.5 × 18 cm).

Collection
Irving and Natalie Forman, Chicago, Illinois.

Provenance
Lo Giudice Gallery, Chicago, Illinois; Dr. Jerome Forman, Chicago, Illinois.

Exhibitions
Lo Giudice Gallery, Chicago, Illinois. *Hard and Soft: Recent Sculpture*. 1970.

The Solomon R. Guggenheim Museum, New York, New York. *John Chamberlain: A Retrospective Exhibition*, cat. no. 94. December 23, 1971–February 20, 1972.

Donald Young Gallery, Chicago, Illinois. *Group Show*. May–June 1984.

365

Penthouse #70 1969
Paper and polyester resin
5 × 6½ × 4½ in.
(12.5 × 16.5 × 11.5 cm).

Collection
Frank Gehry, Santa Monica, California.

366

Penthouse #71 1969
Paper and resin
4½ × 5 × 5 in.
(11.5 × 12.5 × 12.5 cm).

Collection
Freide and Rubin Gorewitz, West Nyack, New York, 1969; acquired directly from the artist.

367

Penthouse #72 1969
Paper and resin
4 × 7 × 5 in. (10 × 18 × 12.5 cm).

Collection
David Prentice, New York, New York; acquired directly from the artist.

368

Penthouse #73 1969
Paper, resin, and watercolor
7 × 8½ × 6 in.
(18 × 21.5 × 15 cm).

Provenance
Jim Jacobs, New York, New York, 1969; acquired directly from the artist.

Exhibitions
The Solomon R. Guggenheim Museum, New York, New York. *John Chamberlain: A Retrospective Exhibition*, cat. no. 91, color illus. p. 42. December 23, 1971–February 20, 1972.

Notes
The sculpture is believed to be in existence; however, its whereabouts have been unknown since the time of the Guggenheim exhibition.

369

Penthouse #74 1969
Paper, resin, and watercolor
5 × 6 × 6½ in.
(12.5 × 15 × 16.5 cm).

Collection
George L. and Dorothy A. Sturman, Las Vegas, Nevada, 1969–70.

Provenance
Walter Kelly Gallery, Chicago, Illinois.

370

Penthouse #75 1969
Paper, resin, and watercolor
6 × 6 × 5 in. (15 × 15 × 12.5 cm).

Provenance
Leo Castelli Gallery, New York, New York; Mr. and Mrs. Michael Sonnabend, New York, New York.

Exhibitions
Leo Castelli Gallery, New York, New York. *Benefit Exhibition: Art for the Moratorium*. December 11–13, 1969.

Notes
The sculpture has been destroyed.

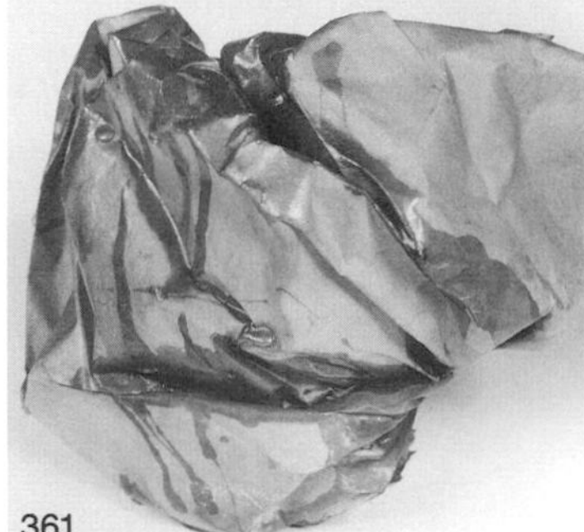
361

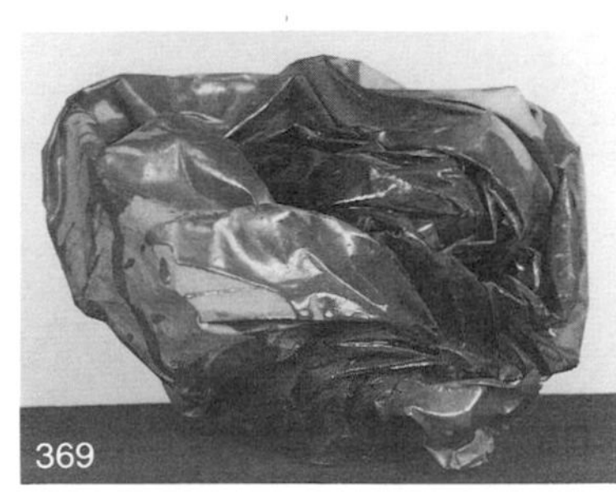
369

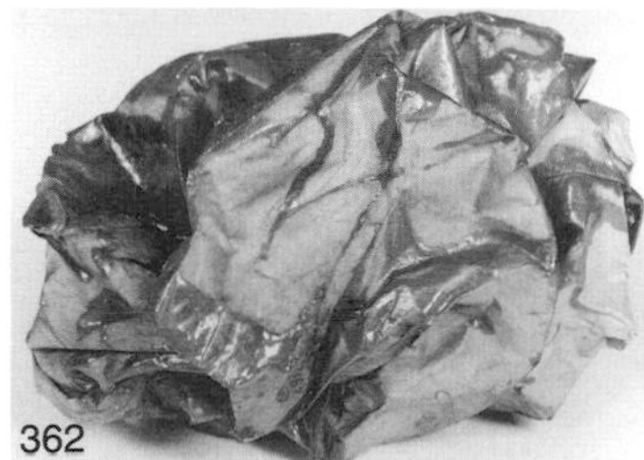
362

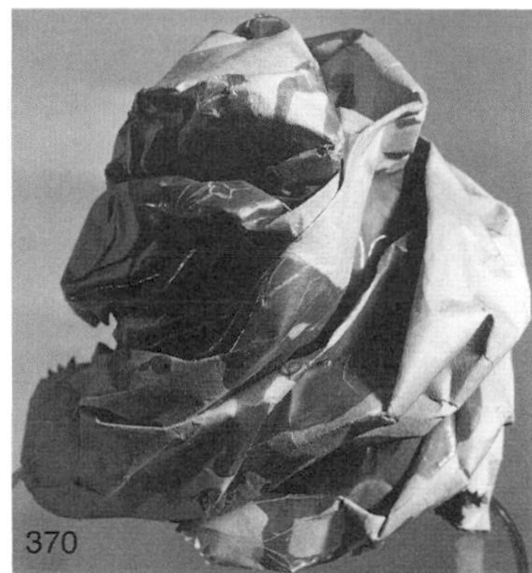
370

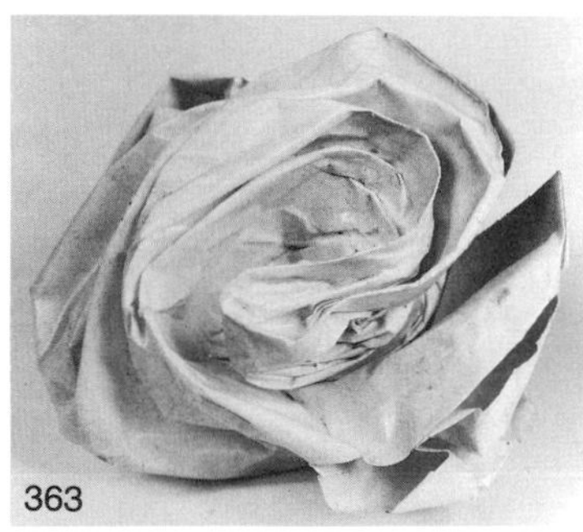
363

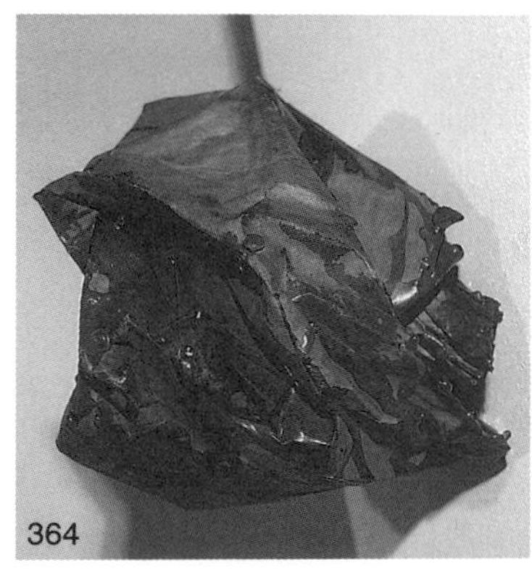
364

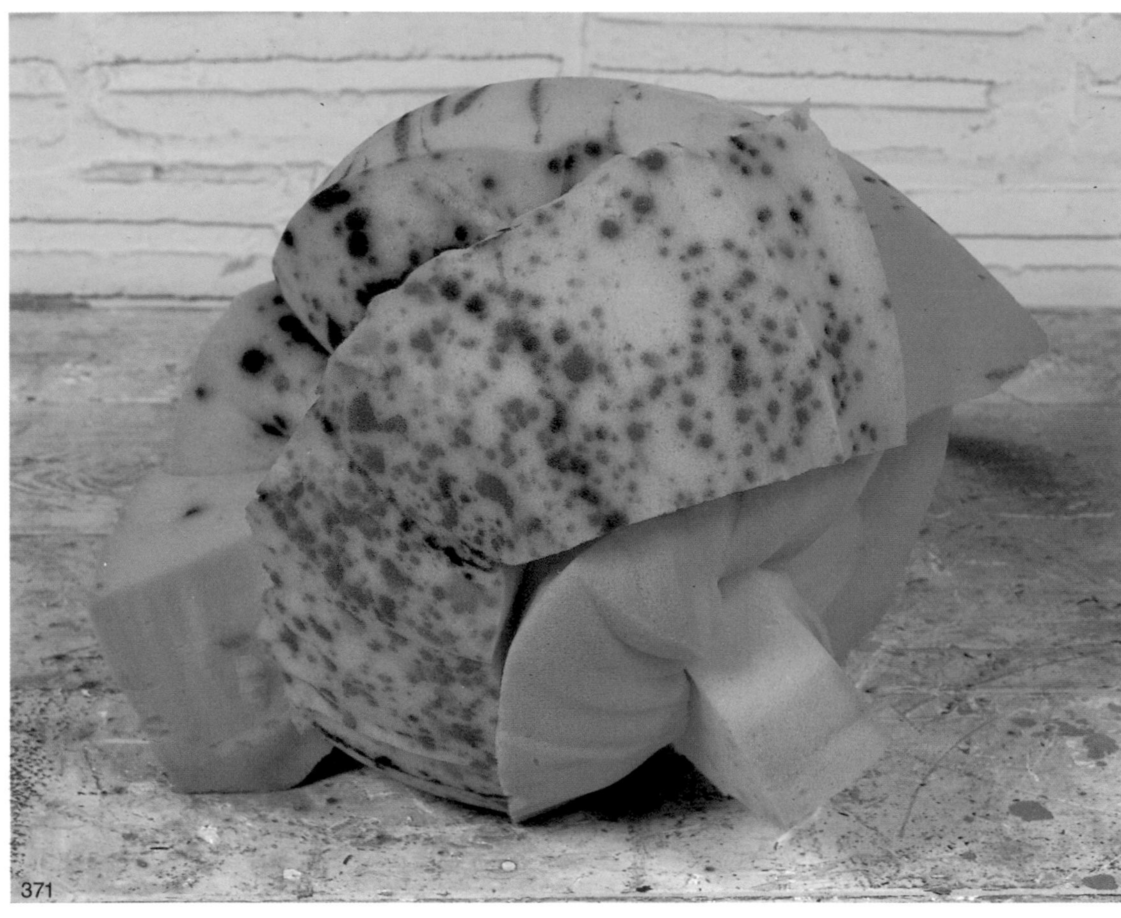
371

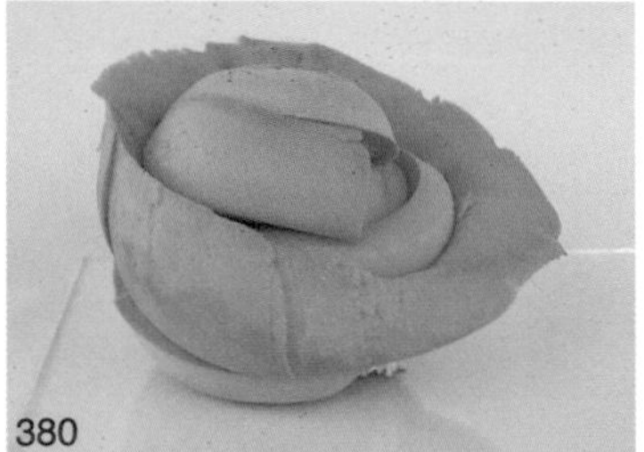
380

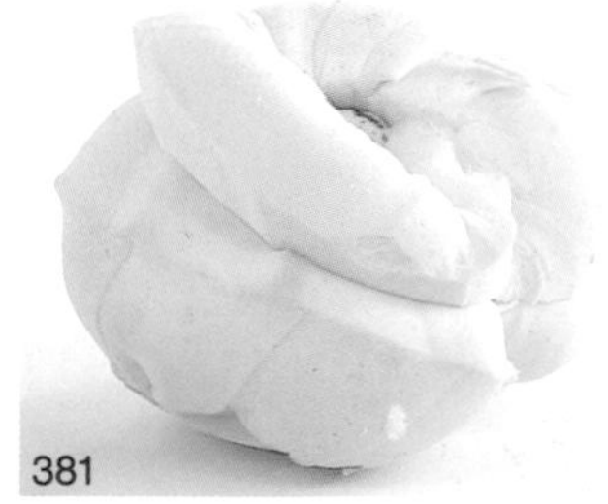
381

371

A 1969–70

Urethane foam, cord, and paint
13½ × 17 × 15½ in.
(34.5 × 43 × 39.5 cm).

Collection

Dia Art Foundation, New York, New York, 1980.

Provenance

Julia Fahey, New York, New York; Lone Star Foundation, New York, New York, 1979.

Exhibitions

The Solomon R. Guggenheim Museum, New York, New York. *John Chamberlain: A Retrospective Exhibition*, cat. no. 95. December 23, 1971–February 20, 1972.

Notes

The sculpture is inscribed on the underside: *A Chamberlain*.

The sculpture was referred to as *Stuffed Dog 10* and incorrectly dated 1973, until the original title was rediscovered in 1984.

372

B 1969–70

Urethane foam
13½ × 24 × 22½ in.
(34 × 61 × 57 cm).

Collection

Present location unknown.

Exhibitions

The Solomon R. Guggenheim Museum, New York, New York. *John Chamberlain: A Retrospective Exhibition*, cat. no. 96. December 23, 1971–February 20, 1972.

Notes

It is likely that this sculpture and "Untitled, 1969–70" (cat. no. 373) are one and the same piece. The relevant markings on that work have faded so that a positive identification cannot be made.

373

Untitled 1969–70

Urethane foam, cord, and paint
13½ × 25½ × 22 in.
(34.5 × 65 × 56 cm).

Collection

Dr. and Mrs. Stanley Fromm, Miami Shores, Florida.

Provenance

Gordon Locksley, Minneapolis, Minnesota; Berenson Gallery, Miami, Florida.

Exhibitions

Fort Lauderdale Museum, Fort Lauderdale, Florida. *South Florida Collects*. February 7–March 6, 1973.

Notes

The sculpture is signed on the underside. This and *B*, 1969–70 (cat. no. 372) are likely one and the same piece.

374

C 1969–70

Urethane foam and cord
12½ × 17 × 11 in.
(32 × 43 × 28 cm).

Collection
Michael Rosenfeld, New York, New York, 1985.

Provenance
Louis Meisel, New York, New York.

Exhibitions
The Solomon R. Guggenheim Museum, New York, New York. *John Chamberlain: A Retrospective Exhibition*, cat. no. 97. December 23, 1971–February 20, 1972.

Christie's East, New York, New York. *Contemporary Art*, cat. no. 137. January 8, 1985.

Notes
The sculpture is signed and dated on the underside: *Chamberlain '70* ©. It has deteriorated considerably.

375

Untitled 1970

Urethane foam and cord
10 × 19 × 14 in.
(25½ × 48 × 35.5 cm).

Collection
Helen Marden, New York, New York, 1970; acquired directly from the artist.

376

Untitled 1970

Urethane foam, cord, and paint
9 × 12 × 24 in.
(23 × 30.5 × 61 cm).

Collection
Dorothy Berenson Blau, Bal Harbour, Florida, 1970.

Provenance
Gordon Locksley, Minneapolis, Minnesota.

Notes
The sculpture is signed on the underside.

377

Untitled 1970

Urethane foam, cord, and paint
10½ × 17 × 15 in.
(26.5 × 43 × 38 cm).

Collection
Private collection, New York, New York.

Notes
The sculpture is signed on the underside: *Cham 70.*

378

Untitled 1970

Urethane foam, cord, and paint
9 × 16 × 14 in.
(23 × 40.5 × 35.5 cm).

Collection
Private collection, New York, New York.

Notes
The sculpture is signed and dated on the underside: *Chamberlain '70.*

379

Babe 1970

Urethane foam with watercolor
13½ × 21 × 17 in.
(34 × 53.5 × 43 cm).

Collection
Collection of the artist, Sarasota, Florida.

The nine sculptures in the *Stuffed Dog* series (cat. nos. 380–388) were made in 1967 and 1970. They were titled as a series by the artist in 1981.

380

Stuffed Dog 1 1967

Urethane foam, cord, and paint
7 × 10 × 9½ in.
(18 × 25.5 × 24 cm).

Collection
Dia Art Foundation, New York, New York, 1980.

Provenance
Gordon Locksley, Minneapolis, Minnesota; Lone Star Foundation, New York, New York, 1978.

Notes
The sculpture is signed and dated on the underside: *Chamberlain '67.*

381

Stuffed Dog 2 1970

Urethane foam, cord, and paint
10 × 12½ × 11 in.
(25.5 × 32 × 28 cm).

Collection
Dia Art Foundation, New York, New York, 1980.

Provenance
Gordon Locksley, Minneapolis, Minnesota; Lone Star Foundation, New York, New York, 1978.

Notes
The sculpture is signed and dated on the underside: *CHAM '70.* It is weighted with lead weights.

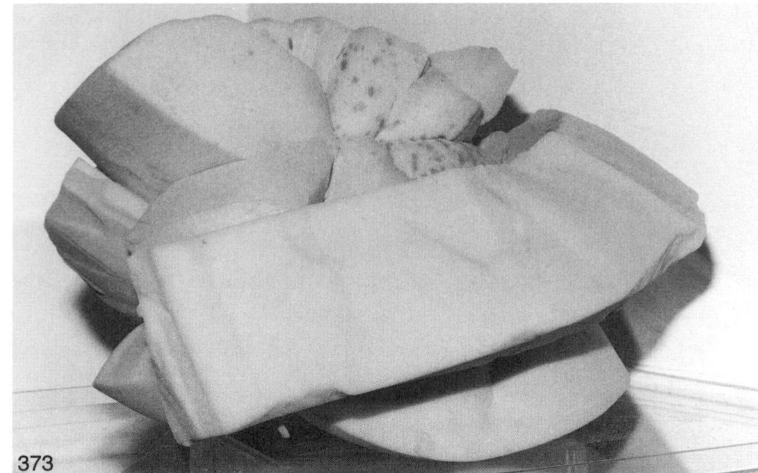
373

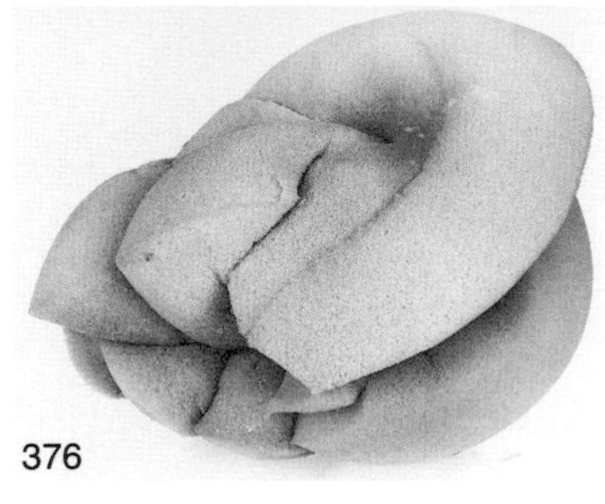
376

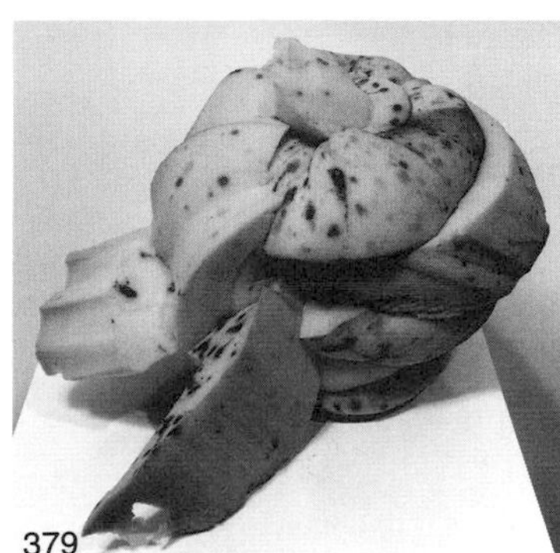
379

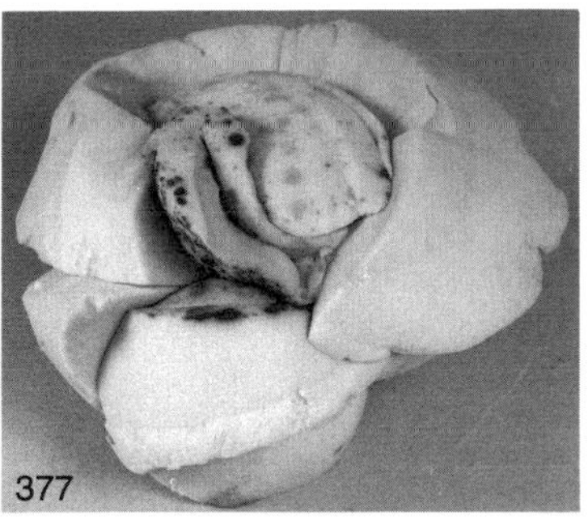
377

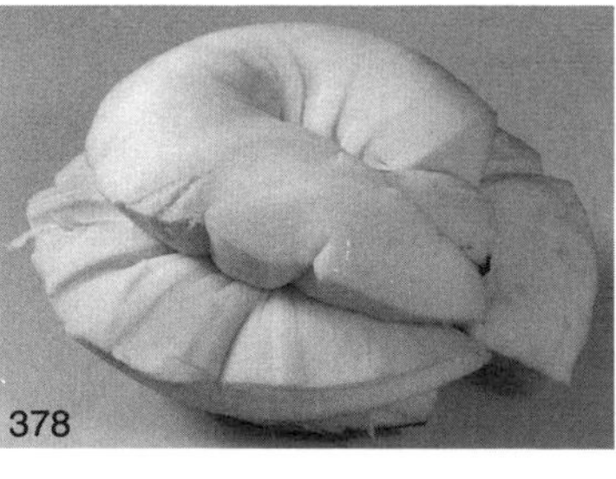
378

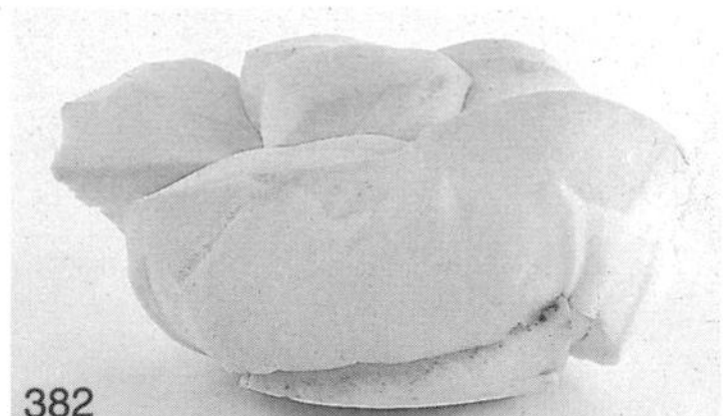
382

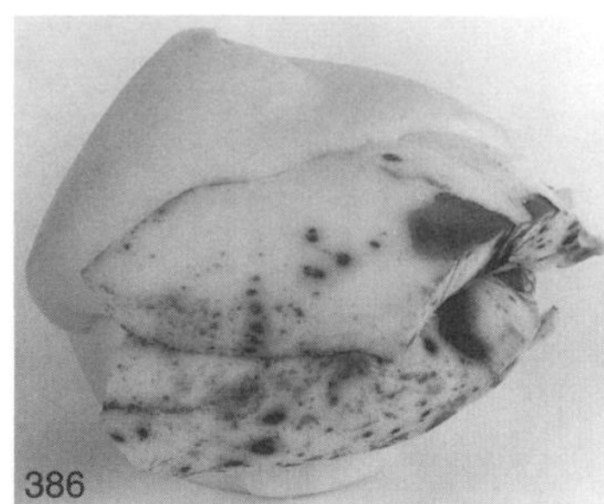
386

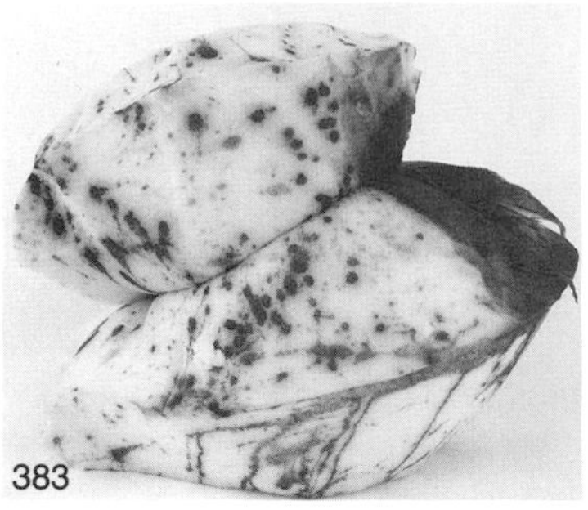
383

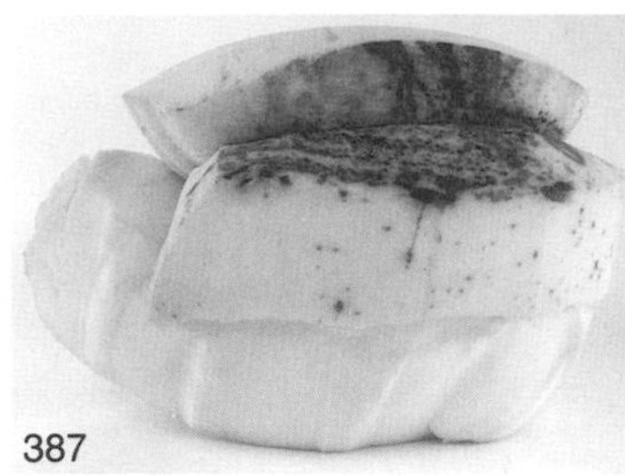
387

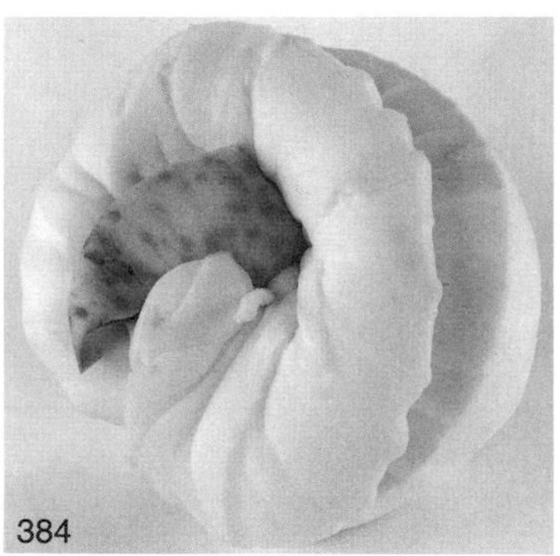
384

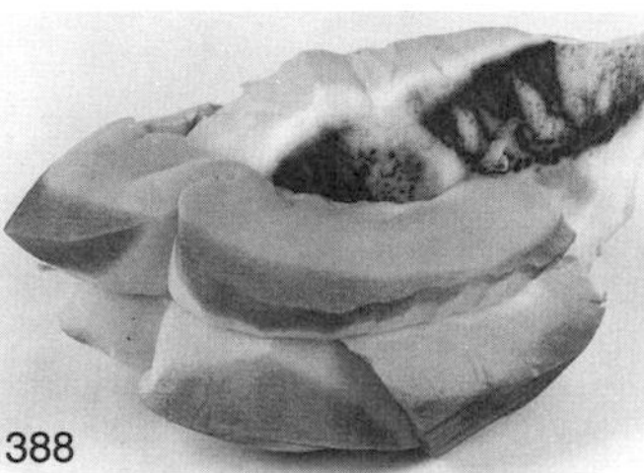
388

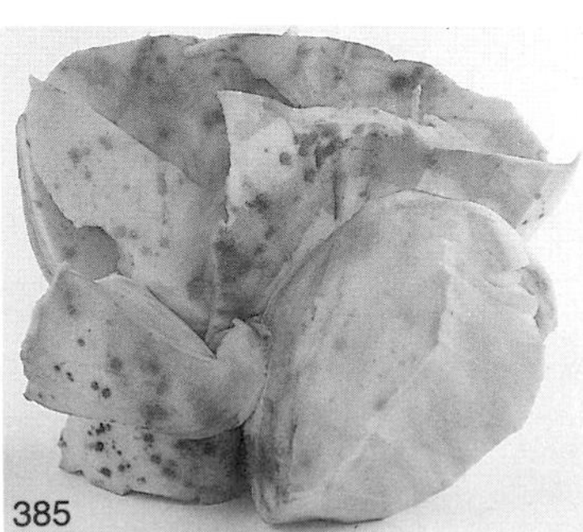
385

382

Stuffed Dog 3 1970

Urethane foam, cord, and paint
8½ × 14½ × 13 in.
(21.5 × 37 × 33 cm).

Collection

Dia Art Foundation, New York, New York, 1980.

Provenance

Gordon Locksley, Minneapolis, Minnesota; Lone Star Foundation, New York, New York, 1978.

383

Stuffed Dog 4 1970

Urethane foam, cord, and paint
10½ × 14 × 14 in.
(26.5 × 35.5 × 35.5 cm).

Collection

Dia Art Foundation, New York, New York, 1980.

Provenance

Gordon Locksley, Minneapolis, Minnesota; Lone Star Foundation, New York, New York, 1978.

384

Stuffed Dog 5 1970

Urethane foam, cord, and paint
11 × 13 × 12 in.
(28 × 33 × 30.5 cm).

Collection

Dia Art Foundation, New York, New York, 1980.

Provenance

Gordon Locksley, Minneapolis, Minnesota; Lone Star Foundation, New York, New York, 1978.

Notes

The sculpture is signed and dated on the underside.

385

Stuffed Dog 6 1970

Urethane foam, cord, and paint
11 × 15½ × 14½ in.
(28 × 39.5 × 37 cm).

Collection

Dia Art Foundation, New York, New York, 1980.

Provenance

Gordon Locksley, Minneapolis, Minnesota; Lone Star Foundation, New York, New York, 1978.

386

Stuffed Dog 7 1970

Urethane foam, cord, and paint
10½ × 15 × 14½ in.
(26.5 × 38 × 37 cm).

Collection

Dia Art Foundation, New York, New York, 1980.

Provenance

Gordon Locksley, Minneapolis, Minnesota; Lone Star Foundation, New York, New York, 1978.

Notes

The sculpture is signed and dated on the underside: *CHAM '70*.

387

Stuffed Dog 8 1970

Urethane foam, cord, and paint
12½ × 18 × 16 in.
(31.5 × 45.5 × 40.5 cm).

Collection

Dia Art Foundation, New York, New York, 1980.

Provenance

Gordon Locksley, Minneapolis, Minnesota; Lone Star Foundation, New York, New York, 1978.

Notes

The sculpture is signed and dated by the artist on the underside: *CHAM '70*.

388

Stuffed Dog 9 1970

Urethane foam, cord, paint, and flocking
12 × 21 × 20 in.
(30.5 × 53.5 × 51 cm).

Collection

Dia Art Foundation, New York, New York, 1980.

Provenance

Gordon Locksley, Minneapolis, Minnesota; Lone Star Foundation, New York, New York, 1978.

These Plexiglas sculptures (cat. nos. 389–411) were made in East Los Angeles in 1970. Fabricated Plexiglas boxes were melted in walk-in ovens, where they were manipulated by Chamberlain at the moment of collapse. The pieces were then coated with various minerals, using the vacuum coater in the studio of the artist Larry Bell. A second series (cat. nos. 412–416) was made in 1970–71, when Chamberlain was living in Little Sycamore Canyon, California.

Most of the sculptures were named after towns and regions in Northern Arizona.

389

Dinnebito 1970

Mineral-coated synthetic polymer resin
25 × 55 × 38 in.
(63.5 × 139.5 × 96.5 cm).

Provenance

Lo Giudice Gallery, New York, New York.

Exhibitions

The Solomon R. Guggenheim Museum, New York, New York. *John Chamberlain: A Retrospective Exhibition*, cat. no. 100, illus. p. 90. December 23, 1971–February 20, 1972.

The Contemporary Arts Center, Cincinnati, Ohio. *Ponderosa Collection*. May 3–June 24, 1974.

Notes

According to the artist, the sculpture was destroyed while in the possession of the Lo Giudice Gallery, New York, New York.

390

Dot-Klish 1970

Mineral-coated synthetic polymer resin
18½ × 23½ × 19½ in.
(47 × 59.5 × 49.5 cm).

Collection

Mr. and Mrs. Michael Sonnabend, New York, New York.

Provenance

Leo Castelli Gallery, New York, New York.

391

Hano 1970

Mineral-coated synthetic polymer resin
30 × 37 × 34 in.
(76 × 94 × 86.5 cm).

Collection

The New Museum of Contemporary Art, New York, New York, 1983; not accessioned.

Provenance

Leo Castelli Gallery, New York, New York; Giuseppe Agrati, Rome; Leo Castelli Gallery, New York, New York.

Exhibitions

Leo Castelli Gallery, New York, New York. *John Chamberlain*. April 17–May 8, 1971.

The Solomon R. Guggenheim Museum, New York, New York. *John Chamberlain: A Retrospective Exhibition*, cat. no. 101, illus. p. 88. December 23, 1971–February 20, 1972.

References

"From Various Exhibitions of Last Season," *Art International*, vol. 15, no. 8 (October 1971), illus. p. 33.

392

Jeddito 1970

Mineral-coated synthetic polymer resin
26½ × 42½ × 30 in.
(67.5 × 108 × 76 cm).

Collection

Mr. and Mrs. Michael Sonnabend, New York, New York.

Provenance

Leo Castelli Gallery, New York, New York.

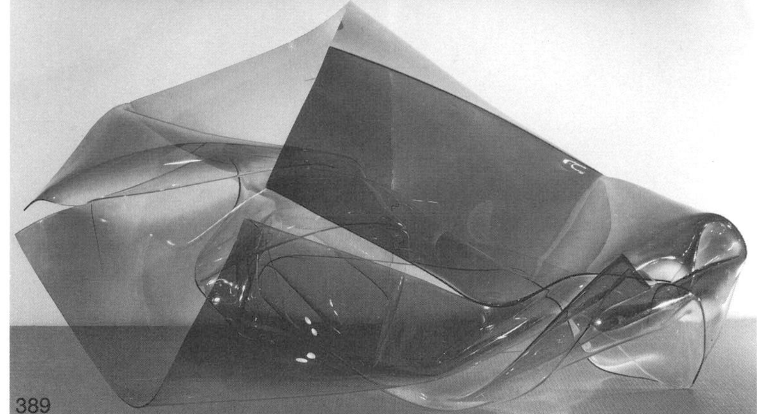
389

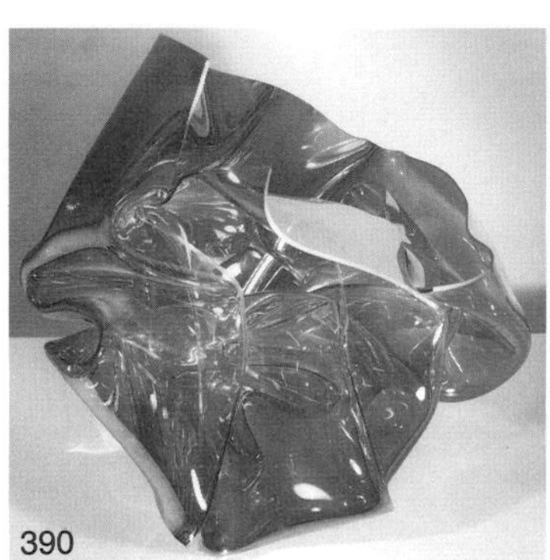
390

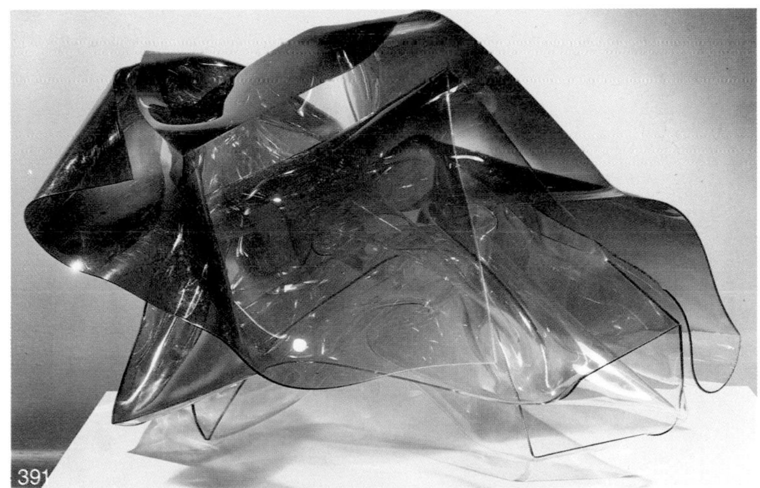
391

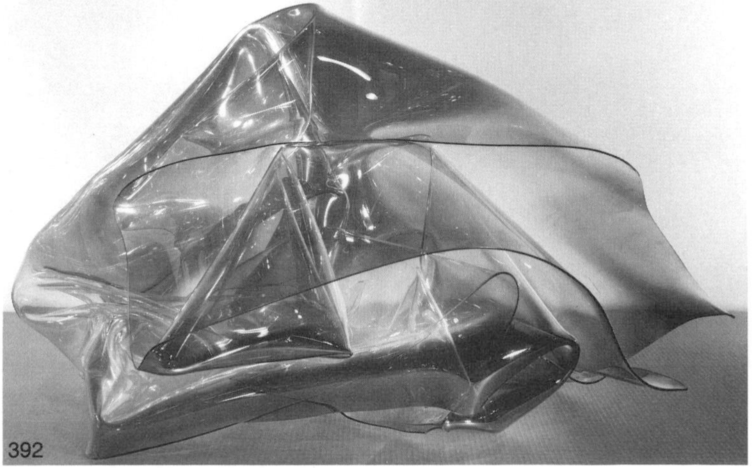
392

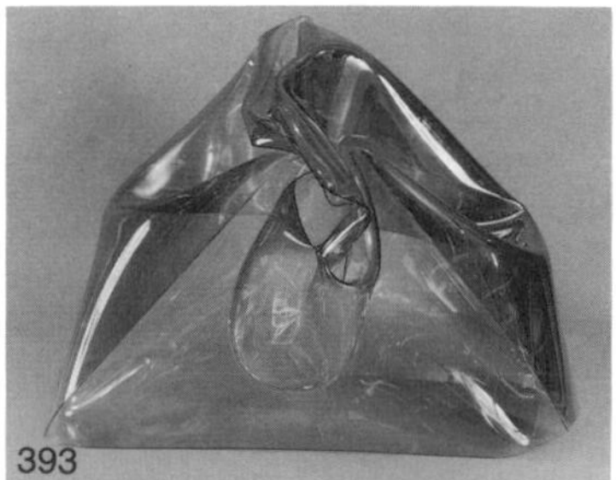

393

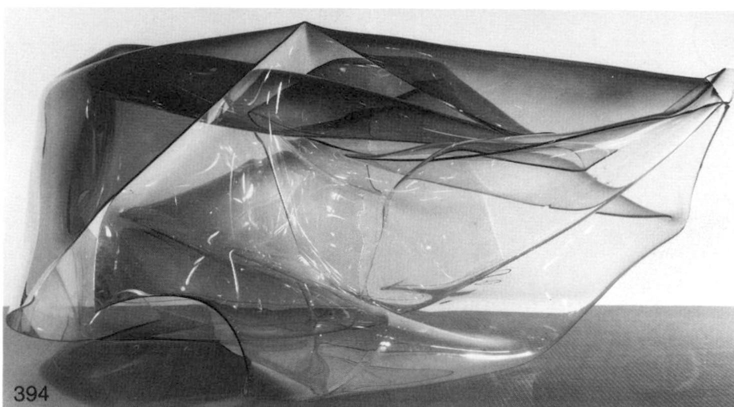

394

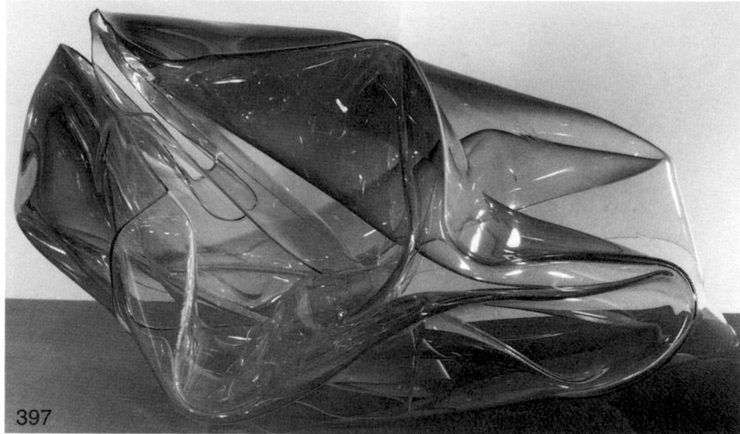

397

393

Luna, Luna, Luna (In Memory of Elaine Chamberlain) 1970

Mineral-coated synthetic polymer resin

30½ × 44 × 34 in.
(77.5 × 112 × 86.5 cm).

Collection

Dia Art Foundation, New York, New York, 1980.

Provenance

Lone Star Foundation, New York, New York, 1977.

Exhibitions

The Solomon R. Guggenheim Museum, New York, New York. *John Chamberlain: A Retrospective Exhibition*, cat. no. 102, color illus. cover, listed as "Untitled." December 23, 1971–February 20, 1972.

Notes

The sculpture was titled by the artist in 1979.

394

Moenkopi 1970

Mineral-coated synthetic polymer resin

24 × 55 × 44 in.
(61 × 139.5 × 112 cm).

Collection

Present location unknown.

Exhibitions

Leo Castelli Gallery, New York, New York. *John Chamberlain*. April 17–May 8, 1971.

The Aldrich Museum of Contemporary Art, Ridgefield, Connecticut. *Highlights of the 1970–1971 Season*, cat. no. 15. June 27–September 19, 1971.

395

Na-An-Tee 1970

Mineral-coated synthetic polymer resin

29 × 61 × 35 in.
(73.5 × 155 × 89 cm), original dimensions.

Collection

Madison Art Center, Madison, Wisconsin, 1976; gift from the estate of Robert B. Mayer.

Provenance

Leo Castelli Gallery, New York, New York, 1970; Mr. and Mrs. Robert B. Mayer, Chicago, Illinois, 1971.

Exhibitions

Leo Castelli Gallery, New York, New York. *John Chamberlain*. April 17–May 8, 1971.

Madison Art Center, Madison, Wisconsin. *Selections from the Permanent Collection*. February 22–March 28, 1980.

References

"From Various Exhibitions of Last Season," *Art International*, vol. 15, no. 8 (October 1971), p. 33, illus.

Notes

According to the Mayers, the sculpture was damaged while in shipment from New York to their home in Winnetka, Illinois. A triangular piece approximately 10 × 13 inches was broken off. The Mayers kept the sculpture and later donated it in its damaged state to the Madison Art Center. The sculpture has been exhibited frequently at the Madison Art Center in this condition.

396

Oraibi 1970

Mineral-coated synthetic polymer resin

27 × 45 × 49 in.
(68.5 × 114.5 × 124.5 cm).

Collection

Collection of the artist, Sarasota, Florida.

Exhibitions

The Solomon R. Guggenheim Museum, New York, New York. *John Chamberlain: A Retrospective Exhibition*, cat. no. 99, illus. p. 88. December 23, 1971–February 20, 1972.

References

The Aldrich Museum of Contemporary Art, Ridgefield, Connecticut. *Highlights of the 1970–1971 Season*, illus. June 27–September 19, 1971.

Phyllis Tuchman, "An Interview with John Chamberlain," *Artforum*, vol. 10, no. 6 (February 1972), illus. p. 42.

397

Polacca 1970

Mineral-coated synthetic polymer resin

27 × 46 × 39 in.
(68.5 × 117 × 99 cm).

Collection

Alan Power, Nevada City, California; acquired directly from the artist.

Exhibitions

The Solomon R. Guggenheim Museum, New York, New York. *John Chamberlain: A Retrospective Exhibition*, cat. no. 103, illus. p. 87. December 23, 1971–February 20, 1972.

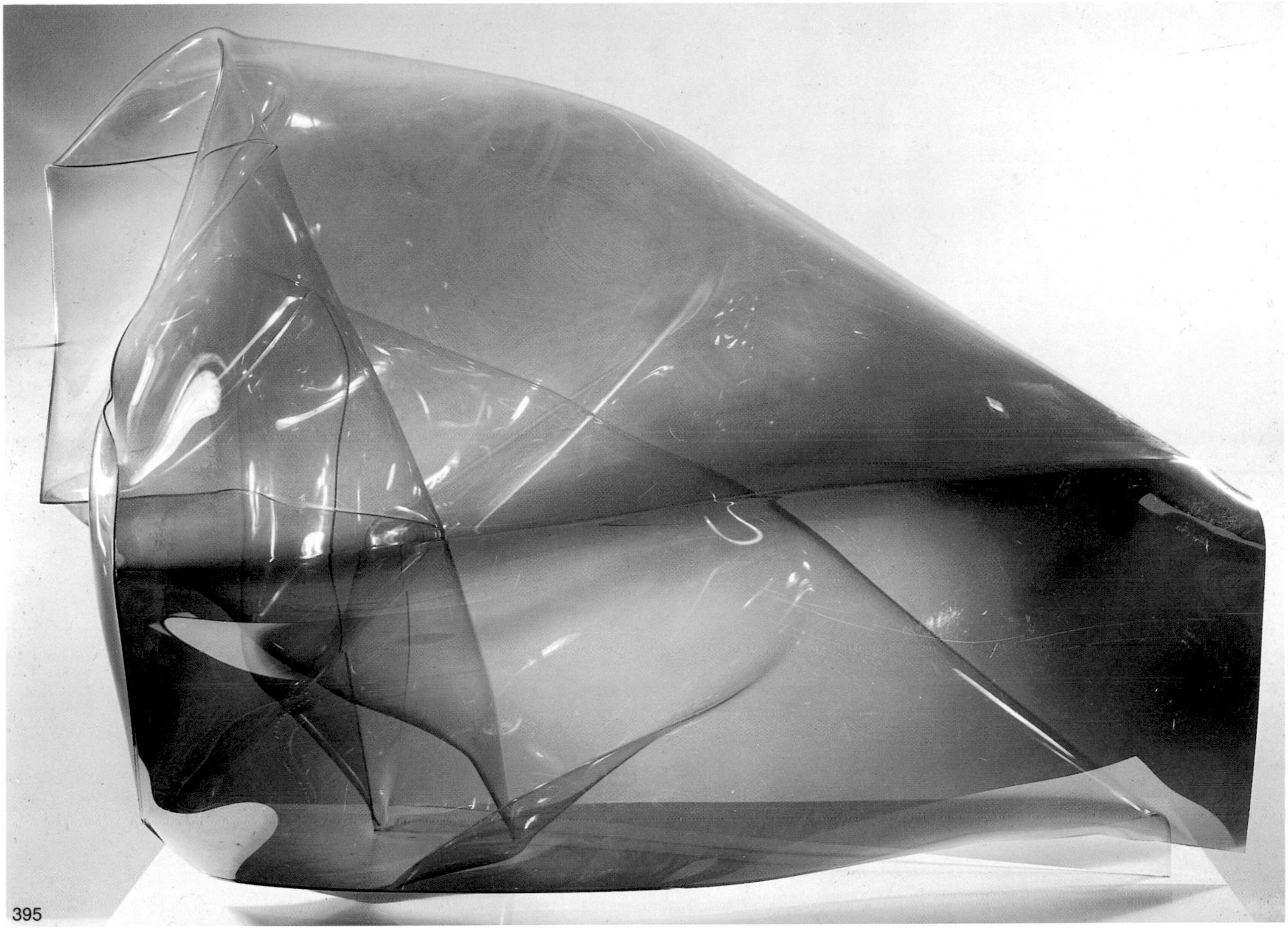

395

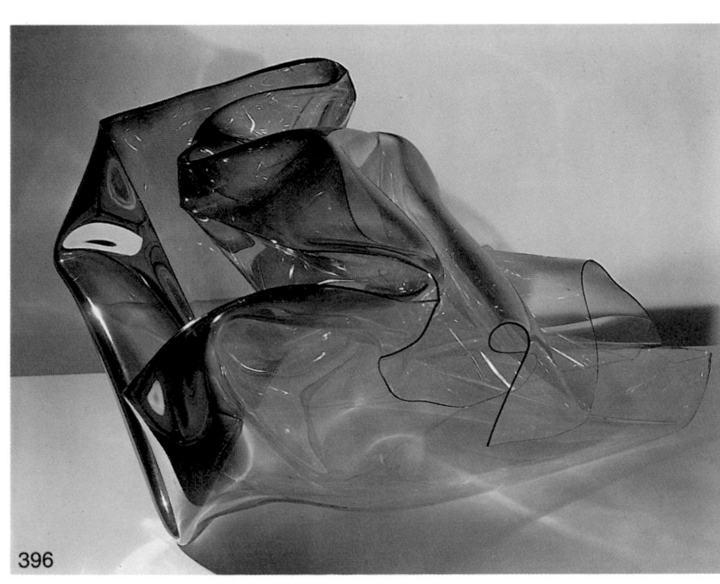

396

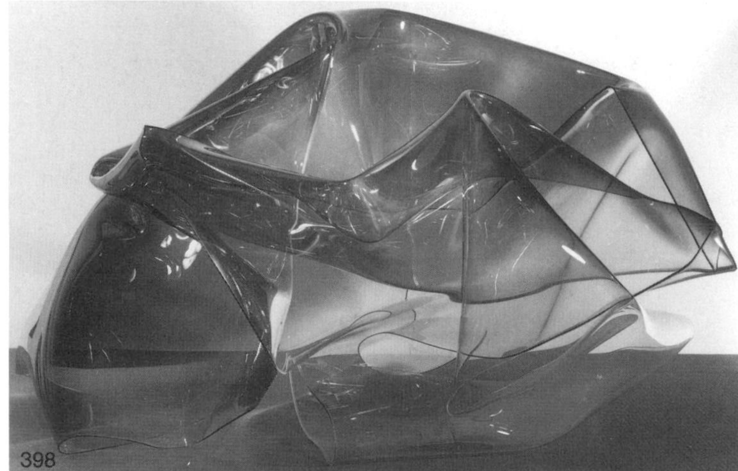
398

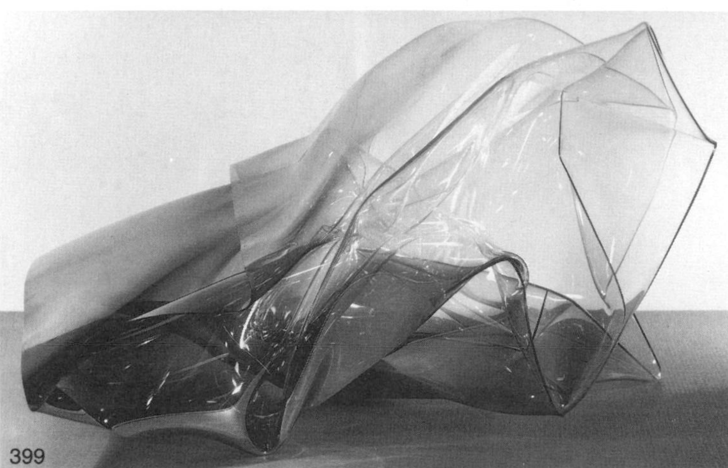
399

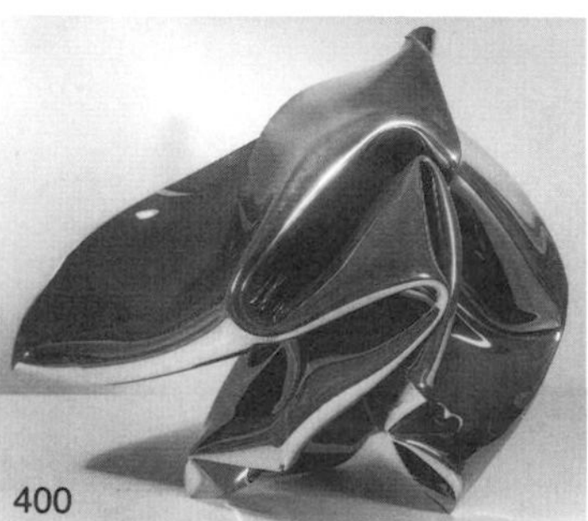
400

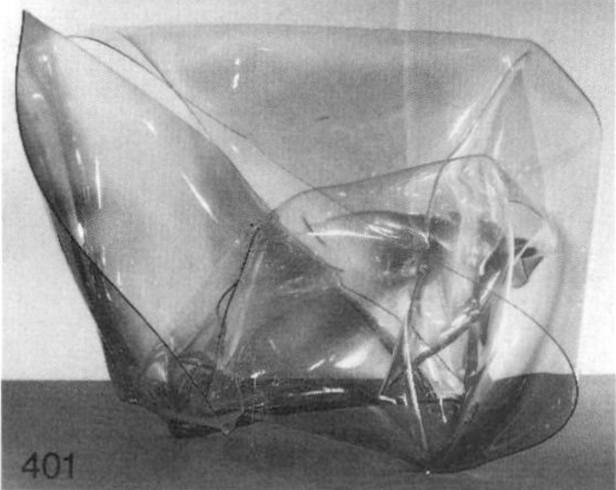
401

398

Shongopovi 1970

Mineral-coated synthetic polymer resin
30 × 58 × 58 in.
(76 × 147.5 × 147.5 cm).

Exhibitions

Leo Castelli Gallery, New York, New York. *John Chamberlain.* April 17–May 8, 1971.

The Aldrich Museum of Contemporary Art, Ridgefield, Connecticut. *Highlights of the 1970–1971 Season*, cat. no. 14. June 27–September 19, 1971.

The Solomon R. Guggenheim Museum, New York, New York. *John Chamberlain: A Retrospective Exhibition*, cat. no. 98, illus. p. 89, incorrectly listed as *Shungospavi*. December 23, 1971–February 20, 1972.

References

Elizabeth C. Baker, "Reviews and Previews," *Art News*, vol. 70, no. 4 (Summer 1971), illus. p. 11.

Notes

The sculpture was accidentally destroyed in 1984, while in the possession of the artist.

399

Teec-Nos-Pos 1970

Mineral-coated synthetic polymer resin
26 × 55 × 44 in.
(66 × 140 × 112 cm).

Collection

Dia Art Foundation, New York, New York, 1980.

Provenance

Leo Castelli Gallery, New York, New York; Gordon Locksley, Minneapolis, Minnesota; Lone Star Foundation, New York, New York, 1979.

Exhibitions

Leo Castelli Gallery, New York, New York. *John Chamberlain.* April 17–May 8, 1971.

Christie, Manson & Woods International, Inc., New York, New York. *Contemporary Art*, cat. no. 35, illus. p. 41. May 18, 1979.

Notes

The sculpture was listed as "Untitled, c. 1970" in the Christie's catalogue. In order to give the sculpture a title, Chamberlain decided in 1979 to call it *Gallup*. It has been referred to as such while in the collections of the Lone Star Foundation and the Dia Art Foundation. There is no record of another sculpture titled *Gallup*.

400

Tonalea 1970

Mineral-coated synthetic polymer resin
19½ × 15 × 24 in.
(49.5 × 38 × 61 cm).

Collection

Max Palevsky, Los Angeles, California, 1971.

Provenance

Leo Castelli Gallery, New York, New York.

401

Zihi-Dush-Jhini 1970

Mineral-coated synthetic polymer resin
33 × 45 × 37 in.
(84 × 114.5 × 94 cm).

Provenance

Lo Giudice Gallery, New York, New York.

Exhibitions

Leo Castelli Gallery, New York, New York. *John Chamberlain.* April 17–May 8, 1971.

The Solomon R. Guggenheim Museum, New York, New York. *John Chamberlain: A Retrospective Exhibition*, cat. no. 104, illus. p. 90. December 23, 1971–February 20, 1972.

References

Michael Andre and Erika Rothenberg, eds., *The Poets' Encyclopedia*, vol. 4, no. 4/vol. 5 (New York, Unmuzzled Ox Editions, 1979), illus. p. 179.

Notes

According to the artist, the sculpture was destroyed while in the possession of the Lo Giudice Gallery, New York, New York.

402

Untitled 1970

Mineral-coated synthetic polymer resin

Dimensions unknown.

Notes

The sculpture, sometimes known as *Prototype #1*, has been destroyed.

403

Untitled 1970

Mineral-coated synthetic polymer resin

15½ × 26 × 14 in.
(39.5 × 66 × 35.5 cm).

Collection

Freide and Rubin Gorewitz, West Nyack, New York, 1972; acquired directly from the artist.

404

Untitled 1970

Mineral-coated synthetic polymer resin

Dimensions unknown.

Notes

The sculpture, sometimes known as *Prototype #2*, has been destroyed.

405

Untitled 1970

Mineral-coated synthetic polymer resin

37½ × 36 × 36 in.
(95 × 91.5 × 91.5 cm).

Collection

Neil Williams, Sagaponack, New York, 1970; acquired directly from the artist.

406

Untitled 1970

Mineral-coated synthetic polymer resin

28 × 47 × 39 in.
(71 × 119.5 × 99 cm).

Collection

Alan Power, Nevada City, California; acquired directly from the artist.

407

Untitled 1970

Mineral-coated synthetic polymer resin

16 × 22½ × 21 in.
(40.5 × 57 × 53.5 cm).

Collection

Private collection, New York, New York.

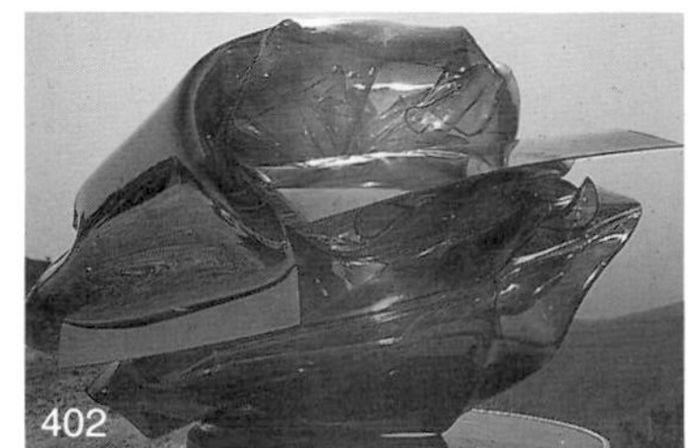
402

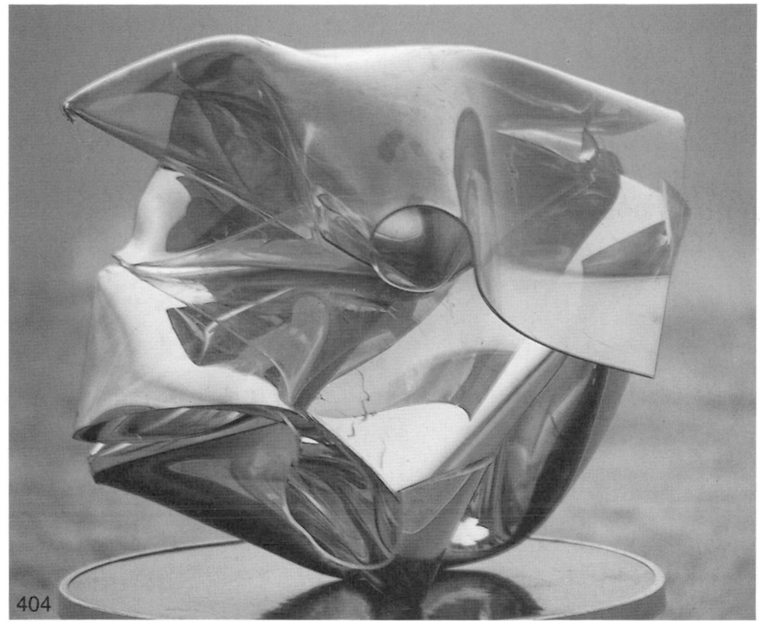
404

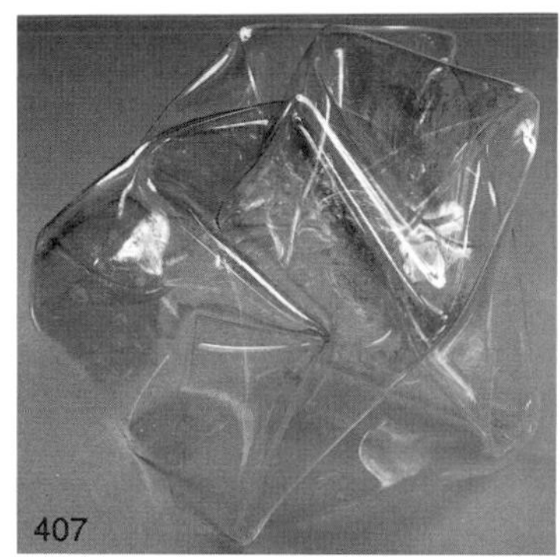
407

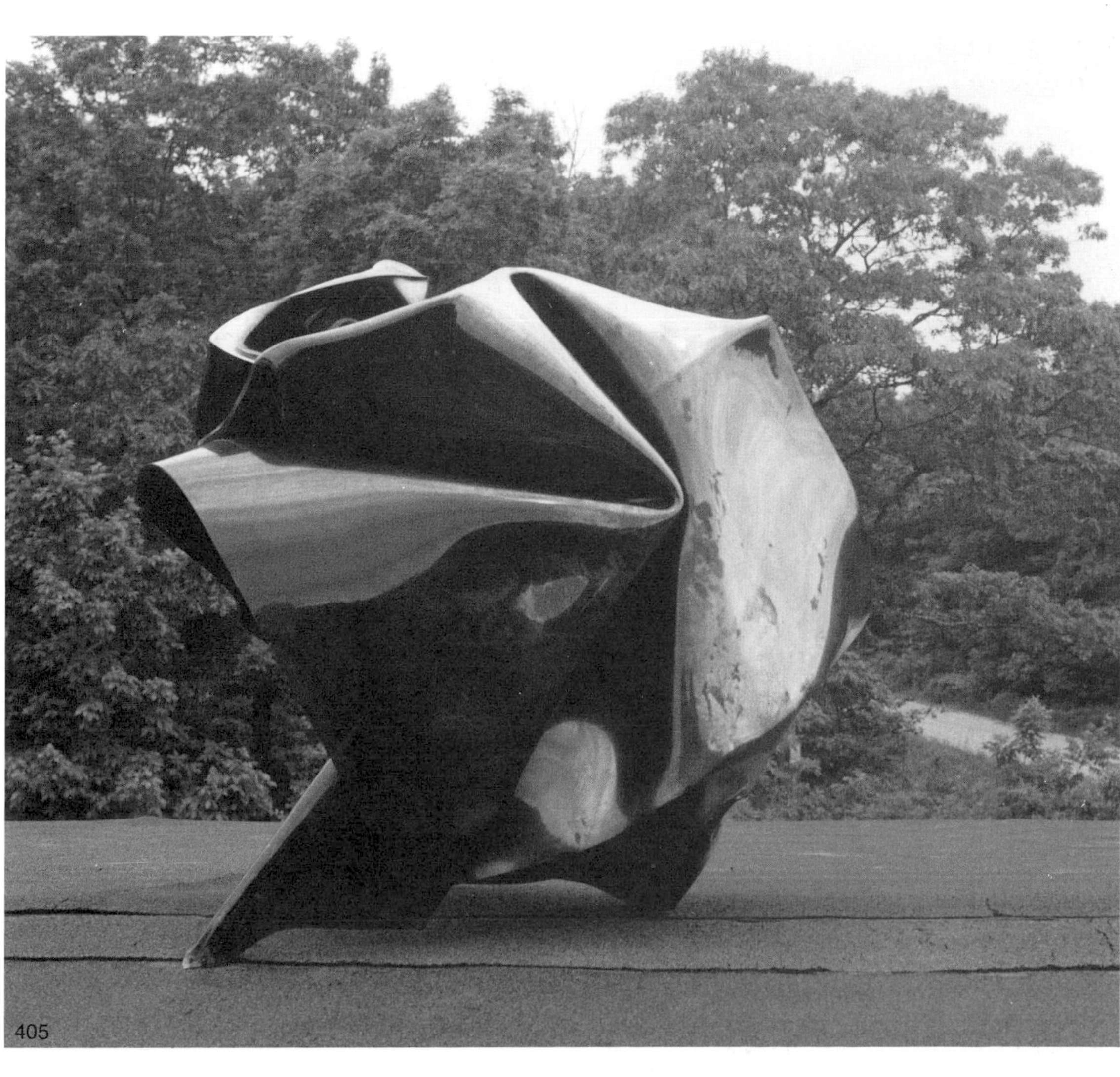
405

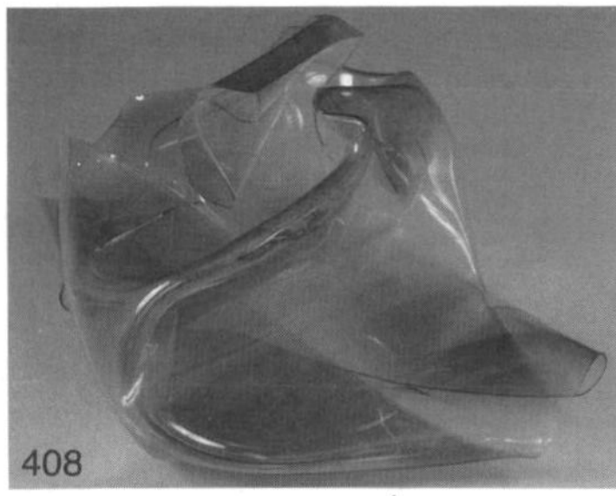
408

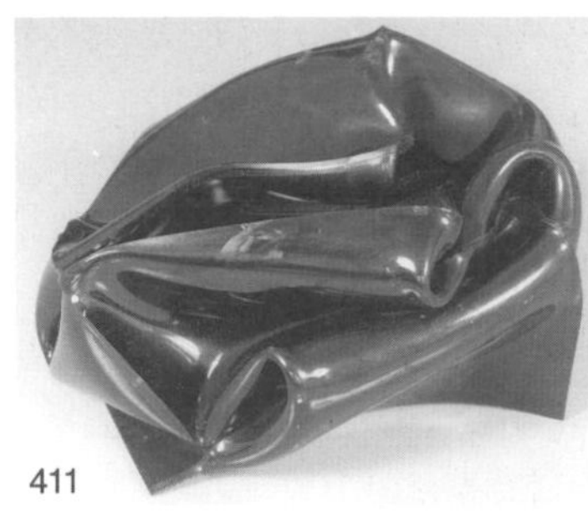
411

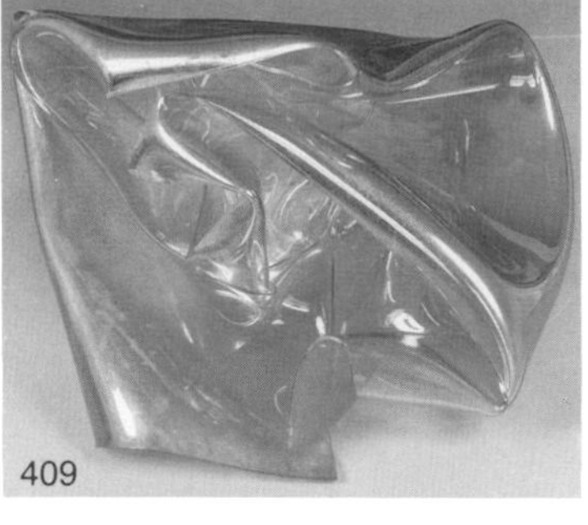
409

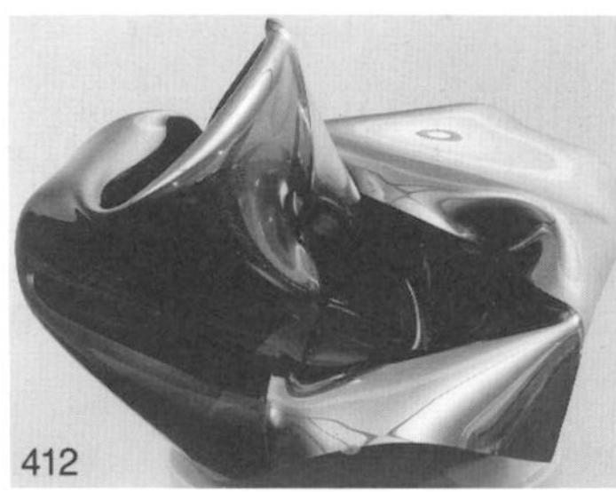
412

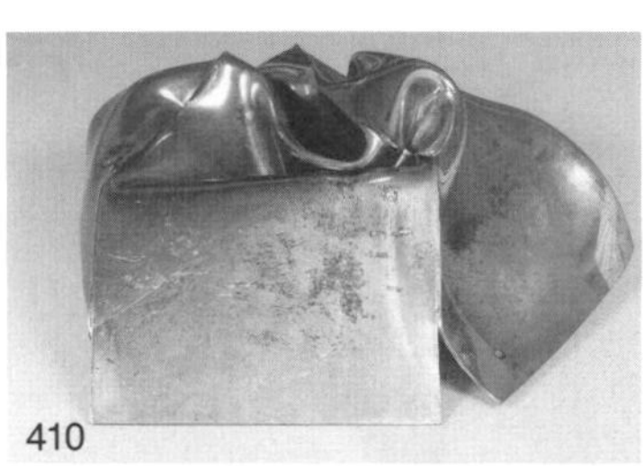
410

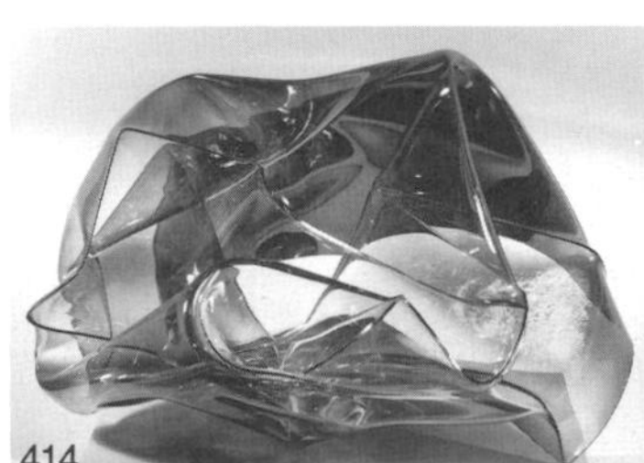
414

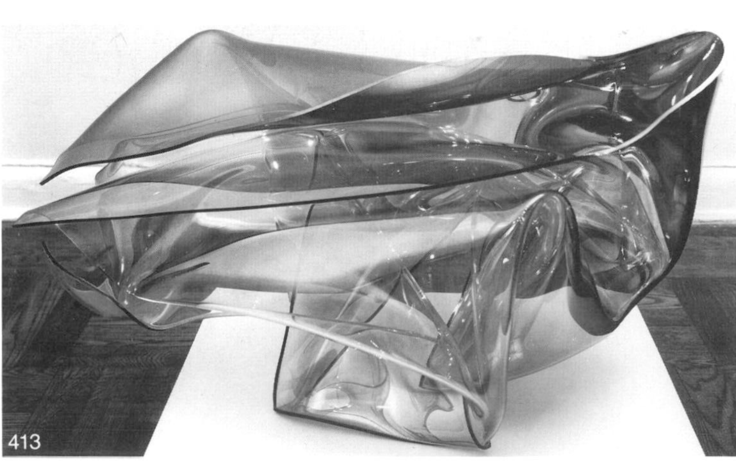
413

408

Untitled 1970
Mineral-coated synthetic polymer resin
13½ × 28½ × 25½ in.
(34.5 × 72.5 × 65 cm).

Collection
Collection of the artist, Sarasota, Florida.

Notes
According to the artist, the sculpture is in a state of disrepair.

409

Untitled 1970
Mineral-coated synthetic polymer resin
17 × 20 × 15 in.
(43 × 51 × 38 cm).

Collection
Private collection, New York, New York.

410

Untitled 1970
Mineral-coated synthetic polymer resin
10 × 24 × 22 in.
(25.5 × 61 × 56 cm).

Collection
Private collection, New York, New York.

411

Untitled 1970
Mineral-coated synthetic polymer resin
9½ × 17½ × 15½ in.
(24 × 44.5 × 39.5 cm).

Collection
Private collection, New York, New York.

412

Untitled 1970–71
Mineral-coated synthetic polymer resin
16½ × 24 × 24 in.
(42 × 61 × 61 cm).

Collection
Private collection, Bethesda, Maryland, 1971.

Provenance
Leo Castelli Gallery, New York, New York.

Exhibitions
Leo Castelli Gallery, New York, New York. *John Chamberlain*. April 17–May 8, 1971.

The Corcoran Gallery of Art, Washington, D.C. *Ten Years—The Friends of the Corcoran/Twentieth Century American Artists*, cat. no. 13. October 23–November 21, 1971.

413

Untitled 1970–71
Mineral-coated synthetic polymer resin
15½ × 23 × 23 in.
(39.5 × 58.5 × 58.5 cm).

Collection
Leo Castelli Gallery, New York, New York, 1976.

Provenance
Leo Castelli Gallery, New York, New York; O. K. Harris Works of Art, New York, New York; Mr. and Mrs. Bruce Berger, New York, New York.

Exhibitions
Leo Castelli Gallery, New York, New York. *John Chamberlain*. April 17–May 8, 1971.

414

Untitled 1970–71
Mineral-coated synthetic polymer resin
16 × 24 × 21 in.
(40.5 × 61 × 53.5 cm).

Collection
Present location unknown.

Notes
The only evidence of the existence of this sculpture is that it was entered in the Castelli registry in 1971.

415

Untitled c. 1970–71
Mineral-coated synthetic polymer resin
15½ × 25½ × 21 in.
(39.5 × 65 × 53.5 cm).

Collection
Present location unknown.

Notes
Castelli gallery records indicate that the sculpture is damaged.

416

Untitled 1970–71
Mineral-coated synthetic polymer resin
13½ × 28 × 17½ in.
(34 × 71 × 44.5 cm).

Collection
Present location unknown.

Exhibitions
Leo Castelli Gallery, New York, New York. *John Chamberlain*. April 17–May 8, 1971.

Notes
Castelli gallery records indicate that the sculpture is damaged.

417

N.D.W. 1971

Painted and chromium-plated steel
50 × 66 × 62 in.
(127 × 167.5 × 157.5 cm).

Collection

Present location unknown.

Provenance

Leo Castelli Gallery, New York, New York; Lo Giudice Gallery, New York, New York.

Exhibitions

The Solomon R. Guggenheim Museum, New York, New York. *John Chamberlain: A Retrospective Exhibition*, cat. no. 106. December 23, 1971–February 20, 1972.

Indianapolis Museum of Art, Indianapolis, Indiana. *Painting and Sculpture Today*. April 26–June 4, 1972.

418

Untitled c. 1971

Painted and chromium-plated steel
50 × 54 × 30 in.
(127 × 137 × 76 cm).

Collection

Allan Stone, New York, New York.

Provenance

Tania Neufeld, New York, New York; O. K. Harris Works of Art, New York, New York.

In 1972 Chamberlain began a series of sculptures made of lacquer- and resin-coated aluminum foil. The industrial-weight aluminum foil was formed into balls and then compressed and wadded. These were then sprayed with auto lacquer and polyester resin. A group of these works was first exhibited at the Castelli Gallery from December 8, 1973 to January 12, 1974.

The Castelli registry provides the only actual record of the aluminum-foil sculptures. Many have been lost or destroyed over the years; as recently as 1983 a number were destroyed by the artist. Because of the highly flexible nature of the material, some of the sculptures have lost their original shapes, thereby dramatically changing their dimensions. For these reasons it has been very difficult to identify works that have turned up later without their original titles.

The following entries (cat. nos. 419–447) are listed as they appear in the Castelli registry, and are accompanied by photographs of the works in their original state.

419

Asarabaca 1973

Aluminum foil with acrylic lacquer and polyester resin
22 × 25½ × 27 in.
(56 × 64.5 × 68.5 cm).

Collection

Mark Twain Bancshares, Inc., Saint Louis, Missouri, 1973.

Provenance

Leo Castelli Gallery, New York, New York; Richard Bellamy, New York, New York; Adam and Judith Aronson, Saint Louis, Missouri.

420

Barba-Aron 1973

Aluminum foil with acrylic lacquer and polyester resin
33 × 65 × 50 in.
(84 × 165 × 127 cm).

Collection

Allen Memorial Art Museum, Oberlin College, Oberlin, Ohio, 1975; gift of John Chamberlain in honor of Ellen Johnson.

Exhibitions

Leo Castelli Gallery, New York, New York. *John Chamberlain*. December 8, 1973–January 12, 1974.

Leo Castelli Gallery, New York, New York. *Benefit Exhibition for the Allen Memorial Art Museum, Oberlin College*. April 2–5, 1975.

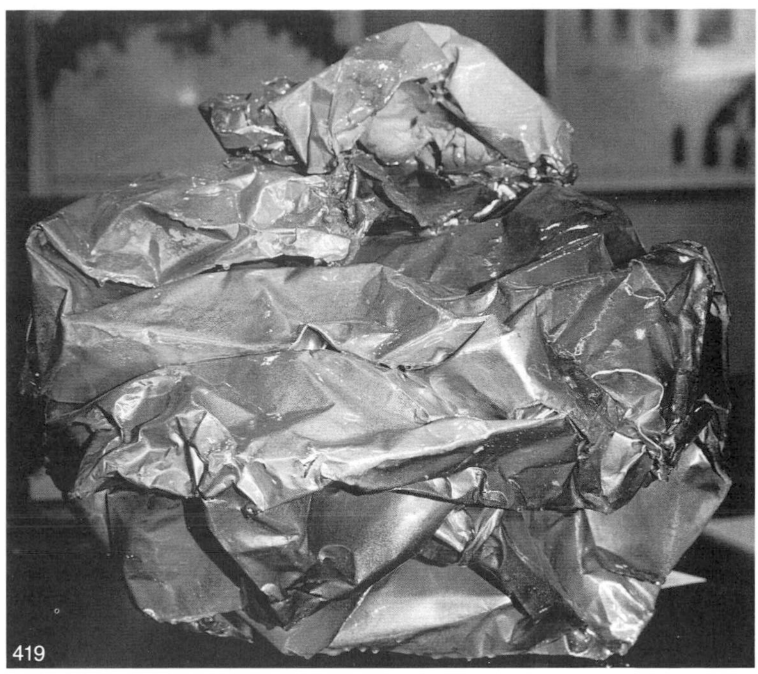

419

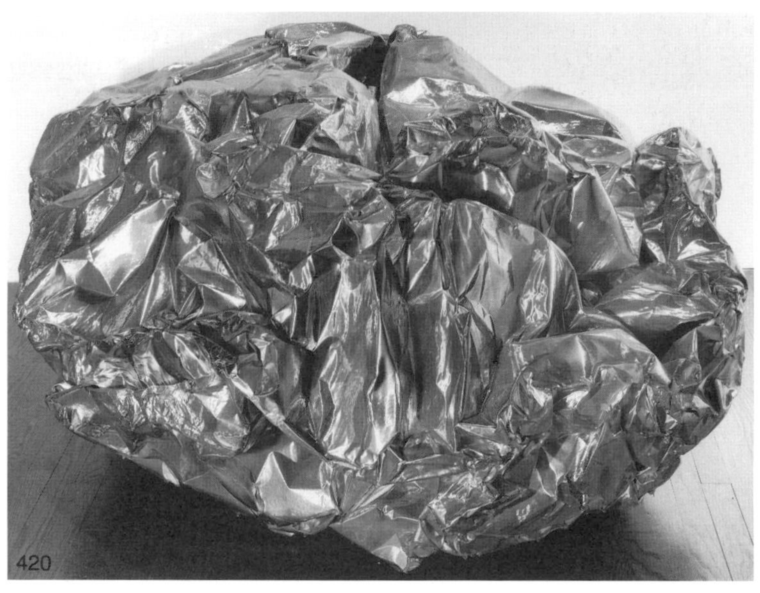

420

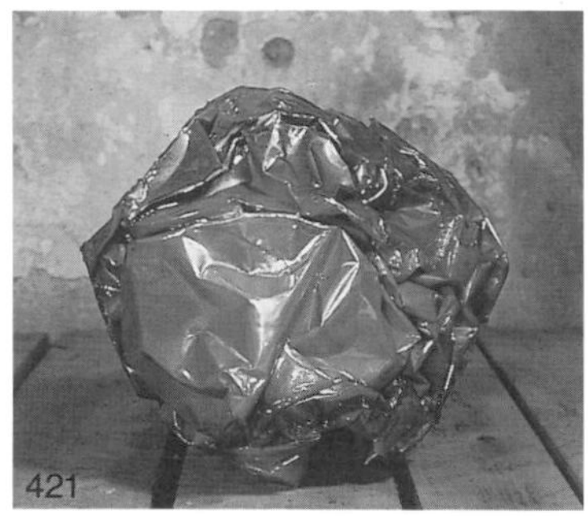
421

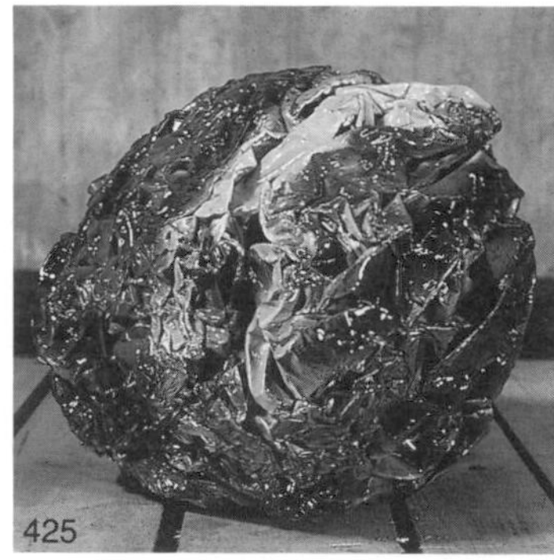
425

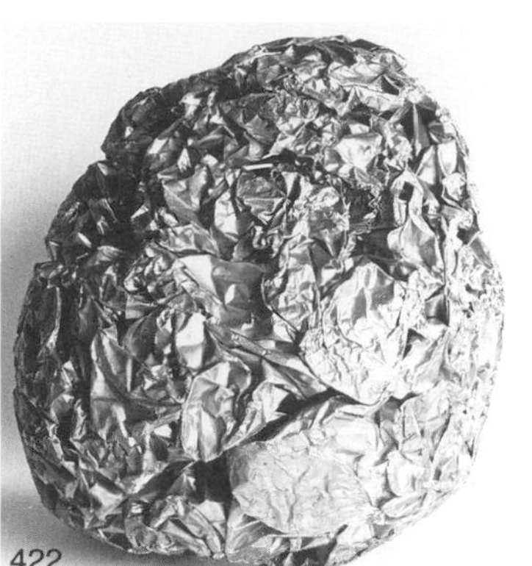
422

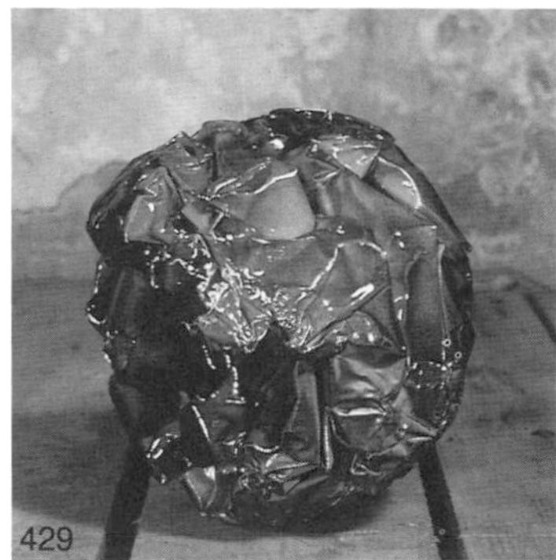
429

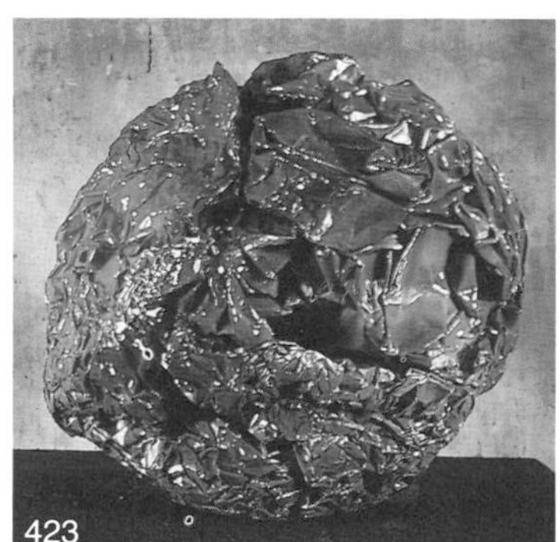
423

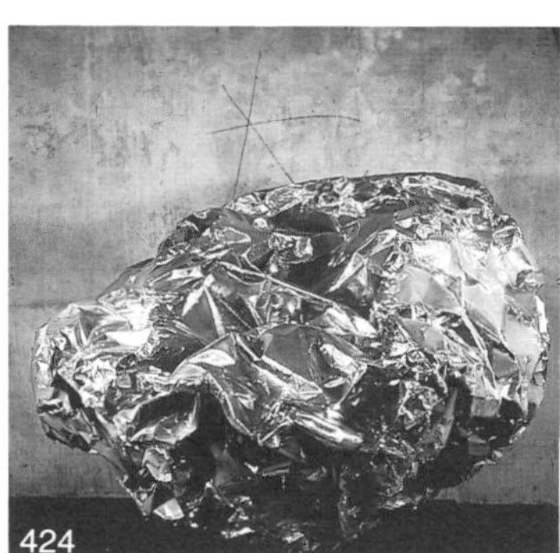
424

Sotheby Parke-Bernet, Inc., New York, New York. *Important Postwar and Contemporary Art*, cat. no. 25, illus. April 9, 1975.

421

Bugle 1973

Aluminum foil with acrylic lacquer and polyester resin
10½ × 12 × 12½ in.
(26.5 × 30.5 × 32 cm).

Collection
Present location unknown.

Provenance
Leo Castelli Gallery, New York, New York; Bo Alveryd, Kävlinge, Sweden; Christev Jacobsson, Sweden.

422

Dogstooth Violet 1973

Aluminum foil with acrylic lacquer and polyester resin
25 × 26½ × 32½ in.
(63.5 × 67.5 × 82.5 cm).

Collection
Armand P. Arman, New York, New York, 1975.

Provenance
Jack H. Klein, New York, New York.

Exhibitions
Leo Castelli Gallery, New York, New York. *John Chamberlain*. December 8, 1973–January 12, 1974.

423

Fleabane (Marsh) 1973

Aluminum foil with acrylic lacquer and polyester resin
17 × 19 × 23 in.
(43 × 48 × 58.5 cm).

Collection
Present location unknown.

424

Hare's Foot 1973

Aluminum foil with acrylic lacquer and polyester resin
34 × 46 × 47 in.
(86.5 × 117 × 119.5 cm).

Collection
Present location unknown.

Provenance
Leo Castelli Gallery, New York, New York; Galerie Ostergren, Malmö, Sweden.

425

Heart's Ease 1972–73

Aluminum foil with acrylic lacquer and polyester resin
12½ × 12 × 18 in.
(31.5 × 30.5 × 45.5 cm).

Collection
Present location unknown.

Provenance
Leo Castelli Gallery, New York, New York; Galerie Ostergren, Malmö, Sweden.

426

Lovage 1972

Aluminum foil with acrylic lacquer and polyester resin
45 × 67 × 59 in.
(114.5 × 170 × 150 cm).

Collection
Present location unknown.

Exhibitions
Leo Castelli Gallery, New York, New York. *John Chamberlain*. December 8, 1973–January 12, 1974.

427

Mandrake 1973

Aluminum foil with acrylic lacquer and polyester resin
29 × 39 × 32 in.
(73.5 × 99 × 81.5 cm).

Collection
Present location unknown.

Provenance
Malcolm Morley, New York, New York, 1973; Elizabeth Wiener, New York, New York.

Exhibitions
Auction 393, New York, New York. *Contemporary Art*, cat. no. 54, illus. May 26, 1976.

428

Marshmallow 1973

Aluminum foil with acrylic lacquer and polyester resin
35 × 63 × 59 in.
(89 × 160 × 150 cm).

Collection
Present location unknown.

Exhibitions
Leo Castelli Gallery, New York, New York. *John Chamberlain*. December 8, 1973–January 12, 1974.

429

Medlar 1973

Aluminum foil with acrylic lacquer and polyester resin
8 × 9 × 8 in.
(20.5 × 23 × 20.5 cm).

Collection
Richard Bellamy, New York, New York, 1973; acquired directly from the artist.

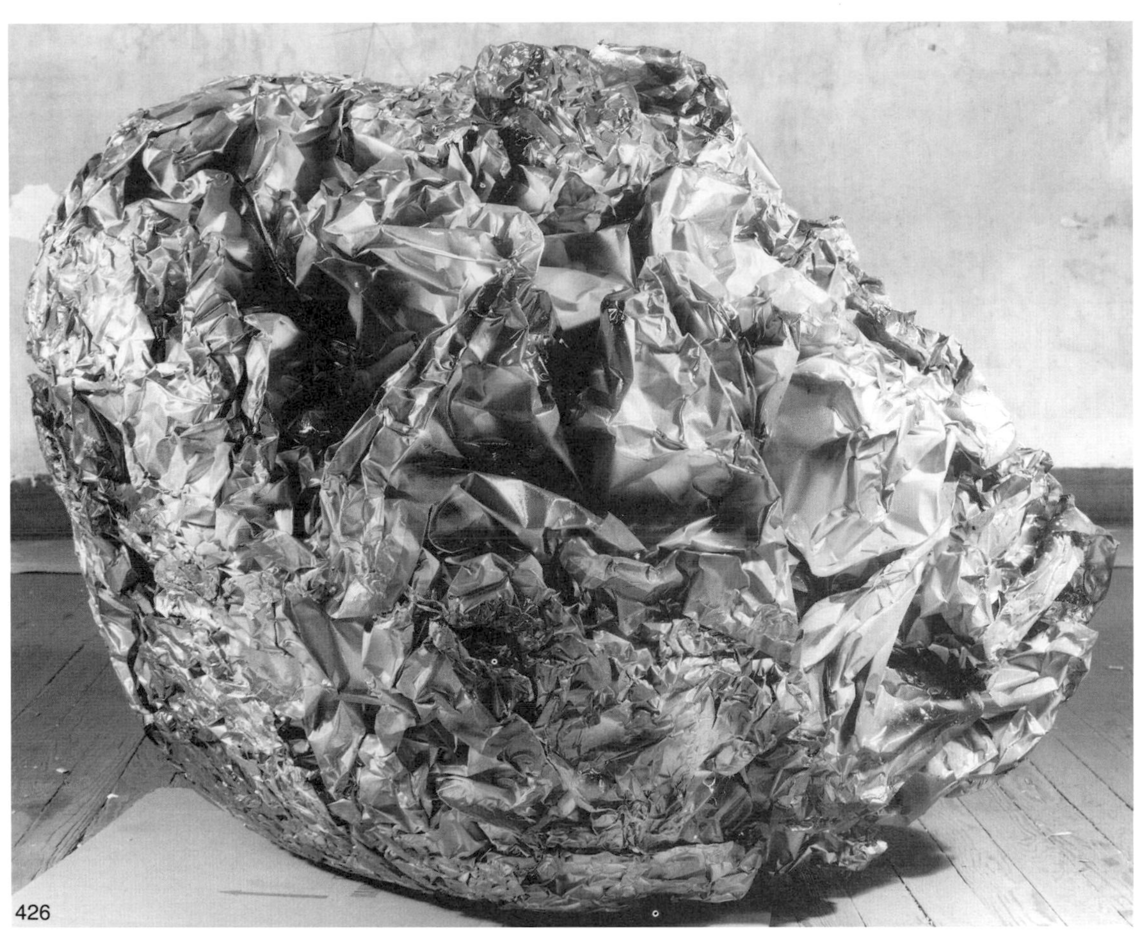

426

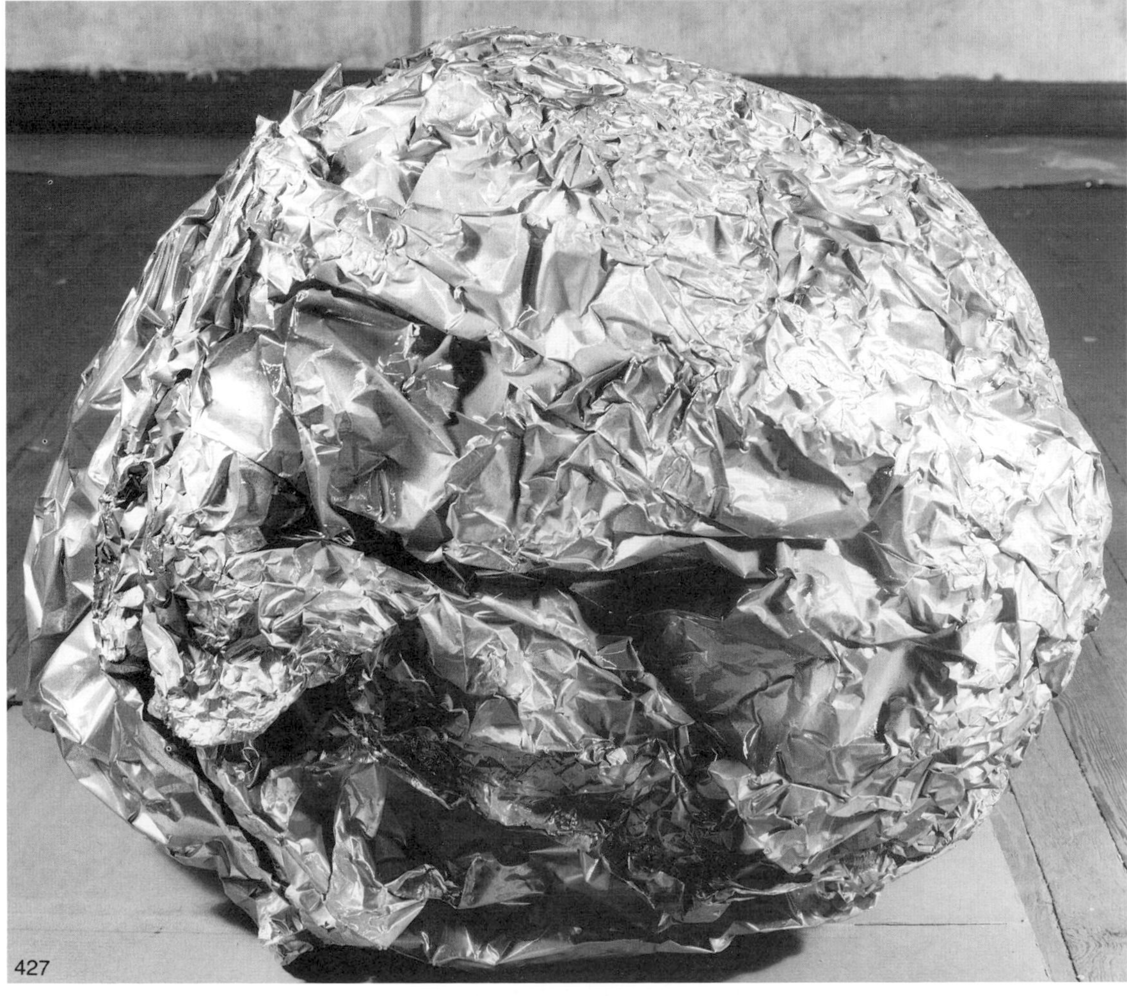

427

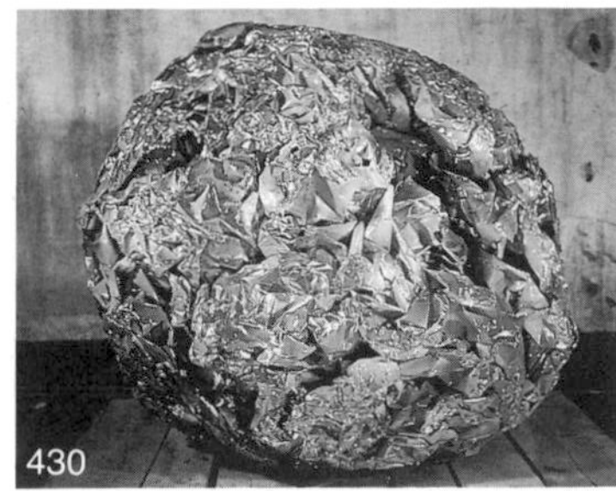
430

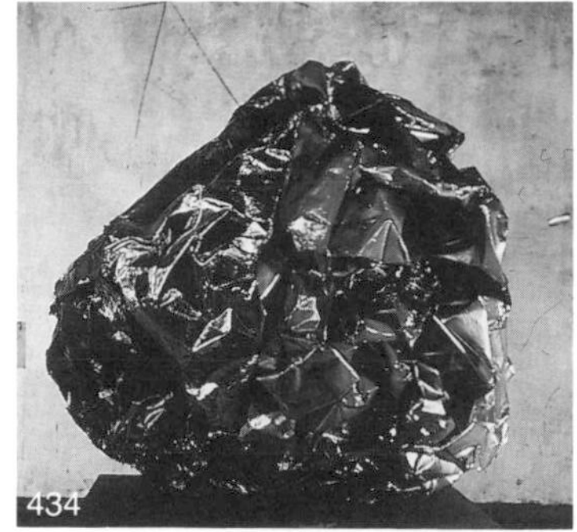
434

431

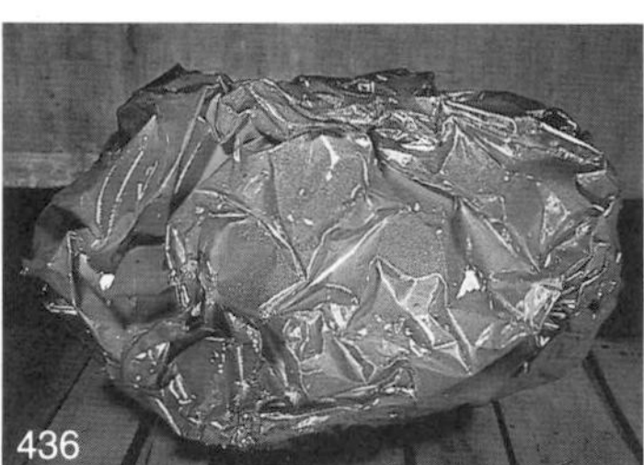
436

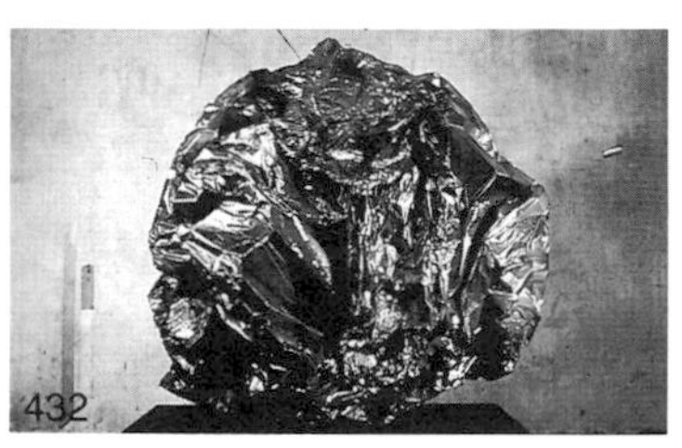
432

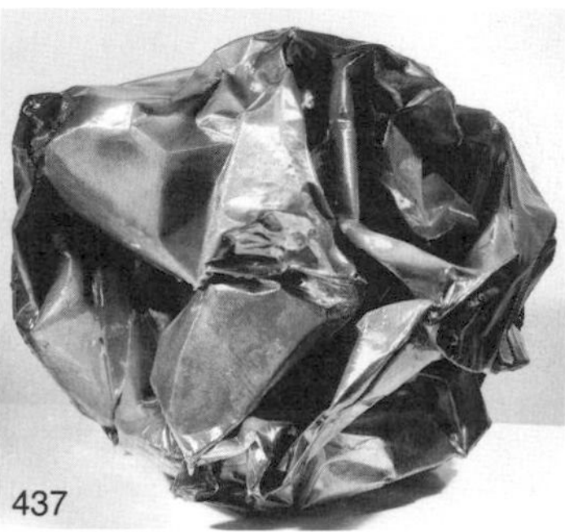
437

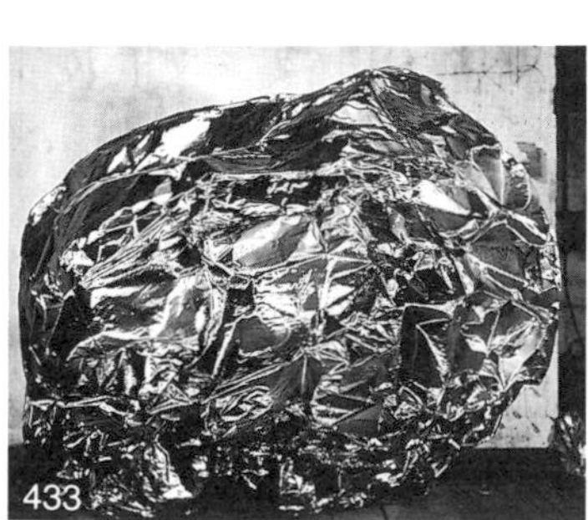
433

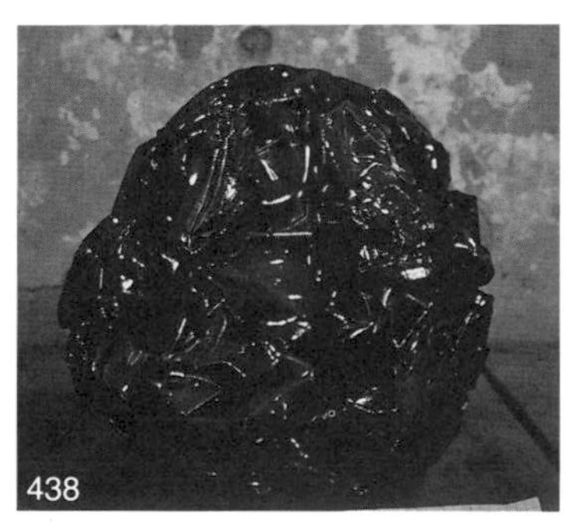
438

430

Navew 1973
Aluminum foil with acrylic lacquer and polyester resin
37 × 38 × 34 in.
(94 × 96.5 × 86.5 cm).

Collection
Present location unknown.

Exhibitions
Leo Castelli Gallery, New York, New York. *John Chamberlain*. December 8, 1973–January 12, 1974.

431

Peter's Wort 1973
Aluminum foil with acrylic lacquer and polyester resin
22½ × 23 × 32 in.
(57 × 58.5 × 81.5 cm).

Collection
Present location unknown.

432

Rampion 1972–73
Aluminum foil with acrylic lacquer and polyester resin
27 × 31 × 29 in.
(68.5 × 78.5 × 73.5 cm).

Collection
Present location unknown.

Provenance
Leo Castelli Gallery, New York, New York; Galerie Ostergren, Malmö, Sweden.

433

Red Fitching 1973
Aluminum foil with acrylic lacquer and polyester resin
58½ × 81 × 74 in.
(148.5 × 205.5 × 188 cm).

Collection
Collection of the artist, Sarasota, Florida.

Exhibitions
Leo Castelli Gallery, New York, New York. *John Chamberlain*. December 8, 1973–January 12, 1974.

434

Samphire 1973
Aluminum foil with acrylic lacquer and polyester resin
32 × 37½ × 31 in.
(81.5 × 95 × 78.5 cm).

Collection
Present location unknown.

Exhibitions
Leo Castelli Gallery, New York, New York. *John Chamberlain*. December 8, 1973–January 12, 1974.

435

Scull Cap 1973
Aluminum foil with acrylic lacquer and polyester resin
42 × 69 × 59 in.
(106.5 × 175.5 × 150 cm).

Collection
Present location unknown.

Exhibitions
Leo Castelli Gallery, New York, New York. *John Chamberlain*. December 8, 1973–January 12, 1974.

436

Simson (Blue) 1973
Aluminum foil with acrylic lacquer and polyester resin
19½ × 25½ × 22 in.
(49.5 × 65 × 56 cm).

Collection
Present location unknown.

437

Skirret 1973
Aluminum foil with acrylic lacquer and polyester resin
18½ × 23 × 22 in.
(47 × 58.5 × 56 cm).

Collection
Mr. and Mrs. David Levin, Terre Haute, Indiana.

Provenance
Leo Castelli Gallery, New York, New York; Hokin Gallery, Inc., Bay Harbour Islands, Florida.

438

Smallage 1973
Aluminum foil with acrylic lacquer and polyester resin
10 × 11½ × 10½ in.
(25.5 × 29 × 26.5 cm).

Collection
Adam and Judith Aronson, Saint Louis, Missouri, 1973.

Provenance
Leo Castelli Gallery, New York, New York.

439

Solomon's Seal 1973

Aluminum foil with acrylic lacquer and polyester resin
30 × 52 × 47 in.
(76 × 132 × 119.5 cm).

Collection

Collection of the artist, Sarasota, Florida.

Exhibitions

Leo Castelli Gallery, New York, New York. *John Chamberlain*. December 8, 1973–January 12, 1974.

Leo Castelli Gallery, New York, New York. *Autumn Group Exhibition*. September 13–27, 1975.

440

Squill 1973

Aluminum foil with acrylic lacquer and polyester resin
39 × 61 × 41 in.
(99 × 155 × 104 cm).

Collection

Present location unknown.

441

Sweet Betty 1972

Aluminum foil with acrylic lacquer and polyester resin
7½ × 8½ × 8½ in.
(19 × 21.5 × 21.5 cm).

Collection

Present location unknown.

442

Uva 1973

Aluminum foil with acrylic lacquer and polyester resin
40 × 59 × 42 in.
(101.5 × 150 × 106.5 cm).

Collection

Present location unknown.

Exhibitions

Leo Castelli Gallery, New York, New York. *John Chamberlain*. December 8, 1973–January 12, 1974.

443

Vipers Bugloss 1973

Aluminum foil with acrylic lacquer and polyester resin
49 × 76 × 68 in.
(124.5 × 193 × 173 cm).

Collection

Present location unknown.

Exhibitions

Leo Castelli Gallery, New York, New York. *John Chamberlain*. December 8, 1973–January 12, 1974.

Newport Monumenta, Newport, Rhode Island. August 1974.

444

Yew 1973

Aluminum foil with acrylic lacquer and polyester resin
25 × 31 × 21½ in.
(63.5 × 78.5 × 54.5 cm).

Collection

Present location unknown.

445

Untitled 1973

Aluminum foil with acrylic lacquer and polyester resin
12 × 15 × 15 in.
(30.5 × 38 × 38 cm).

Collection

Mr. and Mrs. Saul A. Dubinsky, Saint Louis, Missouri, 1974.

Provenance

Leo Castelli Gallery, New York, New York.

Exhibitions

Leo Castelli Gallery, New York, New York. *John Chamberlain*. December 8, 1973–January 12, 1974.

References

Nancy Foote, "John Chamberlain at Castelli," *Art in America*, vol. 62, no. 2 (March/April 1974), p. 105, color illus.

446

Untitled 1973

Aluminum foil with acrylic lacquer and polyester resin
15½ × 18 × 17 in.
(39.5 × 45.5 × 43 cm).

Collection

Present location unknown.

Notes

It is noted in the Castelli registry that the sculpture was at the Museum of Modern Art penthouse for exhibition and sale. No dates or further information are available.

447

Untitled 1973

Aluminum foil with acrylic lacquer and polyester resin
12 × 16 × 13 in.
(30.5 × 40.5 × 33 cm).

Collection

Present location unknown.

Exhibitions

Leo Castelli Gallery, New York, New York. *John Chamberlain*. December 8, 1973–January 12, 1974.

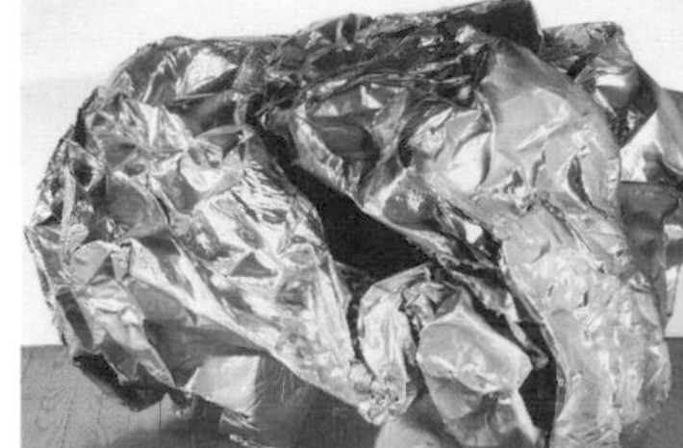
439

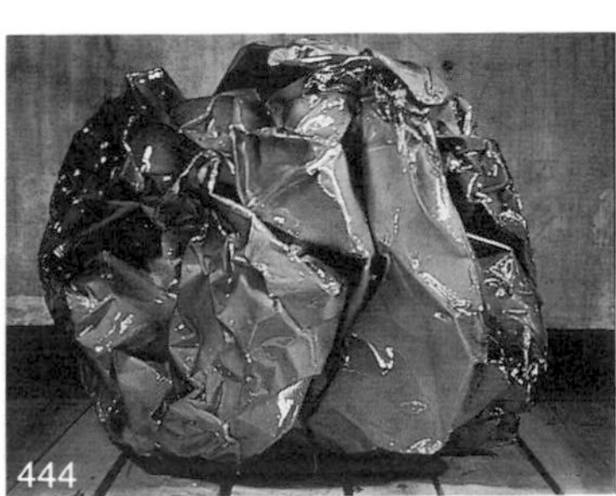
444

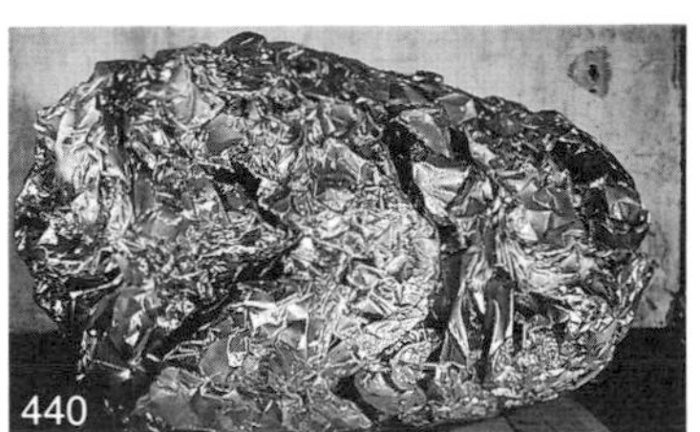
440

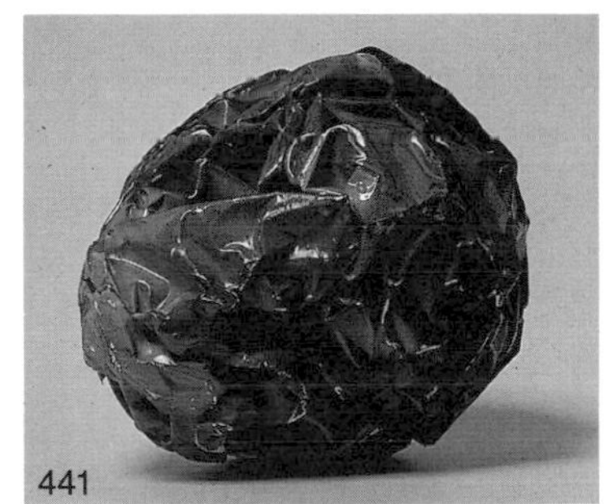
441

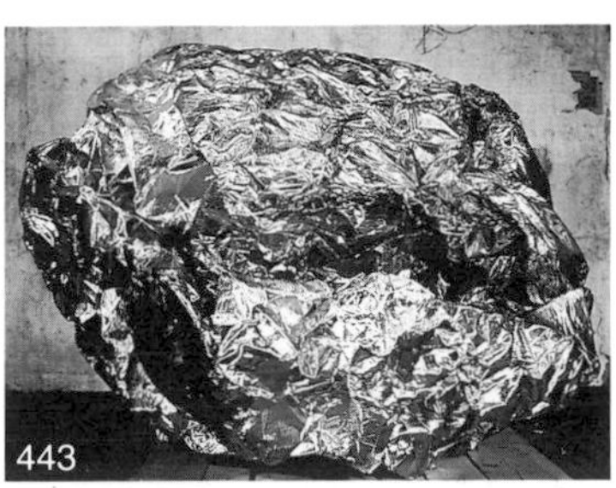
443

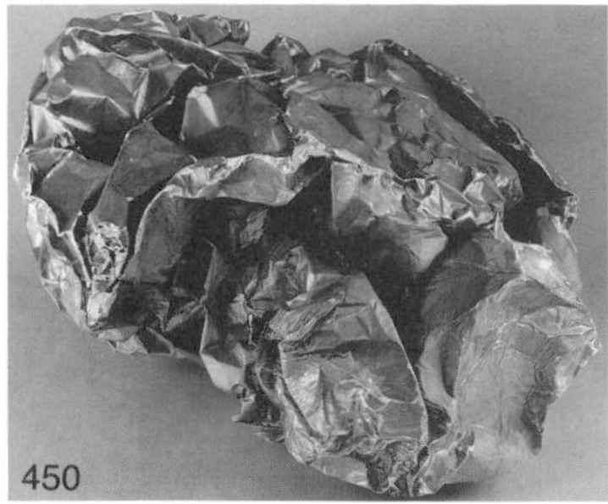
450

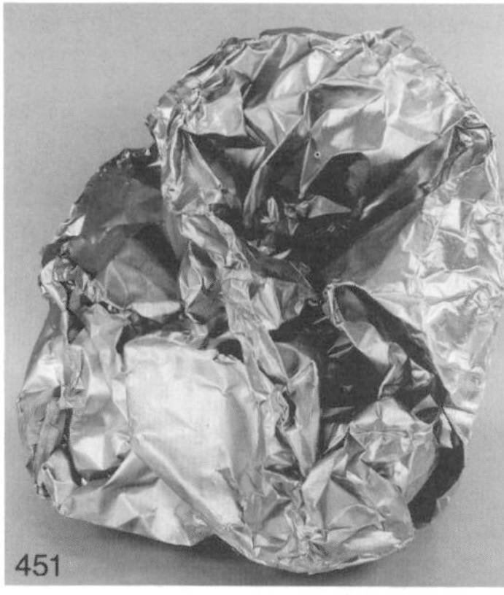
451

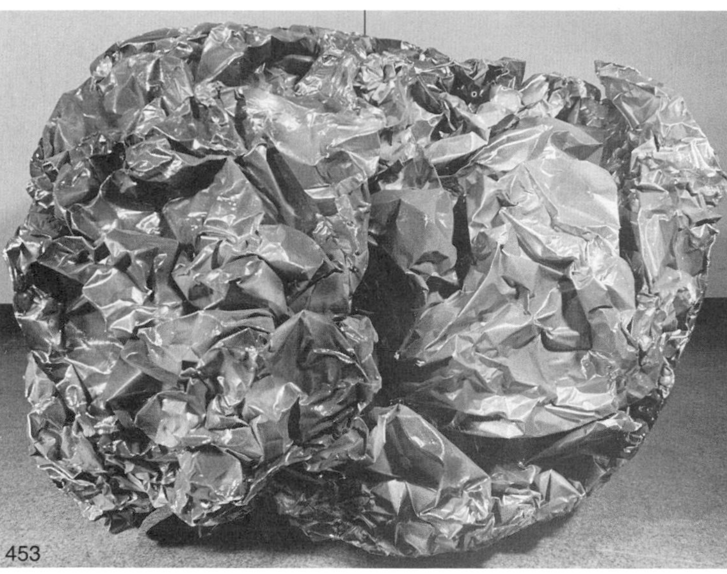
453

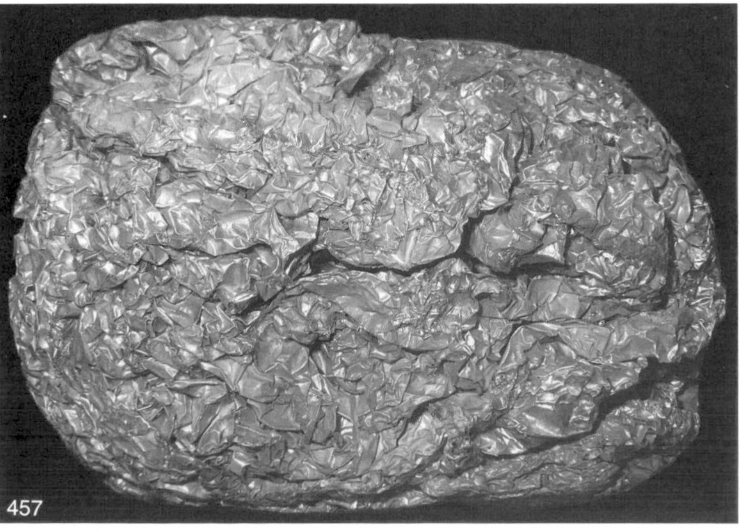
457

There is reason to believe that the following sculptures (cat. nos. 448–457) correspond to entries in the Castelli registry. However, sufficient evidence does not exist to connect them positively.

448

Golden Smell 1973
Aluminum foil
35 × 64 × 61 in.
(89 × 162.5 × 155 cm).

Collection
Dia Art Foundation, New York, New York, 1980.

Exhibitions
Dia Art Foundation, Essex, Connecticut. *Chamberlain Gardens, Essex*. May–November 1982 and May 1983.

Notes
The sculpture was titled by the artist in 1981.

449

Jam and Chunk 1973
Aluminum foil with polyester resin and paint
10 × 13 × 11 in.
(25.5 × 33 × 28 cm).

Collection
Dia Art Foundation, New York, New York, 1981.

Provenance
Julia A. Fahey, New York, New York; Lone Star Foundation, New York, New York, 1979.

Notes
The sculpture was titled by the artist in 1981.

450

Joe and Mary 1973
Aluminum foil with polyester resin and paint
36 × 67½ × 53 in.
(91.5 × 171.5 × 134.5 cm).

Collection
Dia Art Foundation, New York, New York, 1981.

Provenance
Lone Star Foundation, New York, New York, 1977.

Notes
The sculpture was titled by the artist in 1981.

451

Lucy and Ricky 1973
Aluminum foil with acrylic lacquer and polyester resin
44 × 60 × 50 in.
(112 × 152.5 × 127 cm).

Collection
Dia Art Foundation, New York, New York, 1980.

Provenance
Urban Archaeology, New York, New York; Lone Star Foundation, New York, New York, 1979.

452

Peteundclit 1973
Aluminum foil with acrylic lacquer and polyester resin
26 × 45 × 50 in.
(66 × 114.5 × 127 cm).

Collection
Collection of the artist, Sarasota, Florida.

References
Documenta 7/Kassel, vol. 1 (Kassel, West Germany: D + V Paul Dierichs, GmbH, 1982), illus. p. 36.

Gary Indiana, "John Chamberlain's Irregular Set," *Art in America*, vol. 71, no. 10 (November 1983), p. 214, color illus. p. 213.

Notes
The sculpture was titled by the artist in 1981. It bears a resemblance to *Hare's Foot*, cat. no. 428, although no positive correspondence has been determined.

453

Untitled 1973
Aluminum foil with acrylic lacquer and polyester resin
43 × 71 × 68 in.
(109 × 180.5 × 172.5 cm).

Collection
Walter P. Chrysler, Jr., New York, New York; on loan to the Chrysler Museum, Norfolk, Virginia.

Provenance
Richard Librizzi, New York, New York.

Exhibitions
The Chrysler Museum, Norfolk, Virginia. *Three Hundred Years of American Art in the Chrysler Museum*, illus. p. 235. March 1–July 4, 1976.
The Chrysler Museum, Norfolk, Virginia. *Large or Small, Bronze or Wood, Painted or Plain: Problems and Solutions in Sculpture*, illus. p. 21. July 9–September 13, 1981.

Notes
The sculpture bears a very close resemblance to *Squill*, cat. no. 440, although no positive correspondence has been determined.

454

Untitled 1973
Aluminum foil with acrylic lacquer and polyester resin
14 × 8 × 8 in.
(35.5 × 20 × 20 cm).

Collection
Jim Jacobs, New York, New York, 1977; acquired directly from the artist.

455

Untitled 1973
Aluminum foil with acrylic lacquer and polyester resin
14 × 8 × 8 in.
(35.5 × 20 × 20 cm).

Collection
Jim Jacobs, New York, New York, 1977; acquired directly from the artist.

456

Untitled 1973
Aluminum foil with acrylic lacquer and polyester resin
28 × 59 × 49 in.
(71 × 150 × 124.5 cm).

Collection
Allan Stone, New York, New York.

Notes
The sculpture is in a state of disrepair.

457

Untitled 1973
Aluminum foil with acrylic lacquer and polyester resin
24 × 38 × 38 in.
(61 × 96.5 × 96.5 cm).

Collection
Dr. and Mrs. Robert Magoon, Miami Beach, Florida, 1978.

Provenance
Ronald Feldman Gallery, New York, New York; John C. Stoller & Co., Minneapolis, Minnesota; Dorothy-Berenson Blau, Bay Harbour Islands, Florida.

References
Christopher Hemphill, "A Matter of Mood: An Expression of Contemporary Sensibility," *Architectural Digest*, vol. 39, no. 5 (May 1982), color illus. p. 172, incorrectly referred to as *Ball*.

Notes
The sculpture bears a resemblance to *Navew*, cat. no. 430, although no positive correspondence has been determined.

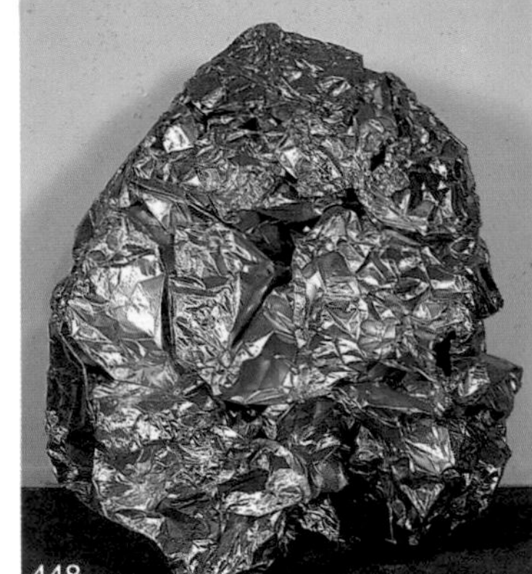
448

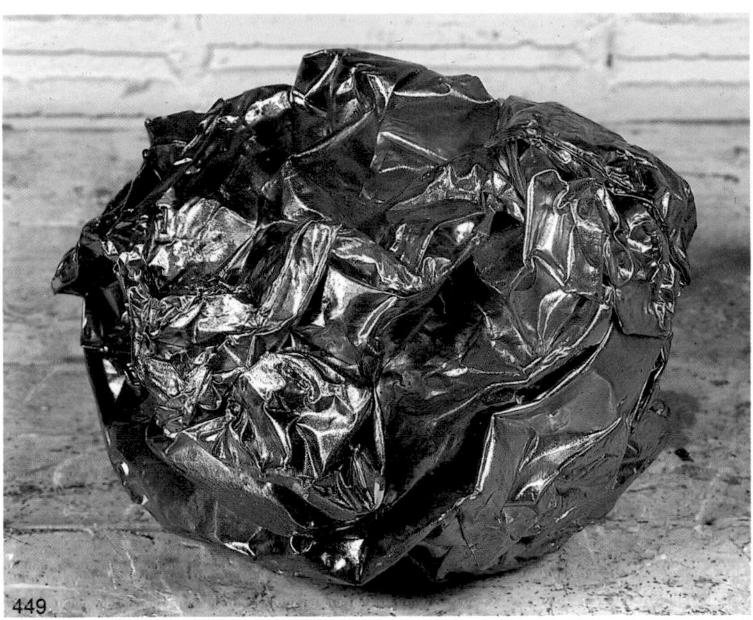
449

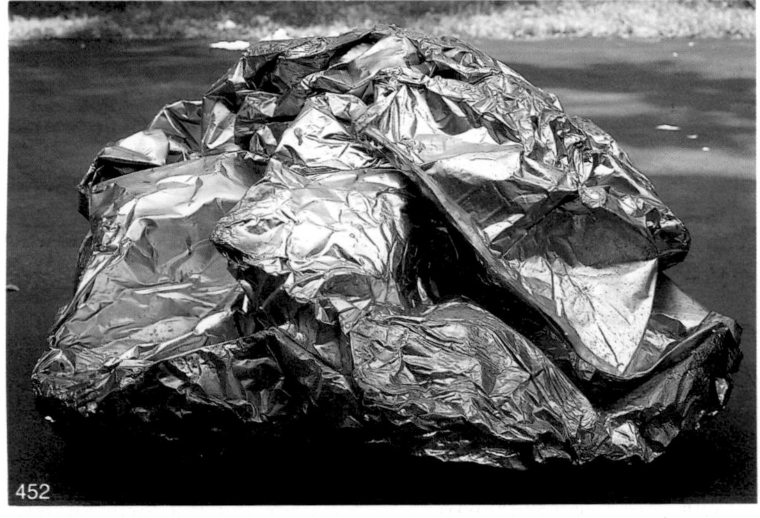
452

A few aluminum-foil sculptures (cat. nos. 458–466) are known to exist or are documented in Chamberlain's records but not in the Castelli registry.

458

Feverfew (Sea) 1972–73
Aluminum foil with acrylic lacquer and polyester resin
12 × 14 × 11 in.
(30.5 × 35.5 × 28 cm).

Collection
Present location unknown.

459

Feverfew (Sweet) 1972
Aluminum foil with acrylic lacquer and polyester resin
11 × 14 × 11 in.
(28 × 35.5 × 28 cm).

Collection
Present location unknown.

460

Untitled 1973
Aluminum foil with acrylic lacquer and polyester resin
13½ × 19½ × 17½ in.
(34 × 49.5 × 44.5 cm).

Collection
Collection of the artist, Sarasota, Florida.

461

Untitled 1973
Aluminum foil with acrylic lacquer and polyester resin
13 × 19½ × 18 in.
(33 × 50 × 45.5 cm).

Collection
Collection of the artist, Sarasota, Florida.

462

Untitled 1973
Aluminum foil with acrylic lacquer and polyester resin
18 × 21 × 17 in.
(45.5 × 53.5 × 43 cm).

Collection
Collection of the artist, Sarasota, Florida.

463

Untitled 1973
Aluminum foil with acrylic lacquer and polyester resin
14½ × 20 × 19 in.
(37 × 51 × 48.5 cm).

Collection
Collection of the artist, Sarasota, Florida.

464

Untitled 1973
Aluminum foil with acrylic lacquer and polyester resin
19 × 22½ × 25 in.
(48.5 × 57 × 63.5 cm).

Collection
Collection of the artist, Sarasota, Florida.

465

Untitled 1973
Aluminum foil with acrylic lacquer and polyester resin
11½ × 12 × 11 in.
(29 × 30.5 × 28 cm).

Collection
Ellen Cohen, New York, New York, 1976; acquired directly from the artist.

466

Untitled 1973
Aluminum foil with acrylic lacquer and polyester resin
17 × 19½ × 17½ in.
(43 × 50 × 44.5 cm).

Collection
Collection of the artist, Sarasota, Florida.

Between 1972 and 1974 Chamberlain made many tiny aluminum-foil pieces. Their dimensions range from 3 × 3 × 3 in. to 7 × 7 × 7 in. (7.5 × 7.5 × 7.5 cm to 18 × 18 × 18 cm), and they were considered studies or playful objects as gifts for friends. They are not reproduced or catalogued in this catalogue raisonné. A few more of these tiny foil pieces appear again in the early 1980s, some of them earlier works that have been redone. They are characterized by a heavy treatment of paint, rather than the thin veils of translucent lacquer on the earlier pieces.

The *Texas Pieces* (cat. nos. 467–478) were begun in 1972, in Amarillo, Texas, at the ranch of Stanley Marsh III. A number of the sculptures were completed at the ranch in later years. They are titled after towns and counties in western Texas. Nine of the twelve in the series have been installed permanently at the Art Museum of the Pecos in Marfa, Texas.

467

Bushland-Marsh 1972–73
Painted and chromium-plated steel
68½ × 90 × 83½ in.
(174 × 228.5 × 212 cm).

Collection
Private collection, New York, New York; on loan to Dia Art Foundation, New York, New York, 1983.

Provenance
Philip Johnson, New Canaan, Connecticut.

Exhibitions
Contemporary Arts Museum, Houston, Texas. *John Chamberlain: Recent Sculpture*, cat. no. 4, illus. February 14–March 17, 1975. Traveled to Saint Louis Botanical Gardens, Saint Louis, Missouri. March 29–April 29, 1975; Minneapolis Institute of Arts, Minneapolis, Minnesota. June 15–August 14, 1975.

Dia Art Foundation, Manhattan Psychiatric Center, Ward's Island, New York, New York. *John Chamberlain at Ward's Island*. October 1977–September 1978.

Dia Art Foundation, the Art Museum of the Pecos, Marfa, Texas. *An Exhibition of Sculpture by John Chamberlain*. From May 7, 1983.

References
John Brod Peters, "John Chamberlain's Sculptures," *Saint Louis Globe-Democrat*, April 26–27, 1975.

In Amarillo, Texas (Amarillo, Texas: Stanley Marsh III, 1975), color illus.

Chamberlain (Bern: Kunsthalle Bern and Van Abbemuseum, Eindhoven, Netherlands, 1979), illus. p. 50.

Notes
The sculpture is also known as *Bushland-Marsh III*.

468

Canyon Road Shell 1972–73
Painted and chromium-plated steel
60 × 65 × 75 in.
(152.5 × 165 × 190.5 cm).

Collection
Private collection, New York, New York.

Exhibitions
Hammarskjold Plaza Sculpture Garden, New York, New York. *John Chamberlain: Texas Pieces*. November 1973–March 1974.

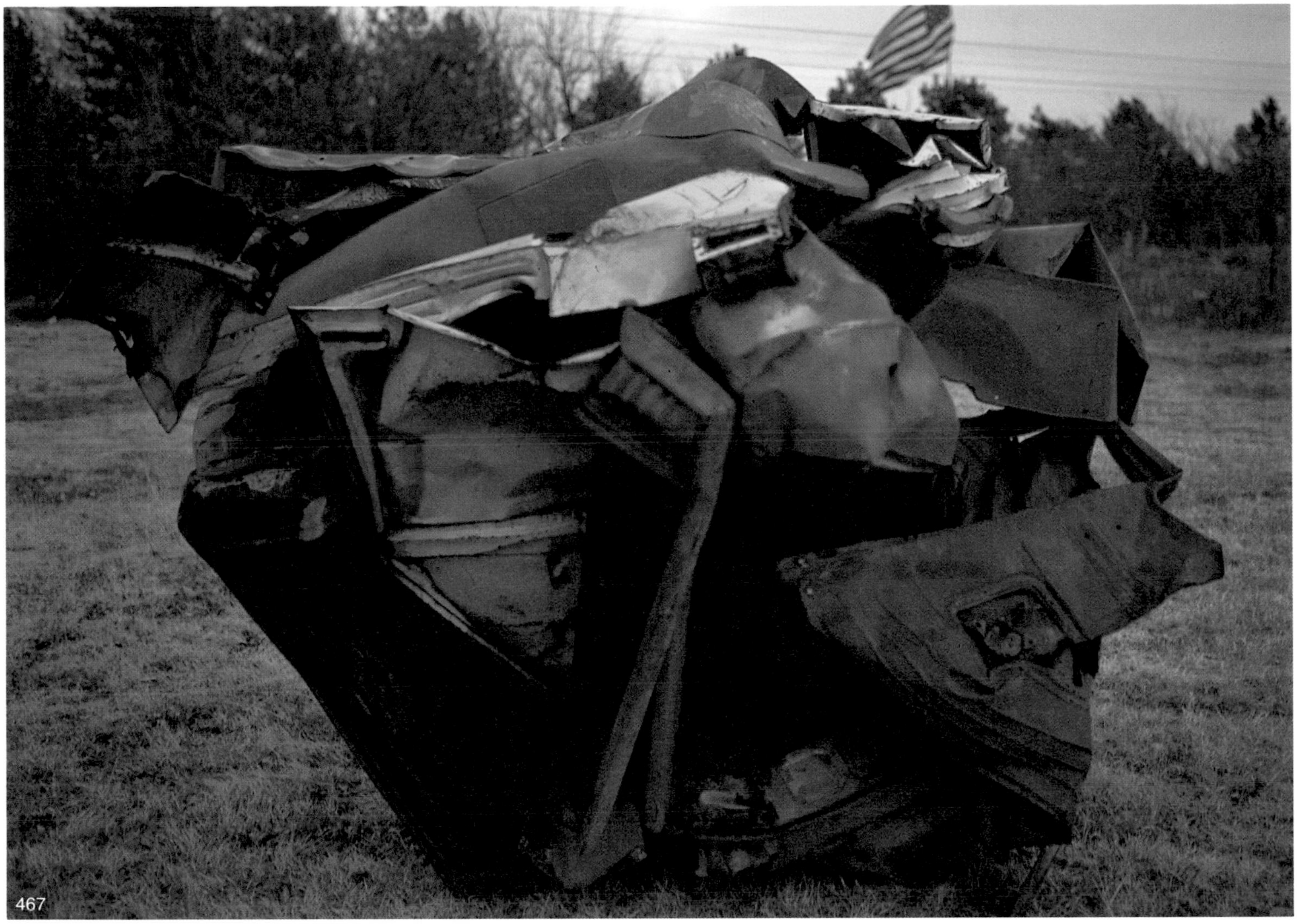

467

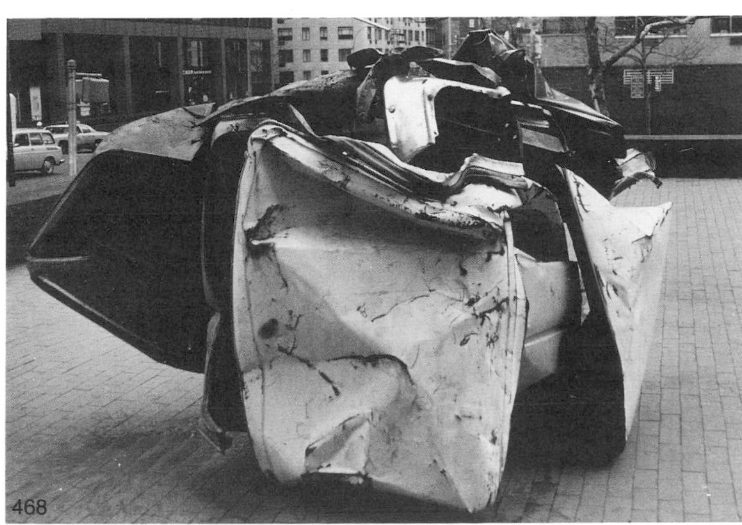

468

469

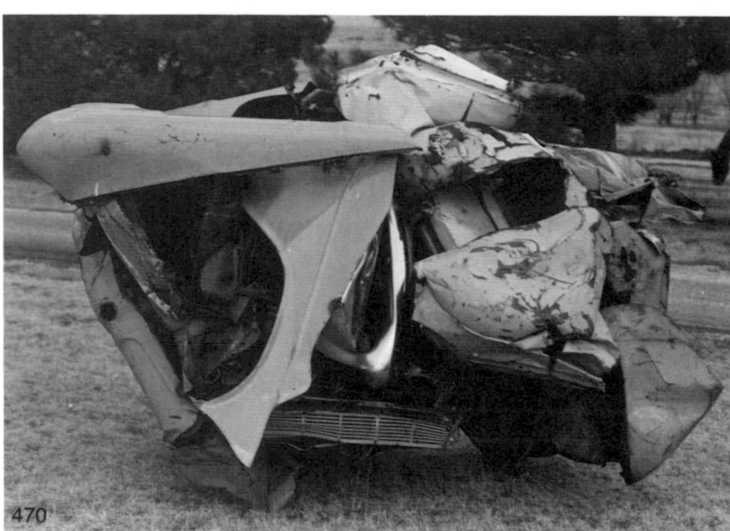

470

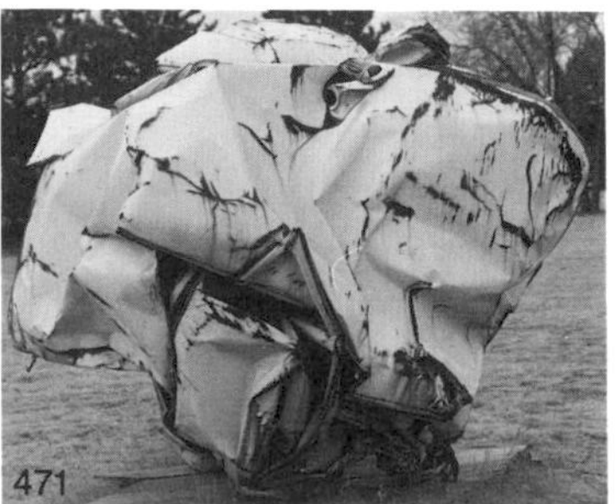

471

469

Capote Peak 1972–74

Painted and chromium-plated steel
114 × 85 × 162 in.
(289.5 × 216 × 411.5 cm).

Provenance

Private collection, New York, New York.

Exhibitions

Contemporary Arts Museum, Houston, Texas. *John Chamberlain: Recent Sculpture*, cat. no. 7, illus. February 14–March 17, 1975. Traveled to Saint Louis Botanical Gardens, Saint Louis, Missouri. March 29–April 29, 1975; Minneapolis Institute of Arts, Minneapolis, Minnesota. June 15–August 14, 1975.

References

Jane Bell, "John Chamberlain: New Sculpture," *Arts*, vol. 49, no. 10 (June 1975), pp. 88-89.

In Amarillo, Texas (Amarillo, Texas: Stanley Marsh III, 1975), illus.

Notes

According to the last owners, the sculpture has been destroyed.

470

Chili Terlingua 1972–74

Painted and chromium-plated steel
69½ × 82 × 104 in.
(176.5 × 208 × 264 cm).

Collection

Private collection, New York, New York; on loan to Dia Art Foundation, New York, New York, 1983.

Exhibitions

Contemporary Arts Museum, Houston, Texas. *John Chamberlain: Recent Sculpture*, cat. no. 5, illus. February 14–March 17, 1975. Traveled to Saint Louis Botanical Gardens, Saint Louis, Missouri. March 29–April 29, 1975; Minneapolis Institute of Arts, Minneapolis, Minnesota. June 15–August 14, 1975.

Dia Art Foundation, Manhattan Psychiatric Center, Ward's Island, New York, New York. *John Chamberlain at Ward's Island.* October 1977–September 1978.

Dia Art Foundation, the Art Museum of the Pecos, Marfa, Texas. *An Exhibition of Sculpture by John Chamberlain.* From May 7, 1983.

References

Jane Bell, "John Chamberlain: New Sculpture," *Arts*, vol. 49, no. 10 (June 1975), pp. 88–89.

In Amarillo, Texas (Amarillo, Texas: Stanley Marsh III, 1975), cover illus.

Chamberlain (Bern: Kunsthalle Bern and Van Abbemuseum, Eindhoven, Netherlands, 1979), illus. p. 53.

471

Falfurrias 1972

Painted steel
58 × 96 × 83 in.
(147.5 × 244 × 211 cm).

Collection

Private collection, New York, New York; on loan to Dia Art Foundation, New York, New York, 1983.

Provenance

Stanley Marsh III, Amarillo, Texas.

Exhibitions

Hammarskjold Plaza Sculpture Garden, New York, New York. *John Chamberlain: Texas Pieces.* November 1973–March 1974.

Contemporary Arts Museum, Houston, Texas. *John Chamberlain: Recent Sculpture*, cat. no. 3, illus. February 14–March 17, 1975. Traveled to Saint Louis Botanical Gardens, Saint Louis, Missouri. March 29–April 29, 1975; Minneapolis Institute of Arts, Minneapolis, Minnesota. June 15–August 14, 1975.

Dia Art Foundation, Manhattan Psychiatric Center, Ward's Island, New York, New York. *John Chamberlain at Ward's Island.* October 1977–September 1978.

Dia Art Foundation, the Art Museum of the Pecos, Marfa, Texas. *An Exhibition of Sculpture by John Chamberlain.* From May 7, 1983.

References

Charlotte Moser, "Chamberlain Sculpture is Major Coup for Museum," *Houston Chronicle*, February 15, 1975.

John Brod Peters, "John Chamberlain's Sculptures," *Saint Louis Globe-Democrat*, April 26–27, 1975.

Jane Bell, "John Chamberlain: New Sculpture," *Arts*, vol. 49, no. 10 (June 1975), illus. pp. 88–89.

Saint Paul Dispatch, June 18, 1975, illus.

Hayden Herrera, "John Chamberlain at the Houston Contemporary Arts Museum," *Art in America*, vol. 63, no. 5 (September/October 1975), pp. 105–6.

In Amarillo, Texas (Amarillo, Texas: Stanley Marsh III, 1975), color illus.

Chamberlain (Bern: Kunsthalle Bern and Van Abbemuseum, Eindhoven, Netherlands, 1979), illus. p. 51.

Notes

The sculpture is also known as *Falfurrias (Marshmellow)*.

472

Glasscock-Notrees 1972–74

Painted and chromium-plated steel
53 × 71 × 67 in.
(134.5 × 180.5 × 170 cm).

Collection

Private collection, New York, New York; on loan to Dia Art Foundation, New York, New York, 1983.

Exhibitions

Contemporary Arts Museum, Houston, Texas. *John Chamberlain: Recent Sculpture*, cat. no. 6. February 14–March 17, 1975. Traveled to Saint Louis Botanical Gardens, Saint Louis, Missouri. March 29–April 29, 1975; Minneapolis Institute of Arts, Minneapolis, Minnesota. June 15–August 14, 1975.

Dia Art Foundation, Manhattan Psychiatric Center, Ward's Island, New York, New York. *John Chamberlain at Ward's Island*. October 1977–September 1978.

Dia Art Foundation, the Art Museum of the Pecos, Marfa, Texas. *An Exhibition of Sculpture by John Chamberlain*. From May 7, 1983.

References

The Minneapolis Star, June 16, 1975, illus.

In Amarillo, Texas (Amarillo, Texas: Stanley Marsh III, 1975), illus.

Chamberlain (Bern: Kunsthalle Bern and Van Abbemuseum, Eindhoven, Netherlands, 1979), illus. p. 52.

473

International 500 1972–73

Painted and chromium-plated steel
58 × 60 × 63 in.
(147.5 × 152.5 × 160 cm).

Collection

Private collection, New York, New York; on loan to Dia Art Foundation, New York, New York, 1983.

Exhibitions

Dia Art Foundation, Manhattan Psychiatric Center, Ward's Island, New York, New York. *John Chamberlain at Ward's Island*. October 1977–September 1978.

Dia Art Foundation, the Art Museum of the Pecos, Marfa, Texas. *An Exhibition of Sculpture by John Chamberlain*. From May 7, 1983.

References

Chamberlain (Bern: Kunsthalle Bern and Van Abbemuseum, Eindhoven, Netherlands, 1979), illus. p. 50.

474

Iraan Crockett 1972–75

Painted and chromium-plated steel
67 × 82½ × 76 in.
(170 × 209.5 × 193 cm).

Collection

Private collection, New York, New York; on loan to Dia Art Foundation, New York, New York, 1983.

Exhibitions

Contemporary Arts Museum, Houston, Texas. *John Chamberlain: Recent Sculpture*, cat. no. 9, illus. February 14–March 17, 1975. Traveled to Saint Louis Botanical Gardens, Saint Louis, Missouri. March 29–April 29, 1975; Minneapolis Institute of Arts, Minneapolis, Minnesota. June 15–August 14, 1975.

Dia Art Foundation, Manhattan Psychiatric Center, Ward's Island, New York, New York. *John Chamberlain at Ward's Island*. October 1977–September 1978.

Dia Art Foundation, the Art Museum of the Pecos, Marfa, Texas. *An Exhibition of Sculpture by John Chamberlain*. From May 7, 1983.

References

In Amarillo, Texas (Amarillo, Texas: Stanley Marsh III, 1975), illus.

Chamberlain (Bern: Kunsthalle Bern and Van Abbemuseum, Eindhoven, Netherlands, 1979), illus. p. 53.

475

Old Anson Impact 1972

Painted and chromium-plated steel
67 × 84 × 97 in.
(170 × 213.5 × 246.5 cm).

Collection

Mr. and Mrs. Alvin Lubetkin, Houston, Texas.

Exhibitions

Contemporary Arts Museum, Houston, Texas. *John Chamberlain: Recent Sculpture*, cat. no. 2, illus. February 14–March 17, 1975. Traveled to Saint Louis Botanical Gardens, Saint Louis, Missouri. March 29–April 29, 1975; Minneapolis Institute of Arts, Minneapolis, Minnesota. June 15–August 14, 1975.

Contemporary Arts Museum, Houston, Texas. *In Our Time: Houston's Contemporary Arts Museum 1948–1982*. October 23, 1982–January 2, 1983.

References

In Amarillo, Texas (Amarillo, Texas: Stanley Marsh III, 1975), illus.

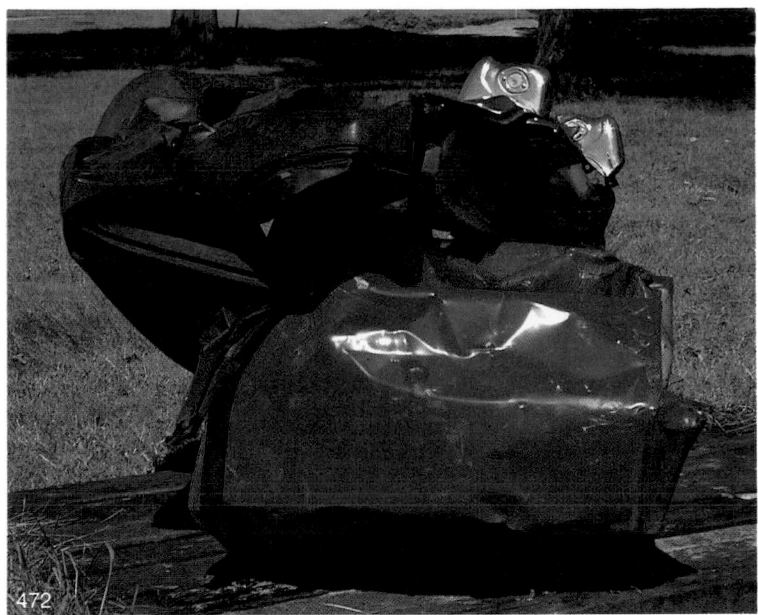
472

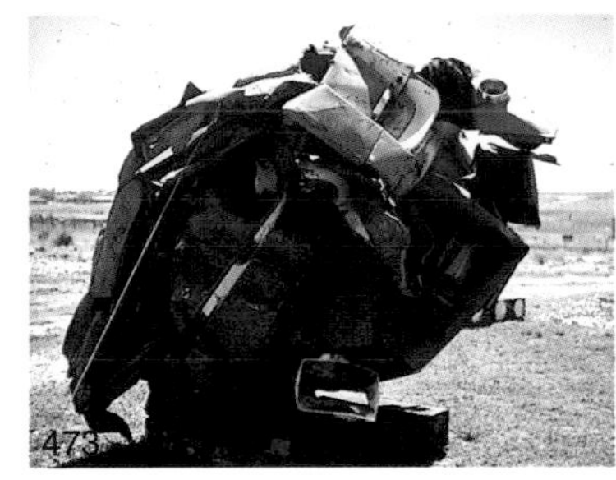
473

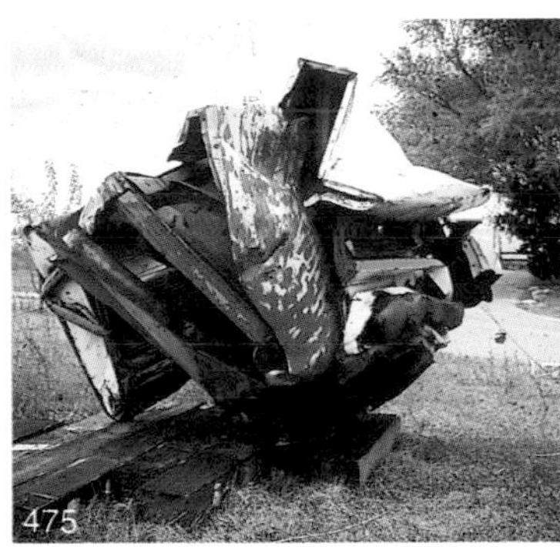
475

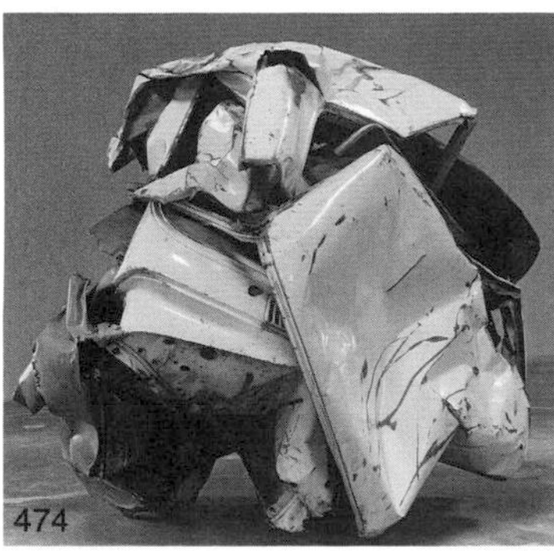
474

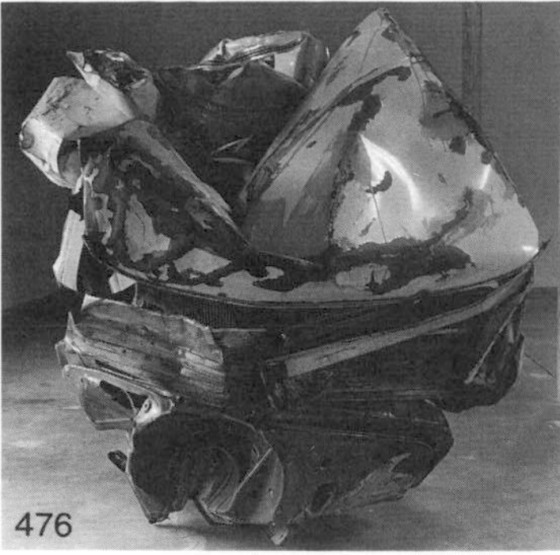
476

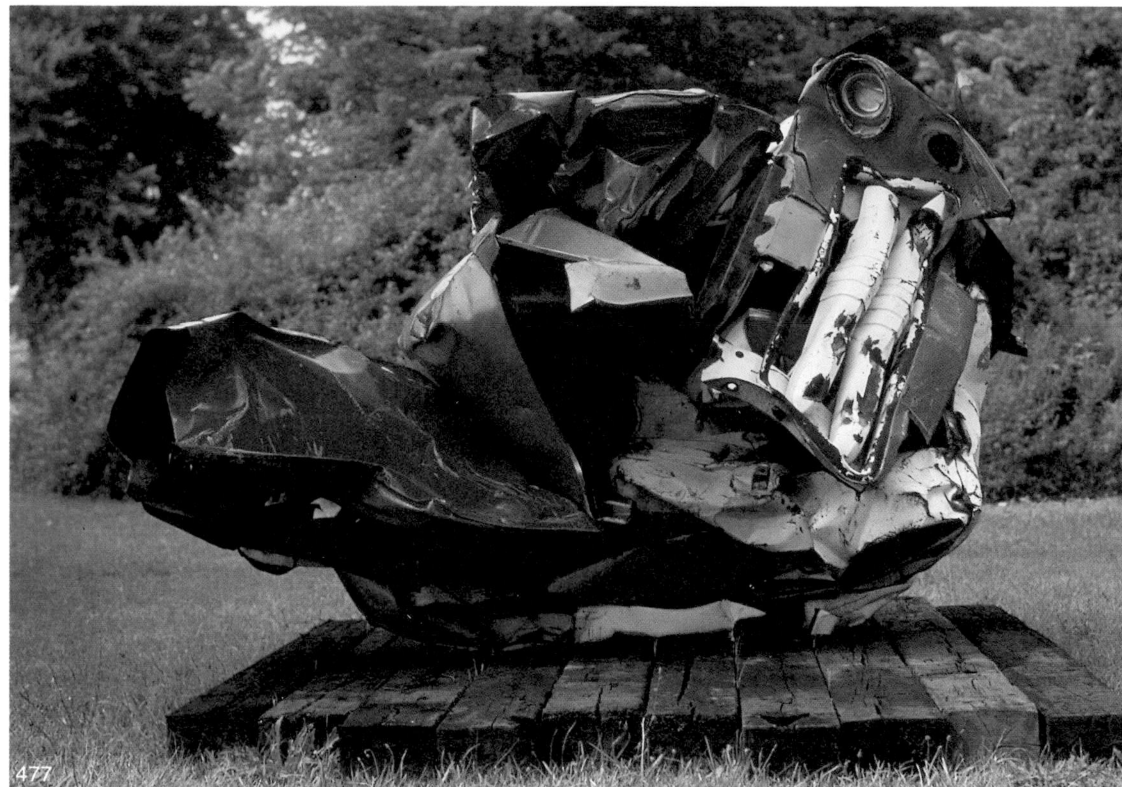
477

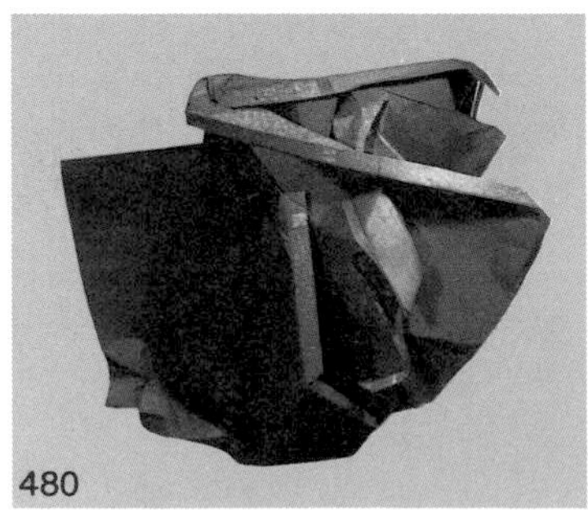
480

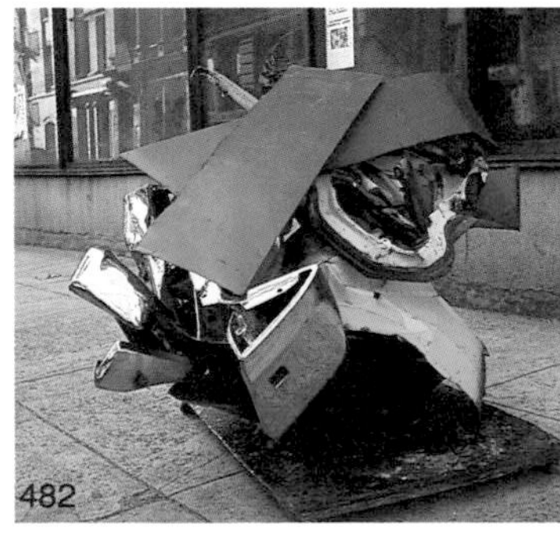
482

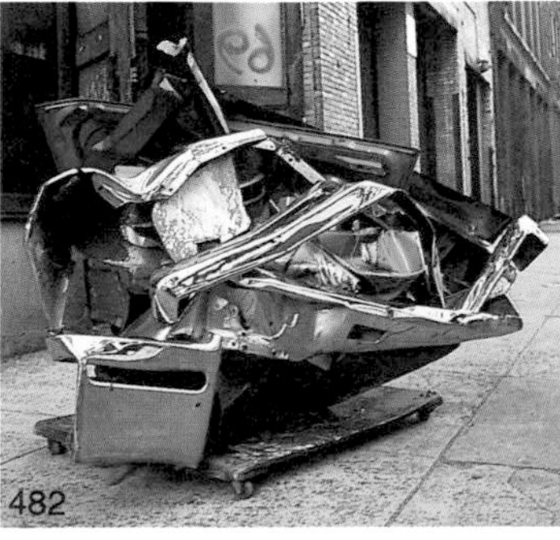
482

476

Panna-Normanna 1972

Painted and chromium-plated steel
67 × 86 × 103 in.
(170 × 218.5 × 261.5 cm).

Collection

Private collection, New York, New York; on loan to Dia Art Foundation, New York, New York, 1983.

Exhibitions

Contemporary Arts Museum, Houston, Texas. *John Chamberlain: Recent Sculpture*, cat. no. 1. February 14–March 17, 1975. Traveled to Saint Louis Botanical Gardens, Saint Louis, Missouri. March 29–April 29, 1975; Minneapolis Institute of Arts, Minneapolis, Minnesota. June 15–August 14, 1975.

Dia Art Foundation, Manhattan Psychiatric Center, Ward's Island, New York, New York. *John Chamberlain at Ward's Island.* October 1977–September 1978.

Dia Art Foundation, the Art Museum of the Pecos, Marfa, Texas. *An Exhibition of Sculpture by John Chamberlain.* From May 7, 1983.

References

In Amarillo, Texas (Amarillo, Texas: Stanley Marsh III, 1975), illus.

Chamberlain (Bern: Kunsthalle Bern and Van Abbemuseum, Eindhoven, Netherlands, 1979), illus. p. 51.

477

Papalote Goliad 1972–75

Painted and chromium-plated steel
67½ × 91½ × 128 in.
(171.5 × 232.5 × 325 cm).

Collection

Private collection, New York, New York; on loan to Dia Art Foundation, New York, New York, 1983.

Exhibitions

Contemporary Arts Museum, Houston, Texas. *John Chamberlain: Recent Sculpture*, cat. no. 8, illus. February 14–March 17, 1975. Traveled to Saint Louis Botanical Gardens, Saint Louis, Missouri. March 29–April 29, 1975; Minneapolis Institute of Arts, Minneapolis, Minnesota. June 15–August 14, 1975.

Dia Art Foundation, Manhattan Psychiatric Center, Ward's Island, New York, New York. *John Chamberlain at Ward's Island.* October 1977–September 1978.

Dia Art Foundation, the Art Museum of the Pecos, Marfa, Texas. *An Exhibition of Sculpture by John Chamberlain.* From May 7, 1983.

References

Hayden Herrera, "Houston Contemporary Arts Museum Exhibition," *Art in America*, vol. 63, no. 5 (September/October 1975), color illus. p. 105.

In Amarillo, Texas (Amarillo, Texas: Stanley Marsh III, 1975), illus.

Chamberlain (Bern: Kunsthalle Bern and Van Abbemuseum, Eindhoven, Netherlands, 1979), illus. p. 52.

James Huheey, *Diversity and Periodicity* (New York: Harper and Row, 1981), illus. p. 26.

478

Tapawingo 1972

Painted and chromium-plated steel
68 × 103 × 126 in.
(173 × 261.5 × 320 cm).

Collection

Dia Art Foundation, New York, New York, 1980; acquired directly from the artist.

Exhibitions

Hammarskjold Plaza Sculpture Garden, New York, New York. *John Chamberlain: Texas Pieces*. November 1973–March 1974.

Dia Art Foundation, the Art Museum of the Pecos, Marfa, Texas. *An Exhibition of Sculpture by John Chamberlain*. From May 7, 1983.

479

Coco La Pee P 1970–73

Painted and chromium-plated steel
61 × 82 × 74 in.
(155 × 208 × 188 cm).

Collection

Mr. and Mrs. Allan Stone, Purchase, New York, 1979.

Provenance

Walter Kelly Gallery, Chicago, Illinois; Silverman Collection, Santa Fe, New Mexico.

480

Crushed Hors D'oeuvre 1970–73

Galvanized and stainless steel
58 × 75 × 91 in.
(147.5 × 190.5 × 231 cm).

Collection

Jerald Ordover, New York, New York, 1974; acquired directly from the artist.

Notes

The sculpture was originally titled *Stuffed Ordover*, and was retitled by the artist in 1983.

481

Shamoonia 1969–73

Painted and chromium-plated steel
19 × 34 × 27 in.
(48.5 × 86.5 × 68.5 cm).

Collection

Harry and Linda Macklowe, New York, New York, 1974; acquired directly from the artist.

482

Viking Fluff 1972–73

Painted and chromium-plated steel
34 × 62 × 60 in.
(86.5 × 157.5 × 152.5 cm).

Collection

Present location unknown.

Provenance

Leo Castelli Gallery, New York, New York, 1973.

Notes

It appears that the sculpture may have been destroyed, since parts of it seem to be incorporated into *Hard Alee*, 1975, cat. no. 517.

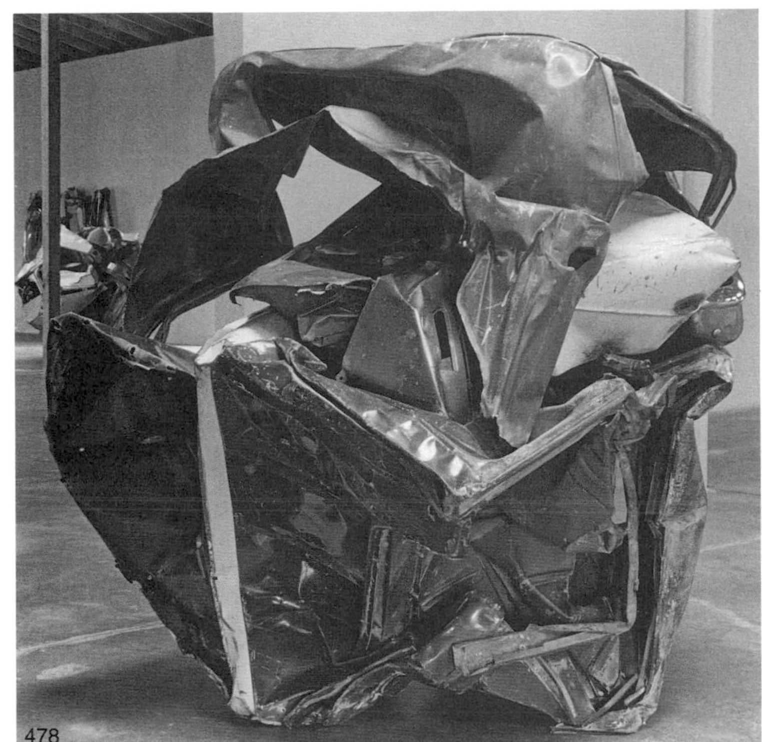
478

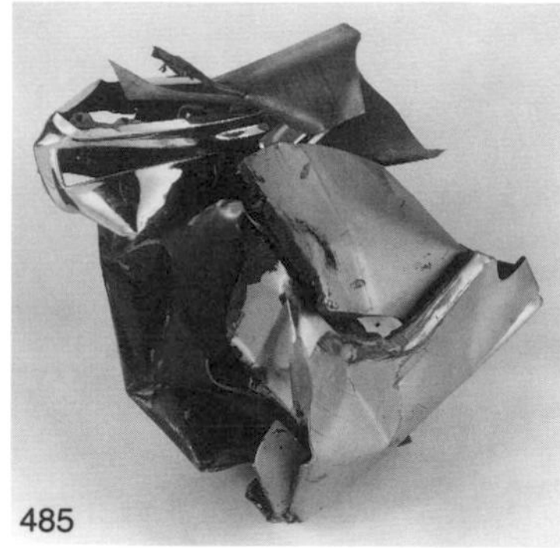
485

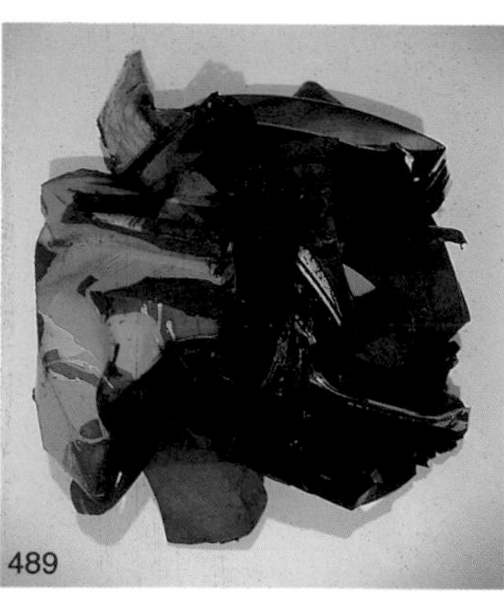
489

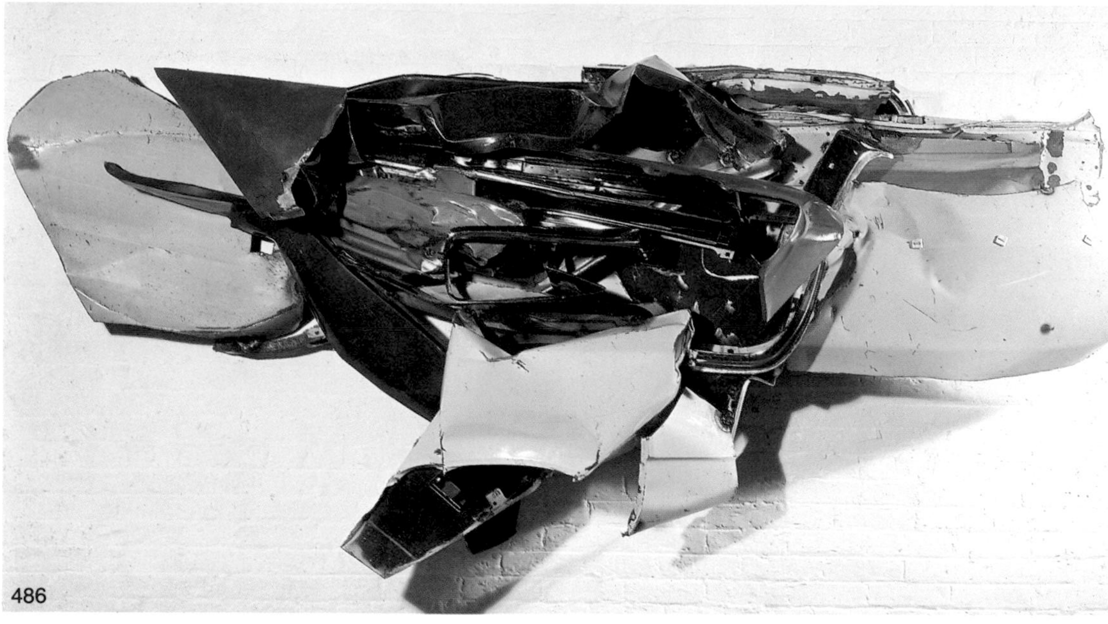
486

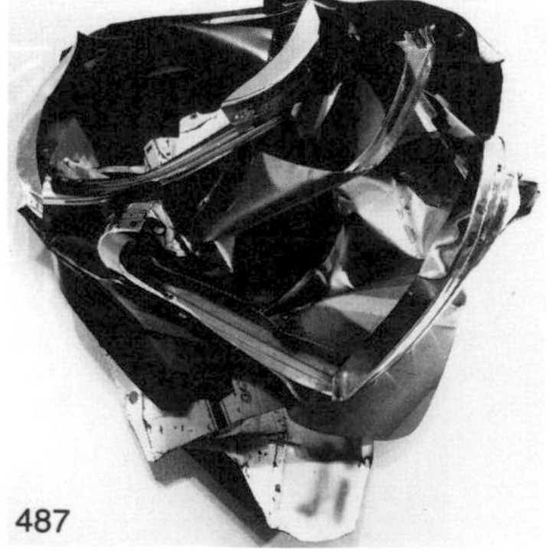
487

483

Untitled 1973

Painted and chromium-plated steel
37 × 31 × 33 in.
(94 × 78.5 × 84 cm).

Collection

Mr. and Mrs. Allan Stone, Purchase, New York.

Provenance

Walter Kelly Gallery, Chicago, Illinois; Mr. and Mrs. Sidney Kohl, Milwaukee, Wisconsin.

Exhibitions

Walter Kelly Gallery, Chicago, Illinois. *John Chamberlain*. December 1974–January 1975.

The School of the Art Institute of Chicago, Chicago, Illinois. *Visions/ Painting and Sculpture: Distinguished Alumni 1945 to the Present*, cat. no. 32, illus. pl. 15. October 7–December 10, 1976.

484

Untitled 1973

Painted and chromium-plated steel
Dimensions unknown.

Collection

Present location unknown.

Provenance

Allan Stone Gallery, New York, New York; The Mayor Gallery, London, 1975; private collection, Illinois, 1975.

485

Box Candy 1974

Painted and chromium-plated steel
40 × 44 × 52 in.
(101.5 × 112 × 132 cm).

Collection

The Saint Louis Art Museum, Saint Louis, Missouri, 1976; gift of Dr. and Mrs. Harold Joseph.

Provenance

Leo Castelli Gallery, New York, New York; Ronald Greenberg Gallery, Saint Louis, Missouri; Dr. and Mrs. Harold Joseph, Saint Louis, Missouri.

Exhibitions

Ronald Greenberg Gallery, Saint Louis, Missouri. *John Chamberlain*. April 6–29, 1975.

The Saint Louis Art Museum, Saint Louis, Missouri. *A Celebration of Acquisitions: Gifts and Purchases, 1975–1979*. December 2, 1979–January 6, 1980.

486

Char-Willie 1974

Painted and chromium-plated steel
53 × 111 × 22 in.
(134.5 × 282 × 56 cm).

Collection
Present location unknown.

Provenance
Leo Castelli Gallery, New York, New York; Gordon Locksley, Minneapolis, Minnesota.

References
Jane Bell, "John Chamberlain: New Sculpture," *Arts*, vol. 49, no. 10 (June 1975), color illus. p. 89.

H. H. Arnason, *History of Modern Art: Painting, Sculpture, Architecture* (Englewood Cliffs, New Jersey: Prentice-Hall, and New York: Abrams, rev. ed., 1977), p. 607, illus. p. 608, pl. 1079.

487

Dancing Duke 1974

Painted and chromium-plated steel
52½ × 49 × 32½ in.
(133.5 × 124.5 × 82.5 cm).

Collection
Dallas Museum of Fine Arts, Dallas, Texas, 1975; gift of Dr. and Mrs. Harold J. Joseph, Saint Louis, Missouri, in honor of Mr. and Mrs. Max Walen, Fort Worth, Texas.

Provenance
Ronald Greenberg Gallery, Saint Louis, Missouri.

Exhibitions
Ronald Greenberg Gallery, Saint Louis, Missouri. *John Chamberlain.* April 6–29, 1975.

488

Double-Hooded Jim 1974

Painted and chromium-plated steel
41 × 62 × 40 in.
(104 × 157.5 × 101.5 cm).

Collection
Mr. and Mrs. Harold Blatt, Saint Louis, Missouri, 1976.

Provenance
Ronald Greenberg Gallery, Saint Louis, Missouri.

Exhibitions
Ronald Greenberg Gallery, Saint Louis, Missouri. *John Chamberlain.* April 6–29, 1975.

489

Galaxie 500 (Revisited Sort of) 1974

Painted and chromium-plated steel
43 × 46½ × 24 in.
(109 × 118 × 61 cm).

Collection
Sharon Ullman, New York, New York.

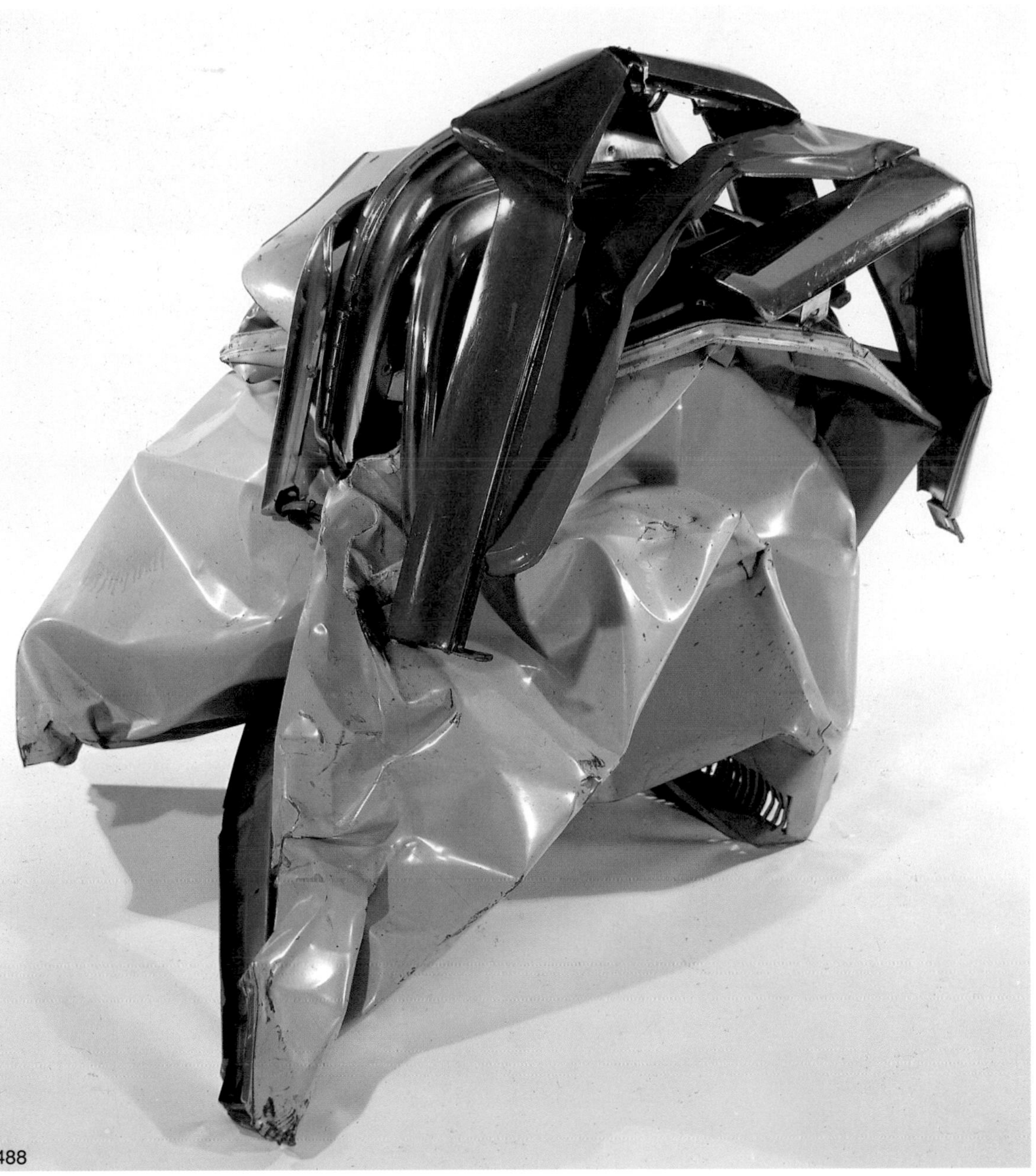

488

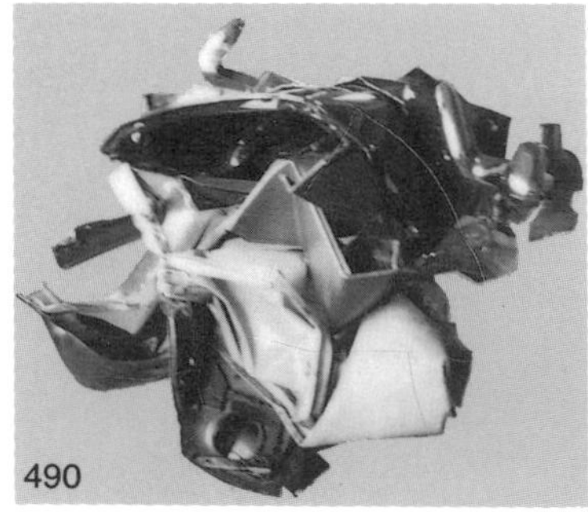
490

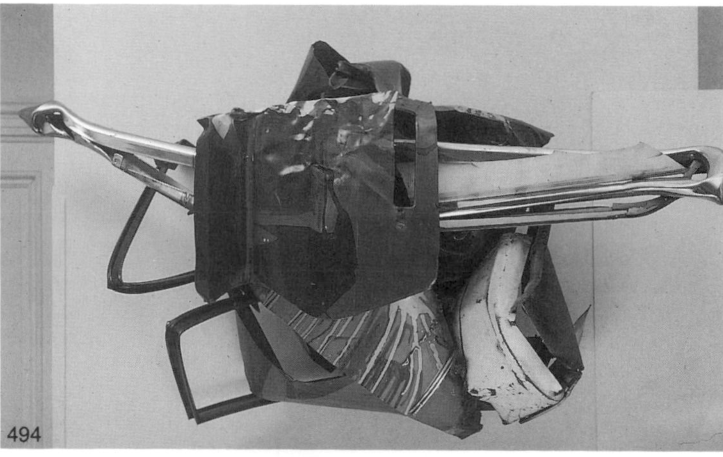
494

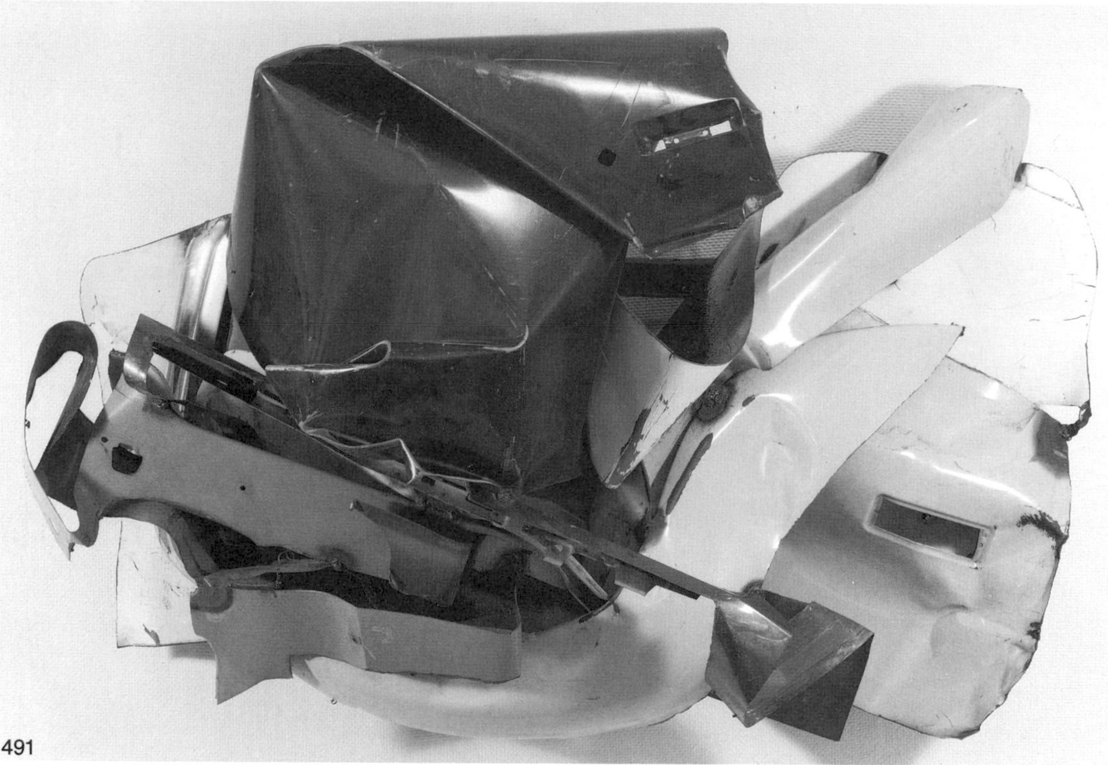
491

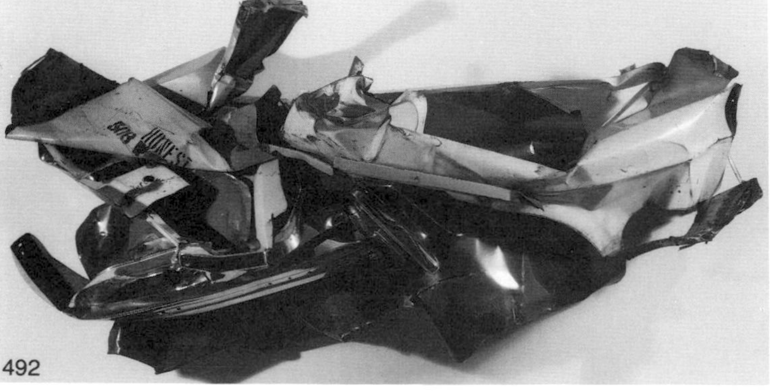
492

490

Gold Rose 1974

Painted and chromium-plated steel
44 × 50 × 49 in.
(112 × 127 × 124.5 cm).

Collection
Present location unknown.

Provenance
Aaron Drizzdorf, New York, New York.

491

Hanging Herm 1974

Painted and chromium-plated steel
41 × 64 × 24½ in.
(104 × 162.5 × 62 cm).

Collection
Washington University Gallery of Art, Saint Louis, Missouri, 1976; gift of Mr. Gene Spector.

Provenance
Ronald Greenberg Gallery, Saint Louis, Missouri, 1975; Mr. Gene Spector, 1975.

Exhibitions
Ronald Greenberg Gallery, Saint Louis, Missouri. *John Chamberlain*. April 6–29, 1975.

Washington University Gallery of Art, Saint Louis, Missouri. *Summer Selections*. May 24–August 31, 1979.

Washington University Gallery of Art, Saint Louis, Missouri. *Nineteenth- and Twentieth-Century American Paintings*. June 2–July 27, 1980.

References
Illustrated Checklist of the Collection: Paintings, Sculpture and Works on Paper (Saint Louis: Washington University Gallery of Art, 1981), p. 24, illus. p. 25.

492

Honest 508 1973–74

Painted and chromium-plated steel
37 × 78 × 25 in.
(94 × 198 × 63.5 cm).

Collection
Present location unknown.

Provenance
Leo Castelli Gallery, New York, New York; Bo Alveryd, Kävlinge, Sweden.

Exhibitions
Leo Castelli Gallery, New York, New York. *In Three Dimensions—Group Sculpture Show*. September 21–October 12, 1974.

493

Ivory Joe 1974/77
Painted and chromium-plated steel
33½ × 62½ × 68 in.
(85 × 159 × 172.5 cm).

Collection
The Pacesetter Corporation, Omaha, Nebraska, 1983.

Provenance
Julia Fahey, New York, New York, 1974; Sharon Ullman, New York, New York, 1976; Jon Leon Gallery, New York, New York, 1982.

Exhibitions
Robert L. Kidd Galleries, Birmingham, Michigan. *John Chamberlain*, illus. brochure. May 21–June 18, 1983.

Notes
In 1977 Chamberlain restored *Ivory Joe*, making significant changes in the sculpture's appearance. The restored sculpture is reproduced here.

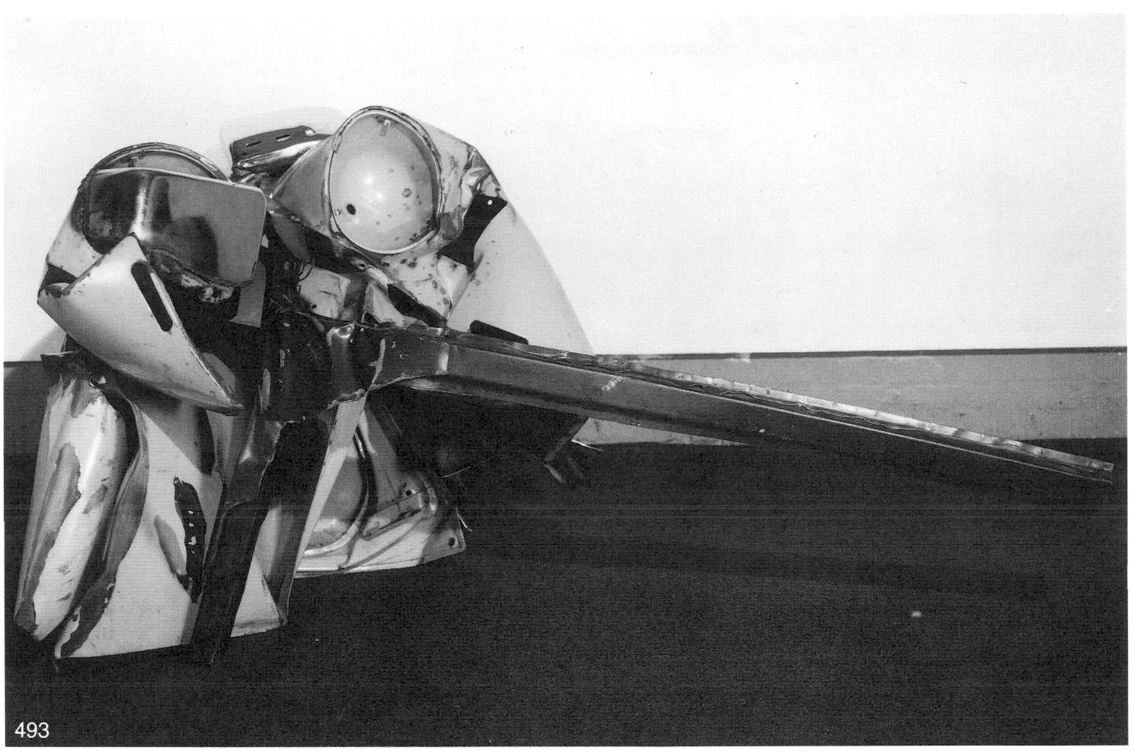

493

494

P. E. Island 1974
Painted and chromium-plated steel
29 × 43 × 11 in.
(73.5 × 109 × 28 cm).

Notes
This work was destroyed by the artist, and parts were incorporated into *Added Pleasure*, 1982. (See cat. no. 683.)

495

Pickled Papoose 1974
Painted and chromium-plated steel
44 × 59 × 32½ in.
(112 × 150 × 82.5 cm).

Collection
Sydney and Frances Lewis, Richmond, Virginia.

Provenance
Leo Castelli Gallery, New York, New York.

496

Red Zinger 1974
Painted and chromium-plated steel
45 × 86 × 18 in.
(114 × 218.5 × 46 cm).

Collection
Dr. Leonard Leight, Glenview, Kentucky, 1974.

Provenance
O. K. Harris Works of Art, New York, New York.

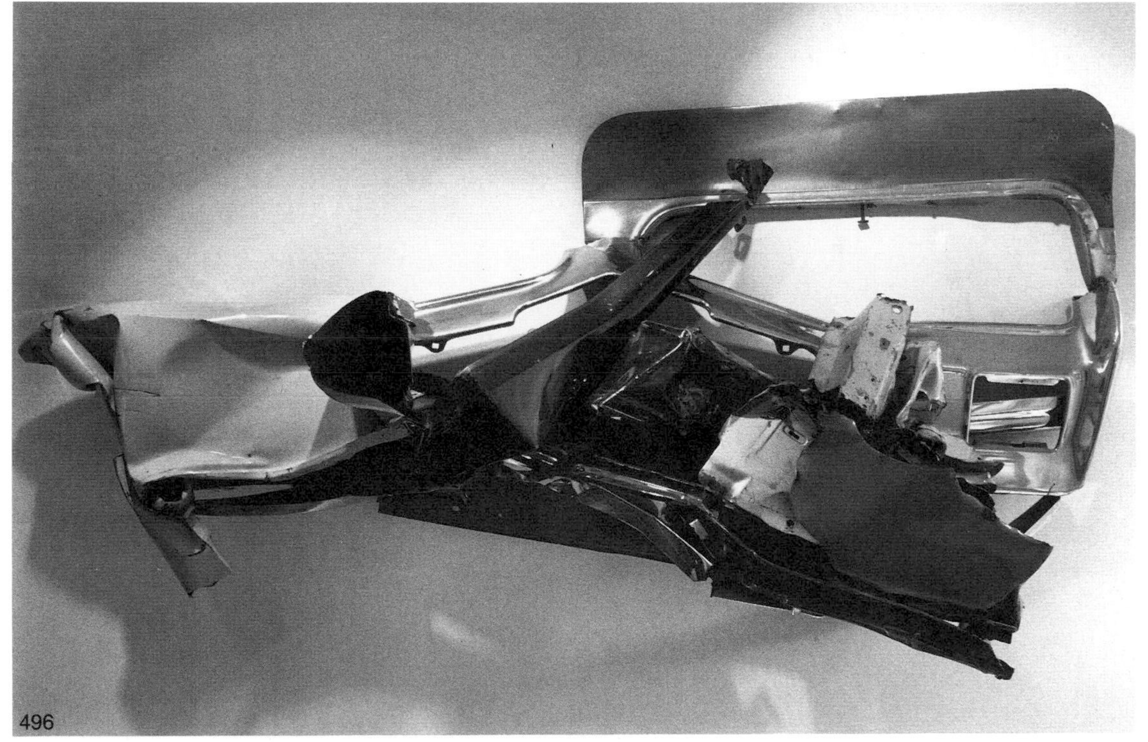

496

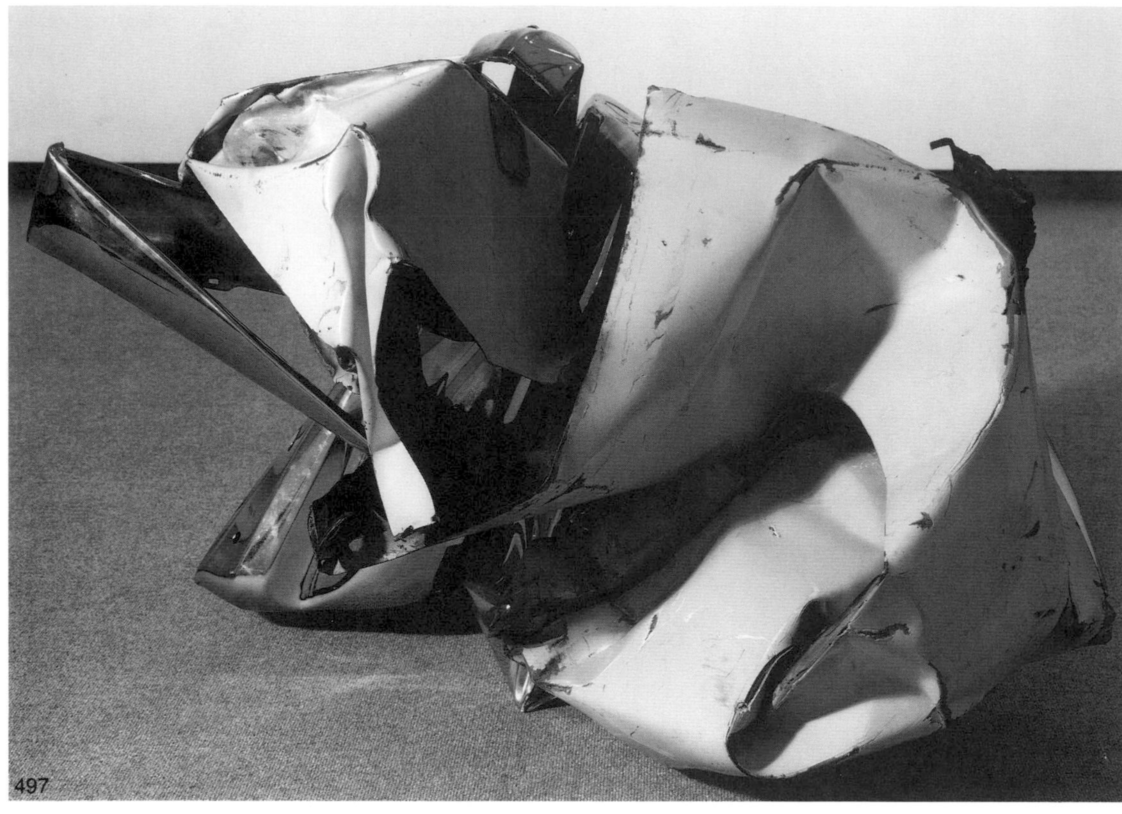
497

497

Scull's Angel 1974

Painted and chromium-plated steel
38 × 39 × 30 in.
(96.5 × 99 × 76 cm).

Collection

Fort Worth Art Museum, Fort Worth, Texas, 1975; gift of Mr. and Mrs. Max Walen.

Provenance

Ronald Greenberg Gallery, Saint Louis, Missouri; Mr. and Mrs. Max Walen, Fort Worth, Texas.

Exhibitions

Ronald Greenberg Gallery, Saint Louis, Missouri. *John Chamberlain*. April 6–29, 1975.

Tyler Museum of Art, Tyler, Texas. *Selections from the Fort Worth Art Museum Permanent Collection*. October 9–November 5, 1978.

498

Speedball 1974

Painted and chromium-plated steel
31½ × 37 × 42 in.
(80 × 94 × 106.5 cm).

Collection

Present location unknown.

499

Who's Afraid of Red, White and Blue (Verkleidung) 1974

Painted and chromium-plated steel
47 × 102 × 19 in.
(119.5 × 259 × 48 cm).

Collection

Harry and Linda Macklowe, New York, New York, 1975; acquired directly from the artist.

500

Williamson Turn 1974

Painted and chromium-plated steel
46 × 37 × 48 in.
(117 × 94 × 122 cm).

Collection

Hanford Yang, New York, New York, 1974; acquired directly from the artist.

Notes

The artist's signature is scratched into the underside of one of the chromium-plated parts.

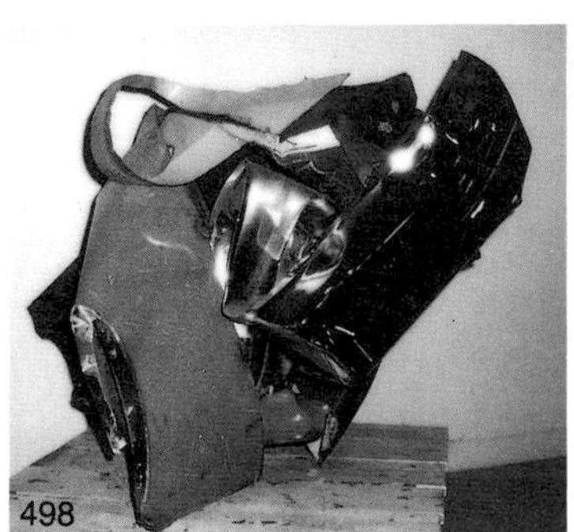
498

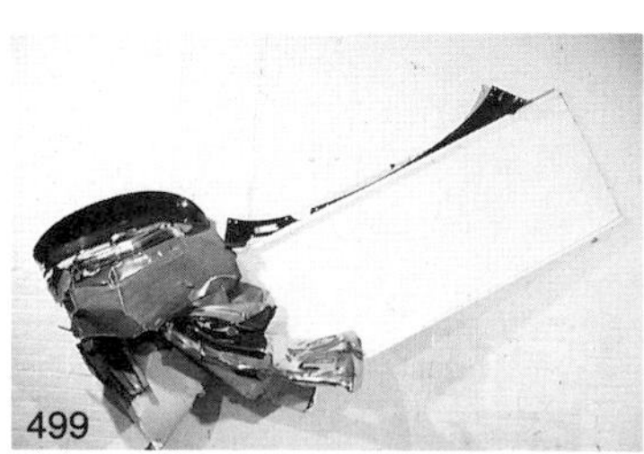
499

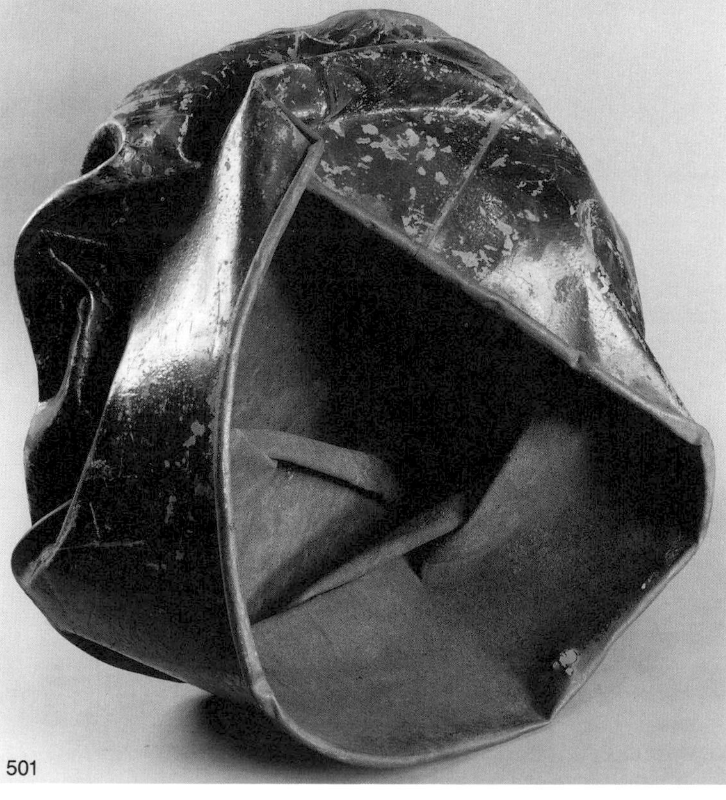
501

In 1974 Chamberlain began a series of works made from painted, compacted oil drums. The single drums are referred to as *Sockets* and the double drums as *Kisses*, although occasionally special titles exist. The series, which continues in 1975, 1977, and 1979 (cat. nos. 501–504, 527, 528, 577–580, 633–642), also includes a small group of miniatures made in 1978 of painted coffee cans (cat. nos. 593–602). These works are grouped at the end of each relevant year. It may be noted that an edition based on these miniatures was produced by Edition der Galerie Heiner Friedrich in Munich in 1978. The thirty reproductions, one of the few editions of objects by Chamberlain in existence, each measure approximately 3½ × 4½ × 4 in. (9 × 11.5 × 10 cm).

501

Socket 1974
Painted steel
25½ × 25½ × 23 in.
(65 × 65 × 58.5 cm).

Collection
Private collection, New York, New York.

Exhibitions
Heiner Friedrich, Inc., New York, New York. *An Exhibition for the War Resisters' League*. 1976.

Dia Art Foundation, New York, New York. *John Chamberlain Sculpture: An Extended Exhibition*. September 22, 1983–February 23, 1985.

502

Kiss 1974
Painted steel
29 × 35 × 28½ in.
(73.5 × 89 × 72.5 cm).

Collection
Marcia Judd Lamb, Lubbock, Texas.

503

Kiss c. 1974
Painted steel
27 × 41 × 24 in.
(68.5 × 104 × 61 cm).

Collection
Dia Art Foundation, New York, New York, 1980.

Provenance
Lone Star Foundation, New York, New York, 1977.

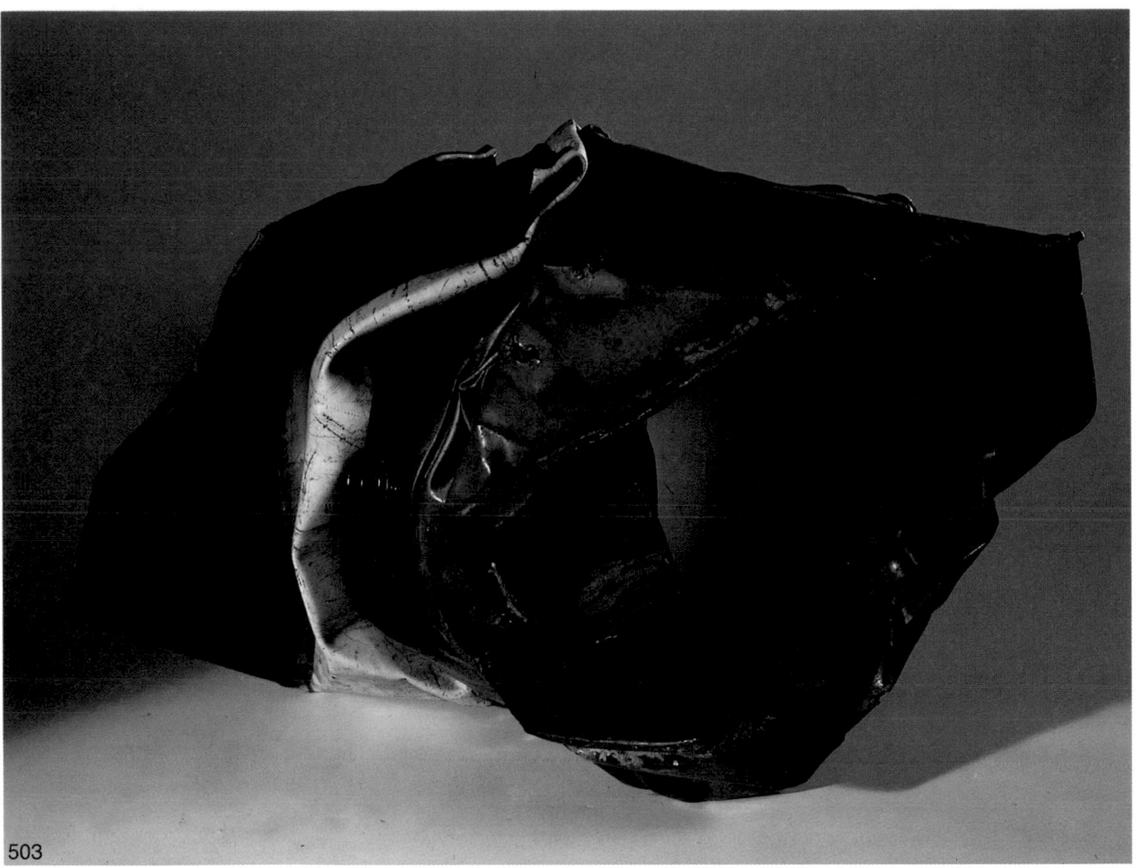

503

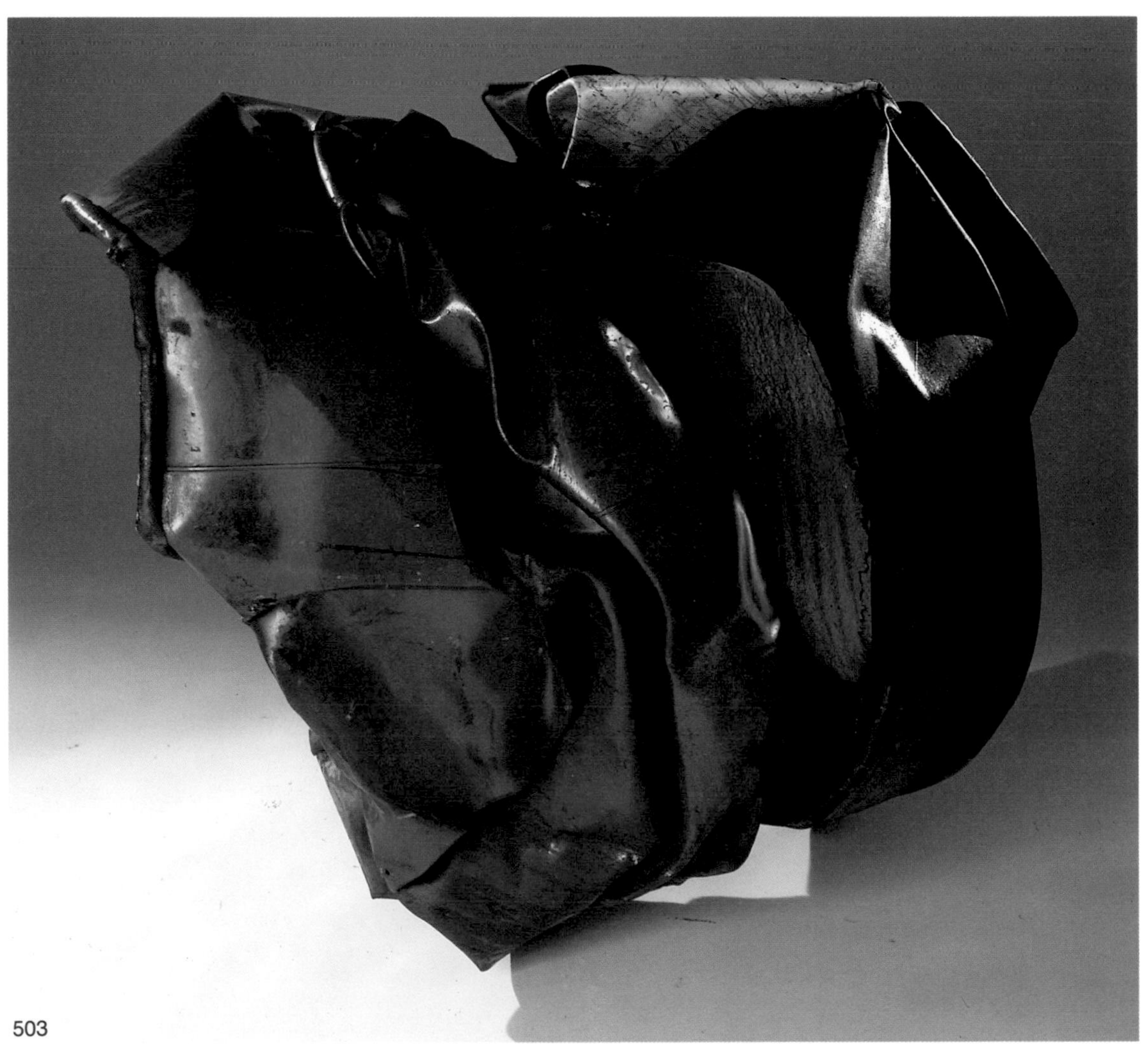

503

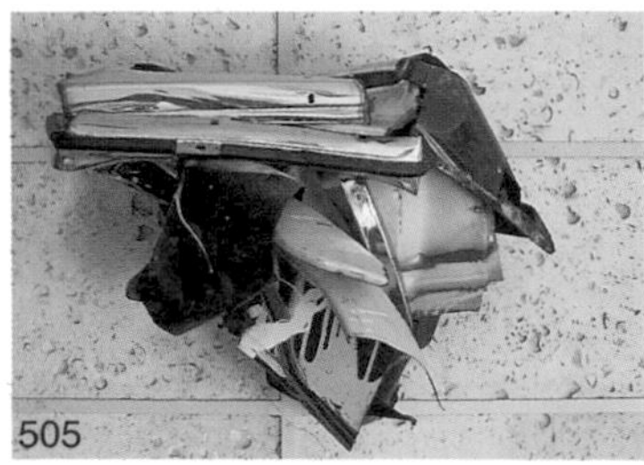
505

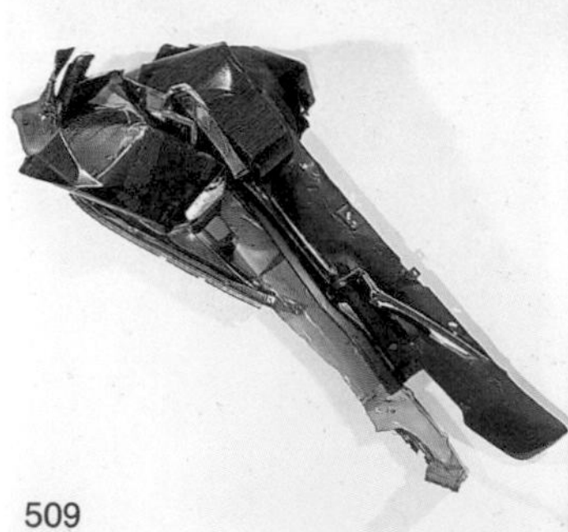
509

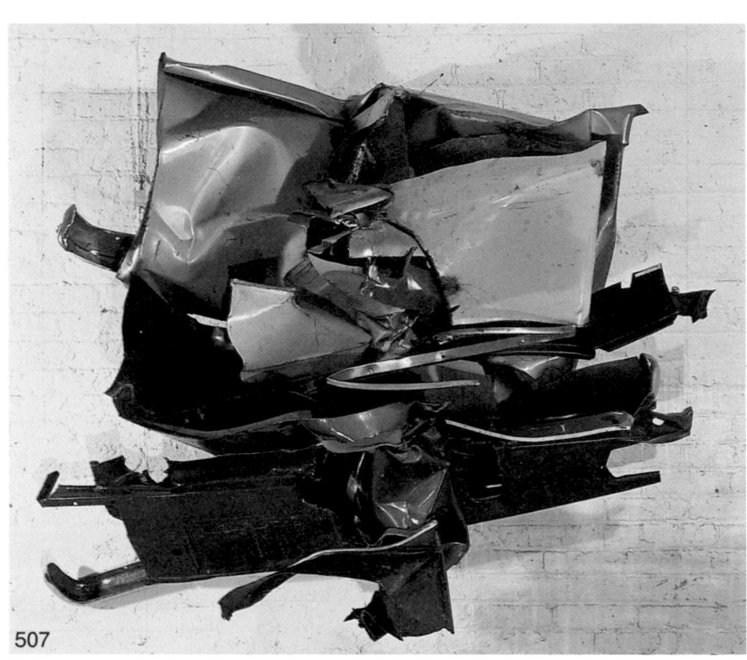
507

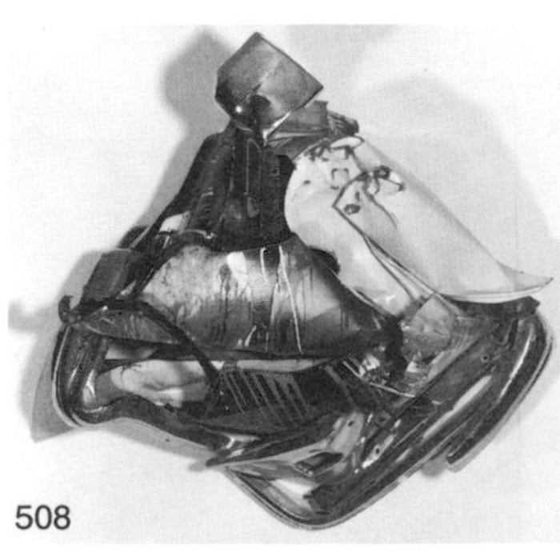
508

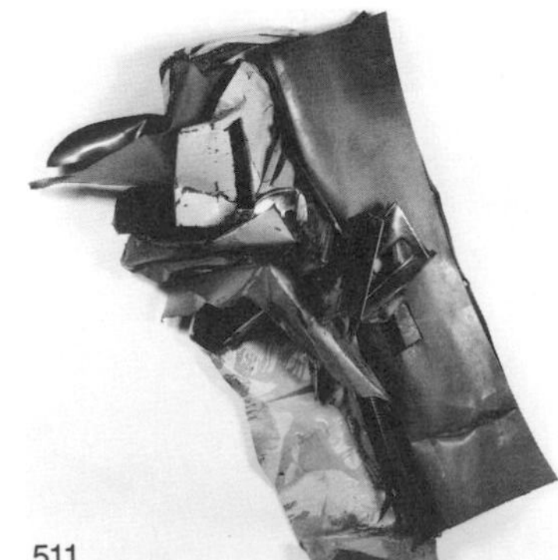
511

504

Pelham IV 1974
Painted steel
20 × 25 × 27 in.
(51 × 63.5 × 68.5 cm).

Collection
Charles Bornstein, New York, New York, 1975; acquired directly from the artist.

Notes
The sculpture was originally titled *I.C.K.*

505

Alan's Piece 1975
Painted and chromium-plated steel
31½ × 39 × 22½ in.
(80 × 99 × 57 cm).

Collection
Edmund Pillsbury, Fort Worth, Texas, 1977.

Provenance
Alan Jacobs, New York, New York; O. K. Harris Works of Art, New York, New York.

506

Black Derby 1975
Painted and chromium-plated steel
Dimensions unknown.

Collection
Present location unknown.

Provenance
Olympia Gallery, Savannah, Georgia, 1975.

507

Blue Flushing 1975
Painted and chromium-plated steel
59 × 63 × 27 in.
(150 × 160 × 68.5 cm).

Collection
Leo Castelli Gallery, New York, New York.

Exhibitions
James Corcoran Gallery, Los Angeles, California. *John Chamberlain.* November 15–December 13, 1975.

Notes
The sculpture was originally titled *Walking Blue*.

508

Bunker Ramos 1975
Painted and chromium-plated steel
61 × 66 × 30 in.
(155 × 167.5 × 76 cm).

Collection
Xavier Fourcade, Inc., New York, New York.

Exhibitions
Akademie der Kunst, Berliner Festwochen, Berlin. *New York—Downtown Manhattan: Soho*. September 5–October 17, 1976.

Hokin Gallery, Bay Harbour Islands, Florida. *Large Sculpture*. October 12–November 8, 1984.

Notes
The sculpture was originally titled *Matta Matta*.

509

Chamouda 1975
Painted and chromium-plated steel
65 × 69 × 23 in.
(165 × 175 × 58.5 cm).

Collection
Barbara Nüsse, Hamburg, 1982.

Provenance

Lorraine Chamberlain, Essex, Connecticut; Thordis Moeller, New York, New York.

Exhibitions

Leo Castelli Gallery, New York, New York. *John Chamberlain*. March 27–April 17, 1976.

The John and Mable Ringling Museum of Art, Sarasota, Florida. *John Chamberlain Reliefs 1960–1982*, illus. p. 41. January 28–March 27, 1983.

510

Colonel Mustard 1975

Painted and chromium-plated steel
20 × 14 × 14 in.
(51 × 35.5 × 35.5 cm).

Collection

Mrs. Jean Martin, New York, New York, 1975; acquired directly from the artist.

511

Daddy-O-Springs 1975

Painted and chromium-plated steel
70 × 66 × 26 in.
(178 × 167.5 × 66 cm).

Collection

Dia Art Foundation, New York, New York, 1980.

Provenance

James Corcoran Gallery, Los Angeles, California, 1980.

Exhibitions

James Corcoran Gallery, Los Angeles, California. *John Chamberlain*. November 15–December 13, 1975.

Dia Art Foundation, New York, New York. *John Chamberlain Sculpture: An Extended Exhibition*. March 19–November 27, 1982.

The John and Mable Ringling Museum of Art, Sarasota, Florida. *John Chamberlain Reliefs 1960–1982*, color illus. p. 39. January 28–March 27, 1983.

Dia Art Foundation, New York, New York. *John Chamberlain Sculpture: An Extended Exhibition*. September 22, 1983–February 23, 1985.

512

Decker & Dicker 1975

Painted and chromium-plated steel
65 × 26½ × 26 in.
(165 × 67.5 × 66 cm).

Collection

Donald and Barbara Jonas, New York, New York, 1978.

Provenance

Neil Cooper, New York, New York.

Exhibitions

The Solomon R. Guggenheim Museum, New York, New York. *American Sculpture from the Permanent Collection*. November 23, 1982–May 8, 1983.

513

Dimmy Jean 1975

Painted and chromium-plated steel
33 × 45 × 27 in.
(84 × 114.5 × 68.5 cm).

Collection

Artists' Rights Today, Inc., New York, New York; acquired directly from the artist.

514

Druid's Cluster (Swish) 1975

Painted and chromium-plated steel
65 × 71 × 20 in.
(165 × 180.5 × 51 cm).

Collection

Private collection, New York, New York.

Provenance

Heiner Friedrich GmbH, Cologne.

Exhibitions

Leo Castelli Gallery, New York, New York. *John Chamberlain*. March 27–April 17, 1976.

Heiner Friedrich GmbH, Cologne. *John Chamberlain*. June–August 1978.

References

Noel Frackman, "John Chamberlain at Castelli Gallery," *Arts*, vol. 50, no. 10 (June 1976), p. 19.

Chicago Review, vol. 30, no. 3 (Winter 1979), color illus. cover.

515

Druid's Future 1975

Painted and chromium-plated steel
46 × 62 × 33 in.
(117 × 157.5 × 84 cm).

Collection

Harry and Linda Macklowe, New York, New York, 1975; acquired directly from the artist.

516

H-A-D Inc. 1975

Painted and chromium-plated steel
57 × 35½ × 32 in.
(145 × 90 × 81.5 cm).

Collection

Gilbert and Lila Silverman, Detroit, Michigan, 1978.

Provenance

Walter Germans, New York, New York; O. K. Harris Works of Art, New York, New York.

Exhibitions

Cranbrook Academy of Art Museum, Bloomfield Hills, Michigan. *The Gilbert and Lila Silverman Collection*, cat. no. 58, illus. p. 35. September 20–November 1, 1981.

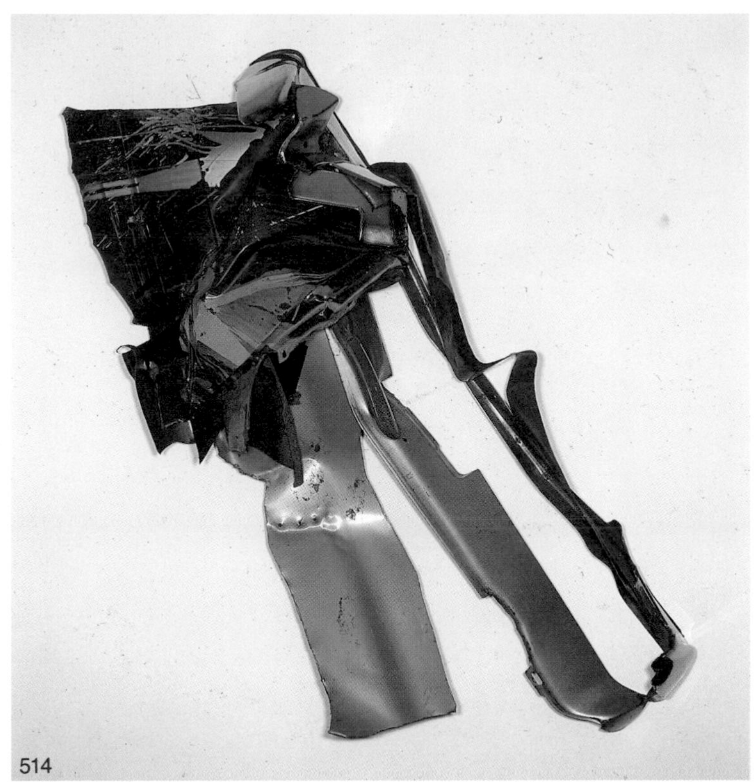

514

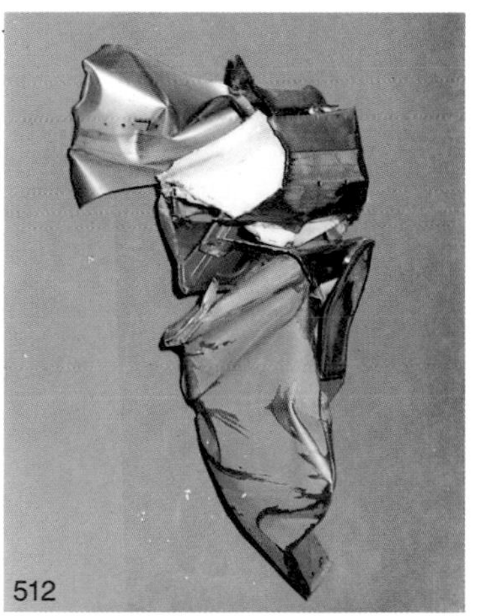

512

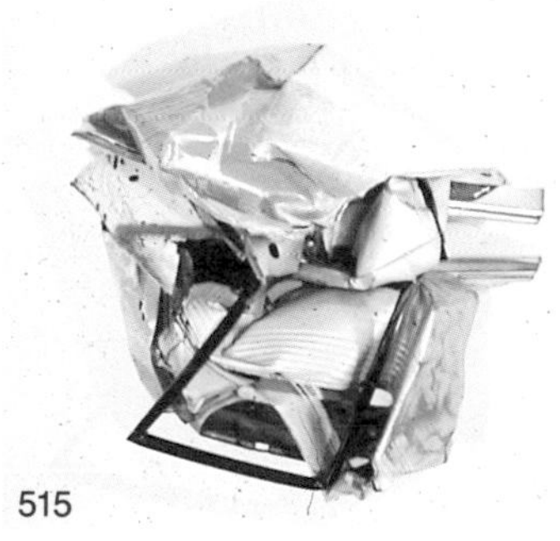

515

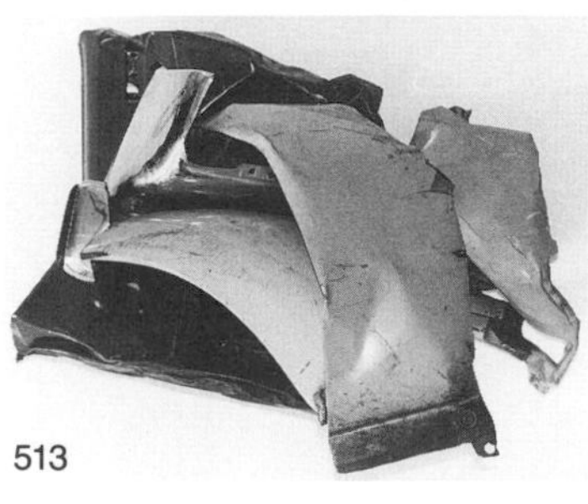

513

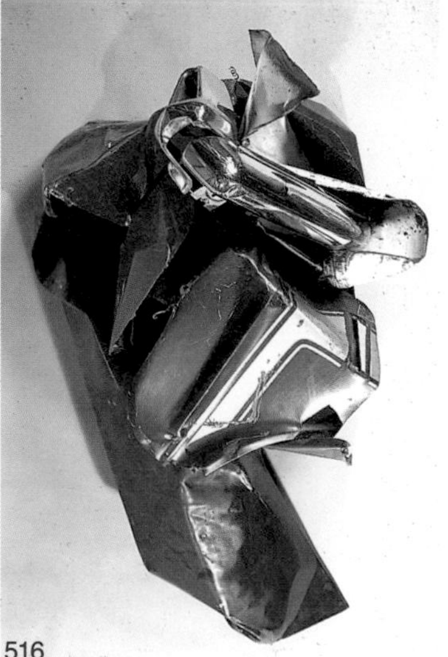

516

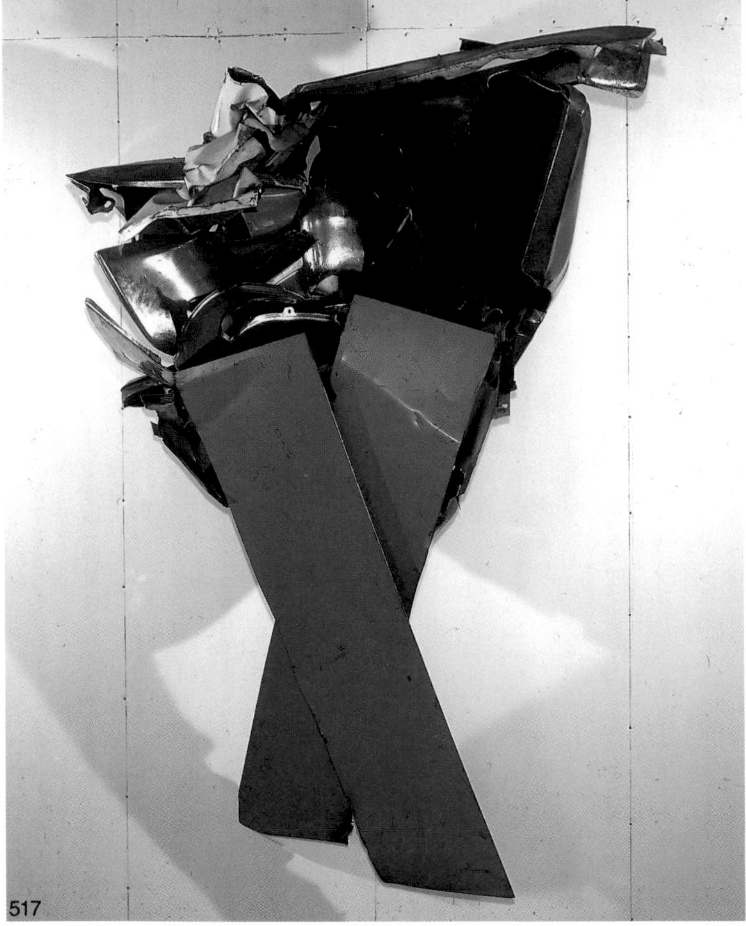
517

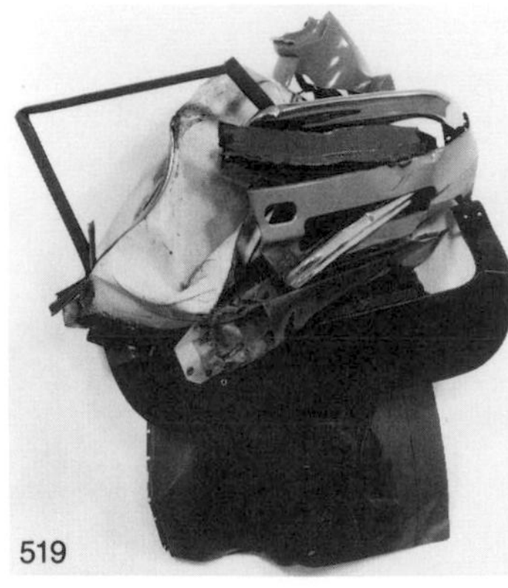
519

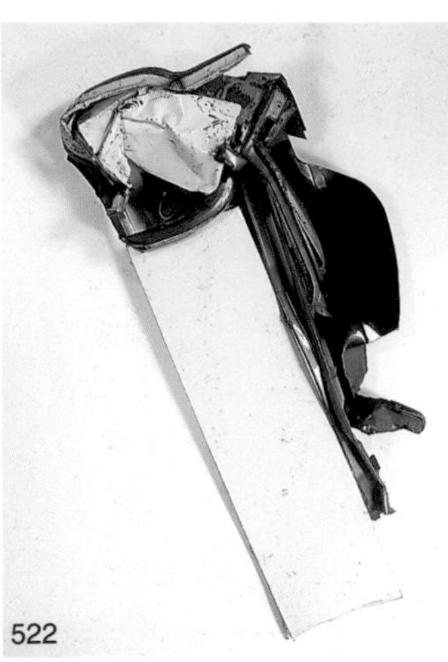
522

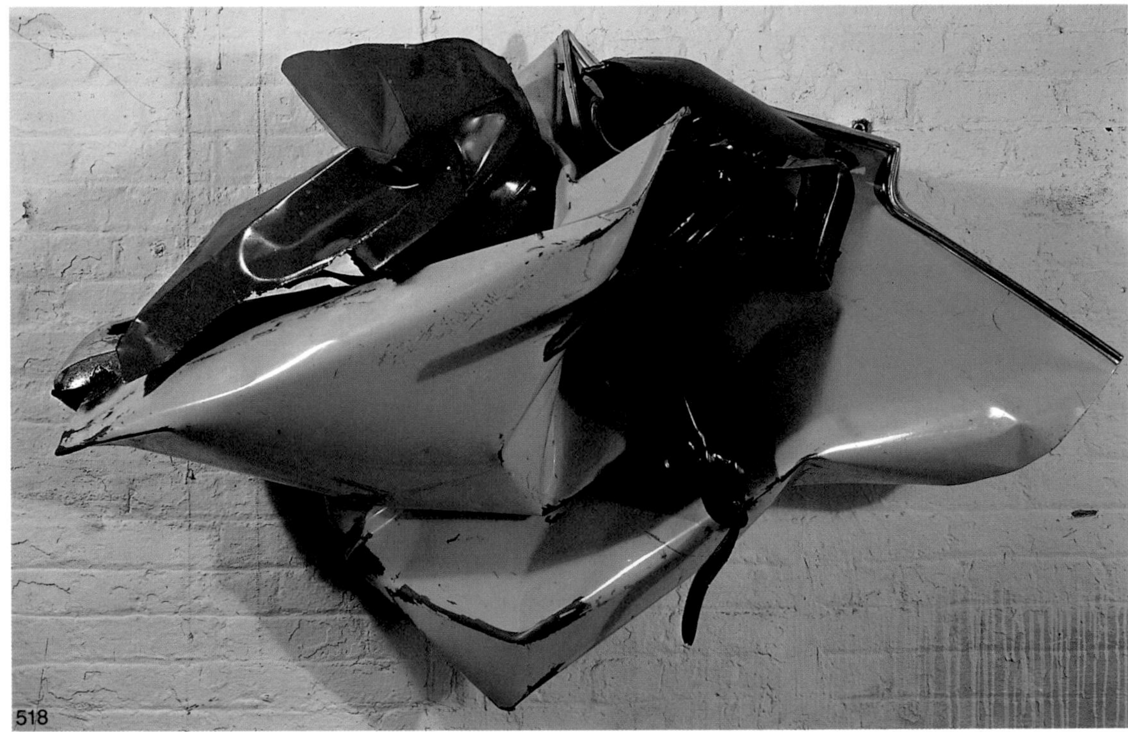
518

517

Hard Alee 1975

Painted and chromium-plated steel
76 × 56½ × 29 in.
(193 × 143.5 × 73.5 cm).

Collection

Edwin Janss, Thousand Oaks, California.

Provenance

James Corcoran Gallery, Los Angeles, California.

Exhibitions

James Corcoran Gallery, Los Angeles, California. *John Chamberlain*. November 15–December 13, 1975.

Sotheby Parke-Bernet, Inc., New York, New York. *Contemporary Paintings, Drawings and Sculpture*, cat. no. 567, color illus. May 15–16, 1980.

The Art Galleries, University of California, Santa Barbara. *John Chamberlain/Alan Saret—Contemporary Sculpture*. March 27–April 19, 1984.

Notes

The sculpture seems to have been made from parts of *Viking Fluff*, 1973, cat. no. 482.

518

Hors d'Oeuvre 1975

Painted and chromium-plated steel
42 × 56 × 27 in.
(106.5 × 142 × 68.5 cm).

Collection

Christophe de Menil, New York, New York.

Provenance

James Corcoran Gallery, Los Angeles, California.

Exhibitions

James Corcoran Gallery, Los Angeles, California. *John Chamberlain*. November 15–December 13, 1975.

519

I, Mencius 1975

Painted and chromium-plated steel
56 × 42 × 22 in.
(142 × 106.5 × 56 cm).

Collection

Dia Art Foundation, New York, New York, 1980.

Provenance

Gordon Locksley, Minneapolis, Minnesota; Lone Star Foundation, New York, New York, 1979.

Exhibitions

Christie, Manson & Woods International, Inc., New York, New York. *Contemporary Art*, cat. no. 129, color illus. p. 105. May 18, 1979.

The John and Mable Ringling Museum of Art, Sarasota, Florida. *John Chamberlain Reliefs 1960–1982*, color illus. p. 31. January 28–March 27, 1983.

Dia Art Foundation, the Art Museum of the Pecos, Marfa, Texas. *An Exhibition of Sculpture by John Chamberlain*. From May 7, 1983.

520

Latino Disco 1975

Painted and chromium-plated steel
44 × 31 × 20 in.
(112 × 78.5 × 50.5 cm).

Collection

Allan Stone, New York, New York, 1977.

Provenance

Leo Castelli Gallery, New York, New York; Margo Leavin Gallery, Los Angeles, California.

Exhibitions

Leo Castelli Gallery, New York, New York. *Summer Group Exhibition*. June 7–September 5, 1975.

The Parrish Art Museum, Southampton, New York. *Forming*, illus., incorrectly listed as *Bullwinkle*, 1961. July 29–September 23, 1984.

521

Mesa Sting 1975

Painted and chromium-plated steel
67½ × 51 × 25 in.
(171.5 × 129.5 × 63.5 cm).

Collection

James Corcoran Gallery, Los Angeles, California, 1975; acquired directly from the artist.

Exhibitions

James Corcoran Gallery, Los Angeles, California. *John Chamberlain*. November 15–December 13, 1975.

James Corcoran Gallery, Los Angeles, California. *Salute to the Museum of Contemporary Art and the Opening of the Temporary Contemporary*. November 19, 1983.

522

Patino Nuevo 1975

Painted and chromium-plated steel
87 × 48 × 17 in.
(221 × 122 × 43 cm).

Collection

Dia Art Foundation, New York, New York, 1980.

Provenance

James Corcoran Gallery, Los Angeles, California.

Exhibitions

James Corcoran Gallery, Los Angeles, California. *John Chamberlain*. November 15–December 13, 1975.

The John and Mable Ringling Museum of Art, Sarasota, Florida. *John Chamberlain Reliefs 1960–1982*, color illus. p. 33. January 28–March 27, 1983.

Dia Art Foundation, the Art Museum of the Pecos, Marfa, Texas. *An Exhibition of Sculpture by John Chamberlain*. From May 7, 1983.

References

Gary Indiana, "John Chamberlain's Irregular Set," *Art in America*, vol. 71, no. 10 (November 1983), p. 214.

523

Pommery 1975

Painted and chromium-plated steel
25 × 36 × 15 in.
(63.5 × 91.5 × 38 cm).

Collection

Present location unknown.

Provenance

Leo Castelli Gallery, New York, New York; Gordon Locksley, Minneapolis, Minnesota.

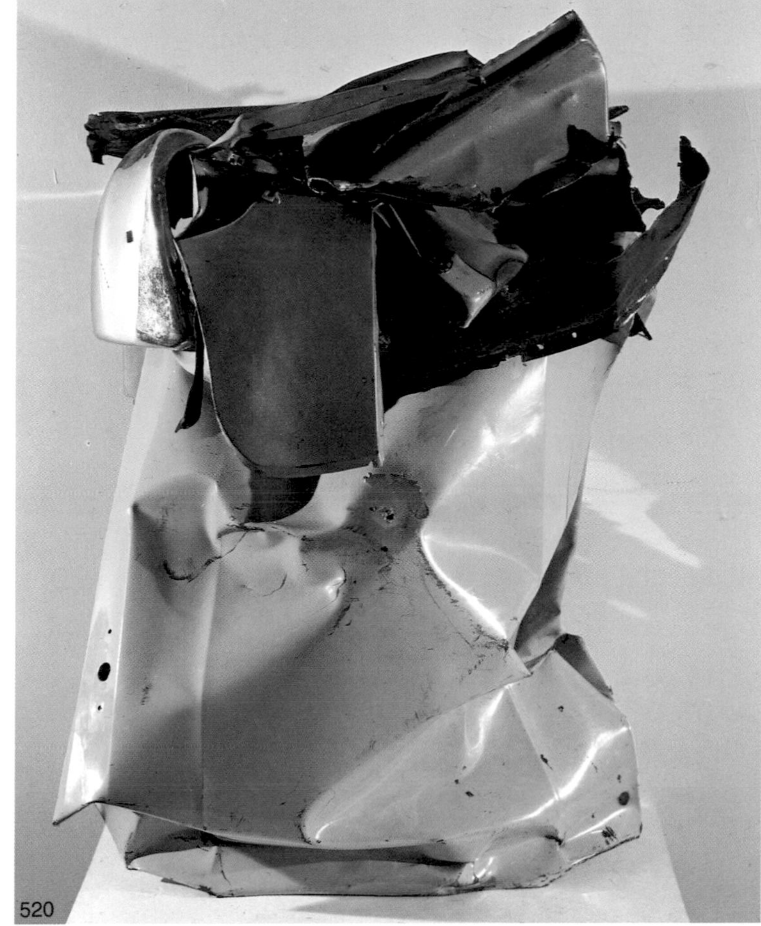
520

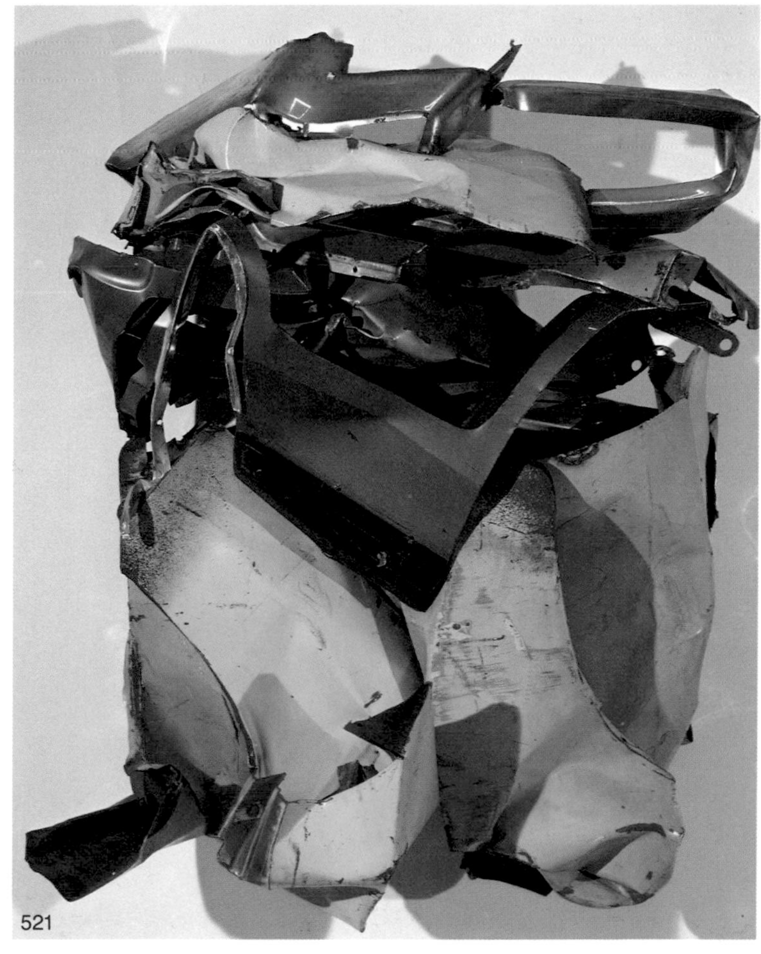
521

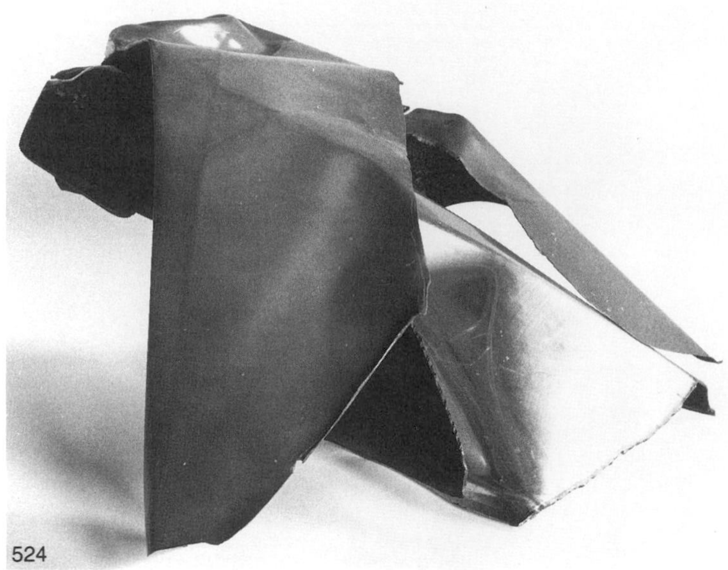
524

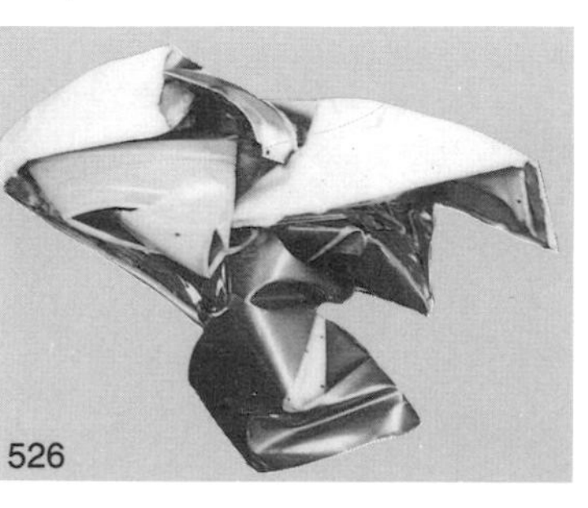
526

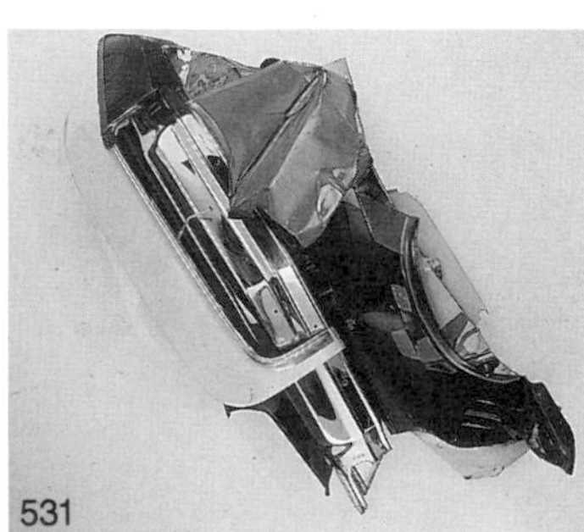
531

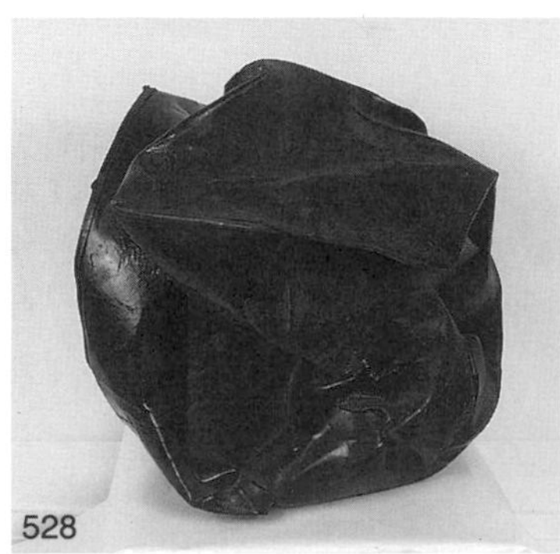
528

524

Sonny Redmond 1975

Painted and chromium-plated steel
14 × 24 × 23 in.
(35.5 × 61 × 58.5 cm).

Collection

Armand P. Arman, New York, New York.

Provenance

Jim Jacobs, New York, New York; Jack H. Klein, New York, New York.

525

Trixie Delight c. 1975

Painted and chromium-plated steel
74 × 58 × 40 in.
(188 × 147.5 × 101.5 cm).

Collection

Stephen Miller, New York, New York, 1982.

Provenance

Sharon Ullman, New York, New York; Jon Leon Gallery, New York, New York, 1982.

526

Yellow Nunn 1975

Painted and chromium-plated steel
45 × 64 × 40 in.
(114.5 × 162.5 × 101.5 cm).

Collection

Present location unknown.

Provenance

Leo Castelli Gallery, New York, New York; Bo Alveryd, Kävlinge, Sweden.

527

Socket 1975

Painted steel
23 × 27½ × 18 in.
(58.5 × 70 × 45.5 cm).

Collection

Private collection, New York, New York; acquired directly from the artist.

528

Socket 1975

Painted steel
24½ × 32 × 19 in.
(62 × 81.5 × 48.5 cm).

Collection

Thordis Moeller, New York, New York; acquired directly from the artist.

529

Bambu 1976

Painted and chromium-plated steel
16 × 22 × 11 in.
(40.5 × 56 × 28 cm).

Collection

Dr. Melvin Silverman, Los Angeles, California.

Provenance

Leo Castelli Gallery, New York, New York; Adler Gallery, Beverly Hills, California.

530

Broke Purple 1976

Painted and chromium-plated steel
36 × 27 × 19½ in.
(91.5 × 68.5 × 49.5 cm).

Collection

Private collection, New York, New York; acquired directly from the artist.

Exhibitions

Heiner Friedrich, Inc., New York, New York. *John Chamberlain*. November 12–December 22, 1977.

The John and Mable Ringling Museum of Art, Sarasota, Florida. *John Chamberlain Reliefs 1960–1982*, color illus. p. 43. January 28–March 27, 1983.

Dia Art Foundation, New York, New York. *John Chamberlain Sculpture: An Extended Exhibition*. September 22, 1983–February 23, 1985.

531

Catlett 1976

Painted and chromium-plated steel
58 × 63 × 22 in.
(147.5 × 160 × 56 cm).

Collection

Present location unknown.

532

Clytie II (Only Women Bleed . . . for Alice) 1976

Painted and chromium-plated steel
59 × 67 × 22 in.
(150 × 170 × 56 cm).

Collection

Private collection, New York, New York.

Provenance

Jesse Chamberlain, New York, New York.

Exhibitions

Leo Castelli Gallery, New York, New York. *John Chamberlain*. March 27–April 17, 1976.

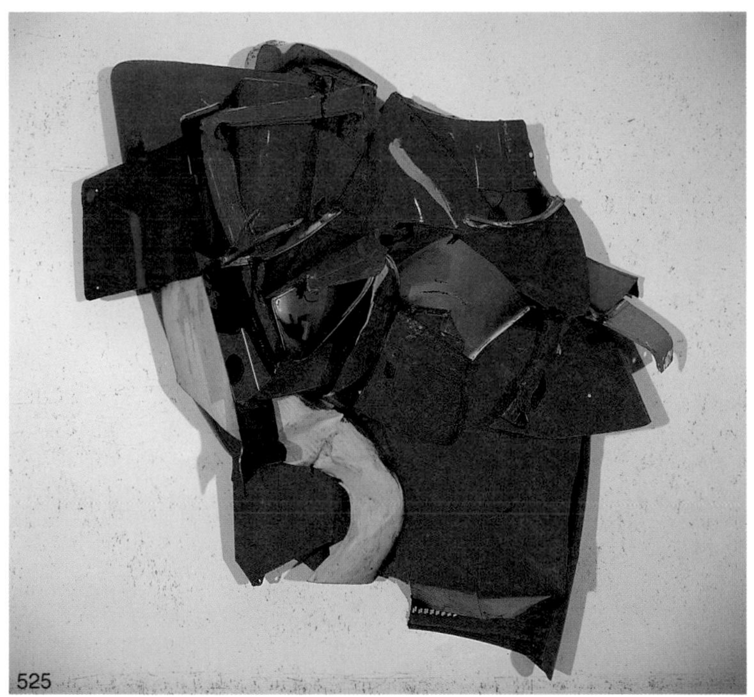
525

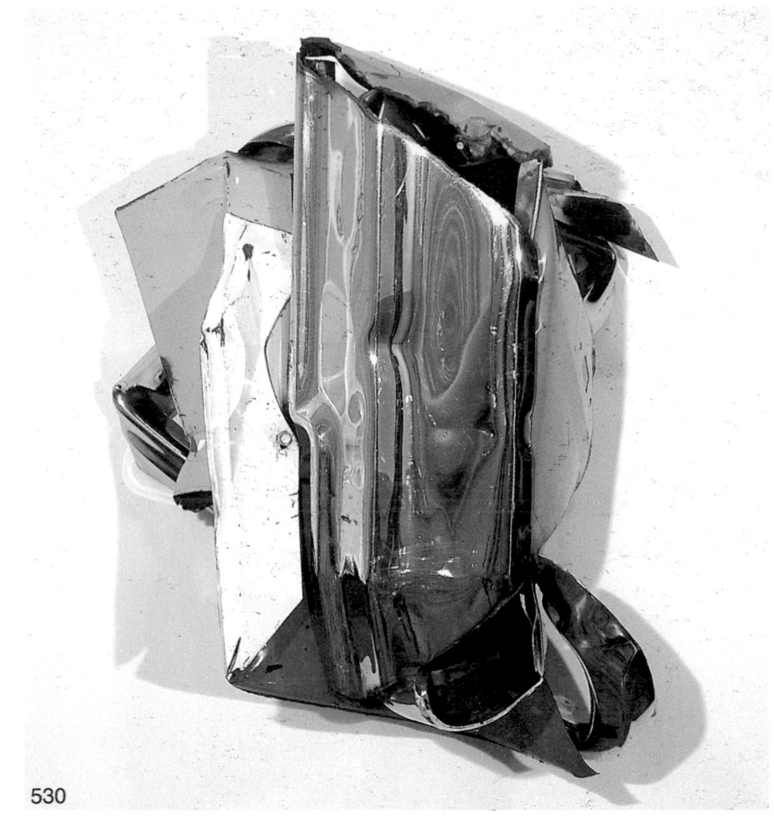
530

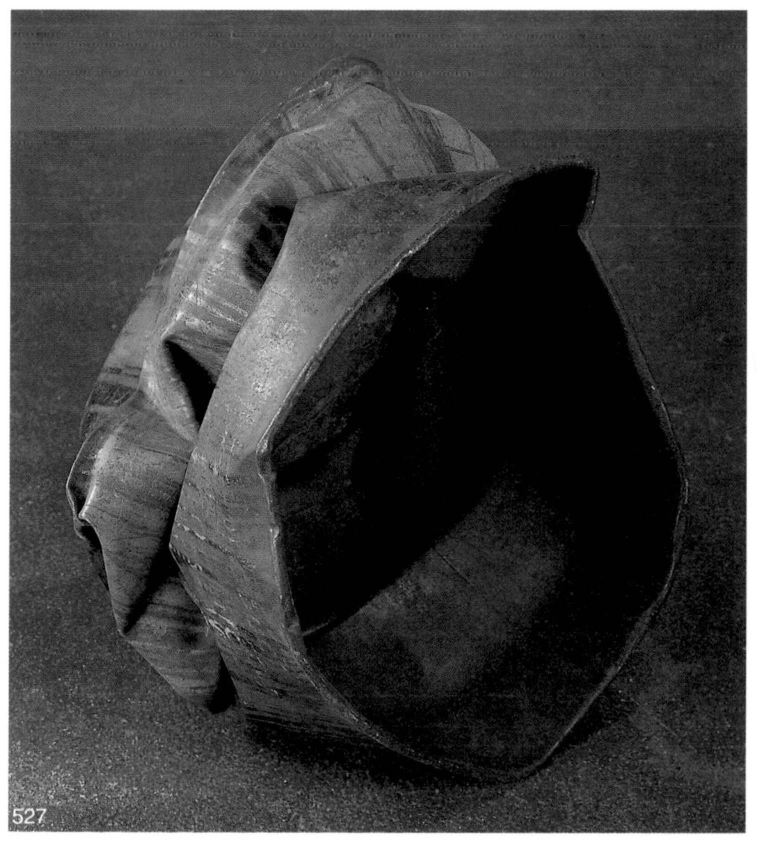
527

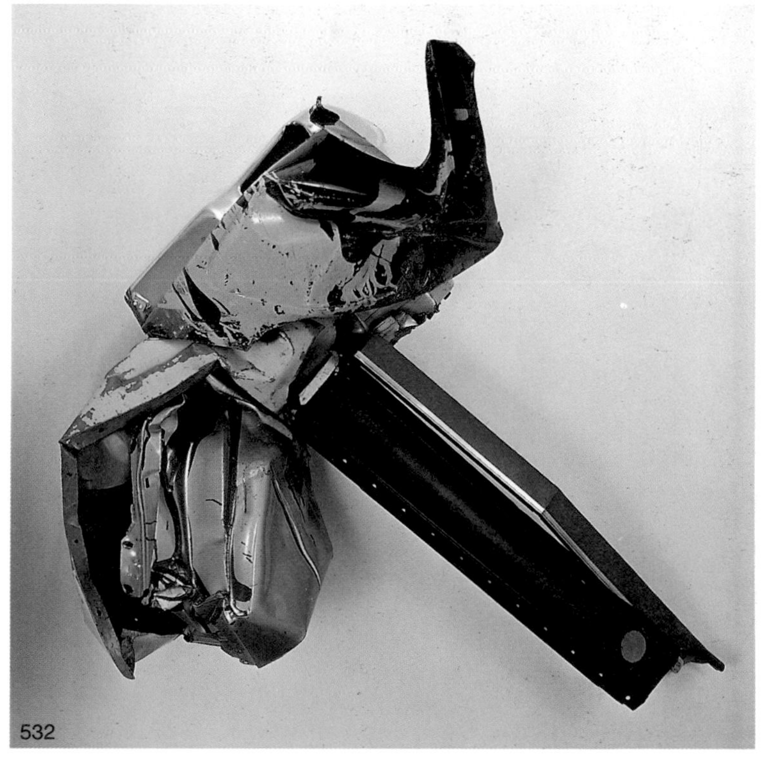
532

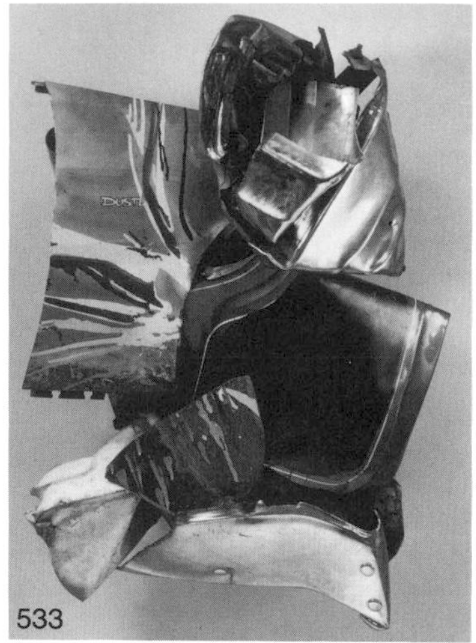
533

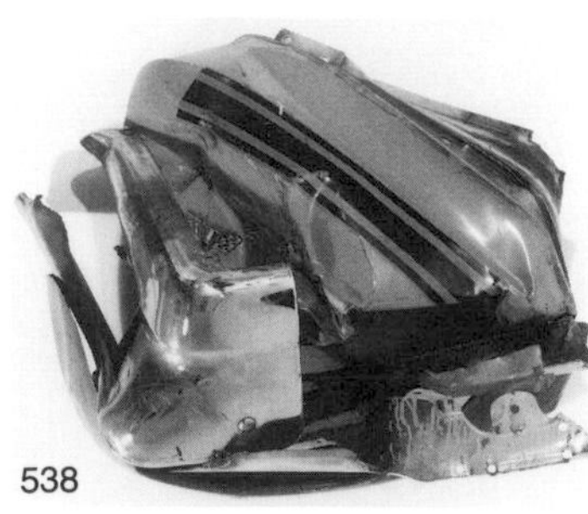
538

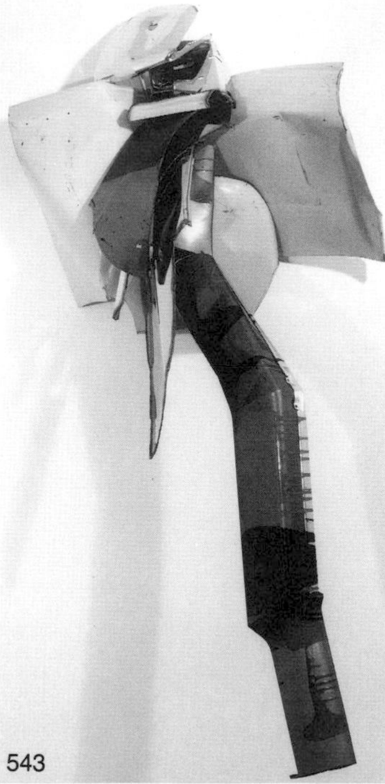
543

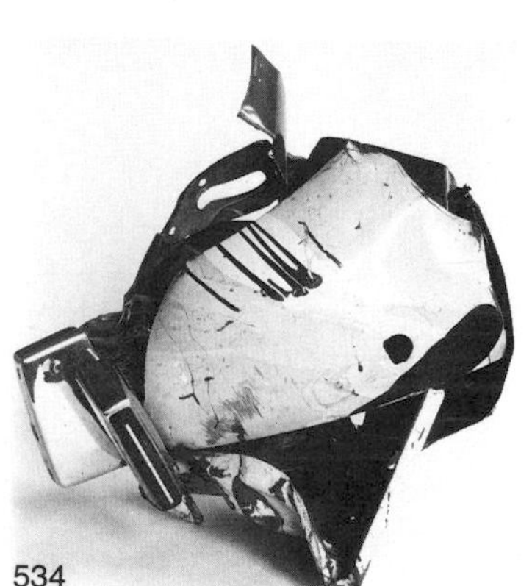
534

533

D. D. Bitch 1976

Painted and chromium-plated steel
56 × 34 × 22 in.
(142 × 86.5 × 56 cm).

Collection

Martin Z. Margulies, Coconut Grove, Florida, 1979.

Provenance

O. K. Harris Works of Art, New York, New York, 1976.

References

Auction 393, New York, New York. *Contemporary Art*, sale no. 4, cat. no. 53, illus. May 26, 1976.

Notes

The sculpture has been known as *Dee Dee Bitch* and *Deep Dish Bitch*.

534

Ethel's Glory 1976

Painted and chromium-plated steel
33 × 31 × 23 in.
(84 × 79 × 58.5 cm).

Collection

Armand P. Arman, New York, New York.

Provenance

Jack H. Klein, New York, New York, 1976.

535

Gennaro 1976

Painted and chromium-plated steel
32 × 27 × 14 in.
(81.5 × 69 × 35.5 cm).

Collection

Private collection, New York, New York, 1976; acquired directly from the artist.

536

Horsepucky 1976

Painted and chromium-plated steel
74 × 43 × 25 in.
(188 × 109 × 63.5 cm).

Collection

Daniel Weinberg Gallery, Los Angeles, California.

Provenance

Alan Power, Nevada City, California.

Exhibitions

Daniel Weinberg Gallery, Los Angeles, California. *The Art Walk Exhibition*. November 1983.

537

Knee Pad Examiner 1976

Painted and chromium-plated steel
54 × 69 × 13 in.
(137 × 175.5 × 33 cm).

Collection

Freide and Rubin Gorewitz, West Nyack, New York, 1976; acquired directly from the artist.

538

Lucy Snaggletooth 1976

Painted and chromium-plated steel
36 × 30 × 21 in.
(91.5 × 76 × 53.5 cm).

Collection

Ralph and Helen Goldenberg, Chicago, Illinois, 1984.

Provenance

O. K. Harris Works of Art, New York, New York; Robert King, New York, New York; Anita Friedman Fine Arts, New York, New York; Solomon and Co., New York, New York; private collection, Scarsdale, New York; Solomon and Co., New York, New York; B. C. Holland and Co., Chicago, Illinois, 1984.

Exhibitions

The Sable-Castelli Gallery, Ltd., Toronto. *Survey—Part I*. February 14–March 6, 1976.

Marissa del Re Gallery, New York, New York. *Found Objects*. June–July 1983.

Notes

The sculpture was known as "Untitled, 1975" while in the possession of Solomon and Co.

539

Monkey Fist 1976

Painted and chromium-plated steel
39 × 24 × 16 in.
(99 × 61 × 40.5 cm).

Collection

Lenore B. Gold, Atlanta, Georgia.

Provenance

Allan Stone, New York, New York; Dr. Jack Kern, New York, New York; James Goodman Gallery, Inc., New York, New York.

540

Mystars 1976

Painted and chromium-plated steel
57 × 47 × 24 in.
(145 × 119.5 × 61 cm).

Collection

Present location unknown.

541

Rio Linda . . . green 1976

Painted and chromium-plated steel
28 × 56 × 27 in.
(71 × 142 × 68.5 cm).

Collection

Douglas Reunzel, New York, New York; acquired directly from the artist.

Exhibitions

Sculpturesites, Amagansett, New York. *Outdoor Sculpture*, site no. 38, illus. 1980–81.

References

Phyllis Braff, "From the Studio," *East Hampton Star*, July 30, 1981.

542

Rooster Starfoot 1976

Painted and chromium-plated steel
90 × 72 × 72 in.
(229.5 × 183 × 183 cm).

Collection

Private collection, New York, New York; acquired directly from the artist.

Exhibitions

Kunsthalle Bern. *Chamberlain*, cat. no. 1, color illus. p. 43. October 12–November 18, 1979. Traveled to Van Abbemuseum, Eindhoven, Netherlands. April 3–May 11, 1980.

Palacio de Cristal, Parque del Retiro, Madrid. *John Chamberlain/Esculturas*, color illus. p. 23. January 26–March 31, 1984.

543

Rosy Future 1976

Painted and chromium-plated steel
74 × 33 × 31 in.
(188 × 84 × 78.5 cm).

Collection

Lorraine Chamberlain, Essex, Connecticut.

Exhibitions

Leo Castelli Gallery, New York, New York. *John Chamberlain*. March 27–April 17, 1976.

Dia Art Foundation, Essex, Connecticut. *Chamberlain Gardens, Essex*. May–November 1982 and May 1983.

The John and Mable Ringling Museum of Art, Sarasota, Florida. *John Chamberlain Reliefs 1960–1982*, color illus. p. 45. January 28–March 27, 1983.

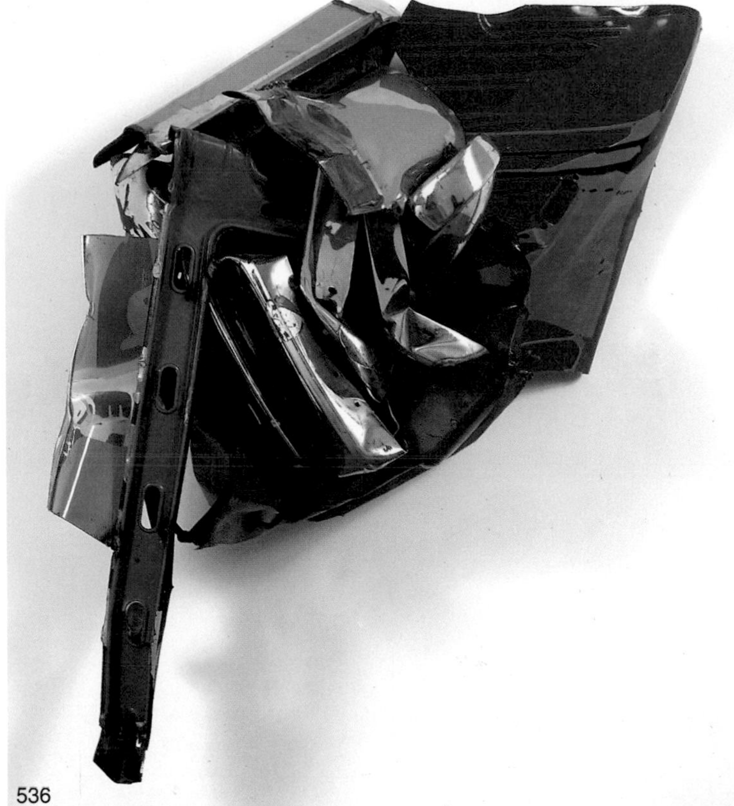
536

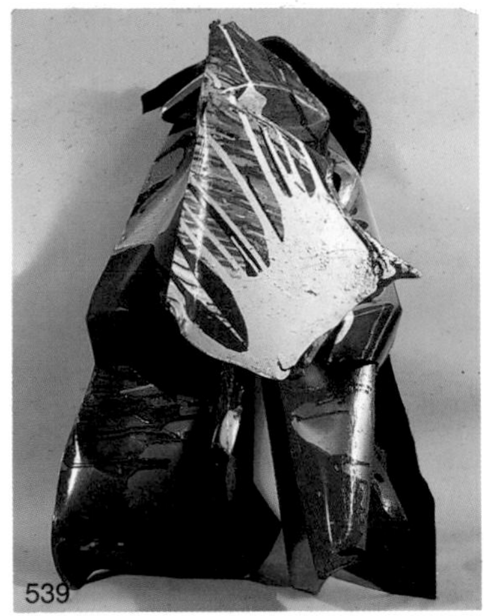
539

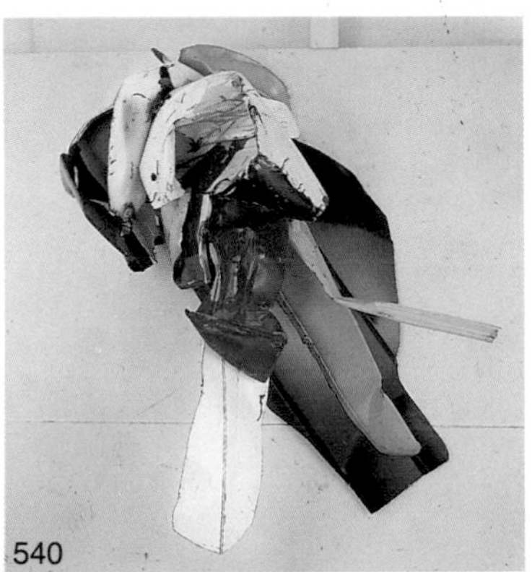
540

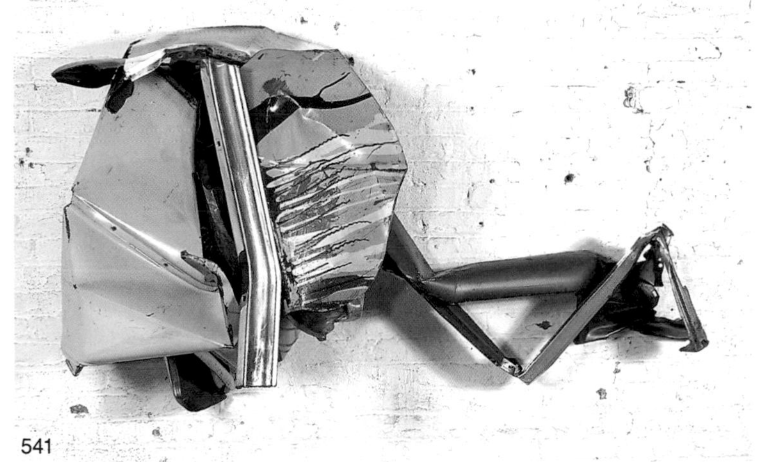
541

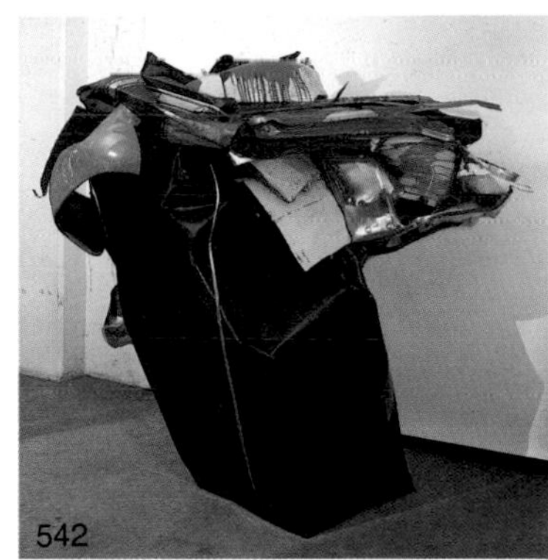
542

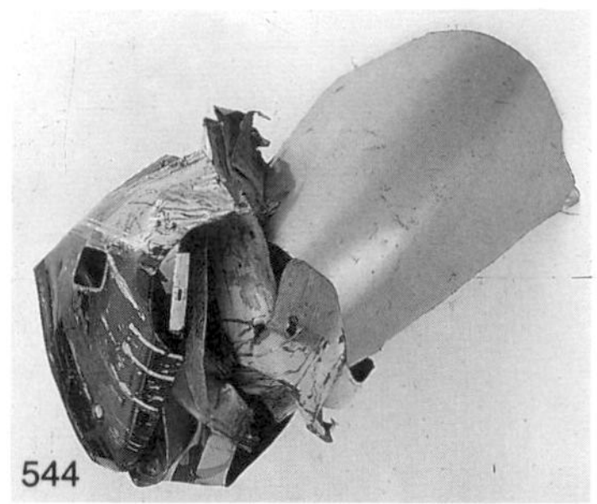
544

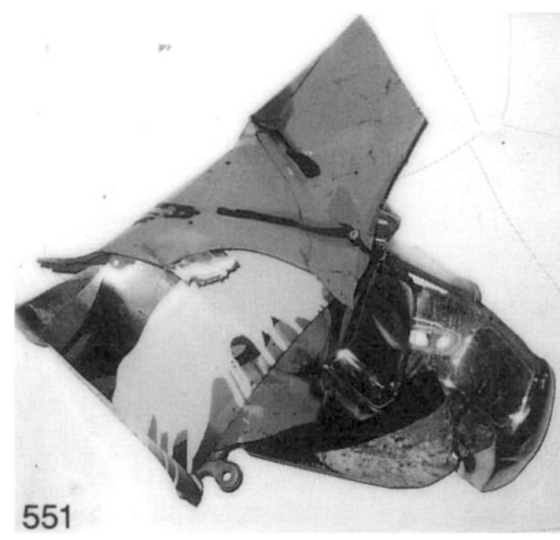
551

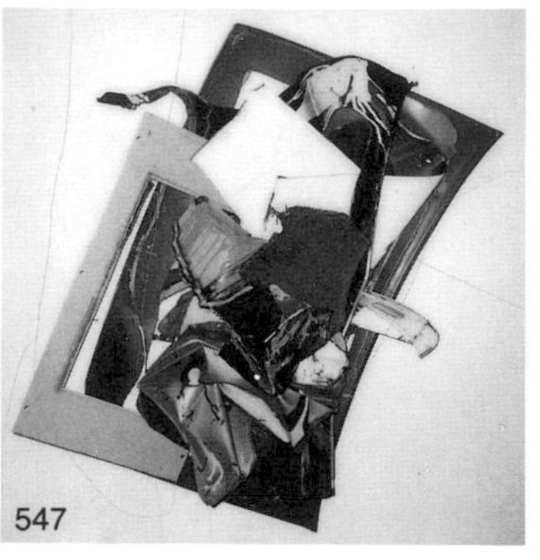
547

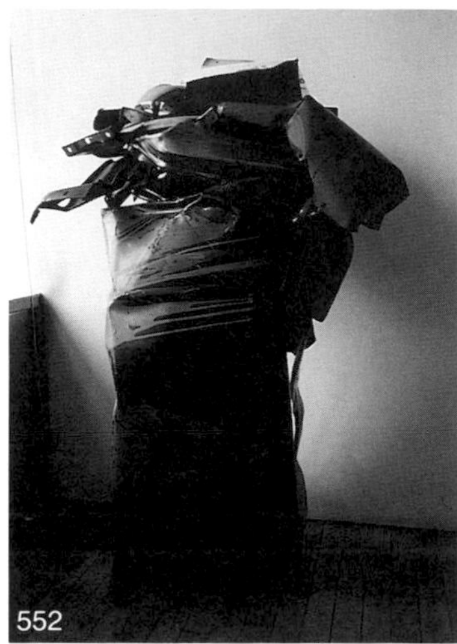
552

544

Silver Plait 1976

Painted and chromium-plated steel
35 × 31 × 25½ in.
(89 × 78.5 × 65 cm).

Collection

Ellen Cohen, New York, New York, 1976; acquired directly from the artist.

545

Stringer 1976

Painted and chromium-plated steel
65 × 67 × 25 in.
(165 × 170 × 63.5 cm).

Collection

Xavier Fourcade, Inc., New York, New York.

Exhibitions

Leo Castelli Gallery, New York, New York. *John Chamberlain*. March 27–April 17, 1976.

Leo Castelli Gallery, New York, New York. *Summer Group Exhibition*. June 12–September 12, 1976.

The John and Mable Ringling Museum of Art, Sarasota, Florida. *John Chamberlain Reliefs 1960–1982*, color illus. p. 47. January 28–March 27, 1983.

Robert L. Kidd Galleries, Birmingham, Michigan. *John Chamberlain*, illus. brochure. May 21–June 18, 1983.

Margo Leavin Gallery, Los Angeles, California. *John Chamberlain*. March 4–30, 1985.

References

Noel Frackman, "John Chamberlain at Castelli Gallery," *Arts*, vol. 50, no. 10 (June 1976), illus. p. 19.

546

Swans-52 1976

Painted and chromium-plated steel
32 × 46 × 16 in.
(81 × 117 × 40.5 cm).

Collection

Present location unknown.

Provenance

Alan Jacobs, New York, New York, 1976.

547

The Faxabrax 1976

Painted and chromium-plated steel
49 × 45 × 26 in.
(124.5 × 114.5 × 66 cm).

Notes

This work was destroyed by the artist.

548

Thors Mahler 1976

Painted and chromium-plated steel
49 × 76 × 29 in.
(124.5 × 193 × 73.5 cm).

Collection

Present location unknown.

549

Wingbone 1976

Painted and chromium-plated steel
52 × 57 × 24 in.
(132 × 145 × 61 cm).

Collection

Present location unknown.

Notes

The only evidence of the existence of this sculpture is that it was entered in the Castelli registry.

550

Zane & Corney 1976

Painted and chromium-plated steel
73 × 56 × 31 in.
(185.5 × 142.5 × 79 cm).

Collection

Teheran Museum of Contemporary Art, Teheran, Iran, 1978.

Exhibitions

Leo Castelli Gallery, New York, New York. *John Chamberlain*. March 27–April 17, 1976.

The New York State Museum, Albany, New York. *New York: The State of Art*, cat. no. 55, illus. p. 44. October 8–November 27, 1977.

Notes

The sculpture was originally titled *Jello Again*.

551

Zapf 1976

Painted and chromium-plated steel
41 × 43 × 20 in.
(104 × 109 × 51 cm).

Collection

Jay I. Kislak, Miami, Florida, 1976; acquired directly from the artist.

552

Untitled 1976

Painted and chromium-plated steel
60 × 24 × 21 in.
(152.5 × 61 × 53.5 cm).

Collection

Paul Hoffman, Naperville, Illinois, 1984.

Provenance

David Crum, New York, New York; O. K. Harris Works of Art, New York, New York.

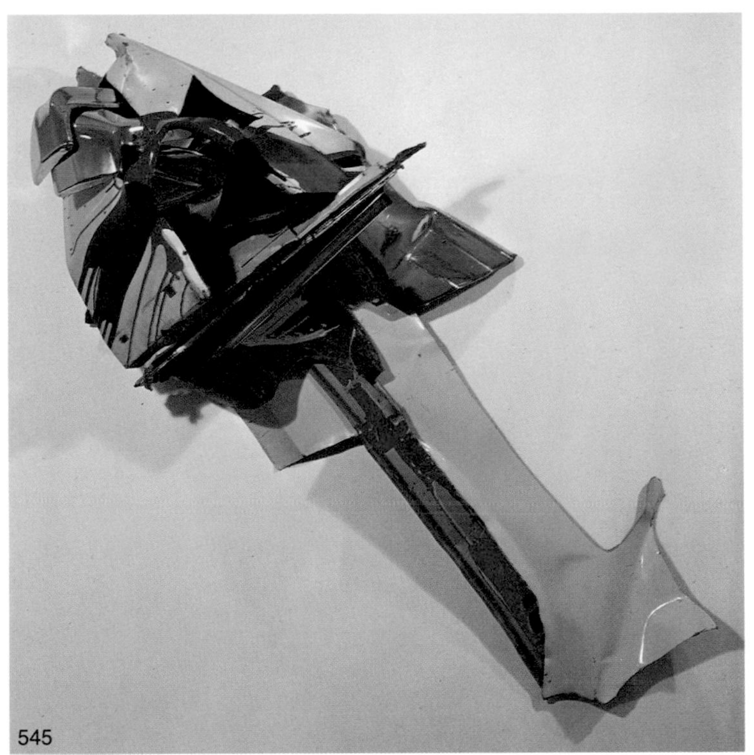
545

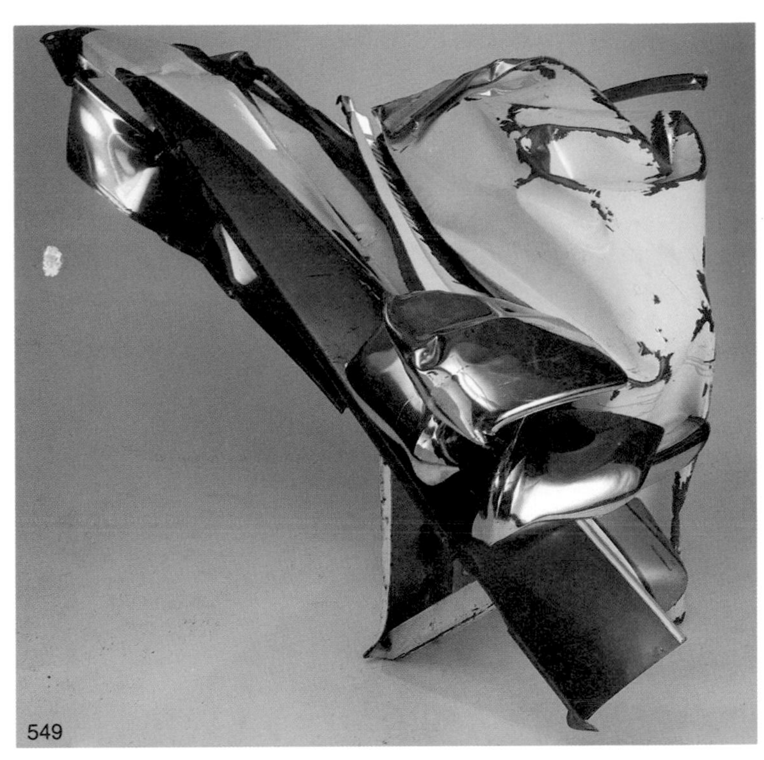
549

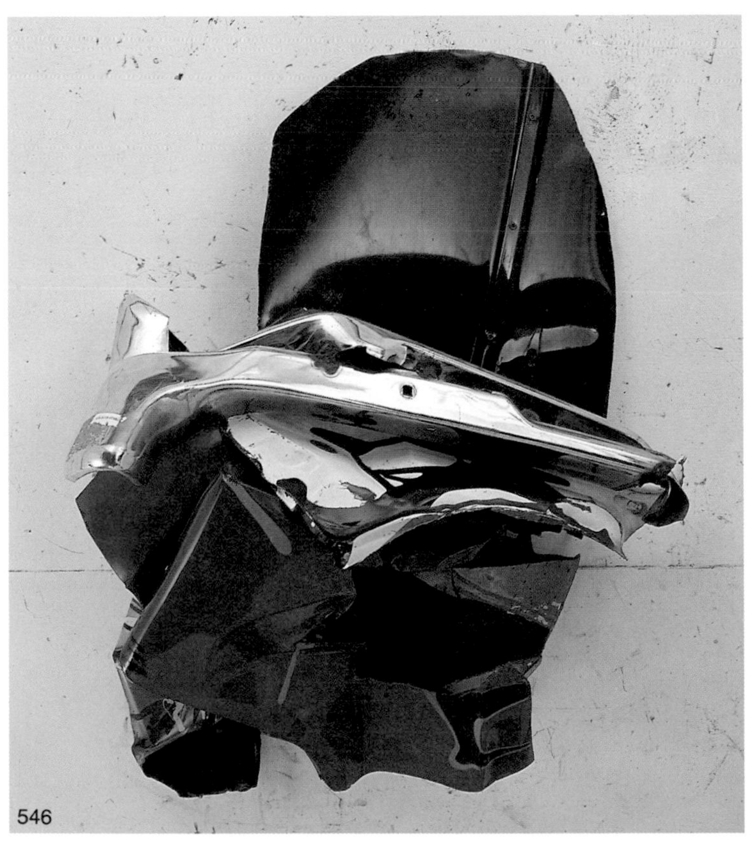
546

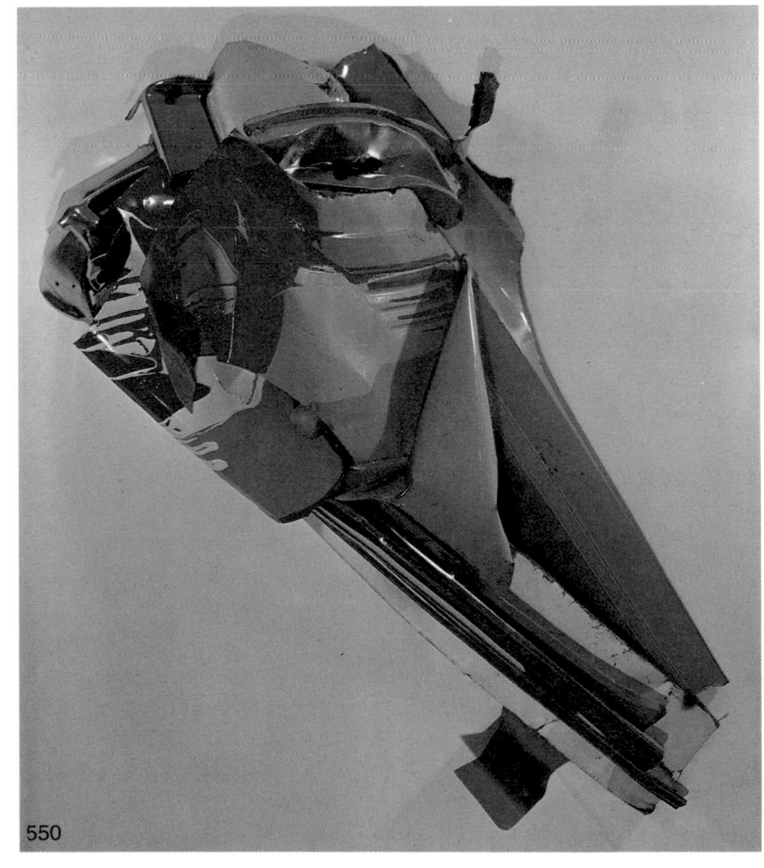
550

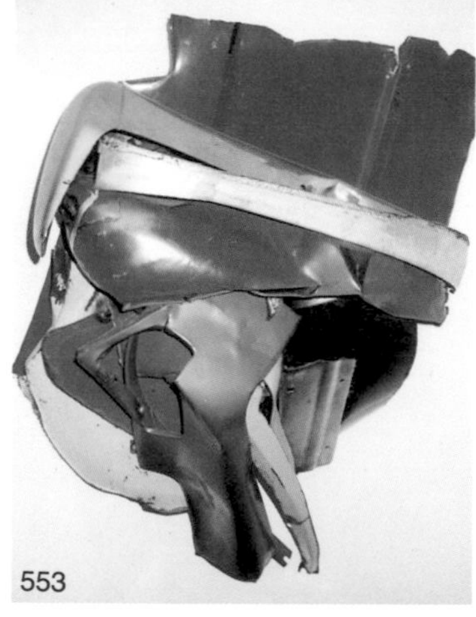
553

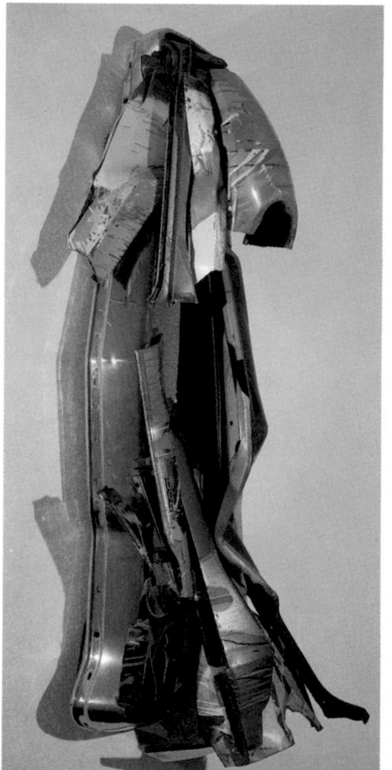
554

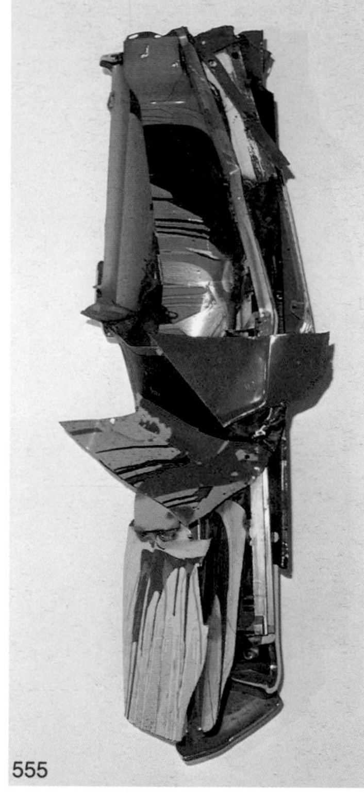
555

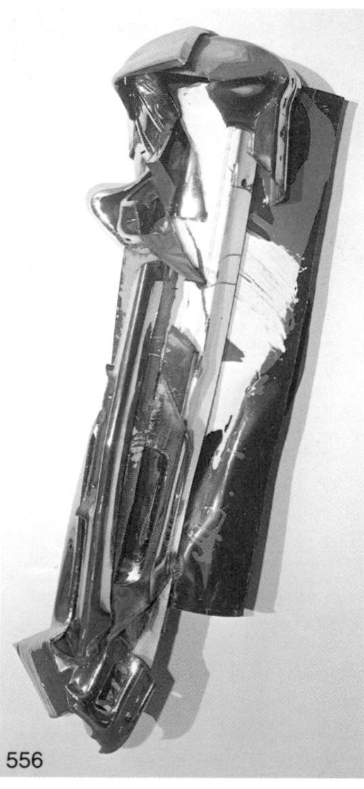
556

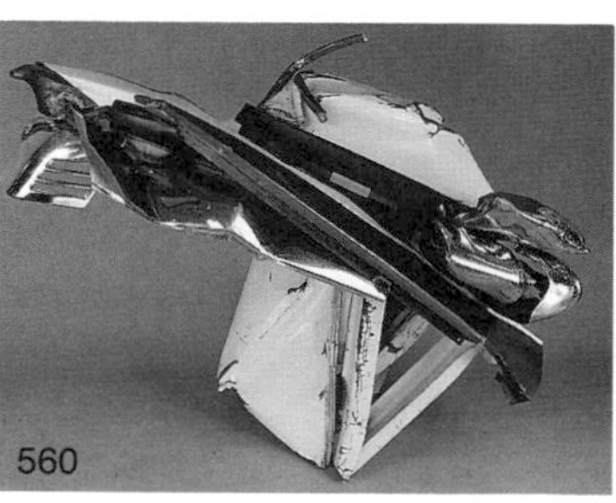
560

553

Untitled 1976

Painted and chromium-plated steel
40 × 30 × 12 in.
(101.5 × 76 × 30.5 cm).

Collection

Mr. and Mrs. Bruce Berger, New York, New York, 1976.

Provenance

O. K. Harris Works of Art, New York, New York.

554

Artur Banres 1977

Painted steel
84 × 30 × 21 in.
(213.5 × 76 × 53.5 cm).

Collection

Menil Collection, Houston, Texas, 1983.

Provenance

Margo Leavin Gallery, Los Angeles, California, 1978.

Exhibitions

Margo Leavin Gallery, Los Angeles, California. *Cast Carved and Constructed: An Exhibition of Contemporary American Sculpture*. August 1–September 19, 1981.

Christie, Manson & Woods International, Inc., New York, New York. *Contemporary Art*, cat. no. 63, illus. p. 63. November 8, 1983.

Notes

Chamberlain donated *Artur Banres* to the Institute for Art and Urban Resources for a benefit raffle at P.S. One, the alternative exhibition space in Long Island City, New York, on February 26, 1978; Margo Leavin acquired the sculpture at that time.

555

Bentley Last 1977

Painted and chromium-plated steel
76 × 28 × 20½ in.
(193 × 71 × 52 cm).

Collection

Private collection, New York, New York.

Provenance

Heiner Friedrich GmbH, Cologne.

Exhibitions

Heiner Friedrich, Inc., New York, New York. *John Chamberlain*. November 12–December 22, 1977.

Mead Art Gallery, Amherst College, Amherst, Massachusetts. *New York Now*. March 9–April 9, 1978.

Heiner Friedrich GmbH, Cologne. *John Chamberlain*. June–August 1978.

Heiner Friedrich GmbH, Cologne. *John Chamberlain*. November 23, 1979–January 20, 1980.

Kunsthaus Zürich. *Reliefs/Formprobleme zwischen Malerei und Skulptur im 20. Jahrhundert*, cat. no. 162, illus. p. 242. August 22–November 2, 1980.

Städtische Kunsthalle, Düsseldorf. *Borofsky, Chamberlain, Dahn, Knoebel*. January 8–18, 1983.

Palacio de Cristal, Parque del Retiro, Madrid. *John Chamberlain/Esculturas*, color illus. p. 35. January 26–March 31, 1984.

556

Chopped Lip 1977

Painted and chromium-plated steel
79 × 27 × 20 in.
(200.5 × 68.5 × 51 cm).

Collection

Anette and Udo Brandhorst, Cologne, 1981.

Provenance

Heiner Friedrich GmbH, Cologne, 1977; Thordis Moeller, New York, New York.

Exhibitions

Heiner Friedrich GmbH, Cologne. *John Chamberlain*. June–August 1978.

Städtische Kunsthalle, Düsseldorf. *Borofsky, Chamberlain, Dahn, Knoebel*. January 8–18, 1983.

References

Heinrich Ehrhardt, ed., *John Chamberlain/Esculturas* (Madrid: Ministerio de Cultura, 1984), color illus. p. 37.

557

Coke Ennyday 1977

Painted and chromium-plated steel
79 × 29½ × 33 in.
(200.5 × 75 × 84 cm).

Collection

Private collection, New York, New York; acquired directly from the artist.

Exhibitions

Dia Art Foundation, New York, New York. *John Chamberlain Sculpture: An Extended Exhibition*. September 22, 1983–February 23, 1985.

Notes

The sculpture was titled by the artist in 1983.

558

Dakota Grass 1976–77

Painted and chromium-plated steel
74 × 26½ × 25 in.
(188 × 67.5 × 63.5 cm).

Collection

Thordis Moeller, New York, New York.

Provenance

Heiner Friedrich GmbH, Cologne.

Exhibitions

Heiner Friedrich GmbH, Cologne. *John Chamberlain*. June–August 1978.

Städtische Kunsthalle, Düsseldorf. *Borofsky, Chamberlain, Dahn, Knoebel*. January 8–18, 1983.

Palacio de Cristal, Parque del Retiro, Madrid. *John Chamberlain/Esculturas*, color illus. p. 25. January 26–March 31, 1984.

559

Flavin Flats 1977

Painted and chromium-plated steel
77 × 37½ × 37 in.
(195.5 × 95.5 × 94 cm).

Collection

Private collection, New York, New York; acquired directly from the artist.

Exhibitions

Dia Art Foundation, New York, New York. *John Chamberlain Sculpture: An Extended Exhibition*. September 22, 1983–February 23, 1985.

560

Flufft 1977

Painted and chromium-plated steel
43 × 59 × 37 in.
(109 × 150 × 94 cm).

Collection

Dia Art Foundation, New York, New York, 1980.

Provenance

Heiner Friedrich, Inc., New York, New York; Lone Star Foundation, New York, New York, 1977.

Notes

The sculpture was titled by the artist in 1982.

561

Full Quartz 1977

Painted and chromium-plated steel
81 × 26 × 19½ in.
(205.5 × 66 × 49.5 cm).

Collection

Thordis Moeller, New York, New York.

Exhibitions

Heiner Friedrich GmbH, Cologne. *John Chamberlain*. June–August 1978.

Kunsthaus Zürich. *Reliefs/Formprobleme zwischen Malerei und Skulptur im 20. Jahrhundert*, cat. no. 161, illus. p. 242. August 22–November 2, 1980.

Städtische Kunsthalle, Düsseldorf. *Borofsky, Chamberlain, Dahn, Knoebel*. January 8–18, 1983.

Van Abbemuseum, Eindhoven, Netherlands. *De Statua*. May 8–June 6, 1983.

Palacio de Cristal, Parque del Retiro, Madrid. *John Chamberlain/Esculturas*, color illus. p. 31. January 26–March 31, 1984.

References

"Journal: John Chamberlain," *Du*, no. 11 (1979), illus. p. 83.

562

Gone to Marfa 1977

Painted and chromium-plated steel
76 × 23 × 29 in.
(193 × 58.5 × 73.5 cm).

Collection

Dia Art Foundation, New York, New York, 1980.

Provenance

Heiner Friedrich, Inc., New York, New York; Lone Star Foundation, New York, New York, 1977.

Exhibitions

The John and Mable Ringling Museum of Art, Sarasota, Florida. *John Chamberlain Reliefs 1960–1982*, not listed in catalogue. January 28–March 27, 1983.

Dia Art Foundation, the Art Museum of the Pecos, Marfa, Texas. *An Exhibition of Sculpture by John Chamberlain*. From May 7, 1983.

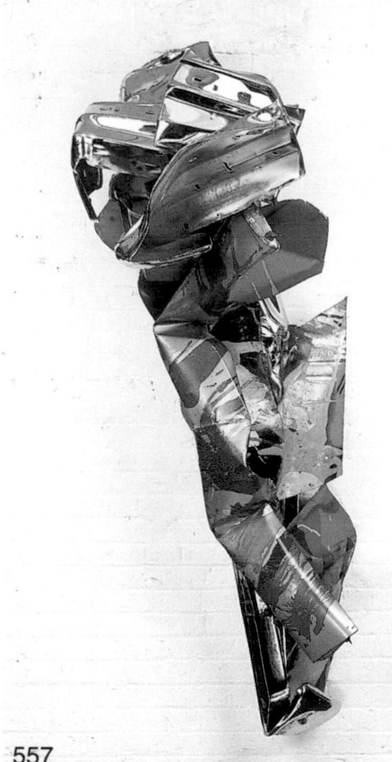

557

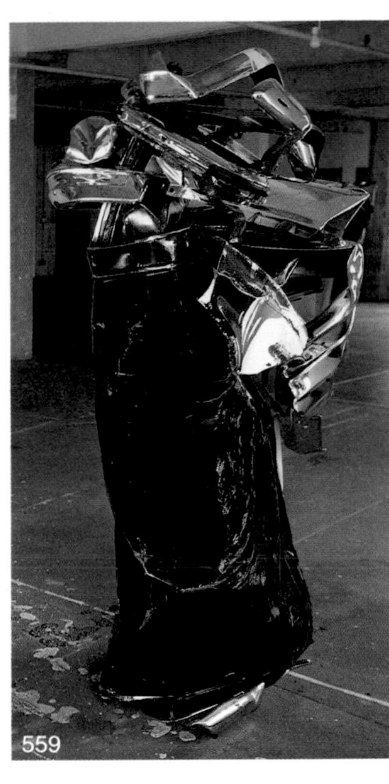

559

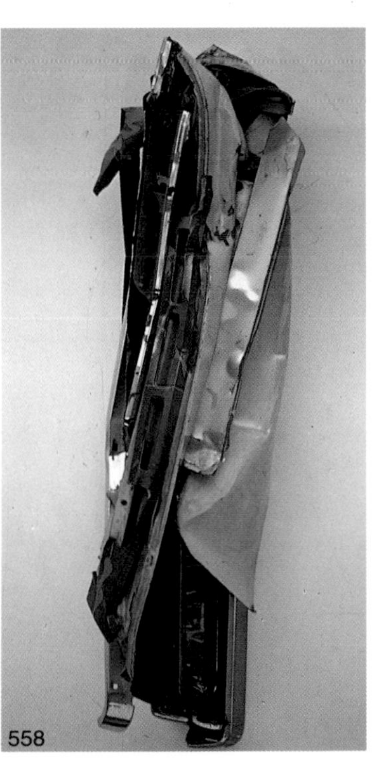

558

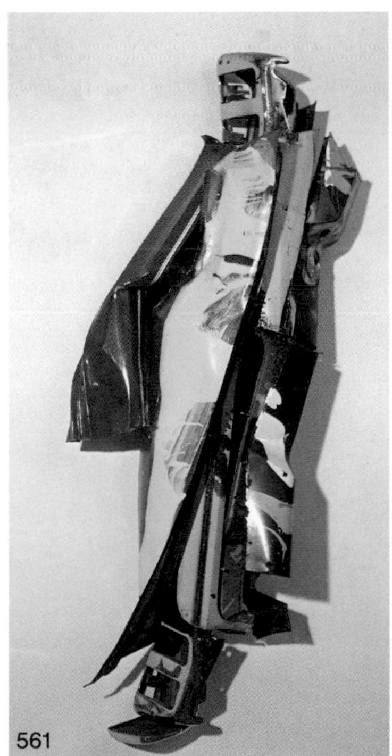

561

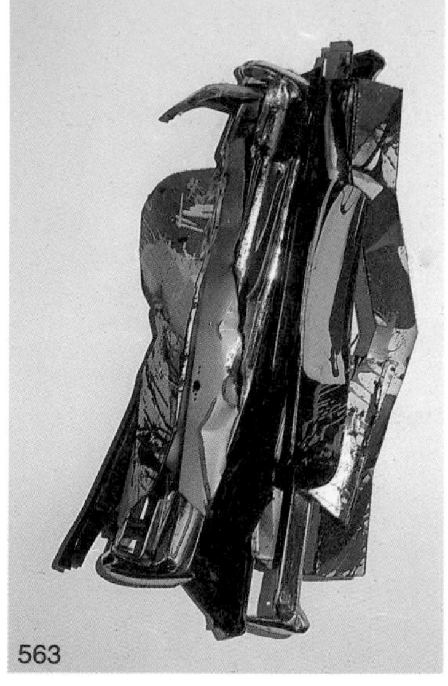
563

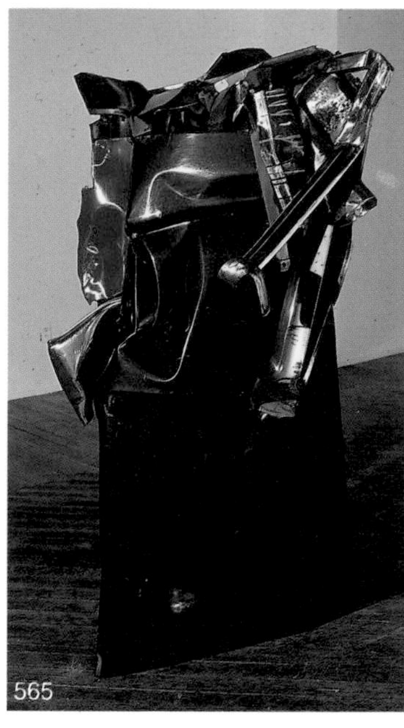
565

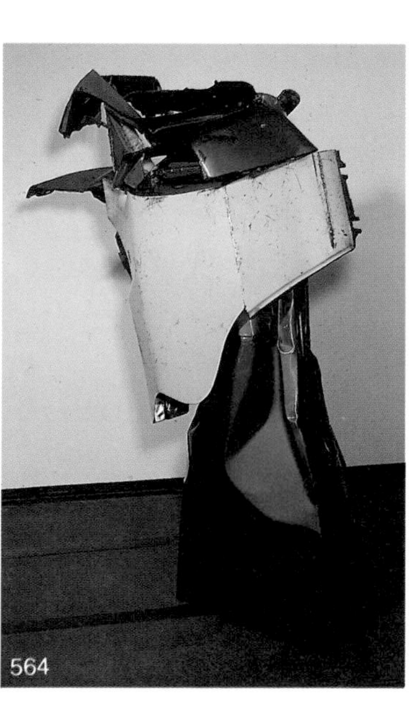
564

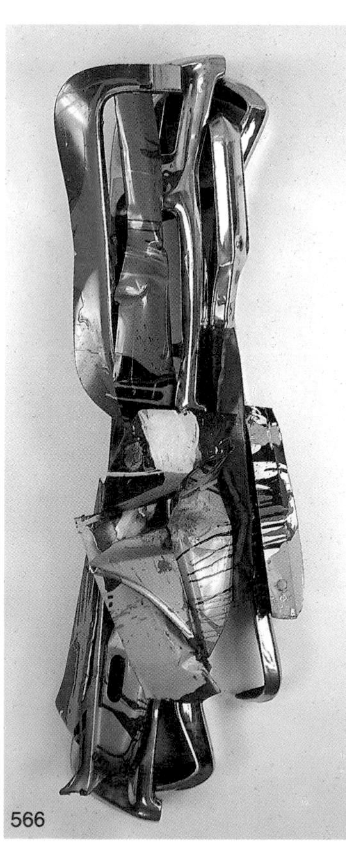
566

563

Kunststecher 1977

Painted and chromium-plated steel
77 × 46 × 23 in.
(195.5 × 117 × 58.5 cm).

Collection

Private collection, New York, New York; on loan to Dia Art Foundation, New York, New York, 1983.

Provenance

Heiner Friedrich, Inc., New York, New York.

Exhibitions

Heiner Friedrich, Inc., New York, New York. *John Chamberlain*. November 12–December 22, 1977.

University of Massachusetts at Amherst, Amherst, Massachusetts. *Sculpture on the Wall*, illus. March 29–May 4, 1980.

Dia Art Foundation, New York, New York. *John Chamberlain Sculpture: An Extended Exhibition*. March 19–November 27, 1982.

The John and Mable Ringling Museum of Art, Sarasota, Florida. *John Chamberlain Reliefs 1960–1982*, color illus. p. 67. January 28–March 27, 1983.

Dia Art Foundation, the Art Museum of the Pecos, Marfa, Texas. *An Exhibition of Sculpture by John Chamberlain*. From May 7, 1983.

References

Chamberlain (Bern: Kunsthalle Bern and Van Abbemuseum, Eindhoven, Netherlands, 1979), illus. p. 47.

564

Leo Castelli 1977

Painted and chromium-plated steel
67½ × 45 × 15 in.
(171.5 × 114.5 × 38 cm).

Collection

Thordis Moeller, New York, New York; acquired directly from the artist.

Exhibitions

Acquavella Gallery, New York, New York. *Postwar American Paintings and Sculpture*. Spring 1977.

Heiner Friedrich GmbH, Cologne. *John Chamberlain*. June–August 1978.

Palacio de Cristal, Parque del Retiro, Madrid. *John Chamberlain/Esculturas*, color illus. p. 29. January 26–March 31, 1984.

Städtische Kunsthalle, Düsseldorf. *Ein anderes Klima*. August 28–October 5, 1984.

Castello di Rivoli, Regione Piemonte, Italy. December 1984–January 1985.

References

Leo Castelli Twenty Years (New York: Leo Castelli, Inc., 1977), cat. no. 370, illus.

"Journal: John Chamberlain," *Du*, no. 11 (1979), illus. p. 83.

565

Magnesium Revolt 1977

Painted and chromium-plated steel
71 × 43 × 42 in.
(180.5 × 109 × 106.5 cm).

Collection

Private collection, New York, New York; acquired directly from the artist.

Exhibitions

Heiner Friedrich, Inc., New York, New York. *John Chamberlain*. November 12–December 22, 1977.

Dia Art Foundation, New York, New York. *John Chamberlain Sculpture: An Extended Exhibition*. March 19–November 27, 1982.

References

Valentin Tatransky, "Arts Reviews," *Arts*, vol. 52, no. 5 (January 1978), p. 27.

566

Paddy's Limbo 1976–77

Painted and chromium-plated steel
51 × 27 × 21 in.
(129.5 × 68.5 × 53.5 cm).

Collection

Dia Art Foundation, New York, New York, 1980.

Provenance

Heiner Friedrich, Inc., New York, New York; Lone Star Foundation, New York, New York, 1978.

Exhibitions

Dia Art Foundation, New York, New York. *John Chamberlain Sculpture: An Extended Exhibition*. March 19–November 27, 1982.

The John and Mable Ringling Museum of Art, Sarasota, Florida. *John Chamberlain Reliefs 1960–1982*, color illus. p. 49. January 28–March 27, 1983.

Dia Art Foundation, the Art Museum of the Pecos, Marfa, Texas. *An Exhibition of Sculpture by John Chamberlain*. From May 7, 1983.

References

Jeanne Silverthorne, "John Chamberlain," *Artforum*, vol. 21, no. 3 (November 1982), p. 75.

Gary Indiana, "John Chamberlain's Irregular Set," *Art in America*, vol. 71, no. 10 (November 1983), color illus. p. 216.

567

Piece Pockets 1977

Painted and chromium-plated steel
80 × 32 × 20 in.
(203 × 81.5 × 51 cm).

Collection

Private collection, New York, New York.

Exhibitions

Heiner Friedrich, Inc., New York, New York. *John Chamberlain*. November 12–December 22, 1977.

Heiner Friedrich GmbH, Cologne. *John Chamberlain*. June–August 1978.

Städtische Kunsthalle, Düsseldorf. *Borofsky, Chamberlain, Dahn, Knoebel*. January 8–18, 1983.

Palacio de Cristal, Parque del Retiro, Madrid. *John Chamberlain/Esculturas*, color illus. p. 33. January 26–March 31, 1984.

References

Edit de Ak, "John Chamberlain at Heiner Friedrich," *Artforum*, vol. 16, no. 6 (February 1978), p. 62.

Chamberlain (Bern: Kunsthalle Bern and Van Abbemuseum, Eindhoven, Netherlands, 1979), illus. p. 47.

568

Rainier Falls 1977

Painted and chromium-plated steel
86 × 36 × 27 in.
(218.5 × 91.5 × 68.5 cm).

Collection

Dia Art Foundation, New York, New York, 1980.

Provenance

Heiner Friedrich GmbH, Cologne; Lone Star Foundation, New York, New York, 1977.

Exhibitions

Dia Art Foundation, New York, New York. *John Chamberlain Sculpture: An Extended Exhibition*, September 22, 1983–February 23, 1985.

569

Rare Meat 1977

Painted and chromium-plated steel
79 × 25 × 27 in.
(200.5 × 63.5 × 68.5 cm).

Collection

Private collection, New York, New York, 1977.

Provenance

Heiner Friedrich, Inc., New York, New York.

Exhibitions

Heiner Friedrich, Inc., New York, New York. *John Chamberlain*. November 12–December 22, 1977.

References

Valentin Tatransky, "Arts Reviews," *Arts*, vol. 52, no. 5 (January 1978), p. 27.

Nina ffrench-frazier, "New York Reviews," *Art News*, vol. 77, no. 2 (February 1978), p. 152.

Donald B. Kuspit, "John Chamberlain at Heiner Friedrich," *Art in America*, vol. 66, no. 4 (July/August 1978) p. 112.

Chamberlain (Bern: Kunsthalle Bern and Van Abbemuseum, Eindhoven, Netherlands, 1979), illus. p. 47.

570

Sabine Knights 1977

Painted and chromium-plated steel
74 × 30½ × 16½ in.
(188 × 77.5 × 42 cm).

Collection

Christophe de Menil, New York, New York.

Provenance

Heiner Friedrich, Inc., New York, New York.

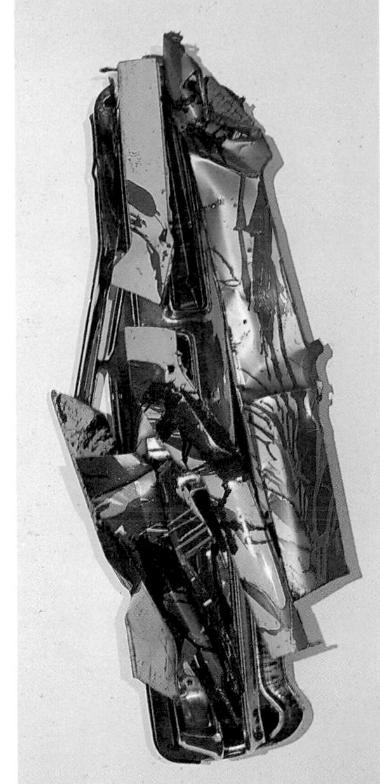
567

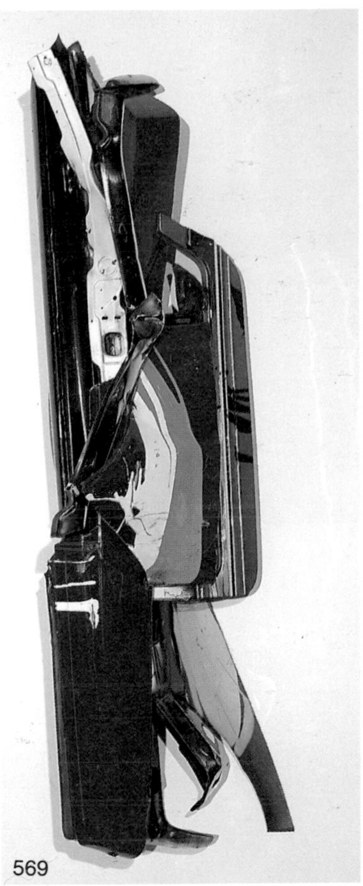
569

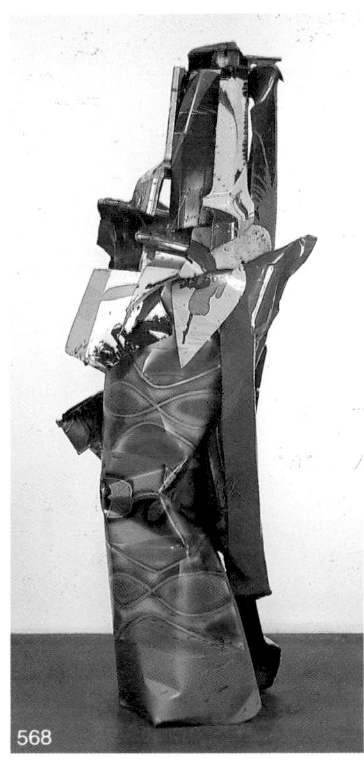
568

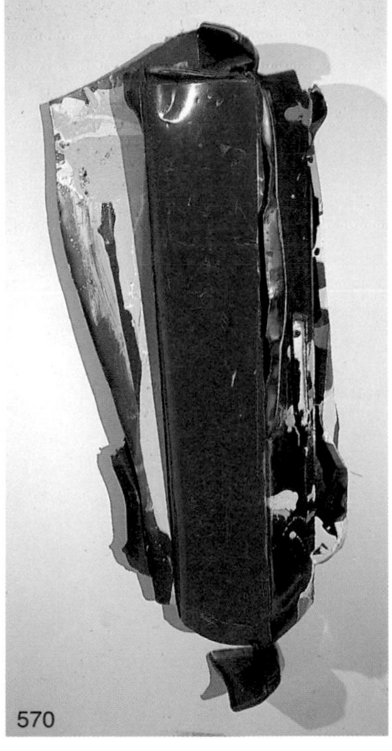
570

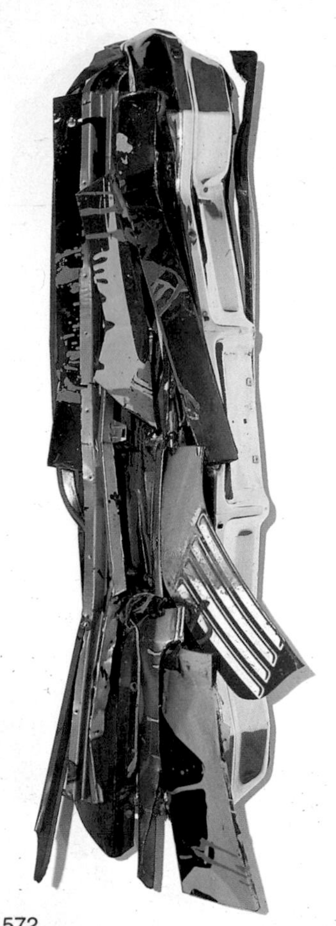

572

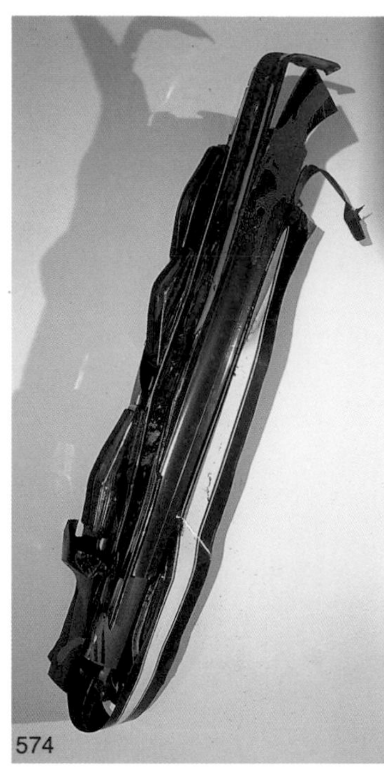

574

573

571

Son of Dudes 1977

Painted and chromium-plated steel
72 × 52 × 38 in.
(183 × 132 × 96.5 cm).

Collection

Christophe de Menil, New York, New York, 1977.

Provenance

Heiner Friedrich, Inc., New York, New York.

Exhibitions

Heiner Friedrich, Inc., New York, New York. *John Chamberlain*. November 12–December 22, 1977.

Kunsthalle Bern. *Chamberlain*, cat. no. 3, color illus. p. 25. October 12–November 18, 1979. Traveled to Van Abbemuseum, Eindhoven, Netherlands. April 3–May 11, 1980.

References

Valentin Tatransky, "Arts Reviews," *Arts*, vol. 52, no. 5 (January 1978), illus. p. 27.

Edit de Ak, "John Chamberlain at Heiner Friedrich," *Artforum*, vol. 16, no. 6 (February 1978), p. 62.

Nina ffrench-frazier, "New York Reviews," *Art News*, vol. 77, no. 2 (February 1978), p. 152.

Donald B. Kuspit, "John Chamberlain at Heiner Friedrich," *Art in America*, vol. 66, no. 4 (July–August 1978), illus. p. 112.

Gary Indiana, "John Chamberlain's Irregular Set," *Art in America*, vol. 71, no. 10 (November 1983), p. 208.

Heinrich Ehrhardt, ed., *John Chamberlain/Esculturas* (Madrid: Ministerio de Cultura, 1984), color illus. p. 39.

572

That You Marty 1977

Painted and chromium-plated steel
78 × 20 × 20½ in.
(198 × 51 × 52 cm).

Collection

Christophe de Menil, New York, New York.

Provenance

Heiner Friedrich, Inc., New York, New York.

Exhibitions

Heiner Friedrich, Inc., New York, New York. *John Chamberlain*. November 12–December 22, 1977.

The Metropolitan Museum of Art, New York, New York. *Summer Loan Exhibition*. July 17–September 30, 1979.

References

Valentin Tatransky, "Arts Reviews," *Arts*, vol. 52, no. 5 (January 1978), p. 27.

Chamberlain (Bern: Kunsthalle Bern and Van Abbemuseum, Eindhoven, Netherlands, 1979), illus. p. 47.

573

Toasted Hitlers (from E. J.) 1977

Painted and chromium-plated steel
86 × 51 × 40 in.
(218.5 × 129.5 × 101.5 cm).

Collection

Dia Art Foundation, New York, New York, 1980.

Provenance

Heiner Friedrich, Inc., New York, New York; Lone Star Foundation, New York, New York, 1977.

Exhibitions

Heiner Friedrich, Inc., New York, New York. *John Chamberlain*. November 12–December 22, 1977.

Kunsthalle Bern. *Chamberlain*, cat. no. 2, color illus. p. 23. October 12–November 18, 1979. Traveled to Van Abbemuseum, Eindhoven, Netherlands. April 3–May 11, 1980.

Heiner Friedrich GmbH, Cologne. *John Chamberlain*. November 23, 1979–January 20, 1980.

Van Abbemuseum, Eindhoven, Netherlands. *De Statua*, color illus. p. 21. May 8–June 6, 1983.

Palacio de Cristal, Parque del Retiro, Madrid. *John Chamberlain/Esculturas*, color illus. p. 27. January 26–March 31, 1984.

Grand Palais, Paris. *La rime et la raison: Les collections Menil (Houston—New York)*, cat. no. 455, illus. p. 389. April 18–July 30, 1984.

References

Valentin Tatransky, "Arts Reviews," *Arts*, vol. 52, no. 5 (January 1978), p. 27.

Nina ffrench-frazier, "New York Reviews," *Art News*, vol. 77, no. 2 (February 1978), color illus. p. 152.

Donald B. Kuspit, "John Chamberlain at Heiner Friedrich," *Art in America*, vol. 66, no. 4 (July–August 1978), p. 112.

Gary Indiana, "John Chamberlain's Irregular Set," *Art in America*, vol. 71, no. 10 (November 1983), p. 214.

574

Wardell Gray Sends His Regards 1977

Painted and chromium-plated steel
77½ × 23½ × 15 in.
(197 × 59.5 × 38 cm).

Collection

Christophe de Menil, New York, New York, 1977.

Provenance

Heiner Friedrich, Inc., New York, New York.

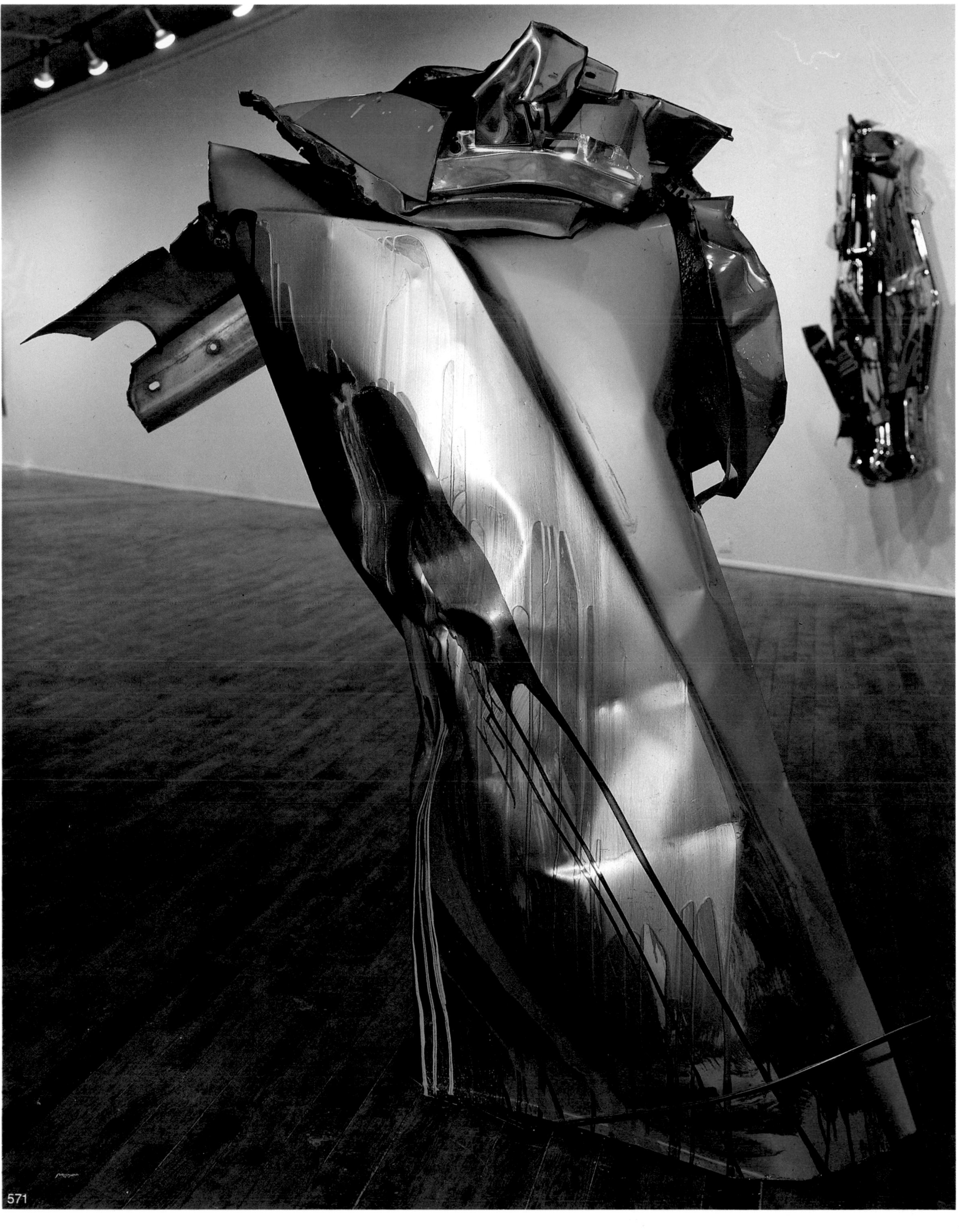

571

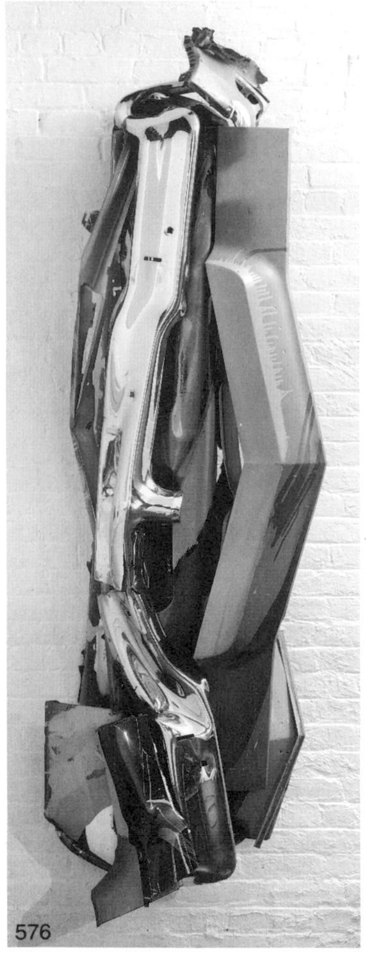
576

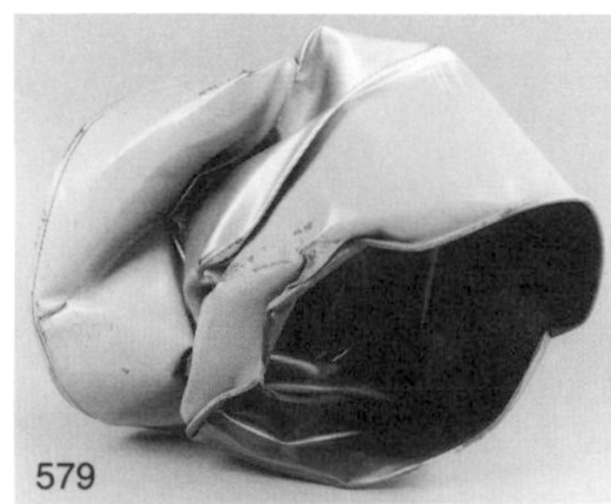
579

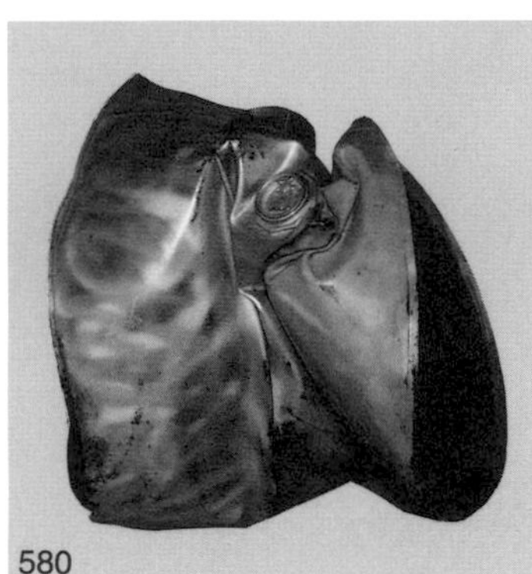
580

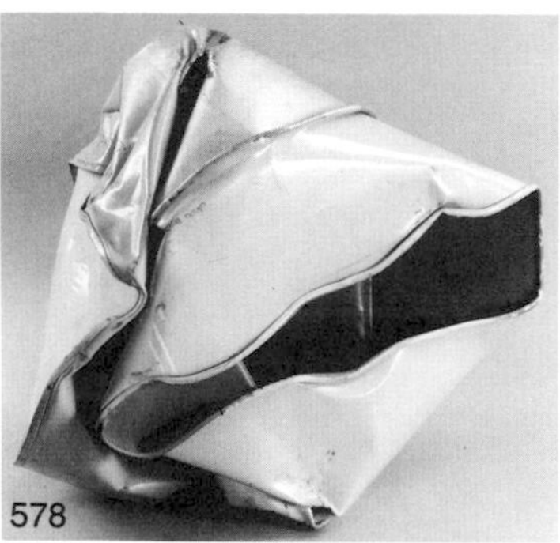
578

575

Yulee Infinger 1977

Painted and chromium-plated steel
47 × 31 × 12 in.
(119.5 × 78.5 × 30.5 cm).

Collection

Collection of the artist, Sarasota, Florida.

576

Untitled 1977

Painted and chromium-plated steel
82 × 23 × 20 in.
(208.5 × 58.5 × 51 cm).

Collection

John Martin Shea, Newport Beach, California.

Provenance

Leo Castelli Gallery, New York, New York; Larry Gagosian Gallery, Los Angeles, California.

Exhibitions

University of South Florida, Tampa, Florida. *Five in Florida/Recent Work by Anuszkiewicz, Chamberlain, Olitski, Rauschenberg, Rosenquist*, color illus. January 7–February 8, 1980.

John and Mable Ringling Museum of Art, Sarasota, Florida. *International Florida Artists Exhibition*, listed. February 26–April 26, 1981.

577

Salanangie 1977

Painted steel
Dimensions unknown.

Collection

Andy Warhol, New York, New York, 1977; acquired directly from the artist.

Notes

This is the first sculpture graffiti-painted by the artist; it was made especially for Andy Warhol.

578

Socket 1977

Painted steel
27 × 32½ × 19 in.
(68.5 × 82.5 × 48.5 cm).

Collection

Private collection, New York, New York; acquired directly from the artist.

579

Socket 1977

Painted steel
28½ × 21 × 33 in.
(72.5 × 53.5 × 84 cm).

Collection

Private collection, New York, New York; acquired directly from the artist.

580

Socket 1977

Painted steel
27 × 28 × 29 in.
(68.5 × 71 × 73.5 cm).

Collection

Collection of the artist, Sarasota, Florida.

581

American Star 1978

Painted and chromium-plated steel
80 × 74½ × 68½ in.
(203 × 189 × 174 cm).

Collection

Museum Moderner Kunst Wien, Österreichische Ludwig-Stiftung, Vienna, 1981.

Provenance

Heiner Friedrich GmbH, Cologne; Professor Doctor Peter Ludwig, Cologne.

Exhibitions

Heiner Friedrich GmbH, Cologne. *John Chamberlain*. June–August 1978.

Palacio de Cristal, Parque del Retiro, Madrid. *John Chamberlain/Esculturas*, cat. p. 63. January 26–March 31, 1984.

References

Sammlung Ludwig (Vienna: Museum Moderner Kunst Wien, 1979), illus.

"Journal: John Chamberlain," *Du*, no. 11 (1979), illus. p. 83.

582

. . . and his hair was perfect 1978

Painted and chromium-plated steel
78 × 50 × 22 in.
(198 × 127 × 56 cm).

Collection

Dia Art Foundation, New York, New York, 1980.

Provenance

Heiner Friedrich, Inc., New York, New York; Lone Star Foundation, New York, New York, 1978.

Exhibitions

Grace Borgenicht Gallery and Terry Dintenfass Gallery, New York, New York. *Twenty Galleries/Twenty Years*, illus. p. 16. January 9–February 4, 1982.

The John and Mable Ringling Museum of Art, Sarasota, Florida. *John Chamberlain Reliefs 1960–1982*, color illus. p. 51. January 28–March 27, 1983.

Dia Art Foundation, New York, New York. *John Chamberlain Sculpture: An Extended Exhibition*. September 22, 1983–February 23, 1985.

583

Fiddler's Foot 1978

Painted and chromium-plated steel
42 × 49½ × 15½ in.
(106.5 × 126 × 39.5 cm).

Collection

Private collection, New York, New York; acquired directly from the artist.

584

Folded Nude 1978

Painted and chromium-plated steel
78 × 76 × 21 in.
(198 × 193 × 53.5 cm).

Collection

Private collection, New York, New York; on loan to Dia Art Foundation, New York, New York, 1983.

Provenance

Heiner Friedrich GmbH, Cologne.

Exhibitions

Dia Art Foundation, New York, New York. *John Chamberlain Sculpture: An Extended Exhibition*. March 19–November 27, 1982.

The John and Mable Ringling Museum of Art, Sarasota, Florida. *John Chamberlain Reliefs 1960–1982*, color illus. p. 61. January 28–March 27, 1983.

Dia Art Foundation, the Art Museum of the Pecos, Marfa, Texas. *An Exhibition of Sculpture by John Chamberlain*. From May 7, 1983.

585

Funn 1978

Painted and chromium-plated steel
80 × 41 × 21 in.
(203 × 104 × 53.5 cm).

Collection

Private collection, New York, New York; acquired directly from the artist.

Exhibitions

Dia Art Foundation, New York, New York. *John Chamberlain Sculpture: An Extended Exhibition*. March 19–November 27, 1982.

The John and Mable Ringling Museum of Art, Sarasota, Florida. *John Chamberlain Reliefs 1960–1982*, color illus. p. 55. January 28–March 27, 1983.

The Butler Institute of American Art, Youngstown, Ohio. *John Chamberlain: Sculpture and Work on Paper*, cat. no. 6. May 1–29, 1983.

References

Duncan Smith, "In the Heart of the Tinman: An Essay on John Chamberlain," *Artforum*, vol. 22, no. 5 (January 1984), illus. p. 42.

586

High Tale 1978

Painted and chromium-plated steel
84½ × 25 × 32 in.
(214.5 × 63.5 × 81.5 cm).

Collection

Private collection, New York, New York; acquired directly from the artist.

Exhibitions

Dia Art Foundation, New York, New York. *John Chamberlain Sculpture: An Extended Exhibition*. March 19–November 27, 1982.

The John and Mable Ringling Museum of Art, Sarasota, Florida. *John Chamberlain Reliefs 1960–1982*, color illus. p. 57. January 28–March 27, 1983.

References

Gary Indiana, "John Chamberlain's Irregular Set," *Art in America*, vol. 71, no. 10 (November 1983), p. 214, color illus. p. 216.

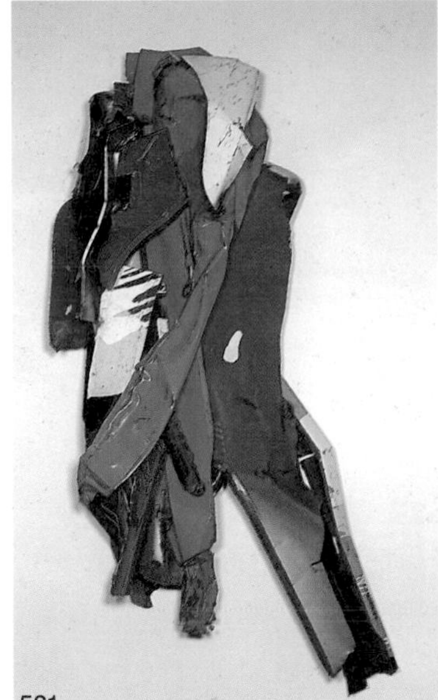
581

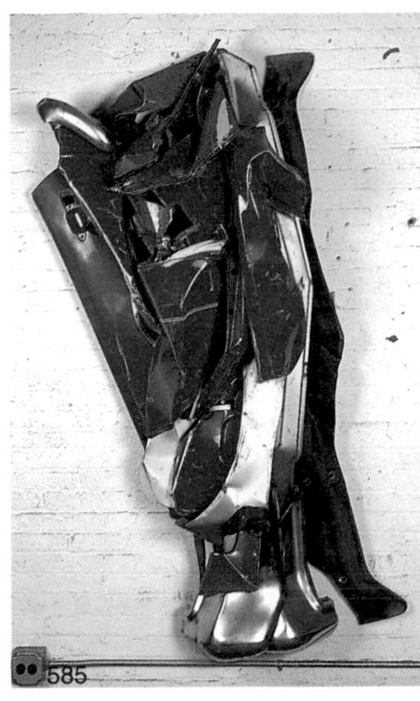
585

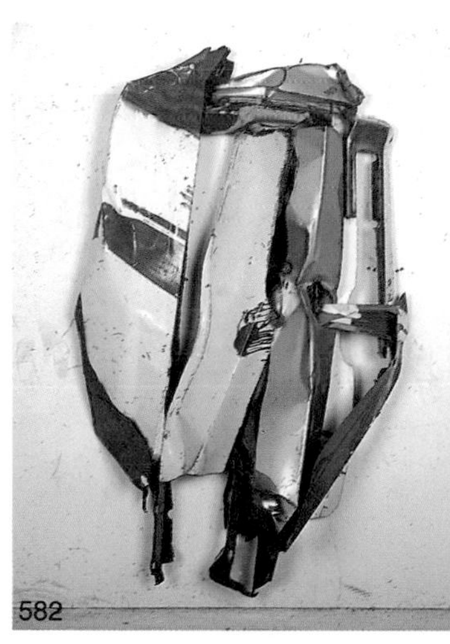
582

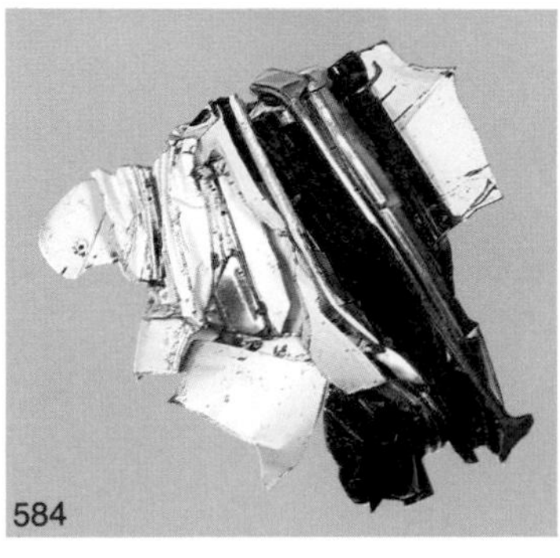
584

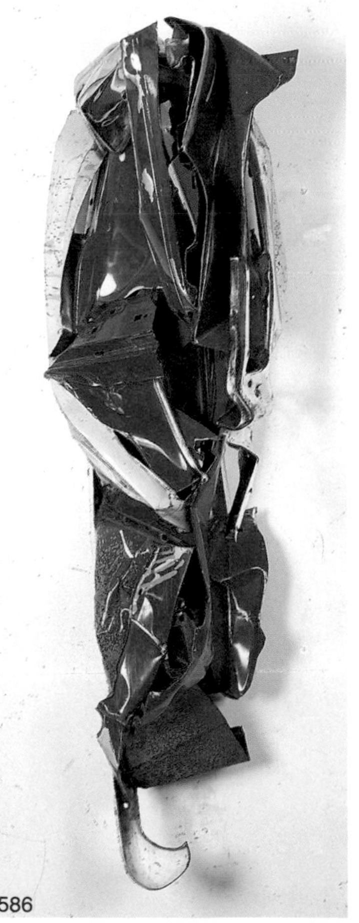
586

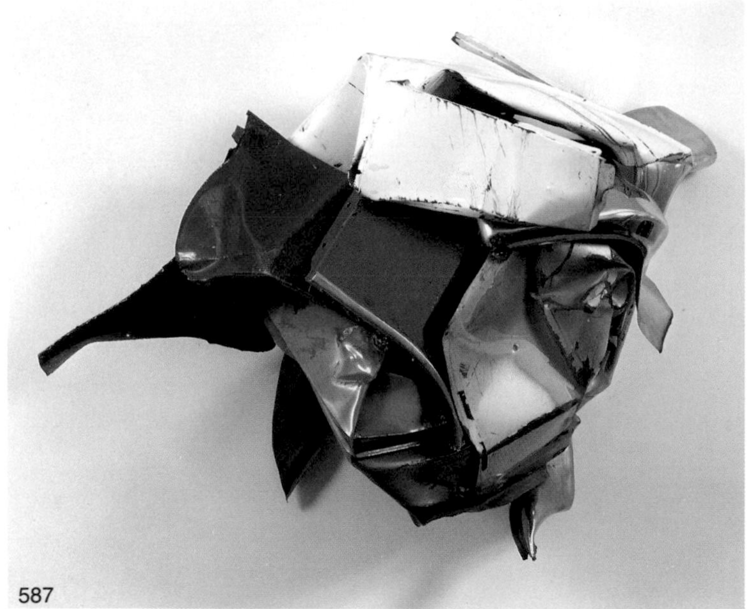

587

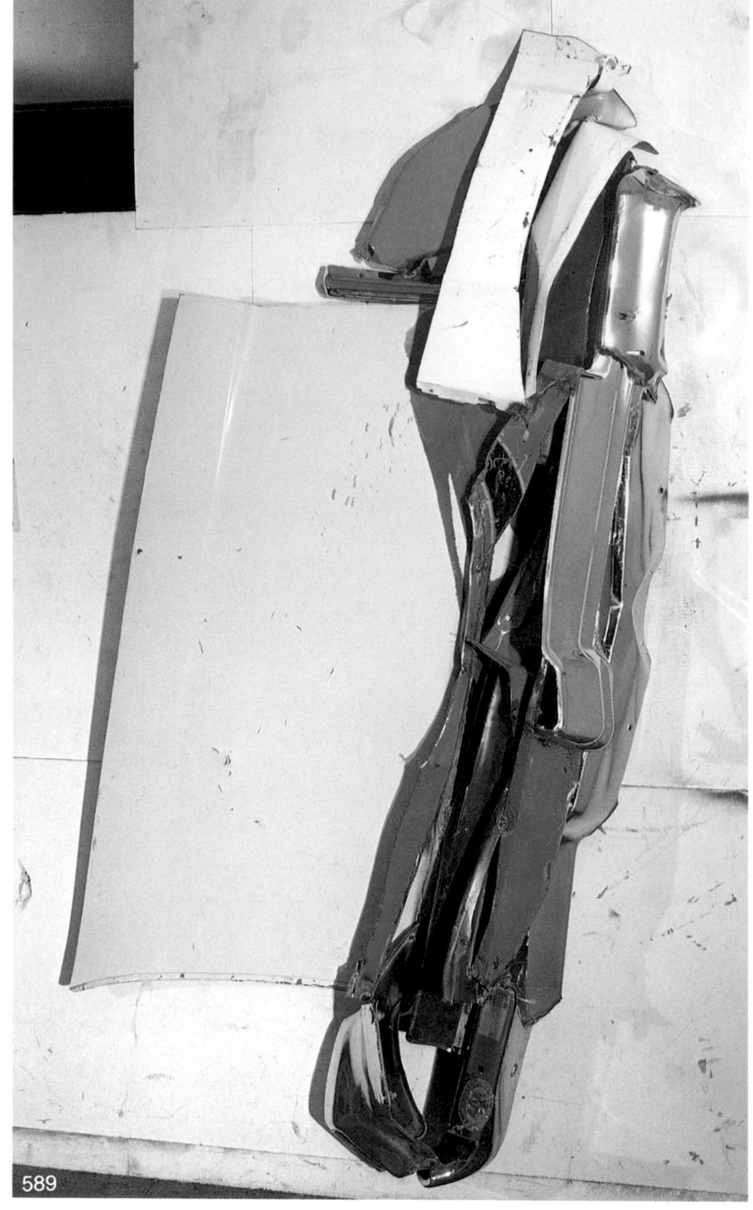

589

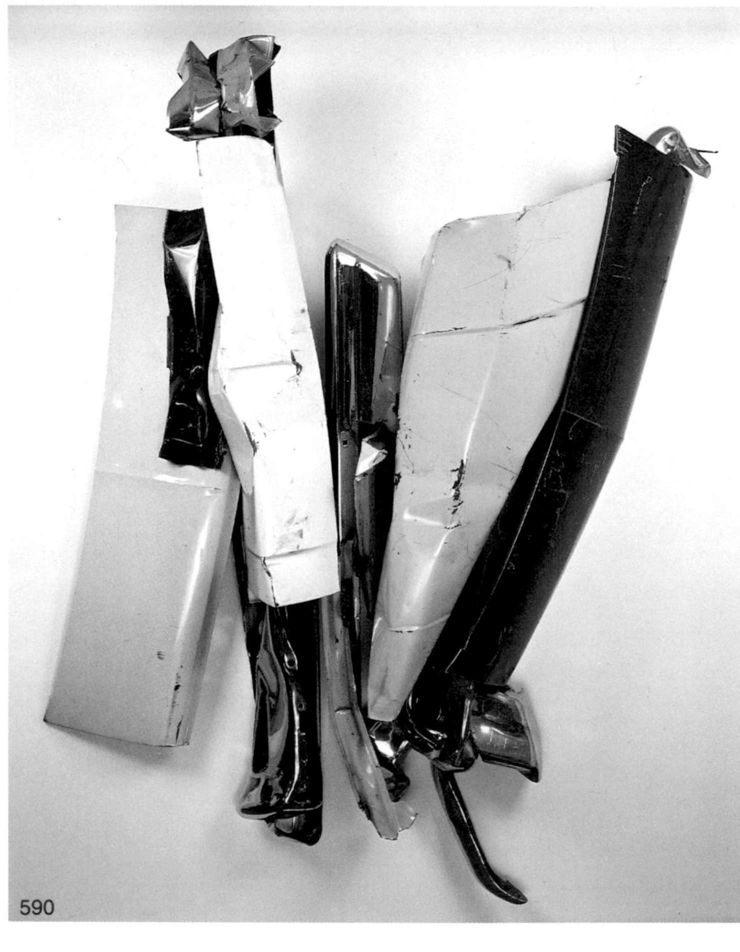

590

587

Lucky You 1978

Painted and chromium-plated steel
31 × 53 × 20 in.
(79 × 134.5 × 51 cm).

Collection

Thordis Moeller, New York, New York.

Exhibitions

The John and Mable Ringling Museum of Art, Sarasota, Florida. *John Chamberlain Reliefs 1960–1982*, color illus. p. 53. January 28–March 27, 1983.

588

Lucky You Too 1978

Painted and chromium-plated steel
32 × 32 × 16 in.
(81.5 × 81.5 × 40.5 cm).

Collection

Lorraine Chamberlain, Essex, Connecticut, 1978; acquired directly from the artist.

589

Maude's Dream 1978

Painted and chromium-plated steel
94 × 54 × 15½ in.
(239 × 137 × 39.5 cm).

Collection

Private collection, New York, New York, 1978; acquired directly from the artist.

Exhibitions

The John and Mable Ringling Museum of Art, Sarasota, Florida. *John Chamberlain Reliefs 1960–1982*, color illus. p. 59. January 28–March 27, 1983.

References

Gary Indiana, "John Chamberlain's Irregular Set," *Art in America*, vol. 71, no. 10 (November 1983), p. 214.

590

Shoemaker's Knife 1978

Painted and chromium-plated steel
89 × 74 × 22 in.
(226 × 188 × 56 cm).

Collection

Private collection, New York, New York; acquired directly from the artist.

Exhibitions

Dia Art Foundation, New York, New York. *John Chamberlain Sculpture: An Extended Exhibition*. March 19–November 27, 1982.

The John and Mable Ringling Museum of Art, Sarasota, Florida. *John Chamberlain Reliefs 1960–1982*, listed. January 28–March 27, 1983.

Dia Art Foundation, New York, New York. *John Chamberlain Sculpture: An Extended Exhibition*. September 22, 1983–February 23, 1985.

591

White Thumb Four 1978

Painted and chromium-plated steel
71½ × 112½ × 32 in.
(181.5 × 286 × 81 cm).

Collection

Mr. and Mrs. Asher B. Edelman, New York, New York, 1984.

Provenance

Thordis Moeller, New York, New York, 1979; I Club, Hong Kong, 1982.

Exhibitions

Leo Castelli Gallery, New York, New York. *Group Exhibition*. October 28–November 18, 1978.

Kunsthalle Bern. *Chamberlain*, cat. no. 4, color illus. p. 31. October 12–November 18, 1979. Traveled to Van Abbemuseum, Eindhoven, Netherlands. April 3–May 11, 1980.

592

Why You 1978

Painted and chromium-plated steel
73 × 38 × 27 in.
(185.5 × 96.5 × 68.5 cm).

Collection

Private collection, New York, New York; acquired directly from the artist.

Exhibitions

Dia Art Foundation, New York, New York. *John Chamberlain Sculpture: An Extended Exhibition*. September 22, 1983–February 23, 1985.

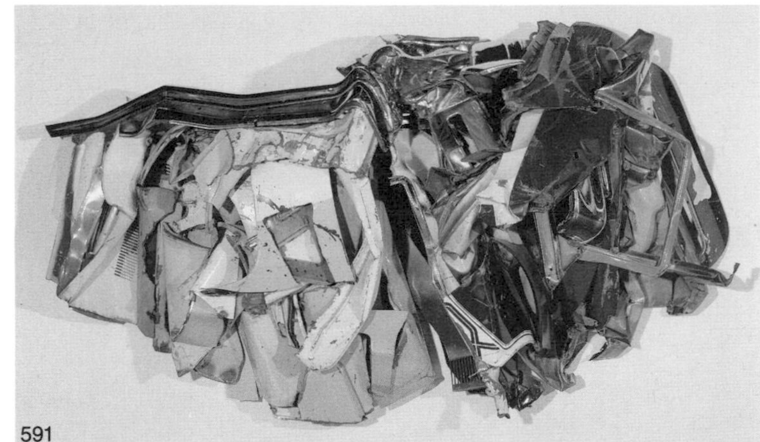

591

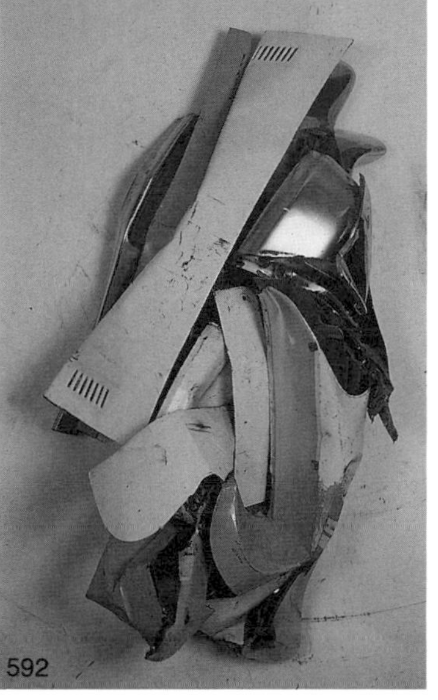

592

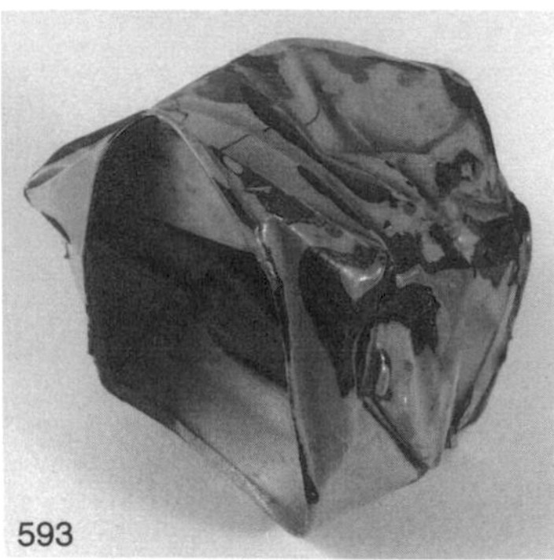
593

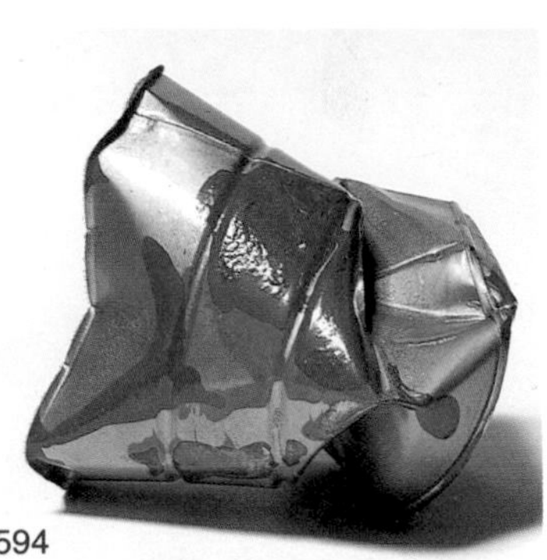
594

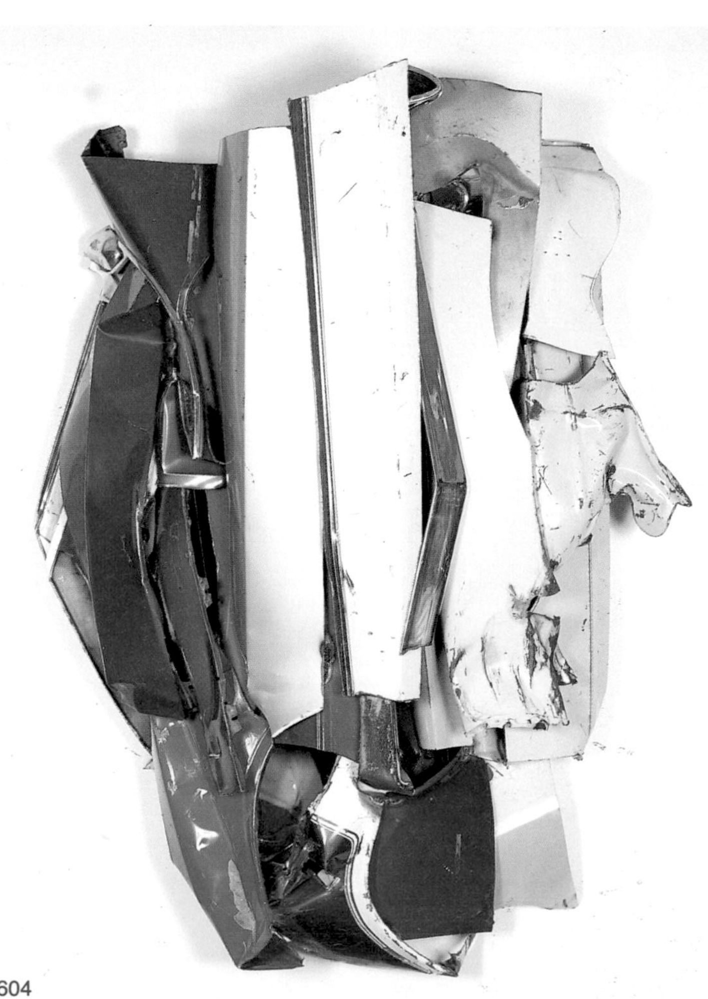
604

The following sculptures (cat. nos. 593–602) are a group of miniature *Sockets* made from crushed coffee cans.

593

Socket #27 1978
Painted aluminum with resin
4½ × 4½ × 3½ in.
(15.5 × 11.5 × 9 cm).

Collection
Private collection, New York, New York, 1978; acquired directly from the artist.

594

Socket 1978
Painted aluminum
4½ × 5 × 4½ in.
(11.5 × 12.5 × 11.5 cm).

Collection
Dia Art Foundation, New York, New York, 1979.

Provenance
Christophe de Menil, New York, New York.

Exhibitions
Cooper-Hewitt Museum of Decorative Arts and Design, Smithsonian Institution, New York, New York. *1979 Benefit Auction*, cat. no. 23, illus. p. 24. May 21, 1979.

595

Socket 1978
Painted aluminum
6 × 3 × 3 in. (15 × 7.5 × 7.5 cm).

Collection
Jim Jacobs, New York, New York, 1977; acquired directly from the artist.

596

Socket 1978
Painted aluminum
3½ × 5½ × 4½ in.
(9 × 14 × 11.5 cm).

Collection
Dia Art Foundation, New York, New York, 1980.

Provenance
Heiner Friedrich, Inc., New York, New York; Lone Star Foundation, New York, New York, 1978.

597

Socket 1978
Painted aluminum
4 × 3½ × 5 in. (10 × 9 × 12.5 cm).

Collection
Dia Art Foundation, New York, New York, 1980.

Provenance
Heiner Friedrich, Inc., New York, New York; Lone Star Foundation, New York, New York, 1978.

598

Socket 1978
Painted aluminum
4½ × 4½ × 4½ in.
(11.5 × 11.5 × 11.5 cm).

Collection
Dia Art Foundation, New York, New York, 1980.

Provenance
Heiner Friedrich, Inc., New York, New York; Lone Star Foundation, New York, New York, 1978.

599

Socket 1978
Painted aluminum
5 × 5½ × 4 in.
(12.5 × 14 × 10 cm).

Collection
Dia Art Foundation, New York, New York, 1980.

Provenance
Heiner Friedrich, Inc., New York, New York; Lone Star Foundation, New York, New York, 1978.

600

Socket 1978
Painted aluminum
4½ × 5 × 5 in.
(11.5 × 12.5 × 12.5 cm).

Collection
Dia Art Foundation, New York, New York, 1980.

Provenance
Heiner Friedrich, Inc., New York, New York; Lone Star Foundation, New York, New York, 1978.

601

Socket 1978
Painted aluminum
4½ × 4 × 4 in.
(11.5 × 10 × 10 cm).

Collection
Dia Art Foundation, New York, New York, 1980.

Provenance
Heiner Friedrich, Inc., New York, New York; Lone Star Foundation, New York, New York, 1978.

602

Socket 1978
Painted aluminum
5 × 5½ × 5 in.
(12.5 × 14 × 12.5 cm).

Collection
Dia Art Foundation, New York, New York, 1980.

Provenance
Heiner Friedrich, Inc., New York, New York; Lone Star Foundation, New York, New York, 1978.

603

Abba Funn 1979

Painted and chromium-plated steel
63 × 69 × 48 in.
(160 × 175 × 122 cm).

Collection

Dia Art Foundation, New York, New York, 1980; acquired directly from the artist.

Exhibitions

Dia Art Foundation, New York, New York. *John Chamberlain Sculpture: An Extended Exhibition*. March 19, 1982–July 30, 1983.

604

Blue Brownie 1979

Painted and chromium-plated steel
85 × 64 × 26 in.
(216 × 162.5 × 66 cm).

Collection

Mrs. Edith Hafter, Soluthurn, Switzerland.

Provenance

Heiner Friedrich GmbH, Cologne.

Exhibitions

Kunsthalle Bern. *Chamberlain*, cat. no. 8, color illus. October 12–November 18, 1979. Traveled to Van Abbemuseum, Eindhoven, Netherlands. April 3–May 11, 1980.

605

Chickmeat 1979

Painted and chromium-plated steel
77 × 106 × 24 in.
(195.5 × 269.5 × 61 cm).

Collection

Dia Art Foundation, New York, New York, 1980; acquired directly from the artist.

Exhibitions

Dia Art Foundation, New York, New York. *John Chamberlain Sculpture: An Extended Exhibition*. March 19–November 27, 1982.

The John and Mable Ringling Museum of Art, Sarasota, Florida. *John Chamberlain, Reliefs 1960–1982*, color illus. p. 77. January 28–March 27, 1983.

Dia Art Foundation, New York, New York. *John Chamberlain Sculpture: An Extended Exhibition*. September 22, 1983–February 23, 1985.

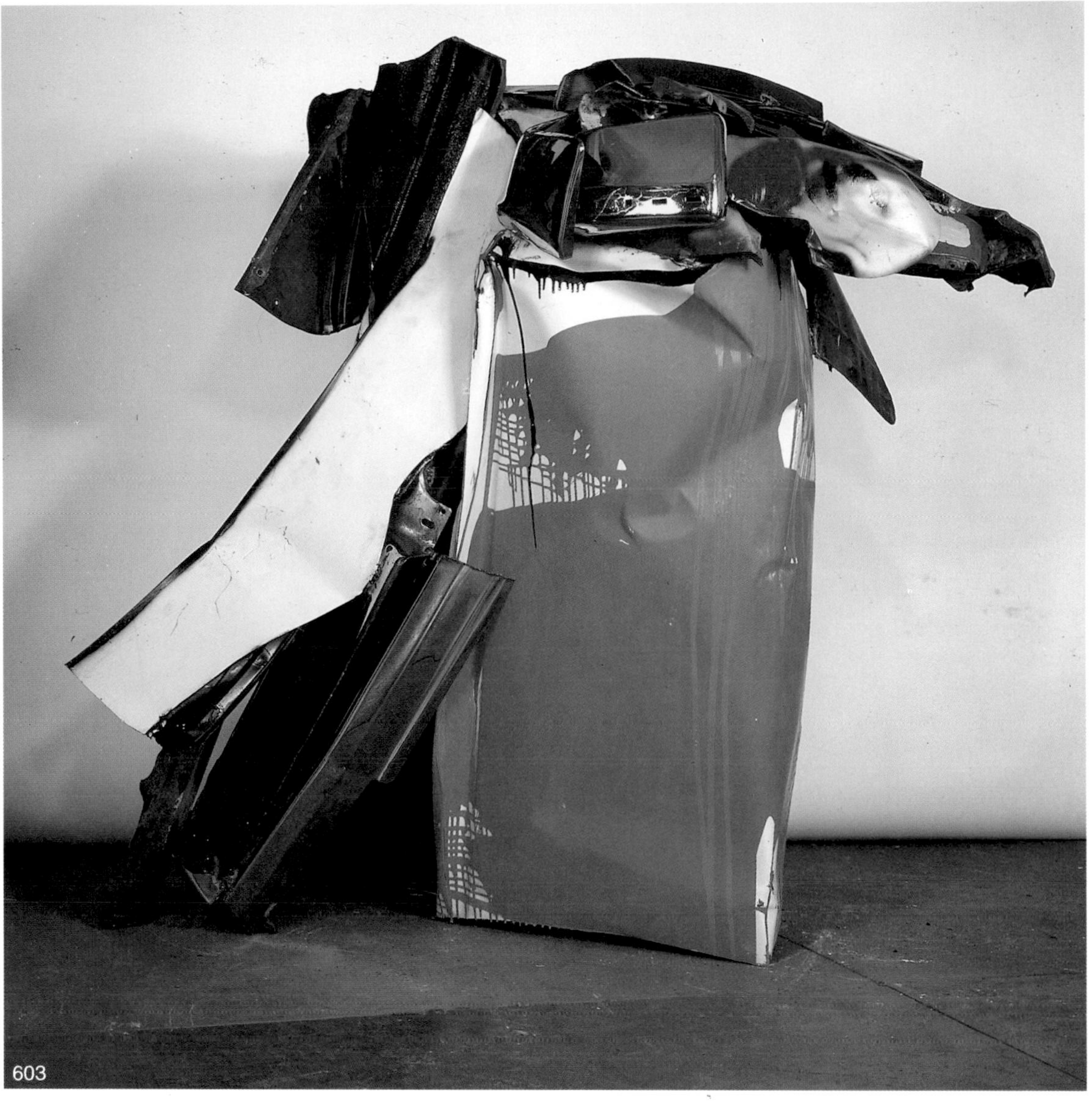

603

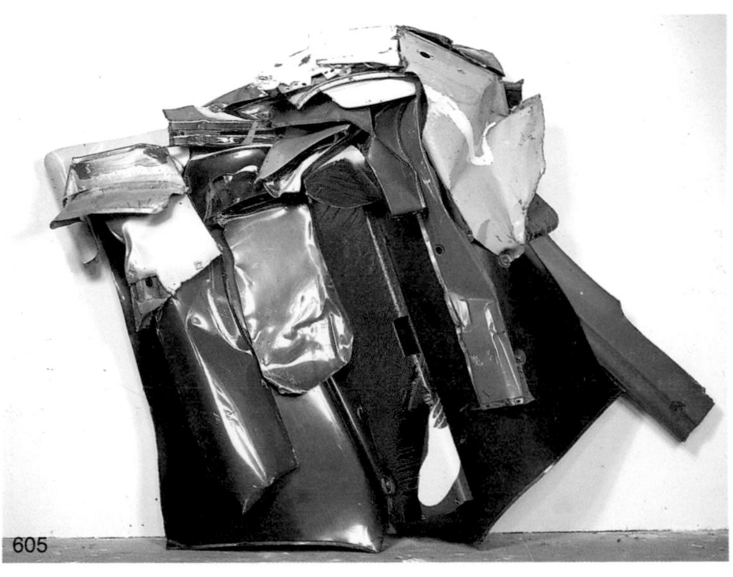

605

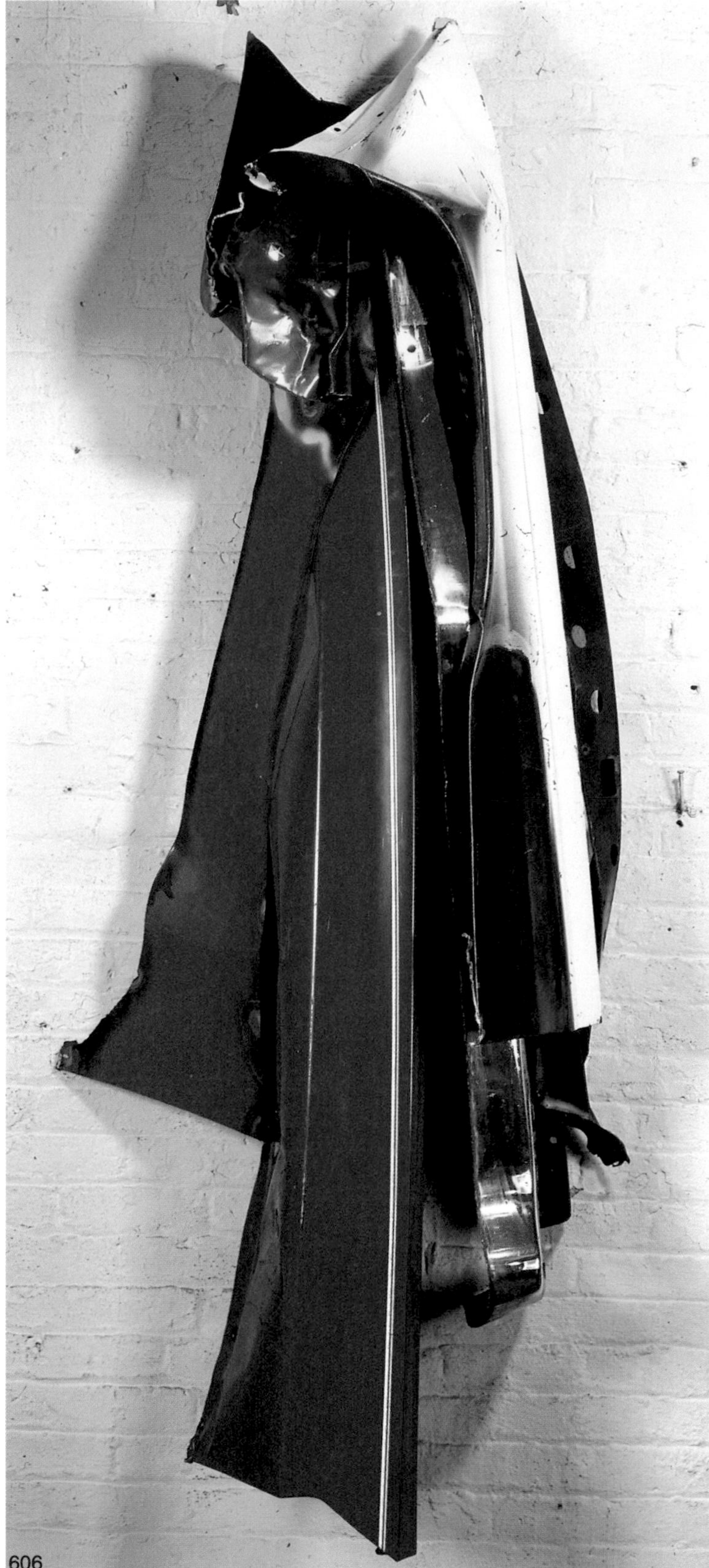
606

606

Creeley's Lookout 1979

Painted and chromium-plated steel
85 × 30 × 16½ in.
(216 × 76 × 42 cm).

Collection

Private collection, New York, New York; acquired directly from the artist.

Exhibitions

Kunsthalle Bern. *Chamberlain*, cat. no. 9, illus. p. 37. October 12–November 18, 1979. Traveled to Van Abbemuseum, Eindhoven, Netherlands, April 3–May 11, 1980.

Palacio de Cristal, Parque del Retiro, Madrid. *John Chamberlain/Esculturas*, color illus. p. 47. January 26–March 31, 1984.

607

Electra Underlace 1979

Painted and chromium-plated steel
85 × 62 × 33 in.
(216 × 157.5 × 84 cm).

Collection

Dia Art Foundation, New York, New York, 1980.

Provenance

Heiner Friedrich GmbH, Cologne.

Exhibitions

Kunsthalle Bern. *Chamberlain*, cat. no. 6, color illus. p. 29. October 12–November 18, 1979. Traveled to Van Abbemuseum, Eindhoven, Netherlands. April 3–May 11, 1980.

Heiner Friedrich GmbH, Cologne. *John Chamberlain*. November 23, 1979–January 20, 1980.

Palacio de Cristal, Parque del Retiro, Madrid. *John Chamberlain/Esculturas*, color illus. p. 43. January 26–March 31, 1984.

Städtische Kunsthalle, Düsseldorf. *Ein anderes Klima*. August 28–October 5, 1984.

608

Four Polished Nails 1979

Painted and chromium-plated steel
56 × 49 × 21 in.
(142 × 124.5 × 53.5 cm).

Collection

Dia Art Foundation, New York, New York, 1980.

Provenance

Lone Star Foundation, New York, New York, 1979.

Exhibitions

Kunsthalle Bern. *Chamberlain*, cat. no. 7, color illus. p. 33. October 12–November 18, 1979. Traveled to Van Abbemuseum, Eindhoven, Netherlands. April 3–May 11, 1980.

Palacio de Cristal, Parque del Retiro, Madrid. *John Chamberlain/Esculturas*, color illus. p. 45. January 26–March 31, 1984.

References

John Chamberlain Reliefs 1960–1982 (Sarasota: The John and Mable Ringling Museum of Art, 1983), color illus. p. 69.

609

Hi Jinks 1979

Painted and chromium-plated steel
39 × 32 × 20 in.
(99 × 81.5 × 51 cm).

Collection

Dia Art Foundation, New York, New York, 1979; acquired directly from the artist.

Exhibitions

Dia Art Foundation, New York, New York. *John Chamberlain Sculpture: An Extended Exhibition*. March 19–November 27, 1982.

The John and Mable Ringling Museum of Art, Sarasota, Florida. *John Chamberlain Reliefs 1960–1982*, color illus. p. 75. January 28–March 27, 1983.

610

Hit Height Lear 1979

Painted and chromium-plated steel
81 × 88 × 31 in.
(205.5 × 223.5 × 78.5 cm).

Collection

Dia Art Foundation, New York, New York, 1980.

Provenance

Heiner Friedrich GmbH, Cologne.

Exhibitions

Kunsthalle Bern. *Chamberlain*, cat. no. 5, color illus. p. 27. October 12–November 18, 1979. Traveled to Van Abbemuseum, Eindhoven, Netherlands. April 3–May 11, 1980.

Heiner Friedrich GmbH, Cologne. *John Chamberlain*. November 23, 1979–January 20, 1980.

Palacio de Cristal, Parque del Retiro, Madrid. *John Chamberlain/Esculturas*, color illus. p. 41. January 26–March 31, 1984.

Grand Palais, Paris. *La rime et la raison: Les collections Menil (Houston—New York)*, cat. no. 456, illus. pp. 75 and 389. April 18–July 30, 1984.

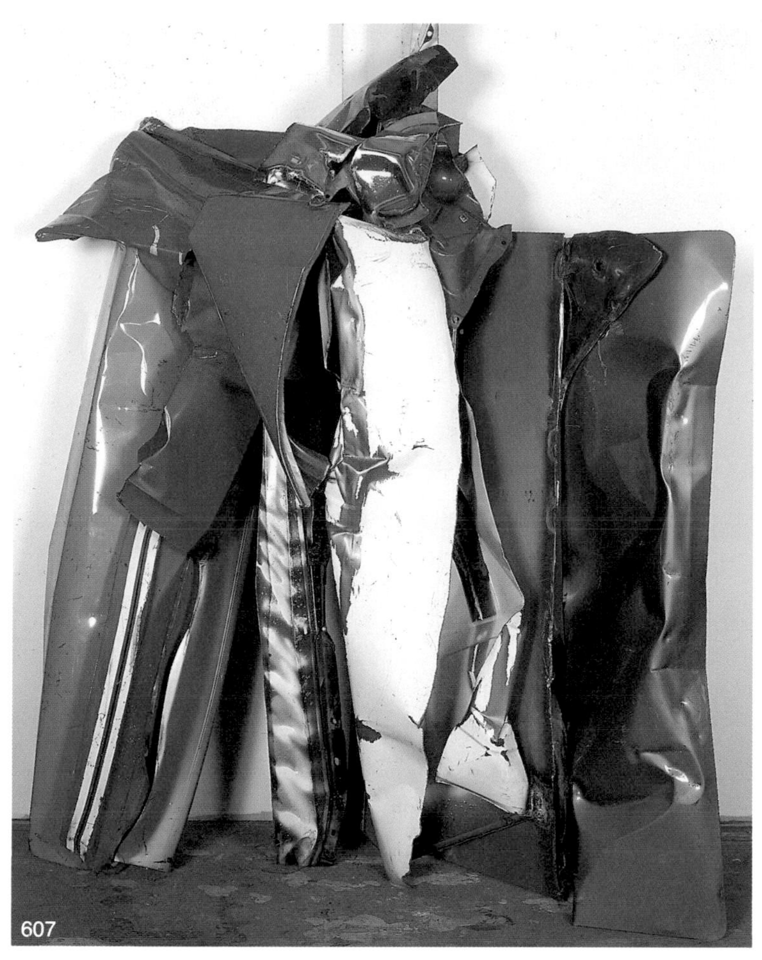
607

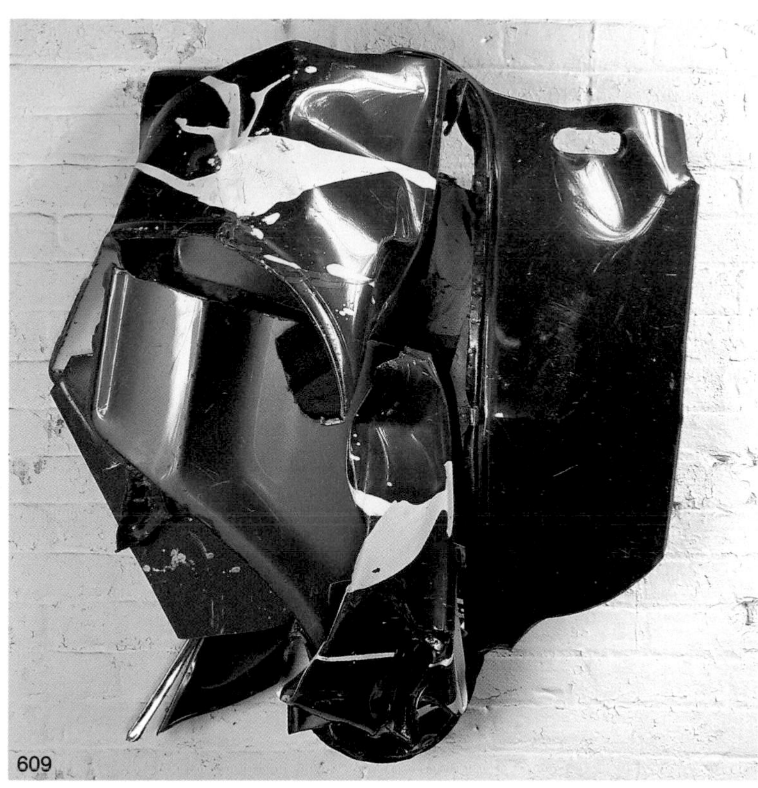
609

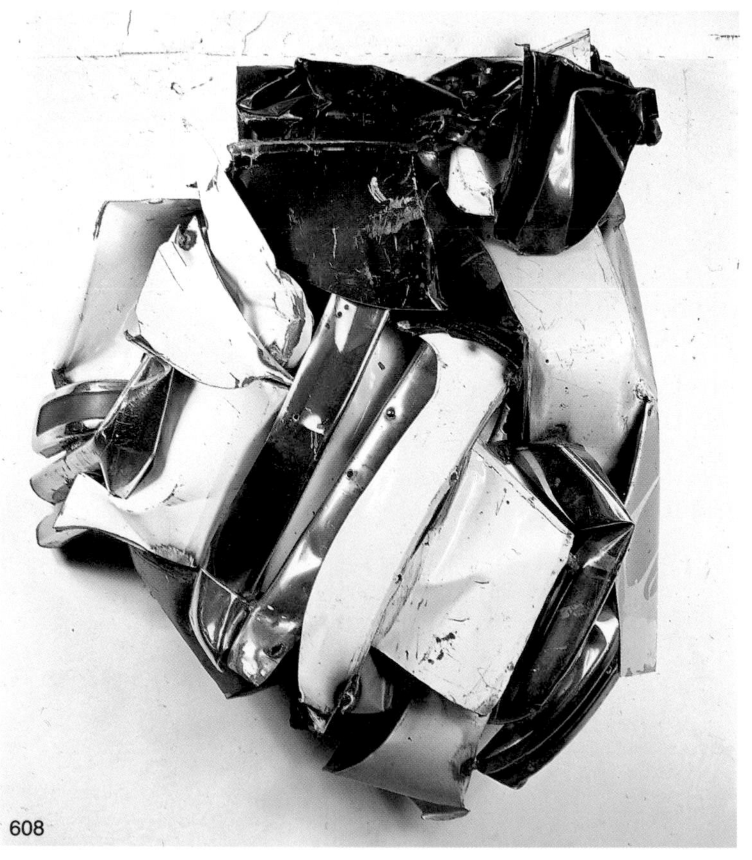
608

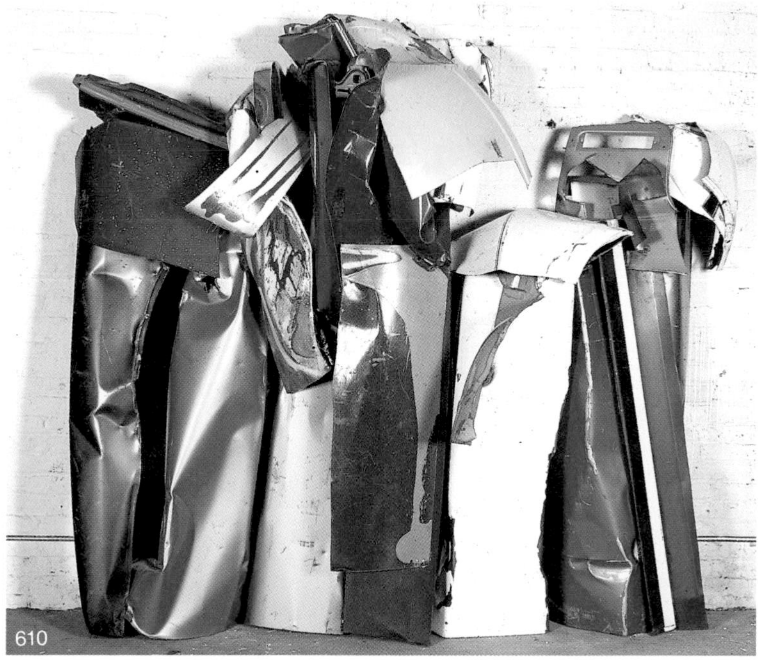
610

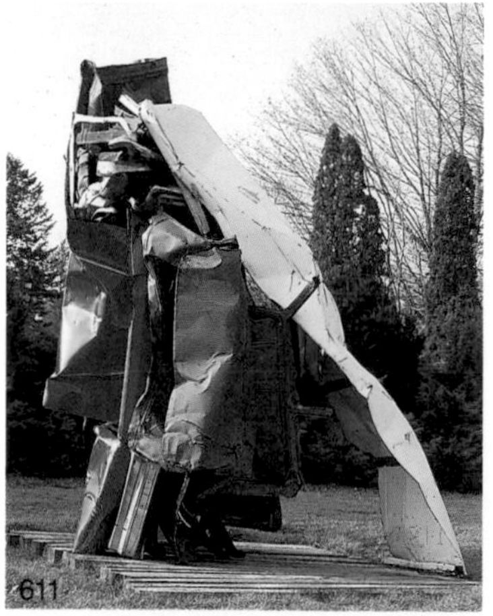
611

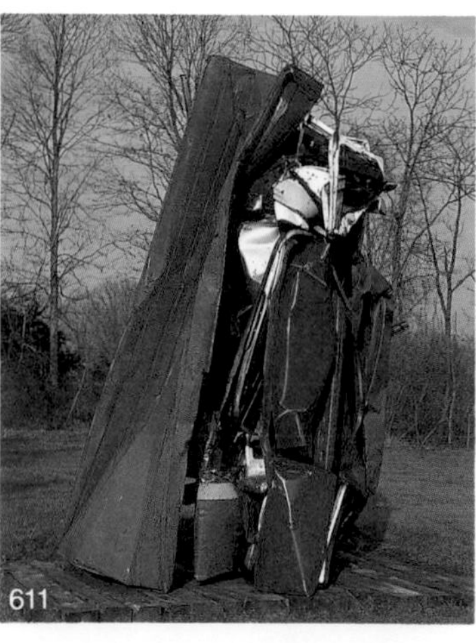
611

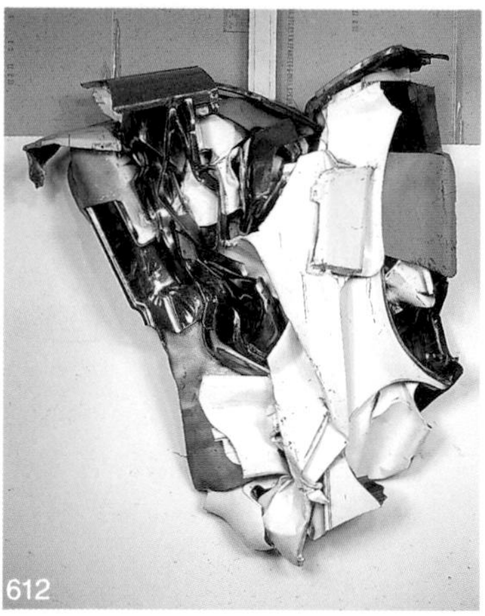
612

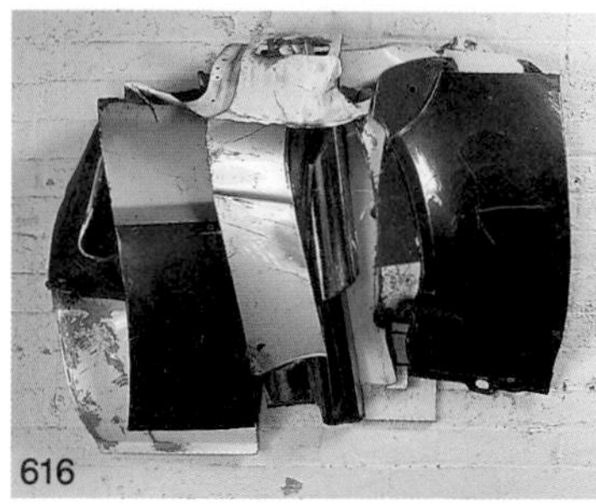
616

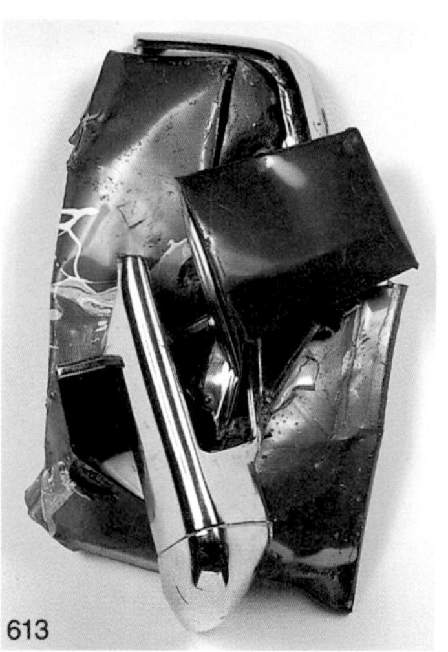
613

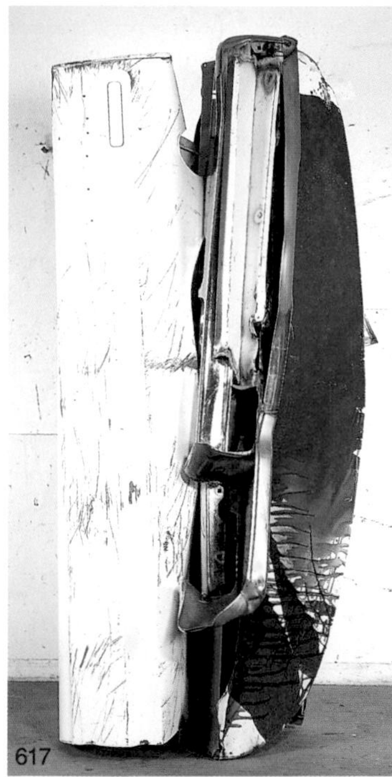
617

611

Luftschloss 1979

Painted and chromium-plated steel
152 × 103 × 83 in.
(386 × 261.5 × 211 cm).

Collection

Dia Art Foundation, New York, New York, 1981; acquired directly from the artist.

Exhibitions

Dia Art Foundation, Essex, Connecticut. *Chamberlain Gardens, Essex*. May–November 1982.

References

Documenta 7/Kassel, vol 1 (Kassel, West Germany: D + V Paul Dierichs, GmbH, 1982), illus. p. 37.

612

One Twin 1979

Painted and chromium-plated steel
65 × 55 × 26 in.
(165 × 139.5 × 66 cm).

Collection

Dia Art Foundation, New York, New York, 1980; acquired directly from the artist.

Exhibitions

Dia Art Foundation, New York, New York. *John Chamberlain Sculpture: An Extended Exhibition*. March 19–November 27, 1982.

The John and Mable Ringling Museum of Art, Sarasota, Florida. *John Chamberlain Reliefs 1960–1982*, color illus. p. 73. January 28–March 27, 1983.

Dia Art Foundation, the Art Museum of the Pecos, Marfa, Texas. *An Exhibition of Sculpture by John Chamberlain*. From May 7, 1983.

613

Portrait of a Nude with a Chrome Fan 1979

Painted and chromium-plated steel
27 × 16 × 10 in.
(68.5 × 40.5 × 25.5 cm).

Collection

Margo Leavin Gallery, Los Angeles, California.

Provenance

Xavier Fourcade, Inc., and Thordis Moeller, New York, New York.

Notes

In 1979 a ceramic edition was made based on this sculpture. Also titled *Portrait of a Nude with a Chrome Fan*, only a few examples from the edition exist.

614

Prez's Blurb 1979

Painted and chromium-plated steel
64½ × 55 × 37½ in.
(164 × 139.5 × 95 cm).

Collection

Dia Art Foundation, New York, New York, 1980; acquired directly from the artist.

Exhibitions

Dia Art Foundation, New York, New York. *John Chamberlain Sculpture: An Extended Exhibition*. March 19–November 27, 1982.

615

Roxanne Loup 1979

Painted and chromium-plated steel
61 × 80 × 42 in.
(155 × 203 × 106.5 cm).

Collection

Dia Art Foundation, New York, New York, 1980; acquired directly from the artist.

Exhibitions

Dia Art Foundation, New York, New York. *John Chamberlain Sculpture: An Extended Exhibition*. March 19, 1982–July 30, 1983.

616

Sashimi Mendoza 1979

Painted and chromium-plated steel
39 × 35 × 22 in.
(99 × 89 × 56 cm).

Collection

Private collection, New York, New York; acquired directly from the artist.

Exhibitions

Dia Art Foundation, New York, New York. *John Chamberlain Sculpture: An Extended Exhibition*. March 19–November 27, 1982.

The John and Mable Ringling Museum of Art, Sarasota, Florida. *John Chamberlain Reliefs 1960–1982*, color illus. p. 63. January 28–March 27, 1983.

Nassau County Museum of Fine Arts, Roslyn, New York. *Sculpture: The Tradition in Steel*. October 9, 1983–January 22, 1984.

617

Softer Sticks 1979

Painted and chromium-plated steel
82 × 40 × 28 in.
(208.5 × 101.5 × 71 cm).

Collection

Dia Art Foundation, New York, New York, 1981; acquired directly from the artist.

Exhibitions

Dia Art Foundation, Essex, Connecticut. *Chamberlain Gardens, Essex*. May–November 1982 and 1983.

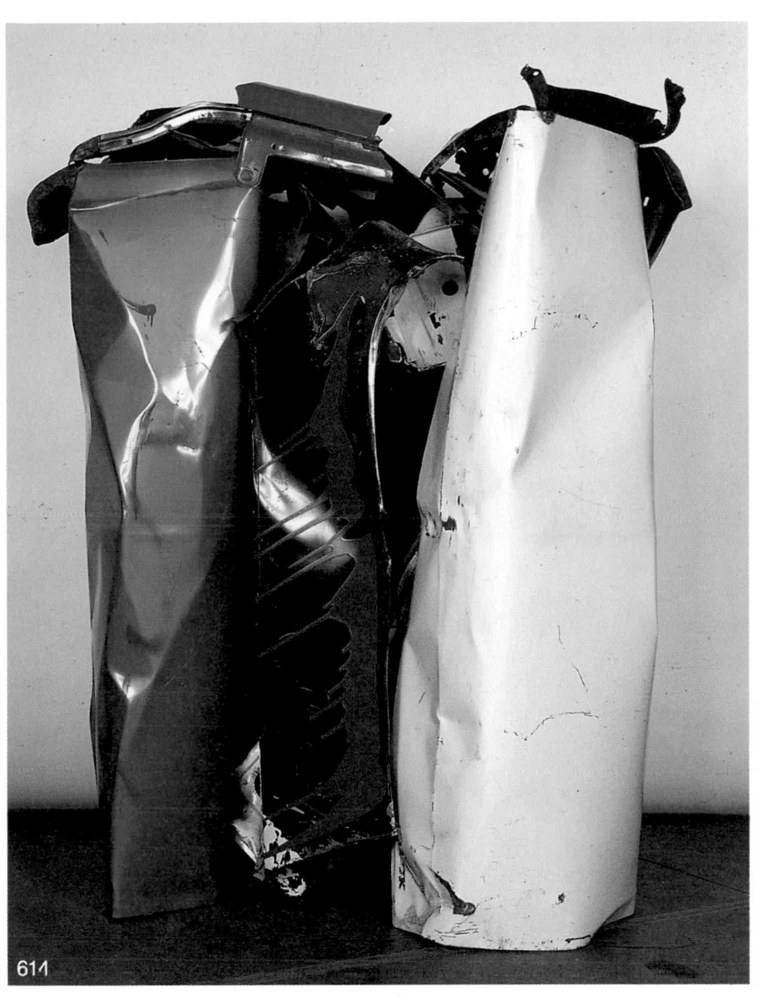
614

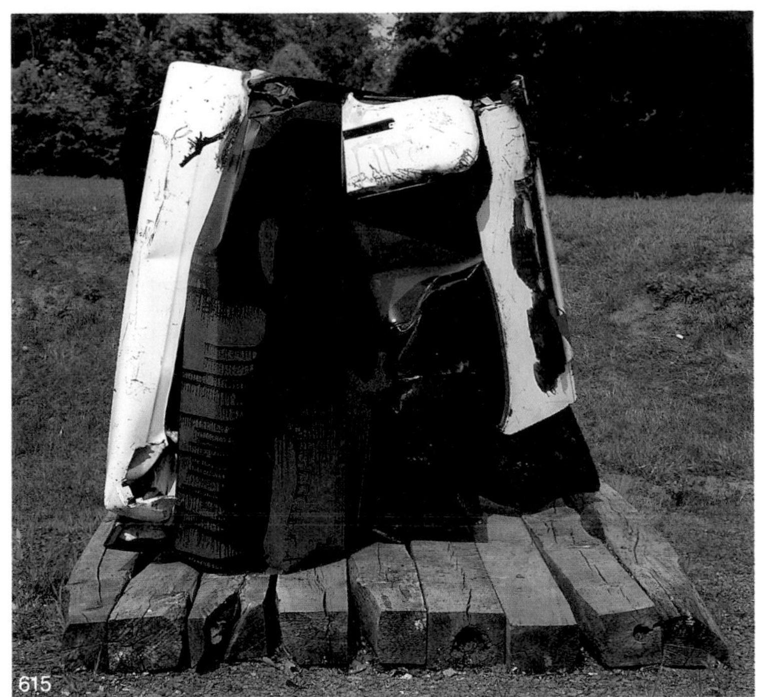
615

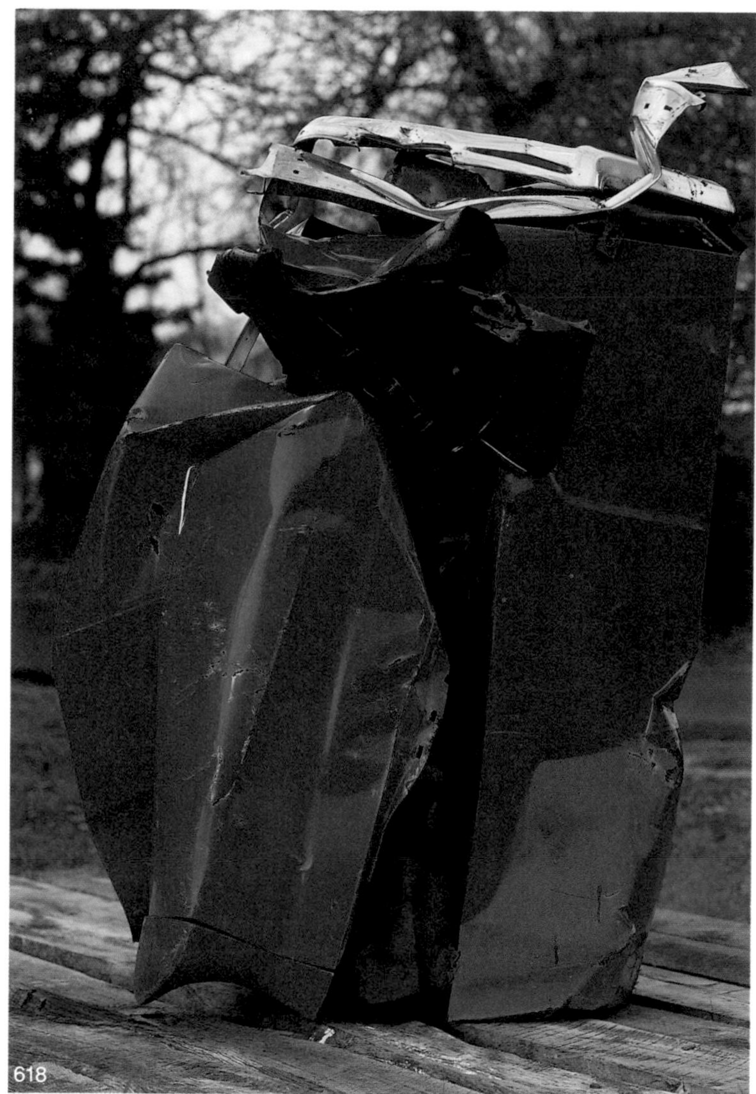

618

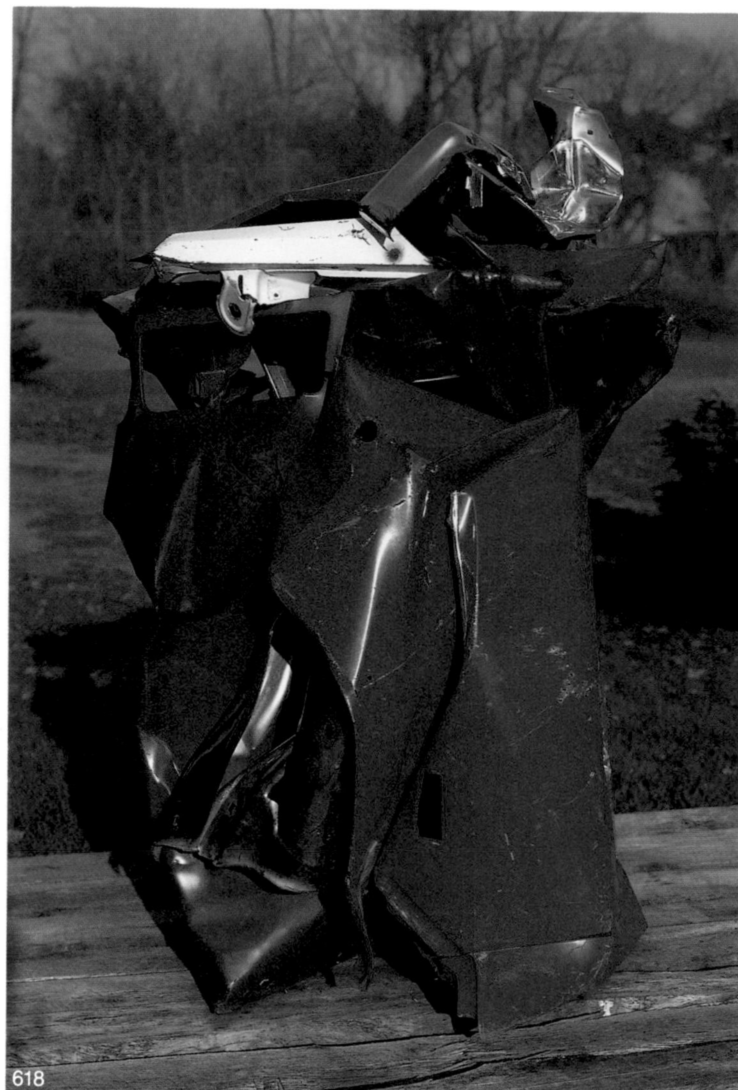

618

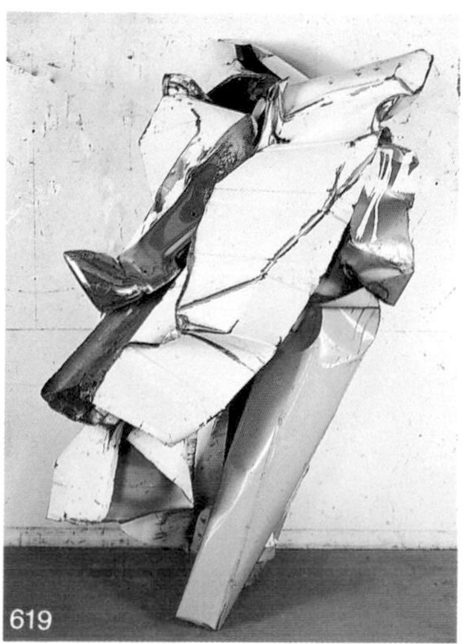

619

618

SWIFT
WI T 1979

Painted and chromium-plated steel
59 × 45½ × 40 in.
(150 × 115.5 × 101.5 cm).

Collection

Dia Art Foundation, New York, New York, 1978; acquired directly from the artist.

Exhibitions

Dia Art Foundation, Essex, Connecticut. *Chamberlain Gardens, Essex.* May–November 1982, 1983, and 1984.

619

The Hot Lady from Bristol 1979

Painted and chromium-plated steel
83 × 51 × 50 in.
(211 × 129.5 × 127 cm).

Collection

Dia Art Foundation, New York, New York, 1979; acquired directly from the artist.

Exhibitions

Dia Art Foundation, New York, New York. *John Chamberlain Sculpture: An Extended Exhibition.* March 19–November 27, 1982.

The John and Mable Ringling Museum of Art, Sarasota, Florida. *John Chamberlain Reliefs 1960–1982*, color illus. p. 71. January 28–March 27, 1983.

Dia Art Foundation, New York, New York. *John Chamberlain Sculpture: An Extended Exhibition.* September 22, 1983–February 23, 1985.

620

Three-Cornered Desire 1979

Painted and chromium-plated steel
70 × 103 × 70 in.
(178 × 261.5 × 178 cm).

Collection

Dia Art Foundation, New York, New York, 1980; acquired directly from the artist.

Exhibitions

Dia Art Foundation, New York, New York. *John Chamberlain Sculpture: An Extended Exhibition.* March 19–November 27, 1982.

The John and Mable Ringling Museum of Art, Sarasota, Florida. *John Chamberlain Reliefs 1960–1982*, color illus. p. 65. January 28–March 27, 1983.

Dia Art Foundation, New York, New York. *John Chamberlain Sculpture: An Extended Exhibition.* September 22, 1983–February 23, 1985.

621

Tongue Pictures 1979

Painted and chromium-plated steel
90 × 63 × 52 in.
(228.5 × 160 × 132 cm).

Collection

Dia Art Foundation, New York, New York, 1981; acquired directly from the artist.

Exhibitions

Dia Art Foundation, Essex, Connecticut. *Chamberlain Gardens, Essex.* May–November 1982, 1983, and 1984.

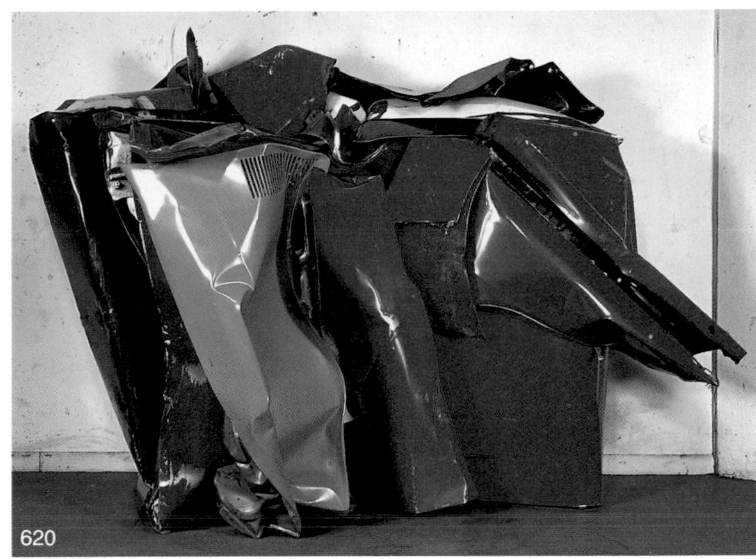
620

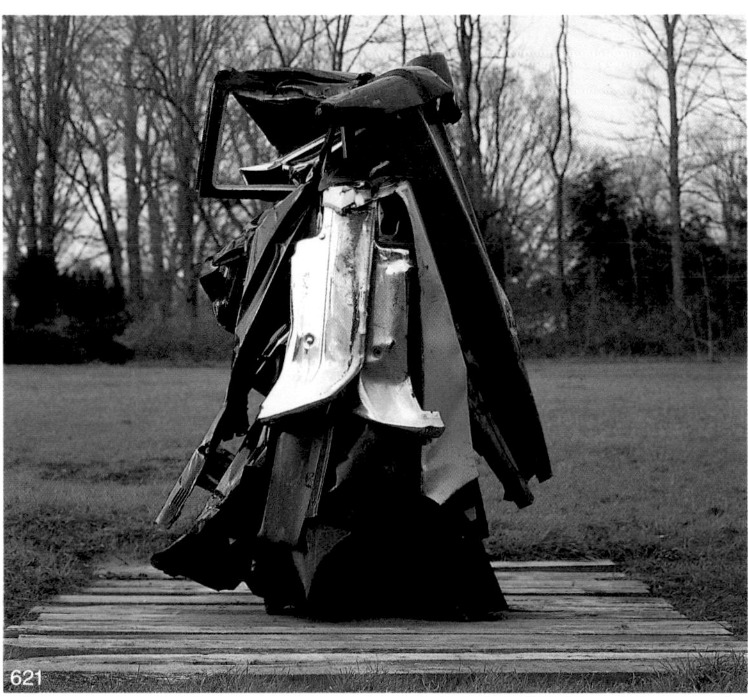
621

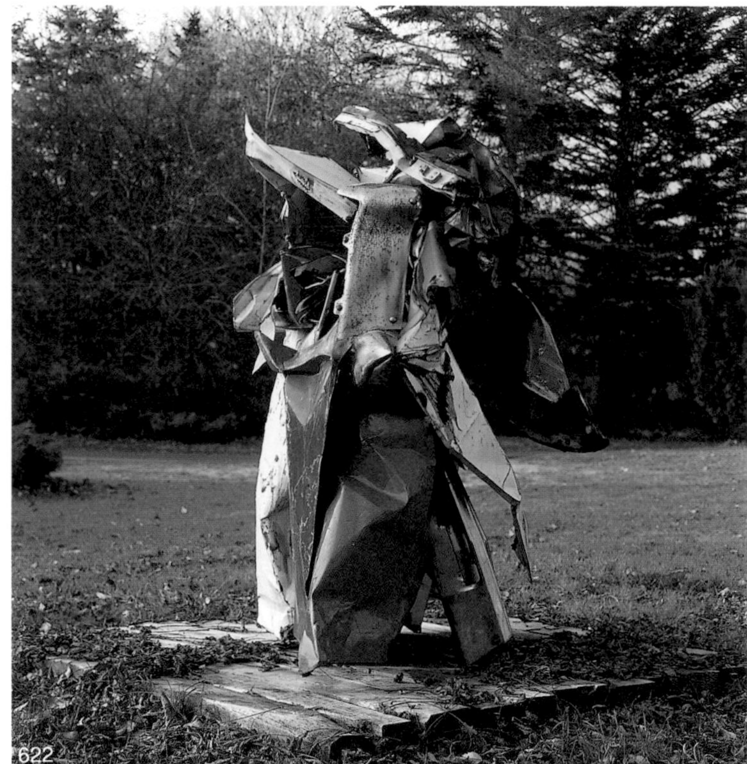
622

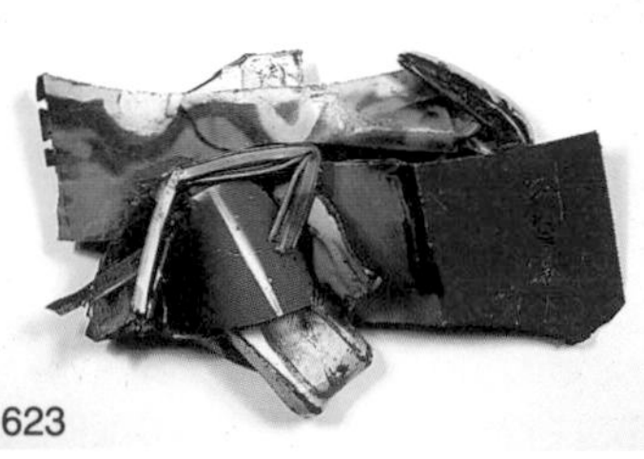
623

622

Two Dark Ladies 1979

Painted and chromium-plated steel
81 × 70 × 63 in.
(206 × 178 × 160 cm).

Collection

Dia Art Foundation, New York, New York, 1981; acquired directly from the artist.

Exhibitions

Dia Art Foundation, Essex, Connecticut. *Chamberlain Gardens, Essex.* May–November 1982, 1983, and 1984.

References

Gary Indiana, "John Chamberlain's Irregular Set," *Art in America*, vol. 71, no. 10 (November 1983), p. 208.

623

Zero Flora 1975–79

Painted and chromium-plated steel
25 × 41 × 10 in.
(63.5 × 104 × 25.5 cm).

Collection

Mr. and Mrs. Richard S. Lane, 1985.

Provenance

Jesse Chamberlain, New York, New York, 1979; Lone Star Foundation, New York, New York, 1980; Dia Art Foundation, New York, New York, 1980.

Exhibitions

The John and Mable Ringling Museum of Art, Sarasota, Florida. *John Chamberlain Reliefs 1960–1982*, color illus. p. 37. January 28–March 27, 1983.

Dia Art Foundation, New York, New York. *John Chamberlain Sculpture: An Extended Exhibition*. September 22, 1983–February 23, 1985.

Sotheby Parke-Bernet, Inc., New York, New York. *Twenty-three Works from the Dia Art Foundation*, cat. no. 19, color illus. November 5, 1985.

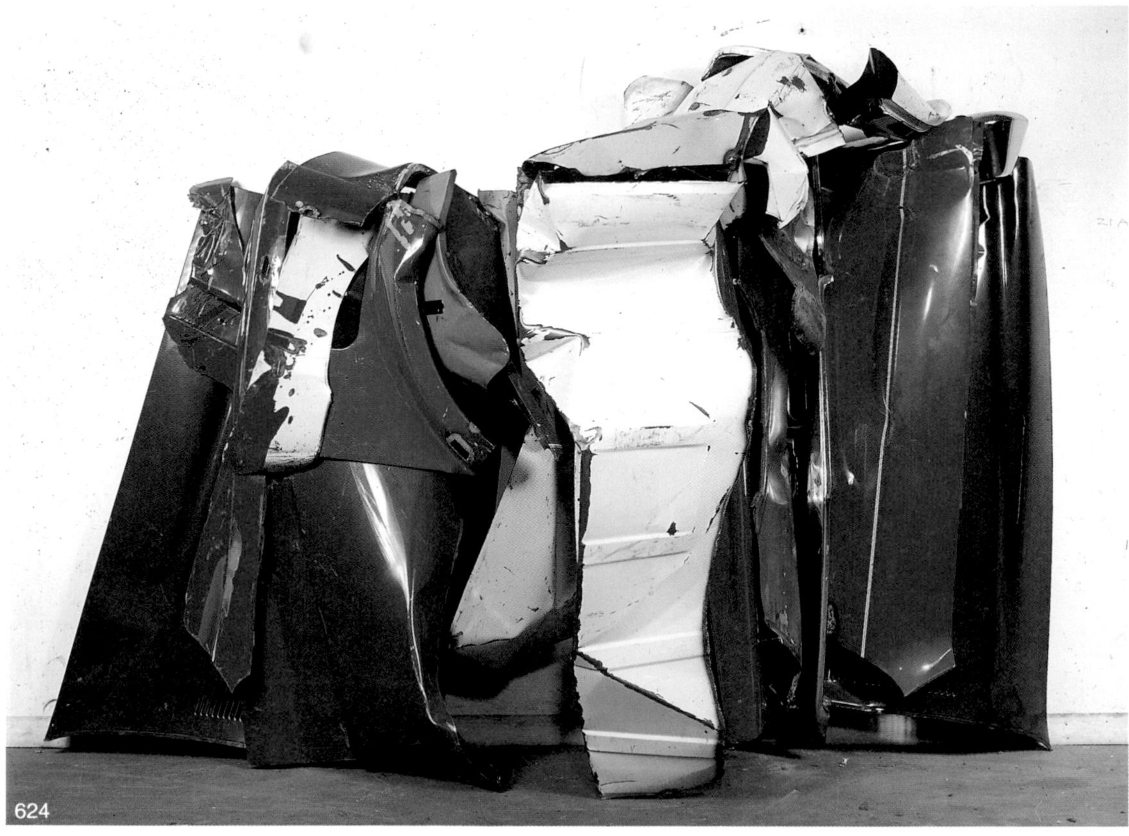
624

624

Zia Lightnin Field Forever 1979

Painted and chromium-plated steel
73 × 106 × 49 in.
(185.5 × 269 × 124.5 cm).

Collection

Dia Art Foundation, New York, New York, 1979; acquired directly from the artist.

Exhibitions

Dia Art Foundation, New York, New York. *John Chamberlain Sculpture: An Extended Exhibition*. March 19, 1982–July 30, 1983.

625

Untitled 1979

Urethane foam and cord
Dimensions unknown.

Collection
Private collection, New York, New York.

Provenance
Heiner Friedrich GmbH, Cologne.

Exhibitions
Heiner Friedrich GmbH, Cologne. *John Chamberlain*. November 23, 1979–January 20, 1980.

626

Untitled 1979

Urethane foam and cord
Dimensions unknown.

Collection
Private collection, New York, New York.

Provenance
Heiner Friedrich GmbH, Cologne.

Exhibitions
Heiner Friedrich GmbH, Cologne. *John Chamberlain*. November 23, 1979–January 20, 1980.

627

Untitled 1979

Urethane foam
6½ × 10½ × 9 in.
(16.5 × 26.5 × 23 cm).

Collection
Heinrich Ehrhardt, Frankfurt, 1979; acquired directly from the artist.

Exhibitions
Heiner Friedrich GmbH, Cologne. *John Chamberlain*. November 23, 1979–January 20, 1980.

628

Untitled 1979

Urethane foam
c. 11½ × 11½ × 11½ in.
(c. 29 × 29 × 29 cm).

Collection
Private collection, New York, New York.

Provenance
Heiner Friedrich GmbH, Cologne

Exhibitions
Heiner Friedrich GmbH, Cologne. *John Chamberlain*. November 23, 1979–January 20, 1980.

629

Untitled 1979

Urethane foam
c. 11½ × 11½ × 11½ in.
(c. 29 × 29 × 29 cm).

Collection
Private collection, New York, New York.

Provenance
Heiner Friedrich GmbH, Cologne.

Exhibitions
Heiner Friedrich GmbH, Cologne. *John Chamberlain*. November 23, 1979–January 20, 1980.

630

Untitled 1979

Urethane foam
c. 11½ × 11½ × 11½ in.
(c. 29 × 29 × 29 cm).

Collection
Private collection, New York, New York.

Provenance
Heiner Friedrich GmbH, Cologne.

Exhibitions
Heiner Friedrich GmbH, Cologne. *John Chamberlain*. November 23, 1979–January 20, 1980.

631

Untitled 1979

Urethane foam
c. 11½ × 11½ × 11½ in.
(c. 29 × 29 × 29 cm).

Collection
Private collection, New York, New York.

Provenance
Heiner Friedrich GmbH, Cologne.

Exhibitions
Heiner Friedrich GmbH, Cologne. *John Chamberlain*. November 23, 1979–January 20, 1980.

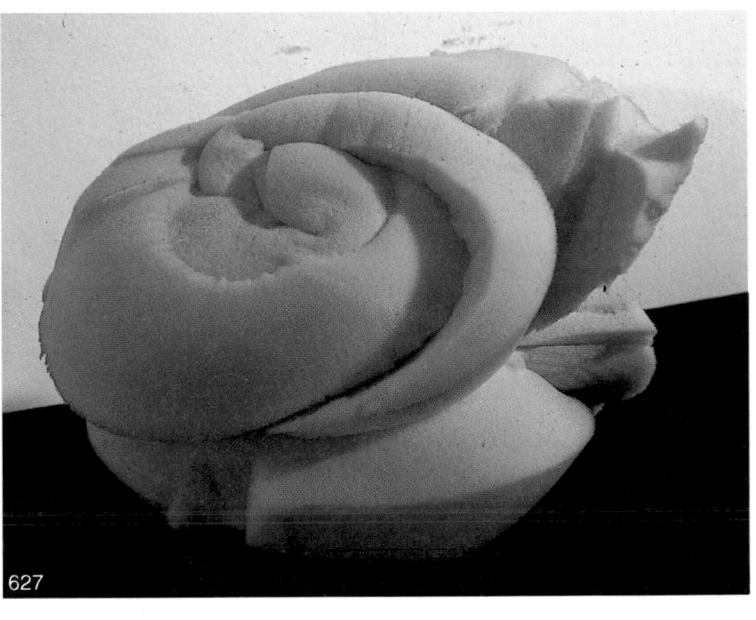

627

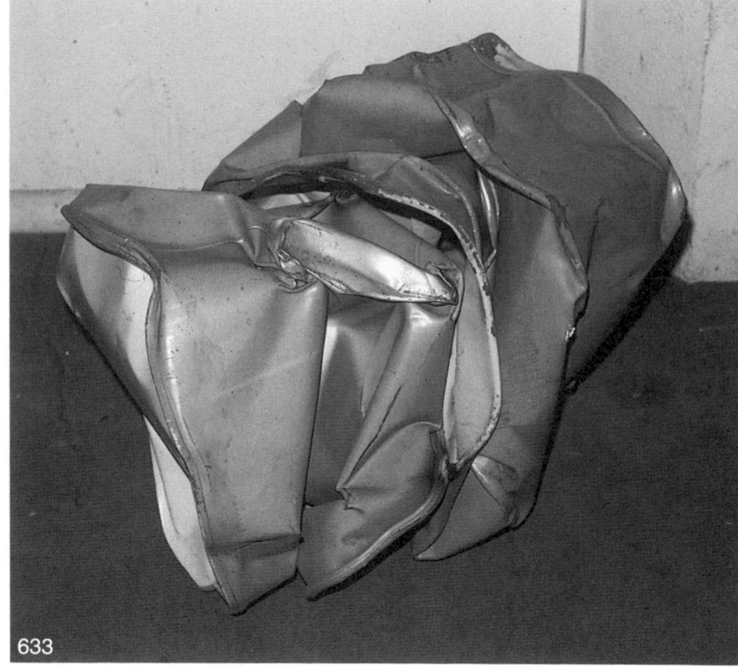
633

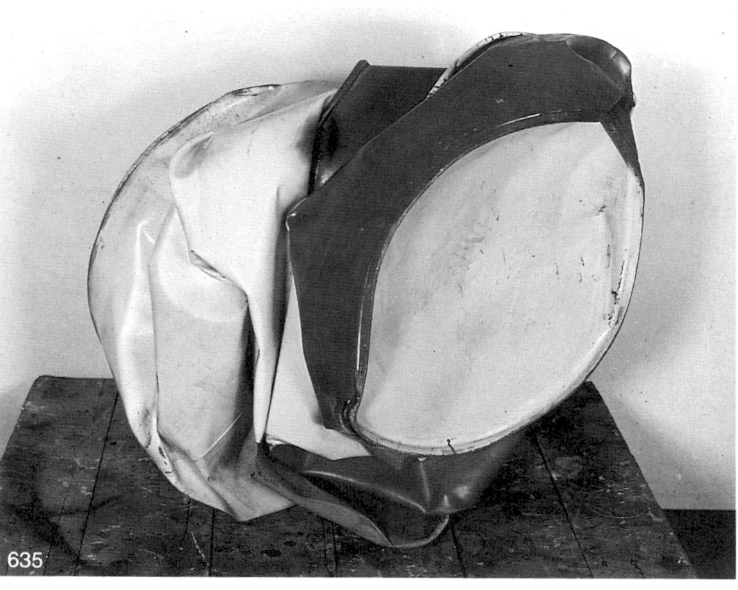
635

632

Untitled 1979
Urethane foam
c. 11½ × 11½ × 11½ in.
(c. 29 × 29 × 29 cm).

Collection
Private collection, New York, New York.

Provenance
Heiner Friedrich GmbH, Cologne.

Exhibitions
Heiner Friedrich GmbH, Cologne. *John Chamberlain*. November 23, 1979–January 20, 1980.

633

P.H.I.P. 1979
Painted steel
27½ × 34½ × 25 in.
(70 × 87.5 × 63.5 cm)

Collection
Private collection, New York, New York; acquired directly from the artist.

634

Kiss #11 1979
Painted steel
24½ × 39 × 20 in.
(62 × 99 × 51 cm).

Collection
Private collection, New York, New York.

Exhibitions
Kunsthalle Bern. *Chamberlain*, cat. no. 10, color illus. p. 41. October 12–November 18, 1979. Traveled to Van Abbemuseum, Eindhoven, Netherlands. April 3–May 11, 1980.

Palacio de Cristal, Parque del Retiro, Madrid. *John Chamberlain/Esculturas*, color illus. p. 55. January 26–March 31, 1984.

Städtische Kunsthalle, Düsseldorf. *Ein anderes Klima*. August 28–October 5, 1984.

635

Kiss #12 1979
Painted steel
30 × 31 × 27 in.
(76 × 78.5 × 68.5 cm).

Collection
Private collection, New York, New York; acquired directly from the artist.

Exhibitions
Kunsthalle Bern. *Chamberlain*, cat. no. 11, color illus. p. 41. October 12–November 18, 1979. Traveled to Van Abbemuseum, Eindhoven, Netherlands. April 3–May 11, 1980.

Palacio de Cristal, Parque del Retiro, Madrid. *John Chamberlain/Esculturas*, color illus. p. 55. January 26–March 31, 1984.

Städtische Kunsthalle, Düsseldorf. *Ein anderes Klima*. August 28–October 5, 1984.

References
Gary Indiana, "John Chamberlain's Irregular Set," *Art in America*, vol. 71, no. 10 (November 1983), color illus. p. 215.

636

Kiss #14 1979
Painted steel
26 × 30 × 32 in.
(66 × 76 × 81 cm).

Collection
Mr. and Mrs. Abe Adler, Los Angeles, California; acquired directly from the artist.

Exhibitions
The Art Galleries, University of California, Santa Barbara. *John Chamberlain/Alan Saret—Contemporary Sculpture*. March 27–April 19, 1984.

637

Kiss #18 1979
Painted steel
27 × 23½ × 24 in.
(68.5 × 59.5 × 61 cm).

Collection
Fred Jahn, Munich, 1984.

Provenance
Peter Buchholz, New York, New York, 1979.

Exhibitions
Sotheby Parke-Bernet, Inc., New York, New York. *Contemporary Painting, Sculpture, Graphic Arts, Tribal Arts: The Little Red Schoolhouse Auction*, cat. no. 25. February 28, 1979.

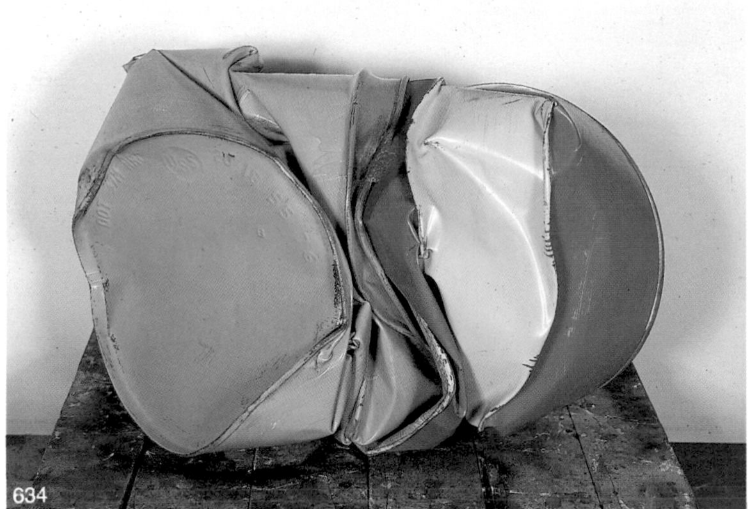
634

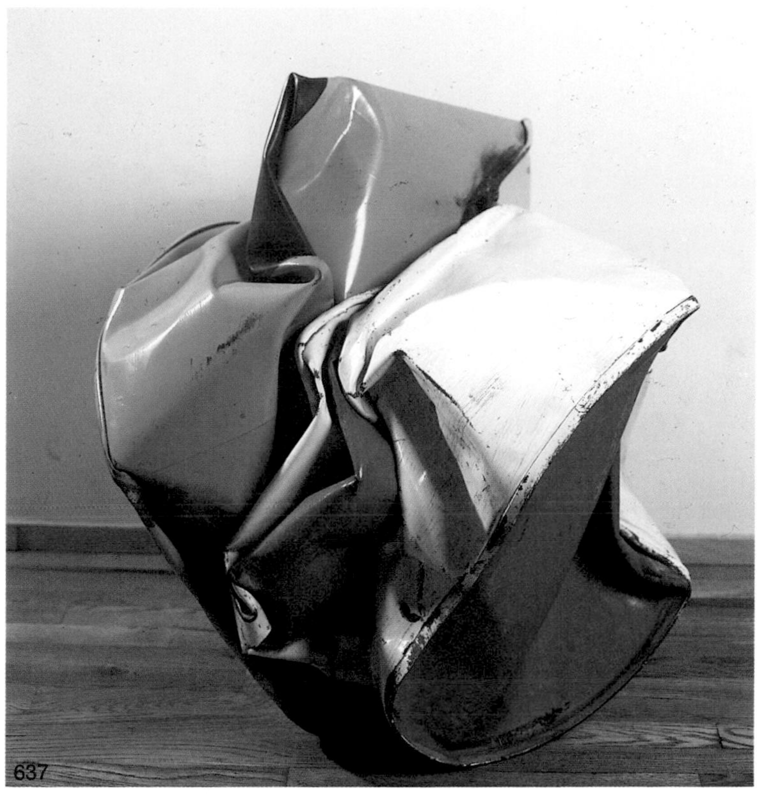
637

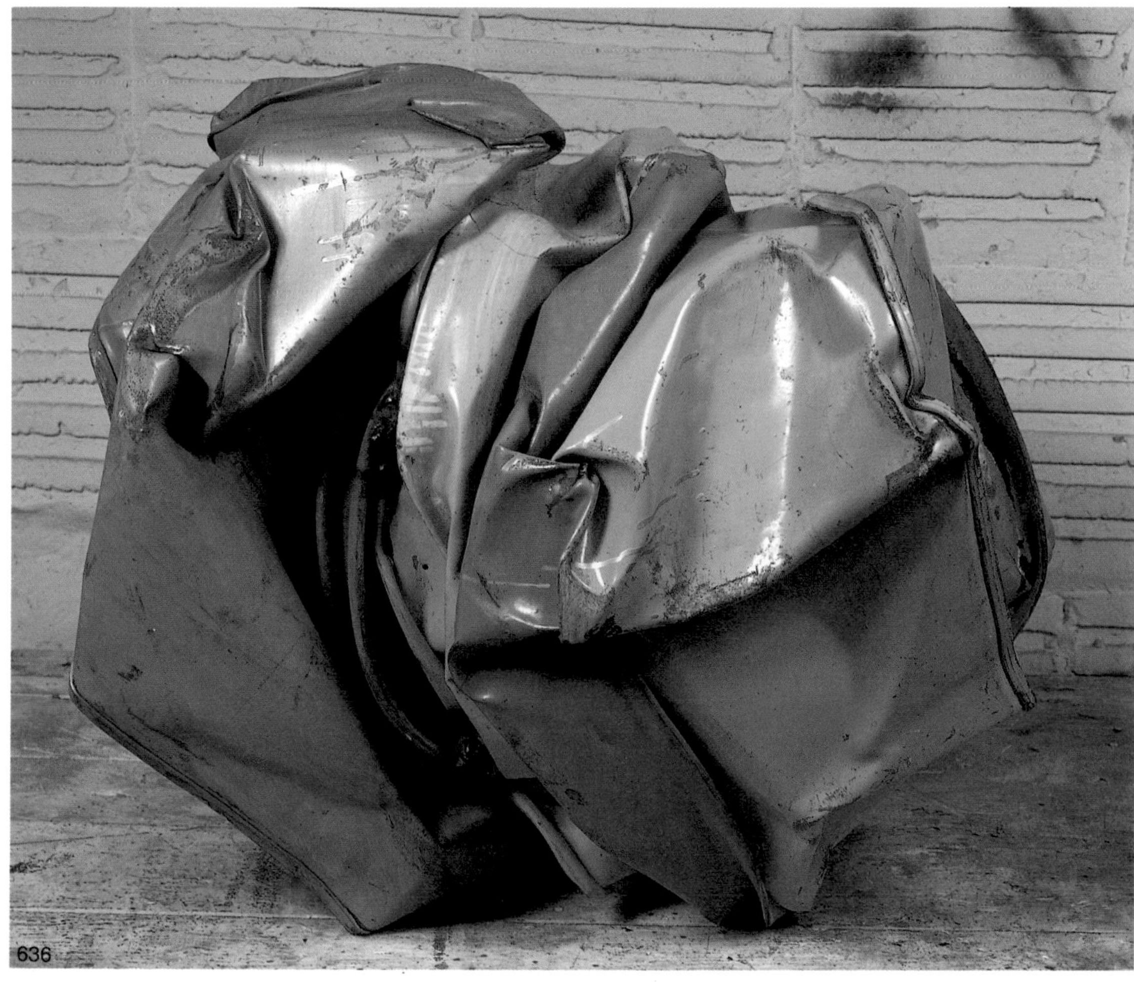
636

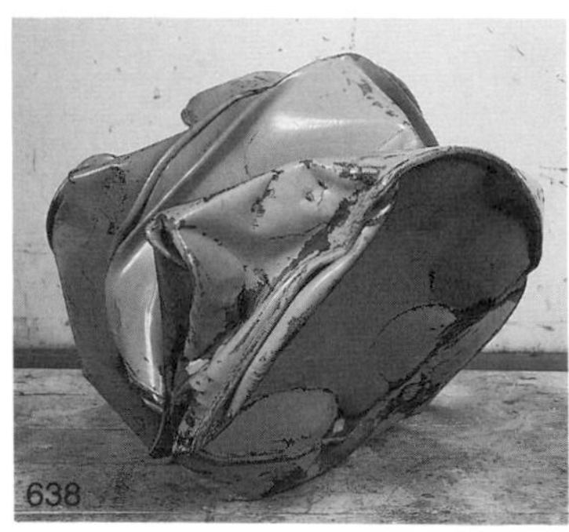
638

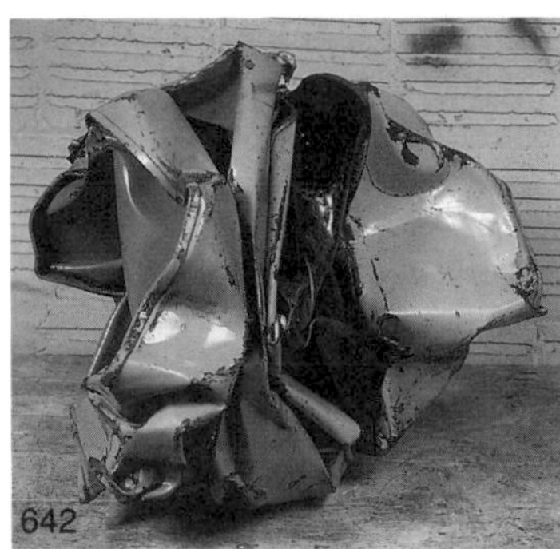
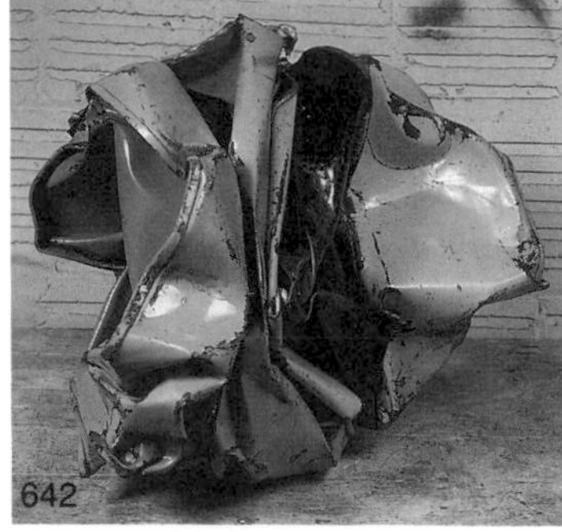
642

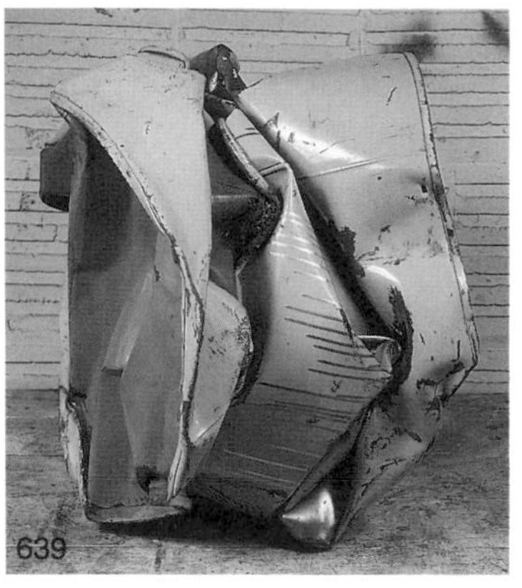
639

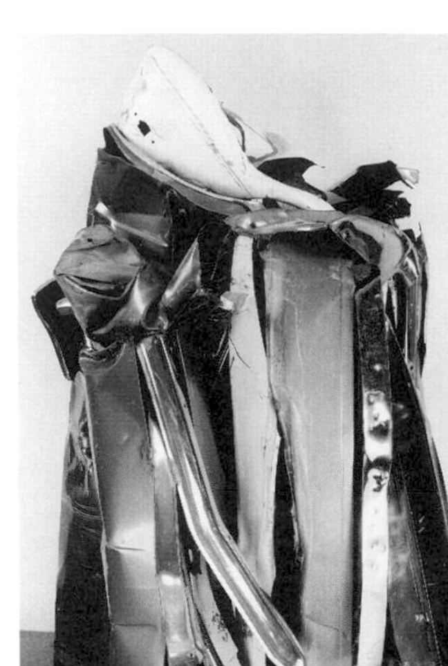
643

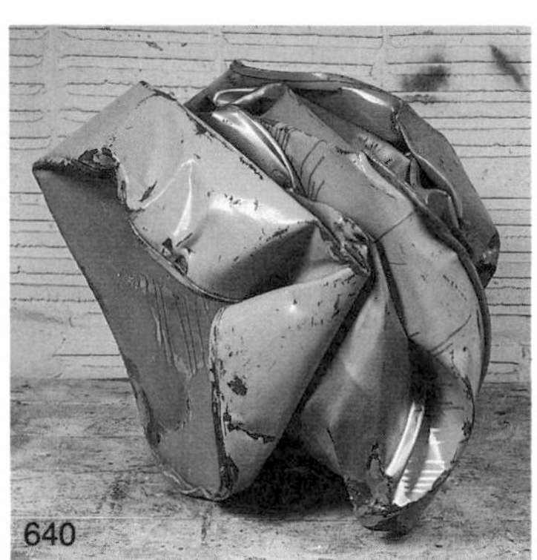
640

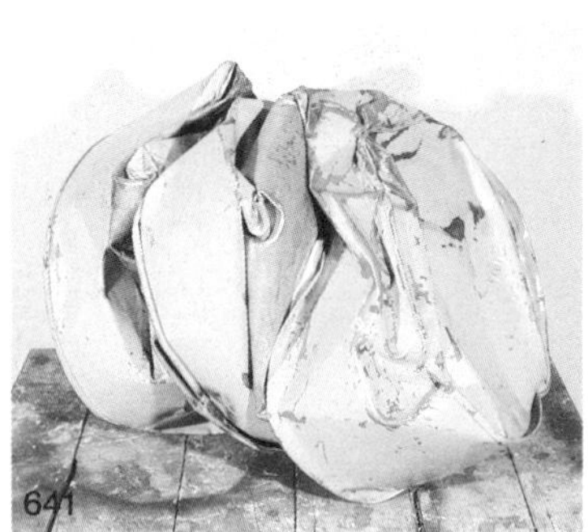
641

638

Kiss #24 1979

Painted steel
26 × 35 × 26 in.
(66 × 89 × 66 cm).

Collection

Private collection, New York, New York; acquired directly from the artist.

References

Chamberlain (Bern: Kunsthalle Bern and Van Abbemuseum, Eindhoven, Netherlands, 1979), color illus. p. 39.

Heinrich Ehrhardt, ed., *John Chamberlain/Esculturas* (Madrid: Ministerio de Cultura, 1984), color illus. p. 53.

639

Kiss #25 1979

Painted steel
25 × 31 × 32 in.
(63.5 × 78.5 × 81 cm).

Collection

Private collection, New York, New York; acquired directly from the artist.

Exhibitions

Kunsthalle Bern. *Chamberlain*, cat. no. 12. October 12–November 18, 1979. Traveled to Van Abbemuseum, Eindhoven, Netherlands. April 3–May 11, 1980.

Palacio de Cristal, Parque del Retiro, Madrid. *John Chamberlain/Esculturas*, listed. January 26–March 31, 1984.

640

Kiss #26 1979

Painted steel
25 × 29 × 20 in.
(63.5 × 73.5 × 51 cm).

Collection

Private collection, New York, New York; acquired directly from the artist.

Exhibitions

Kunsthalle Bern. *Chamberlain*, cat. no. 13. October 12–November 18, 1979. Traveled to Van Abbemuseum, Eindhoven, Netherlands. April 3–May 11, 1980.

Palacio de Cristal, Parque del Retiro, Madrid. *John Chamberlain/Esculturas*, listed. January 26–March 31, 1984.

641

Kiss #27 1979

Painted steel
27 × 32 × 27 in.
(68.5 × 81.5 × 68.5 cm).

Collection

Kathryn Fosdick, New York, New York, 1981; acquired directly from the artist.

References

Chamberlain (Bern: Kunsthalle Bern and Van Abbemuseum, Eindhoven, Netherlands, 1979), color illus. p. 39.

Heinrich Ehrhardt, ed., *John Chamberlain/Esculturas* (Madrid: Ministerio de Cultura, 1984), color illus. p. 53.

642

Kiss #28 1979

Painted steel
25 × 35 × 21 in.
(63.5 × 90 × 53.5 cm).

Collection

Private collection, New York, New York; acquired directly from the artist.

Exhibitions

Kunsthalle Bern. *Chamberlain*, cat. no. 14. October 12–November 18, 1979. Traveled to Van Abbemuseum, Eindhoven, Netherlands. April 3–May 11, 1980.

Palacio de Cristal, Parque del Retiro, Madrid. *John Chamberlain/Esculturas*, listed. January 26–March 31, 1984.

643

Black Satin Custard 1980

Painted and chromium-plated steel
80½ × 60 × 60 in.
(204.5 × 152.5 × 152.5 cm).

Collection

Dia Art Foundation, New York, New York, 1981; acquired directly from the artist.

Exhibitions

Dia Art Foundation, Essex, Connecticut. *Chamberlain Gardens, Essex*. May–November 1982 and 1984.

644

Calla Look 1980

Painted and chromium-plated steel
48 × 42 × 11 in.
(122 × 107 × 28 cm).

Collection

Museum of Contemporary Art, Los Angeles, California, 1982; gift of Donald Judd.

Provenance

Donald Judd, Marfa, Texas.

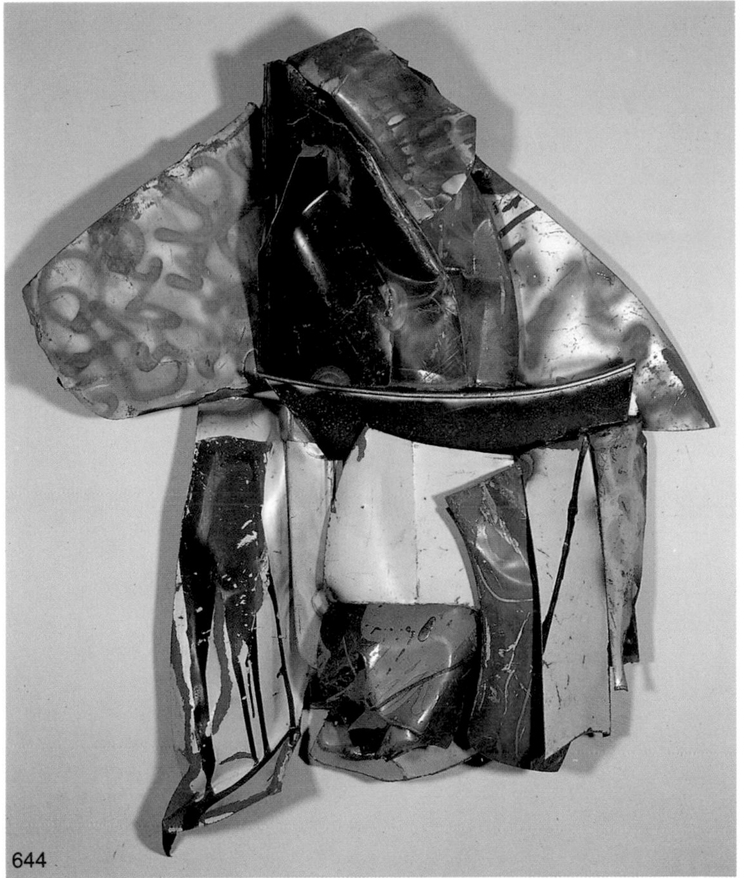

644

645

Coup d'Soup 1980

Painted and chromium-plated steel
102 × 51 × 26 in.
(259 × 129.5 × 66 cm).

Collection

Dia Art Foundation, New York, New York, 1980; acquired directly from the artist.

Exhibitions

Dia Art Foundation, New York, New York. *John Chamberlain Sculpture: An Extended Exhibition*. March 19–November 27, 1982.

The John and Mable Ringling Museum of Art, Sarasota, Florida. *John Chamberlain Reliefs 1960–1982*. January 28–March 27, 1983, color illus. p. 14.

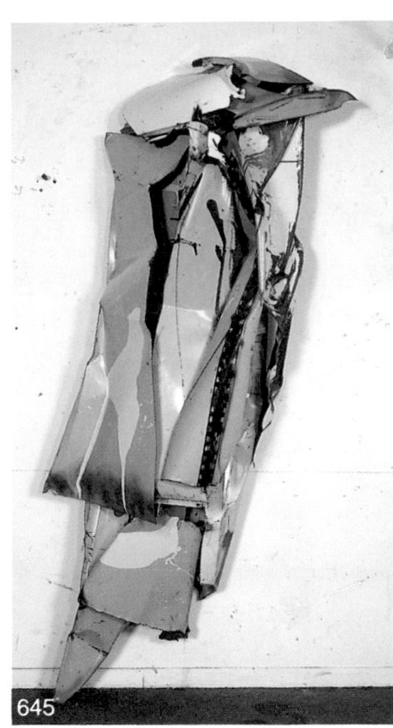

645

646

Idle Worship 1980

Painted and chromium-plated steel
65½ × 81½ × 29 in.
(166.5 × 207 × 73.5 cm).

Collection

Thordis Moeller, New York, New York; acquired directly from the artist.

Exhibitions

Leo Castelli Gallery, New York, New York. *John Chamberlain*. November 27–December 18, 1982.

Fort Wayne Museum of Art, Fort Wayne, Indiana. *Inaugural Exhibition*, color illus. p. 63. April 15–June 30, 1984.

Xavier Fourcade, Inc., New York, New York. *Sculpture*. July 10–September 14, 1984.

Galerie Rudolf Zwirner, Cologne. *John Chamberlain*. November 13–December 31, 1984.

Notes

Idle Worship was originally titled *Kunstliche—Idle Worship*.

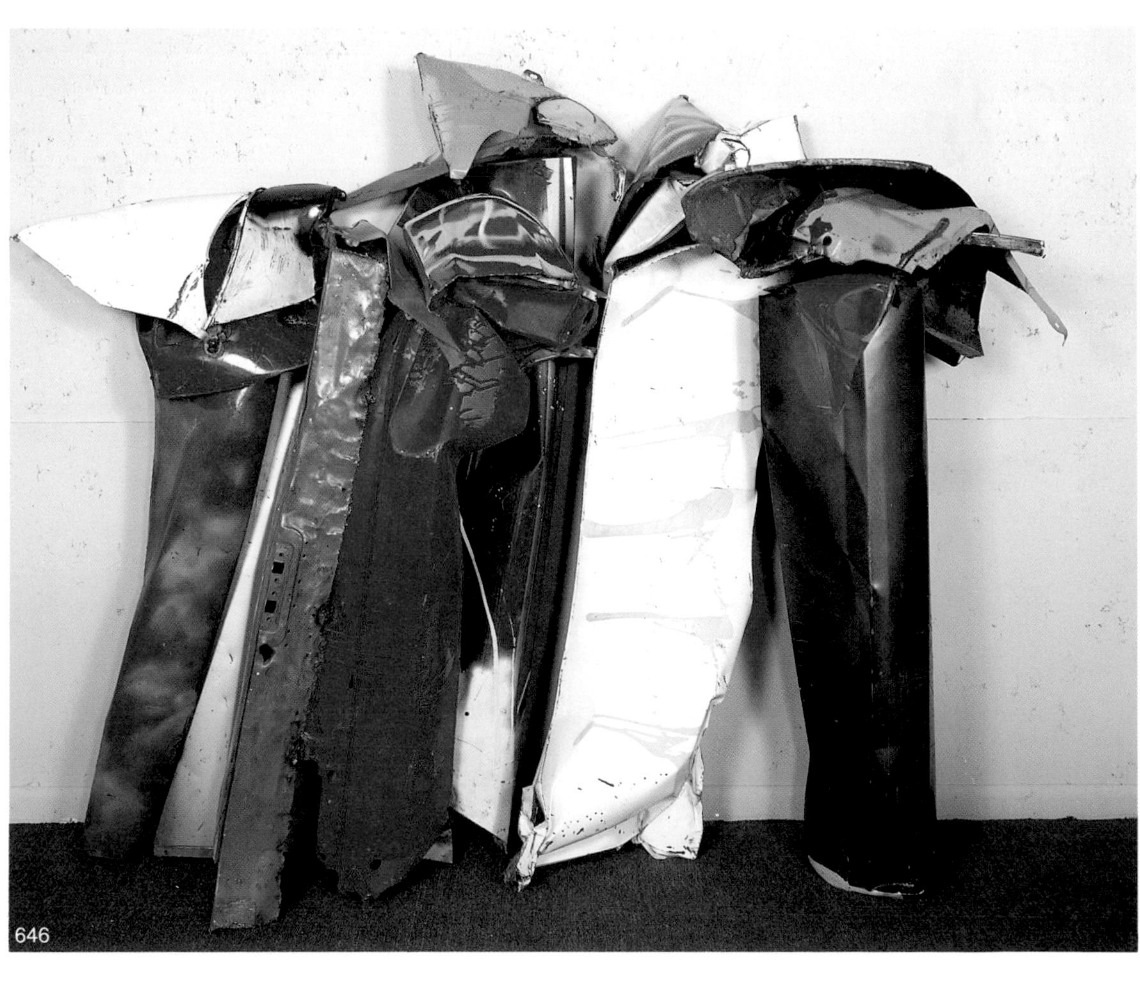

646

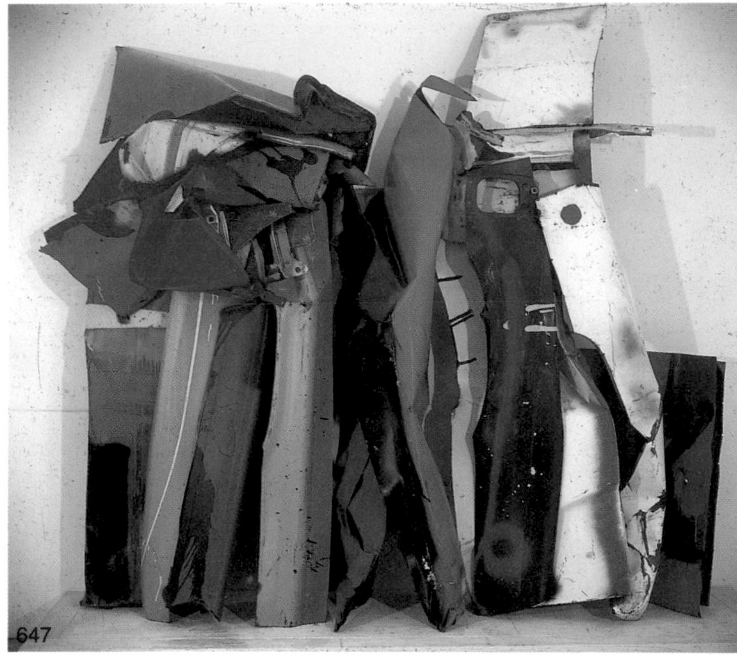
647

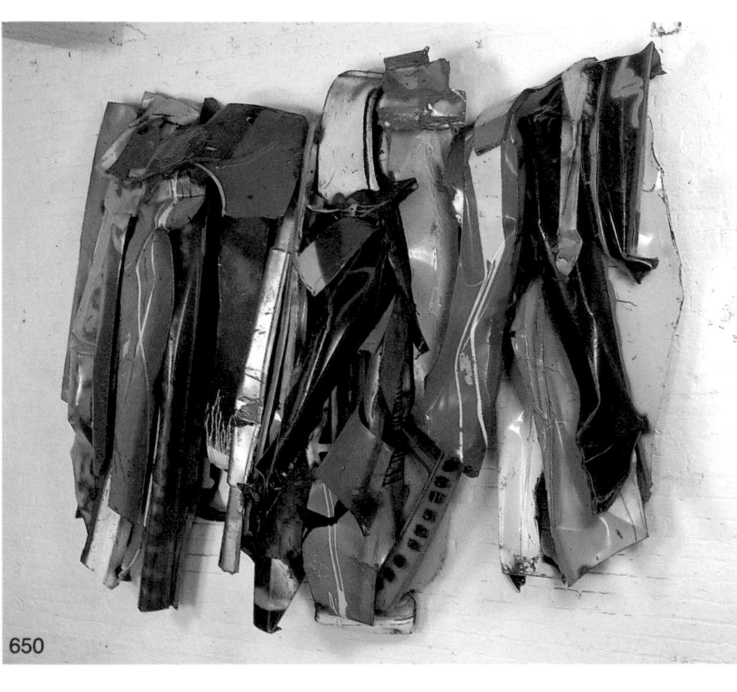
650

647

Isabella's Line 1980

Painted and chromium-plated steel
83 × 84 × 27½ in.
(211 × 213.5 × 70 cm).

Collection

The Pacesetter Corporation, Omaha, Nebraska, 1984.

Provenance

Jon Leon Gallery, New York, New York.

648

Tiny Alice 1980

Painted and chromium-plated steel
74 × 20 × 16 in.
(188 × 51 × 40.5 cm).

Collection

Uli Knecht, Stuttgart.

Provenance

Thordis Moeller, New York, New York.

Exhibitions

The John and Mable Ringling Museum of Art, Sarasota, Florida. *John Chamberlain Reliefs 1960–1982*, color illus. p. 79. January 28–March 27, 1983.

Nassau County Museum of Fine Arts, Roslyn, New York. *Sculpture: The Tradition in Steel*, illus. October 9, 1983–January 22, 1984.

References

Heinrich Ehrhardt, ed., *John Chamberlain/Esculturas* (Madrid: Ministerio de Cultura, 1984), color illus. p. 51.

649

Wandering Bliss Meets Fruit of the Loom (a.k.a. America on Parade) 1980

Painted and chromium-plated steel
71 × 112 × 43 in.
(180.5 × 284.5 × 109 cm).

Collection

Sydney and Rita Adler, Sarasota, Florida, 1980; acquired directly from the artist.

Exhibitions

The John and Mable Ringling Museum of Art, Sarasota, Florida. *International Florida Artists Exhibition*, listed. February 26–April 26, 1981.

Notes

The sculpture is signed.

650

Broken Toe 1980–81

Painted and chromium-plated steel
117½ × 87½ × 20½ in.
(298.5 × 222 × 52 cm).

Collection

Dia Art Foundation, New York, New York, 1981; acquired directly from the artist.

Exhibitions

Dia Art Foundation, New York, New York. *John Chamberlain Sculpture: An Extended Exhibition*. March 19–November 27, 1982.

The John and Mable Ringling Museum, Sarasota, Florida. *John Chamberlain Reliefs 1960–1982*, color illus. p. 81. January 28–March 27, 1983.

Dia Art Foundation, the Art Museum of the Pecos, Marfa, Texas. *An Exhibition of Sculpture by John Chamberlain*. From May 7, 1983.

References

Gary Indiana, "John Chamberlain's Irregular Set," *Art in America*, vol. 71, no. 10 (November 1983), color illus. p. 215.

651

Charcoal Fudge 1981

Painted and chromium-plated steel
72 × 108 × 48 in.
(183 × 274 × 122 cm).

Collection

Xavier Fourcade, Inc., New York, New York.

Exhibitions

Xavier Fourcade, Inc., New York, New York. *John Chamberlain: New Sculpture*, color illus. cover and color illus. February 25–March 31, 1984.

References

Vivien Raynor, "Art," *New York Times*, March 2, 1984.

652

Dumb Name (One for Maurice) 1980–81

Painted and chromium-plated steel
68 × 60 × 32 in.
(173 × 152.5 × 81.5 cm).

Collection

Dia Art Foundation, New York, New York, 1981; acquired directly from the artist.

Exhibitions

Dia Art Foundation, Essex, Connecticut. *Chamberlain Gardens, Essex*. May–November 1982 and 1984.

Dia Art Foundation, New York, New York. *John Chamberlain Sculpture: An Extended Exhibition*. December 10, 1982–July 30, 1983.

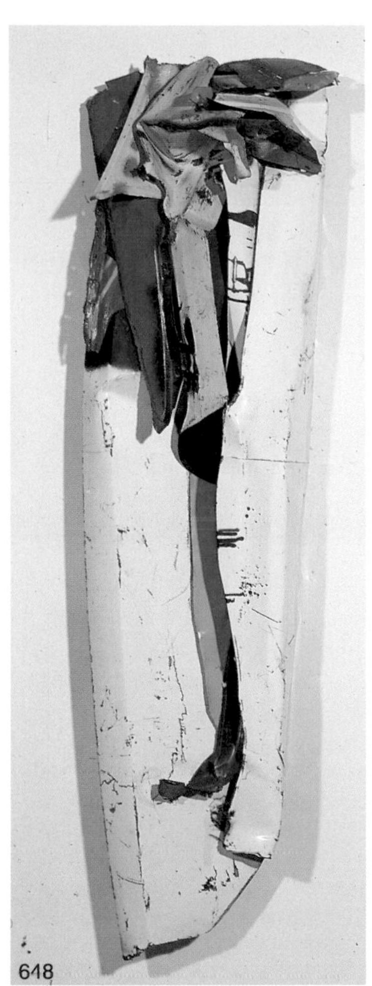

648

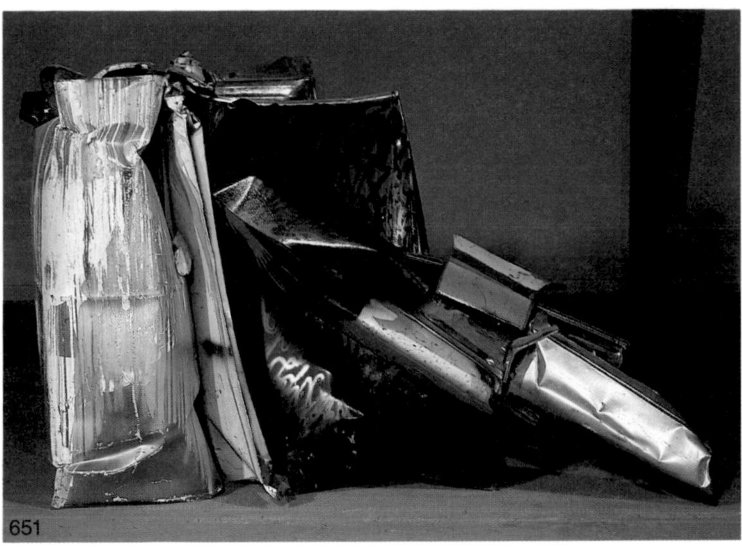

651

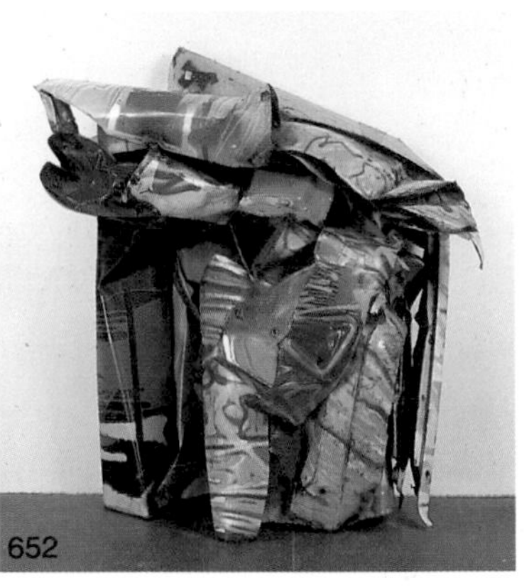

652

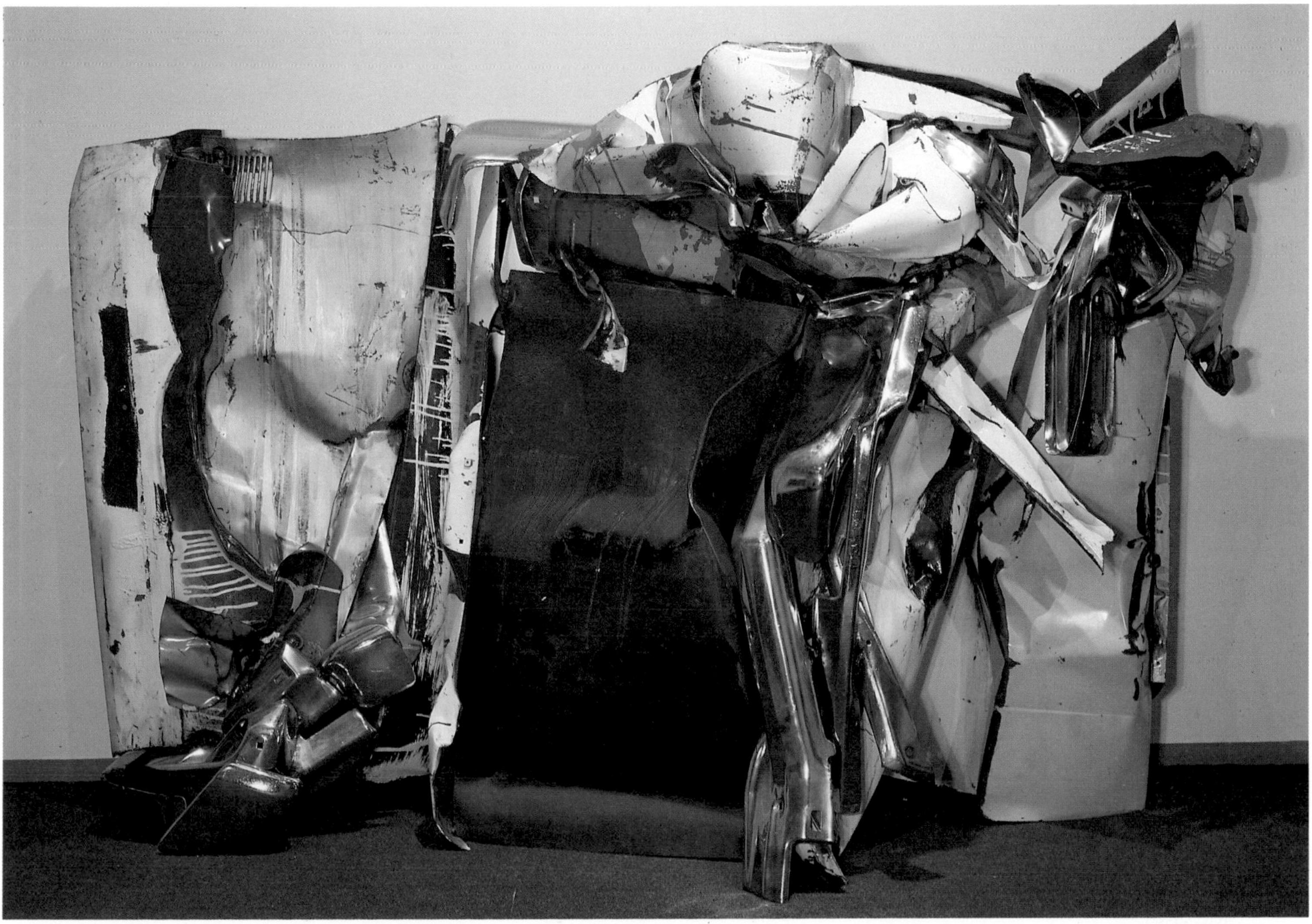

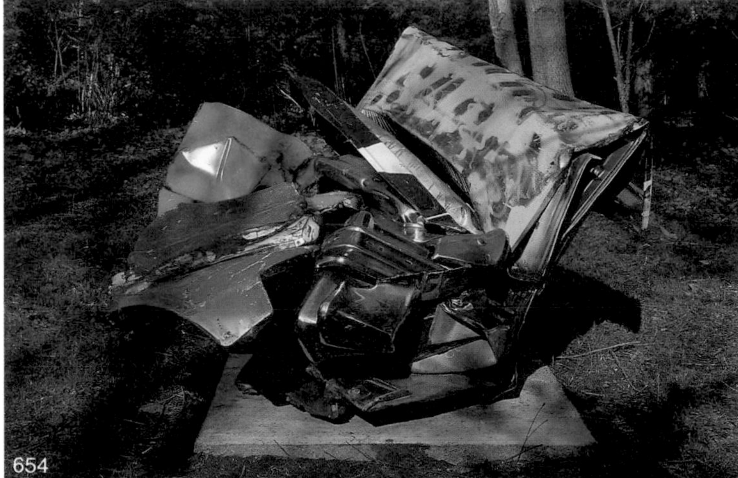
654

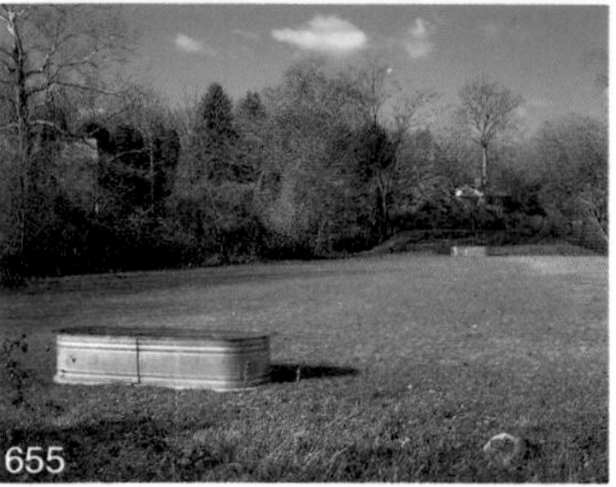
655

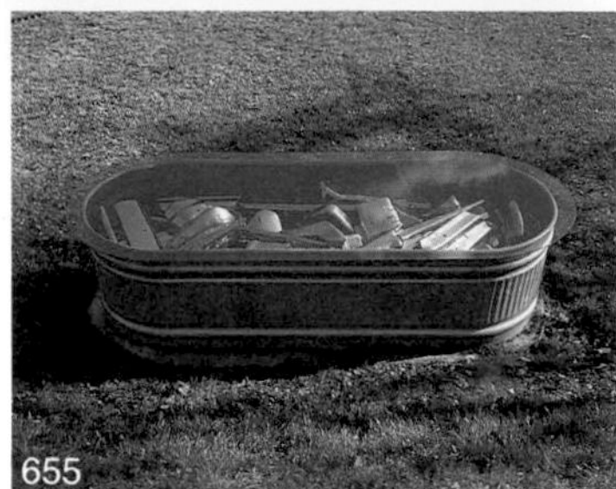
655

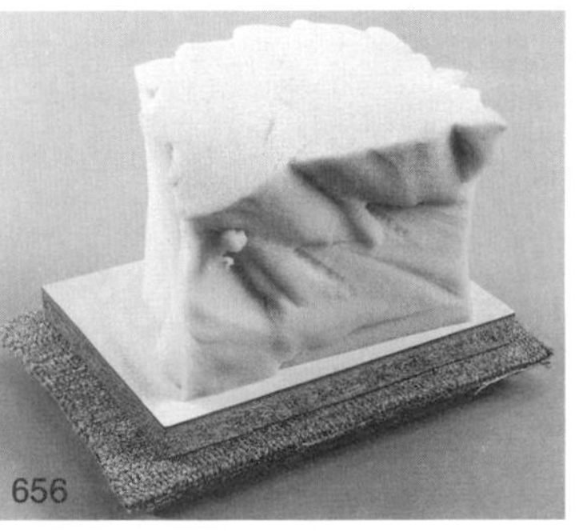
656

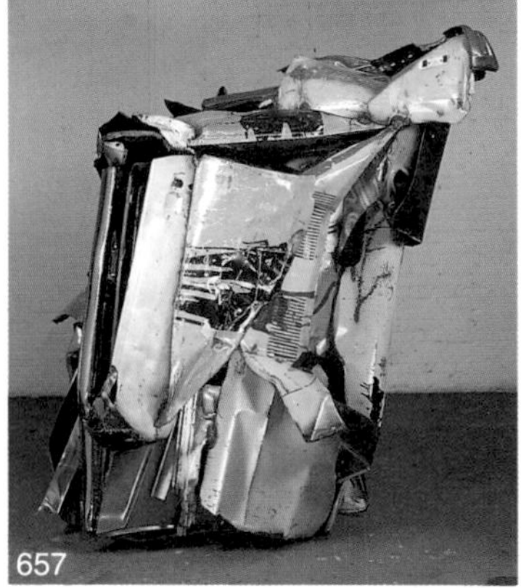
657

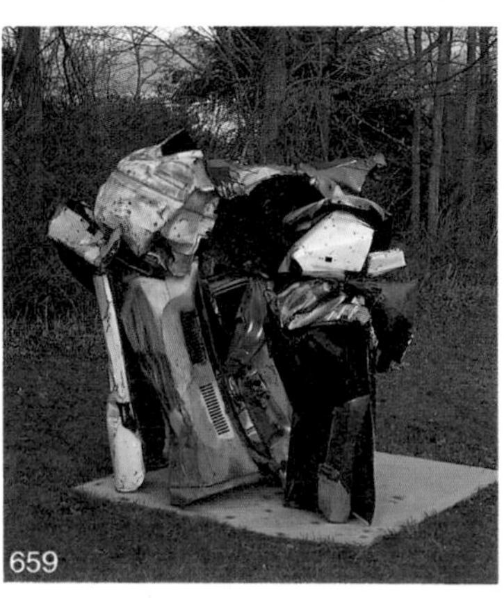
659

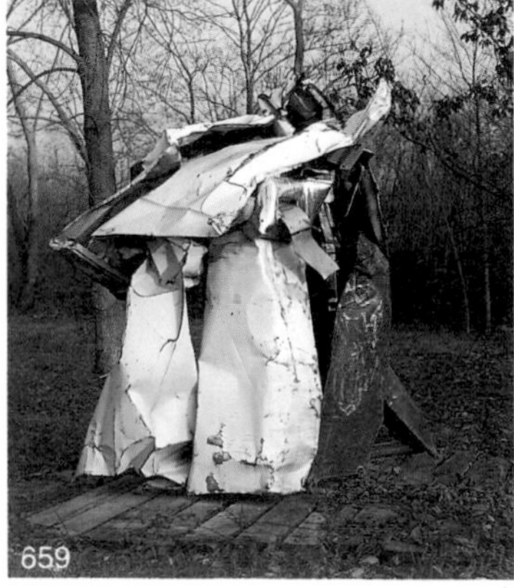
659

653

Grandma's Hat 1981

Painted and chromium-plated steel
72 × 73 × 61 in.
(183 × 185.5 × 155 cm).

Collection

Dia Art Foundation, New York, New York, 1981; acquired directly from the artist.

Exhibitions

Dia Art Foundation, Essex, Connecticut. *Chamberlain Gardens, Essex.* May–November 1982.

Dia Art Foundation, New York, New York. *John Chamberlain Sculpture: An Extended Exhibition.* December 10, 1982–July 30, 1983 and September 22, 1983–February 23, 1985.

References

Gary Indiana, "John Chamberlain's Irregular Set," *Art in America*, vol. 71, no. 10 (November 1983), p. 216.

654

Hurray for Bernie Galvez (3¢ under the Limit) 1981

Painted and chromium-plated steel
43 × 54 × 73 in.
(109 × 137 × 185.5 cm).

Collection

Dia Art Foundation, New York, New York; acquired directly from the artist.

Exhibitions

Dia Art Foundation, Essex, Connecticut. *Chamberlain Gardens, Essex.* May–November 1982, 1983, and 1984.

655

Memorial to Lost Souls at Sea 1980–81

Galvanized and chromium-plated steel, earth, grass, glass, and water, covering an area measuring approximately 135 × 70 feet (41.1 × 21.3 meters), which includes two troughs, one measuring 24 × 96 × 24 in. (61 × 243.5 × 61 cm), the other 24 × 60 × 24 in. (61 × 152.5 × 61 cm).

Collection

Dia Art Foundation, New York, New York, 1981; acquired directly from the artist.

Exhibitions

Dia Art Foundation, Essex, Connecticut. *Chamberlain Gardens, Essex.* May–November 1982, 1983, and 1984.

References

Gary Indiana, "John Chamberlain's Irregular Set," *Art in America*, vol. 71, no. 10 (November 1983), color illus. p. 213.

Notes

This sculpture was made specifically for the exhibition location in Essex, Connecticut. It was dismantled in 1984.

656

Mesa 1981

Urethane foam, wood, and carpet
8 × 11 × 8 in.
(20.5 × 28 × 20.5 cm).

Collection

Dia Art Foundation, New York, New York; acquired directly from the artist.

Exhibitions

Dia Art Foundation, Essex, Connecticut. *Chamberlain Gardens, Essex.* May–November 1982 and 1983.

657

Pigmeat's E♭ Bluesong 1981

Painted and chromium-plated steel
72 × 73 × 61 in.
(183 × 185.5 × 155 cm).

Collection

Dia Art Foundation, New York, New York, 1981; acquired directly from the artist.

Exhibitions

Dia Art Foundation, Essex, Connecticut. *Chamberlain Gardens, Essex.* May–November 1982 and 1984.

Dia Art Foundation, New York, New York. *John Chamberlain Sculpture: An Extended Exhibition.* December 10, 1982–July 30, 1983.

658

Schnoggensie 1981

Painted and chromium-plated steel
112 × 56 × 28 in.
(284.5 × 142 × 71 cm).

Collection

Lorraine Chamberlain, Essex, Connecticut, 1983; acquired directly from the artist.

659

Slippery Axis 1981

Painted and chromium-plated steel
89½ × 87½ × 58½ in.
(227.5 × 222 × 148.5 cm).

Collection

Dia Art Foundation, New York, New York, 1981; acquired directly from the artist.

Exhibitions

Dia Art Foundation, Essex, Connecticut. *Chamberlain Gardens, Essex.* May–November 1982, 1983, and 1984.

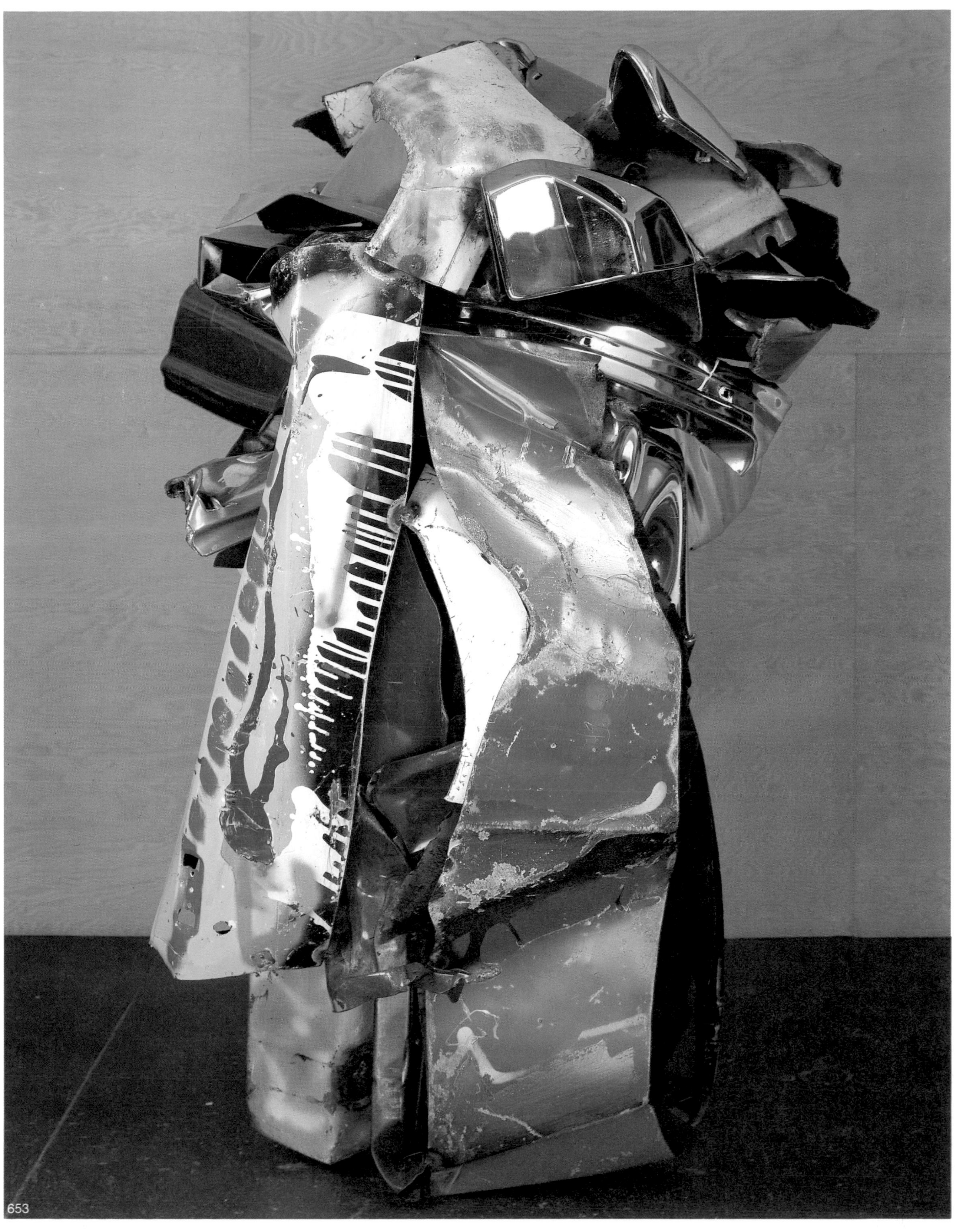

653

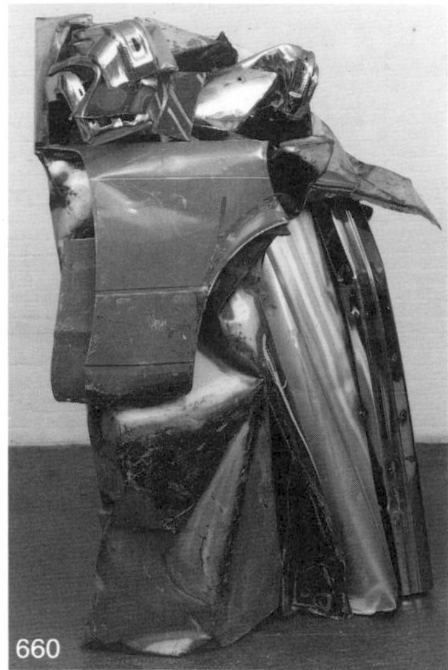
660

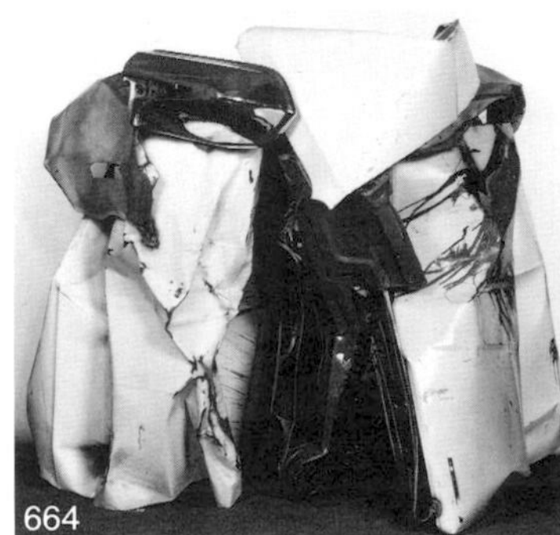
664

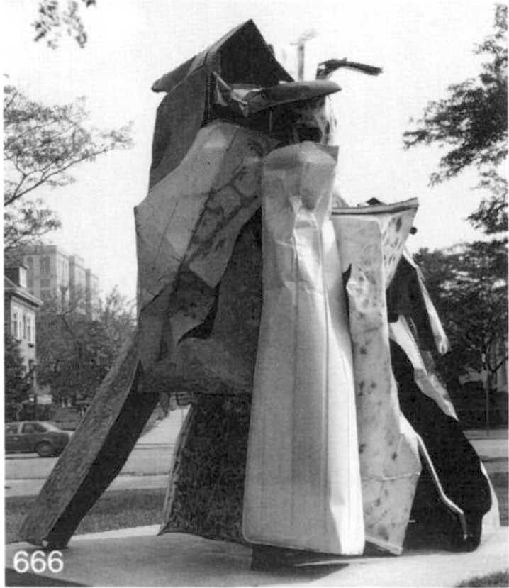
666

660

Slow Dancing to the News 1981
Painted and chromium-plated steel
69 × 59 × 54 in.
(175.5 × 150 × 137 cm).

Collection
Dia Art Foundation, New York, New York, 1981; acquired directly from the artist.

Exhibitions
Dia Art Foundation, Essex, Connecticut. *Chamberlain Gardens, Essex*. May–November 1982.

Dia Art Foundation, New York, New York. *John Chamberlain Sculpture: An Extended Exhibition*. December 10, 1982–July 30, 1983 and September 22, 1983–February 23, 1985.

661

Stoneyknob 1981
Painted and chromium-plated steel
69 × 67 × 40 in.
(175 × 170 × 101.5 cm).

Collection
Dia Art Foundation, New York, New York, 1981; acquired directly from the artist.

Exhibitions
Dia Art Foundation, Essex, Connecticut. *Chamberlain Gardens, Essex*. May–November 1982.

Dia Art Foundation, New York, New York. *John Chamberlain Sculpture: An Extended Exhibition*. December 10, 1982–July 30, 1983.

References
Gary Indiana, "John Chamberlain's Irregular Set," *Art in America*, vol. 71, no. 10 (November 1983), p. 216.

662

Tropical Hot Dog Night 1981
Painted and chromium-plated steel
46 × 47 × 20½ in.
(117 × 119.5 × 52 cm).

Collection
Sabine Knust, Munich, 1982.

Provenance
Thordis Moeller, New York, New York, 1981.

Exhibitions
The John and Mable Ringling Museum of Art, Sarasota, Florida. *John Chamberlain Reliefs 1960–1982*, color illus. p. 83. January 28–March 27, 1983.

Palacio de Cristal, Parque del Retiro, Madrid. *John Chamberlain/Esculturas*, color illus. p. 49. January 26–March 31, 1984.

References
Gary Indiana, "John Chamberlain's Irregular Set," *Art in America*, vol. 71, no. 10 (November 1983), color illus. p. 216.

663

Vandam Billy 1981
Painted and chromium-plated steel
65 × 68 × 42 in.
(165 × 173 × 106.5 cm).

Collection
Xavier Fourcade, Inc., New York, New York, 1985.

Provenance
Dia Art Foundation, New York, New York, 1982.

Exhibitions
Dia Art Foundation, Essex, Connecticut. *Chamberlain Gardens, Essex*. May–November 1982.

Dia Art Foundation, New York, New York. *John Chamberlain Sculpture: An Extended Exhibition*. December 10, 1982–July 30, 1983 and September 22, 1983–February 23, 1985.

Sotheby Parke-Bernet, Inc., *Twenty-three Works from the Dia Art Foundation*, cat. no. 21, color illus. November 5, 1985.

References
Gary Indiana, "John Chamberlain's Irregular Set," *Art in America*, vol. 71, no. 10 (November 1983), p. 216.

664

Voyage En Douce 1980–81
Painted and chromium-plated steel
60½ × 83½ × 60 in.
(153.5 × 212 × 152.5 cm).

Collection
Dia Art Foundation, New York, New York, 1981; acquired directly from the artist.

Exhibitions
Dia Art Foundation, Essex, Connecticut. *Chamberlain Gardens, Essex*. May–November 1982, 1983, and 1984.

665

Winter Editions (Cocola PP) 1981
Painted and chromium-plated steel
84 × 72 × 46 in.
(213.5 × 183 × 117 cm).

Collection
Dia Art Foundation, New York, New York, 1981; acquired directly from the artist.

Exhibitions
Dia Art Foundation, Essex, Connecticut. *Chamberlain Gardens, Essex*. May–November 1982 and 1984.

Dia Art Foundation, New York, New York. *John Chamberlain Sculpture: An Extended Exhibition*. December 10, 1982–July 20, 1983.

666

Deliquescence 1979–81
Painted and chromium-plated steel
192 × 120 × 132 in.
(487.5 × 305 × 335.5 cm).

Collection
United States General Services Administration, 1982; a commissioned work installed on the campus of Wayne State University, Detroit, Michigan.

References
Gary Indiana, "John Chamberlain's Irregular Set," *Art in America*, vol. 71, no. 10 (November 1983), p. 216.

Duncan Smith, "In the Heart of the Tinman: An Essay on John Chamberlain," *Artforum*, vol. 22, no. 5 (January 1984), illus. of maquette, p. 40.

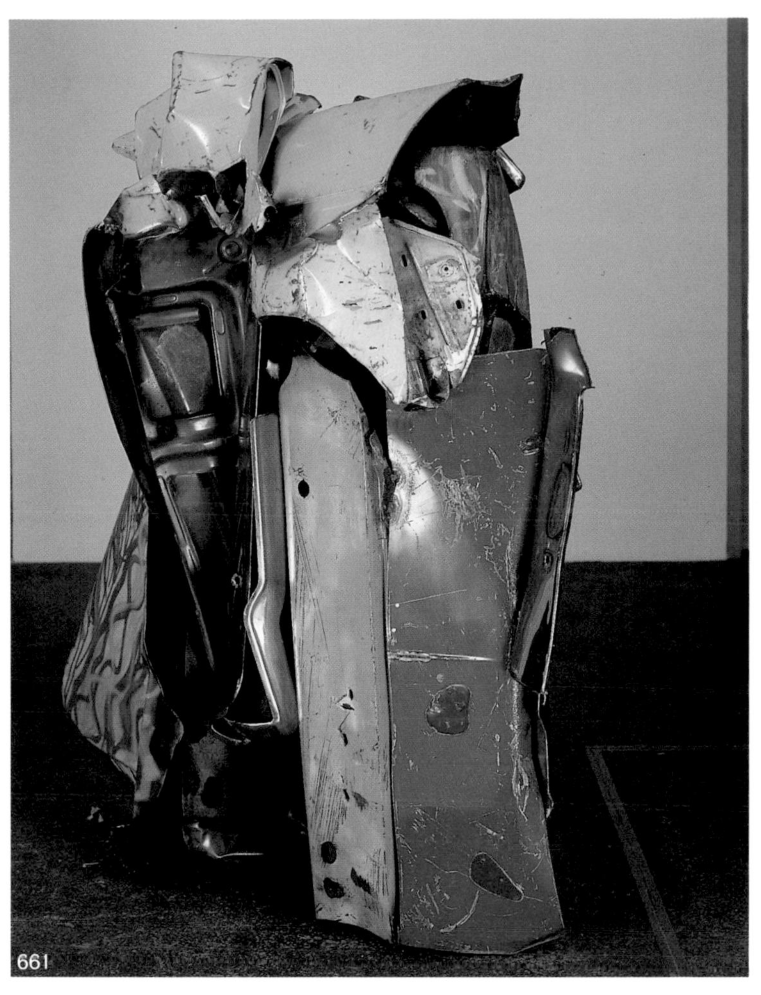
661

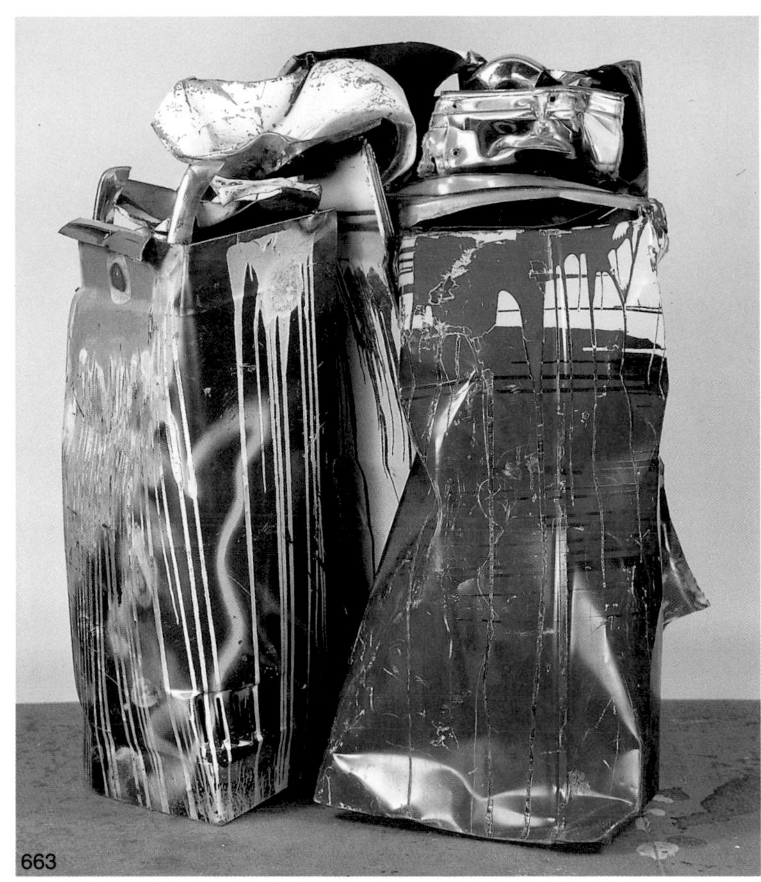
663

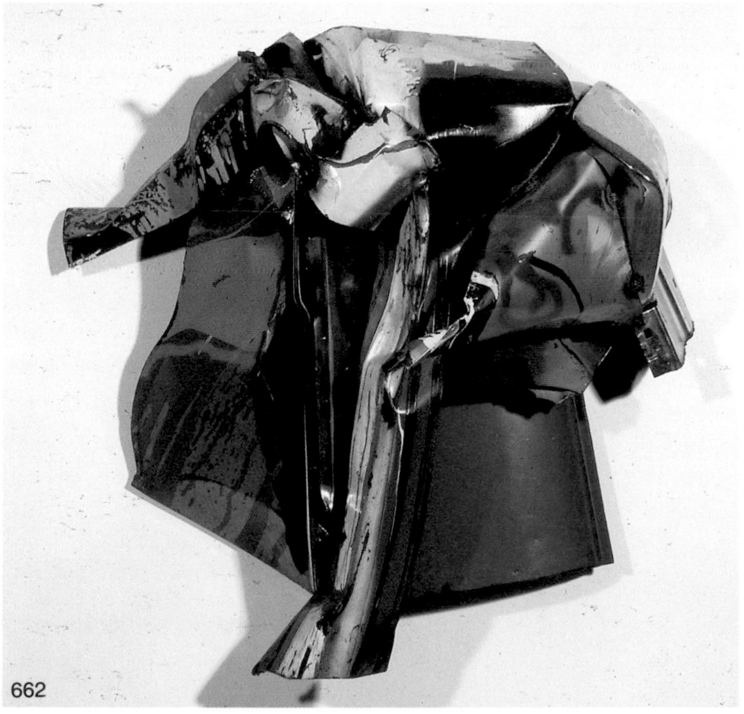
662

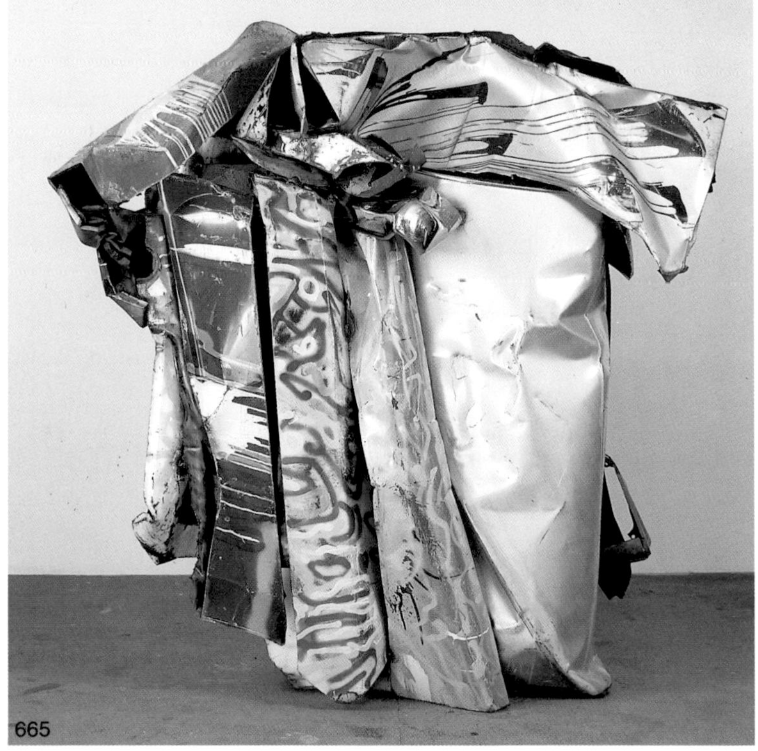
665

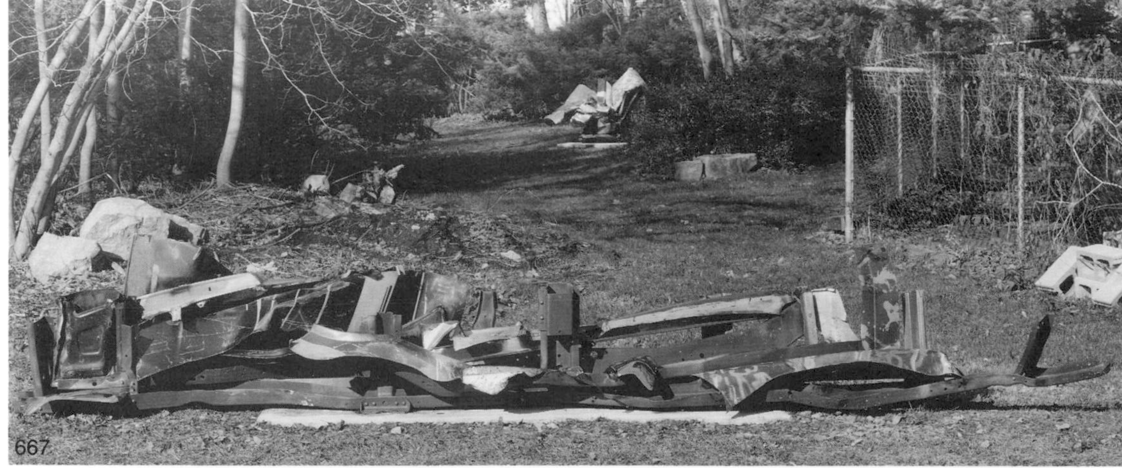
667

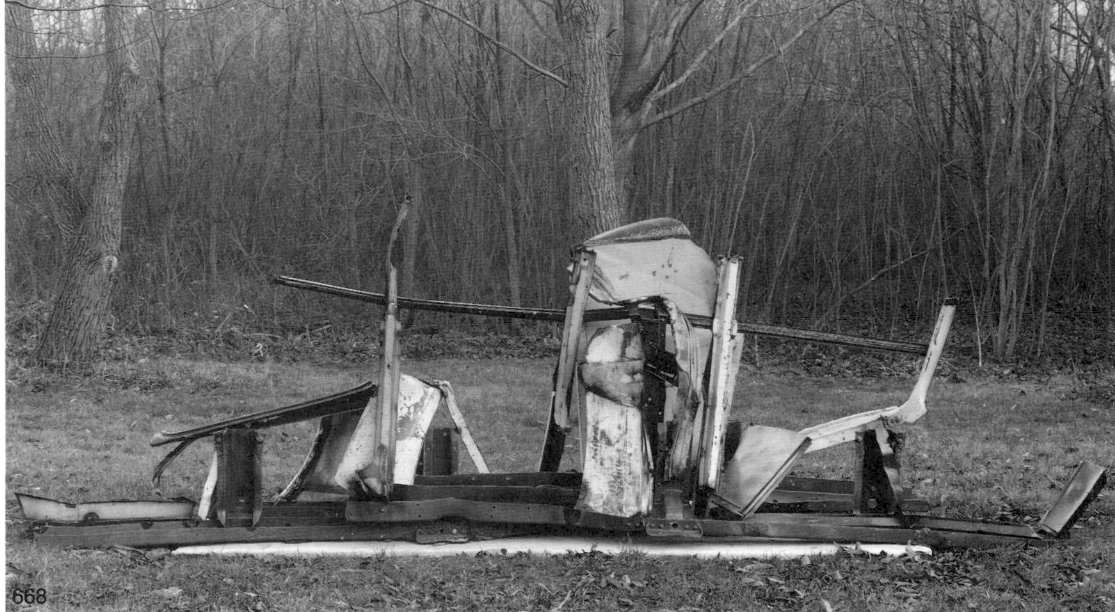
668

In June 1981 Chamberlain was working at an outdoor studio at the back of a junkyard in Osprey, Florida, completing *Deliquescence*, the sculpture in Detroit commissioned by the General Services Administration. (See cat. no. 666.) Automobile-chassis bases were used for the armature of the sixteen-foot sculpture, and many unused lengths of channel steel were piled together in an area of the studio. Chamberlain spotted them one day as he was driving away from the studio and found that they fit a notion of horizontality that had been developing in his mind. This became the basis of the *Armada* series, the first series of low, horizontal floor sculptures, which later came to be known as the *Gondolas*. Of the four works in the *Armada* series, *Bluemoose* was the first made, followed by *Suchard Express*, *Faint Paint*, and *Fiddling Fiddler*. These titles were changed in 1984 to *Gondola Herman Melville*, *Gondola T. S. Eliot*, *Gondola Henry Wadsworth Longfellow*, and *Gondola W. H. Auden*, respectively, in order to make them agree with the titles given to the later *Gondola* series of 1982. This series was titled after poets and fiction writers; Chamberlain had been associated with or introduced to many of them and/or their work at Black Mountain College.

667

Gondola Henry Wadsworth Longfellow 1981

Painted and chromium-plated steel
30 × 202 × 40 in.
(76 × 513 × 101.5 cm).

Collection

Dia Art Foundation, New York, New York, 1981; acquired directly from the artist.

Exhibitions

Dia Art Foundation, Essex, Connecticut. *Chamberlain Gardens, Essex*. May–November 1982, 1983, and 1984.

References

Gary Indiana, "John Chamberlain's Irregular Set," *Art in America*, vol. 71, no. 10 (November 1983), p. 215.

Notes

The sculpture was originally titled *Faint Paint*. It was retitled by the artist in 1984.

668

Gondola Herman Melville 1981

Painted and chromium-plated steel
51 × 170 × 34 in.
(129.5 × 432 × 86.5 cm).

Collection

Dia Art Foundation, New York, New York, 1981; acquired directly from the artist.

Exhibitions

Dia Art Foundation, Essex, Connecticut. *Chamberlain Gardens, Essex.* May–November 1982, 1983, and 1984.

Notes

The sculpture was originally titled *Bluemoose*. It was retitled by the artist in 1984.

669

Gondola T. S. Eliot 1981

Painted and chromium-plated steel
31½ × 215 × 36 in.
(80 × 546 × 91.5 cm).

Collection

Dia Art Foundation, New York, New York, 1981; acquired directly from the artist.

Exhibitions

Dia Art Foundation, Essex, Connecticut. *Chamberlain Gardens, Essex.* May–November 1982, 1983, and 1984.

Notes

The sculpture was originally titled *Suchard Express*. It was retitled by the artist in 1984.

670

Gondola W. H. Auden 1981

Painted and chromium-plated steel
32½ × 212 × 31 in.
(82.5 × 538.5 × 78.5 cm).

Collection

Dia Art Foundation, New York, New York, 1981; acquired directly from the artist.

Exhibitions

Dia Art Foundation, Essex, Connecticut. *Chamberlain Gardens, Essex.* May–November 1982, 1983, and 1984.

Notes

The sculpture was originally titled *Fiddling Fiddler*. It was retitled by the artist in 1984.

671

Gondola Charles Olson 1982

Painted and chromium-plated steel
47 × 205 × 45 in.
(119.5 × 521 × 114.5 cm).

Collection

Xavier Fourcade, Inc., New York, New York.

References

Gary indiana, "John Chamberlain's Irregular Set," *Art in America*, vol. 71, no. 10 (November 1983), color illus. pp. 210–11.

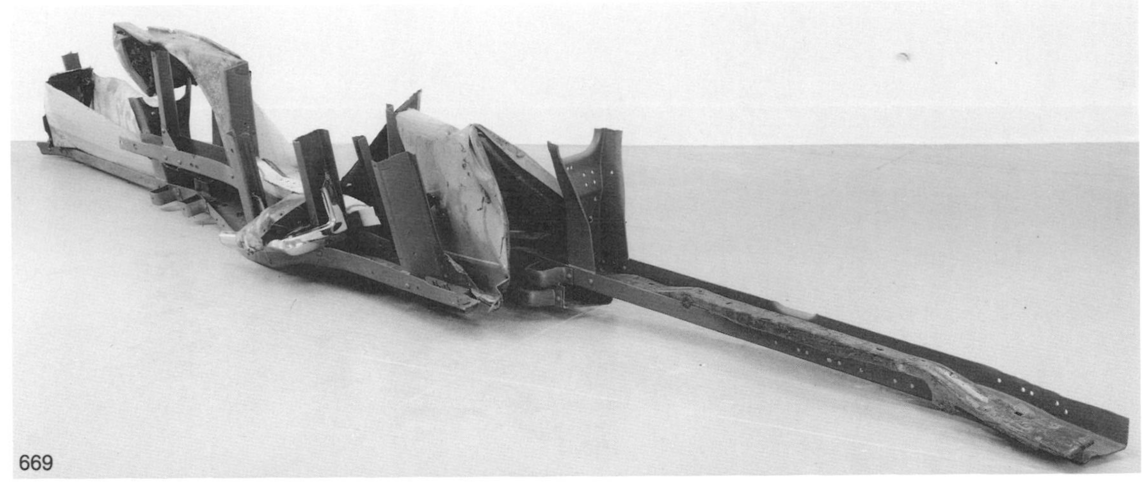

669

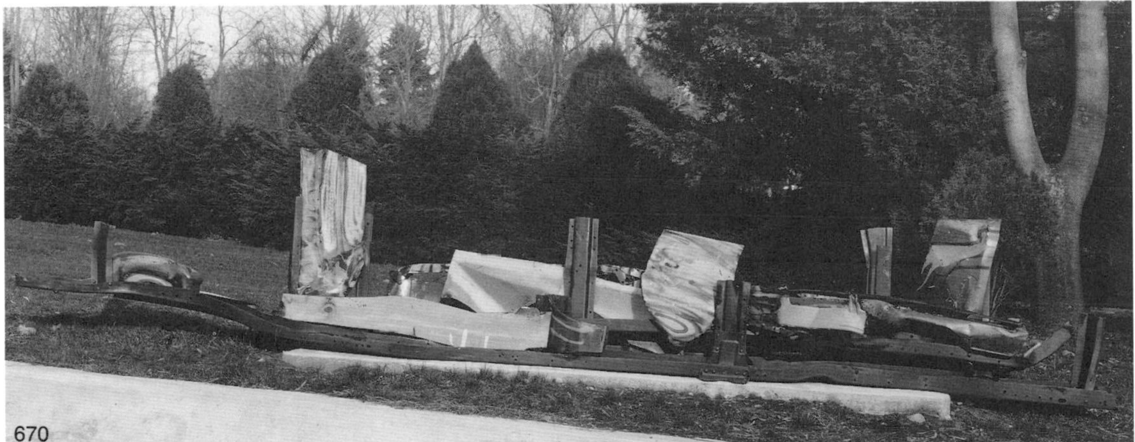

670

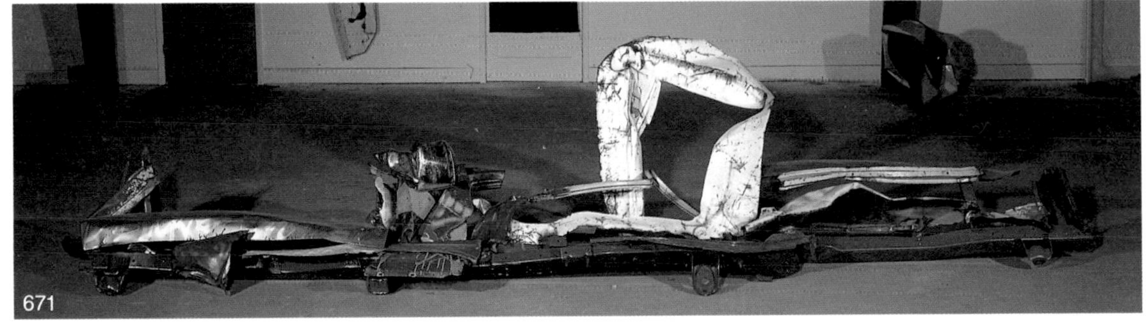

671

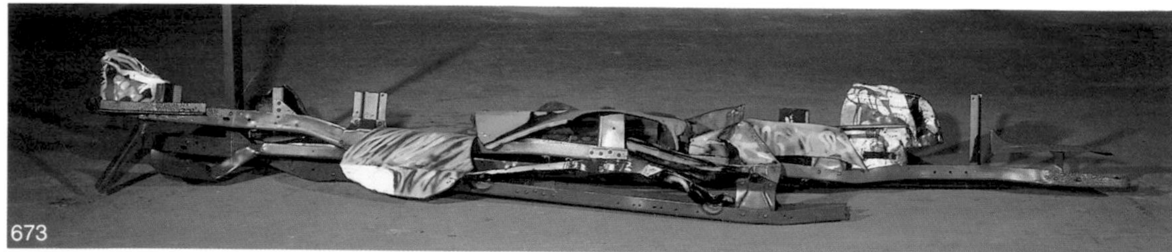
673

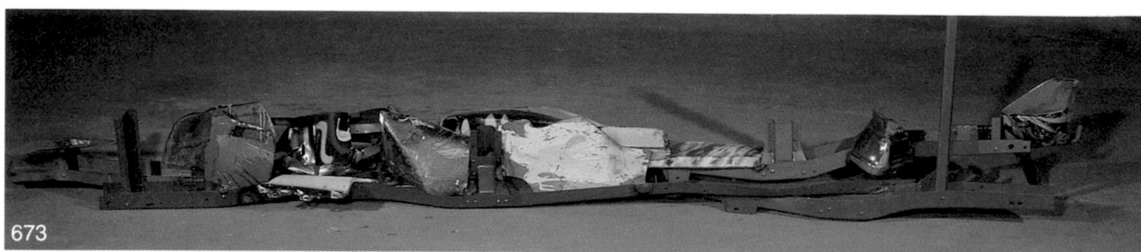
673

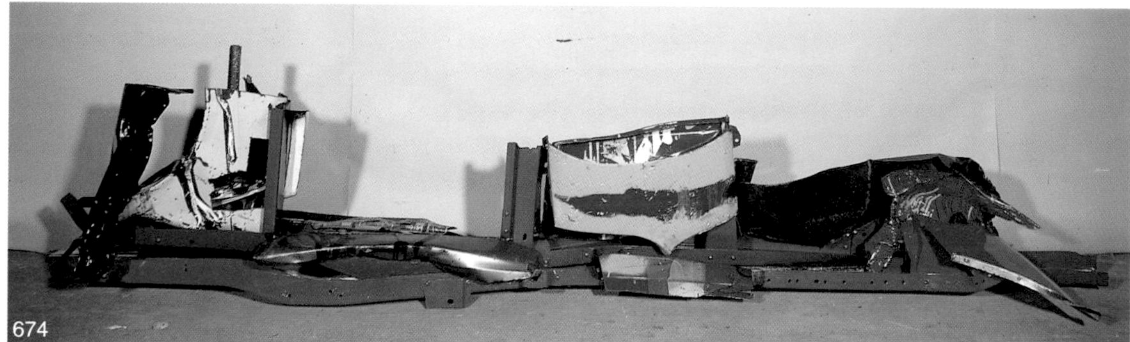
674

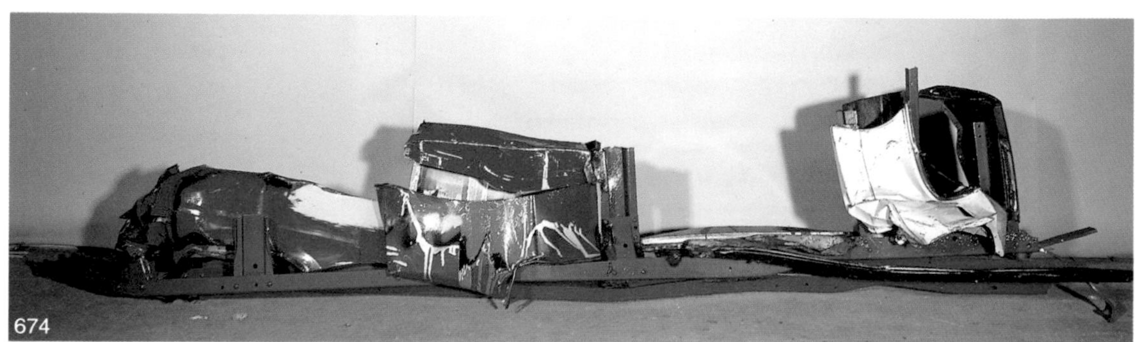
674

672

Gondola Ezra Pound 1982

Painted and chromium-plated steel
29½ × 167 × 73 in.
(75 × 424 × 185.5 cm).

Collection

Xavier Fourcade, Inc., New York, New York.

Exhibitions

Dia Art Foundation, the Art Museum of the Pecos, Marfa, Texas. *An Exhibition of Sculpture by John Chamberlain*. From May 7, 1983.

Notes

The sculpture is signed by the artist. It is in two parts, measuring: 29 × 152 × 44½ in. (74 × 386 × 113 cm) and 29½ × 146½ × 32 in. (75.5 × 372.5 × 81.5 cm).

673

Gondola Hart Crane 1982

Painted and chromium-plated steel
42 × 189 × 37½ in.
(107 × 480 × 95 cm).

Collection

Thordis Moeller, New York, New York, 1985; acquired directly from the artist.

Exhibitions

Kassel, West Germany. *Documenta 7*, vol. 2, illus. p. 79. June 19–August 15, 1982.

Städtische Kunsthalle, Düsseldorf. *Borofsky, Chamberlain, Dahn, Knoebel*. January 8–18, 1983.

Palacio de Cristal, Parque del Retiro, Madrid. *John Chamberlain/Esculturas*, color illus. p. 57. January 26–March 31, 1984.

Notes

Originally called *Gondola Denton*, the sculpture was retitled by the artist in 1983.

674

Gondola Jack Kerouac 1982

Painted and chromium-plated steel
34 × 151 × 30 in.
(86.5 × 383.5 × 76 cm).

Collection

Xavier Fourcade, Inc., New York, New York.

Exhibitions

The Art Galleries, University of California, Santa Barbara. *John Chamberlain/Alan Saret—Contemporary Sculpture*. March 27–April 29, 1984.

Margo Leavin Gallery, Los Angeles, California. *John Chamberlain*. March 4–30, 1985.

References

John Chamberlain: New Sculpture (New York: Xavier Fourcade, Inc., 1984), color illus.

675

Gondola Marianne Moore 1982

Painted and chromium-plated steel
37 × 206 × 33 in.
(94 × 523 × 84 cm).

Collection

Thordis Moeller, New York, New York, 1985; acquired directly from the artist.

Exhibitions

Kassel, West Germany. *Documenta 7*, vol. 2, color illus. p. 79. June 19–August 15, 1982.

Städtische Kunsthalle, Düsseldorf. *Borofsky, Chamberlain, Dahn, Knoebel*. January 8–18, 1983.

Palacio de Cristal, Parque del Retiro, Madrid. *John Chamberlain/Esculturas*, color illus. p. 59. January 26–March 31, 1984.

References

Jean-Christophe Ammann, "Documenta: Reality and Desire," *Flash Art*, no. 109 (November 1982), color illus. p. 38.

Notes

Originally called *Gondola Theodosia*, the sculpture was retitled by the artist in 1983.

676

Gondola Walt Whitman 1981–82

Painted and chromium-plated steel
24 × 162 × 20 in.
(61 × 411.5 × 51 cm).

Collection

Xavier Fourcade, Inc., New York, New York.

677

Gondola William Carlos Williams 1982

Painted and chromium-plated steel
36 × 215 × 47 in.
(91.5 × 546 × 119.5 cm).

Collection

Dia Art Foundation, New York, New York, 1982; acquired directly from the artist.

Exhibitions

Dia Art Foundation, the Art Museum of the Pecos, Marfa, Texas. *An Exhibition of Sculpture by John Chamberlain*. From May 7, 1983.

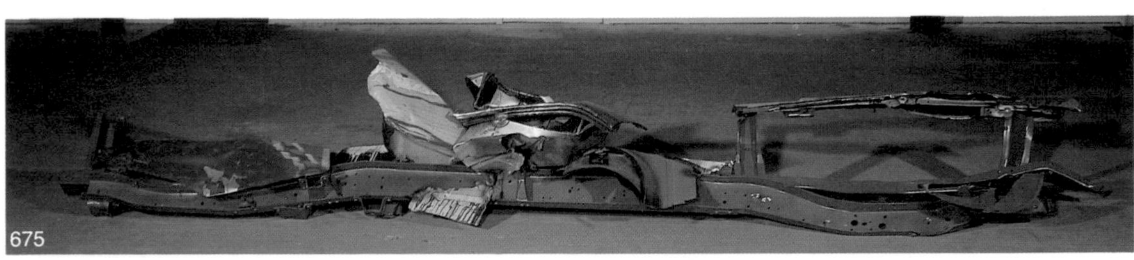
675

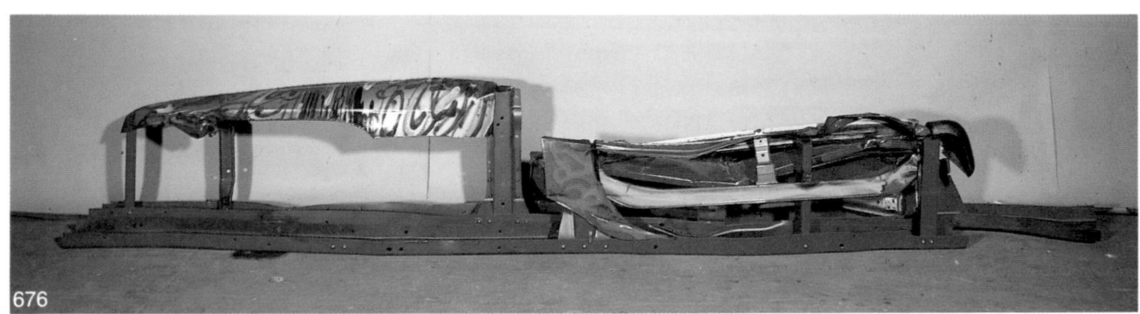
676

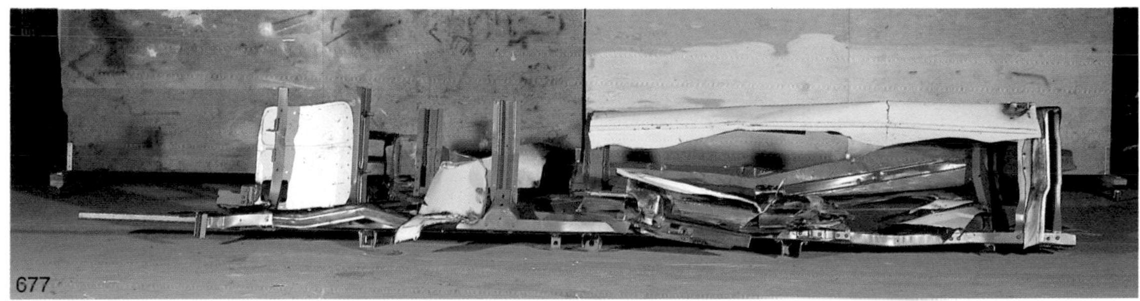
677

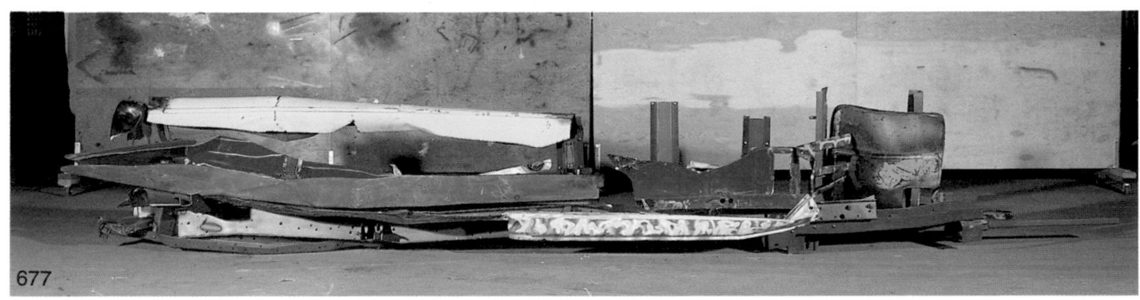
677

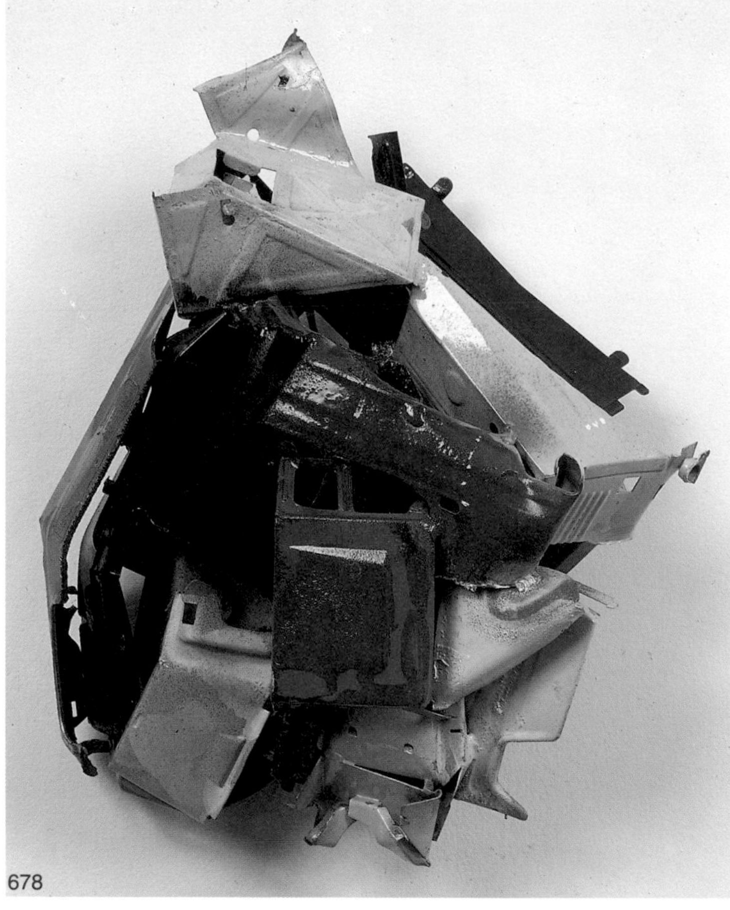
678

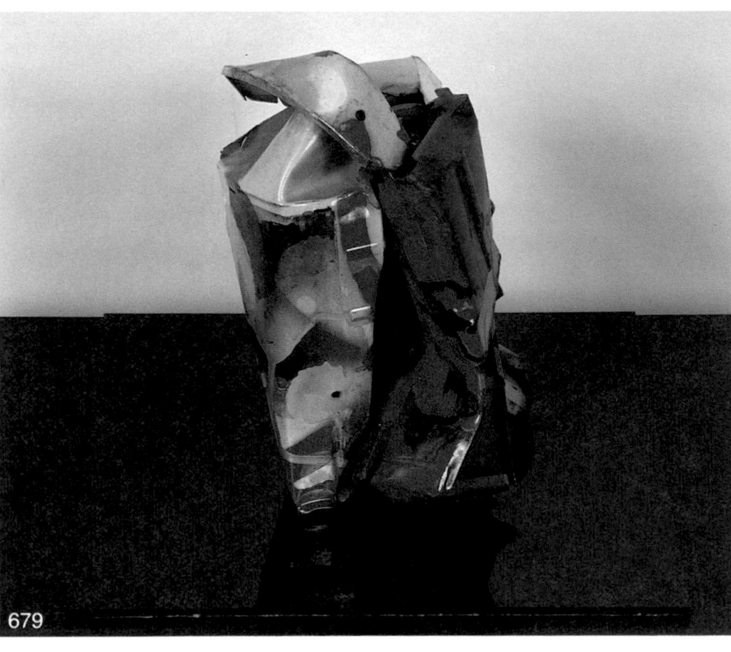
679

In 1981 Chamberlain accumulated a "Tonka Toy junkyard" in his studio in Sarasota, Florida. With these miniature toy parts he began a series of small sculptures called *Tonks*. Each title includes the date of the sculpture and its number in series. A few have been titled without following this system. The *Tonks* appear in the catalogue raisonné grouped at the end of each year.

678

Tonk #0–81 1981

Painted and chromium-plated steel
13 × 10 × 6 in.
(33 × 25.5 × 15.5 cm).

Collection

Thordis Moeller, New York, New York; acquired directly from the artist.

Exhibitions

The Butler Institute of American Art, Youngstown, Ohio. *John Chamberlain: Sculpture and Work on Paper*, cat. no. 11. May 1–29, 1983.

Notes

The sculpture was originally titled *None*. It is the first of the *Tonks*, the pieces made of Tonka Toy parts.

679

Tonk c. 1981

Painted steel
9½ × 8 × 7½ in.
(24 × 20.5 × 19 cm).

Collection

Thordis Moeller, New York, New York; acquired directly from the artist.

680

Tonk c. 1981

Painted steel
6½ × 9 × 5 in.
(16.5 × 23 × 12.5 cm).

Collection

Allan Stone, New York, New York; acquired directly from the artist.

681

Ertl II 1981

Painted steel
17½ × 11½ × 9½ in.
(44.5 × 29 × 24 cm).

Collection

Dr. and Mrs. Steven Feldman, Sarasota, Florida, 1982; acquired directly from the artist.

Notes

Ertl II is a sculpture in the *Tonk* series.

682

Graham's Cracker 1981

Painted steel
8 × 12 × 12 in.
(20.5 × 30.5 × 30.5 cm).

Collection

Edward Leffingwell, Youngstown, Ohio, 1982; acquired directly from the artist.

Exhibitions

The Butler Institute of American Art, Youngstown, Ohio. *John Chamberlain: Sculpture and Work on Paper*, cat. no. 10, illus. p. 20. May 1–29, 1983.

Notes

Graham's Cracker is a sculpture in the *Tonk* series.

683

Added Pleasure 1982

Painted and chromium-plated steel
111 × 53 × 36 in.
(282 × 134.5 × 91.5 cm).

Collection

The John and Mable Ringling Museum of Art, Sarasota, Florida, 1983; acquired directly from the artist.

Exhibitions

The John and Mable Ringling Museum of Art, Sarasota, Florida. *John Chamberlain Reliefs 1960–1982*, color illus. p. 35. January 28–March 27, 1983.

Center for the Fine Arts, Miami, Florida. *In Quest of Excellence*, cat. no. 202, p. 211. January 14–April 22, 1984.

References

Gary Indiana, "John Chamberlain's Irregular Set," *Art in America*, vol. 71, no. 10 (November 1983), color illus. pp. 214, 216.

Notes

Parts of the destroyed sculpture *P. E. Island*, 1974, were incorporated into *Added Pleasure*. See cat. no. 494.

684

A Virgin's Mile 1982

Painted and chromium-plated steel
77 × 72 × 89 in.
(195.5 × 183 × 226 cm).

Collection

Nathan Manilow Sculpture Park, Governors State University, Park Forest South, Illinois, 1982; acquired directly from the artist.

685

Crossed Socks 1982

Painted and chromium-plated steel
124 × 100 × 47 in.
(315 × 254 × 119.5 cm).

Collection

Xavier Fourcade, Inc., New York, New York.

Exhibitions

Leo Castelli Gallery, New York, New York. *John Chamberlain*. November 27–December 18, 1982.

Brüglinger Park, Basel. *Skulptur im 20. Jahrhundert*. June 2–September 30, 1984.

Galerie Rudolf Zwirner, Cologne. *John Chamberlain*. November 13–December 31, 1984.

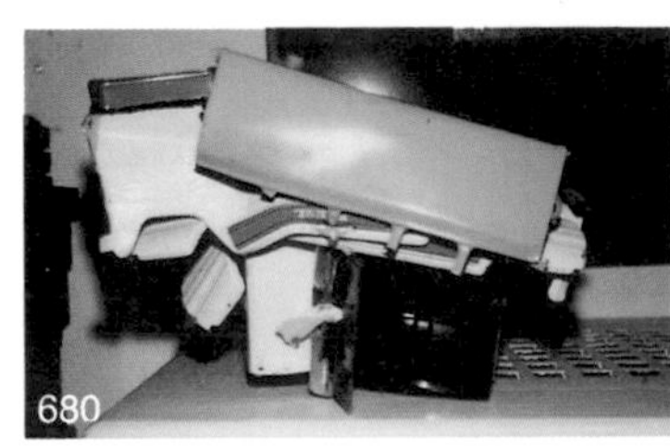

680

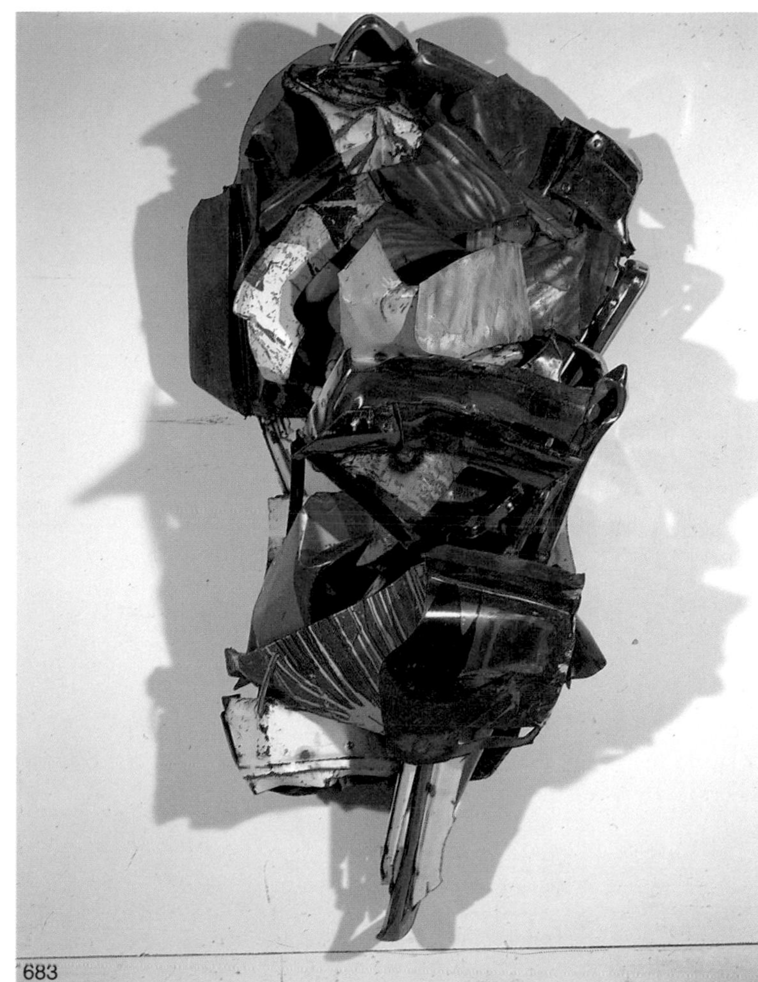

683

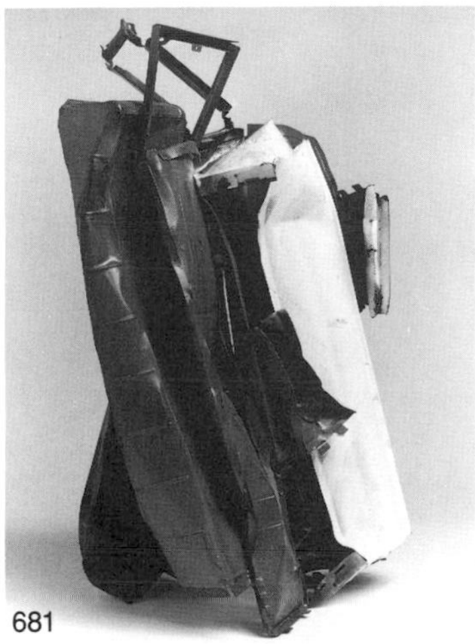

681

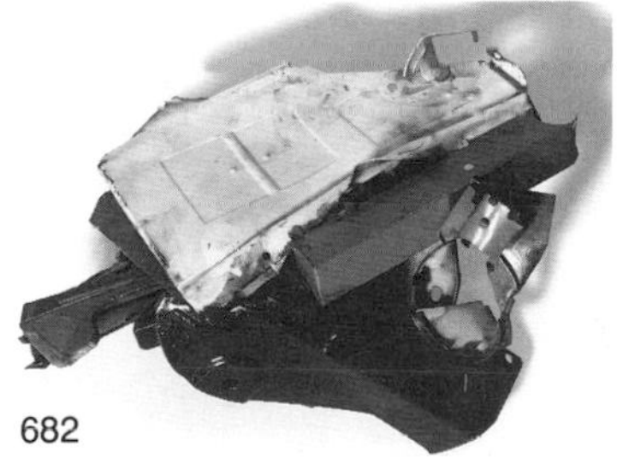

682

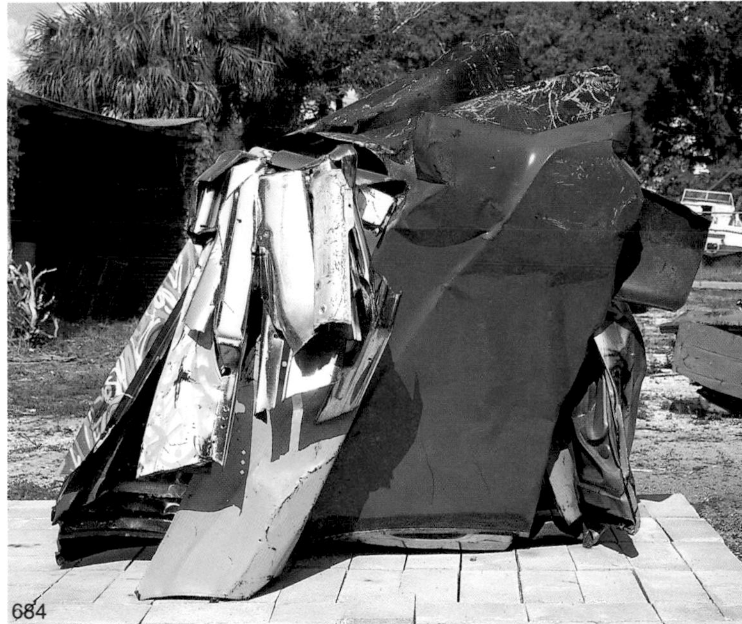

684

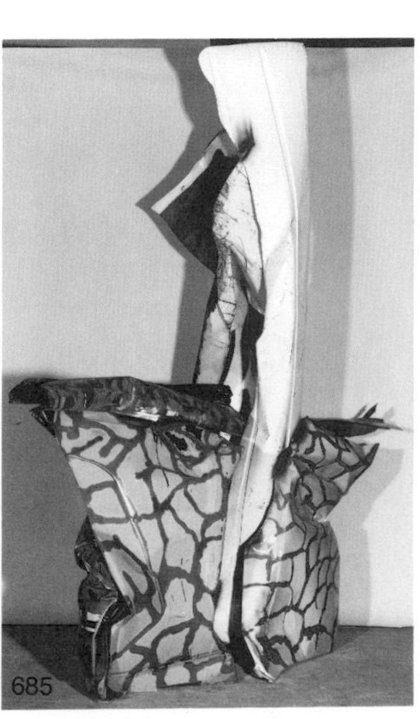

685

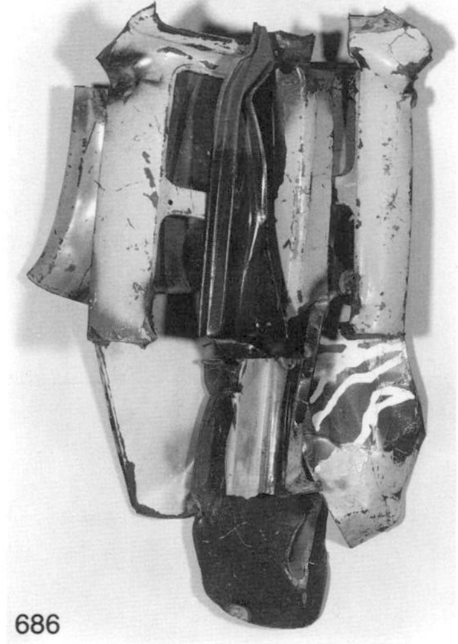
686

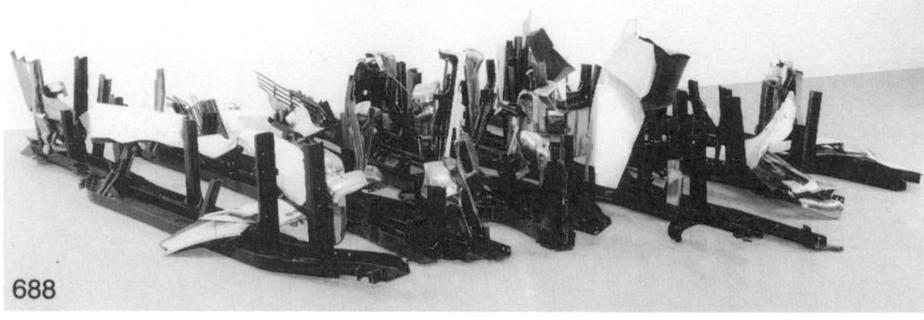
688

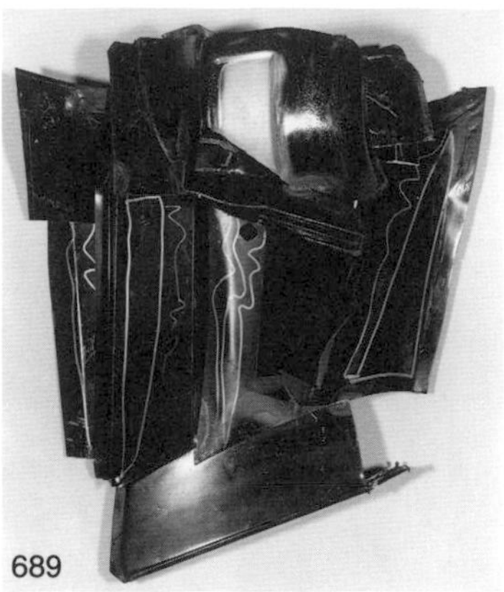
689

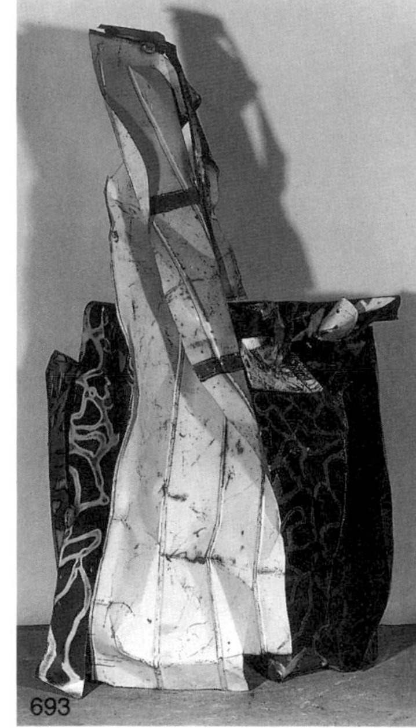
693

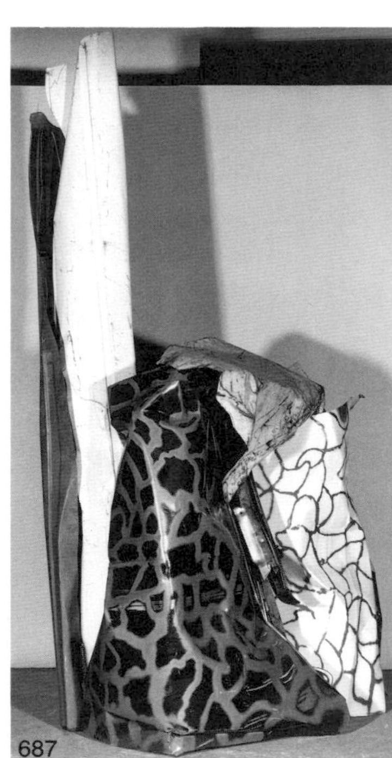
687

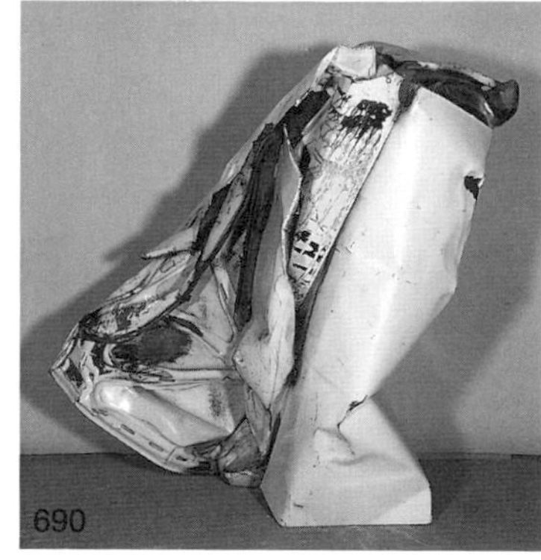
690

686

Crown Top 1982

Painted and chromium-plated steel
38 × 38 × 8 in.
(96.5 × 96.5 × 20.5 cm).

Collection

Xavier Fourcade, Inc., New York, New York.

Exhibitions

Leo Castelli Gallery, New York, New York. *John Chamberlain*. November 27–December 18, 1982.

The Butler Institute of American Art, Youngstown, Ohio. *John Chamberlain: Sculpture and Work on Paper*, cat. no. 7, illus. p. 17. May 1–29, 1983.

L.A. Louver Gallery, Venice, California. *American/European Painting and Sculpture Part II*. November 12–December 24, 1983.

The Art Galleries, University of California, Santa Barbara. *John Chamberlain/Alan Saret—Contemporary Sculpture*. March 27–April 29, 1984.

Margo Leavin Gallery, Los Angeles, California. *John Chamberlain*. March 4–30, 1985.

687

Deadeye Dick 1982

Painted and chromium-plated steel
125 × 74 × 60 in.
(317.5 × 188 × 152.5 cm).

Collection

Xavier Fourcade, Inc., New York, New York.

Exhibitions

Leo Castelli Gallery, New York, New York. *John Chamberlain*. November 27–December 18, 1982.

Oil and Steel Gallery, New York, New York. *Contemporary Painting and Sculpture V: 1957–1984*. September 24–November 30, 1984.

688

Dooms Day Flotilla 1982

Painted and chromium-plated steel
42 × 217 × 205 in.
(106.5 × 551 × 520.5 cm).

Collection

Dia Art Foundation, New York, New York, 1982; acquired directly from the artist.

Notes

The sculpture comprises seven separate units, measuring: 33 × 172 × 36 in. (84 × 437 × 91.5 cm); 28 × 161½ × 29 in. (71 × 410 × 73.5 cm); 40½ × 182½ × 23 in. (103 × 463.5 × 58.5 cm); 36½ × 201 × 26½ in. (93 × 510.5 × 67.5 cm); 41½ × 202 × 26 in. (105.5 × 513 × 66 cm); 40½ × 176 × 36½ in. (103 × 447 × 93 cm); 30 × 165½ × 30 in. (76 × 420.5 × 76 cm).

689

Flawed Logic 1982

Painted and chromium-plated steel
32½ × 30 × 10½ in.
(82.5 × 76 × 26.5 cm).

Collection

Xavier Fourcade, Inc., New York, New York.

Provenance

Lorraine Chamberlain, Essex, Connecticut; acquired directly from the artist.

Exhibitions

Leo Castelli Gallery, New York, New York. *John Chamberlain*. November 27–December 18, 1982.

The Butler Institute of American Art, Youngstown, Ohio. *John Chamberlain: Sculpture and Work on Paper*, cat. no. 8, illus. p. 9. May 1–29, 1983.

Hokin Gallery, Inc., Bay Harbour Islands, Florida. *Large Sculpture*. October 12–November 8, 1984.

690

French Lace 1982

Painted and chromium-plated steel
54 × 34 × 57 in.
(137 × 86.5 × 145 cm).

Collection

Mr. and Mrs. Melvyn J. Estrin, Bethesda, Maryland, 1984.

Provenance

Thordis Moeller, New York, New York; Xavier Fourcade, Inc., New York, New York; Margo Leavin Gallery, Los Angeles, California.

Exhibitions

Marian Goodman Gallery, New York, New York. *A Sculpture Show*. June 15–July 6, 1984.

691

Gomez y Spats 1982

Painted and chromium-plated steel
72 × 64 × 52 in.
(183 × 162.5 × 132 cm).

Notes

The sculpture was destroyed by the artist in 1984.

692

Harp's Parade 1982

Painted and chromium-plated steel
75 × 46 × 24 in.
(190.5 × 117 × 61 cm).

Collection

ART PAC, Washington, D.C., 1982; acquired directly from the artist.

693

Impurient Whey 1982

Painted and chromium-plated steel
109 × 74 × 51 in.
(276.5 × 188 × 129.5 cm).

Collection

Xavier Fourcade, Inc., New York, New York.

Exhibitions

Leo Castelli Gallery, New York, New York. *John Chamberlain*. November 27–December 18, 1982.

Fort Wayne Museum of Art, Fort Wayne, Indiana. *Inaugural Exhibition*, color illus. p. 68. April 15–June 30, 1984.

694

King King Minor 1982

Painted steel
103 × 67 × 46 in.
(261.5 × 170 × 117 cm).

Collection

Dia Art Foundation, New York, New York, 1982; acquired directly from the artist.

Exhibitions

Dia Art Foundation, Essex, Connecticut. *Chamberlain Gardens, Essex*. May–November 1984.

695

Lorelei's Passion 1982

Painted and chromium-plated steel
84 × 60 × 35 in.
(213.5 × 152.5 × 89 cm).

Collection

Xavier Fourcade, Inc., New York, New York.

Exhibitions

Leo Castelli Gallery, New York, New York. *John Chamberlain*. November 27–December 18, 1982.

Robert L. Kidd Galleries, Birmingham, Michigan. *John Chamberlain*, illus. brochure. May 21–June 18, 1983.

Xavier Fourcade, Inc., New York, New York. *John Chamberlain: New Sculpture*, not listed. February 25–March 31, 1984.

Aldrich Museum of Contemporary Art, Ridgefield, Connecticut. *Second Talent*, color illus. September 22–December 29, 1985.

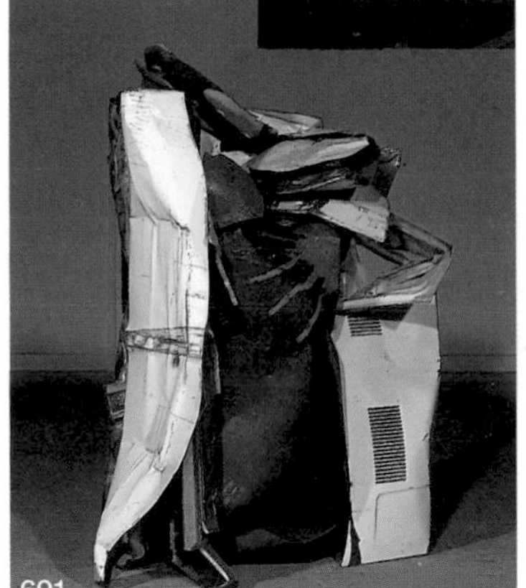
691

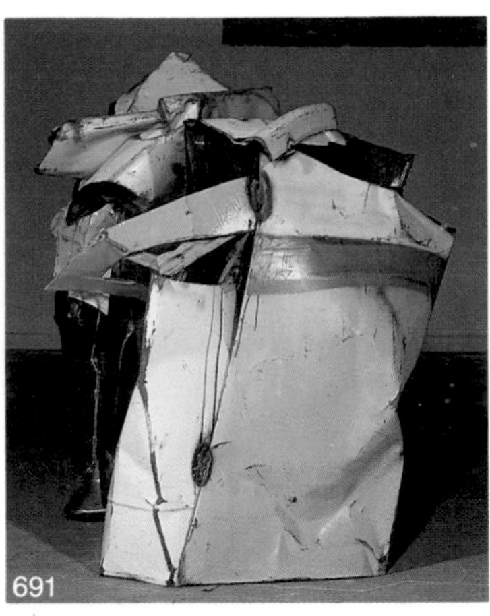
691

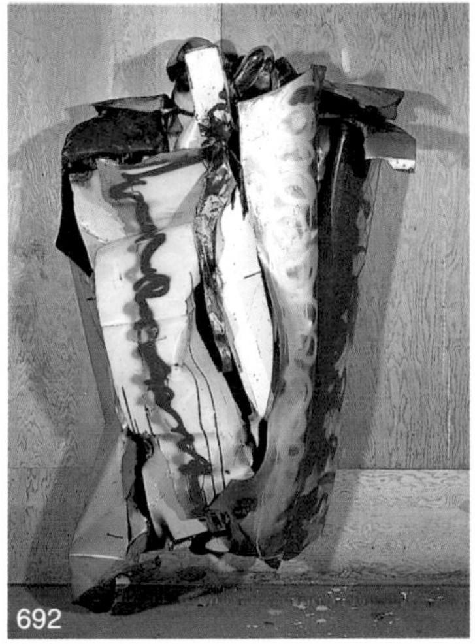
692

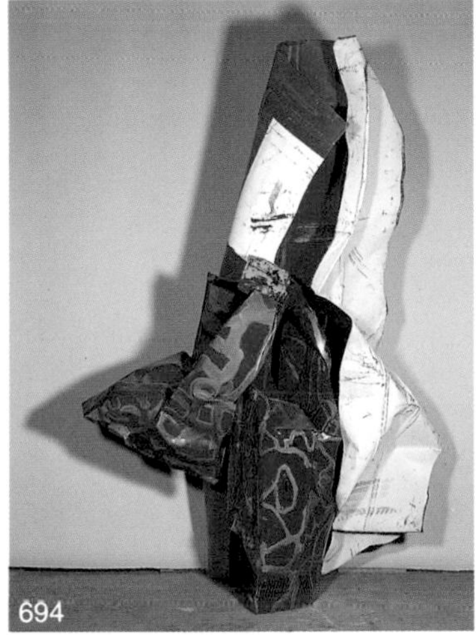
694

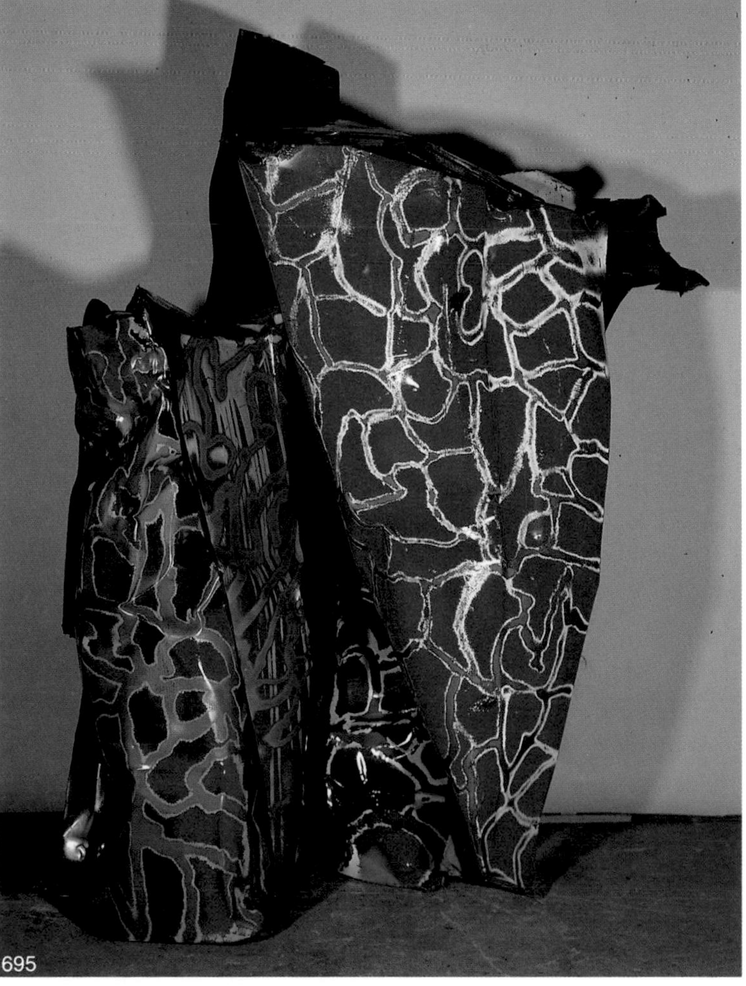
695

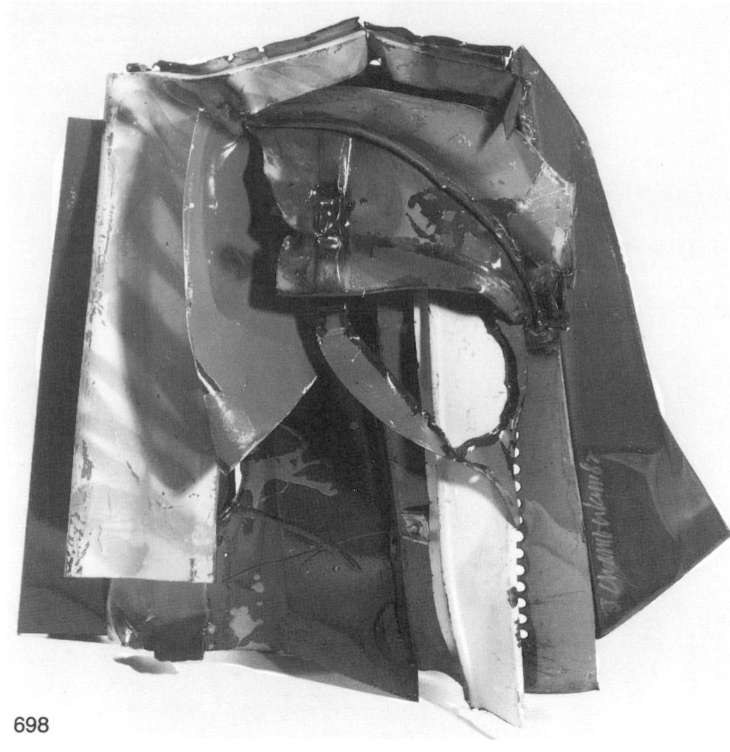

698

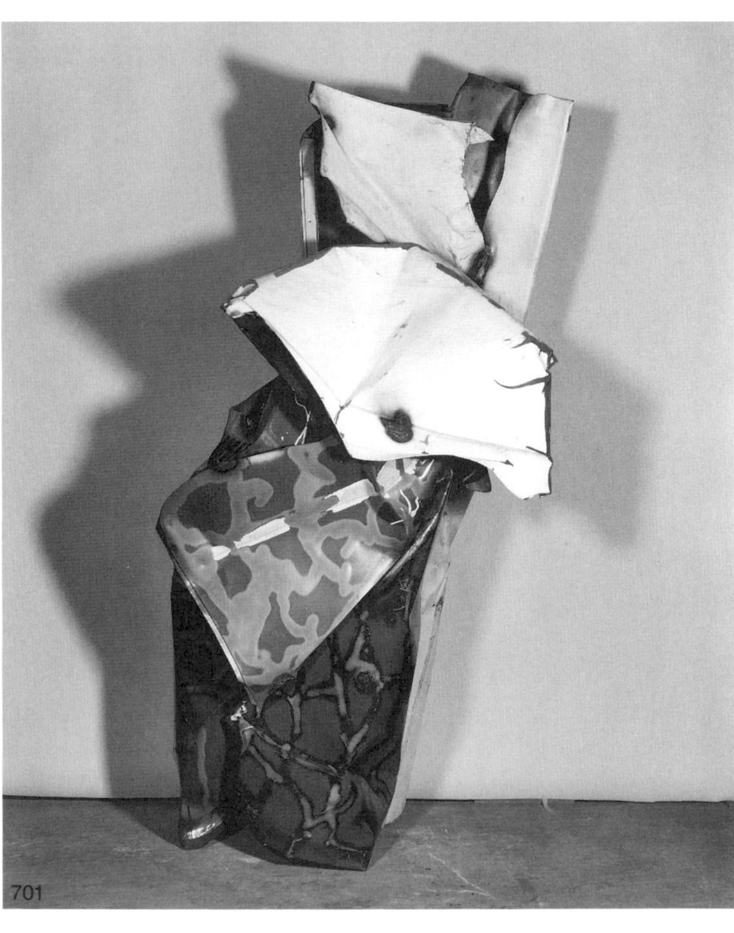

701

696

Mr. Knicely Knicely 1982

Painted and chromium-plated steel
65 × 32 × 21 in.
(165 × 81.5 × 53.5 cm).

Collection

Private collection, New York, New York; acquired directly from the artist.

Exhibitions

Dia Art Foundation, New York, New York. *John Chamberlain Sculpture: An Extended Exhibition*. September 22, 1983–February 23, 1985.

697

Pollo Primavera 1982

Painted and chromium-plated steel
45 × 56 × 37 in.
(114.5 × 142.5 × 94 cm).

Collection

David Budd, New York, New York, 1982; acquired directly from the artist.

Exhibitions

Xavier Fourcade, Inc., New York, New York. *John Chamberlain: New Sculpture*. February 25–March 31, 1984.

698

Samurai Soo 1982

Painted and chromium-plated steel
26 × 27½ × 8½ in.
(66 × 70 × 21.5 cm).

Collection

Mr. and Mrs. Albert Peskin, Los Angeles, California, 1985.

Provenance

Xavier Fourcade, Inc., and Thordis Moeller, New York, New York; Margo Leavin Gallery, Los Angeles, California.

Exhibitions

Leo Castelli Gallery, New York, New York. *John Chamberlain*. November 27–December 18, 1982.

The Butler Institute of American Art, Youngstown, Ohio. *John Chamberlain: Sculpture and Work on Paper*, cat. no. 9, illus. p. 21. May 1–29, 1983.

L.A. Louver Gallery, Venice, California. *American/European Painting and Sculpture Part II*. November 12–December 24, 1983.

The Art Galleries, University of California, Santa Barbara. *John Chamberlain/Alan Saret—Contemporary Sculpture*. March 27–April 29, 1984.

Margo Leavin Gallery, Los Angeles, California. *John Chamberlain*. March 4–30, 1985.

Notes

The sculpture is signed and dated.

699

Small Monument to a Swiss Monument 1979–82

Painted and chromium-plated steel
84 × 171 × 65 in.
(213.5 × 434.5 × 165 cm).

Collection

Dia Art Foundation, New York, New York, 1982; acquired directly from the artist.

Exhibitions

The John and Mable Ringling Museum of Art, Sarasota, Florida. *John Chamberlain Reliefs 1960–1982*, color illus. p. 85. January 28–March 27, 1983.

Dia Art Foundation, New York, New York. *John Chamberlain Sculpture: An Extended Exhibition*. September 22, 1983–February 23, 1985.

References

Gary Indiana, "John Chamberlain's Irregular Set," *Art in America*, vol. 71, no. 10 (November 1983), p. 208.

Notes

See also cat. no. XX (Appendix: Couches), where the sculpture is illustrated in a gallery installation, together with *Thordis' Barge*.

700

The Line Up 1982

Painted and chromium-plated steel
82 × 198½ × 49½ in.
(208 × 504 × 125.5 cm).

Collection

Dia Art Foundation, New York, New York, 1983; acquired directly from the artist.

701

Wongkong Melong 1982

Painted steel
95 × 52 × 49 in.
(241.5 × 132 × 124.5 cm).

Collection

Xavier Fourcade, Inc., New York, New York.

Exhibitions

Leo Castelli Gallery, New York, New York. *John Chamberlain*. November 27–December 18, 1982.

The Parrish Art Museum, Southampton, New York. *Forming*, illus. July 29–September 23, 1984.

References

Gary Indiana, "John Chamberlain's Irregular Set," *Art in America*, vol. 71, no. 10 (November 1983), p. 214, color illus. p. 209.

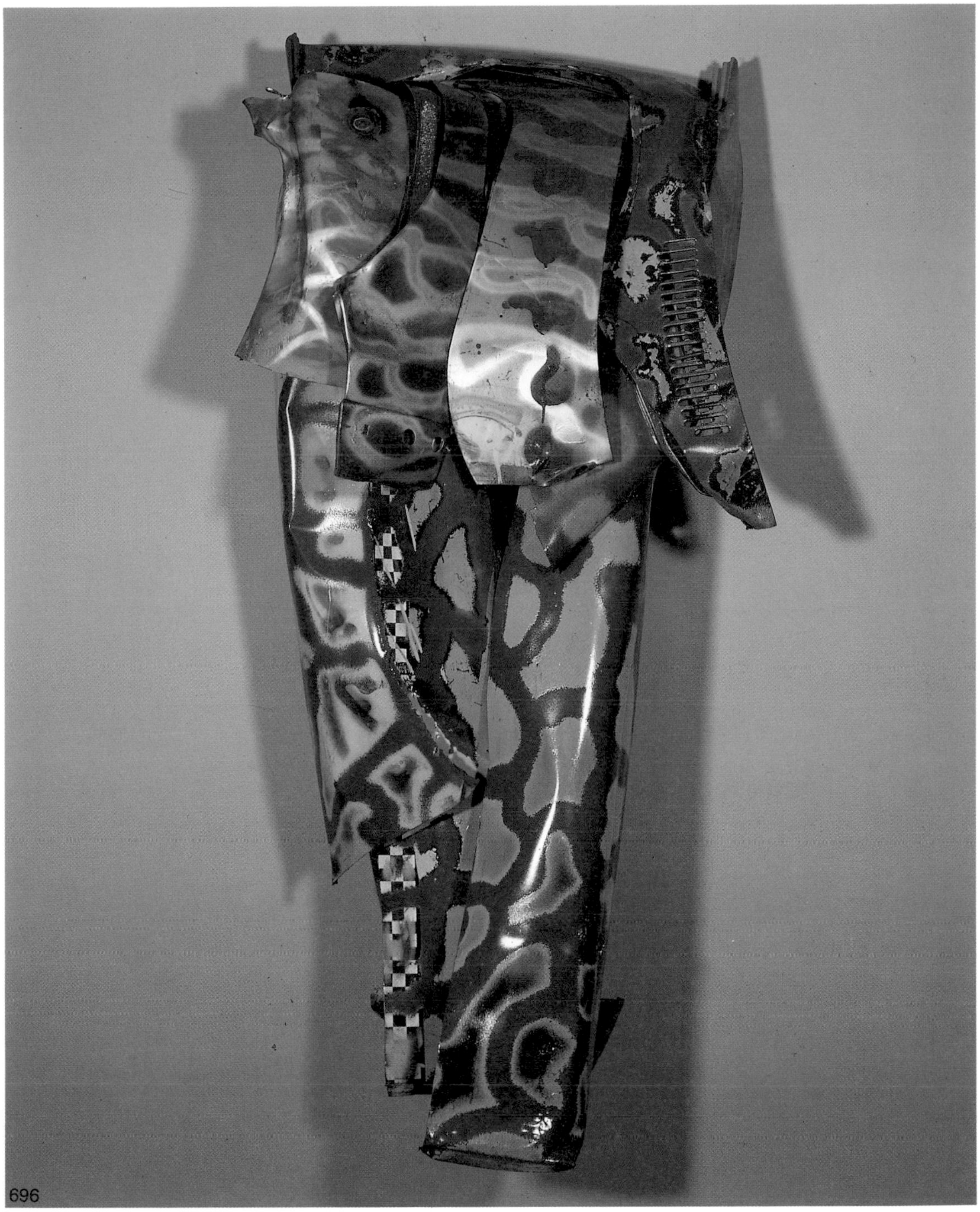

696

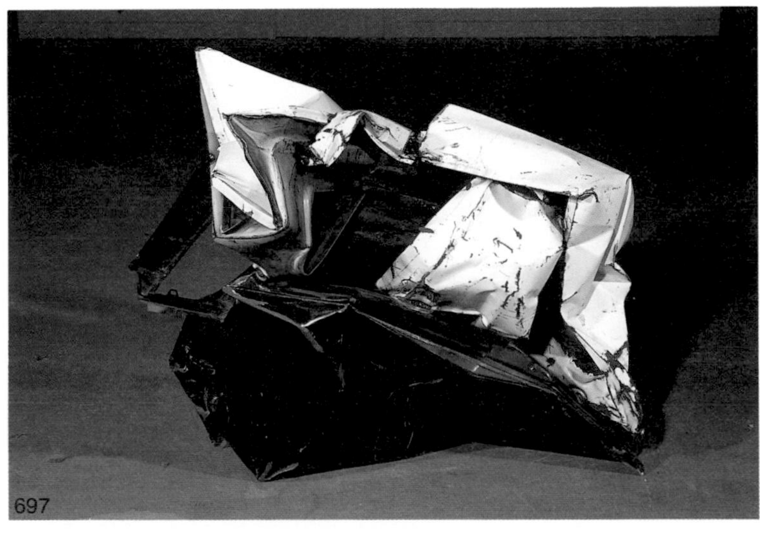

697

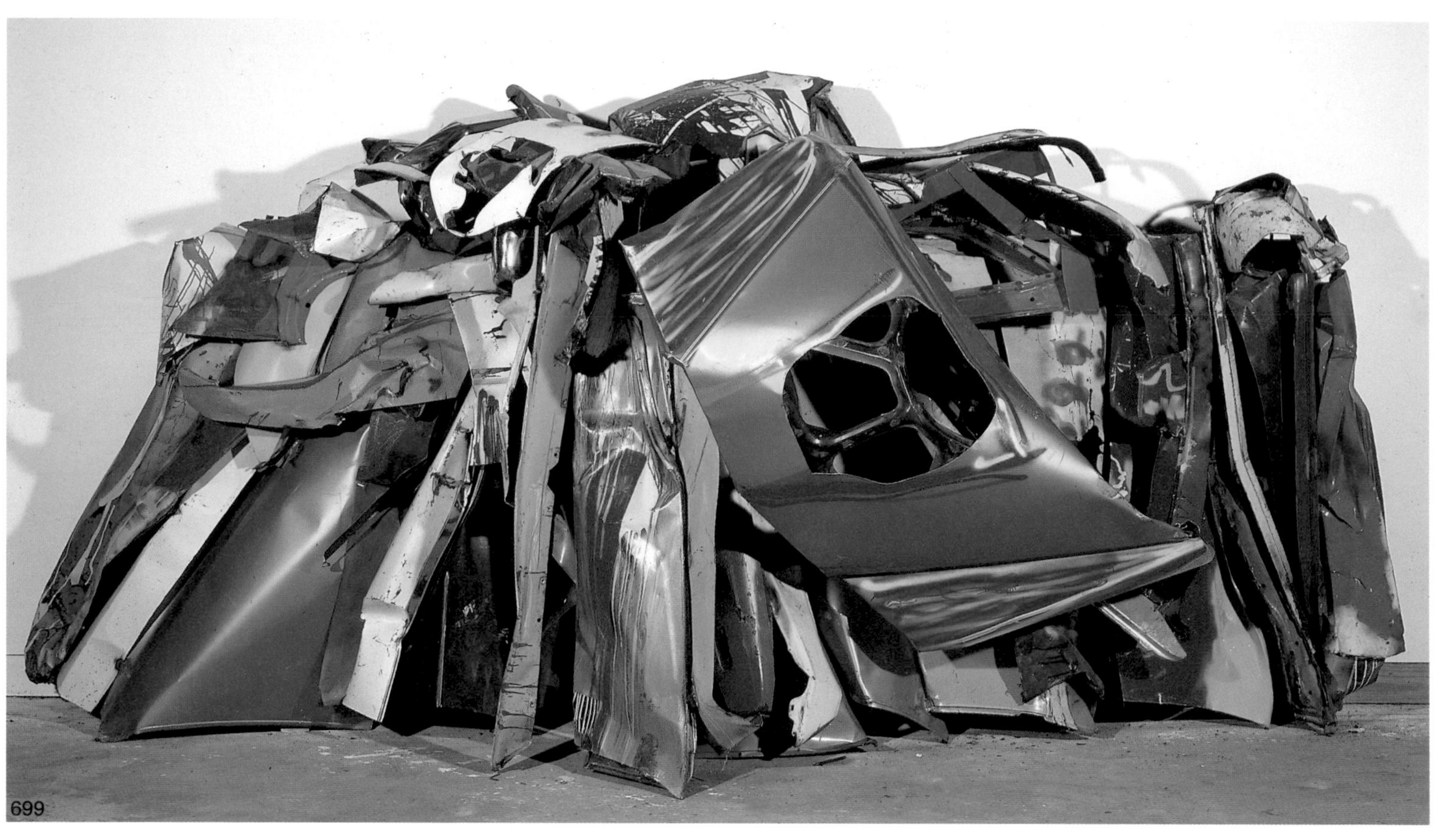

699

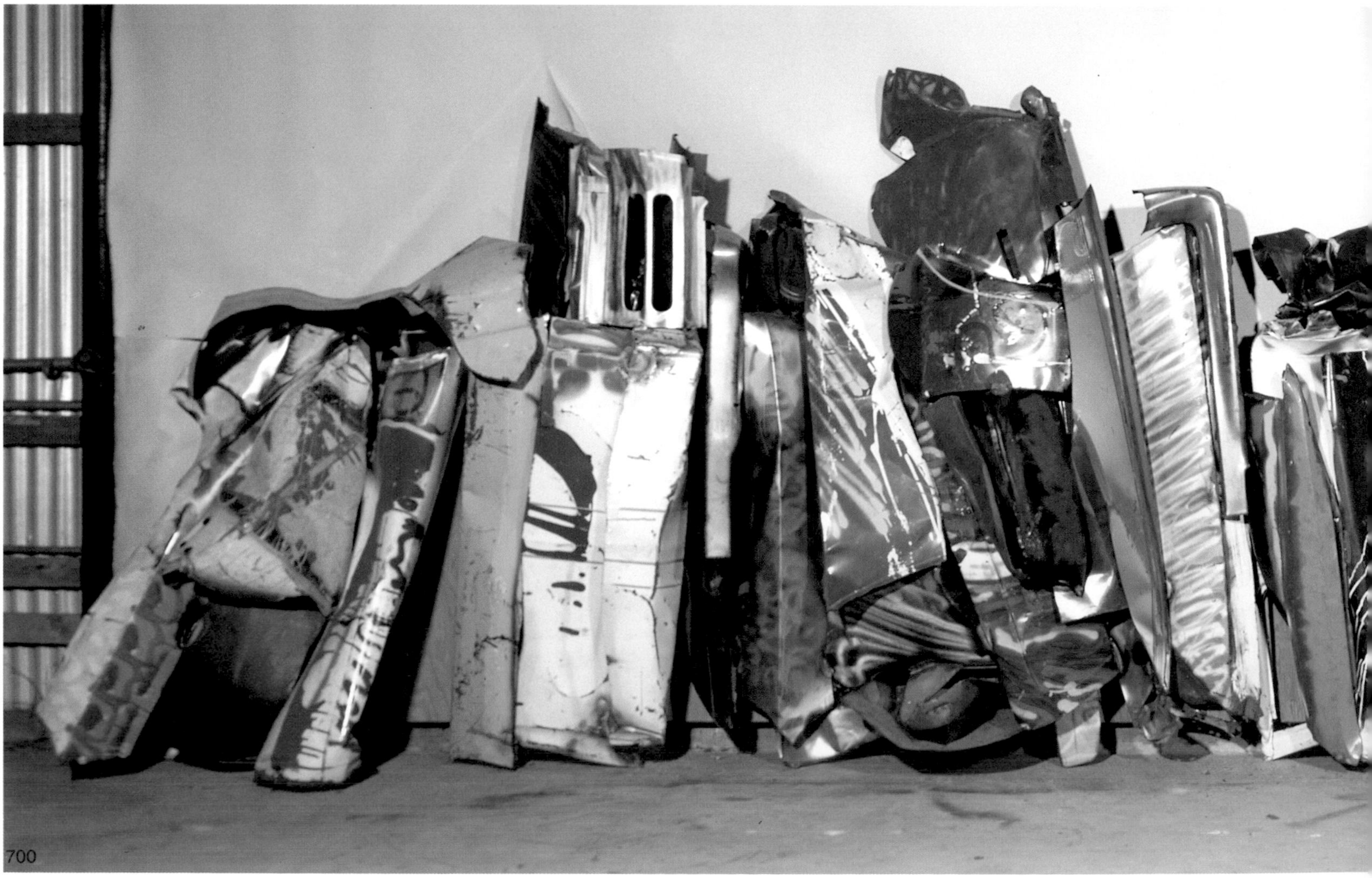

700

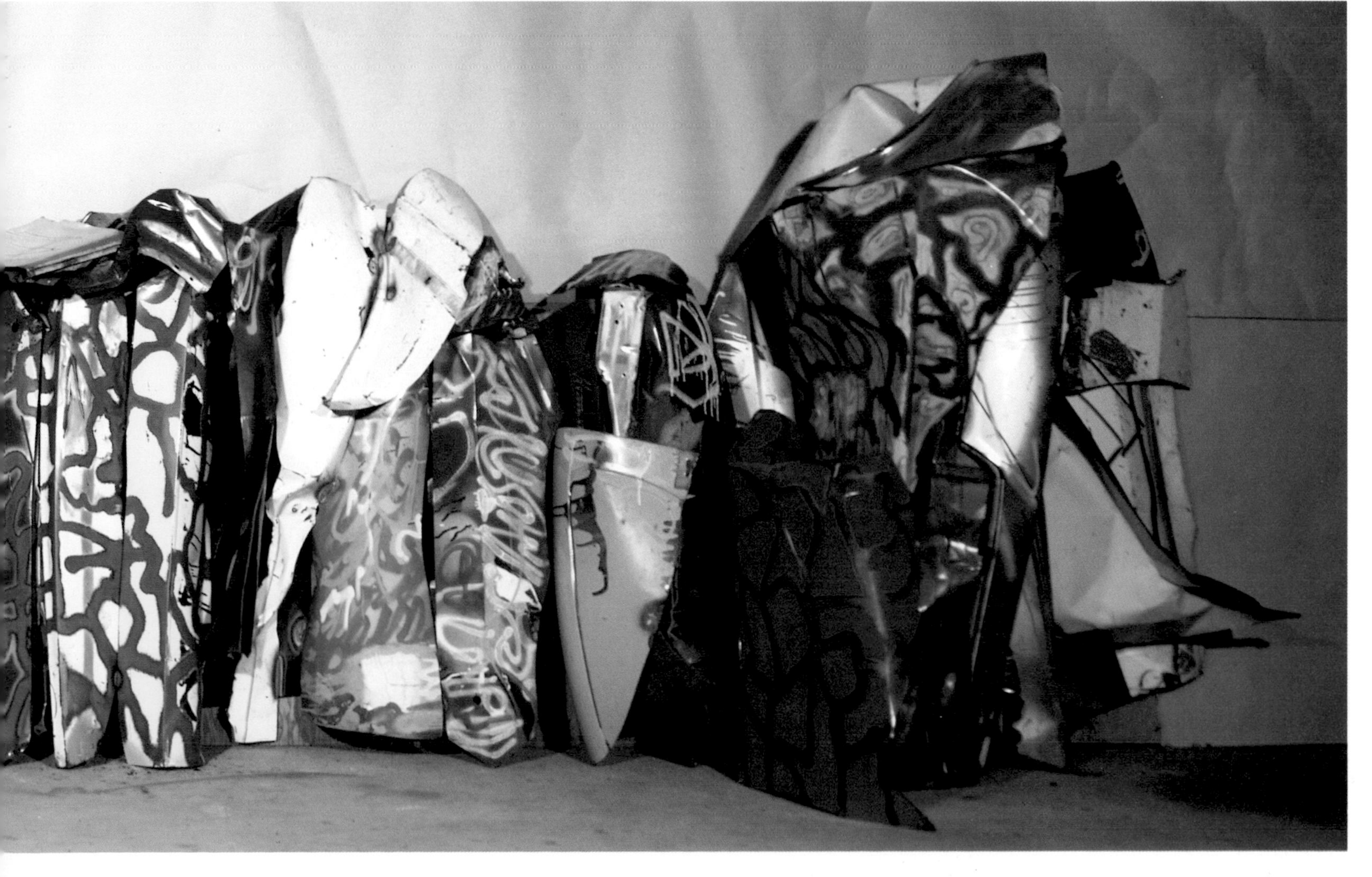

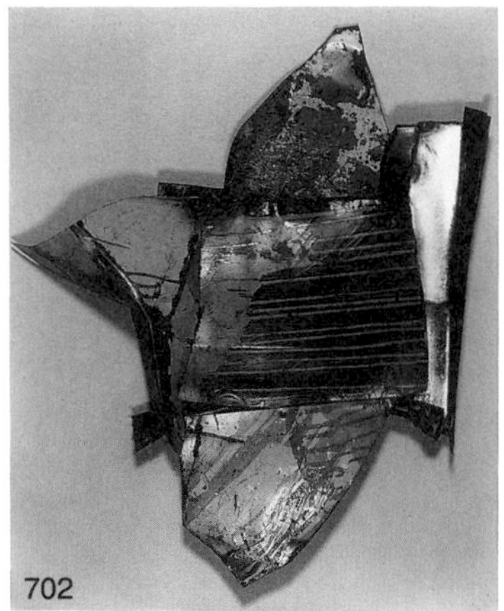
702

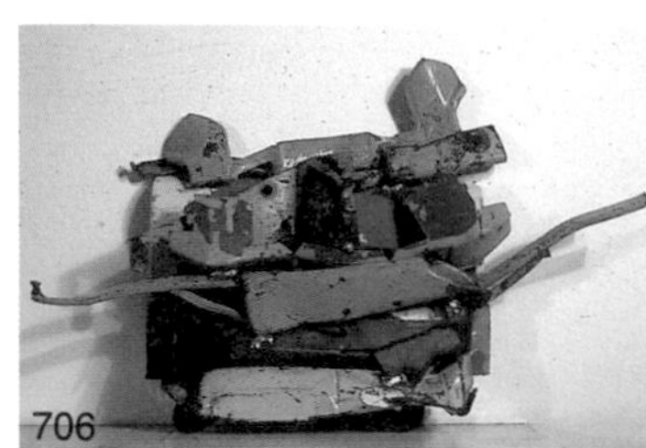
706

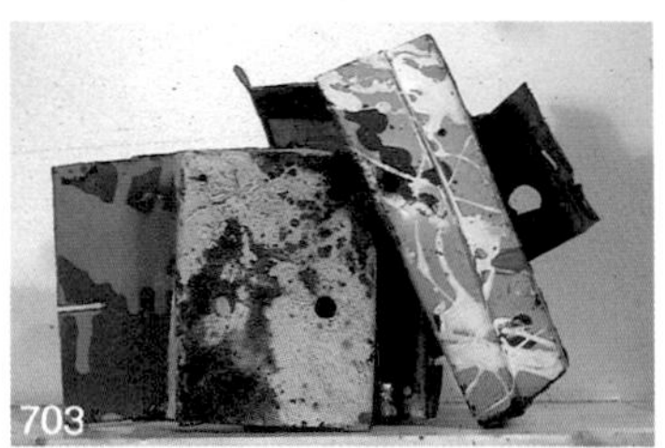
703

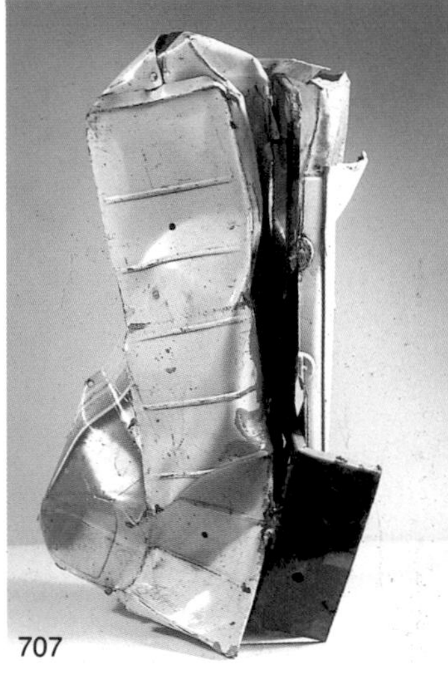
707

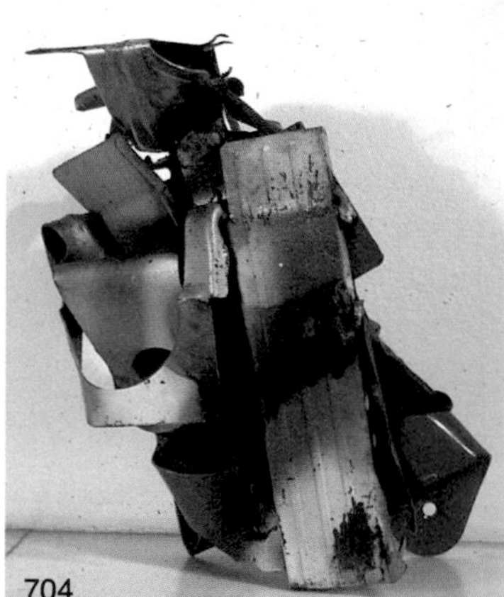
704

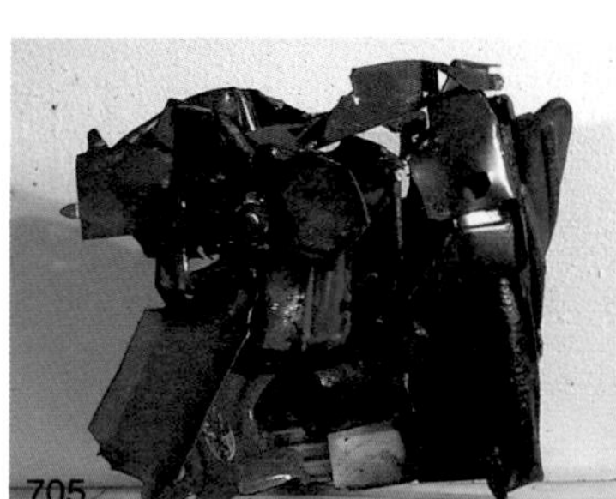
705

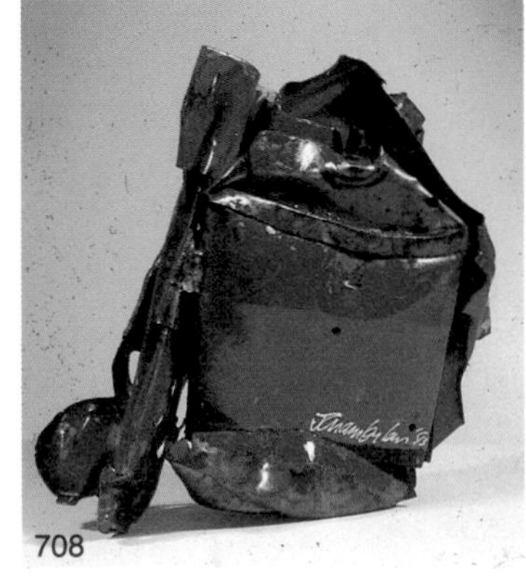
708

702

Wrinkled Porker 1982
Painted and chromium-plated steel
30 × 35 × 7 in. (76 × 89 × 18 cm).

Collection
Leo Castelli Gallery, New York, New York; acquired directly from the artist.

Exhibitions
Leo Castelli Gallery, New York, New York. *John Chamberlain*. November 27–December 18, 1982.

703

Tonk #1–82 1982
Painted steel
6½ × 8½ × 4 in.
(16.5 × 21.5 × 10 cm).

Collection
Collection of the artist, Sarasota, Florida.

Exhibitions
Galerie Helen van der Meij, Amsterdam. *John Chamberlain: Tonks*. April 21–May 24, 1984.

Notes
The sculpture was orginally titled *Tonk #9–82*. It was retitled by the artist in 1983.

704

Tonk #2–82 1982
Painted steel
10 × 6½ × 4½ in.
(25.5 × 16.5 × 11.5 cm).

Collection
William J. Hokin, Chicago, Illinois, 1984.

Provenance
Xavier Fourcade, Inc., and Thordis Moeller, New York, New York; Margo Leavin Gallery, Los Angeles, California.

Exhibitions
L.A. Louver Gallery, Venice, California. *American/European Painting and Sculpture Part II*. November 12–December 24, 1983.

The Art Galleries, University of California, Santa Barbara. *John Chamberlain/Alan Saret—Contemporary Sculpture*. March 27–April 29, 1984.

705

Tonk #3–82 1982
Painted steel
19½ × 7 × 4½ in.
(49.5 × 18 × 11.5 cm).

Collection
Galleriet, Lund, Sweden.

706

Tonk #4–82 1982
Painted steel
2½ × 16 × 9½ in.
(6.5 × 40.5 × 24 cm).

Collection
Mr. and Mrs. Larry Wolf, Beverly Hills, California, 1984.

Provenance
Xavier Fourcade, Inc., and Thordis Moeller, New York, New York; Margo Leavin Gallery, Los Angeles, California.

Exhibitions
L.A. Louver Gallery, Venice, California. *American/European Painting and Sculpture Part II*. November 12–December 24, 1983.

The Art Galleries, University of California, Santa Barbara. *John Chamberlain/Alan Saret—Contemporary Sculpture*. March 27–April 29, 1984.

Notes
The sculpture was originally titled *Tonk #36–82*. It was retitled by the artist in 1983.

707

Tonk #5–82 1982
Painted steel
17 × 11 × 6 in. (43 × 28 × 15 cm).

Collection
Dr. George Monahan, Sarasota, Florida, 1983; acquired directly from the artist.

Exhibitions
Xavier Fourcade, Inc., New York, New York. *John Chamberlain: New Sculpture*. February 25–March 31, 1984.

708

Tonk #6–82 1982
Painted steel
9 × 9½ × 4 in. (23 × 24 × 10 cm).

Collection
Dr. George Monahan, Sarasota, Florida, 1983; acquired directly from the artist.

Notes
The sculpture is signed and dated *J. Chamberlain '82*.

In 1982 Chamberlain made a small series of sculptures of urethane foam that were bound with painted paper and weighted with a bolt. The *High Collar* series, as these small studies were called, were given as gifts to friends and have not been included in the catalogue raisonné.

709

Andrea Florentina Luchezzi 1983
Painted and chromium-plated steel
74 × 38 × 35 in.
(188 × 97 × 89 cm).

Collection
Xavier Fourcade, Inc., New York, New York.

Exhibitions
Xavier Fourcade, Inc., New York, New York. *John Chamberlain: New Sculpture*, color illus. February 25–March 31, 1984.

Galerie Gillespie-Laage-Salomon, Paris. *Transgressions*. February–March 1985.

Galerie Gillespie-Laage-Salomon, Paris. *John Chamberlain*. June 6–July 13, 1985.

710

Archie Ha Ha 1983
Painted and chromium-plated steel
36 × 29½ × 15½ in.
(91 × 75 × 39 cm).

Collection
Owen Morrissey, New York, New York, 1983; acquired directly from the artist.

711

Archurback 1983
Painted and chromium-plated steel
51½ × 35½ × 29 in.
(131 × 90 × 73.5 cm).

Collection
Xavier Fourcade, Inc., New York, New York.

Exhibitions
Robert L. Kidd Galleries, Birmingham, Michigan. *John Chamberlain*, illus. brochure. May 21–June 18, 1983.

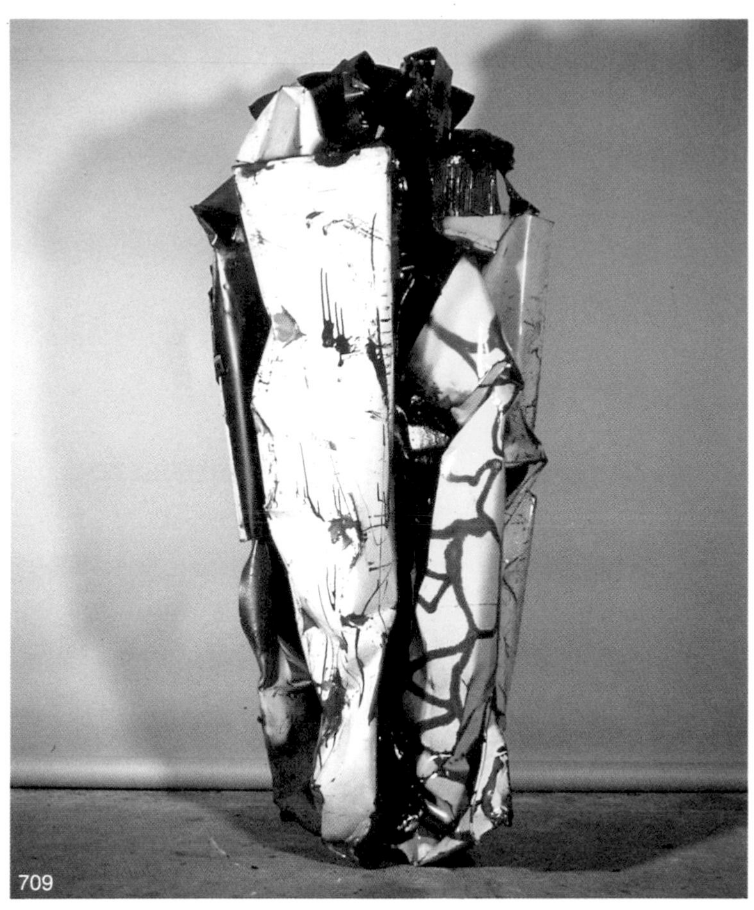
709

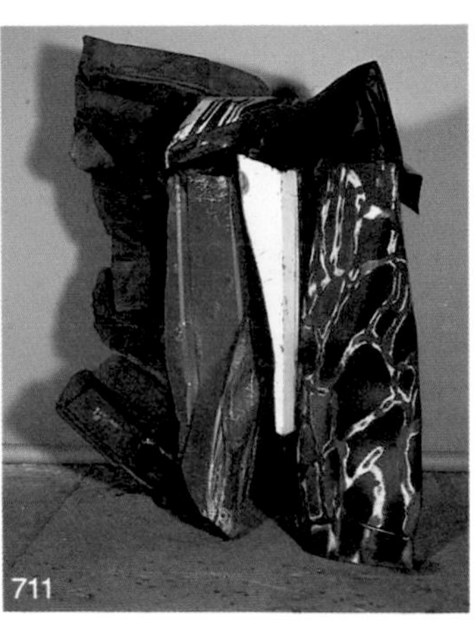
711

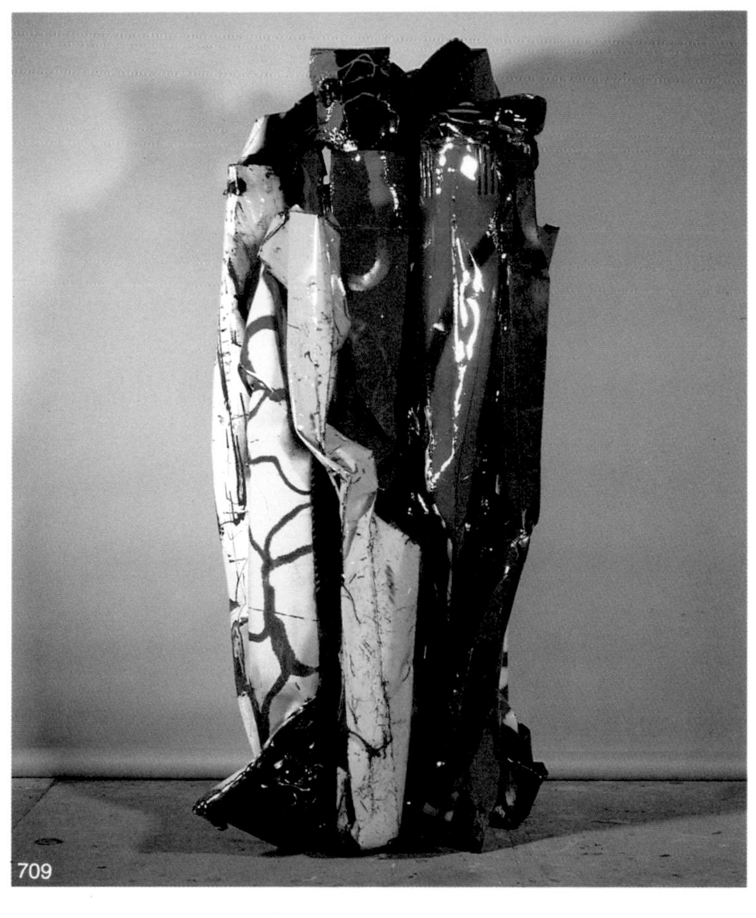
709

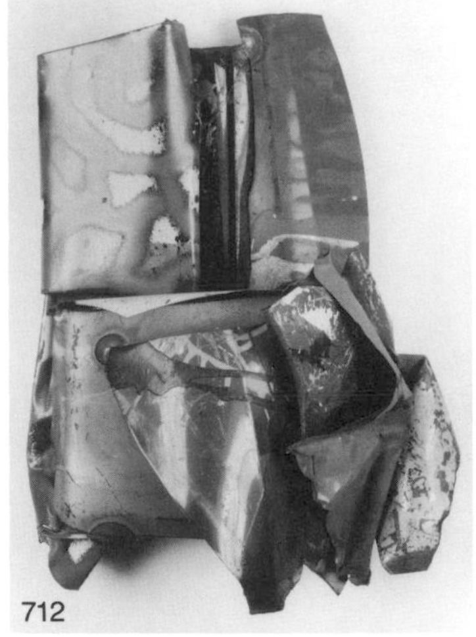
712

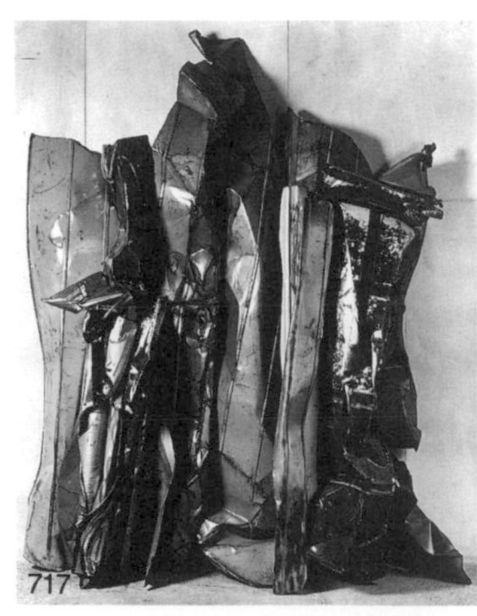
717

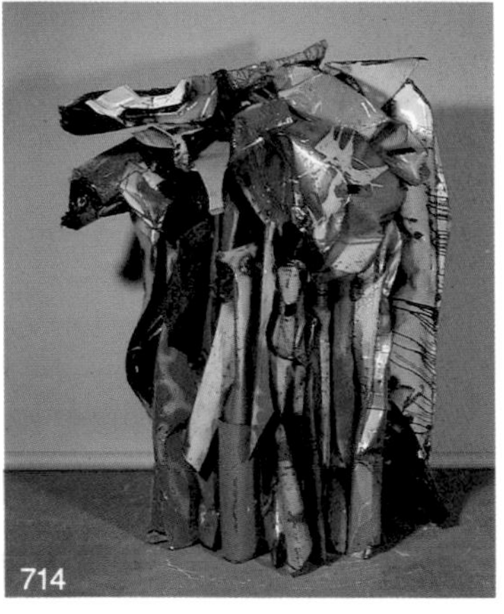
714

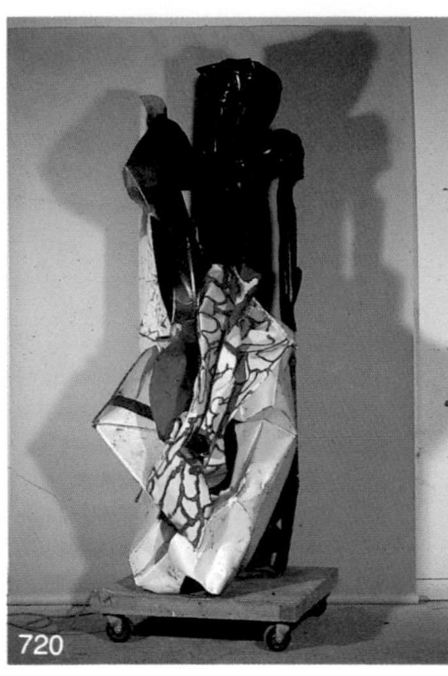
720

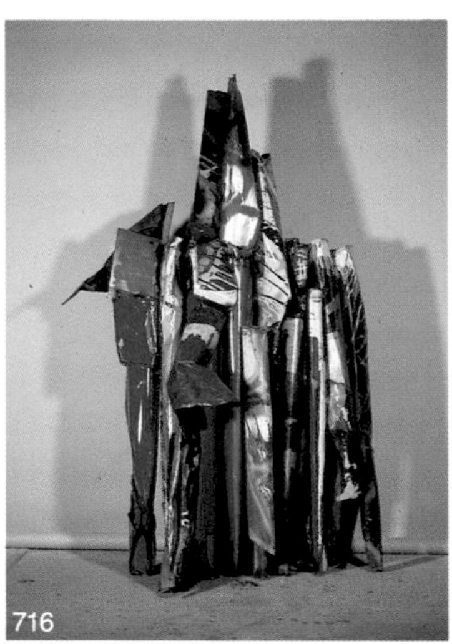
716

712

Available Grace 1983

Painted steel
32½ × 22½ × 13 in.
(82.5 × 57 × 33 cm).

Collection

Private collection, New York, New York; acquired directly from the artist.

713

Battsy Beeker 1983

Painted and chromium-plated steel
15½ × 19½ × 17 in.
(39 × 49.5 × 43 cm).

Collection

Dr. Bernard Kruger, New York, New York, 1983; acquired directly from the artist.

714

Bent Tynes 1983

Painted steel
70 × 55 × 42 in.
(178 × 140 × 107 cm).

Collection

Private collection, New York, New York, 1983; acquired directly from the artist.

Exhibitions

Xavier Fourcade, Inc., New York, New York. *John Chamberlain: New Sculpture*, color illus. February 25–March 31, 1984.

715

Birthday Piece 1983

Painted and chromium-plated steel
36 × 42 × 13 in.
(91.5 × 106.5 × 33 cm).

Collection

Thordis Moeller, New York, New York; acquired directly from the artist.

716

Bugoff Buggo 1983

Painted and chromium-plated steel
84 × 58 × 38 in.
(213.5 × 147.5 × 96.5 cm).

Collection

Xavier Fourcade, Inc., New York, New York.

Exhibitions

Xavier Fourcade, Inc., New York, New York. *John Chamberlain: New Sculpture*, color illus. February 25–March 31, 1984.

Galerie Rudolf Zwirner, Cologne. *John Chamberlain*. November 13–December 31, 1984.

717

City Lux 1983

Painted steel
138 × 114 × 54 in.
(350.5 × 289.5 × 137 cm).

Collection

Collection of the artist; on extended loan to the Whitney Museum of American Art, Philip Morris Building, New York, New York.

Exhibitions

Whitney Museum of American Art, Philip Morris Sculpture Court, New York, New York; a semipermanent exhibition. From April 8, 1983.

References

"The Vasari Diary: The Whitney Calls for Philip Morris," *Art News*, vol. 82, no. 5 (May 1983), p. 19.

718

Dhuha Ditty 1983

Painted and chromium-plated steel
71½ × 51 × 18½ in.
(181.5 × 129.5 × 47 cm).

Collection

Thordis Moeller, New York, New York, 1984; acquired directly from the artist.

Exhibitions

Xavier Fourcade Inc., New York, New York. *John Chamberlain: New Sculpture*. February 25–March 31, 1984.

719

Elixir 1983

Painted steel
138 × 50½ × 48 in.
(350.5 × 128.5 × 122 cm).

Collection

Collection of the artist, Sarasota, Florida.

Exhibitions

Dia Art Foundation, Essex, Connecticut. *Chamberlain Gardens, Essex*. May–November 1984.

720

Fenollosa's Column 1983

Painted and chromium-plated steel
125½ × 53 × 47½ in.
(319 × 135 × 120.5 cm).

Collection

Doris and Charles Saatchi, London, 1984.

Provenance

Xavier Fourcade, Inc., New York, New York.

References

John Chamberlain: New Sculpture (New York: Xavier Fourcade, Inc., 1984), color illus.

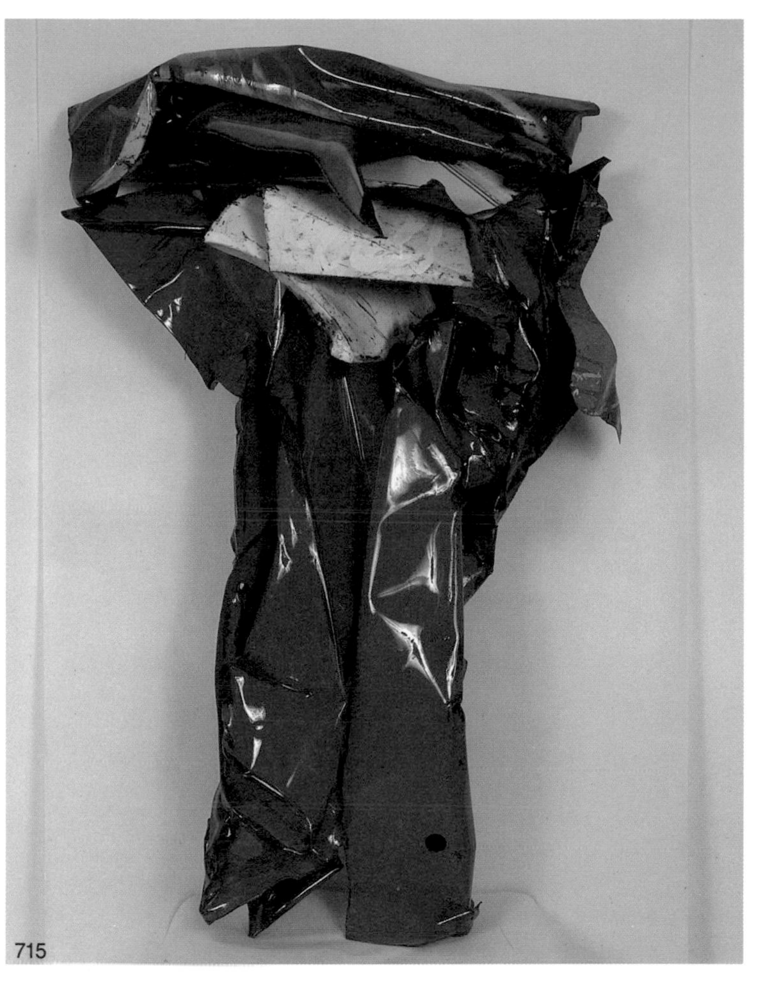
715

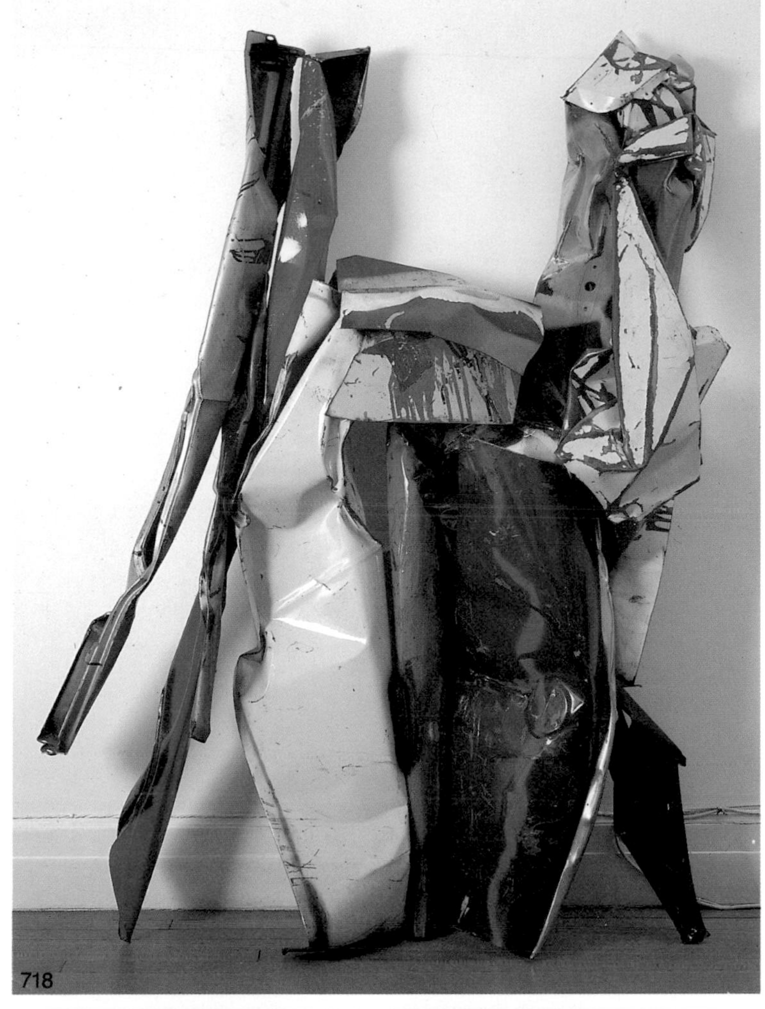
718

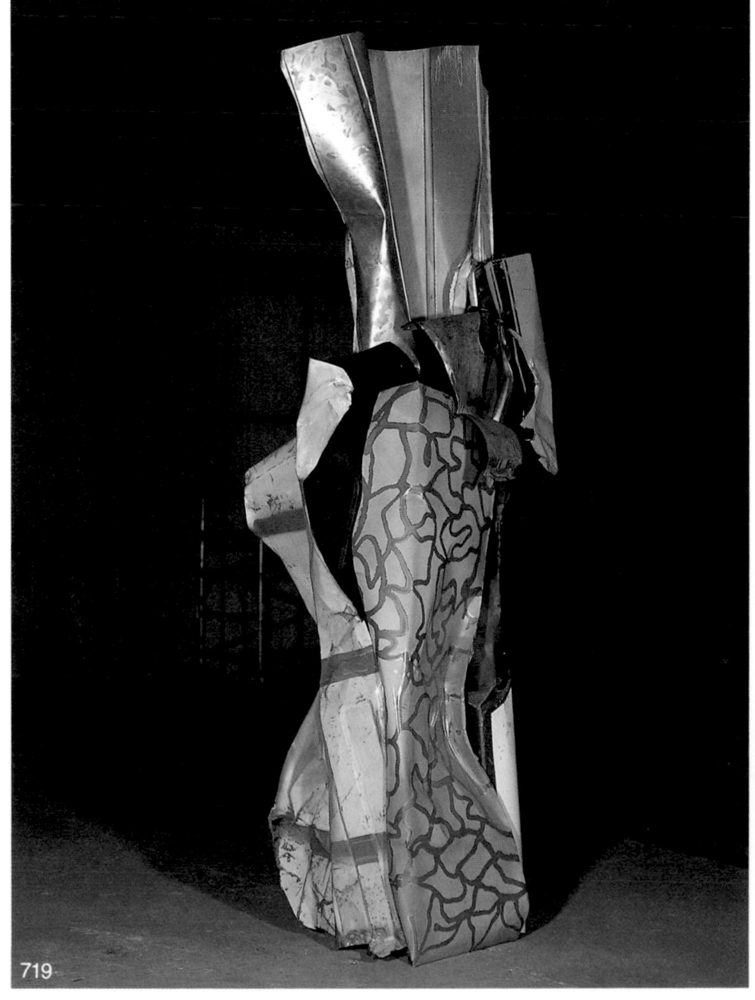
719

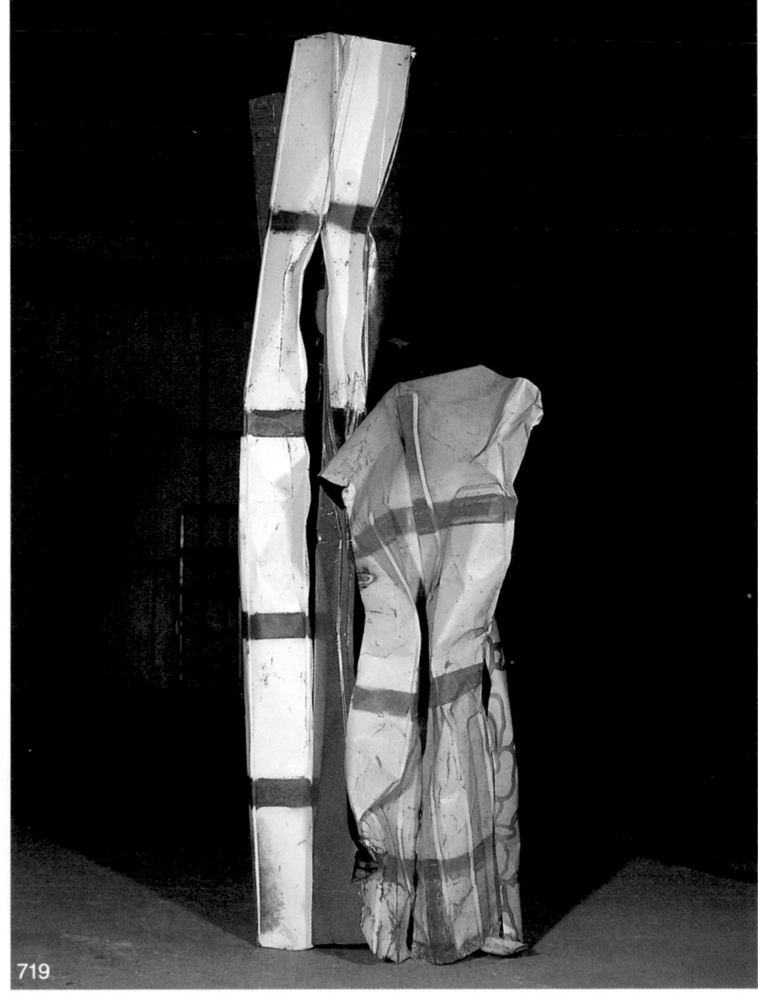
719

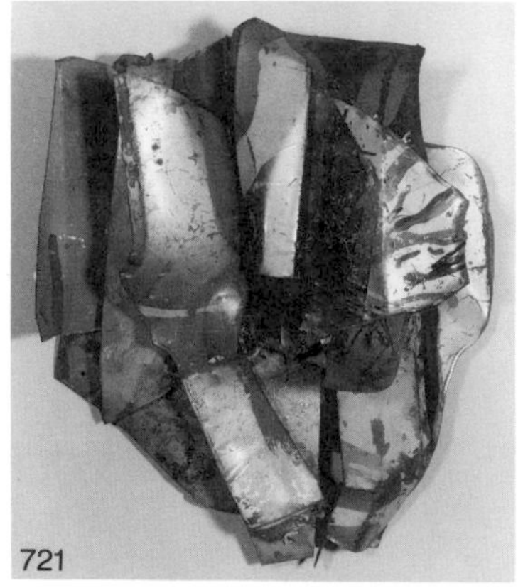
721

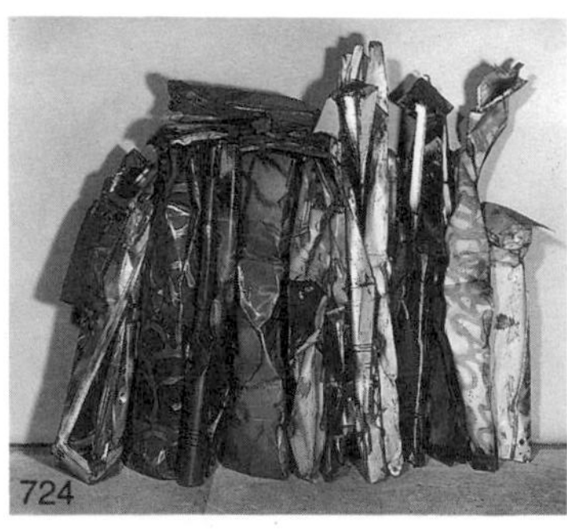
724

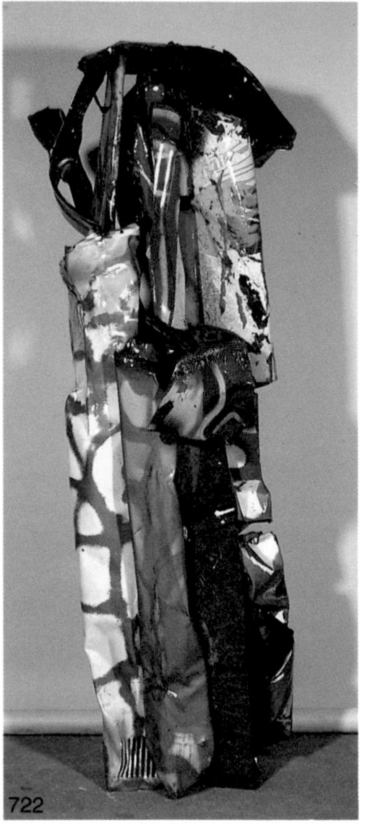
722

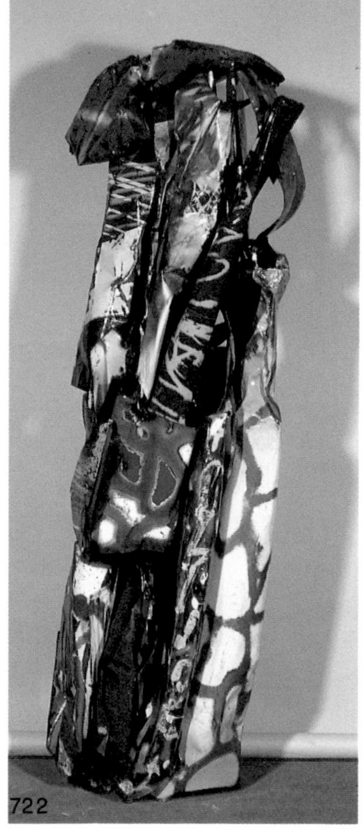
722

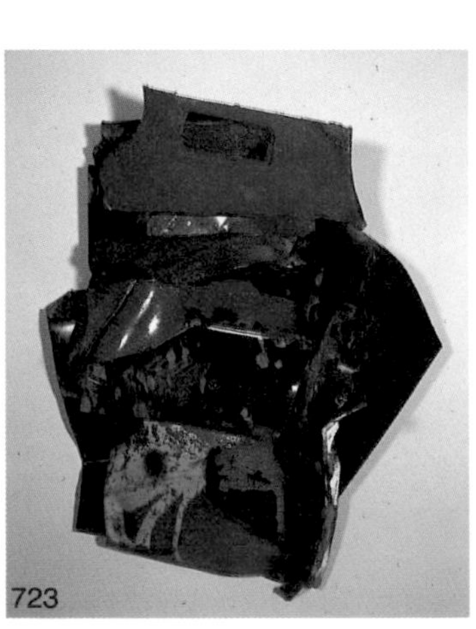
723

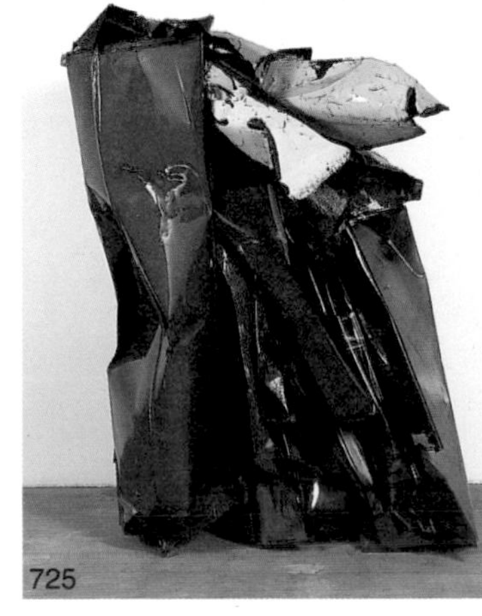
725

721

Fouilly-Puisse 1983
Painted steel
29 × 25 × 9 in.
(74 × 63.5 × 23 cm).

Collection
Xavier Fourcade, Inc., New York, New York.

Exhibitions
Robert L. Kidd Galleries, Birmingham, Michigan. *John Chamberlain*, illus. brochure. May 21–June 18, 1983.

Xavier Fourcade, Inc., New York, New York. *John Chamberlain: New Sculpture*. February 25–March 31, 1984.

Galerie Rudolf Zwirner, Cologne. *John Chamberlain*. November 13–December 31, 1984.

722

Fredrico Alonzo Morelli 1983
Painted steel
63 × 24 × 27 in.
(160 × 61 × 69 cm).

Collection
Galerie Gillespie-Laage-Salomon, Paris, 1984.

Provenance
Xavier Fourcade, Inc., and Thordis Moeller, New York, New York.

Exhibitions
Xavier Fourcade, Inc., New York, New York. *John Chamberlain: New Sculpture*, color illus. February 25–March 31, 1984.

Grand Palais, Paris. *Foire internationale d'art contemporain*. October 20–28, 1984.

Galerie Gillespie-Laage-Salomon, Paris. *John Chamberlain*. June 6–July 13, 1985.

723

In Diana 1983
Painted steel
31½ × 23½ × 8 in.
(80 × 59.5 × 20.5 cm).

Collection
Xavier Fourcade, Inc., New York, New York.

Exhibitions
Robert L. Kidd Galleries, Birmingham, Michigan. *John Chamberlain*, illus. brochure. May 21–June 18, 1983.

Galerie Gillespie-Laage-Salomon, Paris. *John Chamberlain*. June 6–July 13, 1985.

724

Jack Sprat 1983
Painted and chromium-plated steel
65½ × 76 × 20 in.
(166 × 193 × 51 cm).

Collection
Xavier Fourcade, Inc., New York, New York.

Exhibitions
Xavier Fourcade, Inc., New York, New York. *John Chamberlain: New Sculpture*, color illus. February 25–March 31, 1984.

Galerie Rudolf Zwirner, Cologne. *John Chamberlain*. November 13–December 31, 1984.

725

Opian Angel 1983
Painted and chromium-plated steel
73 × 72 × 48 in.
(186 × 183 × 122 cm).

Collection
Mr. and Mrs. Melvyn J. Estrin, Bethesda, Maryland, 1984.

Provenance
Xavier Fourcade, Inc., and Thordis Moeller, New York, New York; Margo Leavin Gallery, Los Angeles, California.

Exhibitions
Xavier Fourcade, Inc., New York, New York. *John Chamberlain: New Sculpture*, color illus. February 25–March 31, 1984.

Margo Leavin Gallery, Los Angeles, California. *American Sculpture*. July 17–August 15, 1984.

726

Pure Drop 1983
Painted and chromium-plated steel
135 × 72 × 36 in.
(343 × 183 × 91.5 cm).

Collection
Doris and Charles Saatchi, London.

Provenance
Xavier Fourcade, Inc., and Thordis Moeller, New York, New York; L.A. Louver Gallery, Venice, California.

Exhibitions
L.A. Louver Gallery, Venice, California. *American/European Painting and Sculpture Part II*. November 12–December 24, 1983.

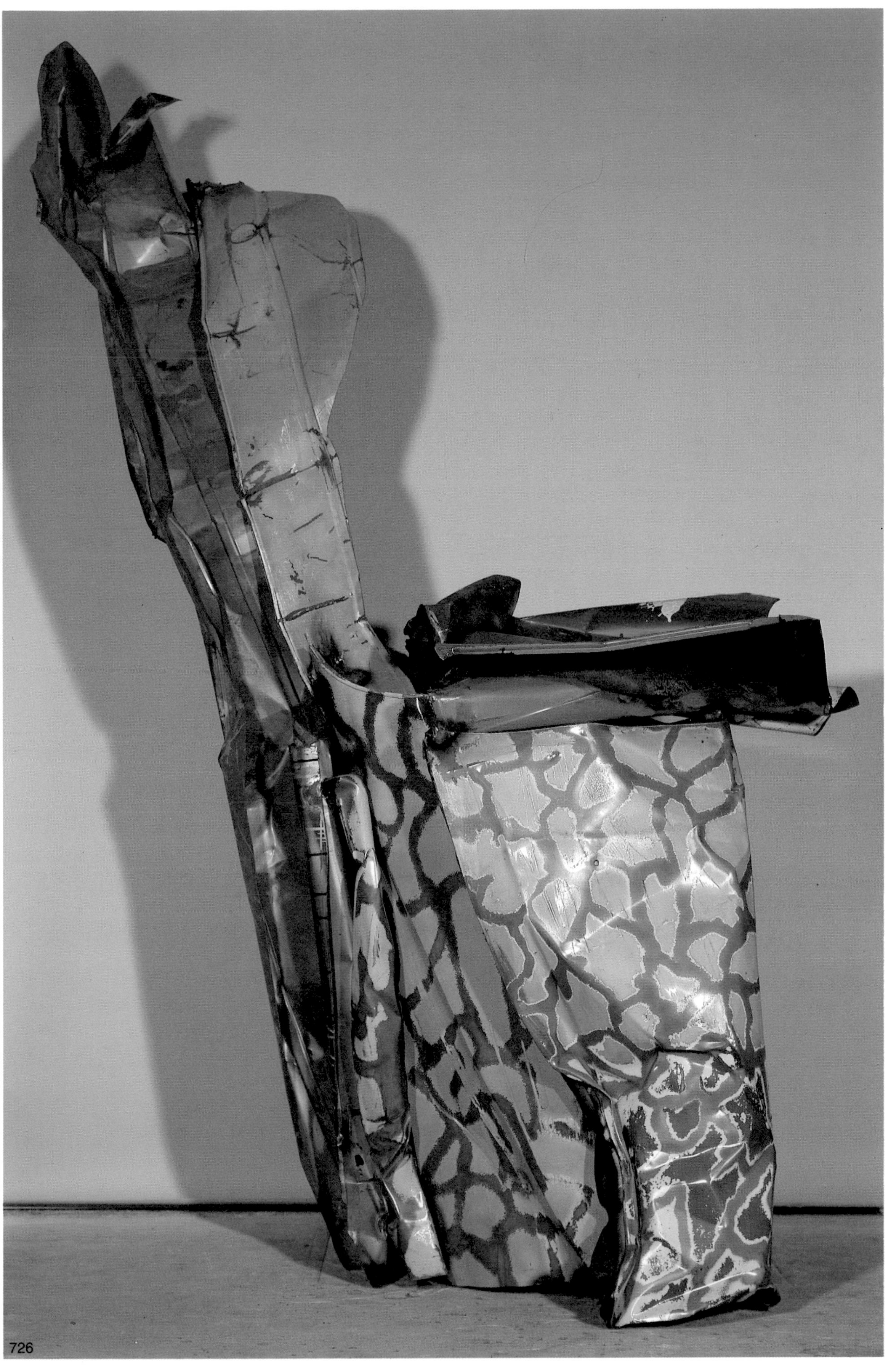

726

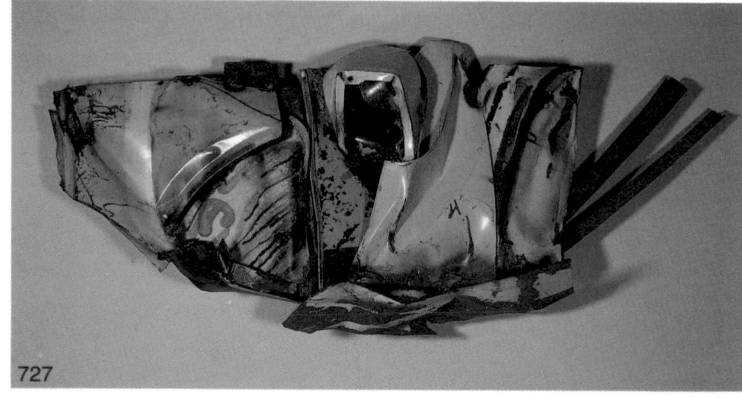
727

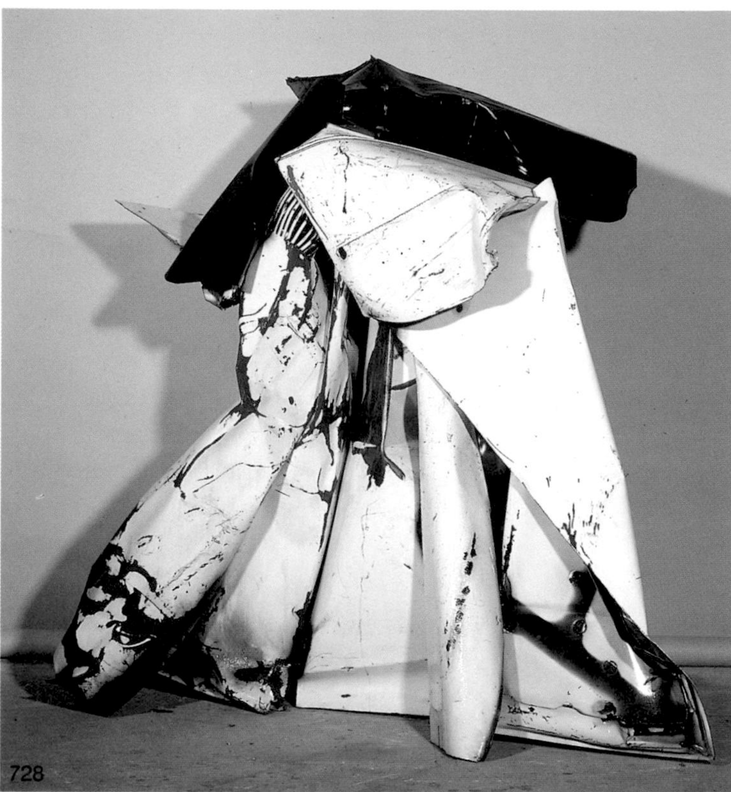
728

727

Rosy Fingered Dawn 1983

Painted and chromium-plated steel
21½ × 55½ × 11½ in.
(54.5 × 141 × 29 cm).

Collection

Mr. and Mrs. Frederick C. Matthaei, Bloomfield Hills, Michigan.

Provenance

Xavier Fourcade, Inc., and Thordis Moeller, New York, New York; Robert L. Kidd Galleries, Birmingham, Michigan.

Exhibitions

Robert L. Kidd Galleries, Birmingham, Michigan. *John Chamberlain*, illus. brochure. May 21–June 18, 1983.

728

Sarducci's Nun ('FLR 4 SEC') 1983

Painted and chromium-plated steel
62½ × 64 × 33 in.
(159 × 162.5 × 84 cm).

Collection

Uli Knecht, Stuttgart.

Provenance

Thordis Moeller, New York, New York, 1984.

729

Slapps 1983

Painted and chromium-plated steel
64½ × 71 × 30 in.
(164 × 180.5 × 76 cm).

Collection

Leo Castelli Gallery, New York, New York; acquired directly from the artist.

Exhibitions

Leo Castelli Gallery, New York, New York. *Sculpture*. Summer 1983.

730

The Archbishop, the Golfer and Ralph 1982–83

Painted and chromium-plated steel
86 × 76 × 33 in.
(218.5 × 193 × 84 cm).

Collection

Philip Johnson, New Canaan, Connecticut.

Provenance

Xavier Fourcade, Inc., and Thordis Moeller, New York, New York.

Exhibitions

Xavier Fourcade, Inc., New York, New York. *In Honor of de Kooning*, color illus. December 8, 1983–January 21, 1984.

Xavier Fourcade, Inc., New York, New York. *John Chamberlain: New Sculpture*, color illus. February 25–March 31, 1984.

731

The Arch of Lumps (A Tribute to an Act of Unclarity, The Vietnam War) 1983

Painted and chromium-plated steel
142 × 64 × 57½ in.
(360.5 × 162.5 × 146 cm).

Collection

Doris and Charles Saatchi, London, 1984.

Provenance

Xavier Fourcade, Inc., and Thordis Moeller, New York, New York.

Exhibitions

Xavier Fourcade, Inc., New York, New York. *John Chamberlain: New Sculpture*, color illus. February 25–March 31, 1984.

References

Heinrich Ehrhardt, ed., *John Chamberlain/Esculturas* (Madrid: Ministerio de Cultura, 1984), color illus.

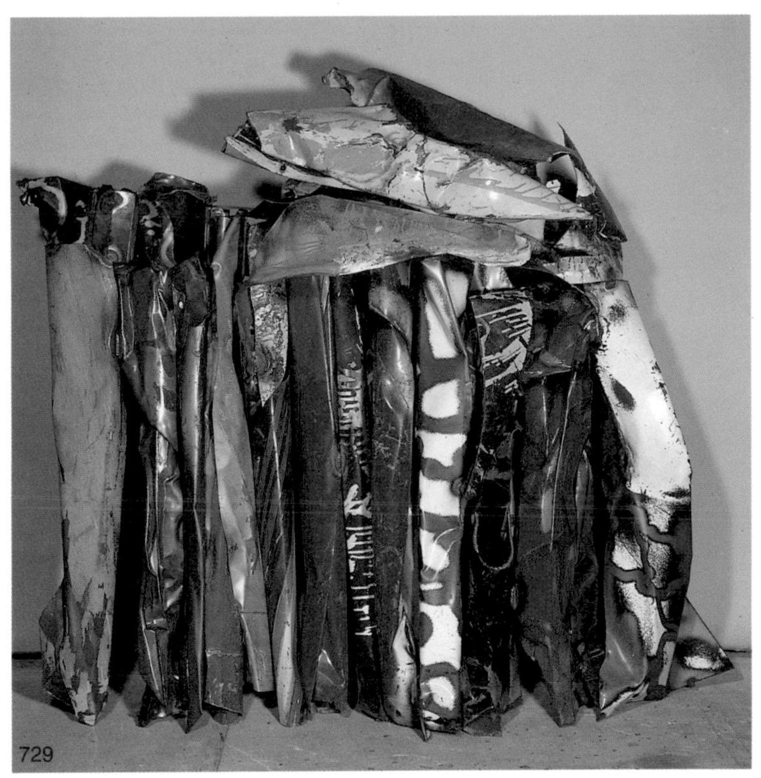
729

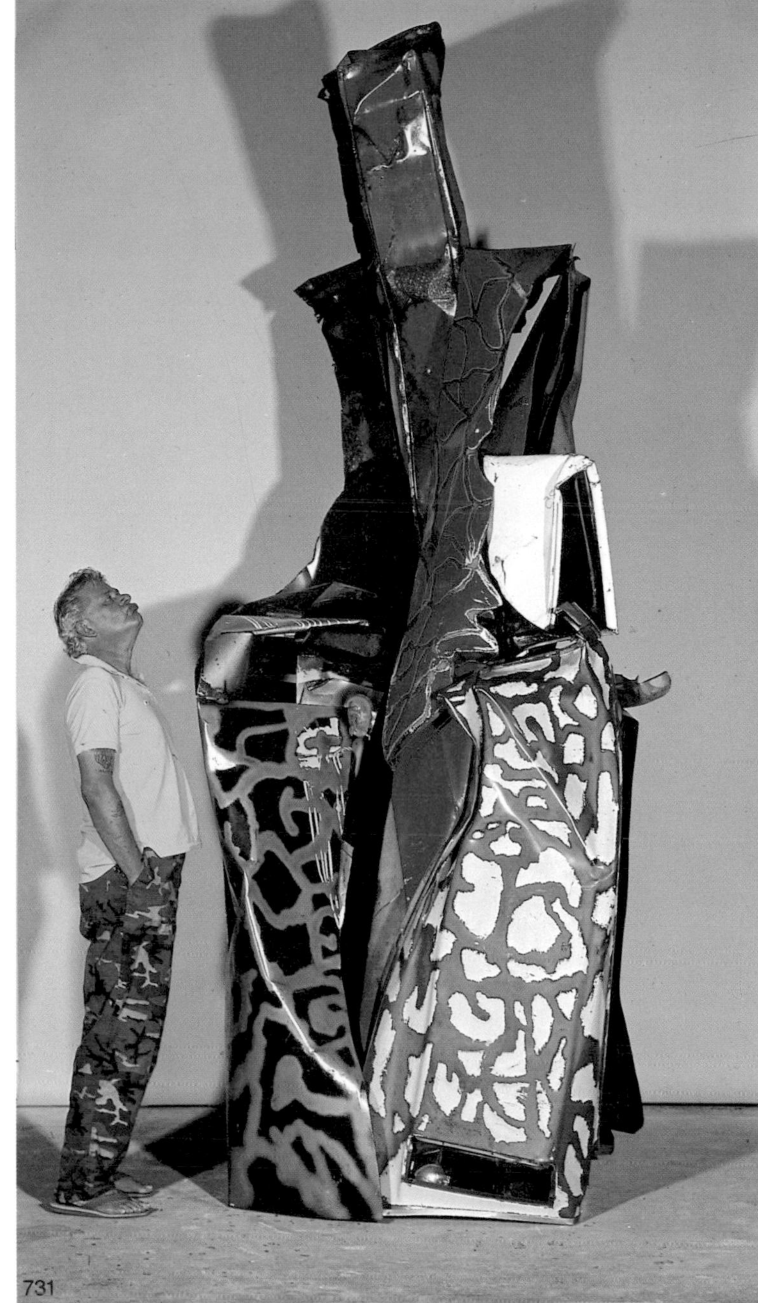
731

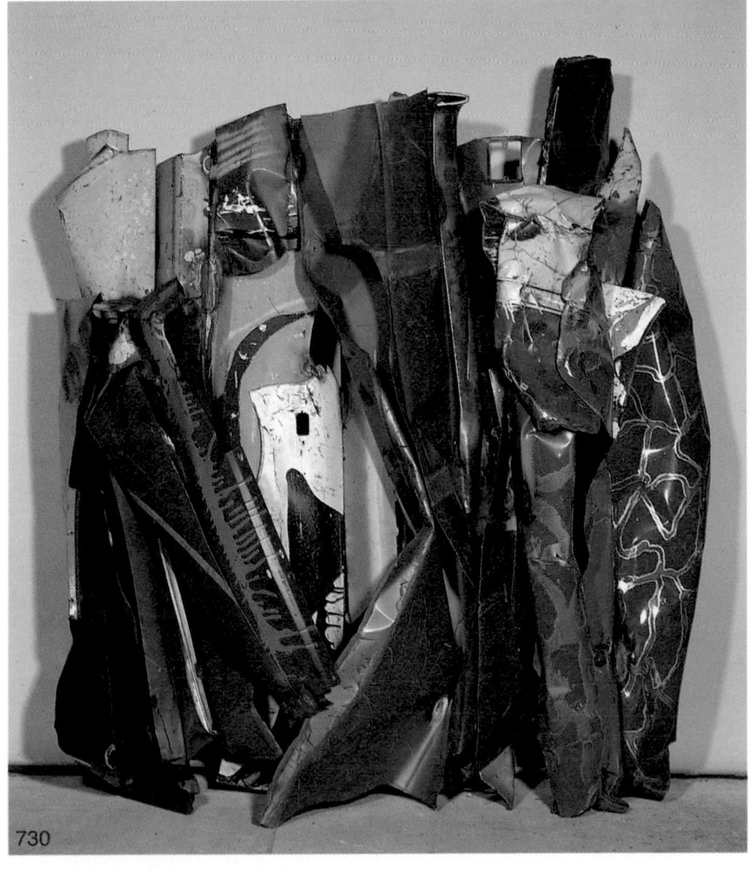
730

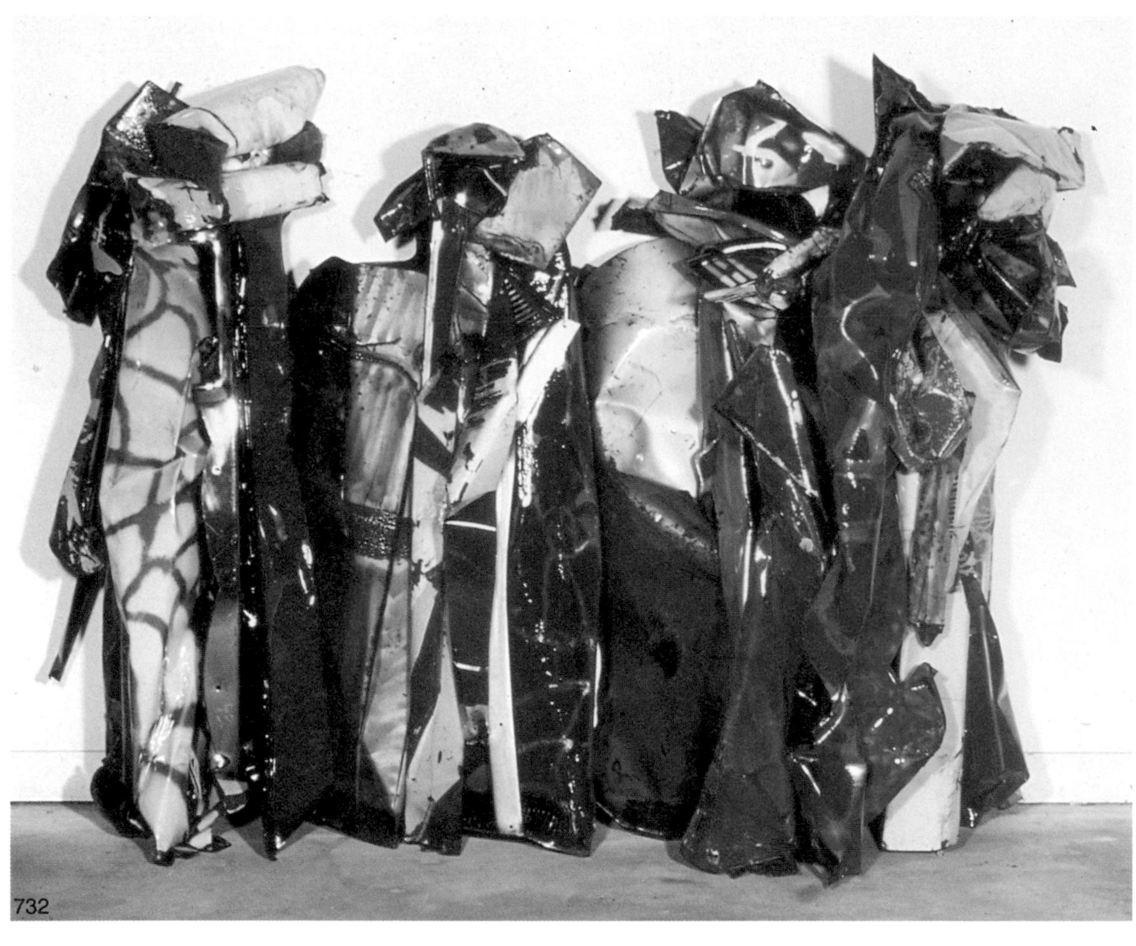
732

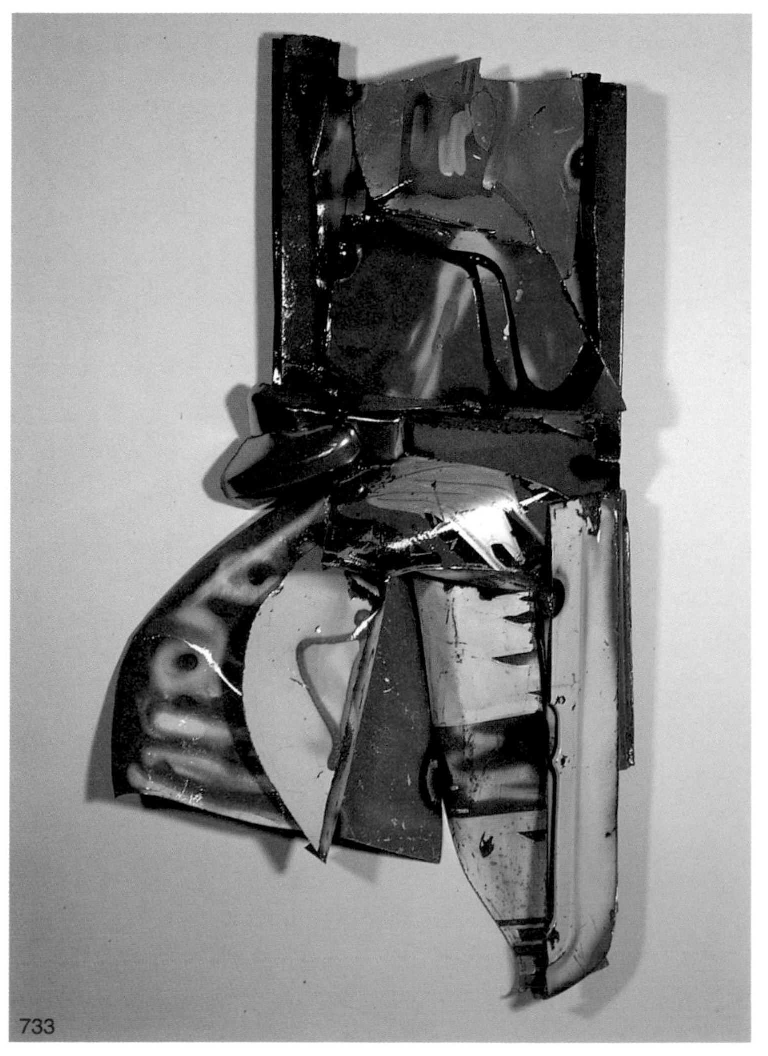
733

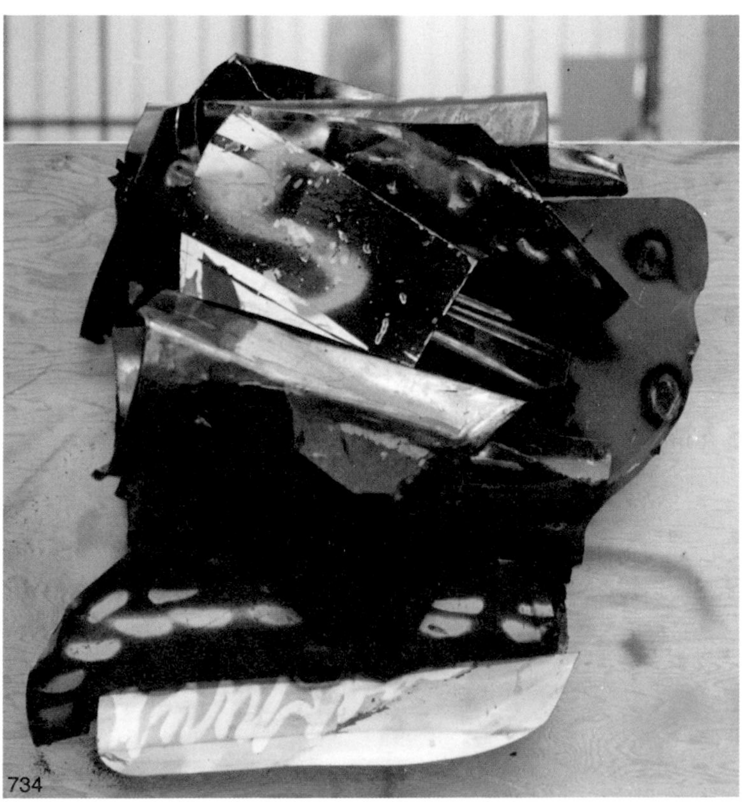
734

732

The Devil and the Deep Blue Sea 1983

Painted and chromium-plated steel
81½ × 107½ × 42 in.
(208 × 273 × 107 cm).

Collection
Xavier Fourcade, Inc., New York, New York.

Exhibitions
Xavier Fourcade, Inc., New York, New York. *John Chamberlain: New Sculpture*, color illus. February 25–March 31, 1984.

Galerie Rudolf Zwirner, Cologne. *John Chamberlain*. November 13–December 31, 1984.

733

Tux Lux 1983

Painted steel
48½ × 25½ × 8 in.
(123 × 65 × 20.5 cm).

Collection
Collection of the artist, Sarasota, Florida.

Exhibitions
Robert L. Kidd Galleries, Birmingham, Michigan, illus. brochure. *John Chamberlain*. May 21–June 18, 1983.

734

Zoomette 1983

Painted and chromium-plated steel
35 × 33 × 10½ in.
(90 × 84 × 26.5 cm).

Collection
Owen Morrissey, New York, New York, 1983; acquired directly from the artist.

A series of five sculptures made in 1983 were known as *Dancing in the Dark* (cat. nos. 735–739). Four were given as gifts by Chamberlain. All numbers in the titles are multiples of nine: 9, 18, 27, and so forth. This is typical of the numbering systems used by the artist.

735

Dancing in the Dark #9 1983

Painted steel
11½ × 11 × 12 in.
(29 × 28 × 30.5 cm).

Collection
Leo Castelli, New York, New York, 1983; acquired directly from the artist.

736

Dancing in the Dark #18 1983

Painted and chromium-plated steel
10 × 14 × 12 in.
(25.5 × 35.5 × 30.5 cm).

Collection
Freide and Rubin Gorewitz, West Nyack, New York, 1983; acquired directly from the artist.

Notes
The sculpture is signed and dated: *Chamberlain '83*.

737

Dancing in the Dark #27 1983

Painted steel
Dimensions unknown.

Collection
Dominique de Menil, Houston, Texas, 1983; acquired directly from the artist.

738

Dancing in the Dark #36 1983

Painted steel
10½ × 18 × 11½ in.
(26.5 × 45.5 × 29 cm).

Collection
Lorraine Chamberlain, Essex, Connecticut, 1983; acquired directly from the artist.

Notes
The sculpture was stolen in 1984.

739

Dancing in the Dark #63 1983

Painted steel
13 × 9 × 12½ in.
(33 × 23 × 31.5 cm).

Collection
Greg Constantine, Berrien Springs, Michigan; acquired directly from the artist.

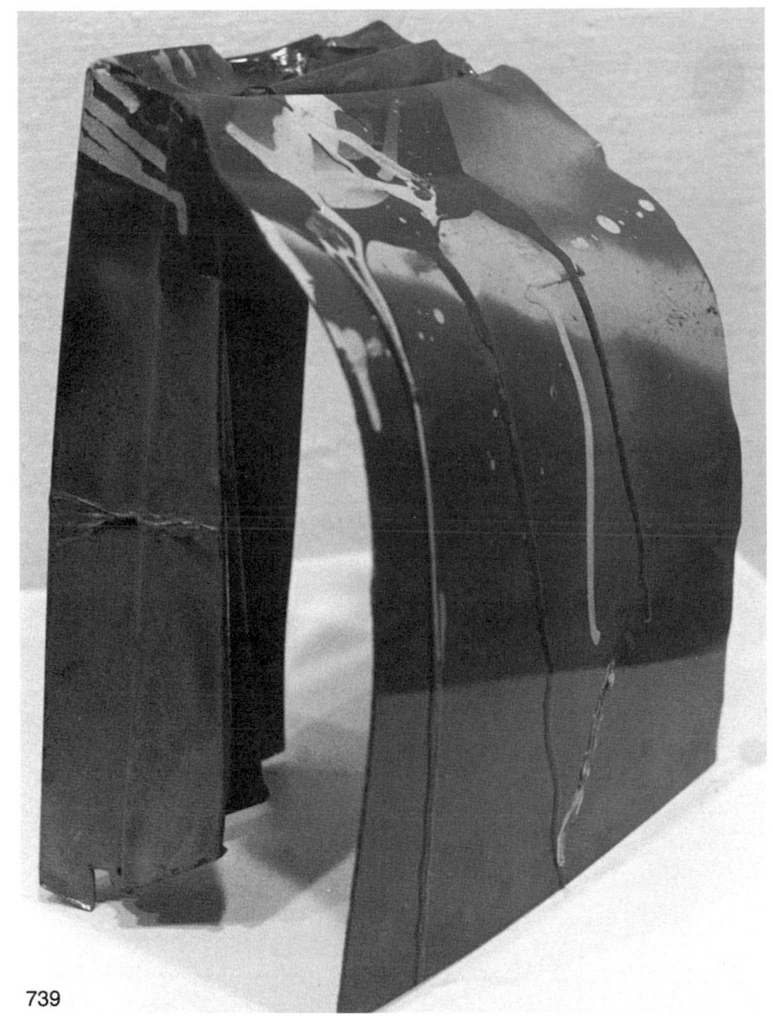

739

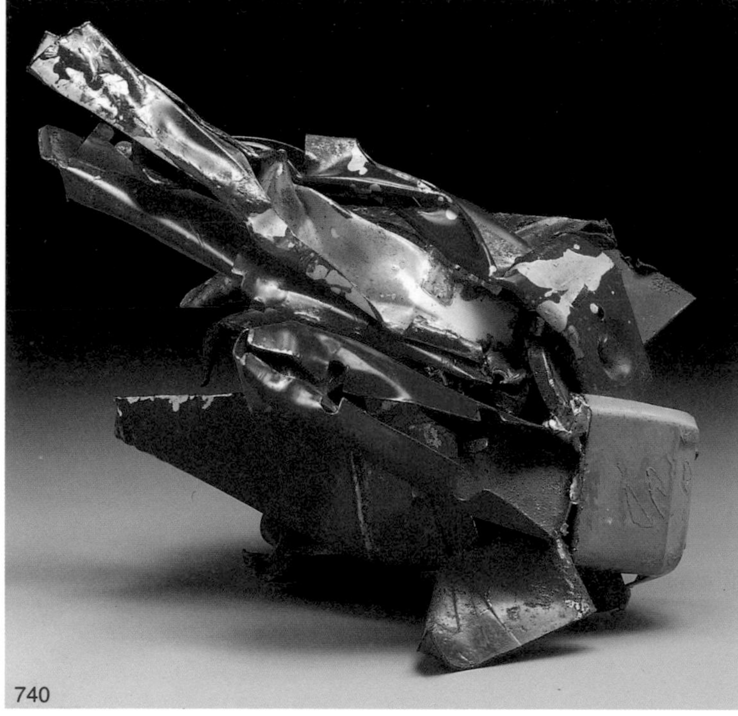
740

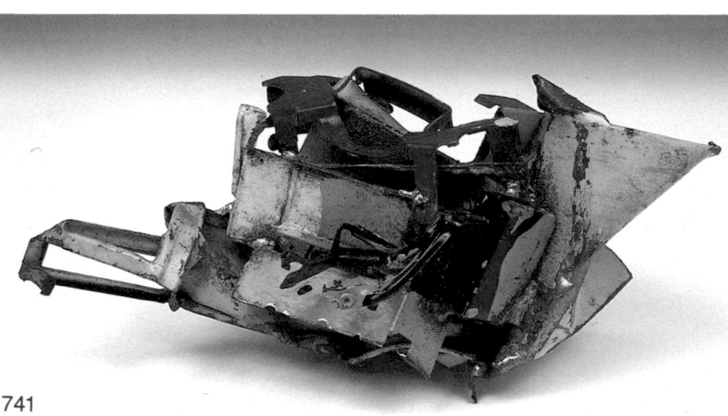
741

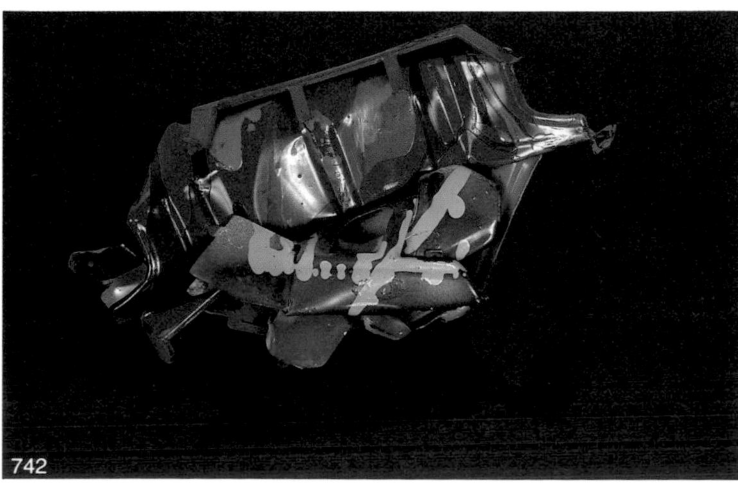
742

740

Tonk #7–83 1983
Painted steel
6 × 10½ × 8 in.
(15 × 26.5 × 20 cm).

Collection
Judge and Mrs. Peter B. Spivak, Grosse Pointe, Michigan, 1983.

Provenance
Xavier Fourcade, Inc., and Thordis Moeller, New York, New York; Marian Goodman Gallery, New York, New York.

Exhibitions
Marian Goodman Gallery, New York, New York. *John Chamberlain*. September 20–October 15, 1983.

Notes
The 1983 numbered *Tonks* begin with *Tonk #7*, which follows *Tonk #6–82* (cat. no. 708).

741

Tonk #8–83 1983
Painted steel
5½ × 10½ × 6½ in.
(14 × 26.5 × 16.5 cm).

Collection
B. C. Holland & Co., Chicago, Illinois, 1985.

Provenance
Xavier Fourcade, Inc., and Thordis Moeller, New York, New York; Margo Leavin Gallery, Los Angeles, California.

Exhibitions
Marian Goodman Gallery, New York, New York. *John Chamberlain*. September 20–October 15, 1983.
Margo Leavin Gallery, Los Angeles, California. *John Chamberlain*. March 4–30, 1985.

742

Tonk #9–83 1983
Painted steel
4½ × 10 × 4½ in.
(11.5 × 25.5 × 11.5 cm).

Collection
Xavier Fourcade, Inc., New York, New York.

743

Tonk #10–83 1983
Painted steel
7½ × 6½ × 5 in.
(19 × 16.5 × 12.5 cm).

Collection
Xavier Fourcade, Inc., New York, New York.

Exhibitions
Galerie Helen van der Meij, Amsterdam. *John Chamberlain: Tonks*. April 21–May 24, 1984.

744

Tonk #11–83 1983
Painted steel
5 × 13½ × 4½ in.
(12.5 × 34 × 11.5 cm).

Collection
Galleriet, Lund, Sweden.

Provenance
Xavier Fourcade, Inc., and Thordis Moeller, New York, New York.

Exhibitions
Marian Goodman Gallery, New York, New York. *John Chamberlain*. September 20–October 15, 1983.

Notes
The sculpture is signed and dated *Chamberlain '83*.

745

Tonk #12–83 1983
Painted steel
5½ × 8½ × 6 in.
(14 × 21.5 × 15 cm).

Collection
Xavier Fourcade, Inc., New York, New York.

Exhibitions
Marian Goodman Gallery, New York, New York. *John Chamberlain*. September 20–October 15, 1983.
Galerie Helen van der Meij, Amsterdam. *John Chamberlain: Tonks*. April 21–May 24, 1984.

746

Tonk #13–83 1983
Painted steel
11½ × 7 × 5½ in.
(29 × 18 × 14 cm).

Collection
Martin Z. Margulies, Coconut Grove, Florida, 1983.

Provenance
Xavier Fourcade, Inc., and Thordis Moeller, New York, New York, 1983; Marian Goodman Gallery, New York, New York, 1983.

Exhibitions
Marian Goodman Gallery, New York, New York. *John Chamberlain*. September 20–October 15, 1983.

747

Tonk #14–83 1983

Painted steel
7½ × 11½ × 11½ in.
(19 × 29 × 29 cm).

Collection
Robert and Susan Sosnick, Bloomfield Hills, Michigan, 1983.

Provenance
Xavier Fourcade, Inc., and Thordis Moeller, New York, New York, 1983; Marian Goodman Gallery, New York, New York, 1983.

Exhibitions
Marian Goodman Gallery, New York, New York. *John Chamberlain*. September 20–October 15, 1983.

748

Tonk #15–83 1983

Painted steel
6 × 9½ × 5½ in.
(15 × 24 × 14 cm).

Collection
Galleriet, Lund, Sweden.

Provenance
Xavier Fourcade, Inc., and Thordis Moeller, New York, New York.

Exhibitions
Marian Goodman Gallery, New York, New York. *John Chamberlain*. September 20–October 15, 1983.

749

Tonk #16–83 1983

Painted steel
7½ × 8½ × 6½ in.
(19 × 21.5 × 16.5 cm).

Collection
Xavier Fourcade, Inc., New York, New York.

750

Tonk #17–83 1983

Painted steel
8½ × 5½ × 4½ in.
(21.5 × 14 × 11.5 cm).

Collection
Present location unknown.

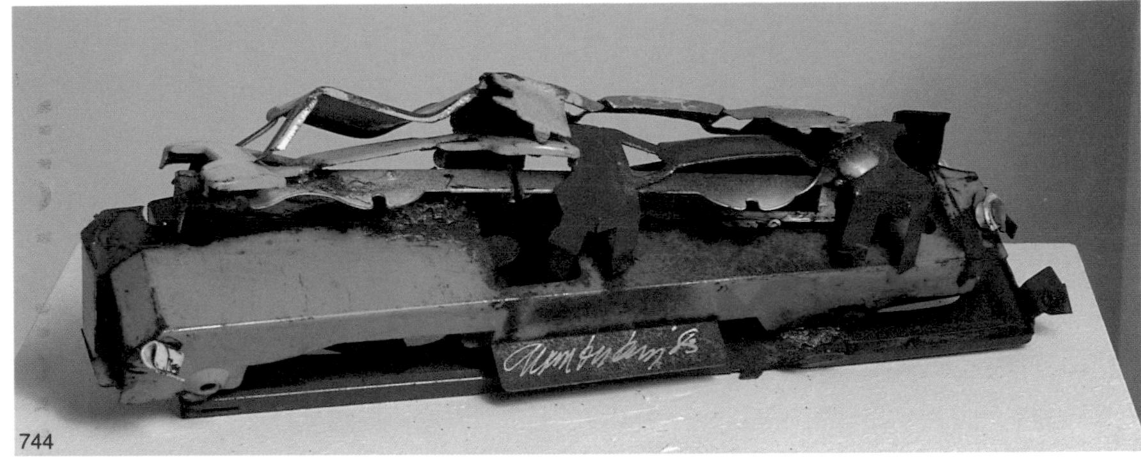
744

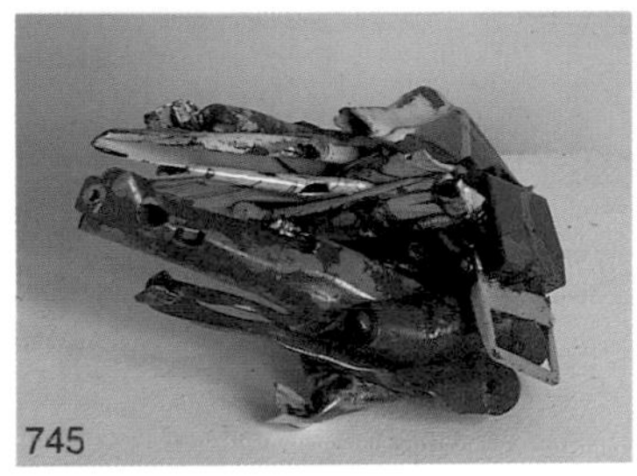
745

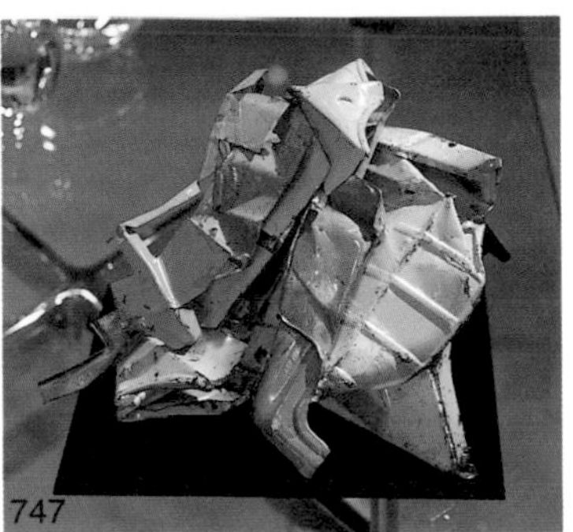
747

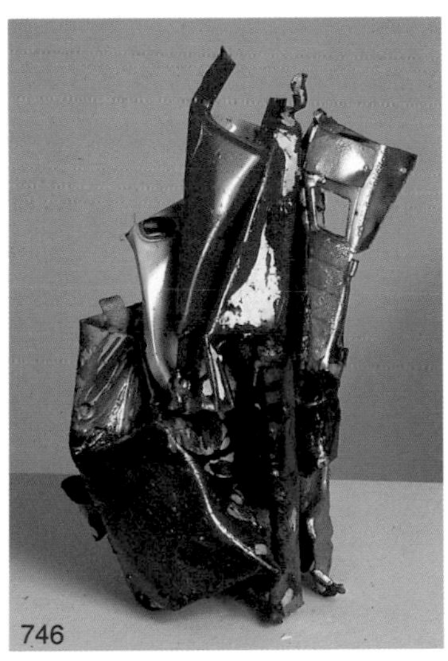
746

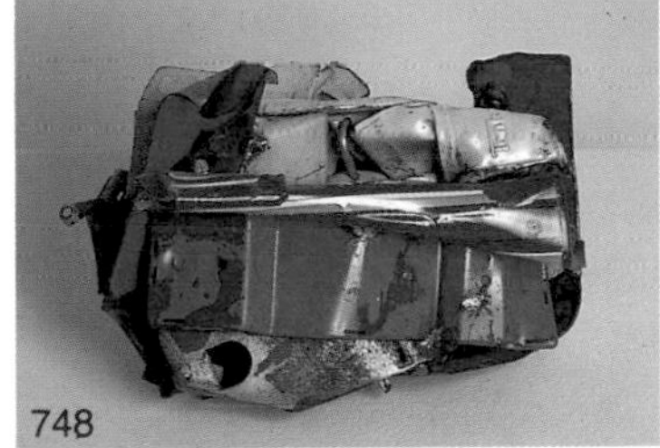
748

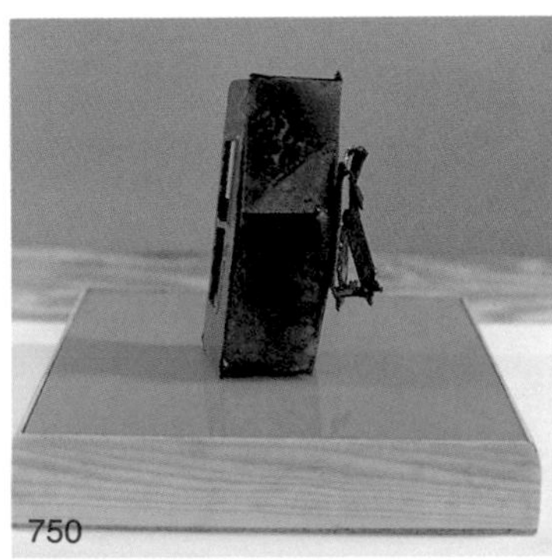
750

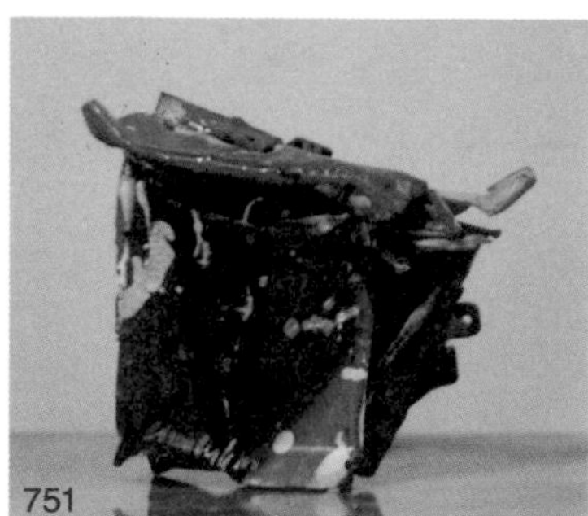
751

751

Tonk #18–83 1983
Painted steel
6 × 7 × 4½ in.
(15 × 17.5 × 11.5 cm).

Collection
John-Charles de Menil, New York, New York, 1984.

Provenance
Xavier Fourcade, Inc., and Thordis Moeller, New York, New York.

Exhibitions
Xavier Fourcade, Inc., New York, New York. *John Chamberlain: New Sculpture*. February 25–March 31, 1984.

752

752

Tonk #19–83 1983
Painted steel
7 × 8 × 5½ in. (18 × 20 × 14 cm).

Collection
Xavier Fourcade, Inc., New York, New York.

Exhibitions
Galerie Helen van der Meij, Amsterdam. *John Chamberlain: Tonks*. April 21–May 24, 1984.

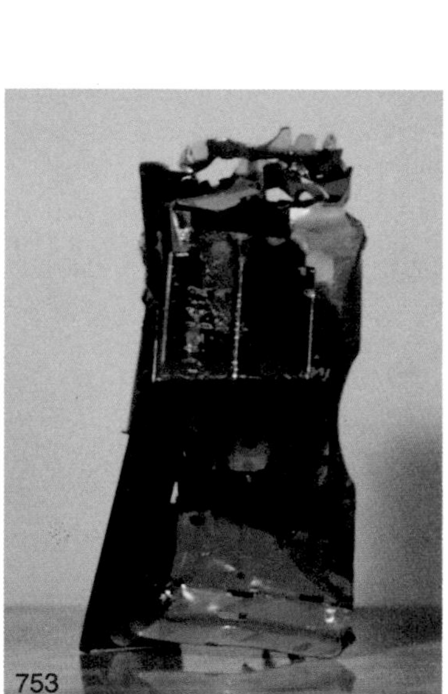
753

753

Tonk #20–83 1983
Painted steel
10 × 5½ × 6 in.
(25.5 × 14 × 15 cm).

Collection
Xavier Fourcade, Inc., New York, New York.

Exhibitions
Hokin Gallery, Inc., Bay Harbour Islands, Florida. *Large Sculpture*. October 12–November 8, 1984.

754

Tonk #21–83 1983
Painted steel
5½ × 8½ × 5½ in.
(14 × 21.5 × 14 cm).

Collection
Peter Fay, South Dartmouth, Massachusetts; acquired directly from the artist.

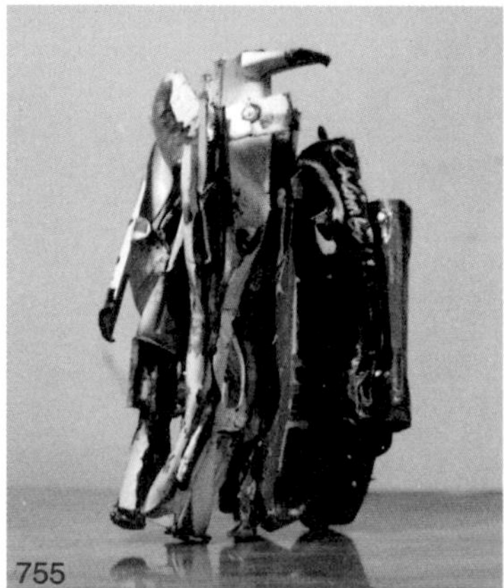
755

755

Tonk #22–83 1983
Painted steel
8½ × 6½ × 4½ in.
(21.5 × 16.5 × 11.5 cm).

Collection
Xavier Fourcade, Inc., New York, New York.

756

Tonk #23–83 1983
Painted steel
6½ × 14½ × 10 in.
(16.5 × 37 × 25.5 cm).

Collection
Xavier Fourcade, Inc., New York, New York.

Exhibitions
Galerie Helen van der Meij, Amsterdam. *John Chamberlain: Tonks*. April 21–May 24, 1984.

References
John Chamberlain: New Sculpture (New York: Xavier Fourcade, Inc., 1984), color illus.

757

Tonk #24–83 1983
Painted steel
11½ × 14 × 7½ in.
(29 × 35.5 × 19 cm).

Collection
Dr. Norman N. Hoffman, Los Angeles, California, 1985.

Provenance
Xavier Fourcade, Inc., and Thordis Moeller, New York, New York; Margo Leavin Gallery, Los Angeles, California.

Exhibitions
Xavier Fourcade, Inc., New York, New York. *John Chamberlain: New Sculpture*. February 25–March 31, 1984.
Margo Leavin Gallery, Los Angeles, California. *John Chamberlain*. March 4–30, 1985.

758

Tonk #27–83 1983
Painted steel
6½ × 15½ × 5 in.
(16.5 × 39.5 × 12.5 cm).

Collection
Xavier Fourcade, Inc., New York, New York.

759

Tonk #28–83 1983
Painted steel
6½ × 5½ × 8½ in.
(16.5 × 14 × 21.5 cm).

Collection
Frances M. Shore, Cincinnati, Ohio, 1984.

Provenance
Hokin Gallery, Inc., Bay Harbour Islands, Florida.

760

Tonk #29–83 1983
Painted steel
5 × 6½ × 20½ in.
(12.5 × 16.5 × 52 cm).

Collection
Xavier Fourcade, Inc., New York, New York.

761

Tonk #30–83 1983
Painted steel
4½ × 6½ × 30½ in.
(11.5 × 16.5 × 77.5 cm).

Collection
Xavier Fourcade, Inc., New York, New York.

Exhibitions
Xavier Fourcade, Inc., New York, New York. *John Chamberlain: New Sculpture*. February 25–March 31, 1984.

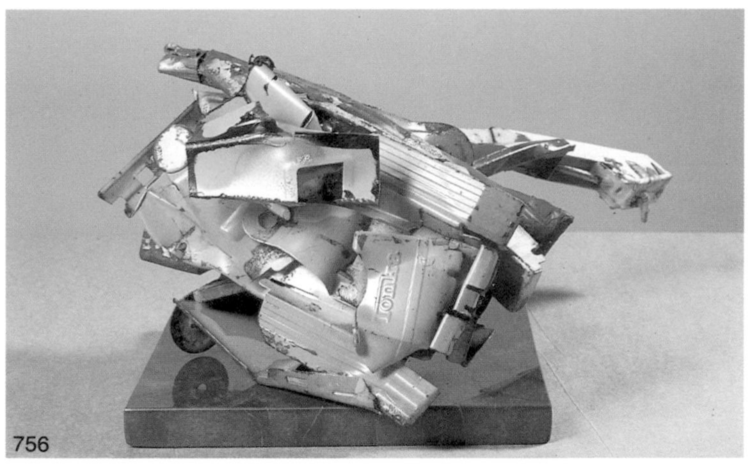
756

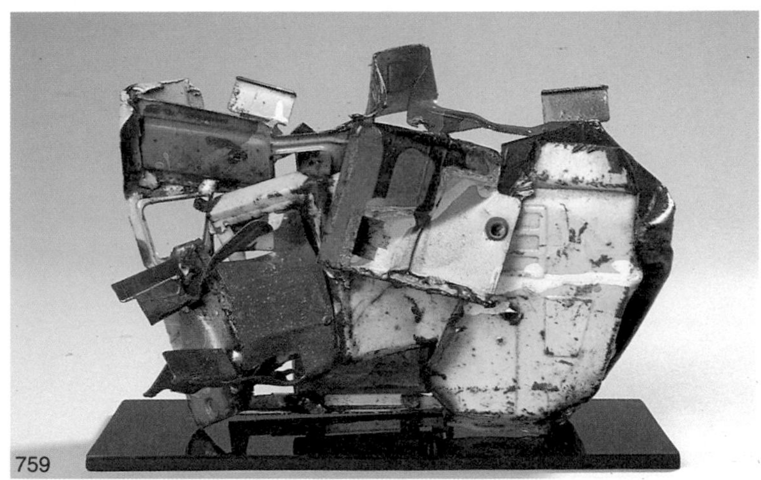
759

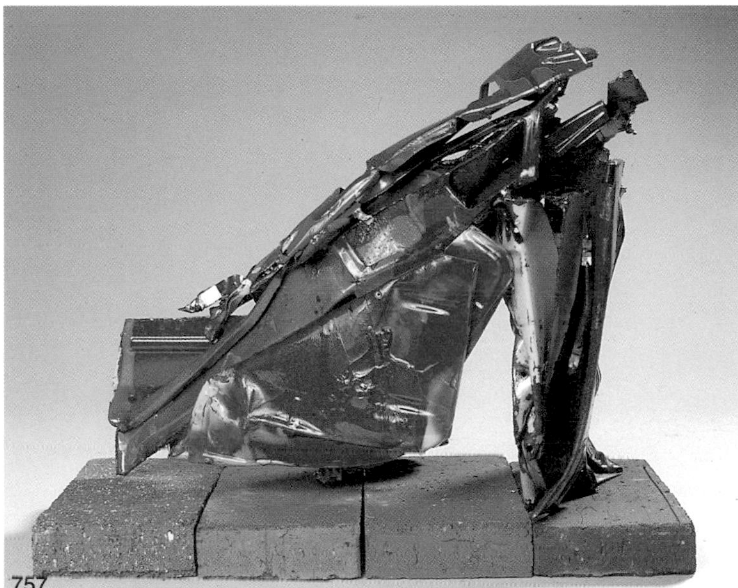
757

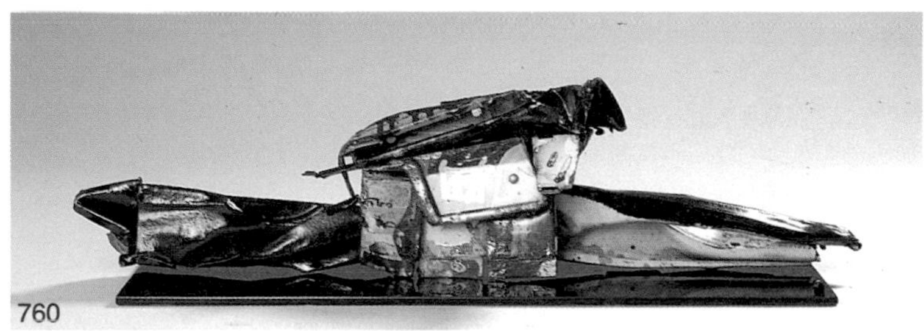
760

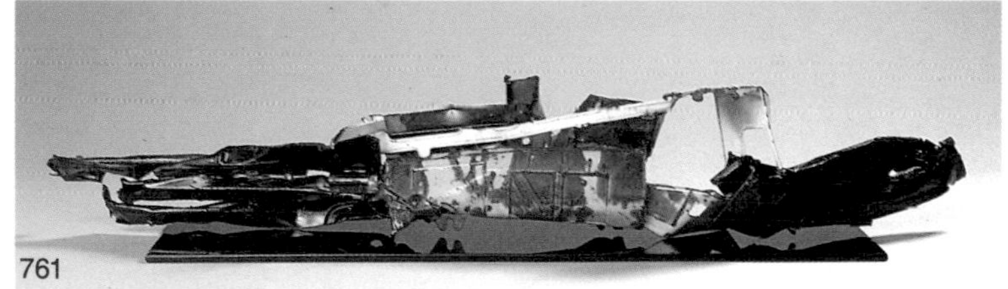
761

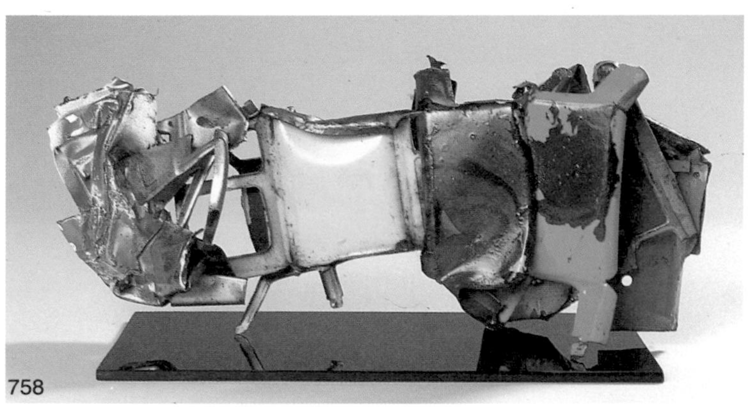
758

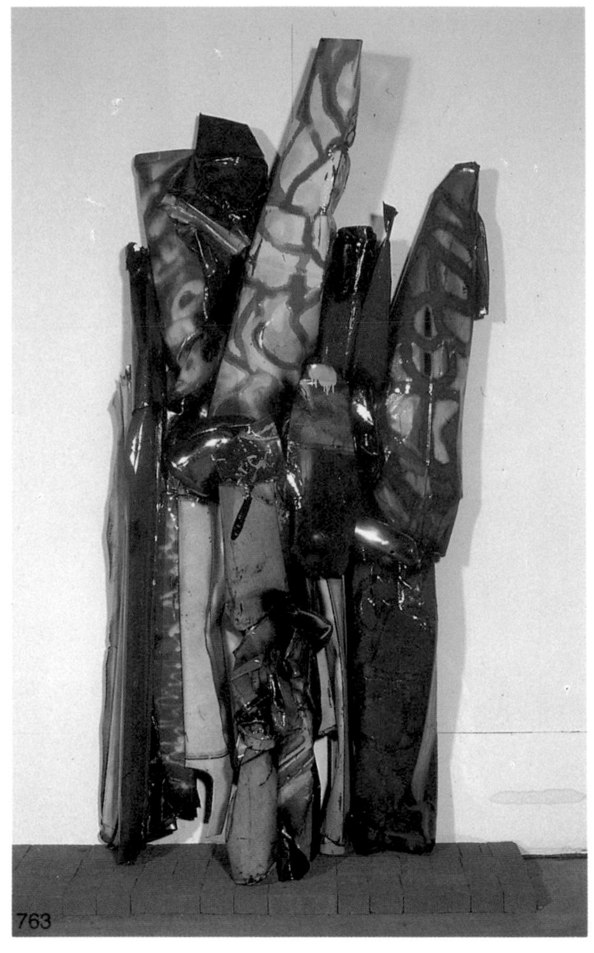
763

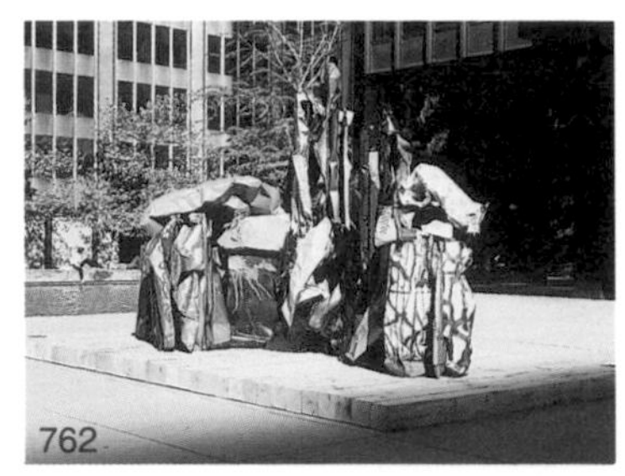
762

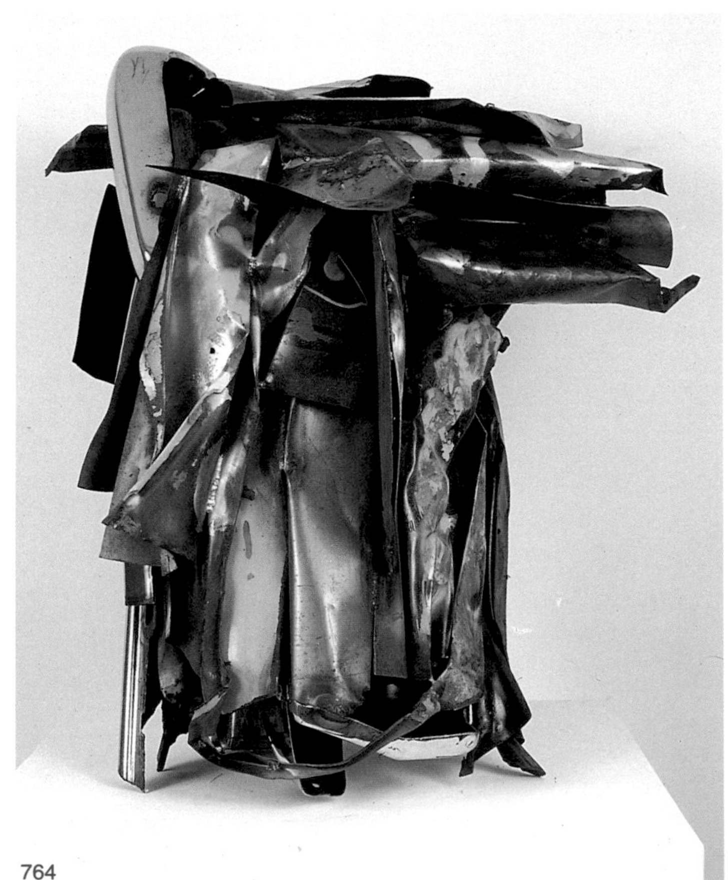
764

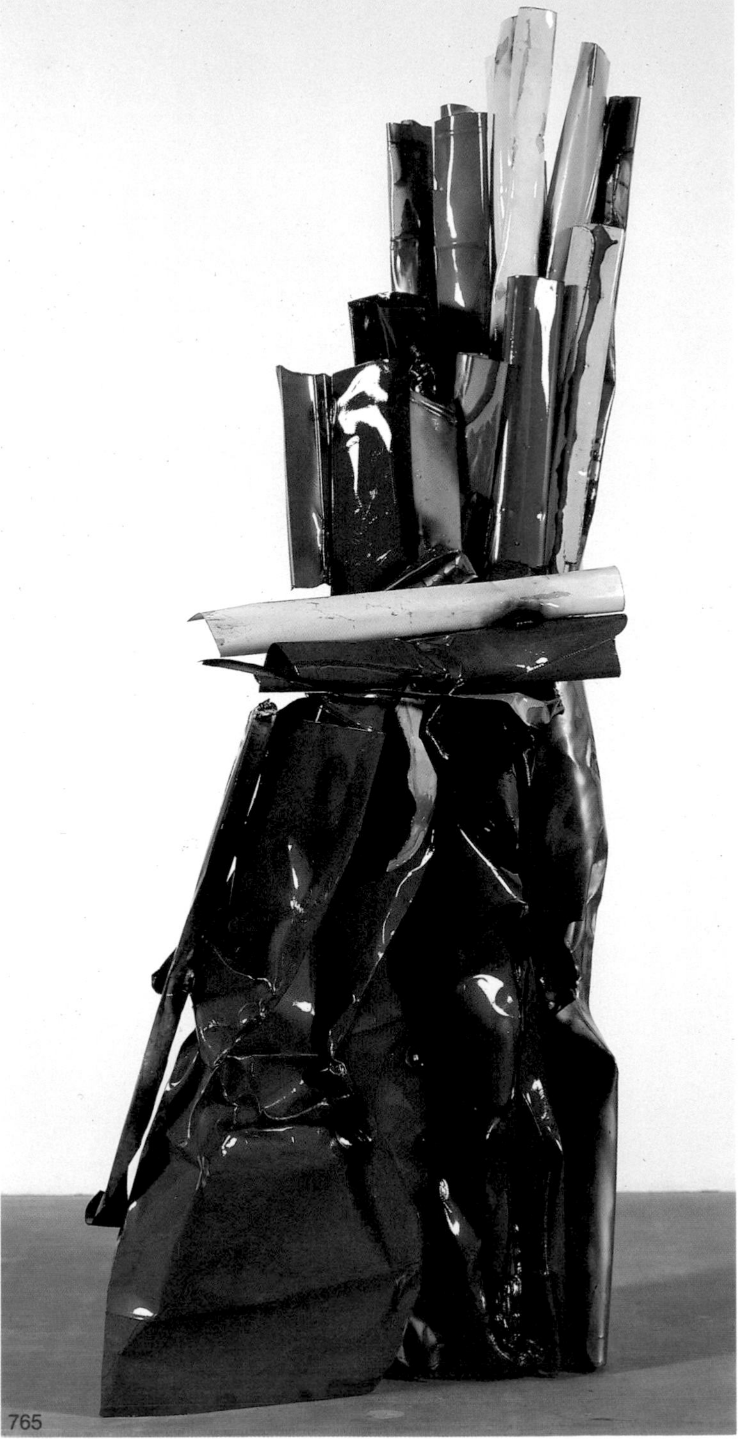
765

762

American Tableau 1984

Painted and chromium-plated steel
144 × 252 × 132 in.
(366 × 640 × 335 cm).

Collection

Menil Collection, Houston, Texas, 1984.

Provenance

Xavier Fourcade, Inc., and Thordis Moeller, New York, New York.

Exhibitions

The Seagram Plaza, New York, New York. September 12–November 10, 1984.

763

Cafe Macedonia 1984

Painted and chromium-plated steel
98 × 49 × 26 in.
(249 × 124.5 × 66 cm).

Collection

Xavier Fourcade, Inc., New York, New York.

Exhibitions

Margo Leavin Gallery, Los Angeles, California. *John Chamberlain*. March 4–30, 1985.

764

Double Dutch 1984

Painted and chromium-plated steel
35 × 30½ × 32 in.
(89 × 77.5 × 81.5 cm).

Collection

Xavier Fourcade, Inc., New York, New York.

Exhibitions

Margo Leavin Gallery, Los Angeles, California. *John Chamberlain*. March 4–30, 1985.

765

Etruscan Romance 1984

Painted and chromium-plated steel
111 × 49 × 31 in.
(282 × 124.5 × 78.5 cm).

Collection

Frederick R. Weisman Foundation of Art, Los Angeles, California, 1985.

Provenance

Xavier Fourcade, Inc., New York, New York; Margo Leavin Gallery, Los Angeles, California.

Exhibitions

Margo Leavin Gallery, Los Angeles, California. *John Chamberlain*. March 4–30, 1985.

766

Glossalia Adagio 1984

Painted and chromium-plated steel
80 × 129 × 72 in.
(203 × 327.5 × 183 cm).

Collection

David Pincus, Wynnewood, Pennsylvania, 1985.

Provenance

Xavier Fourcade, Inc., and Thordis Moeller, New York, New York.

767

Good Friday (An Afternoon Well Spent) 1984

Painted steel
117 × 60 × 19 in.
(297 × 152.5 × 48 cm).

Collection

Xavier Fourcade, Inc., New York, New York.

Exhibitions

Marian Goodman Gallery, New York, New York. *Sculpture*. June 18–July 12, 1985.

768

Infected Eucharist 1984

Painted and chromium-plated steel
109 × 40 × 36 in.
(277 × 101.5 × 91.5 cm).

Collection

Mr. and Mrs. Barry Berkus, Santa Barbara, California, 1985.

Provenance

Xavier Fourcade, Inc., New York, New York; Margo Leavin Gallery, Los Angeles, California.

Exhibitions

Margo Leavin Gallery, Los Angeles, California. *John Chamberlain*. March 4–30, 1985.

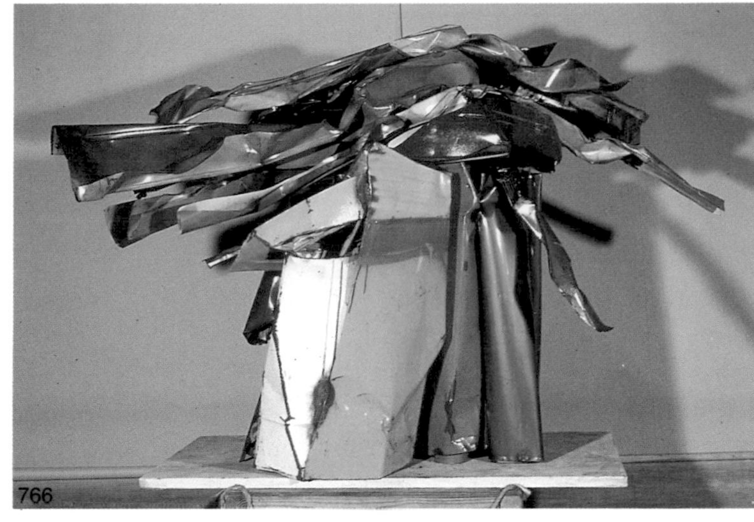
766

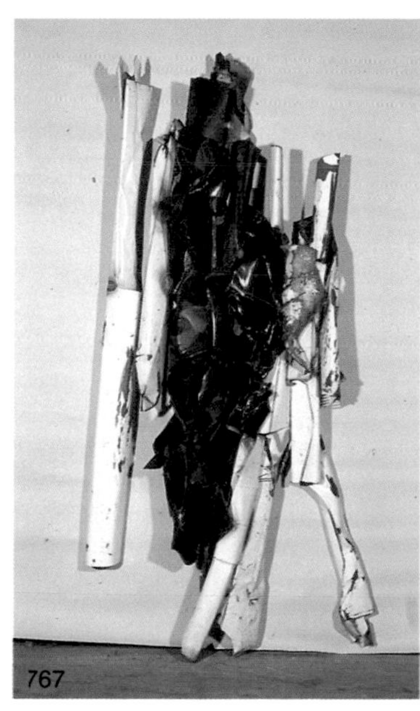
767

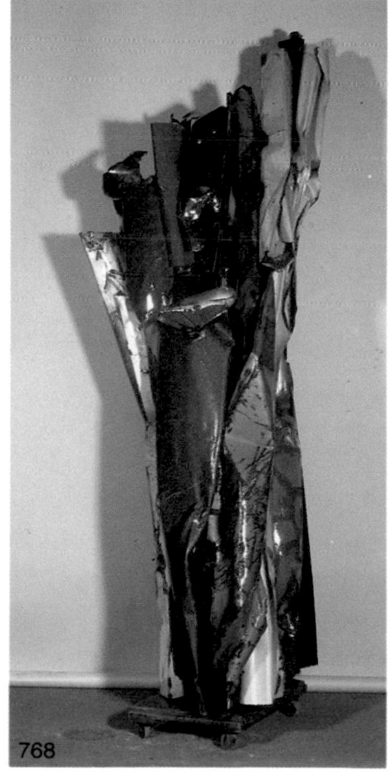
768

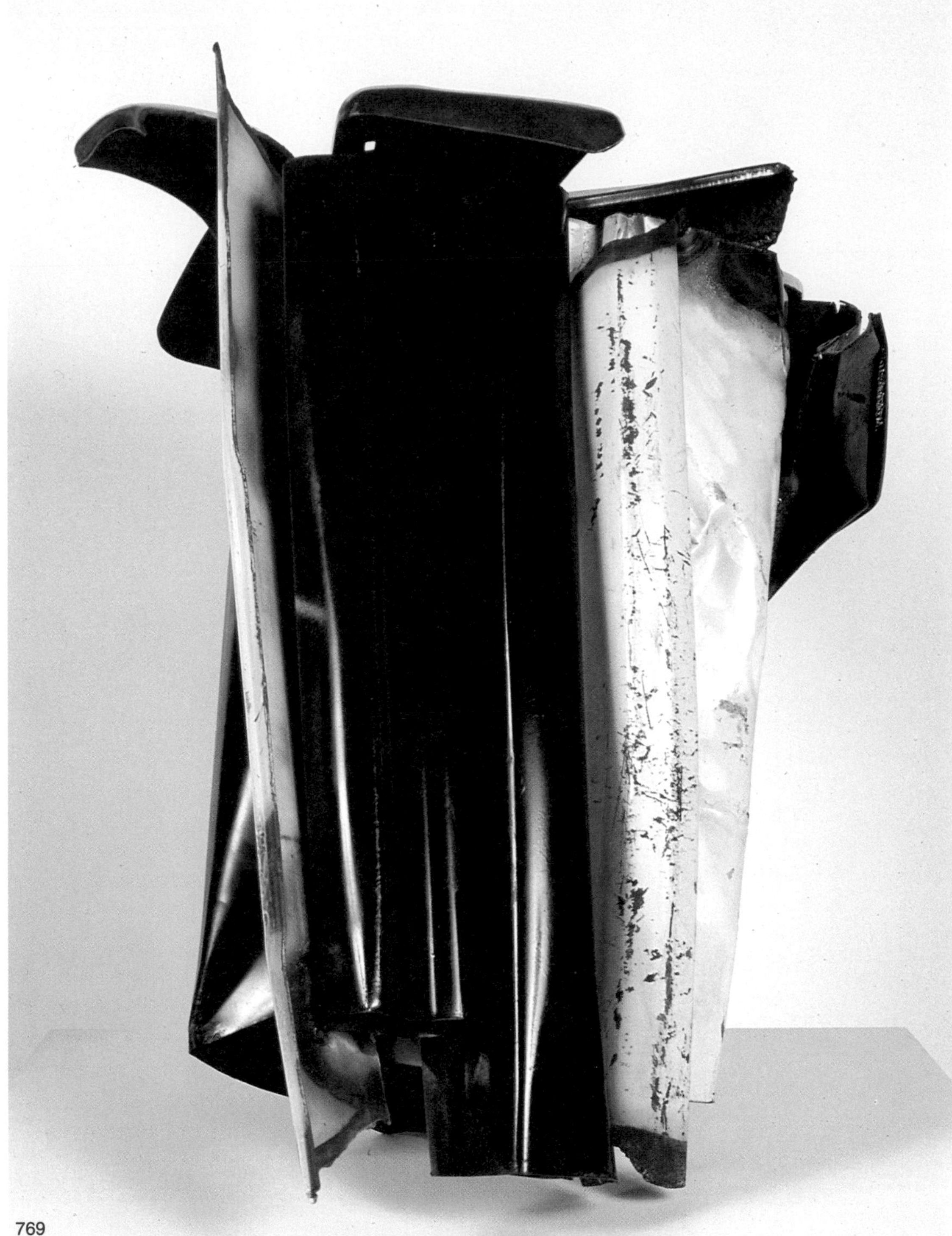
769

769

Looking Good, Billy Ray 1984
Painted and chromium-plated steel
32 × 26 × 27 in.
(81.5 × 66 × 68.5 cm).

Collection
Douglas S. Cramer, Los Angeles, California, 1985.

Provenance
Xavier Fourcade, Inc., New York, New York; Margo Leavin Gallery, Los Angeles, California.

Exhibitions
Margo Leavin Gallery, Los Angeles, California. *John Chamberlain*. March 4–30, 1985.

770

Medina Ataxia 1984
Painted and chromium-plated steel
122 × 46½ × 44 in.
(310 × 118 × 112 cm).

Collection
Xavier Fourcade, Inc., New York, New York.

Exhibitions
Margo Leavin Gallery, Los Angeles, California. *John Chamberlain*. March 4–30, 1985.

771

One Man's Family 1984
Painted and chromium-plated steel
144 × 72 × 72 in.
(366 × 183 × 183 cm).

Collection
Private collection, New York, New York, 1984; acquired directly from the artist.

772

Trumpery Praxis 1984
Painted and chromium-plated steel
126 × 69 × 46 in.
(320 × 175 × 117 cm).

Collection
Xavier Fourcade, Inc., New York, New York.

Exhibitions
Area, New York, New York. *Art*. May 6–June 15, 1985.

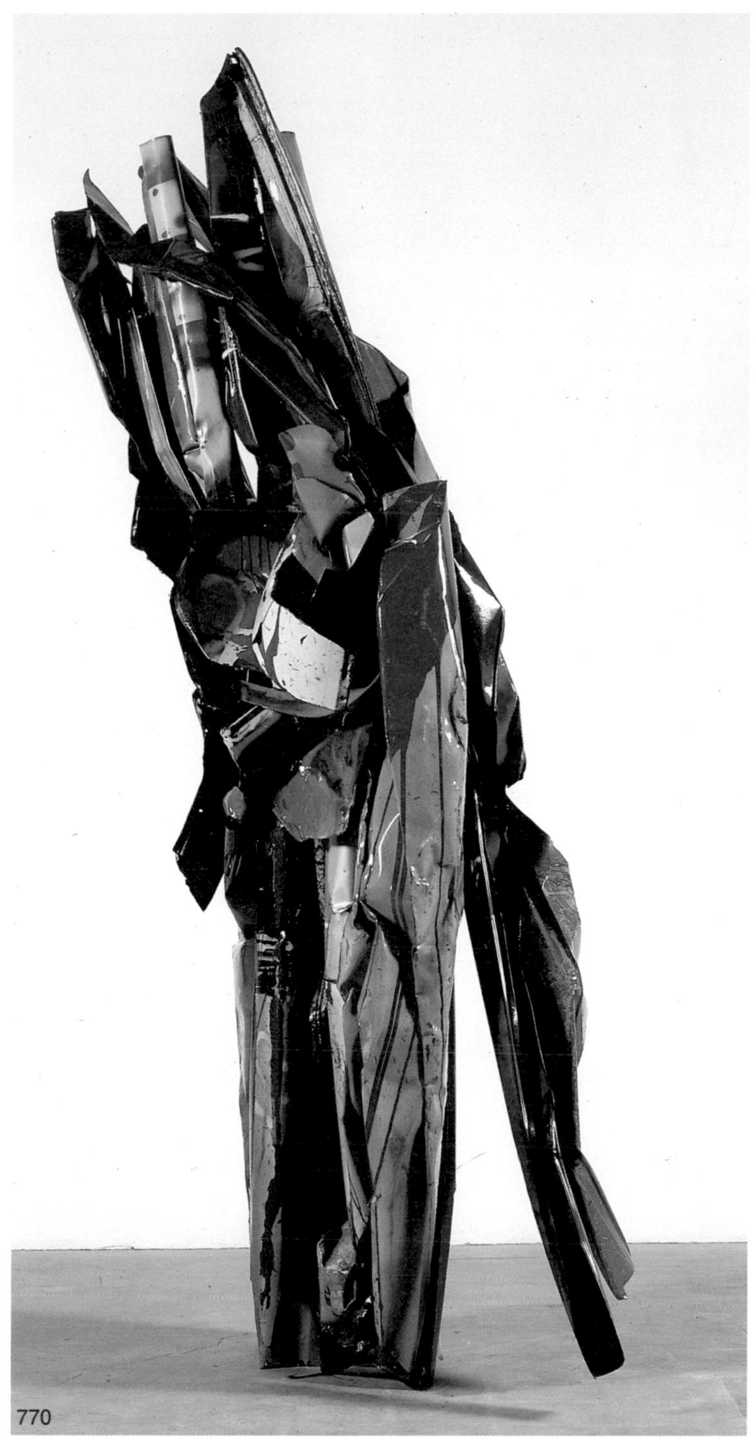

770

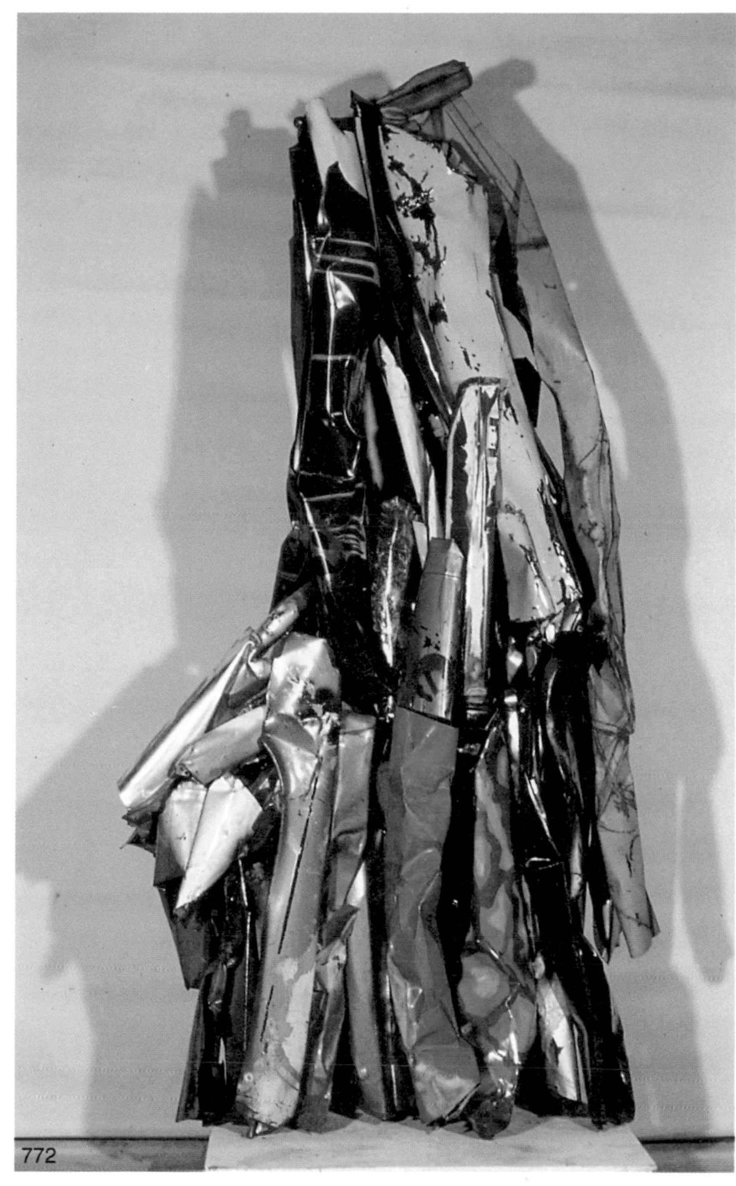

772

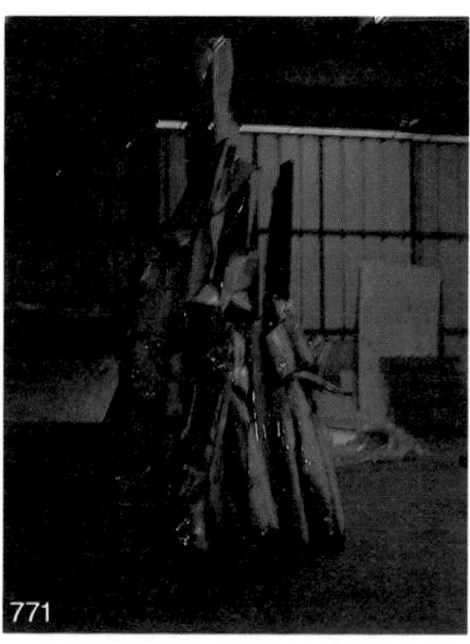

771

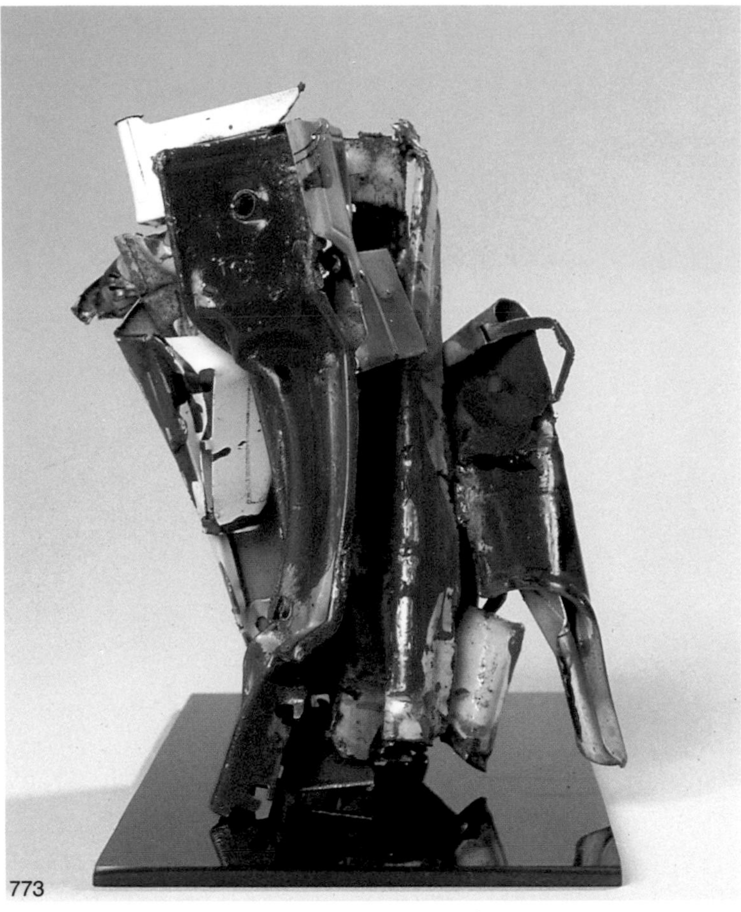

773

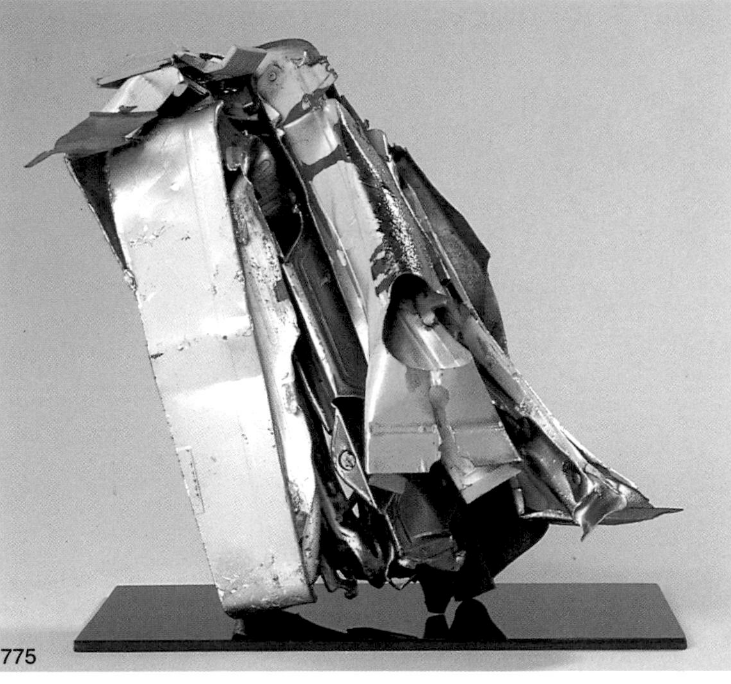

775

773

Tonk #1–84 1984

Painted steel
9 × 8½ × 6½ in.
(23 × 21.5 × 16.5 cm).

Collection

B. C. Holland & Co., Chicago, Illinois, 1985.

Provenance

Xavier Fourcade, Inc., and Thordis Moeller, New York, New York; Margo Leavin Gallery, Los Angeles, California.

Exhibitions

Xavier Fourcade, Inc., New York, New York. *John Chamberlain: New Sculpture*, color illus. February 25–March 31, 1984.

Margo Leavin Gallery, Los Angeles, California. *John Chamberlain*. March 4–30, 1985.

Notes

The 1984 *Tonks* are not numbered in sequence with the 1983 *Tonks, 7–83* through *30–83* (cat. nos. 740–761), but begin the number system again with *Tonk #1–84*.

774

Tonk #2–84 1984

Painted steel
Dimensions unknown.

Collection

Present location unknown.

Notes

It is assumed that there is, or once was, a *Tonk #2–84* although no record of its existence can be found.

775

Tonk #3–84 1984

Painted steel
12½ × 8½ × 12 in.
(32 × 21.5 × 30.5 cm).

Collection

Mr. and Mrs. Harry Altman, Los Angeles, California, 1985.

Provenance

Xavier Fourcade, Inc., and Thordis Moeller, New York, New York; Margo Leavin Gallery, Los Angeles, California.

Exhibitions

Xavier Fourcade, Inc., New York, New York. *John Chamberlain: New Sculpture*, color illus. February 25–March 31, 1984.

Margo Leavin Gallery, Los Angeles, California. *John Chamberlain*. March 4–30, 1985.

776

Tonk #4–84 1984

Painted steel
7½ × 43½ × 11½ in.
(19 × 110.5 × 29 cm).

Collection
Michael and Patricia Auping, Buffalo, New York, 1984; acquired directly from the artist.

Notes
The sculpture is signed.

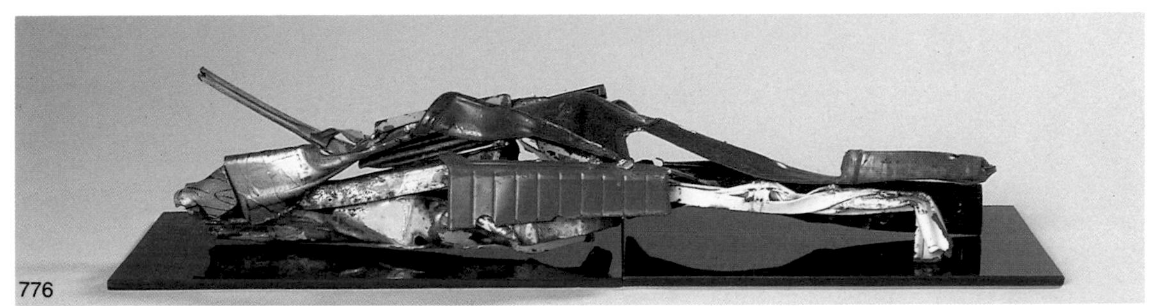

776

777

Tonk #5–84 1984

Painted steel
4½ × 20 × 6 in.
(11.5 × 51 × 15 cm).

Collection
Xavier Fourcade, Inc., New York, New York.

Exhibitions
Xavier Fourcade, Inc., New York, New York. *John Chamberlain: New Sculpture*, color illus. February 25–March 31, 1984.

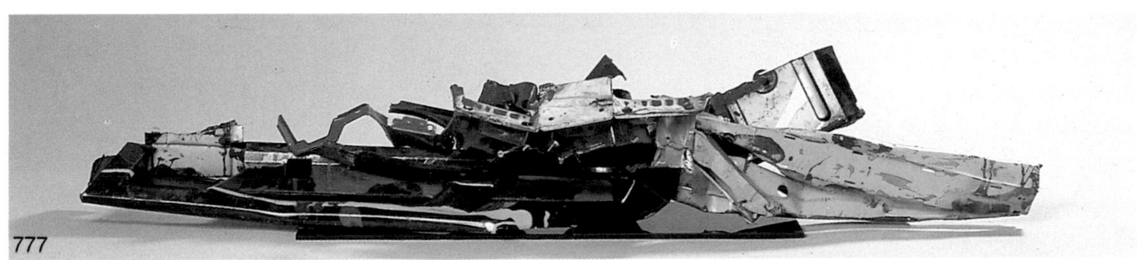

777

778

Tonk #6–84 1984

Painted steel
8½ × 29½ × 9½ in.
(21.5 × 75 × 24 cm).

Collection
Xavier Fourcade, Inc., New York, New York.

Exhibitions
Xavier Fourcade, Inc., New York, New York. *John Chamberlain: New Sculpture*, color illus. February 25–March 31, 1984.

Margo Leavin Gallery, Los Angeles, California. *John Chamberlain*. March 4–30, 1985.

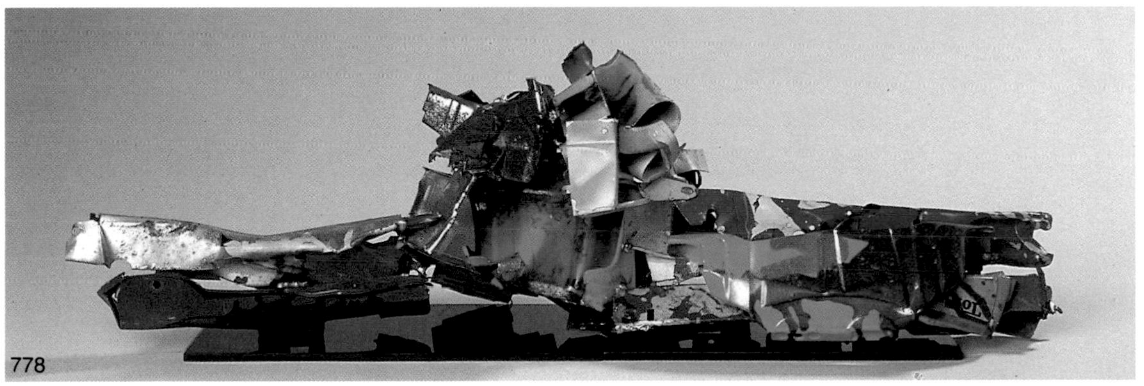

778

779

Tonk #7–84 1984

Painted steel
5½ × 44 × 8½ in.
(14 × 112 × 21.5 cm).

Collection
B. C. Holland & Co., Chicago, Illinois, 1985.

Provenance
Xavier Fourcade, Inc., and Thordis Moeller, New York, New York; Margo Leavin Gallery, Los Angeles, California.

Exhibitions
Xavier Fourcade, Inc., New York, New York. *John Chamberlain: New Sculpture*. February 25–March 31, 1984.

Margo Leavin Gallery, Los Angeles, California. *John Chamberlain*. March 4–30, 1985.

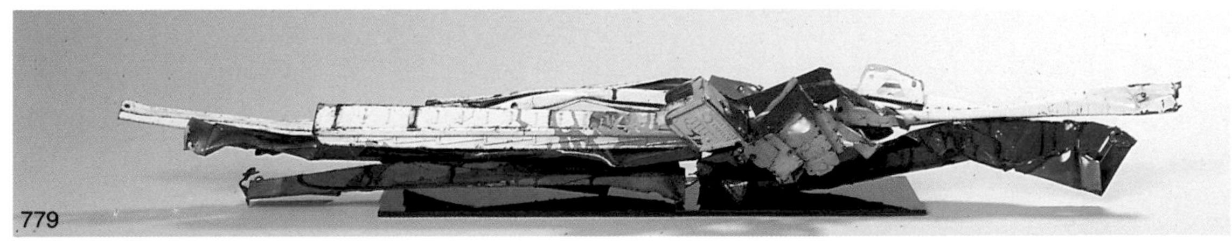

779

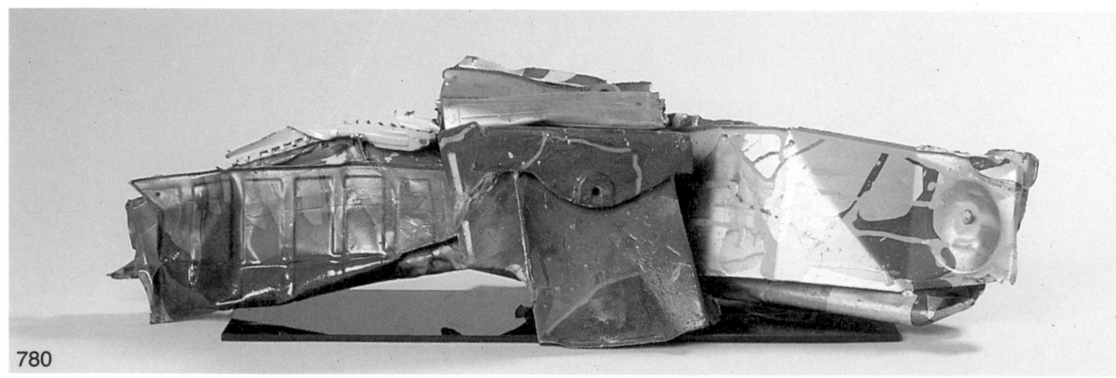
780

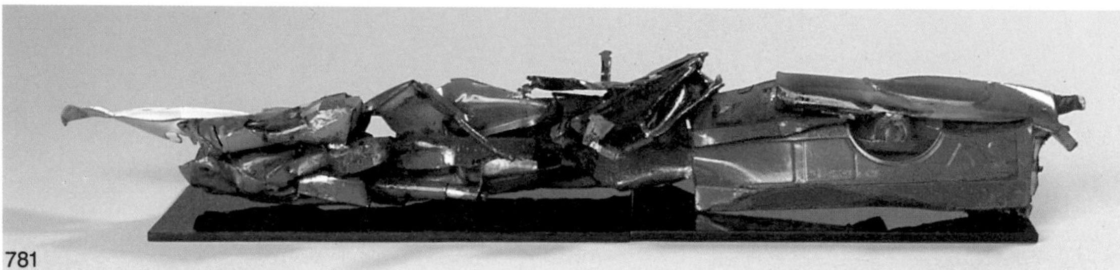
781

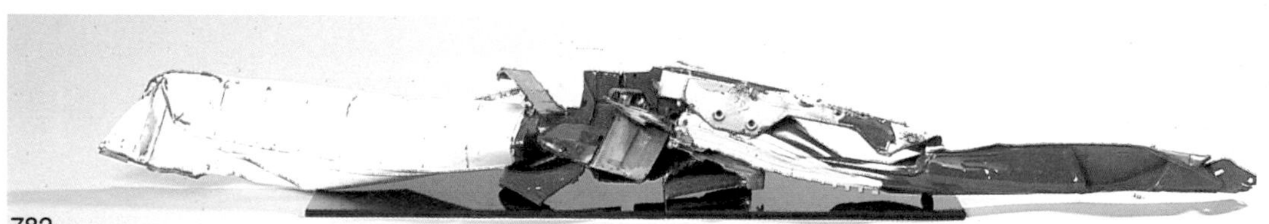
782

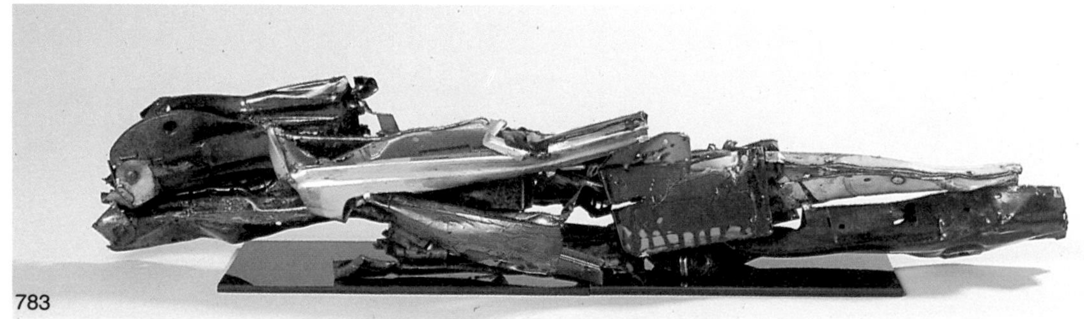
783

780

Tonk #8–84 1984
Painted steel
8 × 32½ × 10 in.
(20 × 82.5 × 25.5 cm).

Collection
Xavier Fourcade, Inc., New York, New York.

Exhibitions
Xavier Fourcade, Inc., New York, New York. *John Chamberlain: New Sculpture*, color illus. February 25–March 31, 1984.

Galerie Helen van der Meij, Amsterdam. *John Chamberlain: Tonks*. April 21–May 24, 1984.

781

Tonk #9–84 1984
Painted steel
4 × 25½ × 6 in.
(10 × 65 × 15 cm).

Collection
Xavier Fourcade, Inc., New York, New York.

782

Tonk #10–84 1984
Painted steel
4½ × 41½ × 6½ in.
(11.5 × 105.5 × 16.5 cm).

Collection
Xavier Fourcade, Inc., New York, New York.

783

Tonk #11–84 1984
Painted steel
6 × 33½ × 8 in.
(15 × 85 × 20 cm).

Collection
Xavier Fourcade, Inc., New York, New York.

Exhibitions
Xavier Fourcade, Inc., New York, New York. *John Chamberlain: New Sculpture*. February 25–March 31, 1984.

Galerie Helen van der Meij, Amsterdam. *John Chamberlain: Tonks*. April 21–May 24, 1984.

784

Arrogance in B♭ 1985
Painted and chromium-plated steel
23½ × 16 × 14 in.
(59.5 × 40.5 × 35.5 cm).

Collection
Xavier Fourcade, Inc., New York, New York.

785

chACE 1985
Painted and chromium-plated steel
42 × 34 × 11 in.
(106.5 × 86.5 × 28 cm).

Collection
Xavier Fourcade, Inc., New York, New York.

786

Feeling Good, Louis 1985
Painted and chromium-plated steel
35 × 23½ × 21 in.
(89 × 58.5 × 54.5 cm).

Collection
Mrs. Marcia Weisman, Los Angeles, California, 1985.

Provenance
Xavier Fourcade, Inc., New York, New York; Margo Leavin Gallery, Los Angeles, California.

Exhibitions
Margo Leavin Gallery, Los Angeles, California. *John Chamberlain*. March 4–30, 1985.

787

Gangster of Love 1985
Painted and chromium-plated steel
90 × 74 × 50 in.
(228.5 × 188 × 127 cm).

Collection
Xavier Fourcade, Inc., New York, New York.

Exhibitions
Margo Leavin Gallery, Los Angeles, California. *John Chamberlain*. March 4–30, 1985.

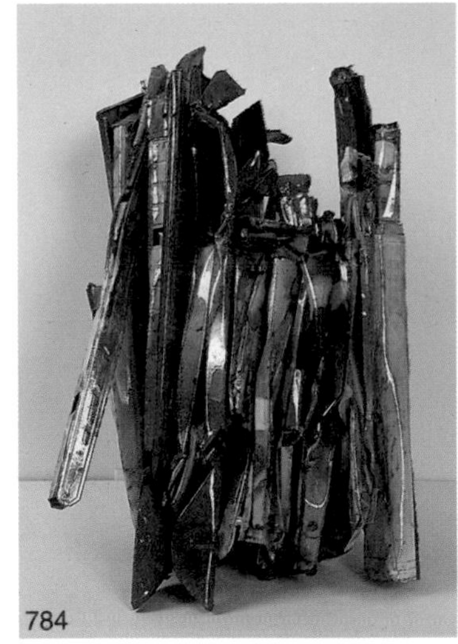
784

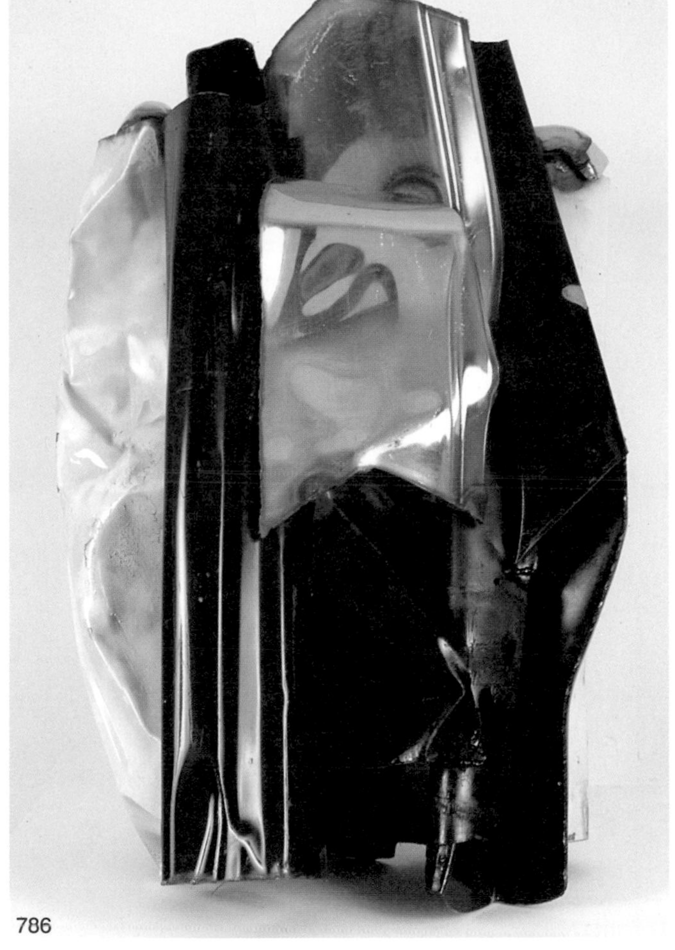
786

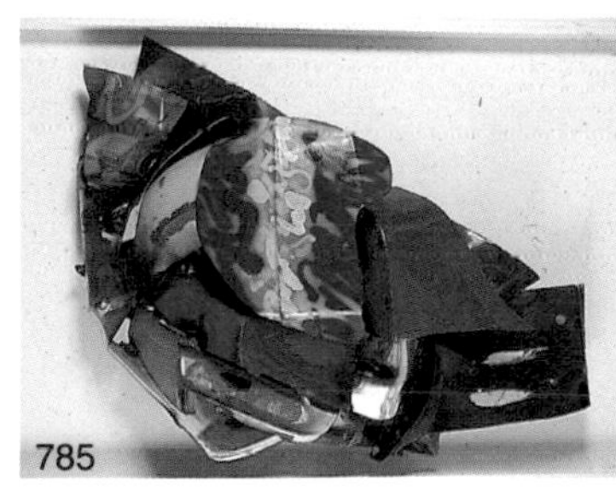
785

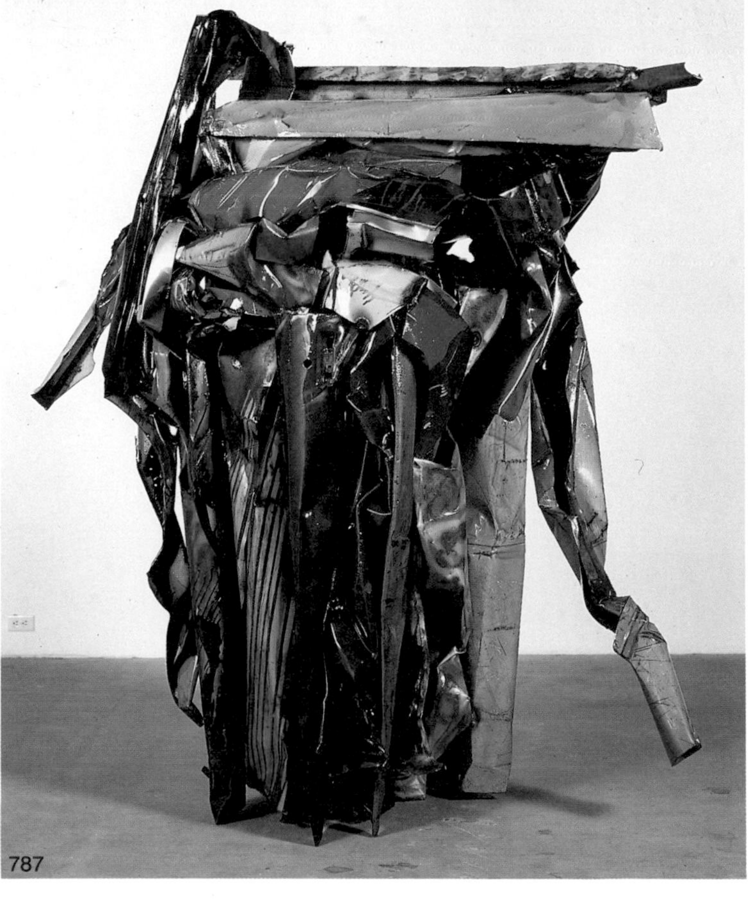
787

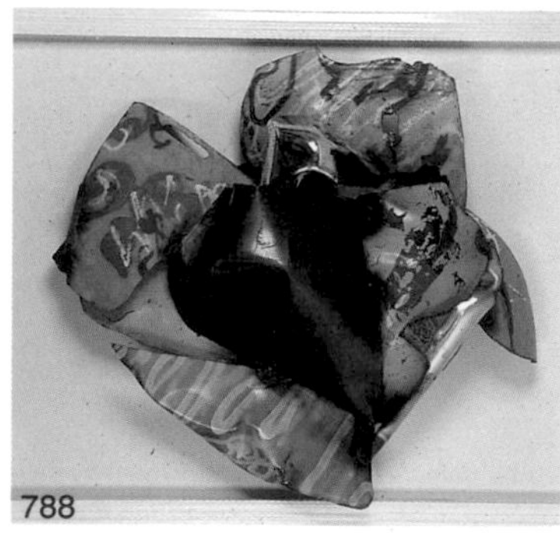
788

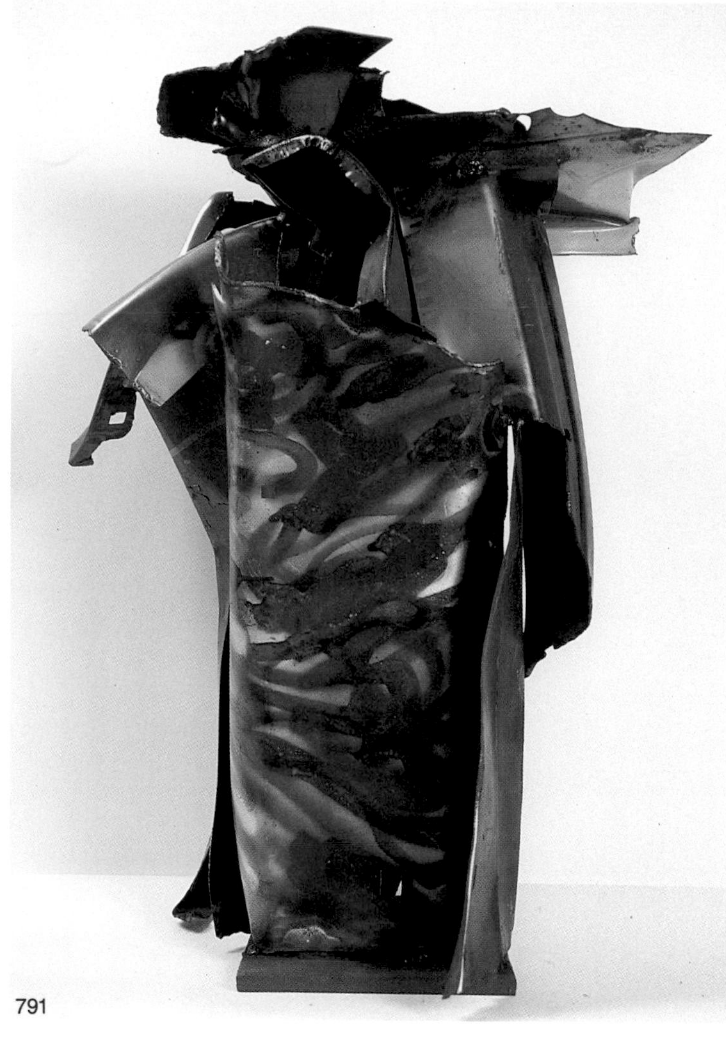
791

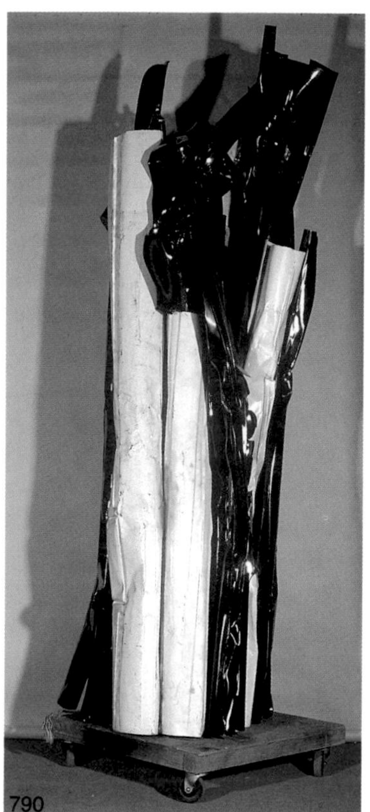
790

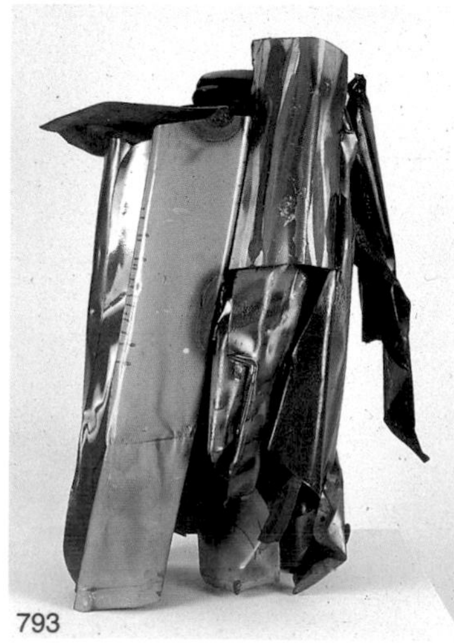
793

788

Garlic Chip 1985
Painted and chromium-plated steel
38 × 35 × 12½ in.
(96.5 × 89 × 32 cm).

Collection
Xavier Fourcade, Inc., New York, New York.

789

Gondola Henry Miller 1985
Painted and chromium-plated steel
36 × 216 × 36 in.
(91.5 × 548.5 × 91.5 cm).

Collection
Sydney and Rita Adler, Sarasota, Florida; acquired directly from the artist.

790

Leaning Tower of Youth 1985
Painted and chromium-plated steel
156 × 48 × 48 in.
(396 × 122 × 122 cm).

Collection
Xavier Fourcade, Inc., New York, New York.

Exhibitions
Chicago Sculpture International, Chicago, Illinois. *Mile–4*. May 9–June 9, 1985.

791

Pink Tennis Shoes 1985
Painted and chromium-plated steel
28 × 20 × 20 in.
(71 × 51 × 51 cm).

Collection
Xavier Fourcade, Inc., New York, New York.

792

Quida 1985
Painted and chromium-plated steel
79 × 62 × 25 in.
(200.5 × 157.5 × 63.5 cm).

Collection
Xavier Fourcade, Inc., New York, New York.

793

Sub Rosa 1985
Painted and chromium-plated steel
38 × 27 × 19 in.
(96.5 × 68.5 × 48.5 cm).

Collection
Xavier Fourcade, Inc., New York, New York.

Exhibitions
Margo Leavin Gallery, Los Angeles, California. *John Chamberlain*. March 4–30, 1985.

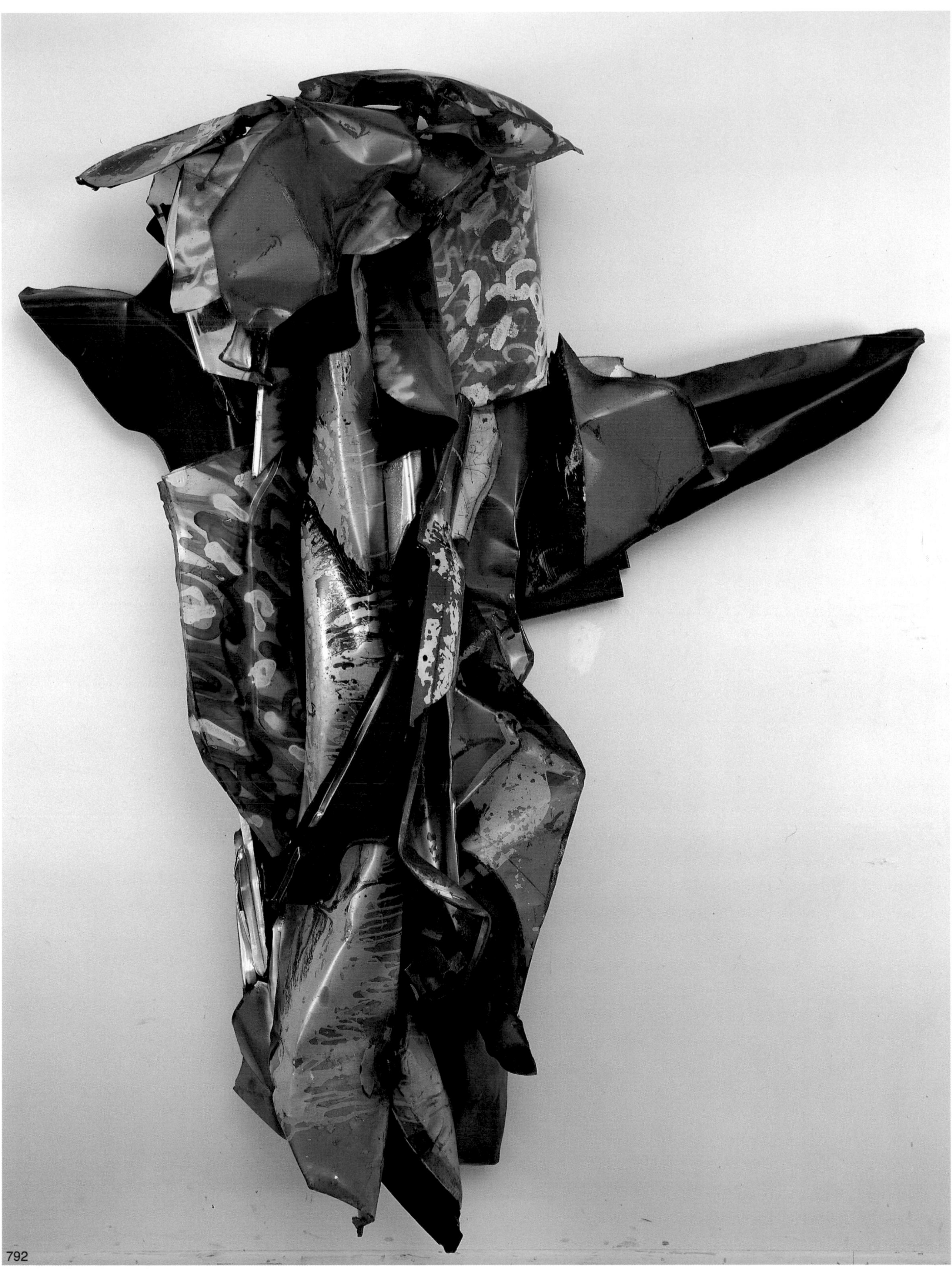

792

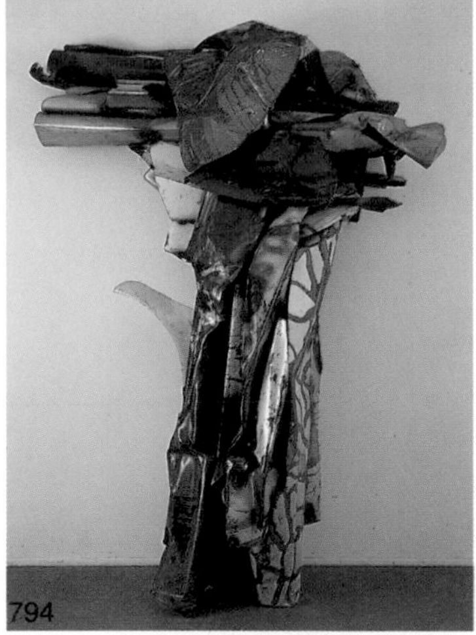
794

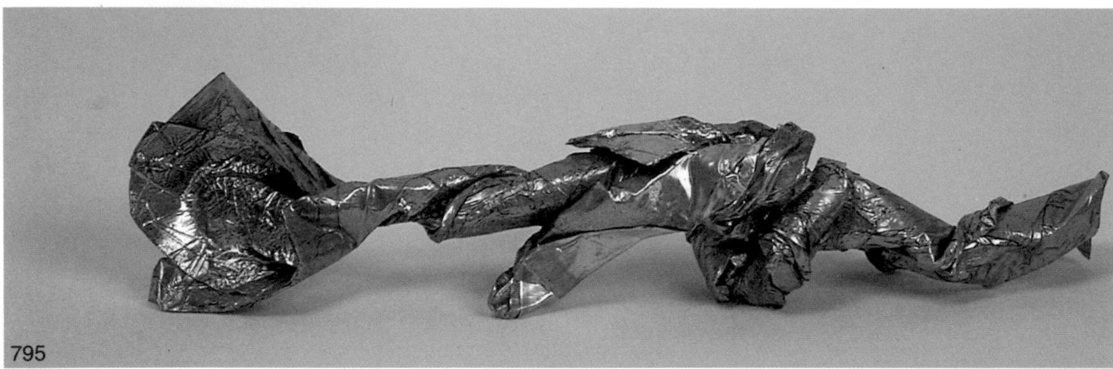
795

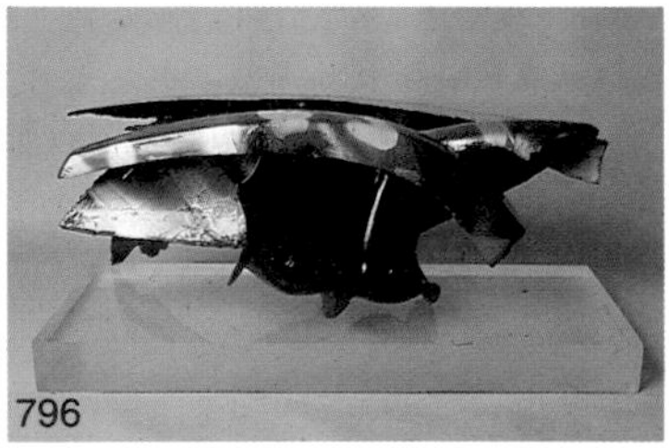
796

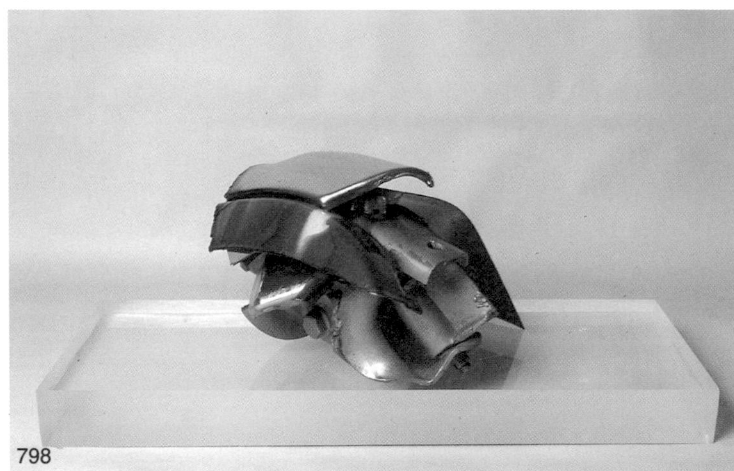
798

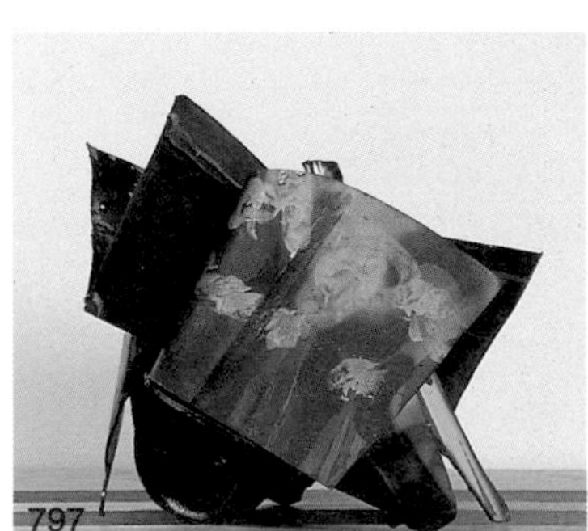
797

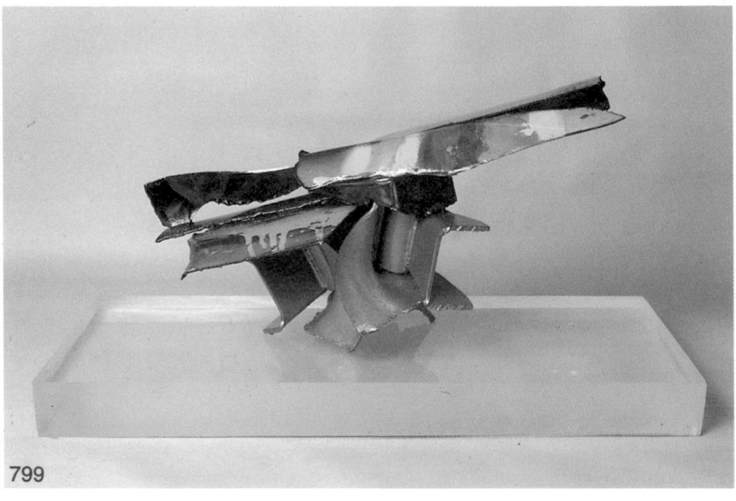
799

794

Tomago 1985
Painted and chromium-plated steel
91 × 68 × 25 in.
(231 × 172.5 × 63.5 cm).

Collection
Xavier Fourcade, Inc., New York, New York.

795

Twisted Comet 1985
Aluminum foil and ink
5½ × 22 × 4 in.
(14 × 55 × 10 cm).

Collection
Collection of the artist, Sarasota, Florida.

Exhibitions
Light Gallery, New York, New York. *The Comet Show.* November 20, 1985–January 21, 1986.

796

Untitled 1985
Painted and chromium-plated steel
8 × 22 × 12 in.
(20.5 × 56 × 30.5 cm).

Collection
Xavier Fourcade, Inc., New York, New York.

Exhibitions
Galerie Gillespie-Laage-Salomon, Paris. *John Chamberlain*. June 6–July 13, 1985.

797

Untitled 1985
Painted and chromium-plated steel
13 × 16 × 13 in.
(33 × 40.5 × 33 cm).

Collection
Xavier Fourcade, Inc., New York, New York.

Exhibitions
Galerie Gillespie-Laage-Salomon, Paris. *John Chamberlain*. June 6–July 13, 1985.

798

Untitled 1985
Painted and chromium-plated steel
7½ × 11 × 11 in.
(19 × 28 × 28 cm).

Collection
Xavier Fourcade, Inc., New York, New York.

799

Untitled 1985
Painted and chromium-plated steel
10½ × 18 × 7½ in.
(26.5 × 46 × 19 cm).

Collection
Xavier Fourcade, Inc., New York, New York.

Appendix: Couches

In 1967, while looking for a place to sit in a studio filled with urethane foam, Chamberlain conceived his first sculpture for seating, a urethane-foam couch. *Judd's Couch*, as it came to be known, marked the beginning of a series of very large sculptures, some of which were exhibited, while others were made specially for friends, and still others were made to order for exhibition spaces.

Couches over 10 feet (3.5 meters) in length are referred to as "barges." The barges made for exhibitions are the only sculptures of this series to be reproduced in the following section.

I

Judd's Couch 1967
Urethane foam
Dimensions unavailable.

Collection
Donald Judd, Marfa, Texas, 1967; acquired directly from the artist.

Notes
This is the first sculpture made for seating. It is very likely that the couch was made from an earlier sculpture, *Chingkanshan*, 1966, cat. no. 246.

Five couches, known as the *Chicago Couches* (cat. nos. II–VI), were made in Chicago for the 1970 exhibition at Lo Giudice Gallery, *Hard and Soft: Recent Sculpture*. One was destroyed in a fire in Chicago and is not listed.

II

Couch 1970
Urethane foam and cord
27 × 72 × 72 in.
(68.5 × 183 × 183 cm).

Collection
Raymond D. Fogelson, Chicago, Illinois, 1972.

Provenance
Lo Giudice Gallery, Chicago, Illinois; Walter Kelly Gallery, Chicago, Illinois.

Exhibitions
Lo Giudice Gallery, Chicago, Illinois. *Hard and Soft: Recent Sculpture*. 1970.

III

Couch 1970
Urethane foam
28 × 77 × 77 in.
(71 × 95.5 × 95.5 cm).

Provenance
Lo Giudice Gallery, Chicago, Illinois, 1970; Mr. and Mrs. Robert B. Mayer, Chicago, Illinois, 1970; The Albright-Knox Art Gallery, Buffalo, New York, 1975, gift of the estate of Robert B. Mayer and Beatrice C. Mayer.

Exhibitions
Lo Giudice Gallery, Chicago, Illinois. *Hard and Soft: Recent Sculpture*. 1970.

Notes
The sculpture was deaccessioned by the Albright-Knox Art Gallery in 1977, due to deterioration and disintegration. It has since been destroyed.

IV

Bellamy's Couch 1970
Urethane foam and cord
Dimensions unknown.

Collection
Present location unknown.

Provenance
Richard Bellamy, New York, New York, 1971.

Exhibitions
Lo Giudice Gallery, Chicago, Illinois. *Hard and Soft: Recent Sculpture*. 1970.

V

Couch 1970
Urethane foam
27 × 72 × 72 in.
(68.5 × 183 × 183 cm).

Collection
Wendy Dunaway, New York, New York, 1972.

Provenance
Lo Giudice Gallery, Chicago, Illinois; Lo Giudice Gallery, New York, New York.

Exhibitions
Lo Giudice Gallery, Chicago, Illinois. *Hard and Soft: Recent Sculpture*. 1970.

A series of couches were made for an exhibition at the Locksley/Shea Gallery in Minneapolis in 1970. The couches were carved by Chamberlain, and he instructed the gallery crew to flock the areas that would not be used for seating. When Chamberlain arrived at the opening of the exhibition, he found that the couches had been flocked with glass adhesive rather than vinyl adhesive. The surfaces therefore cracked upon touch. Chamberlain declared the couches destroyed.

VI

Couch 1970
Urethane foam and cord
34½ × 81 × 79 in.
(87.5 × 205.5 × 200.5 cm).

Collection
Dia Art Foundation, New York, New York, 1980.

Provenance
Gordon Locksley, Minneapolis, Minnesota; Lone Star Foundation, New York, New York, 1978.

VII

Couch 1970
Urethane foam and cord
35 × 80½ × 79 in.
(89 × 204.5 × 200.5 cm).

Collection
Dia Art Foundation, New York, New York, 1980.

Provenance
Gordon Locksley, Minneapolis, Minnesota; Lone Star Foundation, New York, New York, 1978.

VIII

Barge Morley 1970
Urethane foam and cord
26 × 120 × 77 in.
(66 × 305 × 195.5 cm).

Collection
Neith A. Hunter, New York, New York, 1984.

Provenance
Malcolm Morley, New York, New York; Joseph Kosuth, New York, New York.

Exhibitions
Christie's East, New York, New York. *Modern and Contemporary Art*, cat. no. 120 (listed as "*Two Sofas*"). June 10, 1980.

IX

Rocker 1970–71
Urethane foam and cord
Dimensions unknown.

Provenance
David Brown and Jason Croy, New York, New York, 1972; acquired directly from the artist.

Notes
According to the owners, the sculpture has been destroyed.

An unlimited edition of a couch was produced between 1970 and 1971 by a Milanese furniture manufacturer. An original couch carved by Chamberlain was sent to Milan to be copied for production in urethane foam. The fabricators in Milan added a few touches: pillows, which Chamberlain liked, and casters for the couches to roll on, which he eliminated, the idea being that the couches should contain no hard materials.

The edition was published by Daedalus Concepts in New York, and there is no record of the exact number made. Three examples are known to exist in private collections in New York. Each measures 29 × 85 × 81 in. (73.5 × 216 × 205.5 cm) and was signed by the artist.

X

Love seat 1971

Urethane foam and cord
Dimensions unknown.

Collection

Present location unknown.

Provenance

Leo Castelli Gallery, New York, New York.

Exhibitions

Leo Castelli Gallery, New York, New York. *Furniture Designed by Artists*. September 7–23, 1972.

XI

Guggenheim Barge 1971

Urethane foam and cord with video installation
28½ × 307 × 77 in.
(72.5 × 780 × 195.5 cm).

Collection

Walter P. Chrysler, Jr., New York, New York; on loan to the Chrysler Museum, Norfolk, Virginia, 1979.

Provenance

Stanley Jacks, New York, New York; Richard Librizzi, New York, New York.

Exhibitions

The Solomon R. Guggenheim Museum, New York, New York. *John Chamberlain: A Retrospective Exhibition*. December 23, 1971–February 20, 1972.

The Chrysler Museum, Norfolk, Virginia. *Three Hundred Years of American Art at the Chrysler Museum*, p. 235, illus. March 1–July 4, 1976.

References

Elizabeth C. Baker, "The Chamberlain Crunch," *Art News*, vol. 70, no. 10 (February 1972), illus. p. 26.

D. R. A., "Chamberlain Exhibition," *Chrysler Museum Bulletin*, vol. 3, no. 3 (March 1974), illus.

Notes

The *Guggenheim Barge* was made for the rotunda of the Guggenheim Museum, for the artist's retrospective exhibition in 1971–72. The barge was accompanied by two television sets, one at each end, which played a continuous video loop of Chamberlain and his friends playing music at the home of Larry Poons.

Chamberlain offered to donate the barge to the Guggenheim after the exhibition, but the offer was declined. The barge was put into storage at the Guggenheim until July 1, 1972, when it was dispersed; there is no available record of whom it was dispersed to. For several years the barge disappeared, and it was assumed by the artist that it had been destroyed, but subsequently reappeared.

XII

Stockholm Barge 1973

Urethane foam and cord
Dimensions unknown.

Provenance

Moderna Museet, Stockholm.

Exhibitions

Moderna Museet, Stockholm. *New York Collection for Stockholm*. October 27–December 2, 1973.

Notes

The sculpture was created at the Moderna Museet on the occasion of the opening of the *New York Collection* exhibition; it was never finished, although it was on exhibition for one night during the preview reception. According to the artist, it was destroyed.

XIII

Barge Leon 1973

Urethane foam and cord
27 × 122 × 80 in.
(68.5 × 310 × 203 cm).

Collection

Jon Leon, New York, New York, 1973; acquired directly from the artist.

XIV

Stella's Couch 1976

Urethane foam and cord
27 × 95 × 80 in.
(68.5 × 241.5 × 203 cm).

Collection

Frank Stella, New York, New York; acquired directly from the artist.

Notes

The sculpture was made specifically for its location.

XV

Couch Hersey 1977

Urethane foam
48 × 144 × 72 in.
(122 × 366 × 183 cm).

Collection

John Hersey, Millbrook, New York, 1977; acquired directly from the artist.

Notes

The sculpture was made specifically for its location.

XVI

Belcher Barge 1978

Urethane foam and cord
39 × 204 × 77 in.
(99 × 518 × 195.5 cm).

Collection

Collection of the artist, Sarasota, Florida.

Exhibitions

Dia Art Foundation, Essex, Connecticut. *Chamberlain Gardens, Essex*. May–November 1982 and 1983.

XVII

American Barge 1979

Urethane foam and video installation
39½ × 472½ × 157½ in.
(100 × 1200 × 400 cm).

Collection

Dia Art Foundation, New York, New York, 1980.

Provenance

Heiner Friedrich GmbH, Cologne.

Exhibitions

Heiner Friedrich GmbH, Cologne. *John Chamberlain*. November 23, 1979–January 20, 1980.

Van Abbemuseum, Eindhoven, Netherlands. *Chamberlain*. April–May 1980.

Museum der Stadt Köln, Cologne. *Westkunst*. May 30–August 16, 1981.

Palacio de Cristal, Parque del Retiro, Madrid. *John Chamberlain/Esculturas*, illus. p. 61. January 26–March 31, 1984.

References

Nancy Marmer, "Isms on the Rhine," *Art in America*, vol. 69, no. 9 (November 1981), illus. p. 114.

Notes

The fifty-minute videotape that accompanies the sculpture comprises seventy-five commercials taken from American television and ten original satirical commercials made by the artist's friend James Signorelli. It is a continuous loop.

XVIII

Fire and Ice 1979

Urethane foam and video installation
79 × 236½ × 39½ in.
(200.5 × 601 × 100 cm).

Collection

Private collection, New York, New York.

Provenance

Heiner Friedrich GmbH, Cologne.

Exhibitions

Heiner Friedrich GmbH, Cologne. *John Chamberlain*. November 23, 1979–January 20, 1980.

Notes

The sculpture is made from the pieces cut out in the process of making *American Barge* (cat. no. XVII).

The video installation consists of two monitors showing two hours of videotape of a fire burning in a fireplace. The tape has sound and is a continuous loop.

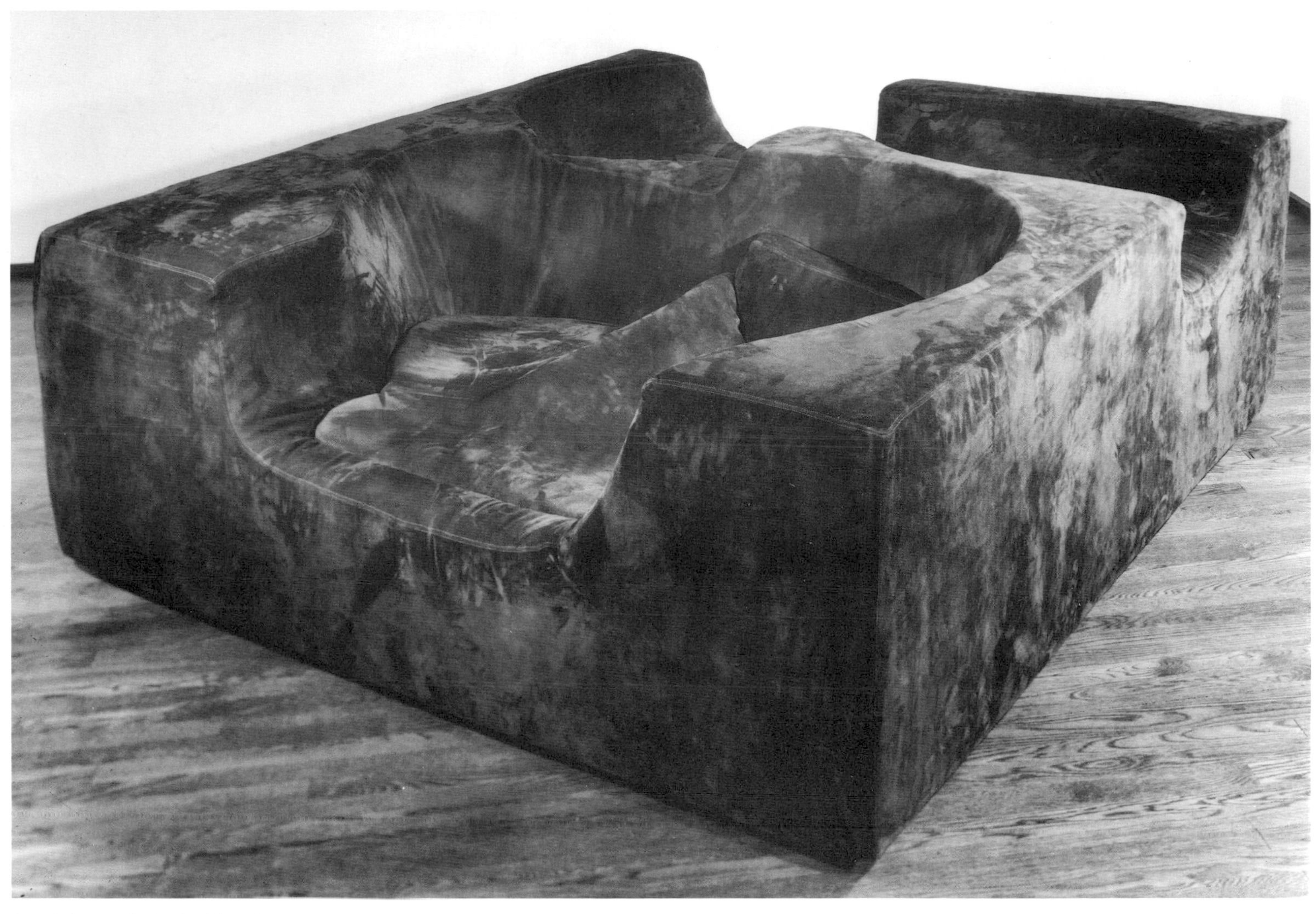

Couch from unlimited edition, Daedalus Concepts, 1970–71.

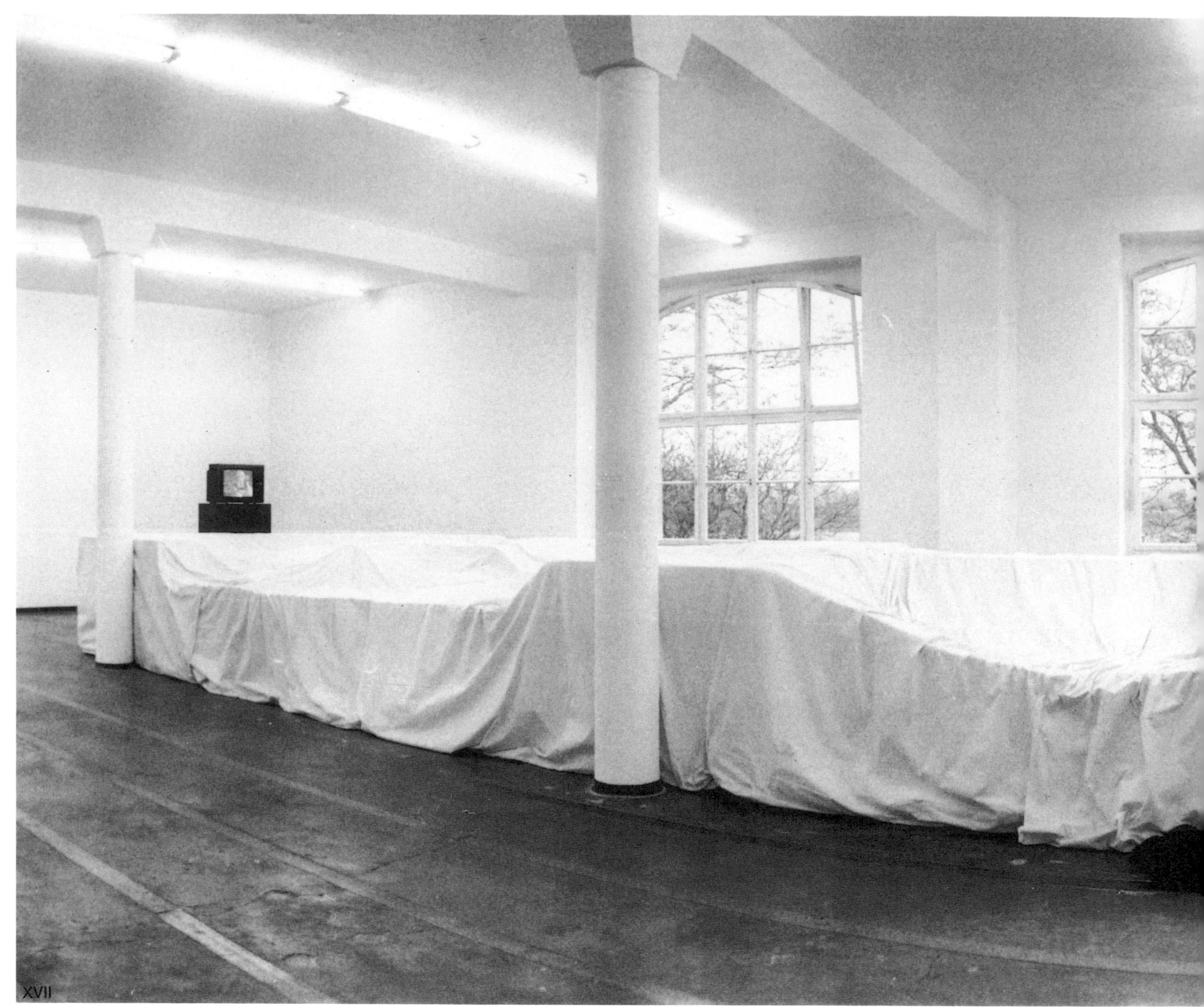

XVII

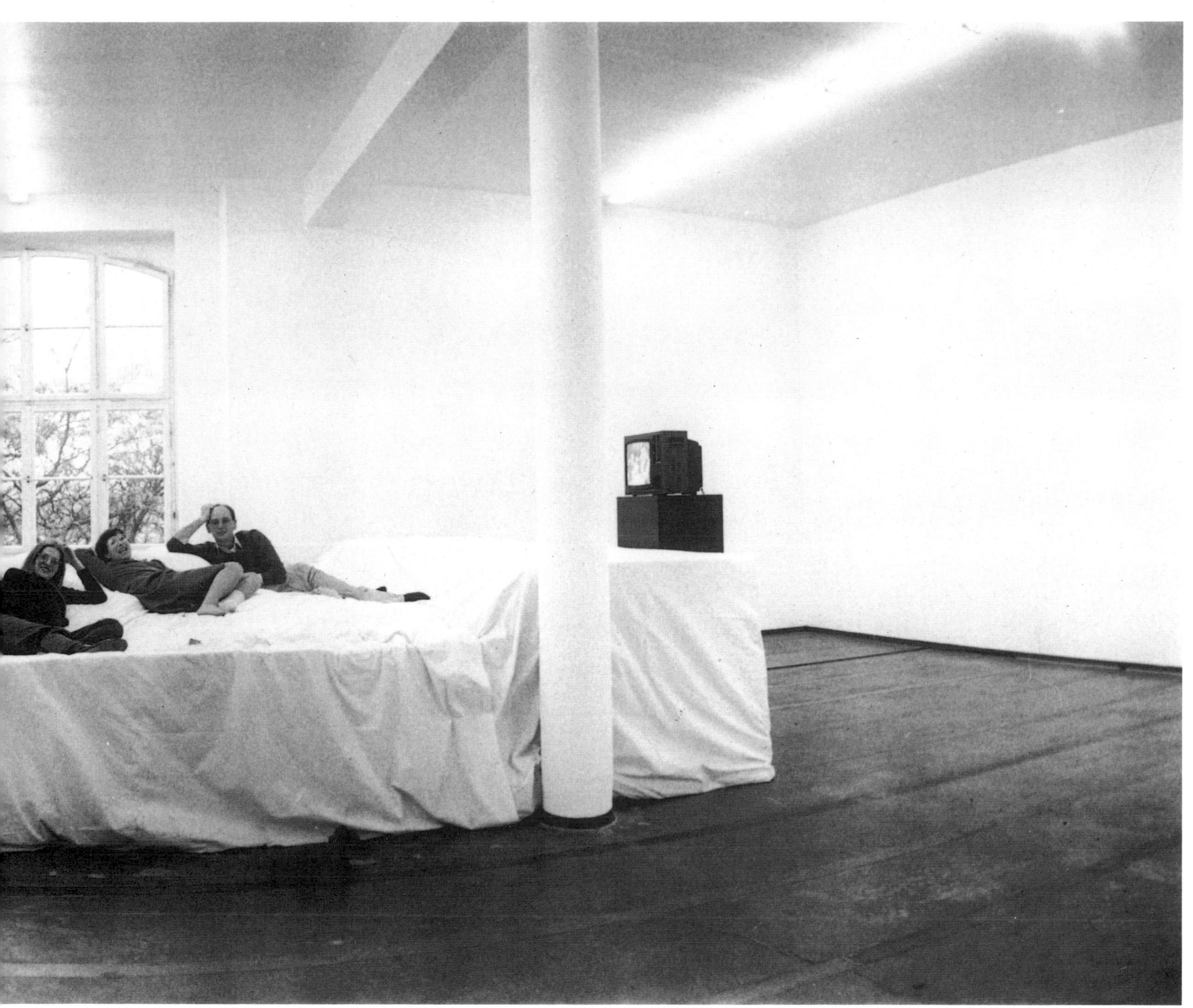

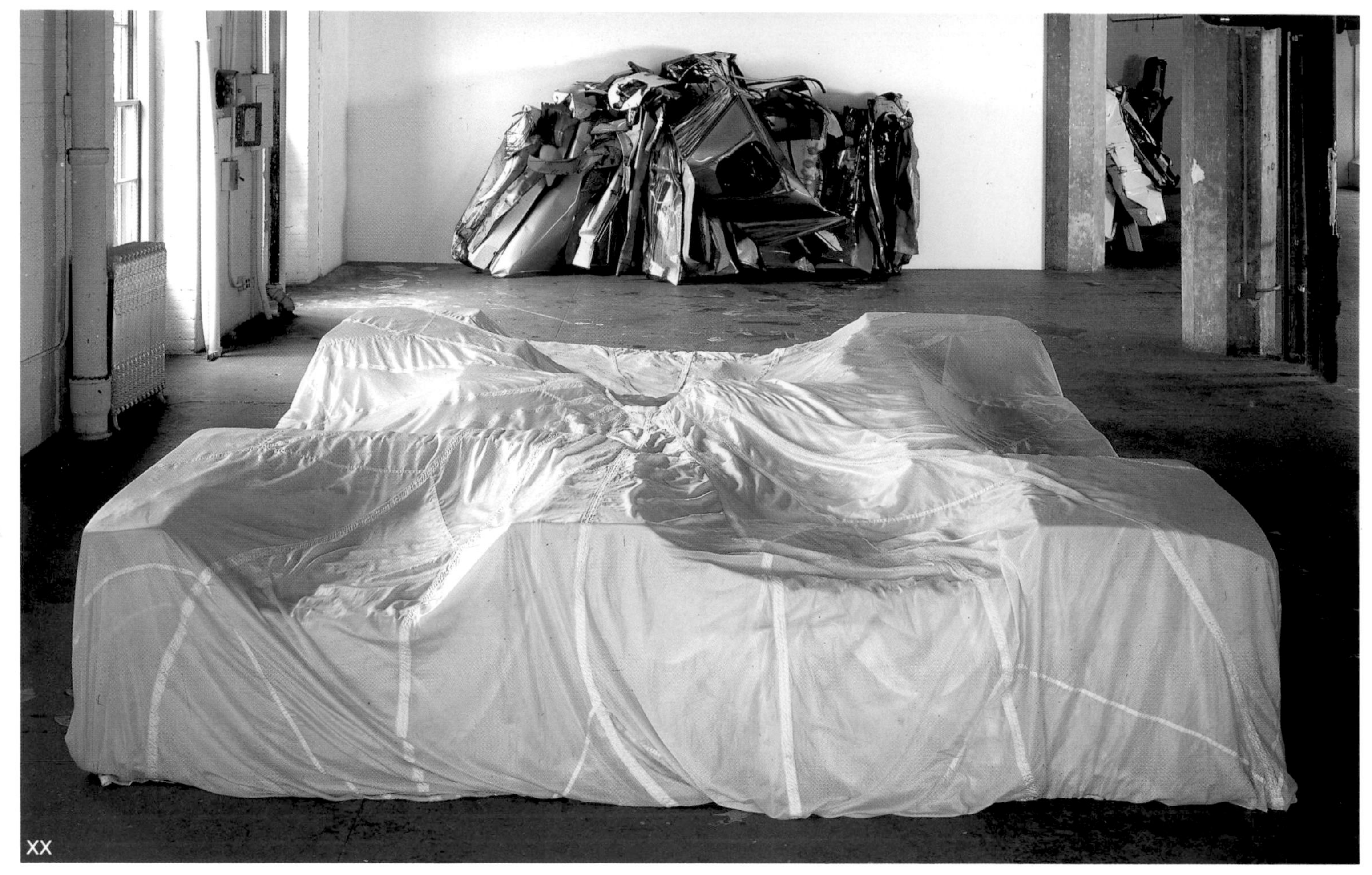

XX

XIX

Freddie's Joint 1979

Urethane foam
39½ × 118 × 79 in.
(100 × 300 × 200.5 cm).

Collection

Friedrich Moeller, New York, New York, 1979; acquired directly from the artist.

Exhibitions

Heiner Friedrich GmbH, Cologne. *John Chamberlain*. November 23, 1979–January 20, 1980.

Notes

The sculpture, which appears to be a set of building blocks of urethane foam, is made from the pieces cut out in the process of making *American Barge* (cat. no. XVII).

XX

Thordis' Barge 1980

Urethane foam and cord
29½ × 138 × 152 in.
(75 × 350.5 × 386 cm).

Collection

Dia Art Foundation, New York, New York, 1984; gift of Thordis Moeller.

Provenance

Thordis Moeller, New York, New York 1980.

Exhibitions

Dia Art Foundation, New York, New York. *John Chamberlain Sculpture: An Extended Exhibition*. March 19–November 27, 1982.

References

Jeanne Silverthorne, "John Chamberlain," *Artforum*, vol. 21, no. 3 (November 1982), p. 75.

Notes

The sculpture was originally made for the residence of Thordis Moeller, New York, New York.

XXI

Chamberlain's Couch 1981

Urethane foam and cord
31 × 80 × 114 in.
(78.5 × 203 × 289.5 cm).

Collection

Collection of the artist, Sarasota, Florida.

XXII

Barge Sylvester 1982

Urethane foam and nylon cord
27 × 170 × 77 in.
(68.5 × 432 × 195.5 cm).

Collection

Julie Sylvester, New York, New York, 1982; acquired directly from the artist.

Notes

The sculpture was made specifically for its location.

XXIII

Barge Marfa 1983

Urethane foam and cord
40 × 240 × 164 in.
(101.5 × 609.5 × 416.5 cm).

Collection

Dia Art Foundation, New York, New York, 1983; acquired directly from the artist.

Exhibitions

Dia Art Foundation, the Art Museum of the Pecos, Marfa, Texas. *An Exhibition of Sculpture by John Chamberlain*. From May 7, 1983.

Notes

The sculpture was made on location, specifically for the exhibition site.

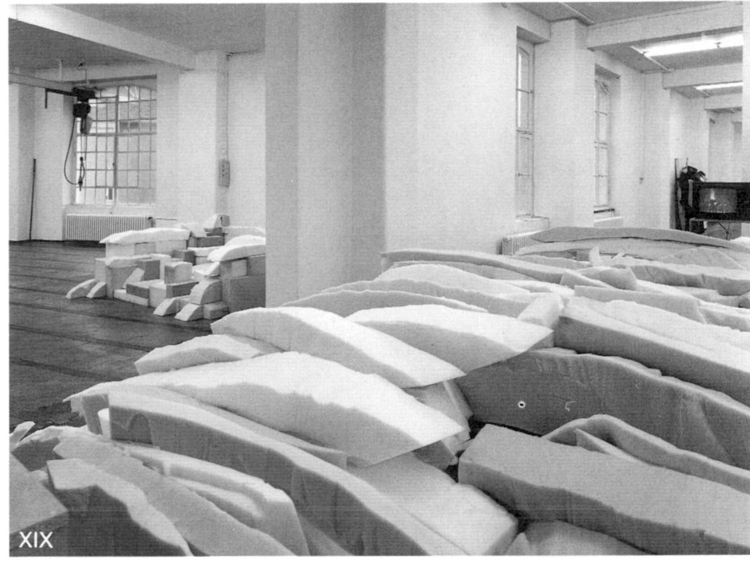

XIX

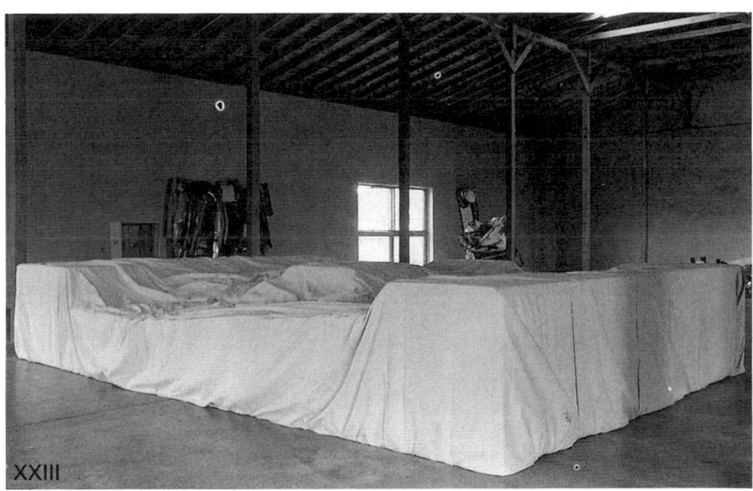

XXIII

Chronology

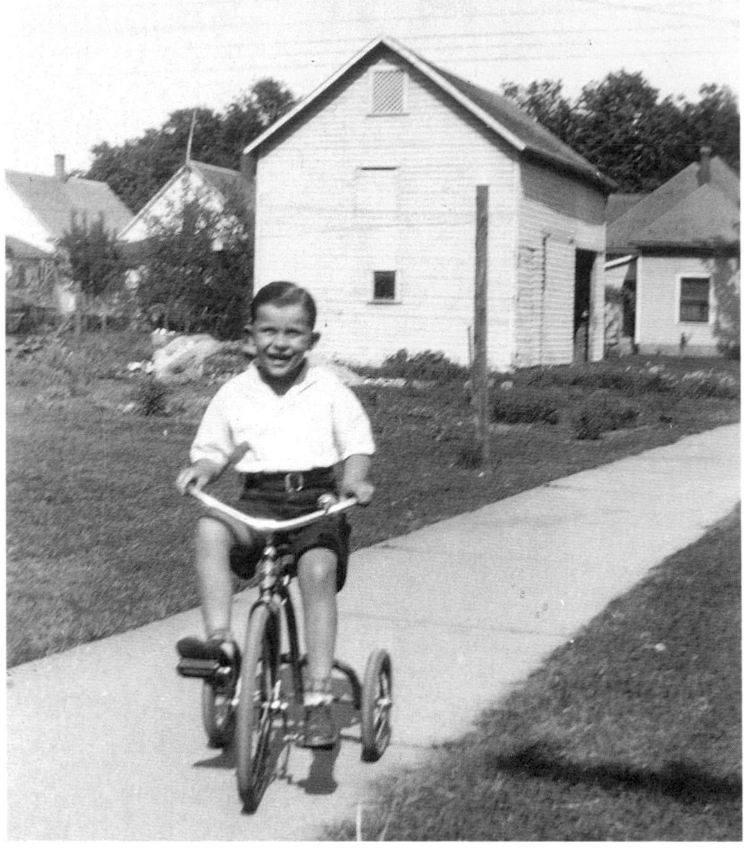

John Chamberlain, Rochester, Indiana, c. 1931–32.

1927
John Angus Chamberlain born April 16, 1927, in Rochester, Indiana, to Mary Francis Waller and Claude Chester Chamberlain.

1931
Moves to Chicago, Illinois; brought up by his maternal grandmother, Edna Brown Waller.

1943
Leaves Chicago. En route to California, joins the U.S. Navy.

1943–46
Serves in the U.S. Navy aboard the aircraft carrier *U.S.S. Tulagi*; tours in the Pacific and Mediterranean.

1948
Moves to Detroit, Michigan; marries Virginia Wooten.

1950
Studies hairdressing in Chicago through the Veterans Administration G.I. Bill.

1951–52
Attends the School of The Art Institute of Chicago.

1953–54
Works as a hairdresser and makeup artist in Chicago.

1955–56
Attends Black Mountain College in North Carolina; meets the poets Charles Olson, Robert Duncan, and Robert Creeley.

1956
Moves to New York; marries Elaine Grulkowski. Birth of first son, Angus Orion Chamberlain, in New York.

1957
First one-person exhibition, at the Wells Street Gallery in Chicago. Makes *Shortstop*, his first sculpture made from auto-body parts, in Southampton, New York, at the home of Larry Rivers.

1958
First exhibition in New York, a two-man exhibition with Joseph Fiore at the Davida Gallery. Included in a group exhibition at the Hansa Gallery, New York. Birth of Jesse Claude Chamberlain, a second son, in New York.

1959
Maintains a studio at Tenth Street and Broadway in New York and lives in Rockland County, New York, through 1961. Included in *Recent Sculpture USA* at the Museum of Modern Art, New York.

1960
First one-man exhibition in New York, at the Martha Jackson Gallery.

1962
Maintains a studio on Cherry Street, New York. Birth of a third son, John Duncan Chamberlain, in New York. First one-man exhibition at the Leo Castelli Gallery, New York.

1963
Moves with his family to Embudo, New Mexico; begins his first series of auto-lacquer and metal-flake paintings. Spends the summer in Topanga Canyon, California.

1965
Returns to New York and maintains a studio at 53 Greene Street.

1966
Follows his family to Santa Fe, New Mexico; teaches graduate students at the University of New Mexico. Receives a John Simon Guggenheim Memorial Foundation Fellowship. Makes a series of fiber glass sculptures based on french-curve drawings. Spends the summer in Malibu, California; begins first instant sculptures, made of urethane foam.

1967
Returns to New York; shares a studio with Neil Williams at 60 Grand Street. Begins galvanized-steel sculptures.

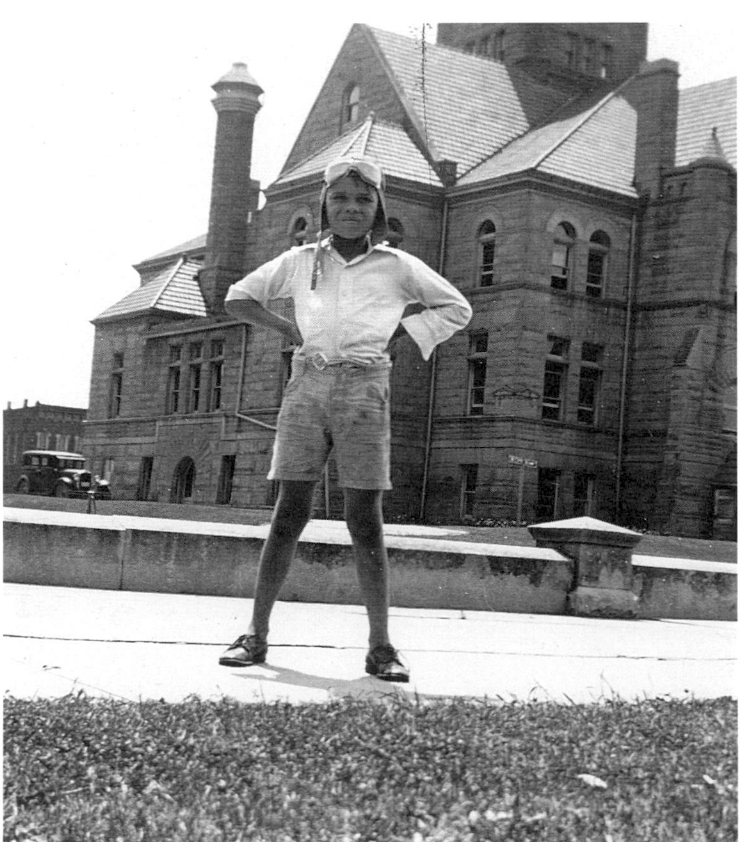

John Chamberlain, Rochester, Indiana, 1937.

1968
Makes his first film, *Wedding Night*, starring Ultra Violet and Taylor Mead, in New York, directed by John Chamberlain and Buddy Wirtshafter, produced by John Chamberlain. *The Secret Life of Hernando Cortez*, a sixteen-millimeter, fifty-four-minute color film starring Ultra Violet and Taylor Mead, made in Valladolla, Mexico, directed by John Chamberlain and produced by Alan Power. Travels to London to make *Wide Point*, a sixteen-millimeter, sixty-minute color film projected on seven screens simultaneously, starring Taylor Mead, directed by John Chamberlain and produced by Alan Power.

1969
Artist in residence at two corporations, in conjunction with the Art and Technology Program of the Los Angeles County Museum: first at Dart Industries, then, for two months, at the Rand Corporation. At Dart, proposes *SniFFter*, an olfactory stimulus-response environment consisting of one hundred bottled smells (adhesive tape, female skin in sun, downtown Las Vegas, wet fur, air at eleven thousand feet in New Mexico); the project is never fully developed. At Rand, a showing of *The Secret Life of Hernando Cortez* causes controversy and is banned and *The Rand Piece* is realized, a thirty-four-page document of questions divided into two sections: What are the circumstances to these responses, and, What is the response to these circumstances? Visiting artist at the University of Wisconsin, Madison. Spends one month at the home of Lewis Manilow in Park Forest South, Illinois; makes a series of white and chrome sculptures. The *Penthouse* series of brown paper-bag sculptures are made in a studio on Park Avenue South in New York.

1970
The Plexiglas pieces are begun in East Los Angeles and vacuum-coated in Larry Bell's studio in Venice, California. Shares a studio with Neil Williams in Little Sycamore Canyon, California, where the *Morgansplit* paintings, a series of some twelve paintings intensely painted on an irregular surface, are made.

1971
Returns to New York and maintains a studio on Wooster Street. *John Chamberlain: A Retrospective Exhibition* opens at the Solomon R. Guggenheim Museum in New York.

1972
Lives and works at the ranch of Stanley Marsh III in Amarillo, Texas, where the group of works known as *The Texas Pieces* is begun. Makes a proposal to the Contemporary Arts Center in Cincinnati for the *Amarillo Piece*, an environment including projected images of a Panhandle feedlot from dawn to dusk, six urethane-foam couches regulated by the mean temperature of Amarillo, an audio of cows and wind, and odors of feedlot and cut hay; the project is never realized.

1973
Death of Elaine Chamberlain in Santa Fe, New Mexico.

1974
Moves to studio at 67 Vestry Street in New York; resumes work with auto-body parts. Maintains that studio until 1980.

1975
The Texas Pieces exhibited at the Contemporary Arts Museum in Houston, outdoors at the Saint Louis Botanical Gardens, Saint Louis, Missouri, and at the Minneapolis Museum of Fine Arts.

1977
Receives a second Guggenheim fellowship. Converts a barn in Essex, Connecticut, into a residence and outdoor studio. Begins taking photographs with a wide-lux camera. Marries Lorraine Belcher in New York.

1979
Receives a commission from the U.S. General Services Administration for the Federal Plaza in Detroit, Michigan.

1980
Moves to Sarasota, Florida.

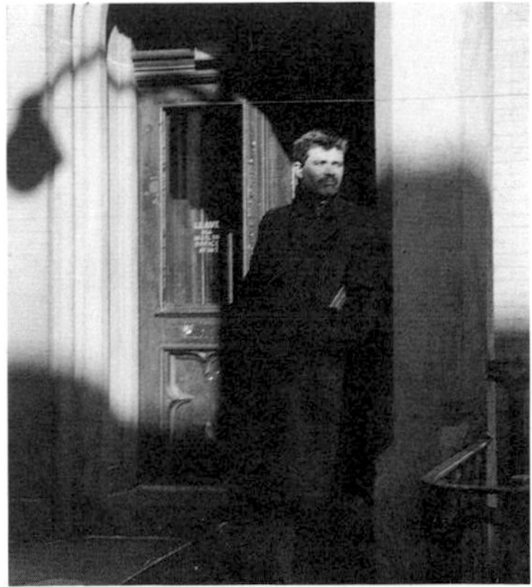

John Chamberlain in front of the Wells Street Gallery in Chicago, 1957.

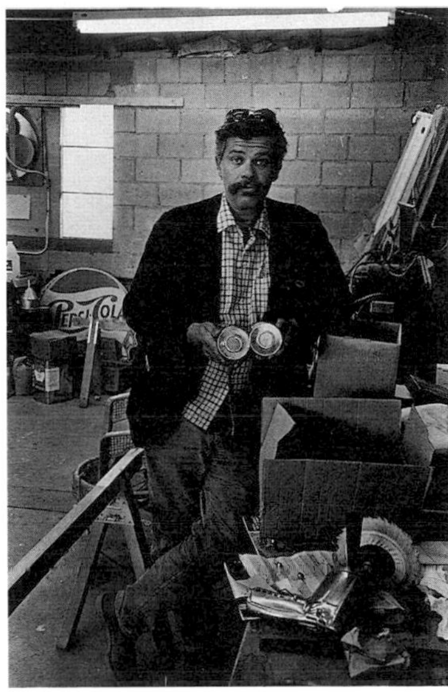

John Chamberlain, Santa Fe, New Mexico, c. 1965.

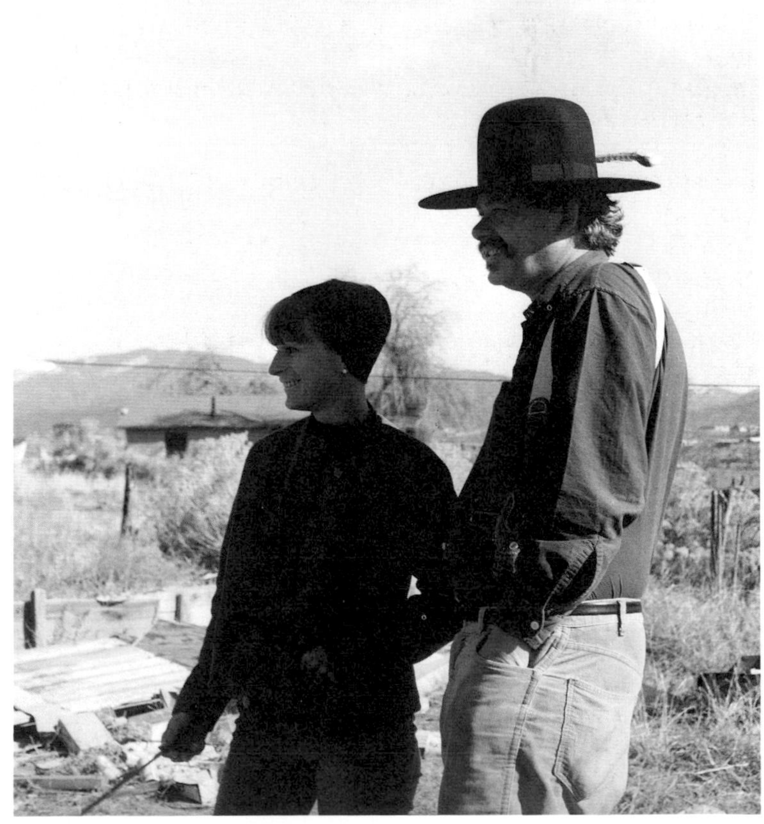

John and Elaine Chamberlain, Santa Fe, New Mexico, c. 1964–65.

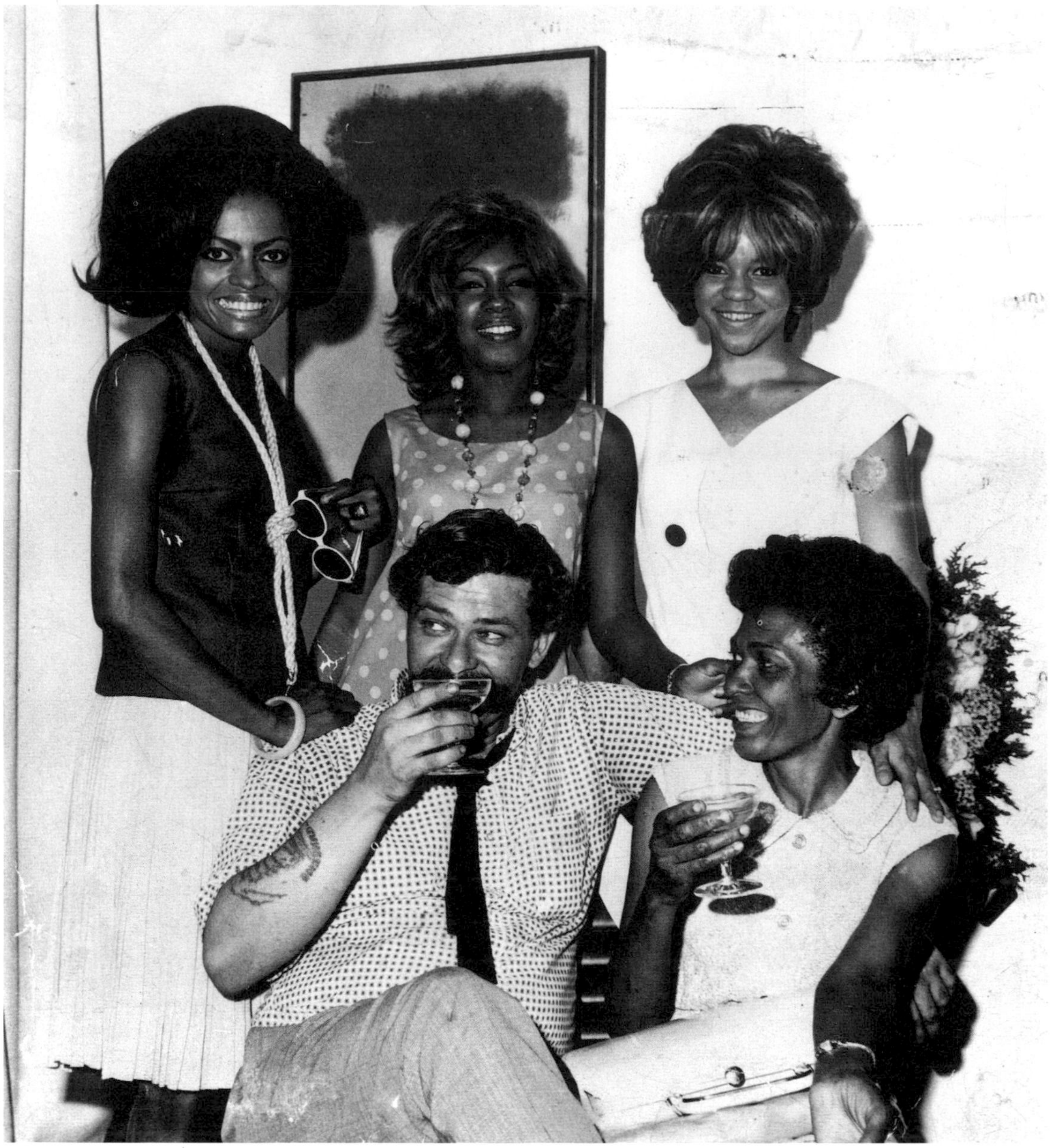

John Chamberlain with Diana Ross and the Supremes, and Diana Ross's mother, New York, New York, 1964.

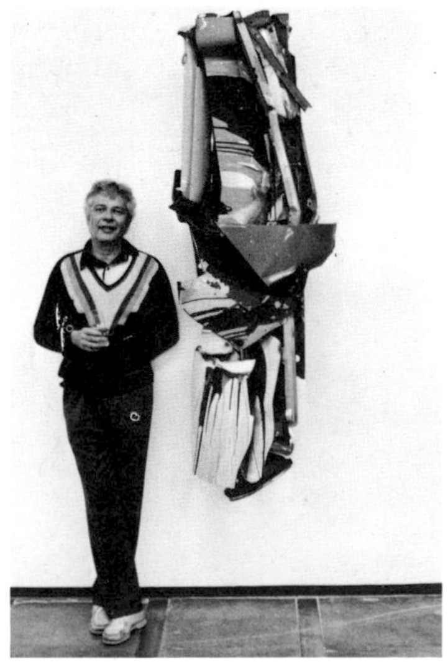

John Chamberlain with *Bentley Last,* 1977 (cat. no. 555), at Galerie Heiner Friedrich, Cologne.

1981
Purchases and lives aboard the houseboat *Ottonello* at the marina in Sarasota, Florida, where his yacht, the *Cocola*, is also moored. Establishes a studio at Tenth Street and Coconut in Sarasota and maintains an outdoor studio in Osprey, Florida, at the end of a junkyard; creates *Deliquescence* and hatches the inspiration for the first *Gondolas*.

1982
Deliquescence installed at the campus of Wayne State University in Detroit, Michigan. An extended exhibition of sculpture is presented by the Dia Art Foundation at the artist's former studio at 67 Vestry Street, New York, until 1985. *Chamberlain Gardens*, an outdoor exhibition of sculpture, is presented by the Dia Art Foundation at the artist's former residence in Essex, Connecticut, until 1984.

1983
An exhibition of his sculpture opens at the Art Museum of the Pecos in Marfa, Texas, sponsored by the Dia Art Foundation.

1984
Receives the Brandeis University Creative Arts award medal in sculpture. *John Chamberlain/Esculturas* exhibition opens at the Palacio Cristal, Parque del Retiro, Madrid. *American Tableau* is presented and installed at the Seagram Plaza in New York.

1985
Artist in Residence, Skowhegan School of Painting and Sculpture, Skowhegan, Maine.

Exhibition History

One-Person Exhibitions

1957
Wells Street Gallery, Chicago, Illinois

1958
Davida Gallery, New York, New York

1960
Martha Jackson Gallery, New York, New York

1962
Leo Castelli Gallery, New York, New York
Dilexi Gallery, San Francisco, California

1963
Pace Gallery, Boston, Massachusetts
Dilexi Gallery, San Francisco, California

1964
Galerie Ileana Sonnabend, Paris, ex. cat.
Leo Castelli Gallery, New York, New York

1965
Leo Castelli Gallery, New York, New York

1966
Dwan Gallery, Los Angeles, California

1967
The Cleveland Museum of Art, Cleveland, Ohio, ex. cat.
Galerie Rudolf Zwirner, Cologne
Galerie Heiner Friedrich, Munich

1969
Leo Castelli Warehouse, New York, New York
Mizuno Gallery, Los Angeles, California

1970
Hard and Soft: Recent Sculpture, Lo Giudice Gallery, Chicago, Illinois
Couches, Locksley/Shea Gallery, Minneapolis, Minnesota

1971
John Chamberlain: A Retrospective Exhibition, The Solomon R. Guggenheim Museum, New York, New York, ex. cat.
Leo Castelli Gallery, New York, New York

1972
John Chamberlain/F______g Couches, Lo Giudice Gallery, New York, New York, in affiliation with Leo Castelli Gallery, New York, New York

1973
Leo Castelli Gallery, New York, New York

1973–74
John Chamberlain: Texas Pieces, Hammarskjold Plaza Sculpture Garden, New York, New York

1974
Walter Kelly Gallery, Chicago, Illinois

1975
John Chamberlain: Recent Sculpture, Contemporary Arts Museum, Houston, Texas; Saint Louis Botanical Gardens, Saint Louis, Missouri; Minneapolis Institute of Arts, Minneapolis, Minnesota, ex. cat.
Ronald Greenberg Gallery, Saint Louis, Missouri
James Corcoran Gallery, Los Angeles, California

1976
Leo Castelli Gallery, New York, New York

1977
View from the Cockpit, Margo Leavin Gallery, Los Angeles, California
Heiner Friedrich, Inc., New York, New York
John Chamberlain: An Exhibition of Sculpture: 1959–1962, The Mayor Gallery, London, ex. cat.

1977–78
The Texas Pieces, presented by the Dia Art Foundation at Manhattan Psychiatric Center, Ward's Island, New York, New York

1978
Heiner Friedrich GmbH, Cologne

1979
Kunsthalle Bern, ex. cat.
Heiner Friedrich GmbH, Cologne

1980
Van Abbemuseum, Eindhoven, Netherlands, ex. cat.

1982
Leo Castelli Gallery, New York, New York
John Chamberlain Sculpture: An Extended Exhibition, Dia Art Foundation, New York, New York
Chamberlain Gardens, Essex, Dia Art Foundation, Essex, Connecticut

1983
John Chamberlain Reliefs 1960–1982, The John and Mable Ringling Museum of Art, Sarasota, Florida, ex. cat.
The Butler Institute of American Art, Youngstown, Ohio, ex. cat.
Robert L. Kidd Galleries, Birmingham, Michigan, illus. brochure
Marian Goodman Gallery, New York, New York
John Chamberlain Sculpture: An Extended Exhibition, Dia Art Foundation, New York, New York
Chamberlain Gardens, Essex, Dia Art Foundation, Essex, Connecticut
The Art Museum of the Pecos, Marfa, Texas, Dia Art Foundation, Marfa, Texas

1984
John Chamberlain/Esculturas, Palacio de Cristal, Parque del Retiro, Madrid, ex. cat
Xavier Fourcade Gallery, New York, New York, ex. cat.
Marian Goodman Gallery, New York, New York
American Tableau, The Seagram Plaza, New York, New York
Galerie Rudolf Zwirner, Cologne
Galerie Helen van der Meij, Amsterdam
John Chamberlain Sculpture: An Extended Exhibition, Dia Art Foundation, New York, New York
Chamberlain Gardens, Essex, Dia Art Foundation, Essex, Connecticut
The Art Museum of the Pecos, Marfa, Texas, Dia Art Foundation, Marfa, Texas

1985
Margo Leavin Gallery, Los Angeles, California
Galerie Gillespie-Laage-Salomon, Paris

Two-Person Exhibitions

1958
Davida Gallery, New York, New York, with Joseph Fiore

1962
Leo Castelli Gallery, New York, New York, with Frank Stella

1963
Robert Fraser Gallery, London, with Richard Stankiewicz

1965
Galerie Rudolf Zwirner, Cologne, with Allan D'Arcangelo

1972
Taft Museum, Cincinnati, Ohio, with Peter Alexander

1976
Locksley/Shea Gallery, Minneapolis, Minnesota, with Cy Twombly

1984
University Art Museum, University of California, Santa Barbara, with Alan Saret

Group Exhibitions

1958

Hansa Gallery, New York, New York

1959

The Enormous Room, Martha Jackson Gallery, New York, New York

Work in Three Dimensions, Leo Castelli Gallery, New York, New York

Hansa Gallery, New York, New York

Recent Sculpture USA, The Museum of Modern Art, New York, New York

1960

Le Nouveau Réalisme, Galerie Rive Droite, Paris

New Forms—New Media I and II, Martha Jackson Gallery, New York, New York, ex. cat.

New Sculpture Group, Stable Gallery, New York, New York

Annual of Sculpture and Drawing, Whitney Museum of American Art, New York, New York

1961

The Museum of Modern Art, New York/Painting and Sculpture Acquisitions, The Museum of Modern Art, New York, New York, ex. cat.

VI Bienal, Museu de Arte Moderna, São Paolo, ex. cat.

The Art of Assemblage, The Museum of Modern Art, New York, New York, ex. cat.

Ways and Means, Houston Contemporary Arts Association, Houston, Texas

The Pittsburgh International Exhibition, Carnegie Institute, Pittsburgh, Pennsylvania

Six Sculptures, Dwan Gallery, Los Angeles, California

Sculpture and Relief, Leo Castelli Gallery, New York, New York

An Exhibition in Progress, Leo Castelli Gallery, New York, New York

Three Young Americans, Allen Memorial Art Museum, Oberlin College, Oberlin, Ohio

1962

International Sculpture Exhibition, Buenos Aires Museum of Modern Art, Buenos Aires

Directions in Modern Sculpture, Providence Arts Club, Providence, Rhode Island

Art since 1950, Seattle World's Fair, Seattle, Washington; Brandeis University, Waltham, Massachusetts

My Country 'Tis of Thee, Dwan Gallery, Los Angeles, California, ex. cat.

Modern Sculpture from the Joseph H. Hirshhorn Collection, The Solomon R. Guggenheim Museum, New York, New York, ex. cat.

Annual of Sculpture and Drawing, Whitney Museum of American Art, New York, New York

Sixty-fifth Annual American Exhibition: Some Directions in Contemporary Painting and Sculpture, The Art Institute of Chicago, Chicago, Illinois, ex. cat.

Leo Castelli Gallery, New York, New York

1963

Six Sculptors, Boston University Art Gallery, Boston, Massachusetts

Zuni Gallery, Buffalo, New York

Sculpture in the Open Air, Battersea Park, London, organized by the Museum of Modern Art, New York, New York, ex. cat.

1er Salon international de galeries-pilotes, Musée Cantonal des Beaux-Arts, Lausanne

Mixed Media and Pop Art, Albright-Knox Art Gallery, Buffalo, New York, ex. cat.

Leo Castelli Gallery, New York, New York

Dwan Gallery, Los Angeles, California

Sculptors of Our Time, Washington Gallery of Modern Art, Washington, D.C.

1964

Twenty-fourth Annual Exhibition by the Society for Contemporary American Art, Art Institute of Chicago, Chicago, Illinois, ex. cat.

Circarama Building, New York State Pavilion at the World's Fair, New York, New York

The Atmosphere of '64, Institute of Contemporary Art, Philadelphia, Pennsylvania

Twenty-nine International Artists, David Mirvish Gallery, Toronto, Canada

Painting and Sculpture of a Decade, The Tate Gallery, London

XXXII Esposizione biennale internationale d'arte, Venice

The Biennale Eight, Institute of Contemporary Art, Boston, Massachusetts, ex. cat.

Recent American Sculpture, The Jewish Museum, New York, New York, ex. cat.

Sculpture Annual, Whitney Museum of American Art, New York, New York

The Classic Spirit in Twentieth-Century Art, Sidney Janis Gallery, New York, New York

Leo Castelli Gallery, New York, New York

1965

Painting and Sculpture Today, Herron Museum of Art, Indianapolis, Indiana, ex. cat.

Painting without a Brush, Institute of Contemporary Art, Boston, Massachusetts

American Sculpture 1900–1965, Flint Institute of Arts, Flint, Michigan

Seven Sculptors, Institute for Contemporary Art, Philadelphia, Pennsylvania

Modern Sculpture USA, The Museum of Modern Art, New York, New York

Virginia Dwan Kondratief Collection, University of California at Los Angeles

Art in Embassies, American Embassy in Mexico City, organized by the Museum of Modern Art, New York, New York

The Weatherspoon Annual Exhibition, Weatherspoon Art Gallery, University of North Carolina at Greensboro, North Carolina

1966

Art of the United States: 1670–1966, Whitney Museum of American Art, New York, New York, ex. cat.

Hommage à Caissa, Cordier and Ekstrom Gallery, New York, New York, organized by Marcel Duchamp for the American Chess Foundation

Contemporary American Sculpture: Selection I, Whitney Museum of American Art, New York, New York, ex. cat.

Flint Invitational, Flint Institute of Arts, Flint, Michigan

Seven Decades, 1895–1965, Cordier and Ekstrom Gallery, New York, New York, organized by the Public Education Association

Annual of Sculpture and Prints, Whitney Museum of American Art, New York, New York

Charles Cowles Gallery, Los Angeles, California

1967

American Sculpture of the Sixties, The Los Angeles County Museum of Art, Los Angeles, California

Ten Years, Leo Castelli Gallery, New York, New York

Sculpture: A Generation of Innovation, The Art Institute of Chicago, Chicago, Illinois

The 1960s: Painting and Sculpture from the Museum Collection, The Museum of Modern Art, New York, New York

The 1967 Pittsburgh International Exhibition of Contemporary Painting and Sculpture, Carnegie Institute, Pittsburgh, Pennsylvania

A Selection from the Collection of Mr. and Mrs. Robert Rowan, University of California, Irvine

New Work, Leo Castelli Gallery, New York, New York

Kunst des 20. Jahrhunderts aus rheinisch-westfälischem Privatbesitz, Städtische Kunsthalle, Düsseldorf, ex. cat.

Homage to Marilyn Monroe, Sidney Janis Gallery, New York, New York, ex. cat.

1968

Sculpture, Murals and Fountains at HemisFair 1968, San Antonio Fair, San Antonio, Texas, ex. cat.

Art in Embassies, American Embassy in Budapest, organized by the Museum of Modern Art, New York, New York

Annual Exhibition of Sculpture, Whitney Museum of American Art, New York, New York

Selections from the Collection of Hanford Yang, The Aldrich Museum of Contemporary Art, Ridgefield, Connecticut

Sammlung Hahn: Zeitgenössische Kunst, Wallraf-Richartz-Museum, Cologne, ex. cat.

Sammlung 1968 Karl Ströher, Galerie-Verein München, Neue Pinakothek, Haus der Kunst, Munich, ex. cat.

Selections from the Collection of Mr. and Mrs. Robert B. Mayer, Museum of Contemporary Art, Chicago, Illinois, ex. cat.

The Contemporary Arts Center, Cincinnati, Ohio

1969

Hard, Soft and Plastic, Wilcox Gallery, Swarthmore College, Swarthmore, Pennsylvania

New Media, New Methods, The Museum of Modern Art, New York, New York

Summer Group Show, Leo Castelli Gallery, New York, New York

Benefit Exhibition: Art for the Moratorium, Leo Castelli Gallery, New York, New York

Contemporary American Sculpture, organized by the Whitney Museum of American Art, New York, New York

Soft Art, New Jersey State Museum, Trenton, New Jersey

Painting and Sculpture Today—1969, Indianapolis Museum of Art, Indianapolis, Indiana, ex. cat.

American Art of the Sixties in Toronto Private Collections, York University, Toronto

Soft Sculpture, American Federation of the Arts Circulating Exhibition

Sammlung 1968 Karl Ströher, Neue Nationalgalerie, Berlin

New York Painting and Sculpture: 1940–1970, The Metropolitan Museum of Art, New York, New York, ex. cat.

An American Report on the Sixties, Denver Art Museum, Denver, Colorado

Castelli at Dayton's, Dayton's Gallery 12, Minneapolis, Minnesota, ex. cat.

1970

The Highway, Institute of Contemporary Art, Philadelphia, Pennsylvania

American Artists of the Nineteen-Sixties, School of Fine and Applied Arts Gallery, Boston, Massachusetts, ex. cat.

Painting and Sculpture Today—1970, Indianapolis Museum of Art, Indianapolis, Indiana, ex. cat.

The Thing as Object, Kunsthalle Nurnberg, Nurnberg

Monumental Art, Contemporary Arts Center, Cincinnati, Ohio, ex. cat.

The Halifax Conference, Nova Scotia College of Art and Design, Halifax

Sculpture Annual, Whitney Museum of American Art, New York, New York

Eisen- und Stahlplastik 1930–1970, Württembergischer Kunstverein, Stuttgart

Contemporary Sculpture from Northwest Collections, Western Washington University, Bellingham, Washington, ex. cat.

Metamorphose des Dinges, Palais des Beaux-Arts, Brussels

Small Sculptures from Cincinnati Collections, Cincinnati Art Museum, Cincinnati, Ohio, ex. cat.

1971

Younger Abstract Expressionists of the Fifties, The Museum of Modern Art, New York, New York

Techniques and Creativity/Selections from Gemini G.E.L., The Museum of Modern Art, New York, New York, ex. cat.

Art around the Automobile, Emily Lowe Gallery, Hofstra University, Hempstead, New York

Prospect '71, Städtische Kunsthalle, Düsseldorf

Lo Giudice Gallery, New York, New York

Martha Jackson Gallery Collection, Seibu Department Store, Tokyo, ex. cat.

Heiner Friedrich GmbH, Cologne

Highlights of the 1970–1971 Season, The Aldrich Museum of Contemporary Art, Ridgefield, Connecticut, ex. cat.

Selections from the Museum Collection and Recent Acquisitions, 1971, The Solomon R. Guggenheim Museum, New York, New York

Wilderness, The Corcoran Gallery of Art, Washington, D.C., ex. cat.

Ten Years—The Friends of the Corcoran/Twentieth Century American Artists, The Corcoran Gallery of Art, Washington, D.C., ex. cat.

1972

Film-Video-Photographs-Projektion, Louisiana Museum, Copenhagen

Painting and Sculpture Today, Indianapolis Museum of Art, Indianapolis, Indiana, ex. cat.

Critics' Choice, Sculpture Center, New York, New York

Recent American Painting and Sculpture, The Albright-Knox Art Gallery, Buffalo, New York, ex. cat.

Summer Group Show, Leo Castelli Gallery, New York, New York

Twentieth Century Sculpture from Southern California Collections, University of California at Los Angeles Art Galleries, Dickson Art Center, Los Angeles, ex. cat.

Wreck, Michael C. Rockefeller Arts Center, Fredonia, New York, ex. cat.

American Art since 1945, Philadelphia Museum of Art, Philadelphia, Pennsylvania, a loan exhibition from the Museum of Modern Art, New York, New York, ex. cat.

New York Collection for Stockholm, Leo Castelli Gallery, New York, New York

Furniture Designed by Artists, Leo Castelli Gallery, New York, New York

Sixties to Seventy-two: American Art from the Collection of Ed Cauduro, Portland Art Museum, Portland, Oregon, ex. cat.

1973

American Art 1948–1973, Seattle Art Museum, Seattle, Washington, ex. cat.

Biennial of Contemporary American Painting and Sculpture, Whitney Museum of American Art, New York, New York

Small Scale Sculpture, Locksley/Shea Gallery, Minneapolis, Minnesota

Sculpture 3—New York Artists on Tour, World Trade Center, New York, New York

Video Tapes by Gallery Artists, Leo Castelli Gallery, New York, New York

Films by Gallery Artists, Leo Castelli Gallery, New York, New York

Selections from the Permanent Collection, Whitney Museum of American Art, New York, New York

Benefit Exhibition for the Committee to Save Venice, Leo Castelli Gallery, New York, New York

New York Collection for Stockholm, Moderna Museet, Stockholm, ex. cat.

South Florida Collects, Fort Lauderdale Museum, Fort Lauderdale, Florida

The Private Collection of Martha Jackson, The University of Maryland Art Gallery, College Park, Maryland, ex. cat.

1974

Poets of the Cities New York and San Francisco 1950–1965, Dallas Museum of Fine Arts and Southern Methodist University, Dallas, Texas, ex. cat.

Large Scale Sculpture Show, Pratt Institute, Brooklyn, New York

Drawings, Leo Castelli Gallery, New York, New York

Six from Castelli (videotapes), de Saisset Art Gallery, University of Santa Clara, Santa Clara, California

The Ponderosa Collection, The Contemporary Arts Center, Cincinnati, Ohio

Works from Change Inc., The Museum of Modern Art, New York, New York

USA on Paper, The Mayor Gallery, London

Wreck, Canton Art Institute, Canton, Ohio

Contemporary American Sculpture, The Society of the Four Arts, Palm Beach, Florida, ex. cat.

Inaugural Exhibition, Hirshhorn Museum and Sculpture Garden, Washington, D.C.

1975

Wreck: A Tragic-Romantic American Theme, The C. W. Post College Art Gallery, Greenvale, New York

Painting, Drawing and Sculpture of the Sixties and Seventies from the Dorothy and Herbert Vogel Collection, Institute of Contemporary Art, Philadelphia, Pennsylvania

Sculpture, American Directions, 1945–1975, National Collection of Fine Arts, Smithsonian Institution, Washington, D.C., ex. cat.

Small Sculpture, The New Gallery, Cleveland, Ohio

Revisione 1, Galleria dell'Ariete, Milan

San Diego Collects, La Jolla Museum of Contemporary Art, La Jolla, California

Sculpture of the 60s, Whitney Museum of American Art, Downtown Branch, New York, New York, ex. cat.

American Art since 1945, Worcester Art Museum, Worcester, Massachusetts, from the collection of the Museum of Modern Art, New York, New York, ex. cat.

Benefit Exhibition for the Allen Memorial Art Museum, Leo Castelli Gallery, New York, New York

Summer Group Show, Leo Castelli Gallery, New York, New York

1976

Survey—Part I, The Sable-Castelli Gallery Ltd., Toronto

Two Hundred Years of American Sculpture, Whitney Museum of American Art, New York, New York, ex. cat.

Inaugural Exhibiton, Zolla/Lieberman Gallery, Chicago, Illinois

An Exhibition for the War Resisters' League, Heiner Friedrich Inc., New York, New York

Newport Art Festival, Newport, Rhode Island

New York—Downtown Manhattan: Soho, Akademie der Kunst, Berliner Festwochen, Berlin

7 + 5: Sculptors in the 1950s, Art Galleries, University of California, Santa Barbara, ex. cat.

Three Hundred Years of American Art in the Chrysler Museum, The Chrysler Museum, Norfolk, Virginia, ex. cat.

Visions/Painting and Sculpture: Distinguished Alumni 1945 to the Present, The School of the Art Institute of Chicago, Chicago, Illinois, ex. cat.

Welded Sculpture, Zabriskie Gallery, New York, New York

Summer Group Show, Leo Castelli Gallery, New York, New York

1977

Two Decades of Exploration: Homage to Leo Castelli on the Occasion of His Twentieth Anniversary, The Art Association of Newport, Newport, Rhode Island

Material of Art: Plastic, Joseloff Gallery, University of Hartford, West Hartford, Connecticut

Pop Plus, Whitney Museum of American Art, Downtown Branch, New York, New York, ex. cat.

Collectors Collect Contemporary: A Selection from Boston Collections, Institute of Contemporary Art, Boston, Massachusetts

Jubilation: American Art during the Reign of Elizabeth II, The Fitzwilliam Museum, Cambridge, ex. cat.

Recent Work, Leo Castelli Gallery, New York, New York

Twentieth-Century American Art from Friends' Collections, Whitney Museum of American Art, New York, New York

New York: The State of Art, The New York State Museum, Albany, New York, ex. cat.

Permanent Collection: Thirty Years of American Art 1945–1975, Whitney Museum of American Art, New York, New York

Works on Paper by Contemporary American Artists, Madison Art Center, Madison, Wisconsin

Recent Acquisitions, The Solomon R. Guggenheim Museum, New York, New York

Timothea Stewart Gallery, Los Angeles, California

1978

Art and the Automobile, Flint Institute of Art, Flint, Michigan

Three Generations: Studies in Collage, Margo Leavin Gallery, Los Angeles, California

Collection: American Sculpture, The Solomon R. Guggenheim Museum, New York, New York

New York Now, Mead Art Gallery, Amherst College, Amherst, Massachusetts

American Art 1950 to the Present, Whitney Museum of American Art, New York, New York

Selections from the Fort Worth Art Museum Permanent Collection, Tyler Museum of Art, Tyler, Texas

Leo Castelli Gallery, New York, New York

1979

Auto Icons, Whitney Museum of American Art, Downtown Branch, New York, New York, ex. cat.

Collection: Art in American after World War II, The Solomon R. Guggenheim Museum, New York, New York

Soft Art Exhibition, Kunsthaus Zurich

Contemporary Art Acquisitions from Sydney and Frances Lewis, Virginia Museum of Fine Arts, Richmond, Virginia

Zum Thema Skulptur, Galerien Maximilianstrasse, Munich

Contemporary Sculpture: Selections from the Collection of the Museum of Modern Art, The Museum of Modern Art, New York, New York, ex. cat.

A Celebration of Acquisitions: Gifts and Purchases, 1975–1979, The Saint Louis Art Museum, Saint Louis, Missouri

Summer Selections, Washington University Gallery of Art, Saint Louis, Missouri

Summer Loan Exhibition, The Metropolitan Museum of Art, New York, New York

1980

Faszination des Objekts, Museum moderner Kunst Wien, Vienna, ex. cat.

Five in Florida, University of South Florida, Tampa, Florida, ex. cat.

Choice of New York, Adler Gallery, Sarasota, Florida

The Guggenheim Collection, 1900–1980, The Solomon R. Guggenheim Museum, New York, New York

Across the Nation: Fine Art for Federal Buildings, 1972–1979, National Collection of Fine Arts, Smithsonian Institution, Washington, D.C.

American Sculpture: Gifts of Howard and Jean Lipman, Whitney Museum of American Art, New York, New York, ex. cat.

Selections from the Permanent Collection, Madison Art Center, Madison, Wisconsin

Nineteenth- and Twentieth-Century American Paintings, Washington University Gallery of Art, Saint Louis, Missouri

Permanent Collection, Fort Worth Art Museum, Fort Worth, Texas

Reliefs/Formprobleme zwischen Malerei und Skulptur in 20. Jahrhundert, Kunsthaus Zurich, ex. cat.

Sculpture on the Wall: Relief Sculpture of the Seventies, University of Massachusetts at Amherst, Amherst, Massachusetts, ex. cat.

1981

Twentieth-Century American Art: Highlights of the Permanent Collection, Whitney Museum of American Art, New York, New York

The Gilbert and Lila Silverman Collection, Cranbrook Academy of Art Museum, Bloomfield Hills, Michigan, ex. cat.

International Florida Artists Exhibition, John and Mable Ringling Museum of Art, Sarasota, Florida, ex. cat.

Westkunst, organized by the Museum der Stadt Köln, Cologne, ex. cat.

1982

Twenty Galleries/Twenty Years, Grace Borgenicht Gallery and Terry Dintenfass Gallery, New York, New York, ex. cat.

Documenta 7, Kassel, West Germany, ex. cat.

Castelli and His Artists/Twenty-Five Years, La Jolla Museum of Contemporary Art, La Jolla, California

American Sculpture from the Permanent Collection, The Solomon R. Guggenheim Museum, New York, New York

Nathan Manilow Sculpture Park, Governors State University, Park Forest South, Illinois

Sculpture from the Vanderbilt Art Collection, Vanderbilt Art Gallery, Nashville, Tennessee

The New York School: Four Decades, Guggenheim Collection and Major Loans, The Solomon R. Guggenheim Museum, New York, New York

1983

Borofsky, Chamberlain, Dahn, Knoebel, Städtische Kunsthalle, Düsseldorf

De Statua, Van Abbemuseum, Eindhoven, Netherlands

American/European Painting and Sculpture Part II, L.A. Louver Gallery, Venice, California

Sculpture: The Tradition in Steel, Nassau County Museum of Fine Arts, Roslyn, New York

In Honor of de Kooning, Xavier Fourcade, Inc., New York, New York, ex. cat.

The Nuclear Age: Tradition and Transition, Phoenix Art Museum, Phoenix, Arizona

Sculpture, Leo Castelli Gallery, New York, New York

Whitney Museum of American Art, Philip Morris Sculpture Court, New York, New York, a semipermanent exhibition

1984

Experiment Sammlung I: Une Collection imaginaire, Kunstmuseum Winterthur, Switzerland, ex. cat.

The First Show: Painting and Sculpture from Eight Collections 1940–1980, Museum of Contemporary Art, Los Angeles, California, ex. cat.

Donald Young Gallery, Chicago, Illinois

La Rime et la raison: Les collections Menil (Houston—New York), Grand Palais, Paris, ex. cat.

Inaugural Exhibition, Fort Wayne Museum of Art, Fort Wayne, Indiana, ex. cat.

A Sculpture Show, Marian Goodman Gallery, New York, New York

Large Sculpture, Hokin Gallery, Bay Harbour Islands, Florida

Forming, The Parrish Art Museum, Southampton, New York, ex. cat.

Ein anderes Klima, Städtische Kunsthalle, Düsseldorf

Sculpture, Xavier Fourcade, Inc., New York, New York

Contemporary Painting and Sculpture V: 1957–1984, Oil and Steel Gallery, New York, New York

American Sculpture, Margo Leavin Gallery, Los Angeles, California

American Sculpture: Three Decades, Seattle Art Museum, Seattle, Washington, ex. cat.

Automobile and Culture, Museum of Contemporary Art, Los Angeles, California, ex. cat.

The Third Dimension, Whitney Museum of American Art, New York, New York, ex. cat.

Castello di Rivoli, Regione Piemonte, Italy

Mile–4, Chicago Sculpture International, Chicago, Illinois

1985

Transgressions, Galerie Gillespie-Laage-Salomon, Paris

Second Talent, Aldrich Museum of Contemporary Art, Ridgefield, Connecticut, ex. cat.

Transformations in Sculpture: Four Decades of American and European Art, The Solomon R. Guggenheim Museum, New York, New York, ex. cat.

Bibliography

The bibliography includes selected listings of the more important monographs, books, and periodicals that contain discussions of John Chamberlain's work. It is by no means exhaustive. Exhibition catalogues are not listed here, but mention of the most important ones is made in the artist's chronological exhibition history: the notation "ex. cat." at the end of an entry there indicates that a catalogue of some significance was published with an exhibition. In most cases, the catalogue title is the same as that of the exhibition it documents.

Monographs

Michael Auping. *John Chamberlain Reliefs 1960–1982.* Sarasota, Florida: John and Mable Ringling Museum of Art Foundation, 1982.

Heinrich Ehrhardt, ed. *John Chamberlain/Esculturas.* Madrid. Ministerio de Cultura, 1984.

Johannes Gachnang, ed. *Chamberlain.* Bern, Switzerland: Kunsthalle Bern, and Eindhoven, Netherlands: Van Abbemuseum, 1979.

Edward Leffingwell. *John Chamberlain Sculpture and Work on Paper.* Youngstown, Ohio: The Butler Institute, 1983.

Diane Waldman. *John Chamberlain: A Retrospective Exhibition.* New York: Solomon R. Guggenheim Foundation, 1971.

Books

Alley, Ronald. *Recent American Art.* London: Tate Gallery, 1969.

Alloway, Lawrence. *Topics in American Art since 1945.* New York: Norton, 1975.

Anderson, Wayne. *American Sculpture in Process: 1930–1970.* Boston: New York Graphic Society, 1975.

Arnason, H. H. *History of Modern Art: Painting, Sculpture, Architecture.* Englewood Cliffs, New Jersey: Prentice-Hall, and New York: Abrams, 1968.

Ashton, Dore. *Modern American Sculpture.* New York: Abrams, 1967.

Baigell, Matthew. *Dictionary of American Art.* New York: Harper and Row, 1979.

Barnett, Vivian Endicott. *Handbook: The Guggenheim Museum Collection, 1900–1980.* New York: The Solomon R. Guggenheim Foundation, 1980.

Buchloh, Benjamin H. D., ed. *Carl Andre—Hollis Frampton/Twelve Dialogues 1962–1963.* Halifax: The Press of the Nova Scotia College of Art and Design, and New York: New York University Press, 1980.

Buell, Charlotte. *Contemporary Art—Exploring Its Roots and Development.* Worcester, Mass.: Davis Publications, 1972.

Calas, Nicolas, and Calas, Elena. *Icons and Images of the Sixties.* New York: Dutton, 1971.

Cummings, Frederick J., and Elam, Charles H., eds. *The Detroit Institute of Art Illustrated Handbook.* Detroit: Wayne State University Press, 1971.

Donald Judd—Complete Writings 1959–1975. Halifax: Press of the Nova Scotia College of Art and Design, and New York: New York University Press, 1975.

Duberman, Martin. *Black Mountain: An Exploration in Community.* New York: Dutton, 1972.

Fleming, William. *Art and Ideas.* New York: Holt, Rinehart and Winston, 1968.

Goldwater, Robert. *What Is Modern Sculpture?* New York: Museum of Modern Art, 1969.

Hamilton, George Heard. *Nineteenth- and Twentieth-Century Art: Painting, Sculpture, Architecture.* New York: Abrams, 1970.

Hammacher, A. M. *The Evolution of Modern Sculpture.* New York: Abrams, 1969.

Hess, Thomas B., and Ashbery, John, eds. *Art News Annual 34: The Avant-Garde.* New York: Macmillan, 1968.

Huheey, James. *Diversity and Periodicity.* New York: Harper and Row, 1981.

Hunter, Sam, and Jacobus, John. *American Art of the Twentieth Century.* New York: Abrams, 1972.

Hunter, Sam, et al. "American Art since 1945," *New Art around the World: Painting and Sculpture.* New York: Abrams, 1966.

Janis, Harriet, and Blesh, Rudi. *Collage: Personalities, Concepts, Techniques.* Philadelphia: Chilton Co., 1962.

Krauss, Rosalind E. *Passages in Modern Sculpture.* New York: Viking, 1977.

Kultermann, Udo. *The New Sculpture.* New York: Praeger, 1968.

Licht, Fred. *History of Western Sculpture/Sculpture: Nineteenth and Twentieth Centuries.* Greenwich, Conn.: New York Graphic Society, 1967.

Lipman, Jean, and Marshall, Richard. *Art about Art.* New York: Dutton, 1978, published in association with Whitney Museum of American Art exhibition, 1978.

Lucie-Smith, Edward. *Late Modern: The Visual Arts since 1945.* New York: Praeger, 1969.

———. *Art Now: From Abstract Expressionism to Superrealism.* New York: Morrow, 1977.

Mahlow, Dietrich. *100 Jahre Metallplastik*; vol. 2. Frankfurt: Metallgesellschaft AG, 1981, p. 171.

Massie, Rebecca. *The Lewis Contemporary Art Fund Collection.* Richmond: Virginia Museum, 1980.

McDarrah, Fred W., and Hess, Thomas B. *The Artist's World.* New York: Dutton, 1961.

Metro International Directory of Contemporary Art. Milan: Editoriale Metro, 1964.

Myron, Robert, and Sundell, Abner. *Modern Art in America.* New York: Crowell-Collier Press, 1971.

Nelson Gallery—Atkins Museum Handbook, vol 1. Fifth edition, 1973.

Phaidon Dictionary of Twentieth-Century Art. Oxford: Phaidon, and New York: Dutton, 1973.

Prown, Jules David, and Rose, Barbara. *American Painting: From the Colonial Period to the Present.* New edition. New York: Rizzoli, 1977.

Read, Herbert. *A Concise History of Modern Sculpture.* New York: Praeger, 1964.

Rose, Barbara. *American Art since 1900: A Critical History.* New York: Praeger, 1967.

Rosenberg, Harold. *Artworks and Packages.* New York: Horizon Press, 1969.

Sammlung Hahn. Vienna: Museum moderner Kunst Wien, 1979.

Sandback, Amy Baker, ed. *Looking Critically: Twenty-One Years of Artforum Magazine.* Ann Arbor: UMI Research Press, 1984.

Sandler, Irving H. *The New York School: The Painters and Sculptors of the Fifties.* New York: Harper and Row, 1978.

Schwartz, Fred R. *Structure and Potential in Art Education.* Waltham, Mass.: Ginn-Blaisdell, 1970.

Selleck, Jack. *Contrast*. Worcester, Mass.: Davis Publications, 1975.

Selz, Peter. *Art in Our Times: A Pictorial History 1890–1980*. New York: Abrams, 1981.

Solomon, Alan, and Mulas, Ugo. *New York: The New Art Scene*. New York: Holt, Rinehart and Winston, 1967.

Warhol, Andy, and Hackett, Pat. *Popism: The Warhol Sixties*. New York, London: Harcourt Brace Jovanovich, 1980.

Wilmerding, John. *American Art*. New York: Pelican, 1976.

Periodicals

A., D. R. "Chamberlain Exhibitions." *Chrysler Museum Bulletin*, vol. 3, no. 3 (March 1974).

A., V. H. "Reviews and Previews." *Art News*, vol. 68, no. 9 (January 1970), p. 12.

Adamson, Jeremy. "American Art of the Sixties in Toronto Private Collections." *Artscanada*, vol. 26, no. 134–35 (August 1969), p. 41.

Ak, Edit de. "John Chamberlain at Heiner Friedrich Gallery." *Artforum*, vol. 16, no. 6 (February 1978), p. 62.

Alloway, Lawrence. "Marilyn as Subject Matter." *Arts*, vol. 42, no. 3 (September/October 1967), p. 30.

———. "Peter Forakis since 1960: Notes on His Retrospective at Windham College, Vermont." *Artforum*, vol. 6, no. 5 (January 1968), p. 25.

"American Sculpture in Paris." *Art in America*, vol. 48, no. 3 (October 1960), p. 97.

Ammann, Jean-Christophe. "Documenta: Reality and Desire." *Flash Art*, no. 109 (November 1982), p. 38.

Anderson, Wayne. "American Sculpture: The Situation in the Fifties." *Artforum*, vol. 5, no. 10 (Summer 1967), pp. 60, 67.

Andre, Michael, and Rothenberg, Erika, eds. *The Poets' Encyclopedia*, vol. 4–5 (New York: Unmuzzled Ox Editions, 1979), pp. 178–79.

Armstrong, Lois. "Los Angeles." *Art News*, vol. 68, no. 8 (December 1969), p. 73.

Ashbery, John. "Art and Artists in Paris." *New York Herald Tribune*, April 14, 1964.

Ashton, Dore. "Art: Two Abstractionists." *New York Times*, January 6, 1960.

———. *Arts and Architecture*, vol. 77, no. 3 (March 1960), p. 11.

———. "La sculpture américaine." *XX siècle*, vol. 22, no. 15 (December 1960), p. 91.

———. "Art." *Arts and Architecture*, vol. 79, no. 3 (March 1962), pp. 6–7.

———. "New York Report." *Kunstwerk*, vol. 16, no. 5 (November 1962), p. 69.

Auping, Michael. "An Interview with John Chamberlain." *Art Papers*, vol. 7, no. 1 (January/February 1983).

Baker, Elizabeth C. "The Secret Life of John Chamberlain." *Art News*, vol. 68, no. 2 (April 1969), pp. 48–51, 63–64.

———. "Reviews and Previews." *Art News*, vol. 70, no. 4 (Summer 1971), p. 11.

———. "The Chamberlain Crunch." *Art News*, vol. 70, no. 10 (February 1972), pp. 26–31.

Baker, Kenneth. "New York." *Artforum*, vol. 9, no. 10 (June 1971), p. 82.

Bannard, Darby. "Cubism, Abstract Expressionism, David Smith." *Artforum*, vol. 6, no. 8 (April 1968), pp. 22–32.

Baracks, Barbara. "John Chamberlain, Leo Castelli Gallery Uptown." *Artforum*, vol. 14, no. 10 (June 1976), p. 70.

Bardeschi, Marco Dezzi. "From Johnson to John Soane." *Domus*, no. 631 (September 1982), pp. 43–48.

Bell, Jane. "John Chamberlain: New Sculpture." *Arts*, vol. 49, no. 10 (June 1975), pp. 88–89.

Benedikt, Michael. "Reviews and Previews." *Art News*, vol. 68, no. 1 (March 1969), p. 14.

Brown, Gordon. "Gallery Previews." *Artvoices*, vol. 3, no. 3 (March 1964).

Burr, James. "Round the Galleries." *Apollo*, vol. 106, no. 186 (August 1977), p. 156.

Butler, Barbara. "Movie Stars and Other Members of the Cast." *Art International*, vol. 4, no. 2–3 (February/March 1960), p. 52.

Canaday, John. "Gargoyles for the Machine Age." *Horizon*, vol. 3, no. 4 (March 1961), p. 112.

———. "John Chamberlain's Sculptures." *New York Times*, April 24, 1971, p. 25.

Caplan, Ralph. "Cars as Collage." *Canadian Art*, vol. 19, no. 1 (January/February 1962), p. 25.

"Chamberlain's Automobiles." *Metro*, no. 2 (May 1961), pp. 90–91.

Chevalier, Denys. "La Sculpture à la XXXIIe Biennale de Venise." *Art International*, vol. 8, no. 7 (September 25, 1964), pp. 42–44.

Choay, Françoise. "Lettre de Paris." *Art International*, vol. 4, no. 5 (December 1, 1960), pp. 35–36.

"Controversy." *People*, November 14, 1983, p. 154.

C[oplans], J[ohn]. "Reviews: John Chamberlain, Dilexi Gallery." *Artforum*, vol. 1, no. 9 (March 1963), pp. 10–11.

———. "Reviews," *Artforum*, vol. 2, no. 10 (April 1964), pp. 38–40.

———. "An Interview with Don Judd." *Artforum*, vol. 9, no. 10 (June 1971), p. 44.

Domingo, Willis. "New York Galleries." *Arts*, vol. 45, no. 8 (Summer 1971), p. 53.

E[dgar], N[atalie]. "John Chamberlain." *Art News*, vol. 60, no. 10 (February 1962), p. 15.

———. "Reviews and Previews." *Art News*, vol. 63, no. 10 (February 1965), p. 13.

Ellenzweig, Allen. "Group Show." *Arts*, vol. 49, no. 8 (April 1975), p. 12.

ffrench-frazier, Nina. "New York Reviews." *Art News*, vol. 77, no. 2 (February 1978), p. 152.

Foote, Nancy. "John Chamberlain at Castelli." *Art in America*, vol. 62, no. 2 (March/April 1974), p. 105.

Frackman, Noel. "John Chamberlain at Castelli Gallery," *Arts*, vol. 50, no. 10 (June 1976), p. 19.

———. "Tracking Frank Stella's Circuit Series." *Arts*, vol. 56, no. 8 (April 1982), pp. 134–37.

Fried, Michael. "New York Letter." *Art International*, vol. 6, no. 8 (October 25, 1962), pp. 72–76.

Friedlander, Albert A. "Sculpture Show Satisfying." *Chicago Daily News*, March 25, 1961.

"From Exhibitions Here and There." *Art International*, vol. 4, no. 1 (January 1960), p. 67.

"From Various Exhibitions of Last Season." *Art International*, vol. 15, no. 8 (October 20, 1971), p. 33.

Fry, Edward F. "Sculpture of the Sixties." *Art in America*, vol. 55, no. 5 (September/October 1967), p. 26.

———. "The Issue of Innovation." *Art News*, vol. 66, no. 6 (October 1967), p. 40.

Gachnang, Johannes. "Bericht einer Reise." *Kunst-Bulletin*, no. 4 (April 1979).

Gassiot-Talabot, Gerald. "La Panoplie de l'oncle Sam à Venise." *Aujourd'hui*, vol. 8, no. 47 (October 1964), p. 32.

Genauer, Emily. "Art and the Artist." *New York Post*, January 8, 1972.

H[ess], T[homas] B. "Editorial: Moses the Art Slayer Wins One Round." *Art News*, vol. 63, no. 2 (April 1964), p. 25.

Hawthorne, Don. "Does the Public Want Public Sculpture?" *Art News*, vol. 81, no. 5 (May 1982), pp. 56–63.

Hemphill, Christopher. "A Matter of Mood: An Expression of Contemporary Sensibility." *Architectural Digest*, vol. 39, no. 5 (May 1982), pp. 172–79.

Henning, Edward B. "An Important Sculpture by John Chamberlain." *The Bulletin of The Cleveland Museum of Art*, vol. 60, no. 8 (October 1973), pp. 242–46.

Herrera, Hayden. "John Chamberlain at the Houston Contemporary Arts Museum." *Art in America*, vol. 63, no. 5 (September/October 1975), pp. 105–6.

Hess, Thomas B. "Collage as an Historical Method." *Art News*, vol. 60, no. 7 (November 1961), p. 70.

Indiana, Gary. "John Chamberlain's Irregular Set." *Art in America*, vol. 71, no. 10 (November 1983), pp. 208–16.

Johnson, Philip. "Young Artists at the Fair and at Lincoln Center." *Art in America*, vol. 52, no. 4 (August 1964), pp. 112, 117.

Joly, Pierre. "Un Palais intérieur." *L'oeil*, no. 201–2 (September/October 1971), p. 46.

"Journal: John Chamberlain." *Du*, no. 11 (1979), p. 83.

J[udd], D[onald]. "In the Galleries." *Arts*, vol. 34, no. 5 (February 1960), p. 57.

———. "In the Galleries." *Arts*, vol. 36, no. 6 (March 1962), p. 48.

———. "Kansas City Report." *Arts*, vol. 38, no. 3 (December 1963), pp. 25–26.

———. "Chamberlain—Another View." *Art International*, vol. 7, no. 10 (January 16, 1964), pp. 38–39.

———. "In the Galleries." *Arts*, vol. 38, no. 10 (September 1964), p. 71.

Jürgen-Fischer, K. "Die NEW Yorker Szene," *Kunstwerk*, vol. 19 (April/June 1966), p. 34.

Kozloff, Max. "New York Letter." *Art International*, vol. 6, no. 2 (March 1962), pp. 57, 63.

———. "Modern Art and the Virtues of Decadence." *Studio*, vol. 174 (November 1967), p. 195.

Kramer, Hilton. "Month in Review." *Arts*, vol. 33, no. 9 (June 1959), p. 48.

———. "Serving a Period Taste." *New York Times*, January 2, 1972, p. 17.

Krauss, Rosalind E. "Boston Letter." *Art International*, vol. 8, no. 1 (February 15, 1964), pp. 32–33.

Kuspit, Donald B. "John Chamberlain at Heiner Friedrich." *Art in America*, vol. 66, no. 4 (July/August 1978), p. 112.

Langsner, Jules. "Los Angeles." *Art News*, vol. 65, no. 9 (January 1967), p. 63.

Larson, Philip. "Cy Twombly/John Chamberlain." *Arts*, vol. 49, no. 10 (June 1975), p. 30.

Lausdale, Nelson. "Huge Sculpture Secretly Commissioned for New York World's Fair." *Artvoices*, vol. 3, no. 3 (March 1964).

Leider, Philip. "A New Medium for John Chamberlain." *Artforum*, vol. 5, no. 6 (February 1967), pp. 48–49.

Lippard, Lucy R. "New York Letter." *Art International*, vol. 9, no. 3 (April 1965), pp. 48, 53.

Lucie-Smith, Edward. "John Chamberlain." *Art and Artists*, vol. 12, no. 5 (September 1977), p. 53.

Lusker, Ron. "New York: The Season in Sculpture." *Craft Horizons*, vol. 31, no. 4 (August 1971), pp. 65–66.

Marmer, Nancy. "Isms on the Rhine." *Art in America*, vol. 69, no. 9 (November 1981), p. 114.

Meadmore, Clement. "Thoughts on Earthworks, Random Distribution, Softness, Horizontality and Gravity." *Arts*, vol. 43, no. 4 (February 1969), pp. 26–27.

Meier, Kurt von. "Violence, Art and the American Way." *Artscanada*, vol. 25, no. 116–17 (April 1968), p. 24.

Mellow, James R. "The 1967 Guggenheim International." *Art International*, vol. 11, no. 10 (December 1967), pp. 51–53.

Morse, John D. "He Returns to Dada." *Art in America*, vol. 48, no. 3 (1960), p. 76.

Mueller, Gregoire. "Points of View: A Taped Conversation with Robert C. Scull." *Arts*, vol. 45, no. 2 (November 1970), p. 39.

New School Art Center Series. "American Private Collections" (1965), pp. 7, 44.

Newsweek (October 15, 1962), p. 110.

The 1969 Compton Yearbook. F. E. Compton Co., 1969, p. 43.

Nordland, Gerald. "West Coast in Review." *Arts*, vol. 36, no. 3 (December 1961), p. 64.

———. "Robert Natkin." *Art International*, vol. 13, no. 8 (October 1969), p. 53.

———. "Los Angeles Newsletter." *Art International*, vol. 20, no. 3–4 (March/April 1976), p. 56.

O'Doherty, Brian. "Art: Transformed Scrap." *New York Times*, January 19, 1962.

Piene, Nan R. "New York: Gallery Notes." *Art in America*, vol. 54, no. 3 (May/June 1966), pp. 108–9.

Plagens, Peter. "Los Angeles." *Artforum*, vol. 8, no. 4 (December 1969), p. 74.

———. "Los Angeles." *Artforum*, vol. 9, no. 2 (October 1970), p. 88.

Pomeroy, Ralph. "Soft Objects at the New Jersey State Museum." *Arts*, vol. 43, no. 5 (March 1969), p. 47.

Porter, Fairfield. "Reviews and Previews." *Art News*, vol. 57, no. 9 (January 1959), p. 17.

Power, Kevin. "Robert Creeley on Art and Poetry." *The Niagara Magazine*, no. 9 (Fall 1978).

"1er Salon international de galeries-pilotes." *Art International*, vol. 7, no. 6 (June 25, 1963), pp. 23–26.

"Il Premio Carnegie 1961." *Domus*, no. 386 (January 1962), p. 26.

Ratcliff, Carter. "New York Letter." *Art International*, vol. 16, no. 2 (February 20, 1972), p. 53.

———. "The 'Art' of Chic." *Saturday Review*, vol. 8, no. 4 (April 1981), pp. 14–15.

Raynor, Vivien. "The Art of Assemblage." *Arts*, vol. 36, no. 2 (November 1961), pp. 18–19.

———. "In the Galleries." *Arts*, vol. 37, no. 3 (December 1962), p. 46.

———. "Art." *New York Times*, March 2, 1984.

Restany, Pierre. "The New Realism." *Art in America*, vol. 51, no. 1 (February 1963), pp. 102–4.

Robbins, Daniel. "Modern Sculpture from the Joseph H. Hirshhorn Collection." *Apollo*, vol. 76, no. 9 (November 1962), pp. 720–21.

Roberts, Colette. "Lettre de New York." *Aujourd'hui*, vol. 7, no. 39, (November 1962), p. 50.

Rose, Barbara. "How to Look at John Chamberlain's Sculpture." *Art International*, vol. 7, no. 10 (January 16, 1964), pp. 36–38.

———. "New York Letter." *Art International*, vol. 8, no. 10 (December 1964), pp. 47–50.

———. "Looking at American Sculpture." *Artforum*, vol. 3, no. 5 (February 1965), p. 30.

———. "On Chamberlain's Interview." *Artforum*, vol. 10, no. 6 (February 1972), pp. 44–45.

Rubin, William. "The International Style: Notes on the Pittsburgh Triennial." *Art International*, vol. 5, no. 9 (November 20, 1961), p. 34.

Rudikoff, Sonya. "New Realists in New York." *Art International*, vol. 7, no. 1 (January 25, 1963), pp. 39–41.

Ruhrberg, Karl. "Museum Ludwig Köln." *Du*, no. 1 (1979), p. 73.

Russell, John. *New York Times*, November 25, 1977.

Russotto, Ellen Romano. "New York." *Craft International*, vol. 3, no. 1 (July/September 1983), p. 43.

S., G. R. "Reviews and Previews." *Art News*, vol. 61, no. 3 (May 1962), p. 55.

S[andler], I[rving] H. "Reviews and Previews." *Art News*, vol. 58, no. 9 (January 1960), p. 18.

———. "Ash Can Revisited: A New York Letter." *Art International*, vol. 4, no. 8 (October 25, 1960), pp. 28–30.

———. "New York Letter." *Art International*, vol. 5, no. 2 (March 1, 1961), p. 43.

———. "New York Letter." *Art International*, vol. 5, no. 9 (November 20, 1961), p. 54.

———. "In the Art Galleries." *New York Post*, January 21, 1962.

———. "Reviews and Previews." *Art News*, vol. 61, no. 8 (December 1962), p. 54.

Sawyer, Kenneth. *Craft Horizons*, vol. 22, no. 3 (May 1962), p. 53.

Schjeldahl, Peter. "The Vicissitudes of Sculpture." *New York Times*, February 9, 1969.

Schulze, Franz. "Collector A. James Speyer." *Art in America*, vol. 55, no. 4 (July/August 1967), p. 40.

Schuyler, James. "Reviews and Previews." *Art News*, vol. 57, no. 2 (April 1958), p. 53.

Schwartz, Barbara. "Letter from New York." *Craft Horizons*, vol. 32, no. 2 (April 1972), p. 58.

———. "New York." *Craft Horizons*, vol. 34, no. 2 (April 1974), p. 48.

———. "New York Sculpture." *Craft Horizons*, vol. 35, no. 1 (February 1975), p. 58.

Seldis, Henry J. "Reporting from L.A." *Artvoices*, vol. 3, no. 4 (April/May 1964).

———. "West Coast Milestone." *Art in America*, vol. 53, no. 2 (April 1965), p. 109.

Senie, Harriet. "Urban Sculpture: Cultural Tokens or Ornaments to Life?" *Art News*, vol. 78, no. 7 (September 1979), p. 198.

Sers, Philippe. "Prendre l'objet pour sujet." *Connaissance des arts*, no. 242 (April 1972), p. 106.

Siegel, Jeanne. "Furniture Designed by Artists for Daedalus Concepts." *Art News*, vol. 71, no. 6 (October 1972), p. 79.

Silverthorne, Jeanne. "John Chamberlain." *Artforum*, vol. 21, no. 3 (November 1982), p. 75.

Slesin, Suzanne. "The New York Artist in Residence." *Art News*, vol. 77, no. 9 (November 1978), pp. 66, 73.

Smith, Duncan. "In the Heart of the Tinman: An Essay on John Chamberlain." *Artforum*, vol. 22, no. 5 (January 1984), pp. 39–43.

Smith, Thomas Macaulay. "Art for the Underground House: A Criticism," *Artvoices*, vol. 4, no. 1 (Winter 1965).

Swenson, Gene R. "Reviews and Previews." *Art News*, vol. 63, no. 5 (September 1964), p. 10.

T., A. "Reviews and Previews." *Art News*, vol. 66, no. 4 (Summer 1967), p. 13.

Tatransky, Valentin. "Arts Reviews." *Arts*, vol. 52, no. 5 (January 1978), p. 27.

Thomsen, Barbara. "Reviews and Previews." *Art News*, vol. 73, no. 2 (February 1974), p. 90.

Tillim, Sidney. "Scale and the Future of Modernism." *Artforum*, vol. 6, no. 2 (October 1967), pp. 14–18.

Tompkins, Calvin. "Profiles (Leo Castelli)." *New Yorker*, May 26, 1980.

Townsend, Benjamin. "Albright-Knox Buffalo: Work in Progress." *Art News*, vol. 65, no. 9 (January 1967), p. 30.

Tuchman, Phyllis. "American Art in Germany: The History of a Phenomenon." *Artforum*, vol. 9, no. 3 (November 1970), p. 58.

———. "An Interview with John Chamberlain." *Artforum*, vol. 10, no. 6 (February 1972), pp. 38–43.

"The Vasari Diary: The Whitney Calls for Philip Morris." *Art News*, vol. 82, no. 5 (May 1983), p. 19.

"Venice: The Biennale XXXII." *Arts*, vol. 38, no. 9 (May/June 1964), pp. 76–77.

Ventura, Anita. "In the Galleries." *Arts*, vol. 32, no. 7 (April 1958), p. 61.

Wasserman, Emily. "Review: New York." *Artforum*, vol. 7, no. 8 (April 1969), pp. 72–74.

Welish, Marjorie. "Chamberlain at the Guggenheim." *Arts*, vol. 46, no. 4 (February 1972), pp. 54–55.

Whelan, Richard. "New Editions." *Art News*, vol. 78, no. 3 (March 1979), p. 44.

Whiteside, Forbes. "Three Young Americans." *Allen Memorial Art Museum Bulletin*, vol. 19, no. 1 (Fall 1961), pp. 52–57.

"The Year in Review for 1973." *The Bulletin of the Cleveland Museum of Art* (February 1974), p. 77.

Zucker, Barbara. "New York Reviews." *Art News*, vol. 75, no. 6 (Summer 1976), p. 175.

Index

Page numbers in *italics* refer to illustrations.

The Museum of Contemporary Art, Los Angeles

Museum Staff

Sue Barrett
Development Secretary

Stephan Bennett
Production Manager

John Bowsher
Chief Preparator

Randall Brockett
Art Handler

Kerry Brougher
Assistant Curator

Lessie Brown
Receptionist

Kerry J. Buckley
Director of Development

Walter Chapman
Facilities and Operations Manager

Carol Chrisong
Bookkeeper

Jacqueline Crist
Assistant Curator

Dory Dutton
Bookstore Manager

Leslie Fellows
Curatorial Secretary

Patrice Fellows
Management Intern

Nancy Fleeter
Controller

Sherri Geldin
Associate Director

Bob Gibson
Art Handler

Betsy Gilbert
Receptionist

Stewart Gilbert
Art Handler

Ann Goldstein
Research Associate

Robin Hanson
Grants Officer

Sylvia Hohri
Public Outreach Coordinator

Susan Jenkins
Curatorial Secretary

Kimberley Kanatani
Education Specialist

Richard Koshalek
Director

Julie Lazar
Curator

Valerie Lee
Senior Accountant

Brian Levitz
Membership Coordinator

Mike Lynch
Ticket Clerk

Leslie Marcus
Support Program Coordinator

Portland McCormick
Registrarial Secretary

Rudy Mercado
Art Handler

Cardie K. Molina
Development Assistant

Randy Mulder
Office and Personnel Manager

Ray Navarro
Bookstore and Ticket Clerk

Marc O'Carroll
Art Handler

Carter Potter
Bookstore and Ticket Clerk

Robin Price
Slide Librarian

Pablo Prietto
Ticket Booth Manager

Jill Quinn
Registrarial Assistant

Pam Richey
Bookstore Assistant

Anna Rodriguez
Bookstore and Ticket Clerk

Nancy Rogers
Administrative Assistant

Alma Ruiz
Executive Assistant

Diana Schwab
Curatorial Secretary

Mo Shannon
Registrar

Howard Singerman
Publications Coordinator

Elizabeth Smith
Assistant Curator

David Temianka
Development Assistant

Julia Brown Turrell
Senior Curator

Gabriela Ulloa
Press Intern

Deborah Voigt
Curatorial Secretary

Holly Wilder
Bookstore and Ticket Clerk

Rhyan Zweifler
Membership Secretary